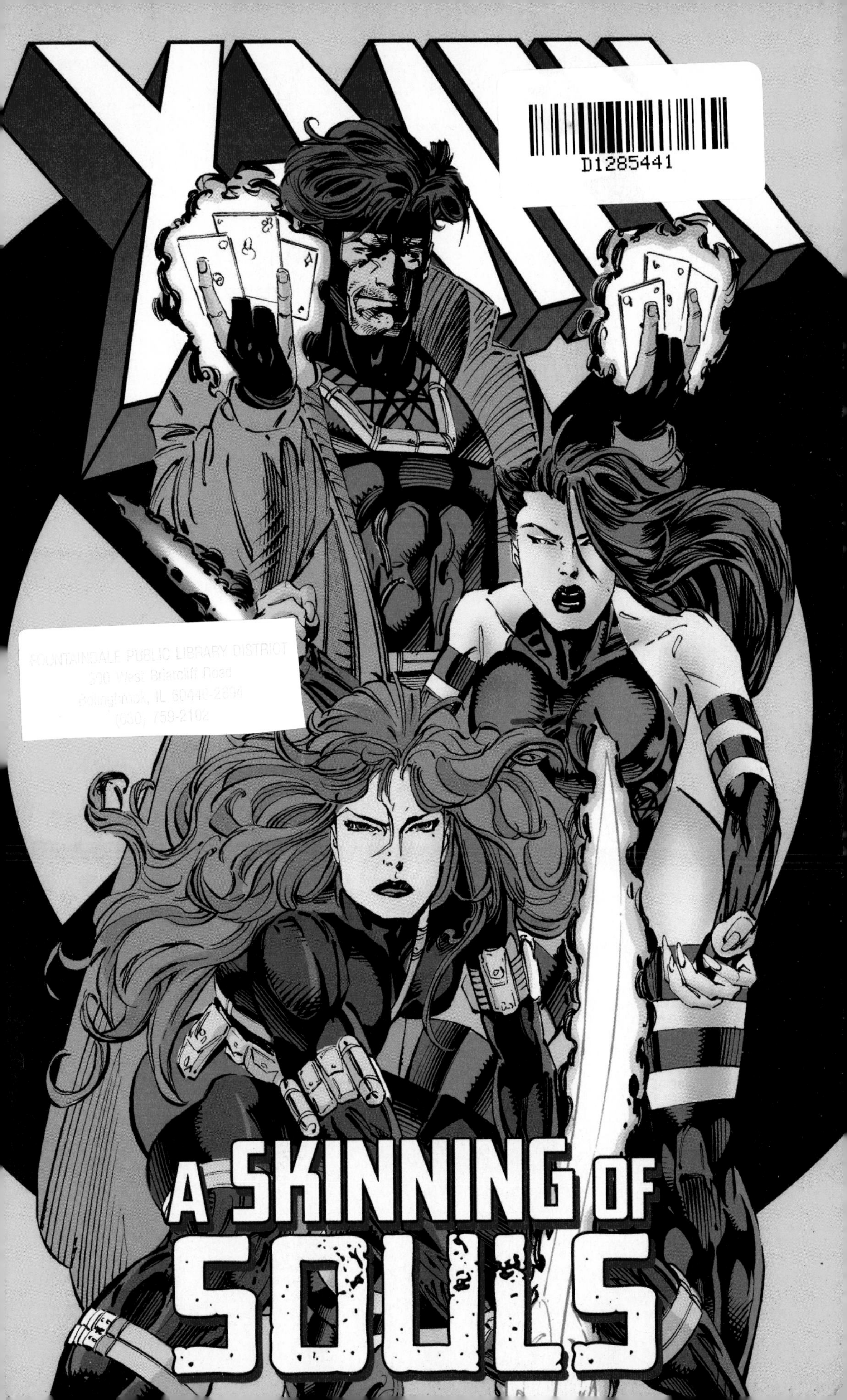
A SKINNING OF
SOULS

WRITERS
FABIAN NICIEZA & **SCOTT LOBDELL** WITH **DAN SLOTT**

PENCILERS
ANDY KUBERT, BRANDON PETERSON, RICHARD BENNETT & **ELIOT R. BROWN** WITH
KRIS RENKEWITZ, HENRY FLINT, STEVE ALEXANDROV & **DARICK ROBERTSON**

INKERS: **MARK PENNINGTON,**
DAN PANOSIAN, BILL SIENKIEWICZ,
RICHARD BENNETT & **ELIOT R. BROWN**
WITH **BOB WIACEK, AL WILLIAMSON,**
MICHAEL GOLDEN, HENRY FLINT,
STEVE ALEXANDROV & **ANDREW PEPOY**

COLORISTS: **JOE ROSAS**
& **PAUL BECTON** WITH **TOM SMITH**
LETTERERS: **CHRIS ELIOPOULOS** & **BILL OAKLEY**
ASSISTANT EDITOR: **LISA PATRICK**
EDITORS: **BOB HARRAS** & **SUZANNE GAFFNEY**
WITH **EVAN SKOLNICK** & **BOBBIE CHASE**

FRONT COVER ARTISTS: **ANDY KUBERT, MARK PENNINGTON** & **MATT MILLA**
BACK COVER ARTISTS: **ANDY KUBERT, MATTHEW RYAN** & **MATT MILLA**

COLLECTION EDITOR: **MARK D. BEAZLEY**
ASSISTANT EDITORS: **ALEX STARBUCK** & **NELSON RIBEIRO**
EDITOR, SPECIAL PROJECTS: **JENNIFER GRÜNWALD**
SENIOR EDITOR, SPECIAL PROJECTS: **JEFF YOUNGQUIST**
RESEARCH & LAYOUT: **JEPH YORK**
PRODUCTION: **COLORTEK, RYAN DEVALL** & **JESSI CHAMPION**
BOOK DESIGNER: **RODOLFO MURAGUCHI**

SVP OF PRINT & DIGITAL PUBLISHING SALES: **DAVID GABRIEL**
EDITOR IN CHIEF: **AXEL ALONSO** CHIEF CREATIVE OFFICER: **JOE QUESADA**
PUBLISHER: **DAN BUCKLEY** EXECUTIVE PRODUCER: **ALAN FINE**

SPECIAL THANKS TO **MIKE HANSEN** & **JOSH SCHWARTZ**

X-MEN: A SKINNING OF SOULS. Contains material originally published in magazine form as X-MEN #17-24, X-MEN: SURVIVAL GUIDE TO THE MANSION and MARVEL SWIMSUIT SPECIAL #2. First printing 2013. ISBN# 978-0-7851-8509-3. Published by MARVEL WORLDWIDE, INC., a subsidiary of MARVEL ENTERTAINMENT, LLC. OFFICE OF PUBLICATION: 135 West 50th Street, New York, NY 10020. Copyright © 1993 and 2013 Marvel Characters, Inc. All rights reserved. All characters featured in this issue and the distinctive names and likenesses thereof, and all related indicia are trademarks of Marvel Characters, Inc. No similarity between any of the names, characters, persons, and/or institutions in this magazine with those of any living or dead person or institution is intended, and any such similarity which may exist is purely coincidental. **Printed in the U.S.A.** ALAN FINE, EVP - Office of the President, Marvel Worldwide, Inc. and EVP & CMO Marvel Characters B.V.; DAN BUCKLEY, Publisher & President - Print, Animation & Digital Divisions; JOE QUESADA, Chief Creative Officer; TOM BREVOORT, SVP of Publishing; DAVID BOGART, SVP of Operations & Procurement, Publishing; C.B. CEBULSKI, SVP of Creator & Content Development; DAVID GABRIEL, SVP of Print & Digital Publishing Sales; JIM O'KEEFE, VP of Operations & Logistics; DAN CARR, Executive Director of Publishing Technology; SUSAN CRESPI, Editorial Operations Manager; ALEX MORALES, Publishing Operations Manager; STAN LEE, Chairman Emeritus. For information regarding advertising in Marvel Comics or on Marvel.com, please contact Niza Disla, Director of Marvel Partnerships, at ndisla@marvel.com. For Marvel subscription inquiries, please call 800-217-9158. **Manufactured between 9/27/2013 and 11/4/2013 by R.R. DONNELLEY, INC., SALEM, VA, USA.**

10 9 8 7 6 5 4 3 2 1

PREVIOUSLY...

The X-Men have suffered several tragedies in recent months. Doug Ramsey, the New Mutants member known as Cypher, was killed in a tragic battle. Soon after, Cyclops' wife Madelyne Pryor was revealed to have been a clone of Jean Grey, created and manipulated by mad geneticist Mr. Sinister specifically to conceive Cyclops' son Nathan Summers. Madelyne snapped, tried to bring a demonic inferno to Earth, and died in the ensuing battle. Colossus' sister Illyana Rasputin, the teleporting Magik, was magically de-aged to childhood in that same event, and returned home to Russia.

Weeks later, Psylocke vanished through the magical Siege Perilous portal. She resurfaced in Japan, having been transformed into an Asian woman via unknown means and manipulated by young crimelord Matsu'o Tsurayaba into becoming the villainous Lady Mandarin. She soon broke free and rejoined the X-Men, but was profoundly changed. Months later, the Darwinist villain Apocalypse and his followers the Dark Riders kidnapped young Nathan Summers, infecting him with a vicious techno-organic virus. A grief-stricken Cyclops was forced to give up Nathan, sending him into the far future in hopes that he could be cured there.

Professor X returned from a lengthy sojourn in outer space, and the X-Men soon faced Magneto — a battle that saw the villain seemingly die, and Banshee quit the team. Matsu'o Tsurayaba's crimelord rival Shinobi Shaw joined the Upstarts, a secretive mutant-killing group moderated by the telepathic Gamesmaster, which wiped out the Hellfire Club's teenage Hellions. Matsu'o gained control of Wolverine's old foe, Russian super-agent Omega Red, and orchestrated the death of Wolverine's true love Mariko Yashida. Tragedy struck Wolverine a second time when he was forced to witness his former lover Silver Fox's death — and soon after, Gambit's estranged wife Bella Donna appeared to die in battle.

Romances bloomed and faded as Storm and Forge split apart, as did Iceman and Opal Tanaka, even as Psylocke found herself attracted to Cyclops, who in turn had rekindled his longtime romance with Jean Grey. The X-Men discovered Colossus' brother Mikhail Rasputin, long thought dead, still alive in another dimension. However, Mikhail's time there had driven him mad, and he soon used his reality-warping powers to kill himself. Meanwhile, the mysterious Cable transformed the New Mutants into the outlaw team X-Force, who clashed repeatedly with the villainous Stryfe and his Mutant Liberation Front. It was soon revealed that both Cable and Stryfe were from the future, and that both men were nearly mirror images of one another.

Stryfe orchestrated a complicated revenge plot against the X-Men, shooting Professor X and hiring Mr. Sinister to kidnap Cyclops and Jean Grey for him. Following Stryfe's complex trail, the X-Men captured X-Force and clashed with Apocalypse, the Dark Riders and the MLF. Rogue's eyes were badly injured, and Mr. Sinister faked his death and retreated. Stryfe tormented Cyclops and Jean, accusing them of betraying and abandoning him, and hinting that he was Cyclops' son Nathan. During the final battle on the moon, Apocalypse seemingly died and Cable and Stryfe were lost, sucked into a time portal before either man's true identity was confirmed. And when Mr. Sinister opened his "payment" from Stryfe, he inadvertently released a strange gas into the atmosphere...

Now, shaken by recent changes, revelations and familial losses, the X-Men try to pick up the pieces and move on. Cyclops, who already lost both parents as a child, grapples with having lost his wife and son. Wolverine has traveled to Russia, tying up a loose end from his secret agent days — and a contingent of X-Men have just picked him up on their way to visit Colossus' family...

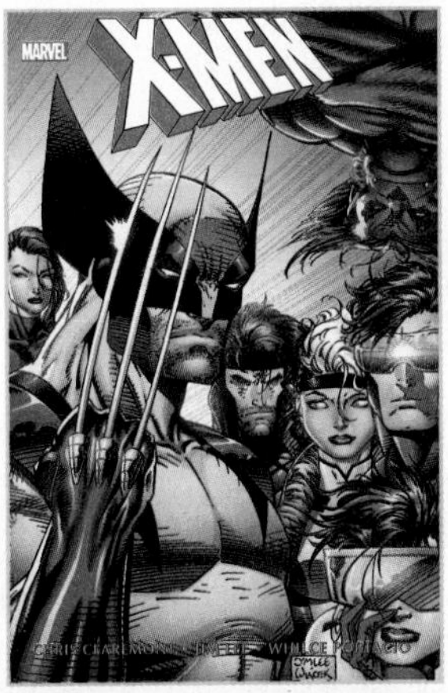
MARVEL
X-MEN

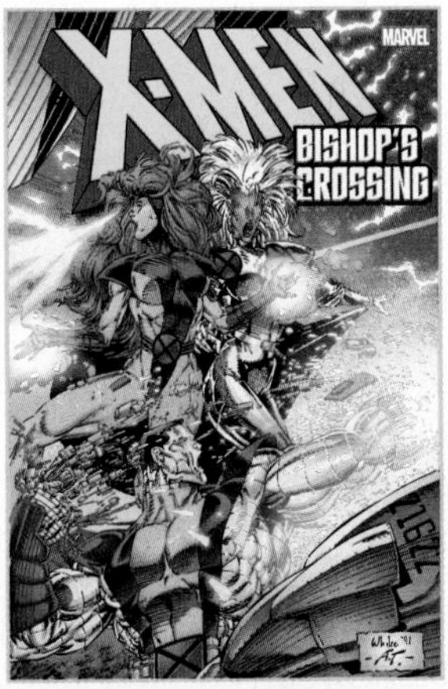
X-MEN
MARVEL
BISHOP'S CROSSING

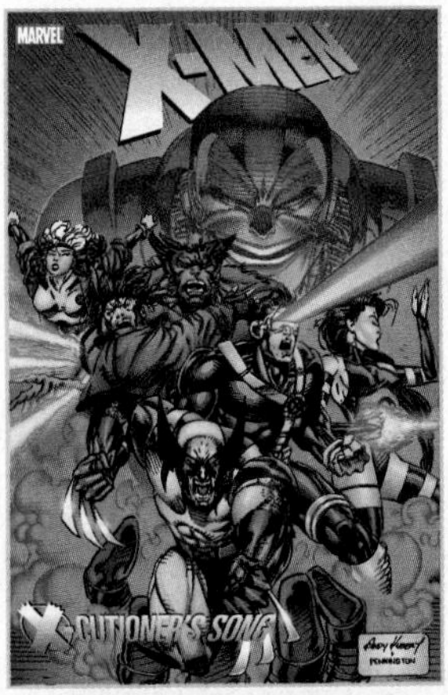
MARVEL
X-MEN
X-CUTIONER'S SONG

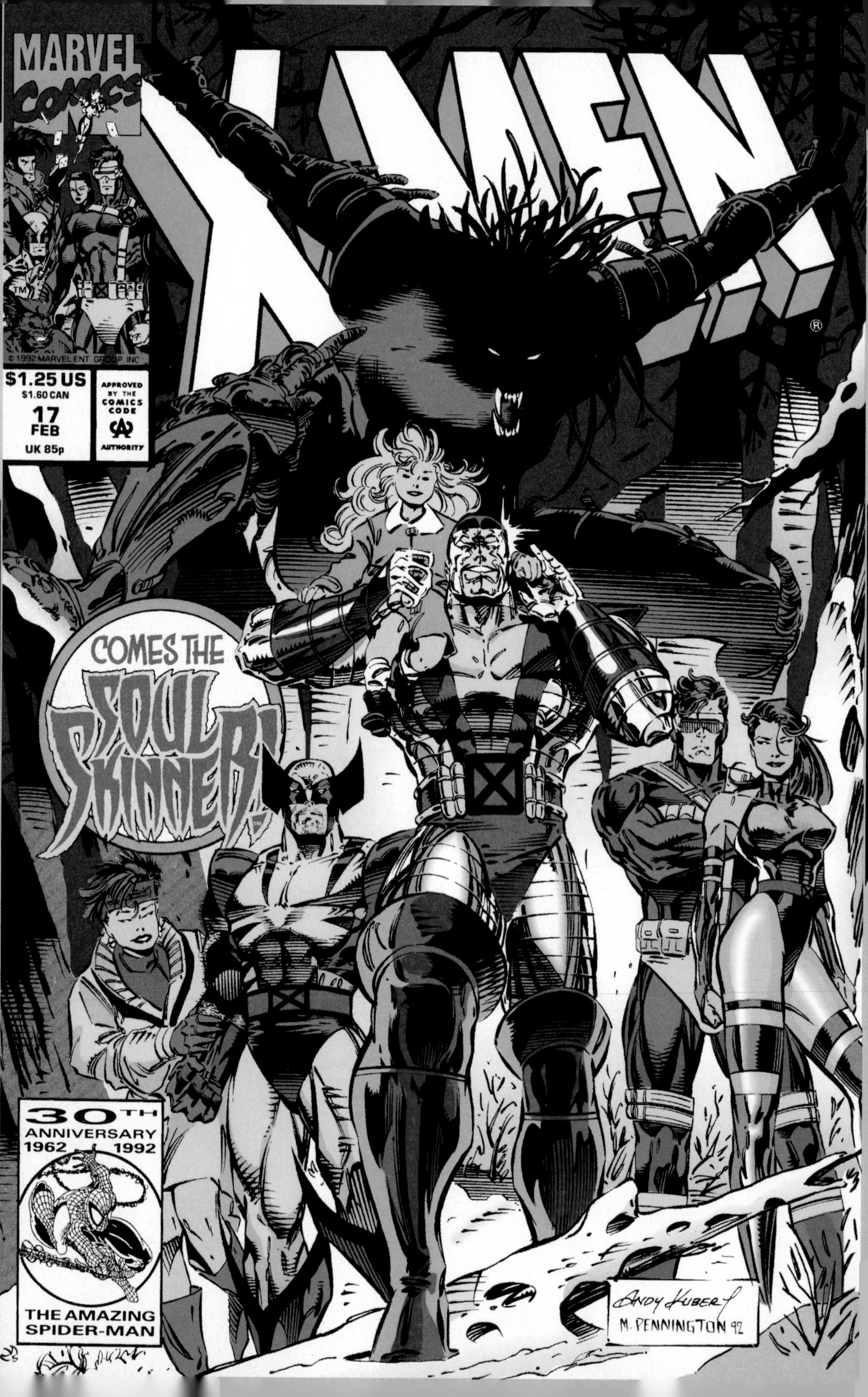
MARVEL COMICS
X-MEN
© 1992 MARVEL ENT. GROUP, INC.
$1.25 US
$1.60 CAN
17
FEB
UK 85p
APPROVED BY THE COMICS CODE AUTHORITY
COMES THE SOUL SKINNER!
30TH ANNIVERSARY 1962 1992
THE AMAZING SPIDER-MAN
ANDY KUBERT
M. PENNINGTON 92

STAN LEE PRESENTS A TALE OF THE X-MEN

A SKINNING OF SOULS
PART ONE: WAITING FOR THE RIPENING

| FABIAN NICIEZA WRITER | ANDY KUBERT PENCILER | MARK PENNINGTON INKER | CHRIS ELIOPOULOS LETTERER | JOE ROSAS COLORIST | BOB HARRAS EDITOR | TOM DeFALCO EDITOR IN CHIEF |

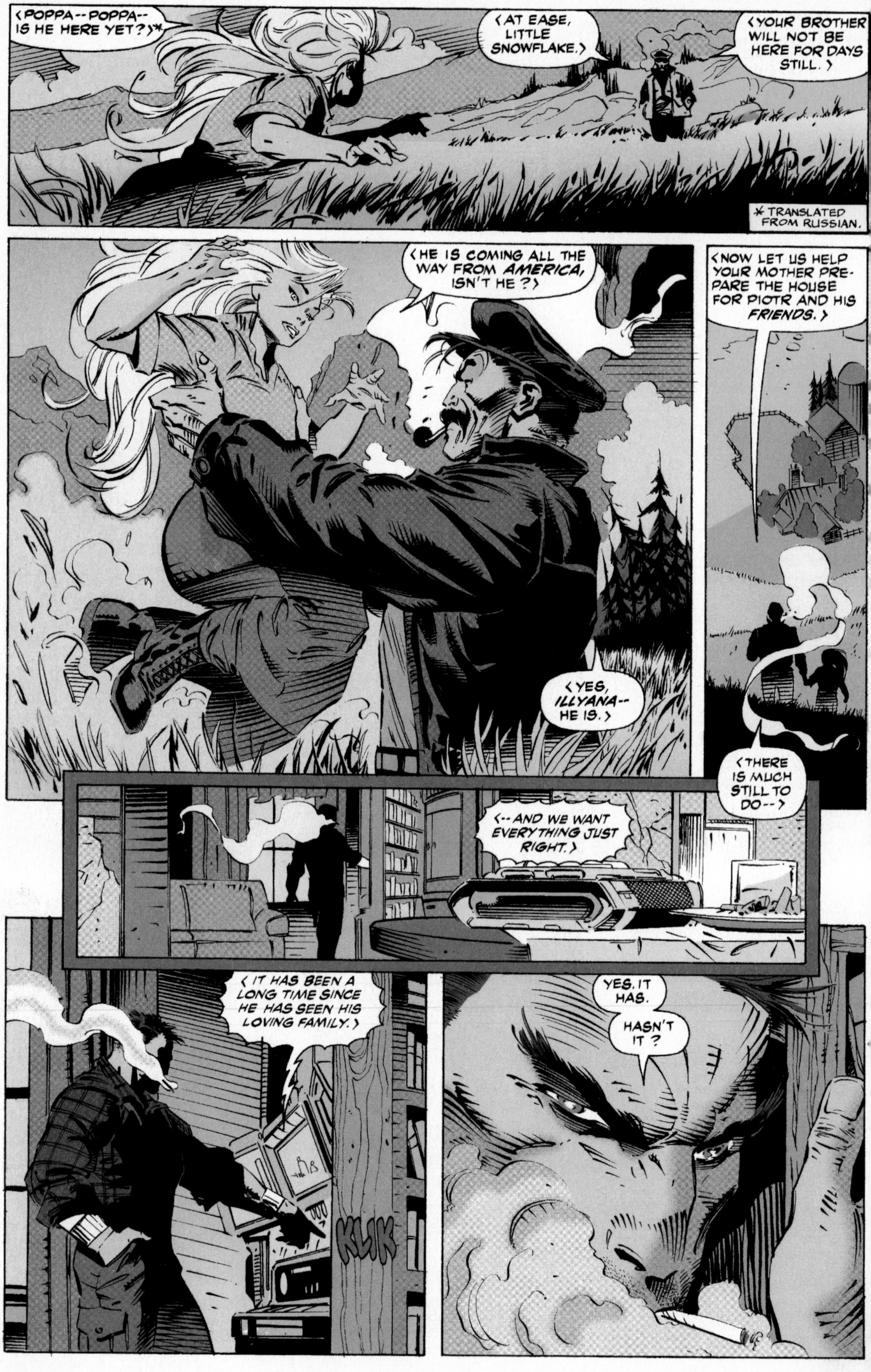
<POPPA--POPPA-- IS HE HERE YET?>*
<AT EASE, LITTLE SNOWFLAKE.>
<YOUR BROTHER WILL NOT BE HERE FOR DAYS STILL.>
*TRANSLATED FROM RUSSIAN.
<HE IS COMING ALL THE WAY FROM AMERICA, ISN'T HE?>
<YES, ILLYANA-- HE IS.>
<NOW LET US HELP YOUR MOTHER PREPARE THE HOUSE FOR PIOTR AND HIS FRIENDS.>
<THERE IS MUCH STILL TO DO-->
<--AND WE WANT EVERYTHING JUST RIGHT.>
<IT HAS BEEN A LONG TIME SINCE HE HAS SEEN HIS LOVING FAMILY.>
KLIK
YES. IT HAS.
HASN'T IT?

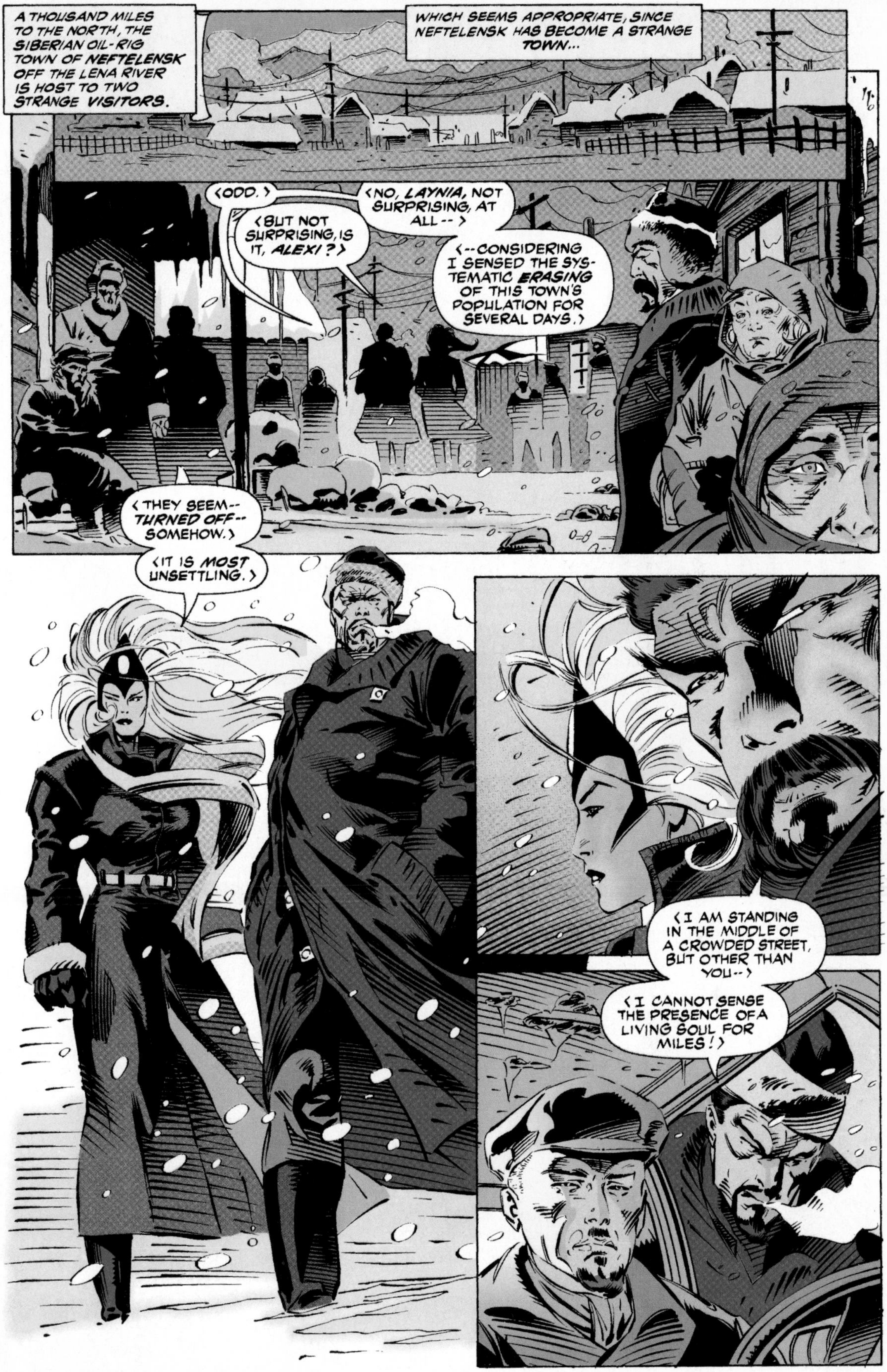
A THOUSAND MILES TO THE NORTH, THE SIBERIAN OIL-RIG TOWN OF NEFTELENSK OFF THE LENA RIVER IS HOST TO TWO STRANGE VISITORS.
WHICH SEEMS APPROPRIATE, SINCE NEFTELENSK HAS BECOME A STRANGE TOWN...
‹ODD.›
‹BUT NOT SURPRISING, IS IT, ALEXI?›
‹NO, LAYNIA, NOT SURPRISING, AT ALL--›
‹--CONSIDERING I SENSED THE SYSTEMATIC ERASING OF THIS TOWN'S POPULATION FOR SEVERAL DAYS.›
‹THEY SEEM--TURNED OFF--SOMEHOW.›
‹IT IS MOST UNSETTLING.›
‹I AM STANDING IN THE MIDDLE OF A CROWDED STREET, BUT OTHER THAN YOU--›
‹I CANNOT SENSE THE PRESENCE OF A LIVING SOUL FOR MILES!›

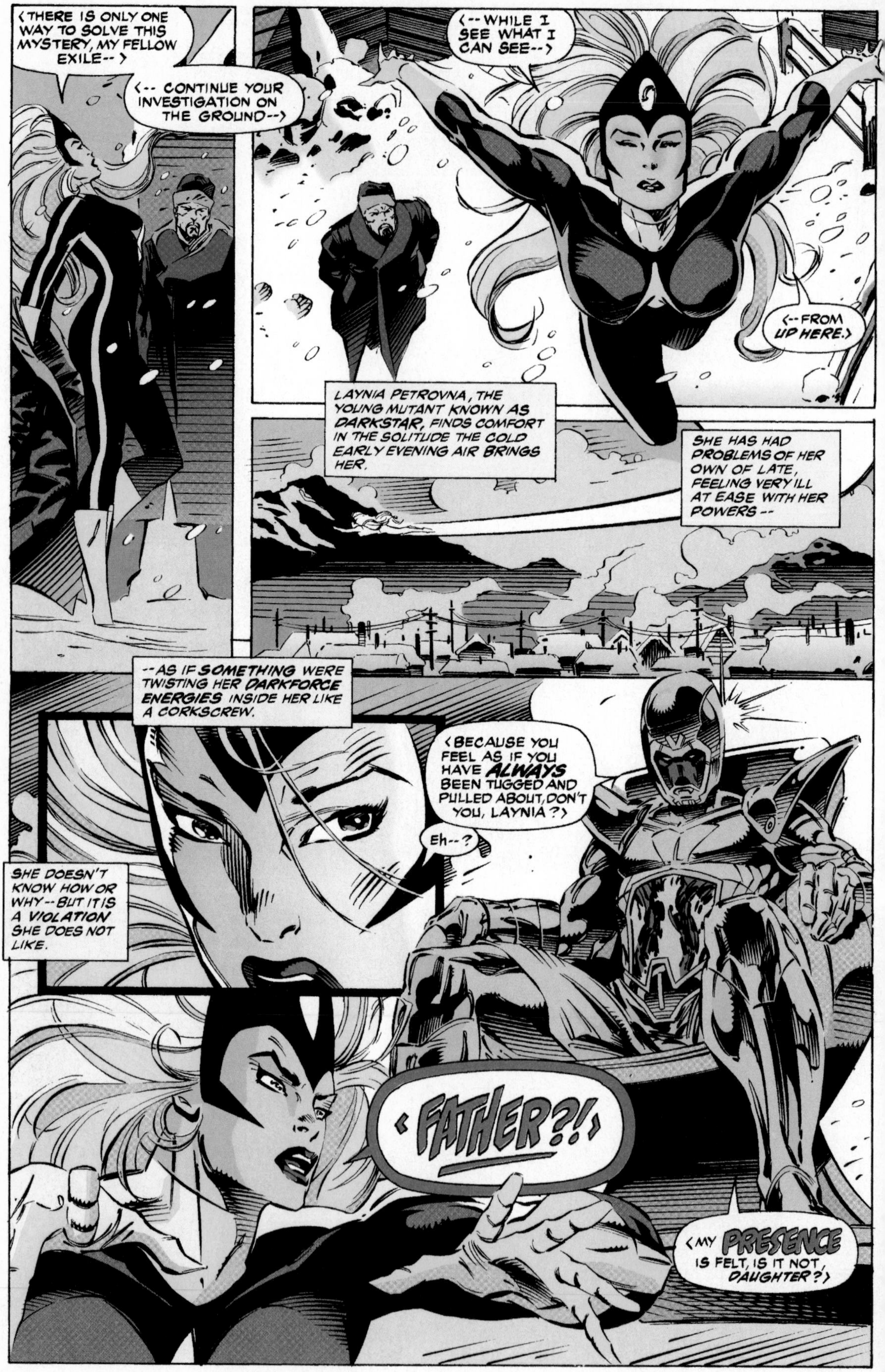
‹THERE IS ONLY ONE WAY TO SOLVE THIS MYSTERY, MY FELLOW EXILE--›
‹-- CONTINUE YOUR INVESTIGATION ON THE GROUND--›
‹--WHILE I SEE WHAT I CAN SEE--›
‹--FROM UP HERE.›
LAYNIA PETROVNA, THE YOUNG MUTANT KNOWN AS DARKSTAR, FINDS COMFORT IN THE SOLITUDE THE COLD EARLY EVENING AIR BRINGS HER.
SHE HAS HAD PROBLEMS OF HER OWN OF LATE, FEELING VERY ILL AT EASE WITH HER POWERS --
--AS IF SOMETHING WERE TWISTING HER DARKFORCE ENERGIES INSIDE HER LIKE A CORKSCREW.
SHE DOESN'T KNOW HOW OR WHY--BUT IT IS A VIOLATION SHE DOES NOT LIKE.
‹BECAUSE YOU FEEL AS IF YOU HAVE ALWAYS BEEN TUGGED AND PULLED ABOUT, DON'T YOU, LAYNIA?›
Eh--?
‹FATHER?!›
‹MY PRESENCE IS FELT, IS IT NOT, DAUGHTER?›

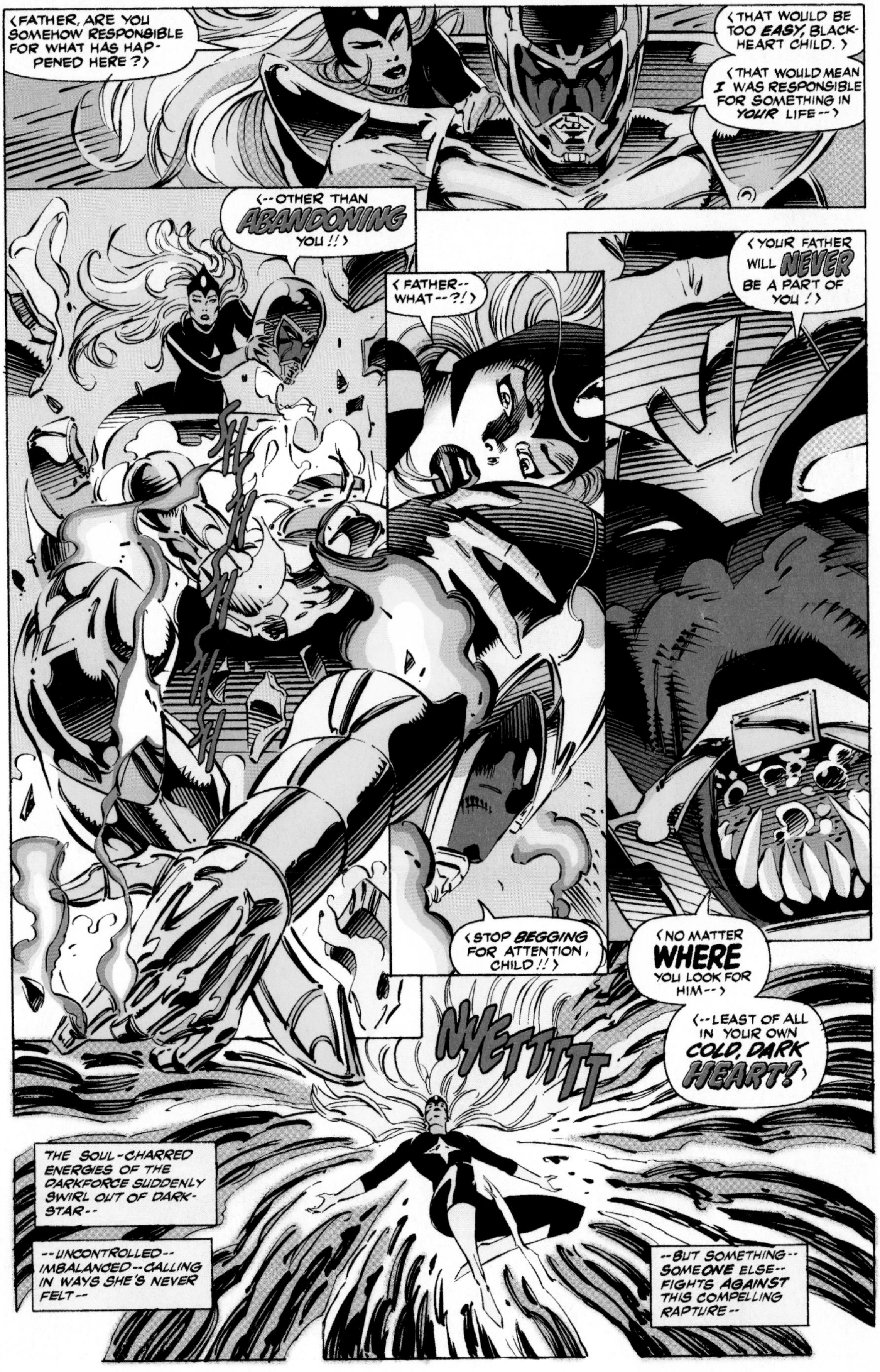
‹FATHER, ARE YOU SOMEHOW RESPONSIBLE FOR WHAT HAS HAP-PENED HERE?›
‹THAT WOULD BE TOO EASY, BLACK-HEART CHILD.›
‹THAT WOULD MEAN I WAS RESPONSIBLE FOR SOMETHING IN YOUR LIFE--›
‹--OTHER THAN ABANDONING YOU!!›
‹FATHER-- WHAT--?!›
‹YOUR FATHER WILL NEVER BE A PART OF YOU!›
‹STOP BEGGING FOR ATTENTION, CHILD!!›
‹NO MATTER WHERE YOU LOOK FOR HIM--›
NYETTTTTT
‹--LEAST OF ALL IN YOUR OWN COLD, DARK HEART!›
THE SOUL-CHARRED ENERGIES OF THE DARKFORCE SUDDENLY SWIRL OUT OF DARK-STAR--
--UNCONTROLLED--IMBALANCED--CALLING IN WAYS SHE'S NEVER FELT--
--BUT SOMETHING--SOMEONE ELSE--FIGHTS AGAINST THIS COMPELLING RAPTURE--

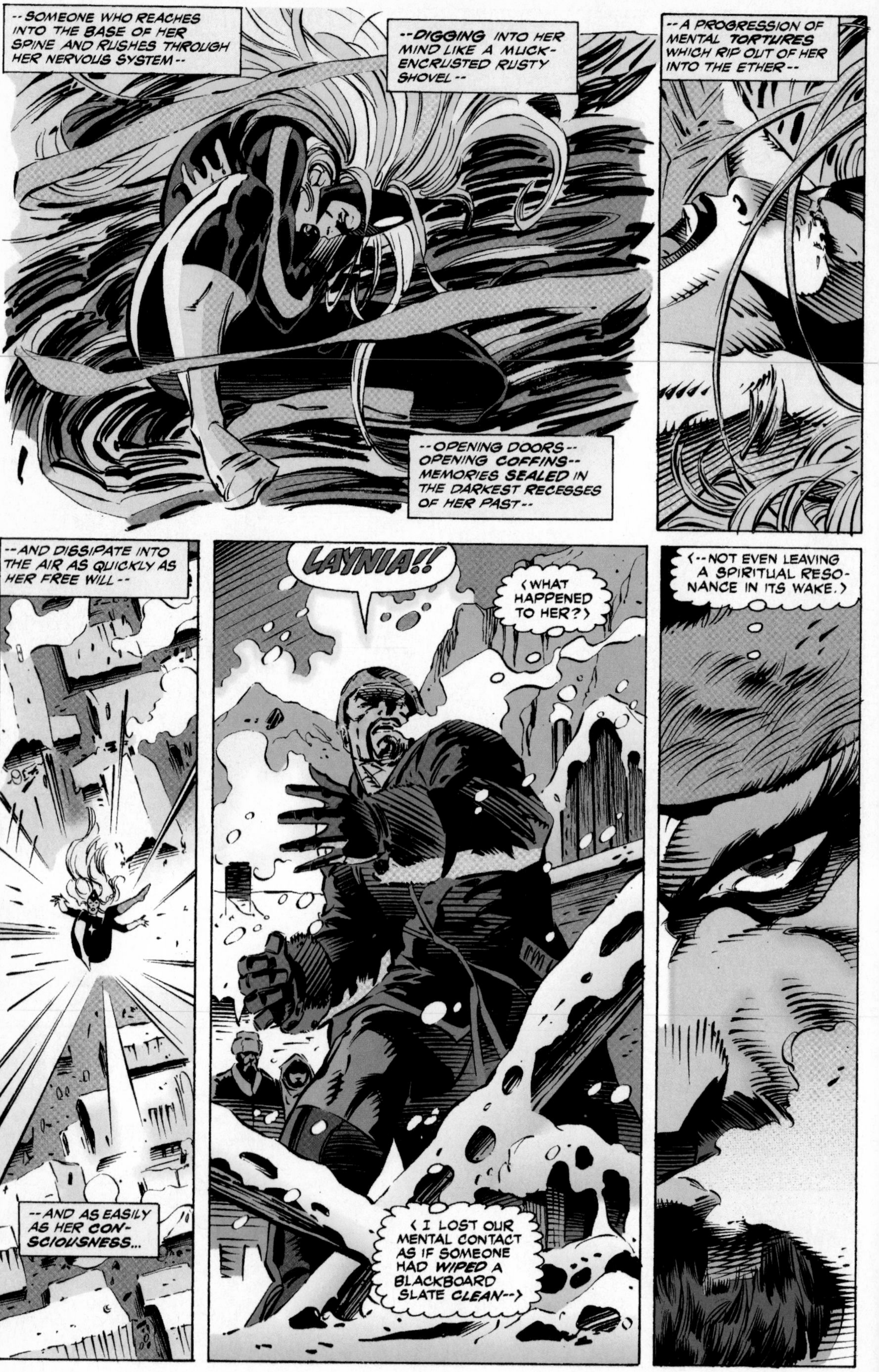
--SOMEONE WHO REACHES INTO THE BASE OF HER SPINE AND RUSHES THROUGH HER NERVOUS SYSTEM--
--DIGGING INTO HER MIND LIKE A MUCK-ENCRUSTED RUSTY SHOVEL--
--OPENING DOORS--OPENING COFFINS--MEMORIES SEALED IN THE DARKEST RECESSES OF HER PAST--
--A PROGRESSION OF MENTAL TORTURES WHICH RIP OUT OF HER INTO THE ETHER--
--AND DISSIPATE INTO THE AIR AS QUICKLY AS HER FREE WILL--
--AND AS EASILY AS HER CONSCIOUSNESS...
LAYNIA!!
<WHAT HAPPENED TO HER?>
<I LOST OUR MENTAL CONTACT AS IF SOMEONE HAD WIPED A BLACKBOARD SLATE CLEAN-->
<--NOT EVEN LEAVING A SPIRITUAL RESONANCE IN ITS WAKE.>

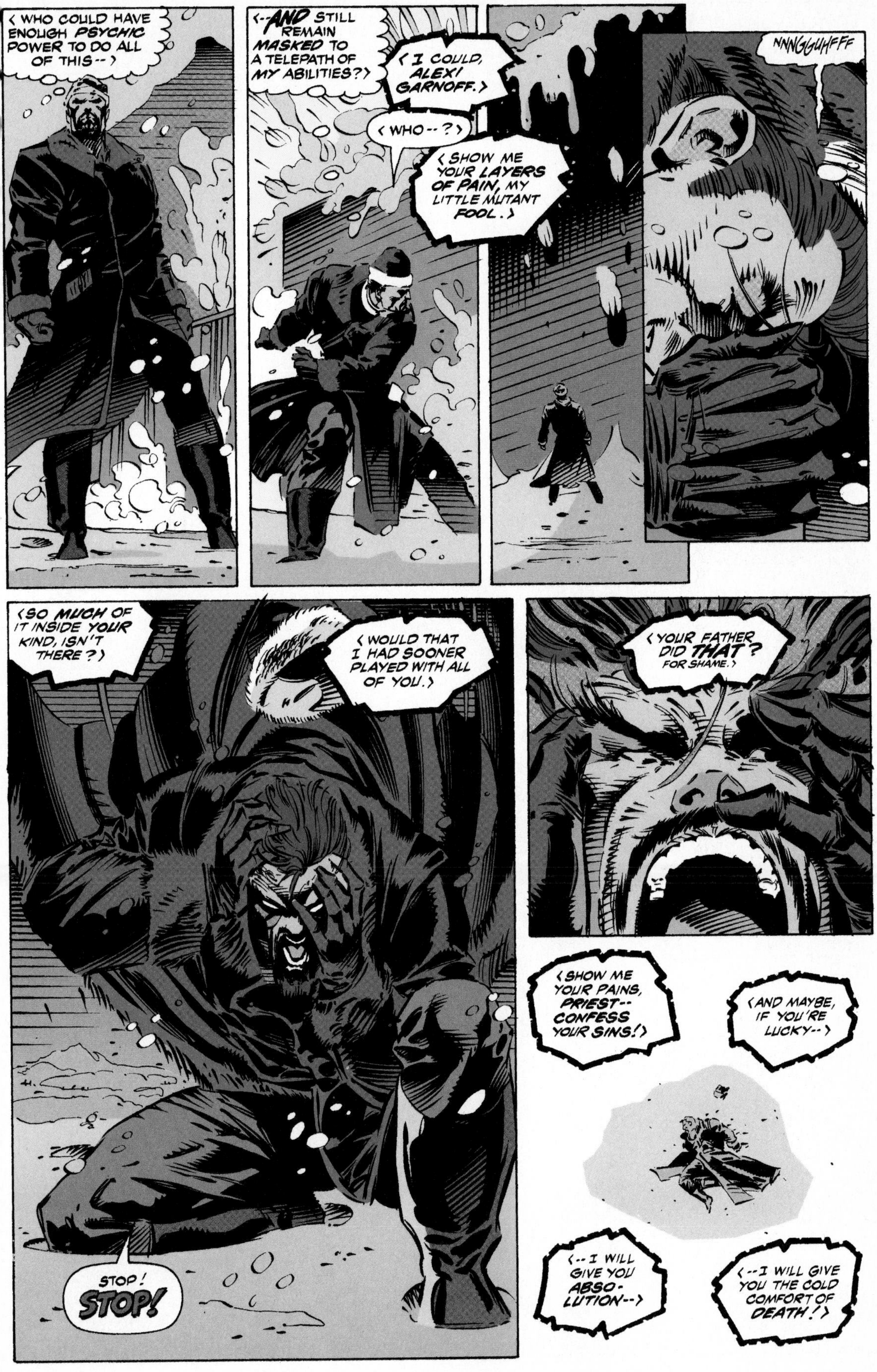

‹ WHO COULD HAVE ENOUGH PSYCHIC POWER TO DO ALL OF THIS-- ›
‹--AND STILL REMAIN MASKED TO A TELEPATH OF MY ABILITIES?›
‹ I COULD, ALEX! GARNOFF. ›
‹ WHO--? ›
‹ SHOW ME YOUR LAYERS OF PAIN, MY LITTLE MUTANT FOOL. ›
NNNGGUHFFF
‹SO MUCH OF IT INSIDE YOUR KIND, ISN'T THERE?›
‹ WOULD THAT I HAD SOONER PLAYED WITH ALL OF YOU! ›
STOP! STOP!
‹ YOUR FATHER DID THAT? FOR SHAME. ›
‹ SHOW ME YOUR PAINS, PRIEST-- CONFESS YOUR SINS! ›
‹AND MAYBE, IF YOU'RE LUCKY--›
‹--I WILL GIVE YOU ABSO-LUTION--›
‹--I WILL GIVE YOU THE COLD COMFORT OF DEATH!›

THREE DAYS LATER, RED SQUARE, MOSCOW...

‹ARE YOU *SURE* ABOUT THIS, *FYODR*?›

‹*ABSOLUTELY*, *VAZHIN.*›

‹THE *ENTIRE* TOWN HAS BEEN CO-OPTED.›

‹*INITIAL* REPORTS INDICATE TWO OF THOSE MUTIE RENE-GADE *EXILES* WENT IN TO FIND OUT WHAT HAPPENED.›

‹WHICH *"MUTIES"* WERE THEY, COLONEL-GENERAL *SHATALOV*?›

‹WHO KNOWS? THEY'RE ALL THE SAME TO ME.›

‹FYODR, YOU *KNOW* HOW I FEEL ABOUT THIS BIGOT...›

‹SHATALOV IS IN CHARGE OF THE *REMONT** PROGRAM, ALEXEI.›

‹YES, I KNOW! AND YOU OF THE *PEOPLE'S PROTECTORATE.**›

* TWO GROUPS REPRESENTING THE REMAINDERS OF THE FORMER *SOVIET SUPER SOLDIERS.* -- BOB-USHKA

‹ARE *EITHER* OF YOU PREPARED TO MOBILIZE YOUR FORCES TO HANDLE THE SITUATION IN NEFTELENSK?›

‹HARDLY. REMONT IS NOT PERMITTED TO WORK INTERNAL MATTERS--›

‹--AND I DON'T FEEL LIKE LOSING MY GROUP!›

‹SO YOU WANT SOMEONE EMINENTLY *EXPENDABLE*--›

‹--WHO WOULD *ONLY* GO INTO A DANGER-ZONE FOR *SELF-SERVING* REASONS, RIGHT?›

‹IT WILL REQUIRE SOME CONVINCING...›

‹...BUT I WILL GET **OMEGA RED** FOR YOU.›

12

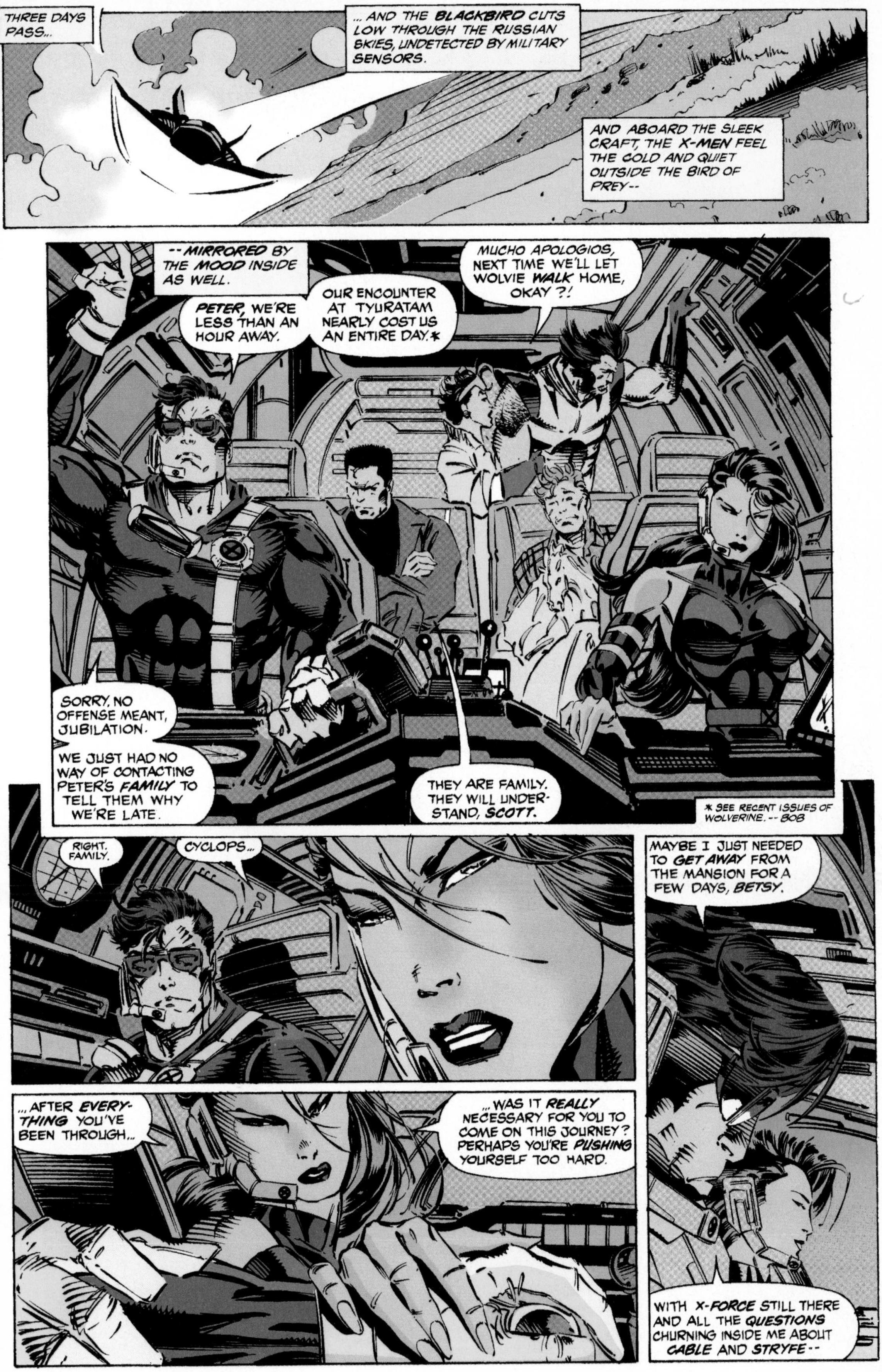
THREE DAYS PASS...
...AND THE BLACKBIRD CUTS LOW THROUGH THE RUSSIAN SKIES, UNDETECTED BY MILITARY SENSORS.
AND ABOARD THE SLEEK CRAFT, THE X-MEN FEEL THE COLD AND QUIET OUTSIDE THE BIRD OF PREY--
--MIRRORED BY THE MOOD INSIDE AS WELL.
PETER, WE'RE LESS THAN AN HOUR AWAY.
OUR ENCOUNTER AT TYURATAM NEARLY COST US AN ENTIRE DAY.*
MUCHO APOLOGIOS, NEXT TIME WE'LL LET WOLVIE WALK HOME, OKAY?!
SORRY, NO OFFENSE MEANT, JUBILATION.
WE JUST HAD NO WAY OF CONTACTING PETER'S FAMILY TO TELL THEM WHY WE'RE LATE.
THEY ARE FAMILY. THEY WILL UNDERSTAND, SCOTT.
* SEE RECENT ISSUES OF WOLVERINE. -- BOB
RIGHT. FAMILY.
CYCLOPS...
...AFTER EVERYTHING YOU'VE BEEN THROUGH...
...WAS IT REALLY NECESSARY FOR YOU TO COME ON THIS JOURNEY? PERHAPS YOU'RE PUSHING YOURSELF TOO HARD.
MAYBE I JUST NEEDED TO GET AWAY FROM THE MANSION FOR A FEW DAYS, BETSY.
WITH X-FORCE STILL THERE AND ALL THE QUESTIONS CHURNING INSIDE ME ABOUT CABLE AND STRYFE--

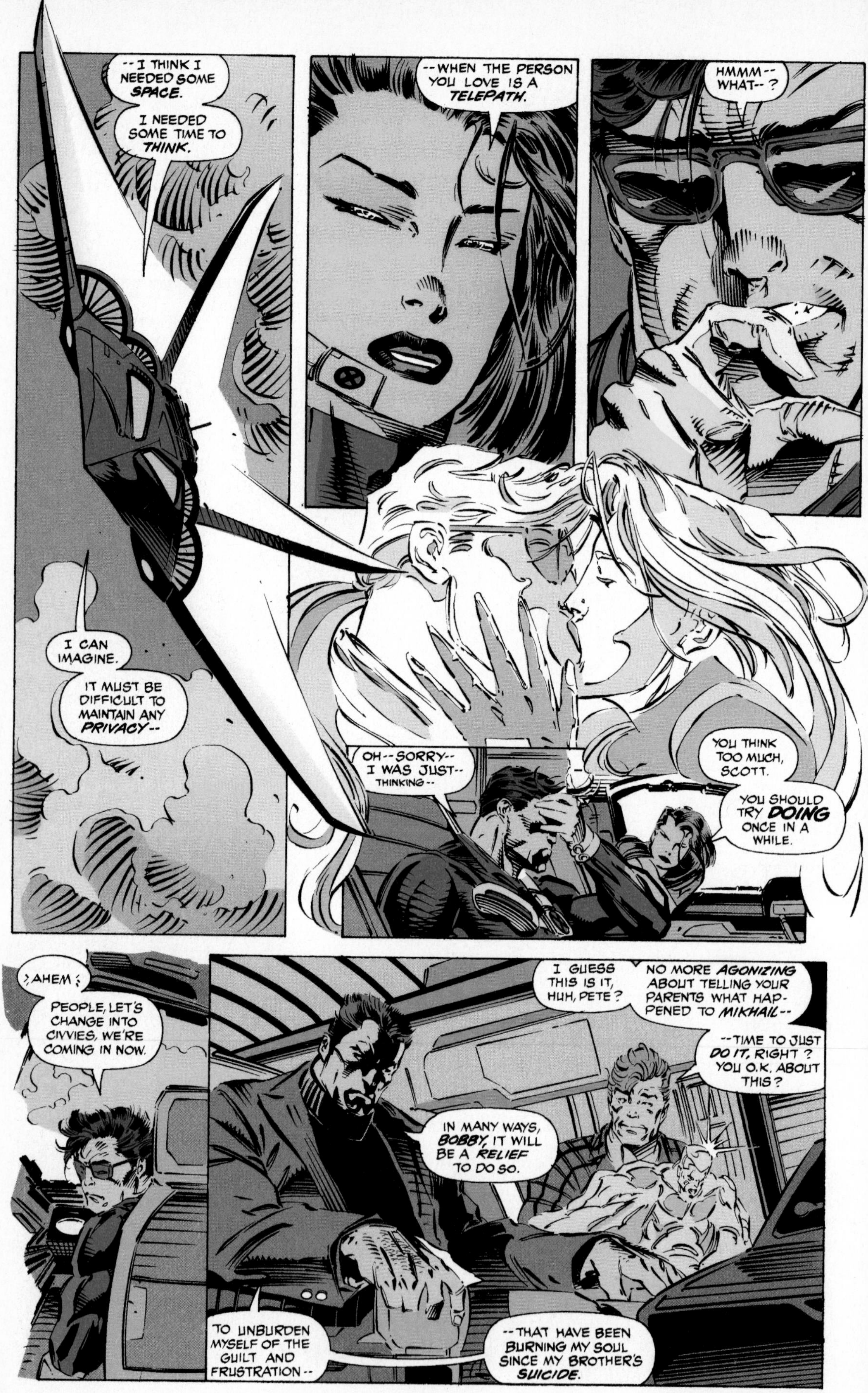
-- I THINK I NEEDED SOME SPACE.
I NEEDED SOME TIME TO THINK.
-- WHEN THE PERSON YOU LOVE IS A TELEPATH.
HMMM -- WHAT -- ?
I CAN IMAGINE.
IT MUST BE DIFFICULT TO MAINTAIN ANY PRIVACY --
OH -- SORRY -- I WAS JUST -- THINKING --
YOU THINK TOO MUCH, SCOTT.
YOU SHOULD TRY DOING ONCE IN A WHILE.
AHEM
PEOPLE, LET'S CHANGE INTO CIVVIES, WE'RE COMING IN NOW.
I GUESS THIS IS IT, HUH, PETE?
NO MORE AGONIZING ABOUT TELLING YOUR PARENTS WHAT HAPPENED TO MIKHAIL --
-- TIME TO JUST DO IT, RIGHT? YOU O.K. ABOUT THIS?
IN MANY WAYS, BOBBY, IT WILL BE A RELIEF TO DO SO.
TO UNBURDEN MYSELF OF THE GUILT AND FRUSTRATION --
-- THAT HAVE BEEN BURNING MY SOUL SINCE MY BROTHER'S SUICIDE.

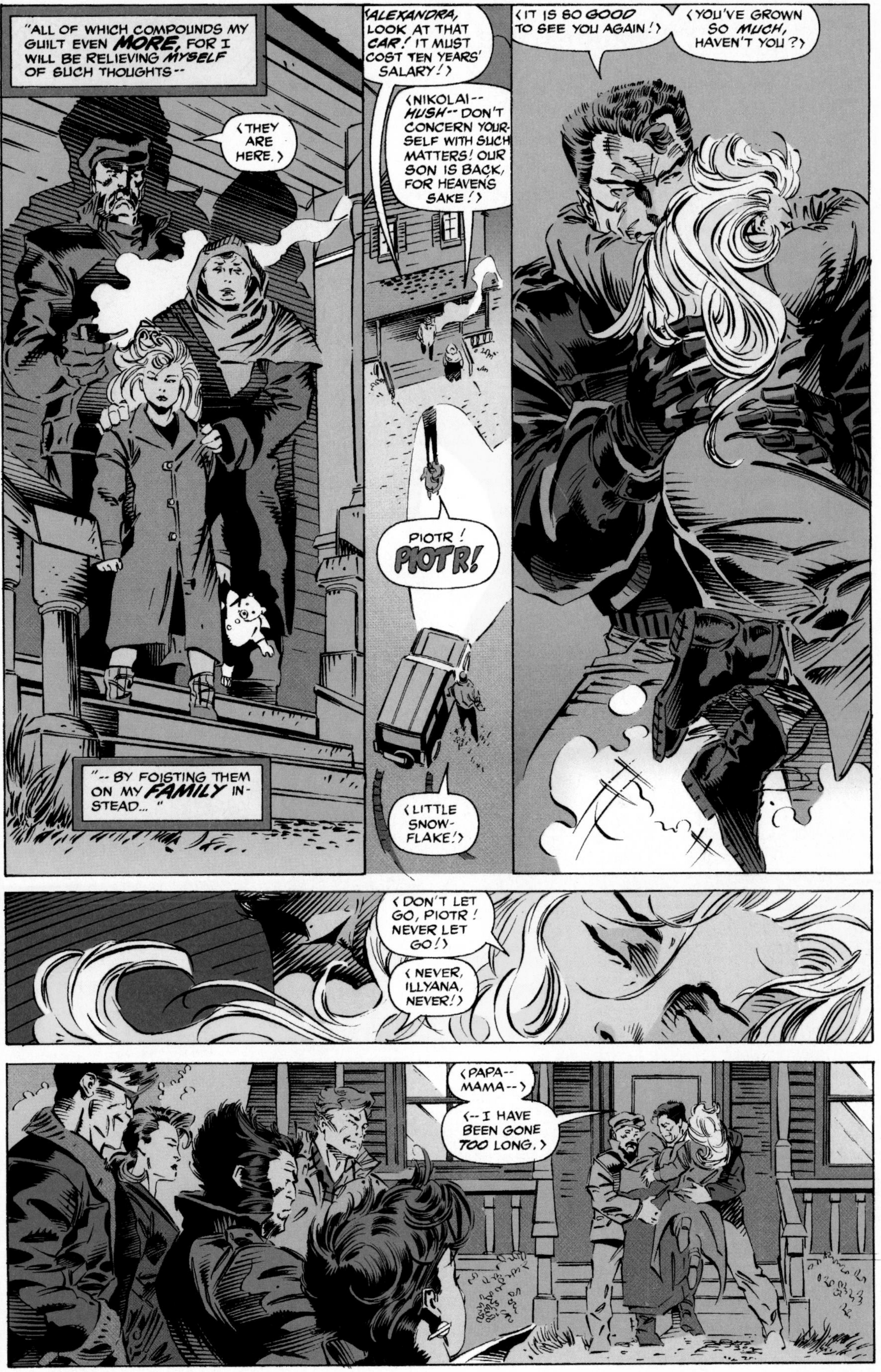
"ALL OF WHICH COMPOUNDS MY GUILT EVEN MORE, FOR I WILL BE RELIEVING MYSELF OF SUCH THOUGHTS--
‹THEY ARE HERE.›
"--BY FOISTING THEM ON MY FAMILY INSTEAD..."
‹ALEXANDRA, LOOK AT THAT CAR! IT MUST COST TEN YEARS' SALARY!›
‹NIKOLAI--HUSH--DON'T CONCERN YOURSELF WITH SUCH MATTERS! OUR SON IS BACK, FOR HEAVEN'S SAKE!›
PIOTR! PIOTR!
‹LITTLE SNOWFLAKE!›
‹IT IS SO GOOD TO SEE YOU AGAIN!›
‹YOU'VE GROWN SO MUCH, HAVEN'T YOU?›
‹DON'T LET GO, PIOTR! NEVER LET GO!›
‹NEVER, ILLYANA, NEVER!›
‹PAPA--MAMA--›
‹--I HAVE BEEN GONE TOO LONG.›

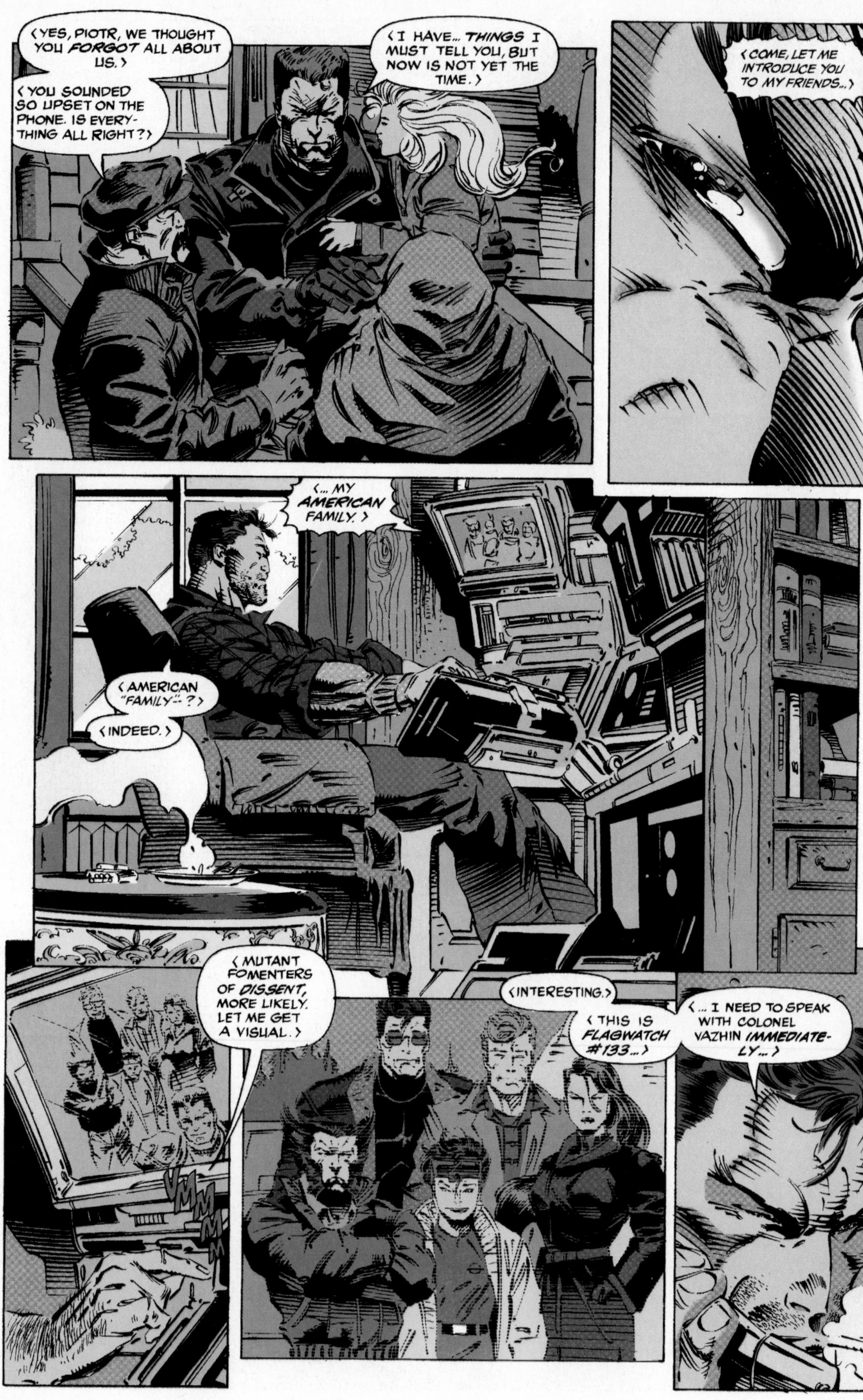
‹YES, PIOTR, WE THOUGHT YOU FORGOT ALL ABOUT US.›
‹YOU SOUNDED SO UPSET ON THE PHONE. IS EVERYTHING ALL RIGHT?›
‹I HAVE... THINGS I MUST TELL YOU, BUT NOW IS NOT YET THE TIME.›
‹COME, LET ME INTRODUCE YOU TO MY FRIENDS...›
‹... MY AMERICAN FAMILY.›
‹AMERICAN "FAMILY"--?›
‹INDEED.›
‹MUTANT FOMENTERS OF DISSENT, MORE LIKELY. LET ME GET A VISUAL.›
VMMMM
‹INTERESTING.›
‹THIS IS FLAGWATCH #133...›
‹... I NEED TO SPEAK WITH COLONEL VAZHIN IMMEDIATELY...›

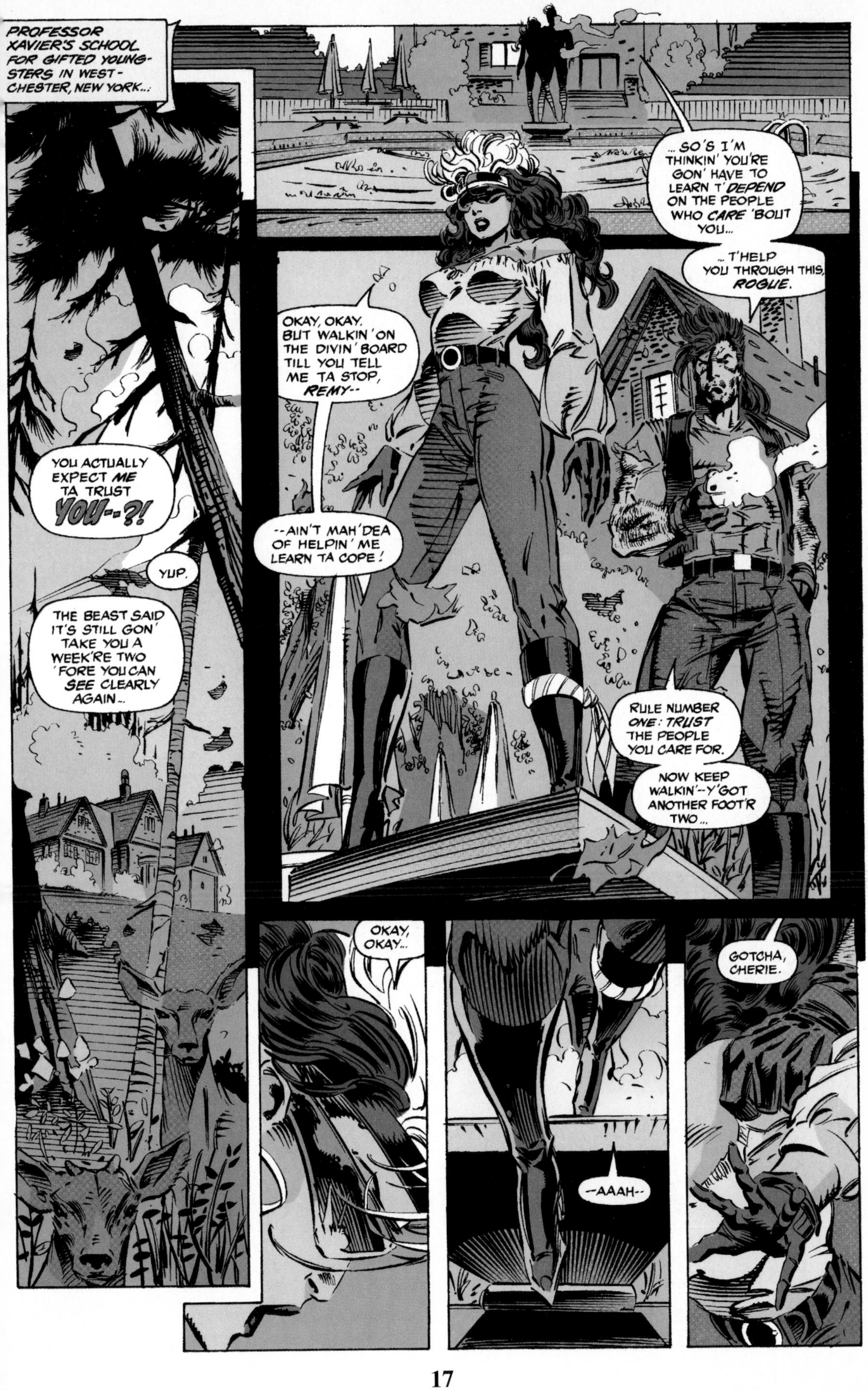
PROFESSOR XAVIER'S SCHOOL FOR GIFTED YOUNGSTERS IN WESTCHESTER, NEW YORK...:
...SO'S I'M THINKIN' YOU'RE GON' HAVE TO LEARN T' DEPEND ON THE PEOPLE WHO CARE 'BOUT YOU...
...T'HELP YOU THROUGH THIS, ROGUE.
OKAY, OKAY. BUT WALKIN' ON THE DIVIN' BOARD TILL YOU TELL ME TA STOP, REMY--
--AIN'T MAH 'DEA OF HELPIN' ME LEARN TA COPE!
YOU ACTUALLY EXPECT ME TA TRUST YOU--?!
YUP.
THE BEAST SAID IT'S STILL GON' TAKE YOU A WEEK'RE TWO 'FORE YOU CAN SEE CLEARLY AGAIN...
RULE NUMBER ONE: TRUST THE PEOPLE YOU CARE FOR.
NOW KEEP WALKIN'--Y'GOT ANOTHER FOOT'R TWO...
OKAY, OKAY...
--AAAH--
GOTCHA, CHERIE.

RULE NUMBER *TWO:* YOU'RE VERY VULNERABLE RIGHT NOW, SO DON' TRUST *ANYONE.*

YOU PLAY A DANGEROUS GAME, *GAMBIT.* BUT THAT SEEMS YOUR SPECIALTY, DOESN'T IT? OF *ALL* MY X-MEN, YOU ARE THE MOST *UNKNOWN* TO ME...

...YOU WANT ROGUE'S LOVE, BUT YOU DON'T WANT TO FALL *IN LOVE* WITH HER, DO YOU?

YOU WANT HER TO DECLARE HERSELF YOURS, BUT YOU WILL NOT *COMMIT TO* HER. WHY?

A DANGEROUS GAME FOR HER, BUT EVEN MORE SO, I FEAR, FOR *YOU.*

CHARLES, DO YOU HAVE A MOMENT?

HANK--?

IF IT'S ABOUT MY REHABILITATION, I PROMISE YOU I AM FOLLOWING YOUR--

I KNOW, PROFESSOR, IT'S NOT ABOUT THAT. IT'S *PERSONAL,* ACTUALLY. IT'S ABOUT ME. I --

HANK, PROFESSOR, PLEASE EXCUSE OUR INTER-RUPTION...

...BUT WE MUST DISCUSS SOME MATTERS WITH *SAM* AND *JAMES.*

ORORO? WHAT IS IT?

HANK AND I WERE--

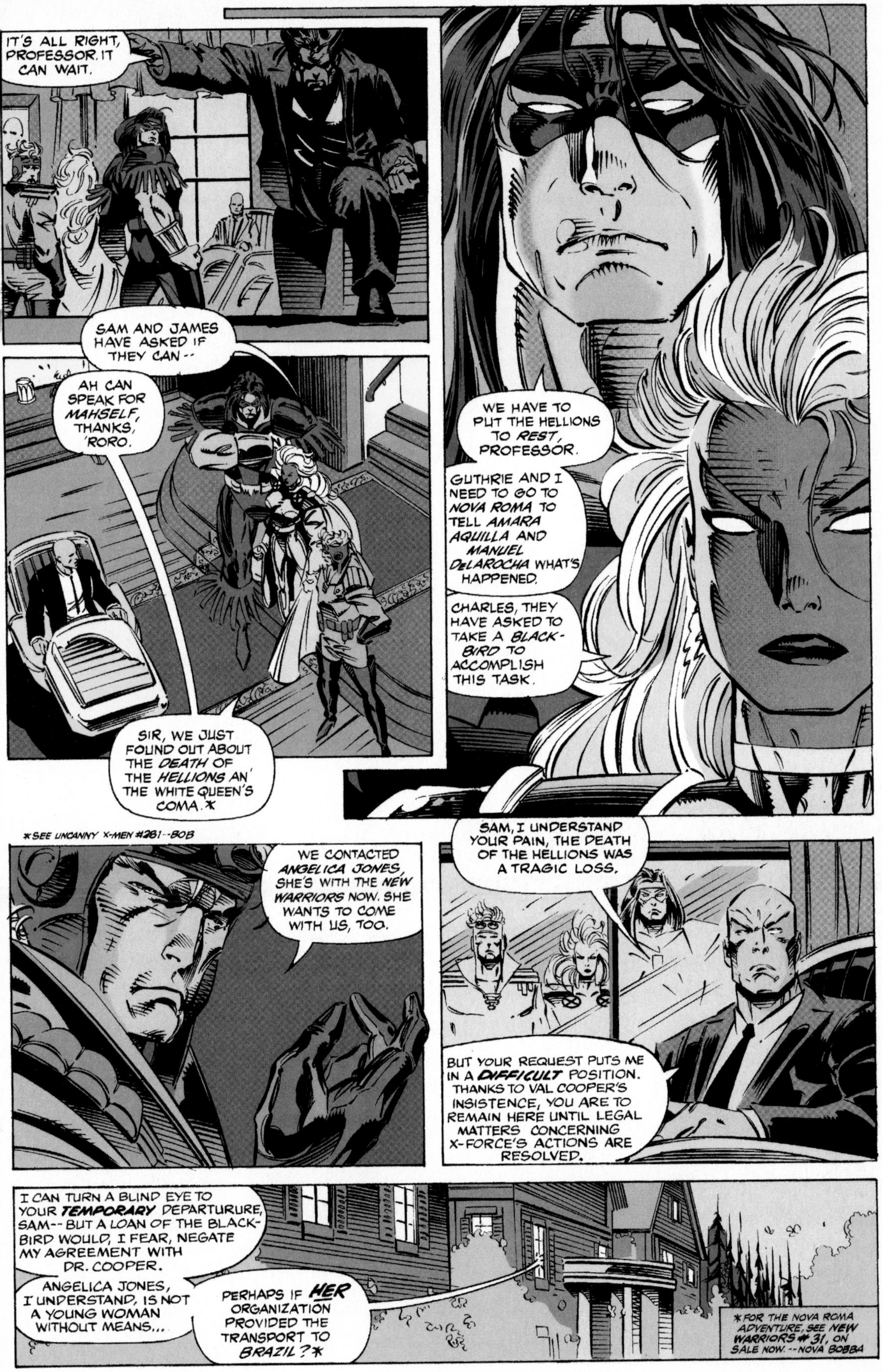
IT'S ALL RIGHT, PROFESSOR. IT CAN WAIT.
WE HAVE TO PUT THE HELLIONS TO REST, PROFESSOR.
GUTHRIE AND I NEED TO GO TO NOVA ROMA TO TELL AMARA AQUILLA AND MANUEL DeLAROCHA WHAT'S HAPPENED.
CHARLES, THEY HAVE ASKED TO TAKE A BLACKBIRD TO ACCOMPLISH THIS TASK.
SAM AND JAMES HAVE ASKED IF THEY CAN--
AH CAN SPEAK FOR MAHSELF, THANKS, 'RORO.
SIR, WE JUST FOUND OUT ABOUT THE DEATH OF THE HELLIONS AN' THE WHITE QUEEN'S COMA.*
*SEE UNCANNY X-MEN #281--BOB
WE CONTACTED ANGELICA JONES, SHE'S WITH THE NEW WARRIORS NOW. SHE WANTS TO COME WITH US, TOO.
SAM, I UNDERSTAND YOUR PAIN, THE DEATH OF THE HELLIONS WAS A TRAGIC LOSS.
BUT YOUR REQUEST PUTS ME IN A DIFFICULT POSITION. THANKS TO VAL COOPER'S INSISTENCE, YOU ARE TO REMAIN HERE UNTIL LEGAL MATTERS CONCERNING X-FORCE'S ACTIONS ARE RESOLVED.
I CAN TURN A BLIND EYE TO YOUR TEMPORARY DEPARTURURE, SAM-- BUT A LOAN OF THE BLACKBIRD WOULD, I FEAR, NEGATE MY AGREEMENT WITH DR. COOPER.
ANGELICA JONES, I UNDERSTAND, IS NOT A YOUNG WOMAN WITHOUT MEANS...
PERHAPS IF HER ORGANIZATION PROVIDED THE TRANSPORT TO BRAZIL?*
*FOR THE NOVA ROMA ADVENTURE, SEE NEW WARRIORS #31, ON SALE NOW. --NOVA BOBBA

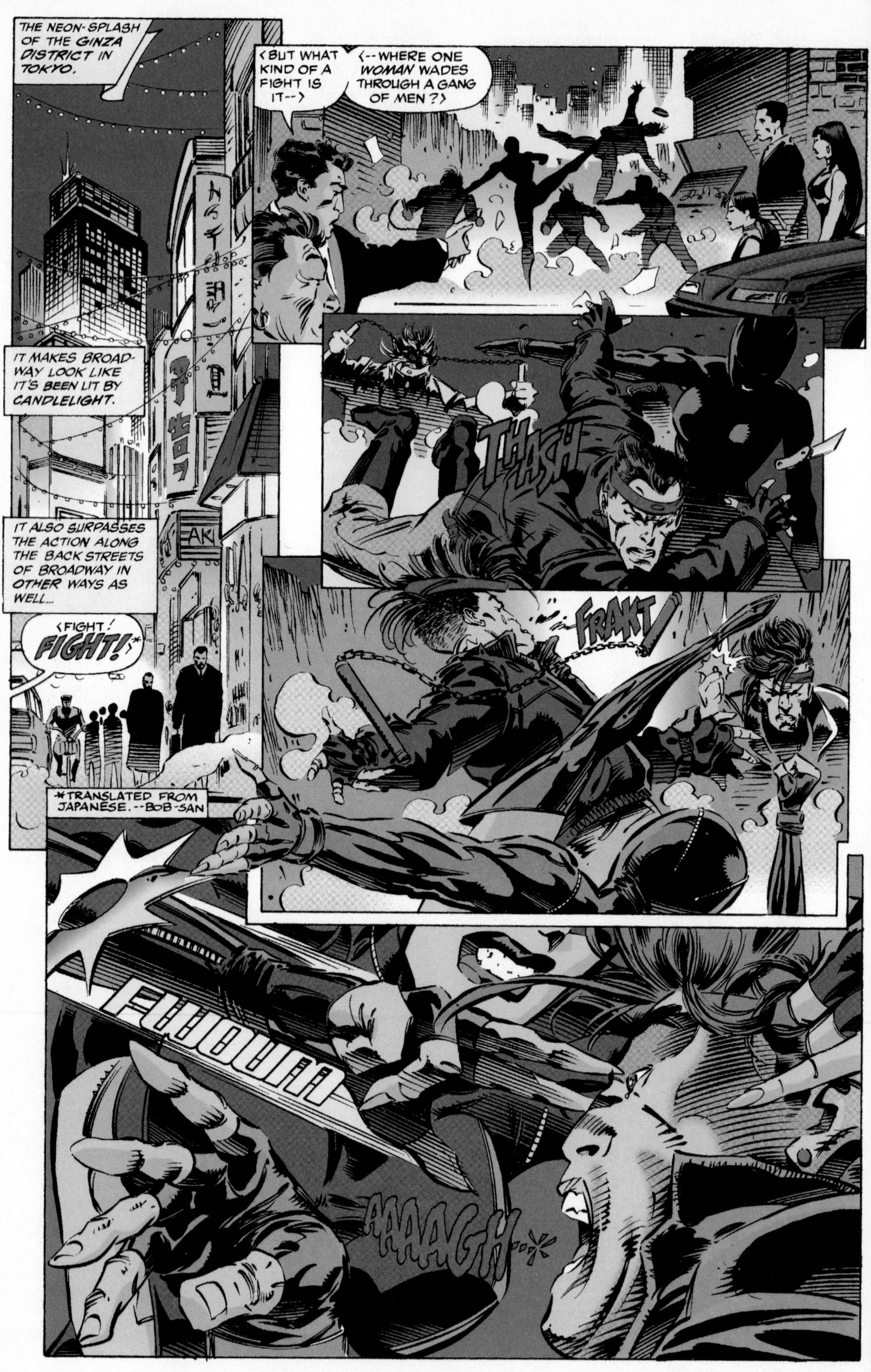
THE NEON-SPLASH OF THE GINZA DISTRICT IN TOKYO.
<BUT WHAT KIND OF A FIGHT IS IT-->
<--WHERE ONE WOMAN WADES THROUGH A GANG OF MEN?>
IT MAKES BROADWAY LOOK LIKE IT'S BEEN LIT BY CANDLELIGHT.
THASH
IT ALSO SURPASSES THE ACTION ALONG THE BACK STREETS OF BROADWAY IN OTHER WAYS AS WELL...
<FIGHT! FIGHT!>*
FRAKT
*TRANSLATED FROM JAPANESE. --BOB-SAN
FWOOMM
AAAAGH

〈 IT IS DONE. 〉

〈 I AM READY. 〉

THE SPECTATORS QUICKLY LEAVE--

ZNRPPP

--AND IF ANY OF THE YOUNG STREET THUGS LYING IN THE ALLEYWAY HAD BEEN LEFT *CONSCIOUS* --

--MAYBE THEY WOULD QUESTION THE SOUNDS OF THEIR NATIVE TONGUE WITH SUCH AN *ODD* ACCENT.

AS IT IS THOUGH, THE NOISE AND LIGHTS OF THE GINZA DISTRICT ARE AS UNTO SILENCE AND *DARKNESS*

--WHEN COMPARED TO THE *PASSION* AND ANGER WHICH BURNS WITHIN THIS STRANGE YOUNG WOMAN...

〈 I AM READY. 〉

〈 THE TIME FOR *REVENGE* HAS COME. 〉

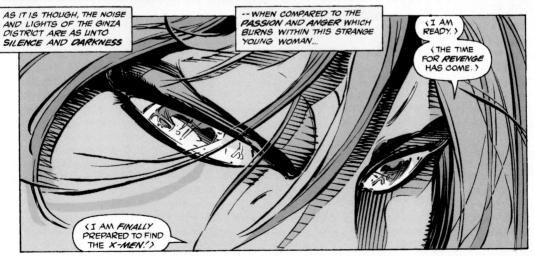

〈 I AM *FINALLY* PREPARED TO FIND THE *X-MEN!* 〉

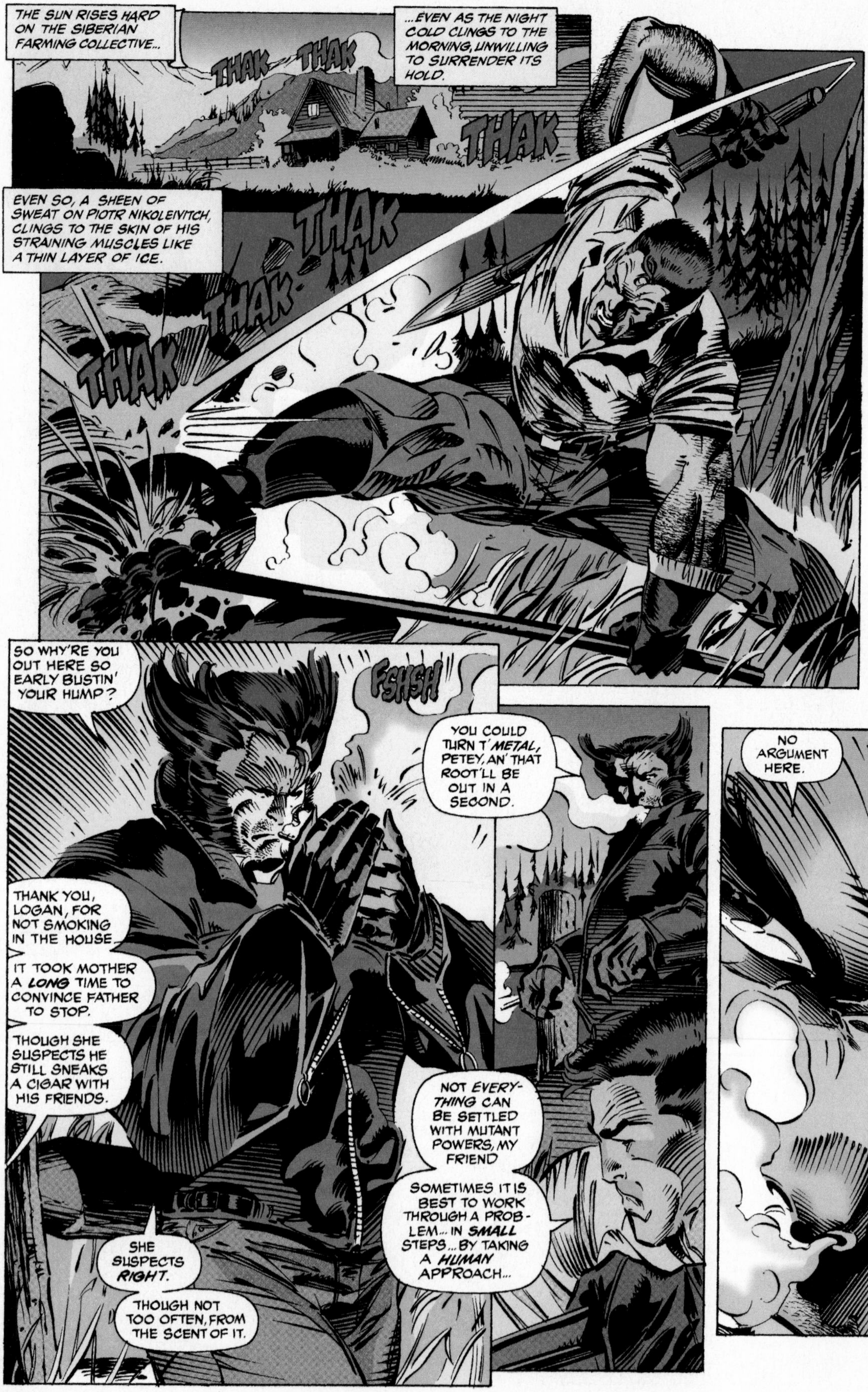
THE SUN RISES HARD ON THE SIBERIAN FARMING COLLECTIVE...
THAK THAK
...EVEN AS THE NIGHT COLD CLINGS TO THE MORNING, UNWILLING TO SURRENDER ITS HOLD.
THAK
EVEN SO, A SHEEN OF SWEAT ON PIOTR NIKOLEIVITCH, CLINGS TO THE SKIN OF HIS STRAINING MUSCLES LIKE A THIN LAYER OF ICE.
THAK
THAK
THAK
SO WHY'RE YOU OUT HERE SO EARLY BUSTIN' YOUR HUMP?
FSHSH!
THANK YOU, LOGAN, FOR NOT SMOKING IN THE HOUSE.
IT TOOK MOTHER A LONG TIME TO CONVINCE FATHER TO STOP.
THOUGH SHE SUSPECTS HE STILL SNEAKS A CIGAR WITH HIS FRIENDS.
SHE SUSPECTS RIGHT.
THOUGH NOT TOO OFTEN, FROM THE SCENT OF IT.
YOU COULD TURN T' METAL, PETEY, AN' THAT ROOT'LL BE OUT IN A SECOND.
NOT EVERYTHING CAN BE SETTLED WITH MUTANT POWERS, MY FRIEND
SOMETIMES IT IS BEST TO WORK THROUGH A PROBLEM... IN SMALL STEPS... BY TAKING A HUMAN APPROACH...
NO ARGUMENT HERE.

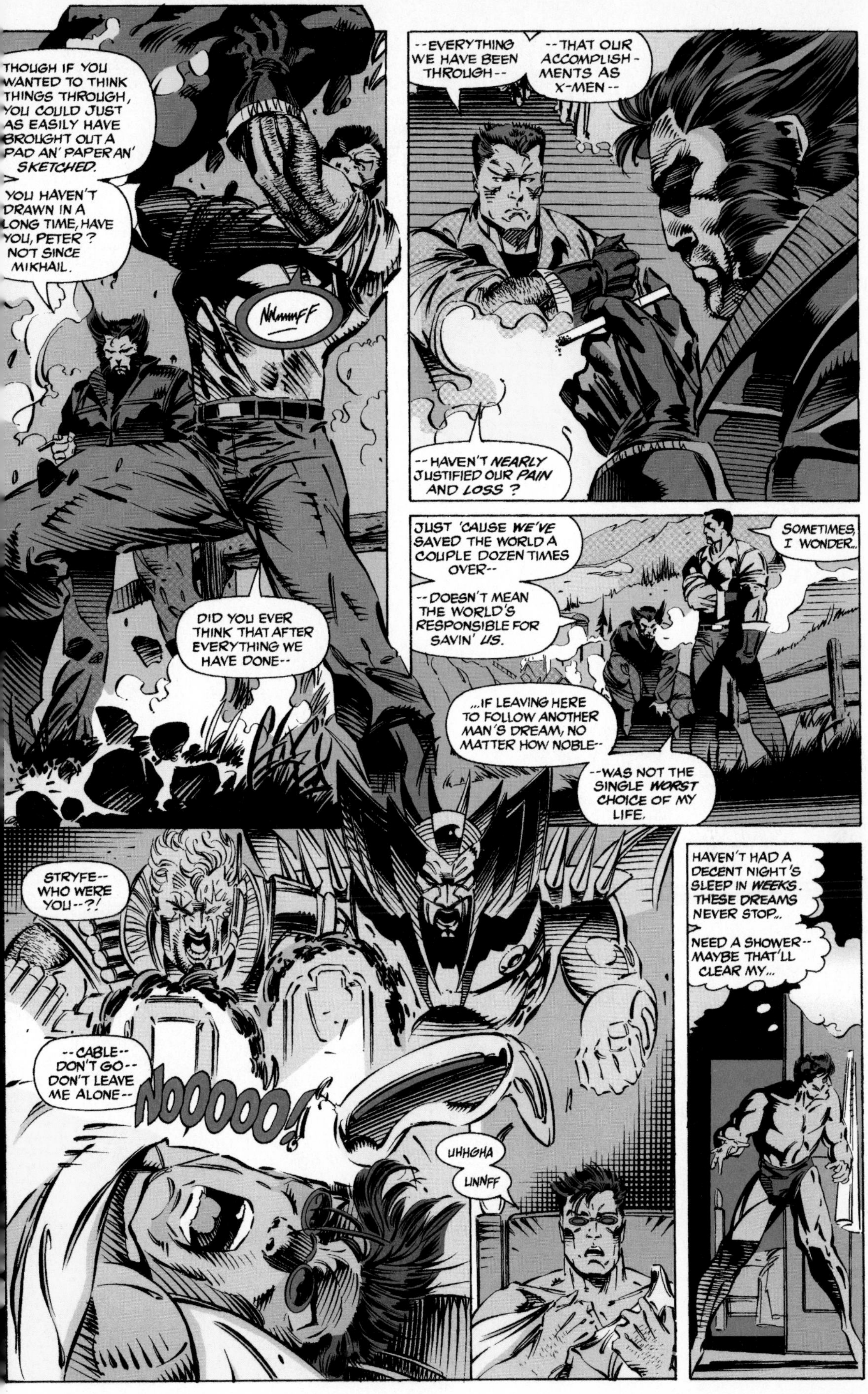
THOUGH IF YOU WANTED TO THINK THINGS THROUGH, YOU COULD JUST AS EASILY HAVE BROUGHT OUT A PAD AN' PAPER AN' SKETCHED.
YOU HAVEN'T DRAWN IN A LONG TIME, HAVE YOU, PETER? NOT SINCE MIKHAIL.
NNmmFF
--EVERYTHING WE HAVE BEEN THROUGH--
--THAT OUR ACCOMPLISH-MENTS AS X-MEN--
--HAVEN'T NEARLY JUSTIFIED OUR PAIN AND LOSS?
DID YOU EVER THINK THAT AFTER EVERYTHING WE HAVE DONE--
JUST 'CAUSE WE'VE SAVED THE WORLD A COUPLE DOZEN TIMES OVER--
--DOESN'T MEAN THE WORLD'S RESPONSIBLE FOR SAVIN' US.
SOMETIMES, I WONDER...
...IF LEAVING HERE TO FOLLOW ANOTHER MAN'S DREAM, NO MATTER HOW NOBLE--
--WAS NOT THE SINGLE WORST CHOICE OF MY LIFE.
STRYFE-- WHO WERE YOU--?!
--CABLE-- DON'T GO-- DON'T LEAVE ME ALONE--
NOOOOO!
UHHGHA
UNNFF
HAVEN'T HAD A DECENT NIGHT'S SLEEP IN WEEKS. THESE DREAMS NEVER STOP...
NEED A SHOWER-- MAYBE THAT'LL CLEAR MY...

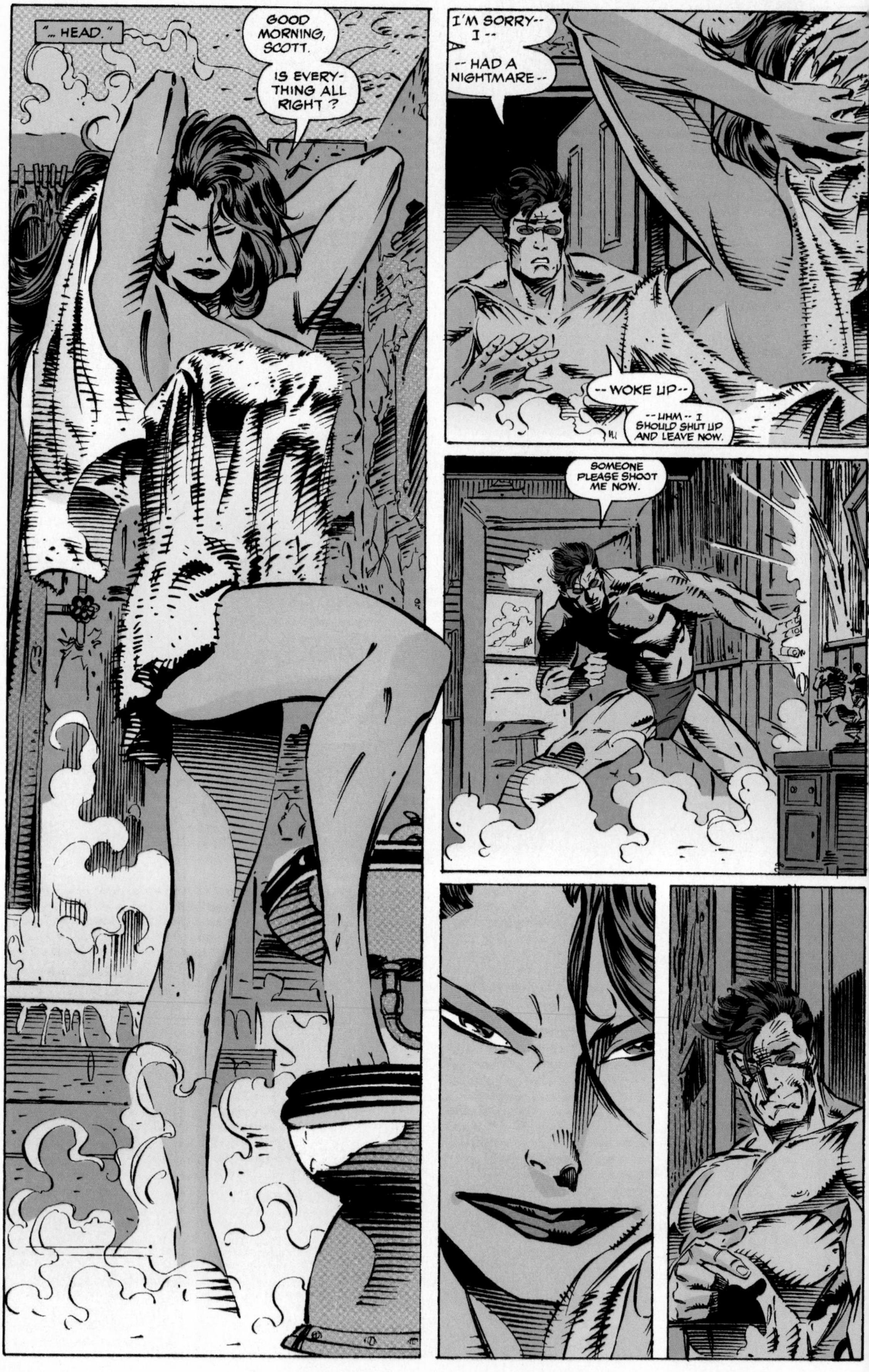
"... HEAD."
GOOD MORNING, SCOTT.
IS EVERYTHING ALL RIGHT?
I'M SORRY-- I --
-- HAD A NIGHTMARE--
-- WOKE UP--
-- UHM -- I SHOULD SHUT UP AND LEAVE NOW.
SOMEONE PLEASE SHOOT ME NOW.

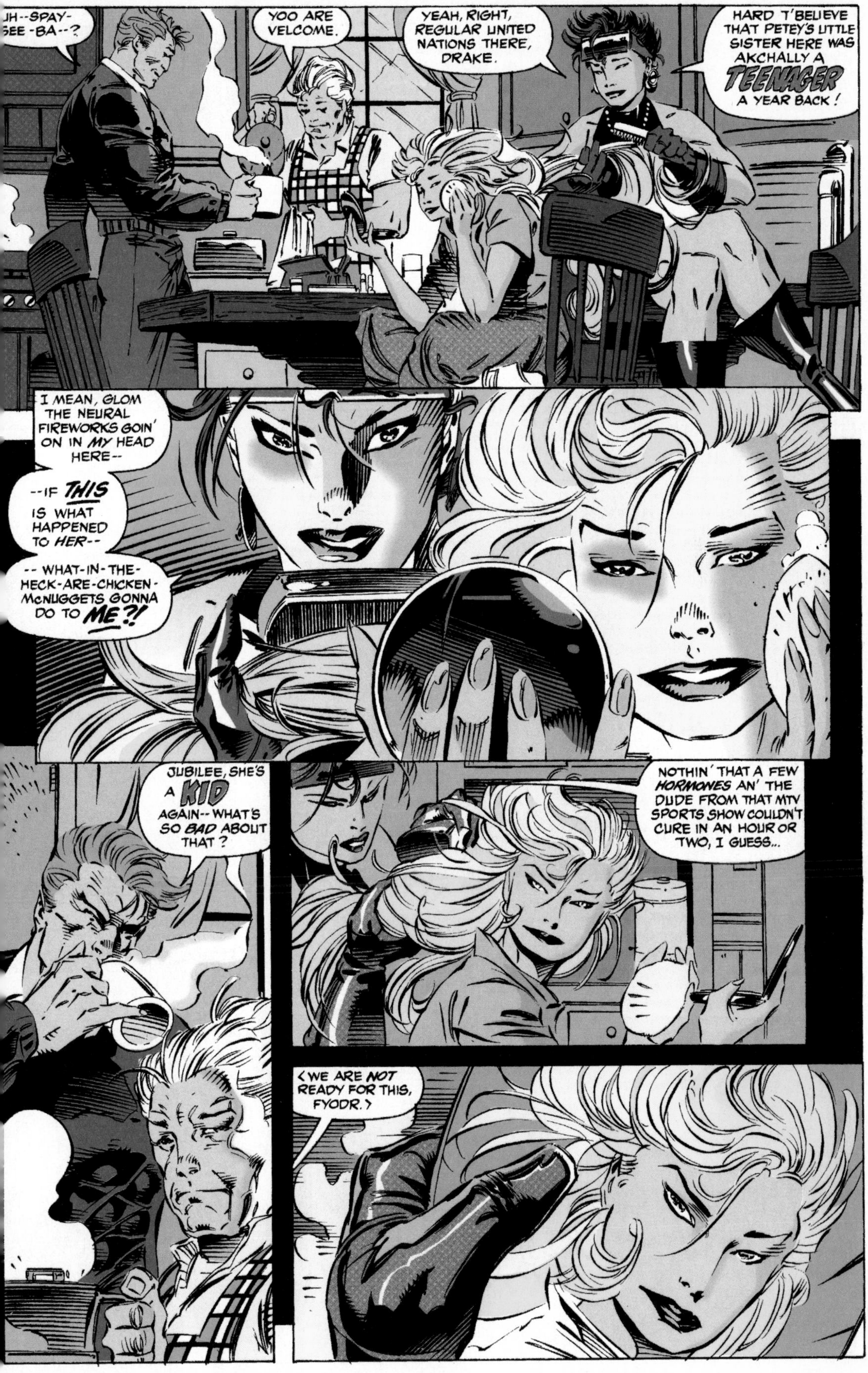
UH--SPAY-SEE-BA--?
YOO ARE VELCOME.
YEAH, RIGHT, REGULAR UNITED NATIONS THERE, DRAKE.
HARD T'BELIEVE THAT PETEY'S LITTLE SISTER HERE WAS AKCHALLY A TEENAGER A YEAR BACK!
I MEAN, GLOM THE NEURAL FIREWORKS GOIN' ON IN MY HEAD HERE--
--IF THIS IS WHAT HAPPENED TO HER--
-- WHAT-IN-THE-HECK-ARE-CHICKEN-McNUGGETS GONNA DO TO ME?!
JUBILEE, SHE'S A KID AGAIN-- WHAT'S SO BAD ABOUT THAT?
NOTHIN' THAT A FEW HORMONES AN' THE DUDE FROM THAT MTV SPORTS SHOW COULDN'T CURE IN AN HOUR OR TWO, I GUESS...
<WE ARE NOT READY FOR THIS, FYODR.>

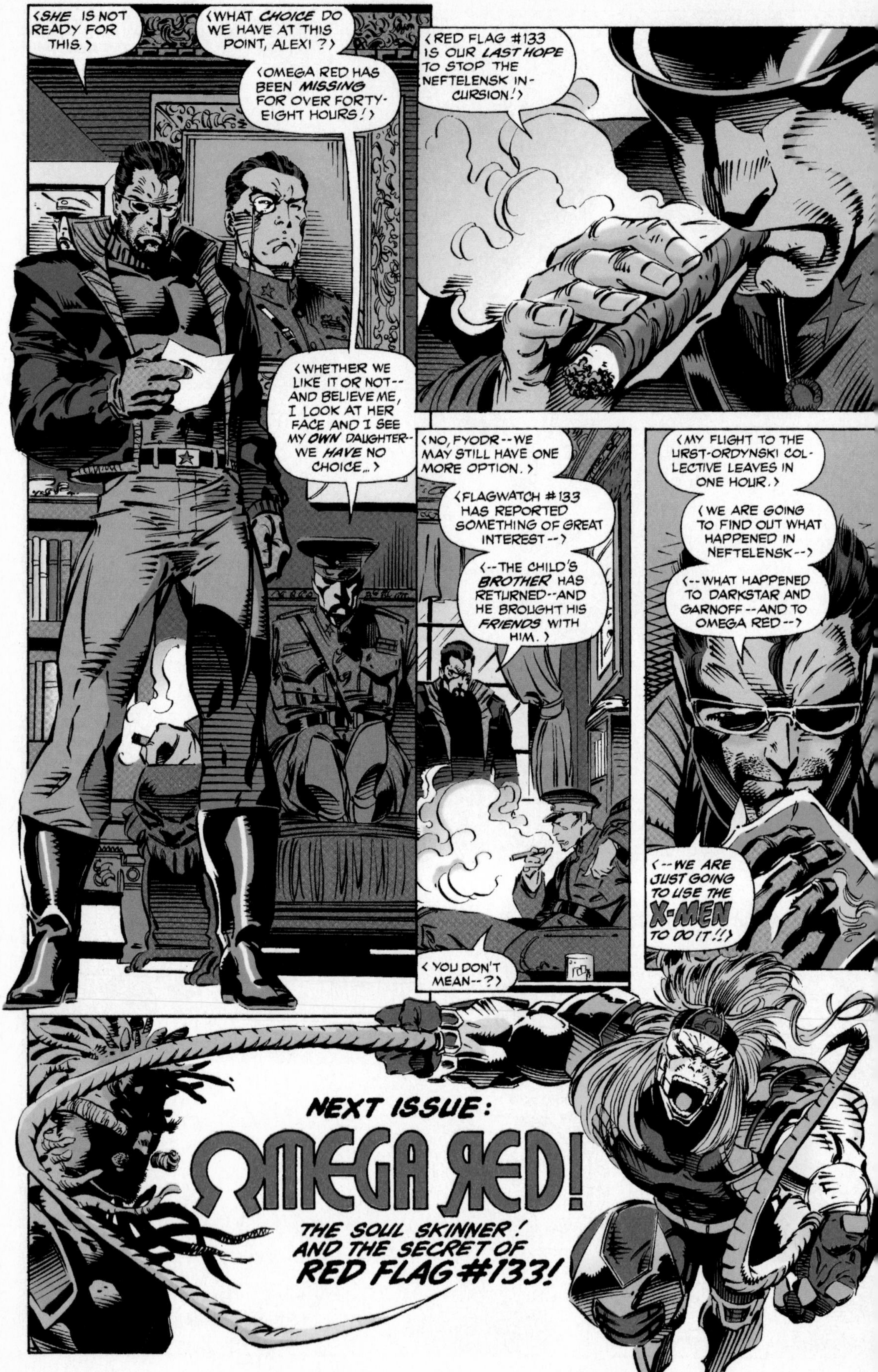

<SHE IS NOT READY FOR THIS.>
<WHAT CHOICE DO WE HAVE AT THIS POINT, ALEXI ?>
<OMEGA RED HAS BEEN MISSING FOR OVER FORTY-EIGHT HOURS!>
<WHETHER WE LIKE IT OR NOT-- AND BELIEVE ME, I LOOK AT HER FACE AND I SEE MY OWN DAUGHTER-- WE HAVE NO CHOICE...>
<RED FLAG #133 IS OUR LAST HOPE TO STOP THE NEFTELENSK INCURSION!>
<NO, FYODR--WE MAY STILL HAVE ONE MORE OPTION.>
<FLAGWATCH #133 HAS REPORTED SOMETHING OF GREAT INTEREST-->
<--THE CHILD'S BROTHER HAS RETURNED--AND HE BROUGHT HIS FRIENDS WITH HIM.>
<YOU DON'T MEAN--?>
<MY FLIGHT TO THE URST-ORDYNSKI COLLECTIVE LEAVES IN ONE HOUR.>
<WE ARE GOING TO FIND OUT WHAT HAPPENED IN NEFTELENSK-->
<--WHAT HAPPENED TO DARKSTAR AND GARNOFF--AND TO OMEGA RED-->
<--WE ARE JUST GOING TO USE THE X-MEN TO DO IT!!>
NEXT ISSUE:
OMEGA RED!
THE SOUL SKINNER! AND THE SECRET OF RED FLAG #133!

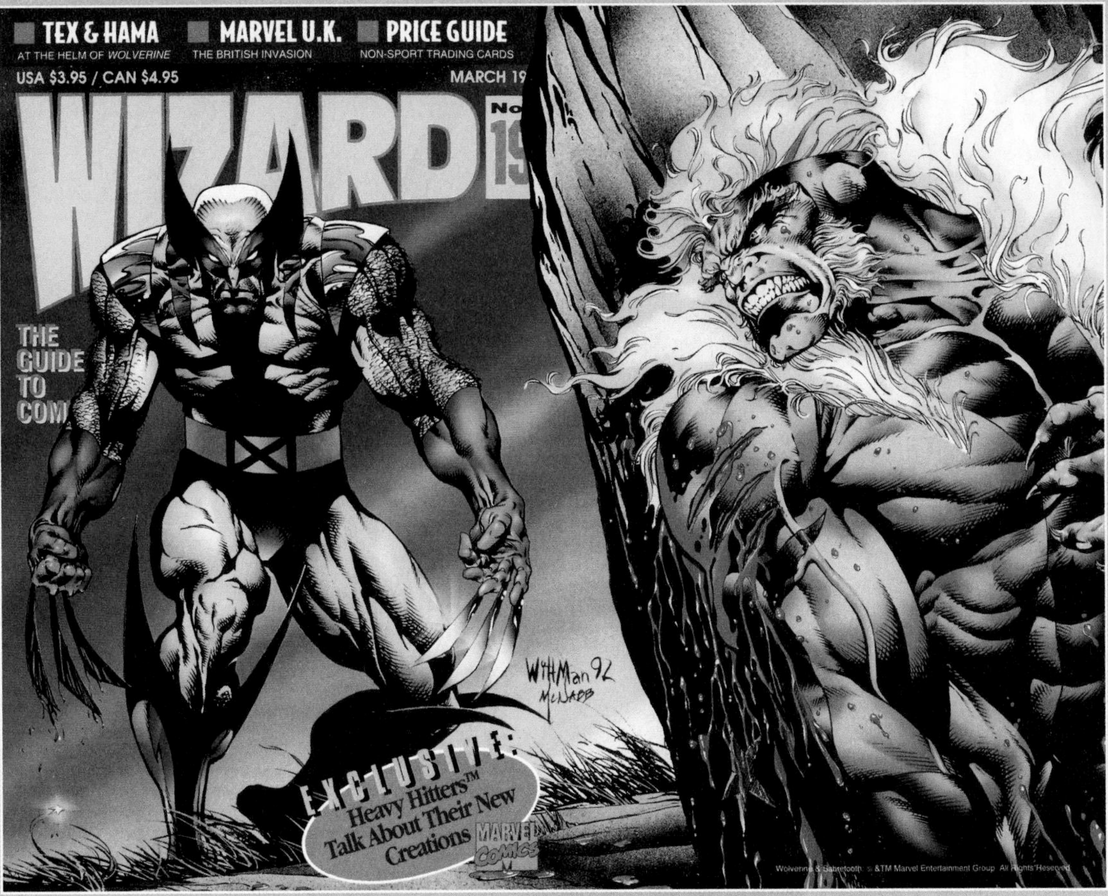
TEX & HAMA
AT THE HELM OF WOLVERINE
MARVEL U.K.
THE BRITISH INVASION
PRICE GUIDE
NON-SPORT TRADING CARDS
USA $3.95 / CAN $4.95
WIZARD
EXCLUSIVE:
Heavy Hitters™ Talk About Their New Creations
MARVEL COMICS

Wizard #19 cover art by Bart "Wittman" Sears & Mark McNabb

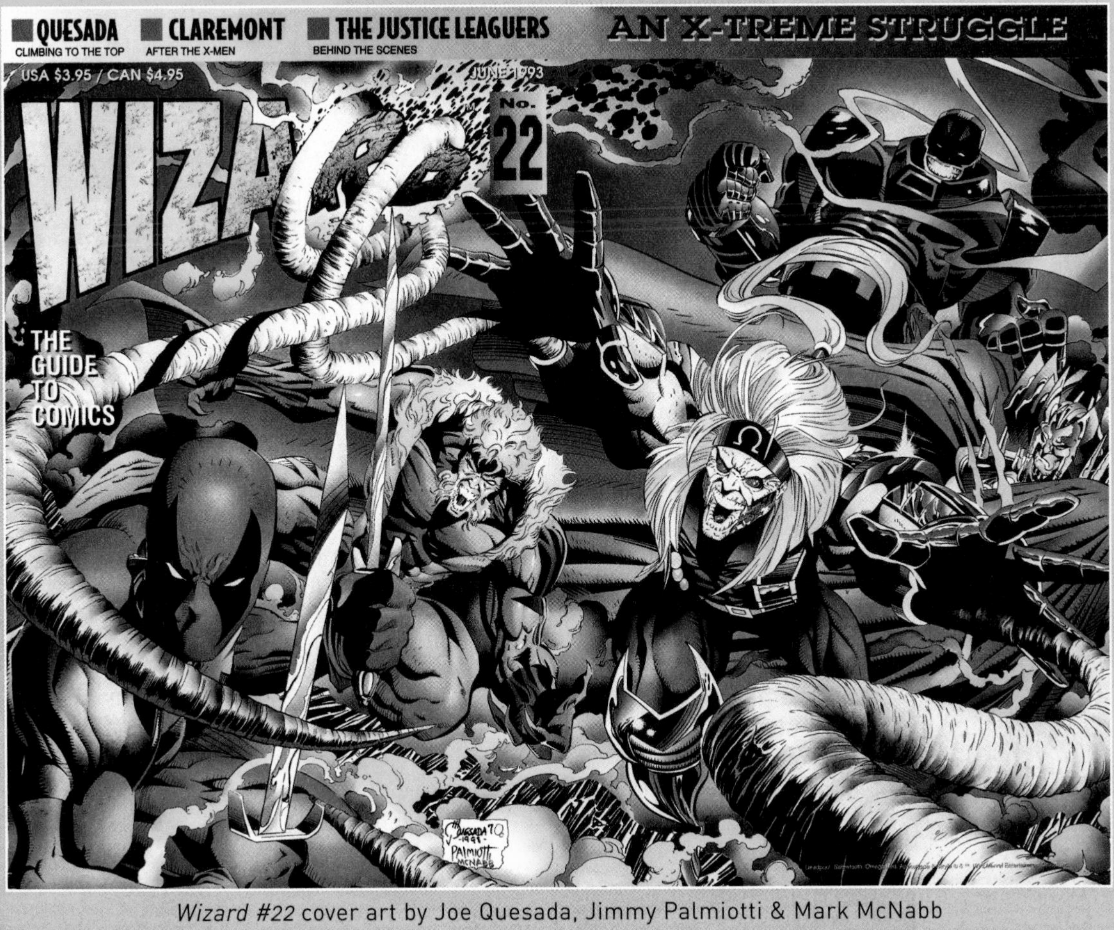
QUESADA
CLIMBING TO THE TOP
CLAREMONT
AFTER THE X-MEN
THE JUSTICE LEAGUERS
BEHIND THE SCENES
AN X-TREME STRUGGLE
USA $3.95 / CAN $4.95
JUNE 1993
No. 22
THE GUIDE TO COMICS

Wizard #22 cover art by Joe Quesada, Jimmy Palmiotti & Mark McNabb

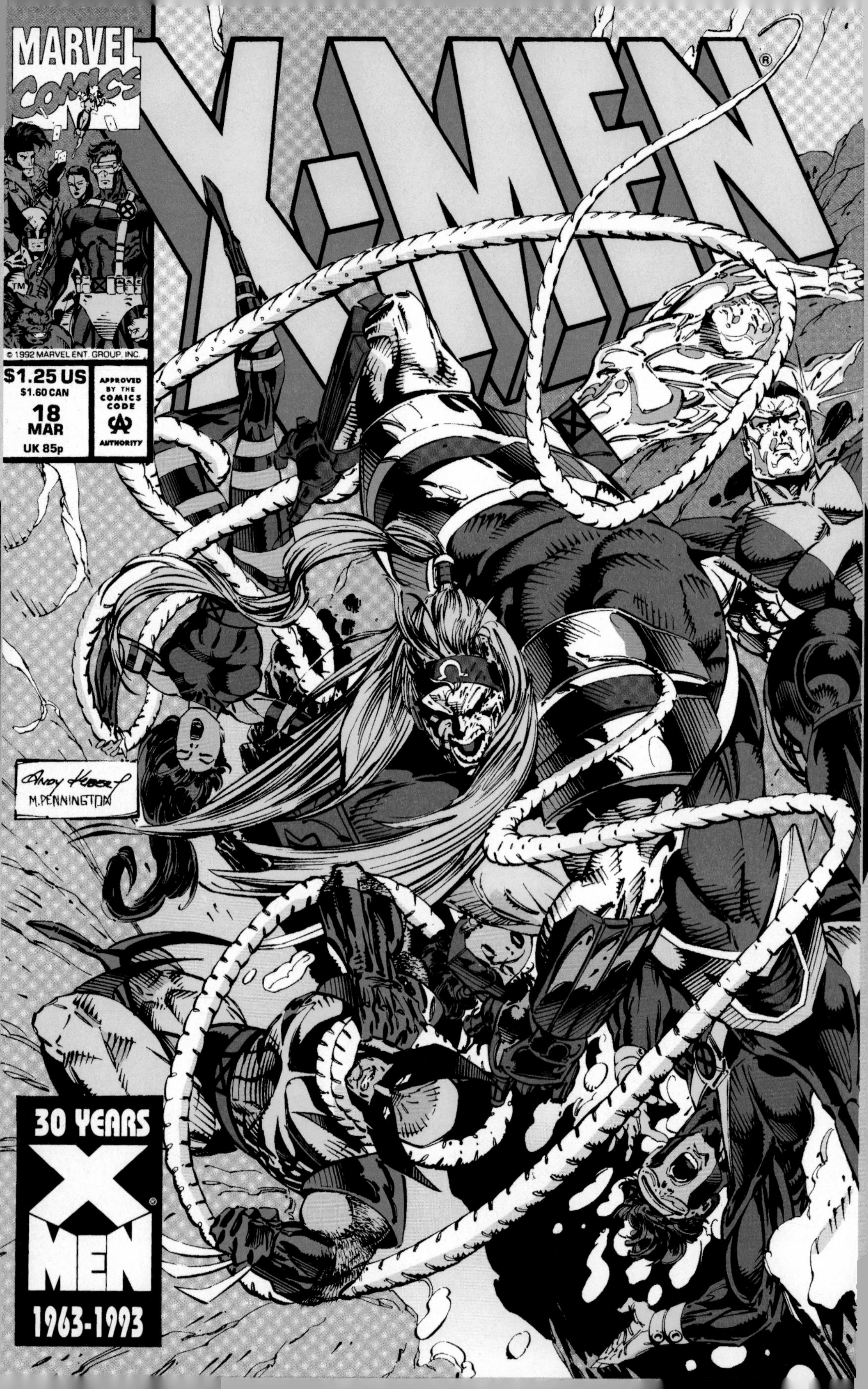
MARVEL COMICS
X-MEN
© 1992 MARVEL ENT. GROUP, INC.
$1.25 US
$1.60 CAN
18
MAR
UK 85p
APPROVED BY THE COMICS CODE AUTHORITY
M. PENNINGTON
30 YEARS
X MEN
1963-1993

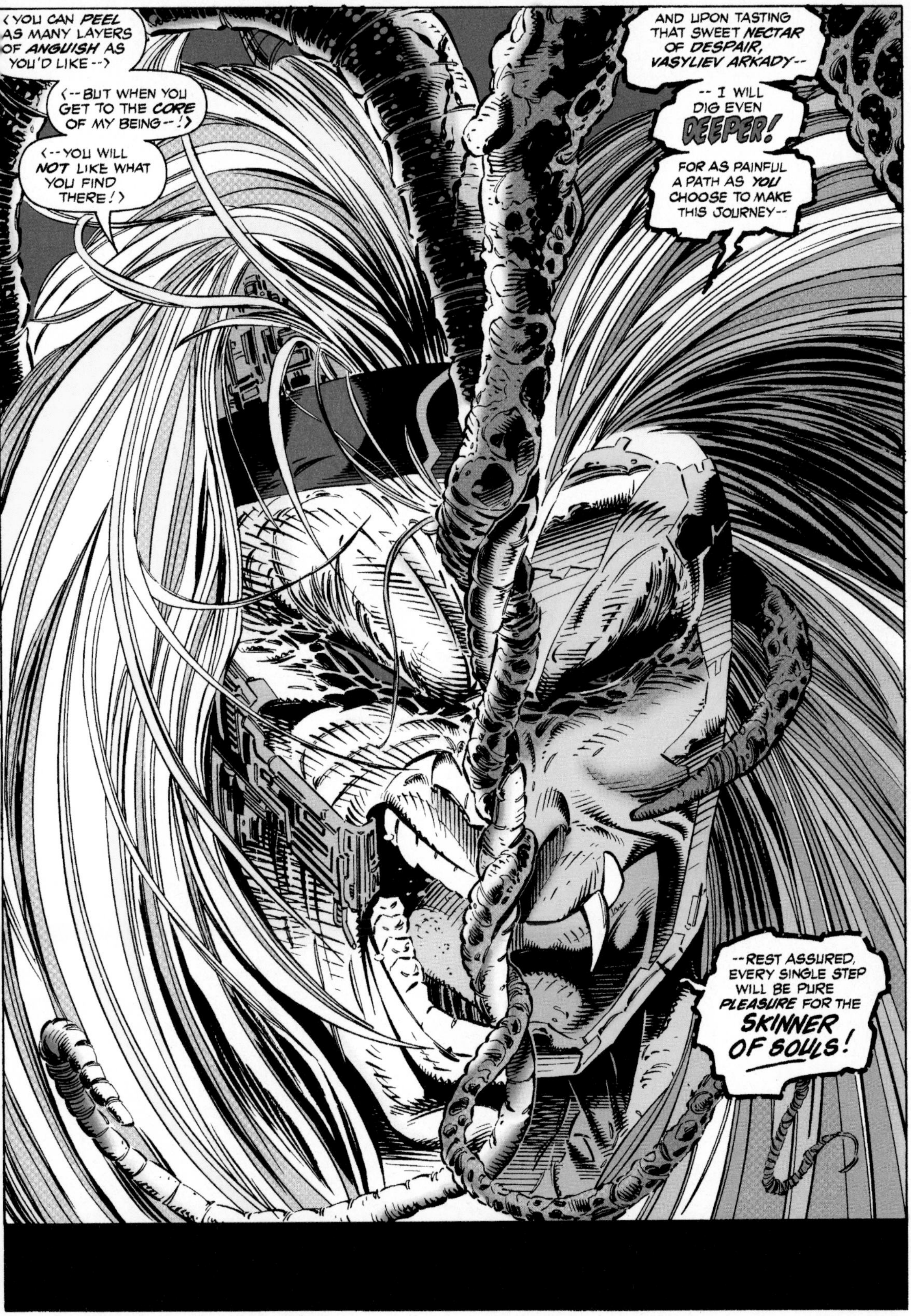
‹YOU CAN PEEL AS MANY LAYERS OF ANGUISH AS YOU'D LIKE--›
‹--BUT WHEN YOU GET TO THE CORE OF MY BEING--!›
‹--YOU WILL NOT LIKE WHAT YOU FIND THERE!›
AND UPON TASTING THAT SWEET NECTAR OF DESPAIR, VASYLIEV ARKADY--
-- I WILL DIG EVEN DEEPER!
FOR AS PAINFUL A PATH AS YOU CHOOSE TO MAKE THIS JOURNEY--
--REST ASSURED, EVERY SINGLE STEP WILL BE PURE PLEASURE FOR THE SKINNER OF SOULS!

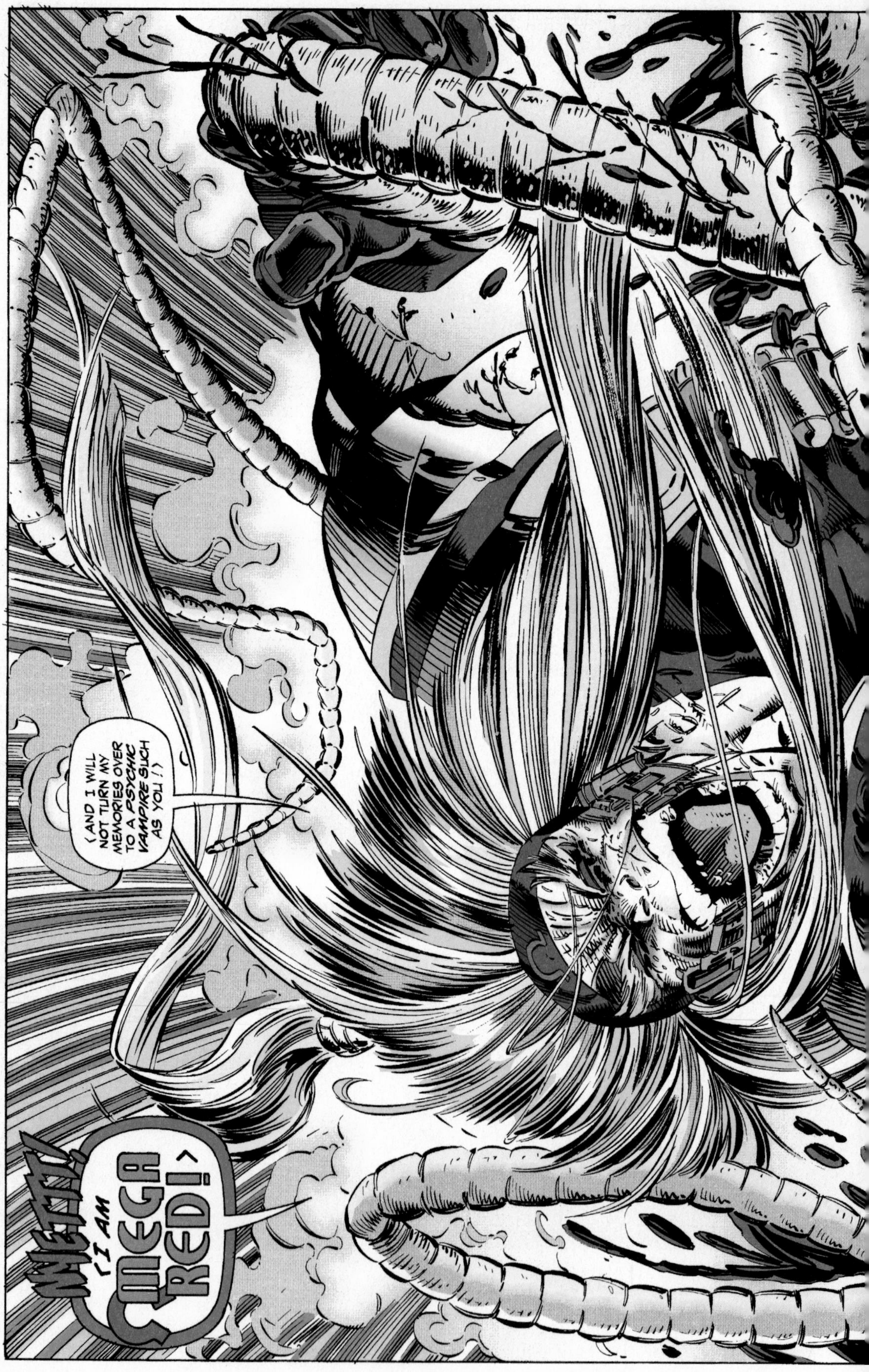
‹ AND I WILL NOT TURN MY MEMORIES OVER TO A PSYCHIC VAMPIRE SUCH AS YOU! ›
‹ I AM OMEGA RED! ›

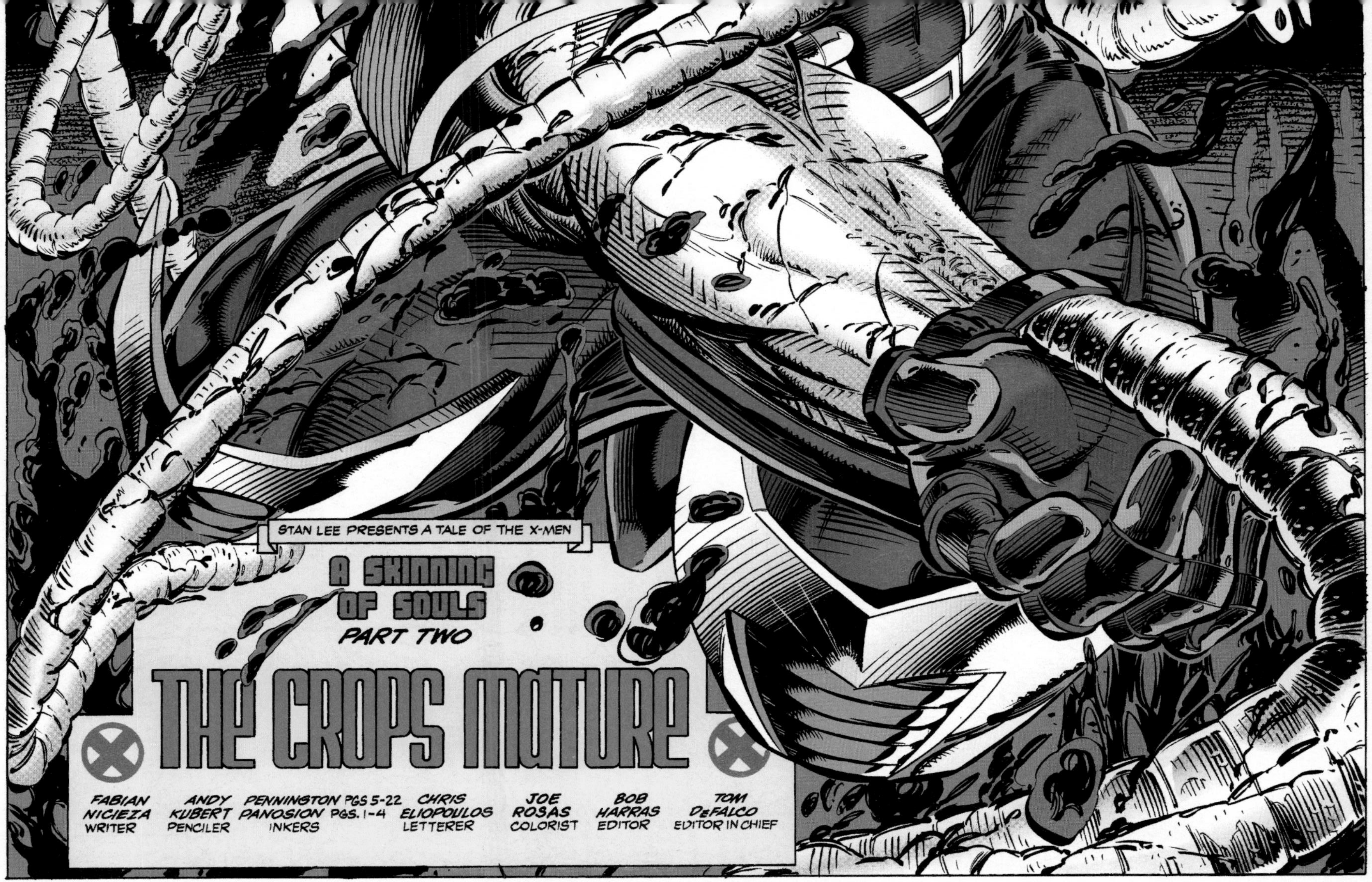

STAN LEE PRESENTS A TALE OF THE X-MEN
A SKINNING OF SOULS
PART TWO
THE CROPS MATURE
FABIAN NICIEZA WRITER
ANDY KUBERT PENCILER
PENNINGTON PGS 5-22 PANOSIAN PGS. 1-4 INKERS
CHRIS ELIOPOULOS LETTERER
JOE ROSAS COLORIST
BOB HARRAS EDITOR
TOM DeFALCO EDITOR IN CHIEF

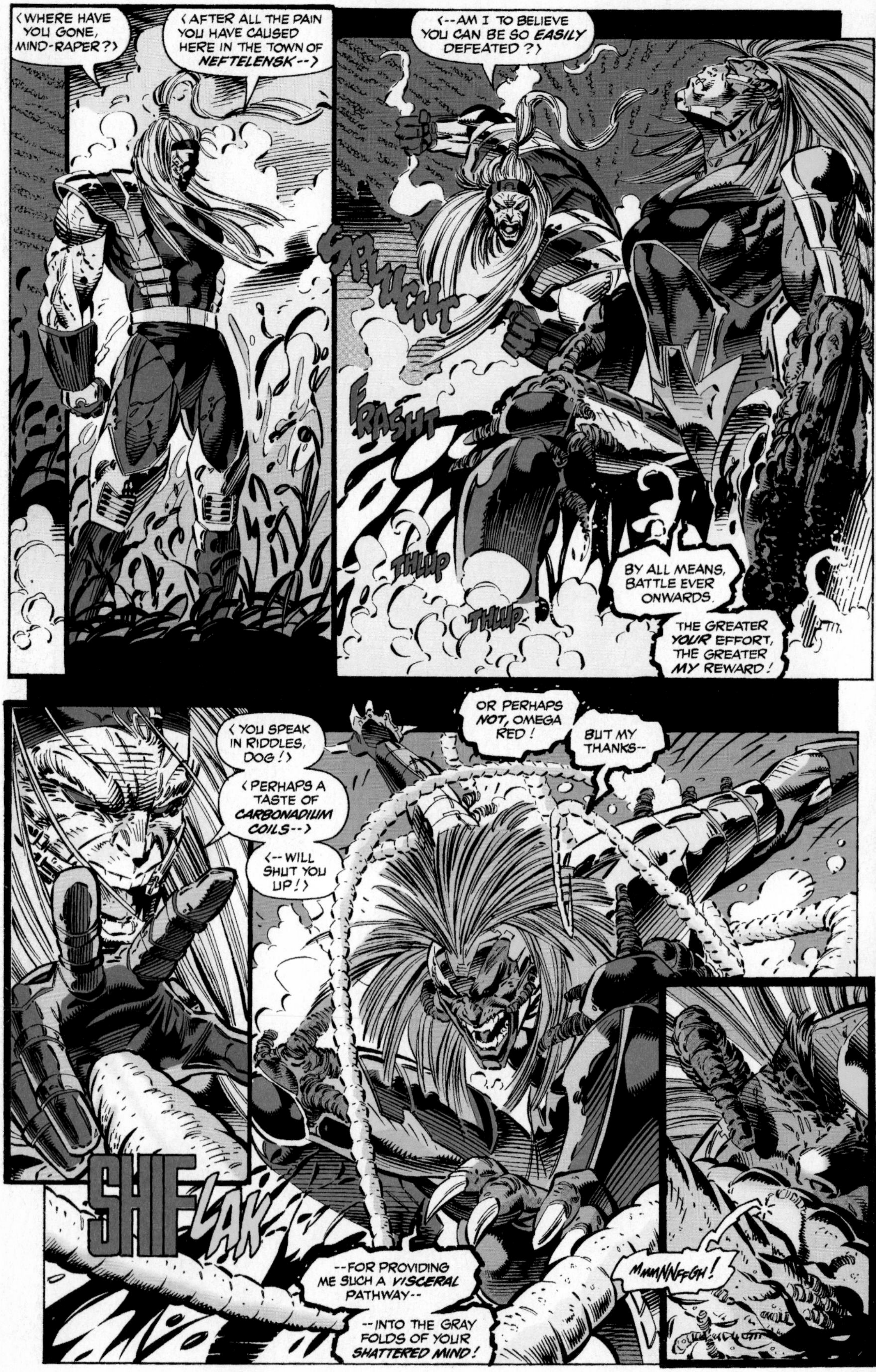

‹WHERE HAVE YOU GONE, MIND-RAPER?›
‹AFTER ALL THE PAIN YOU HAVE CAUSED HERE IN THE TOWN OF NEFTELENSK--›
‹--AM I TO BELIEVE YOU CAN BE SO EASILY DEFEATED?›
FRASHT
THLUP
THLUP
BY ALL MEANS, BATTLE EVER ONWARDS.
THE GREATER YOUR EFFORT, THE GREATER MY REWARD!
‹YOU SPEAK IN RIDDLES, DOG!›
‹PERHAPS A TASTE OF CARBONADIUM COILS--›
‹--WILL SHUT YOU UP!›
OR PERHAPS NOT, OMEGA RED!
BUT MY THANKS--
SHIFLAK
--FOR PROVIDING ME SUCH A VISCERAL PATHWAY--
--INTO THE GRAY FOLDS OF YOUR SHATTERED MIND!
MMMNNFFGH!

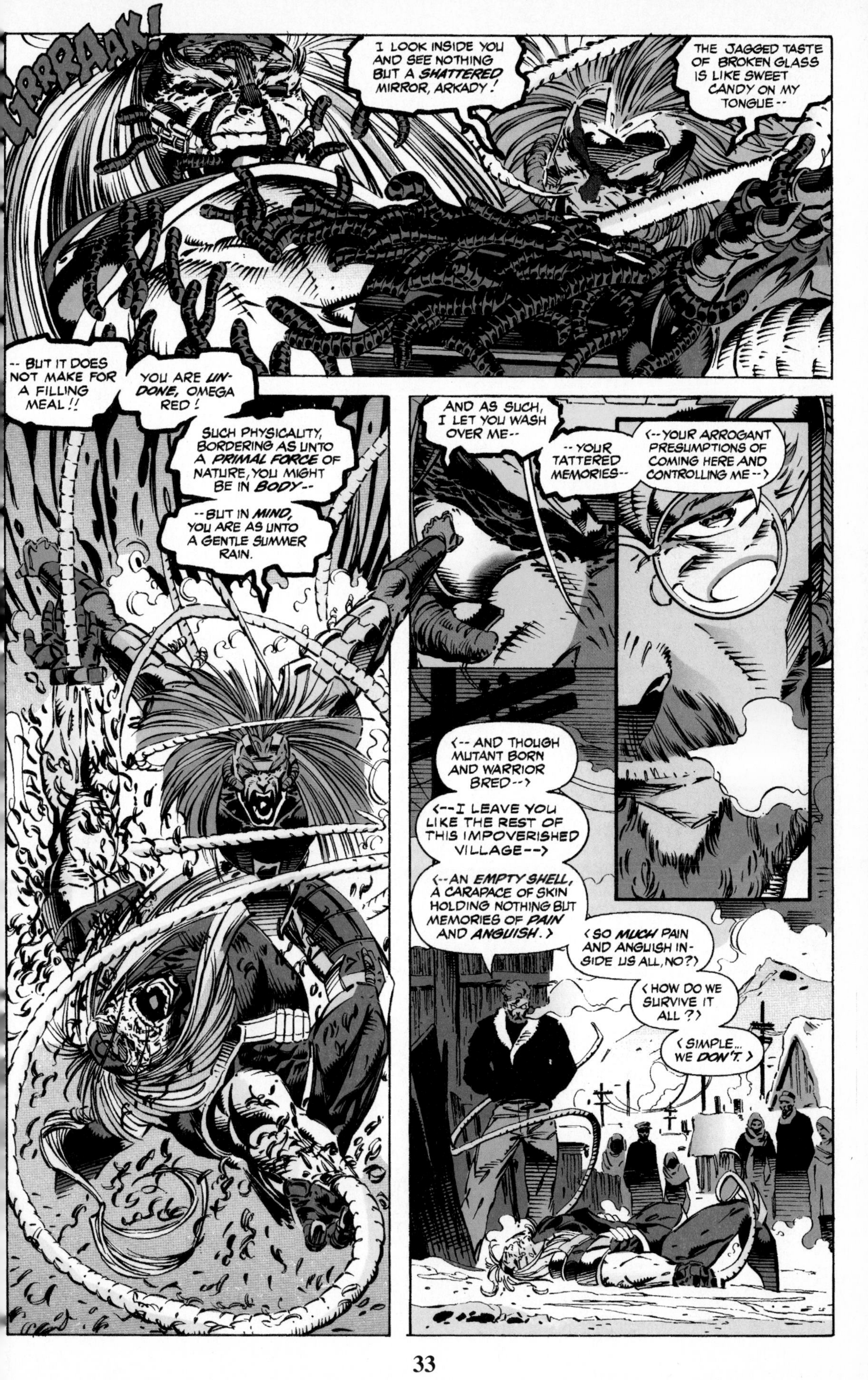
URRRAAK!
I LOOK INSIDE YOU AND SEE NOTHING BUT A SHATTERED MIRROR, ARKADY!
THE JAGGED TASTE OF BROKEN GLASS IS LIKE SWEET CANDY ON MY TONGUE --
-- BUT IT DOES NOT MAKE FOR A FILLING MEAL!!
YOU ARE UN-DONE, OMEGA RED!
SUCH PHYSICALITY, BORDERING AS UNTO A PRIMAL FORCE OF NATURE, YOU MIGHT BE IN BODY--
--BUT IN MIND, YOU ARE AS UNTO A GENTLE SUMMER RAIN.
AND AS SUCH, I LET YOU WASH OVER ME--
--YOUR TATTERED MEMORIES--
<--YOUR ARROGANT PRESUMPTIONS OF COMING HERE AND CONTROLLING ME-->
<-- AND THOUGH MUTANT BORN AND WARRIOR BRED-->
<--I LEAVE YOU LIKE THE REST OF THIS IMPOVERISHED VILLAGE-->
<--AN EMPTY SHELL, A CARAPACE OF SKIN HOLDING NOTHING BUT MEMORIES OF PAIN AND ANGUISH.>
<SO MUCH PAIN AND ANGUISH IN-SIDE US ALL, NO?>
<HOW DO WE SURVIVE IT ALL?>
<SIMPLE... WE DON'T.>

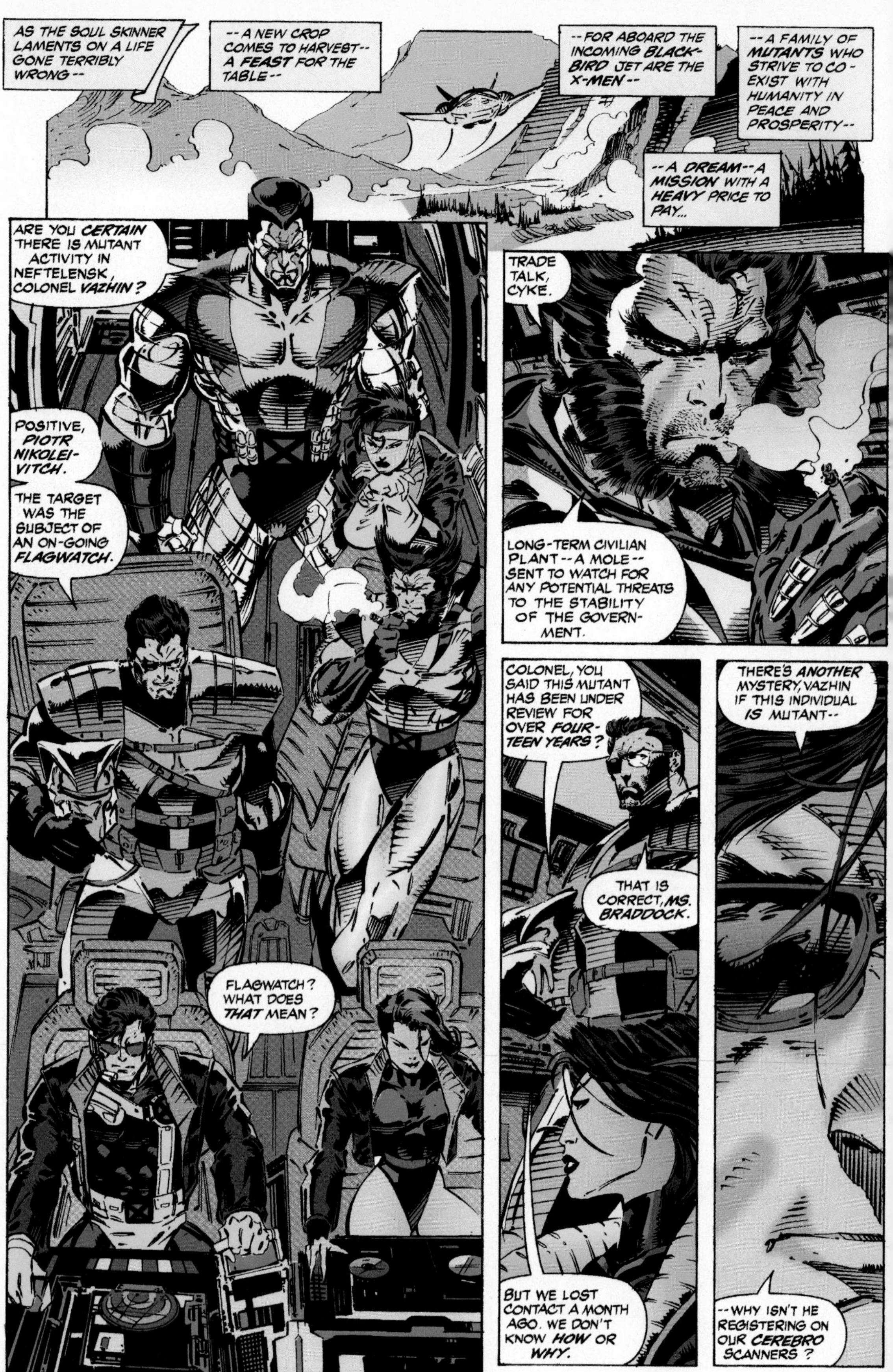

AS THE SOUL SKINNER LAMENTS ON A LIFE GONE TERRIBLY WRONG--
--A NEW CROP COMES TO HARVEST-- A FEAST FOR THE TABLE--
--FOR ABOARD THE INCOMING BLACK-BIRD JET ARE THE X-MEN--
--A FAMILY OF MUTANTS WHO STRIVE TO CO-EXIST WITH HUMANITY IN PEACE AND PROSPERITY--
--A DREAM--A MISSION WITH A HEAVY PRICE TO PAY...
ARE YOU CERTAIN THERE IS MUTANT ACTIVITY IN NEFTELENSK, COLONEL VAZHIN?
POSITIVE, PIOTR NIKOLEI-VITCH.
THE TARGET WAS THE SUBJECT OF AN ON-GOING FLAGWATCH.
FLAGWATCH? WHAT DOES THAT MEAN?
TRADE TALK, CYKE.
LONG-TERM CIVILIAN PLANT--A MOLE--SENT TO WATCH FOR ANY POTENTIAL THREATS TO THE STABILITY OF THE GOVERN-MENT.
COLONEL, YOU SAID THIS MUTANT HAS BEEN UNDER REVIEW FOR OVER FOUR-TEEN YEARS?
THAT IS CORRECT, MS. BRADDOCK.
BUT WE LOST CONTACT A MONTH AGO. WE DON'T KNOW HOW OR WHY.
THERE'S ANOTHER MYSTERY, VAZHIN IF THIS INDIVIDUAL IS MUTANT--
--WHY ISN'T HE REGISTERING ON OUR CEREBRO SCANNERS?

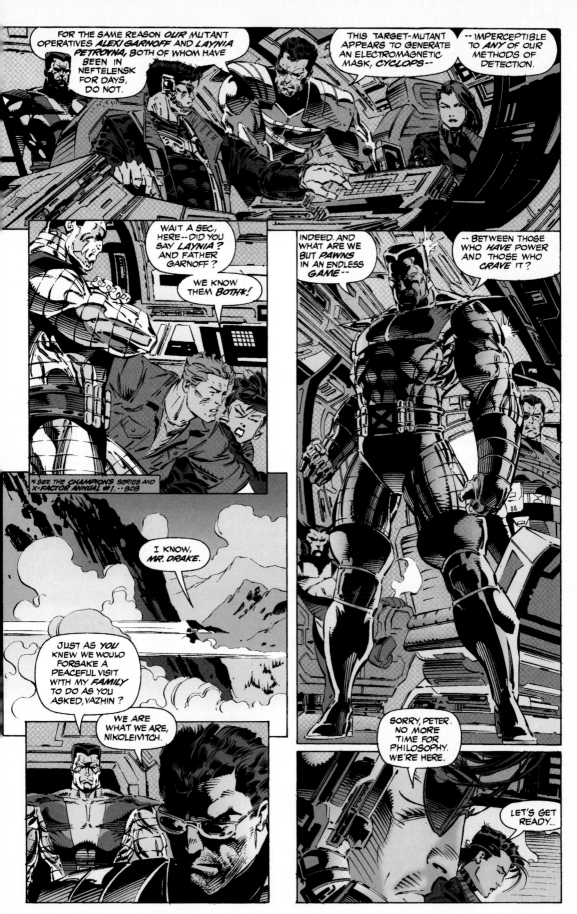

FOR THE SAME REASON *OUR* MUTANT OPERATIVES *ALEXI GARNOFF* AND *LAYNIA PETROVNA*, BOTH OF WHOM HAVE BEEN IN NEFTELENSK FOR DAYS, DO NOT.

THIS TARGET-MUTANT APPEARS TO GENERATE AN ELECTROMAGNETIC MASK, *CYCLOPS*--

-- IMPERCEPTIBLE TO *ANY* OF OUR METHODS OF DETECTION.

WAIT A SEC, HERE-- DID YOU SAY *LAYNIA*? AND FATHER *GARNOFF*?

WE KNOW THEM *BOTH*!

INDEED. AND WHAT ARE WE BUT *PAWNS* IN AN ENDLESS *GAME*--

-- BETWEEN THOSE WHO *HAVE* POWER AND THOSE WHO *CRAVE* IT?

*SEE THE *CHAMPIONS* SERIES AND *X-FACTOR* ANNUAL #1. --BOB

I KNOW, *MR. DRAKE.*

JUST AS *YOU* KNEW WE WOULD FORSAKE A PEACEFUL VISIT WITH MY *FAMILY* TO DO AS YOU ASKED, *VAZHIN*?

WE ARE WHAT WE ARE, *NIKOLEIVITCH.*

SORRY, PETER. NO MORE TIME FOR PHILOSOPHY. WE'RE HERE.

LET'S GET READY...

35

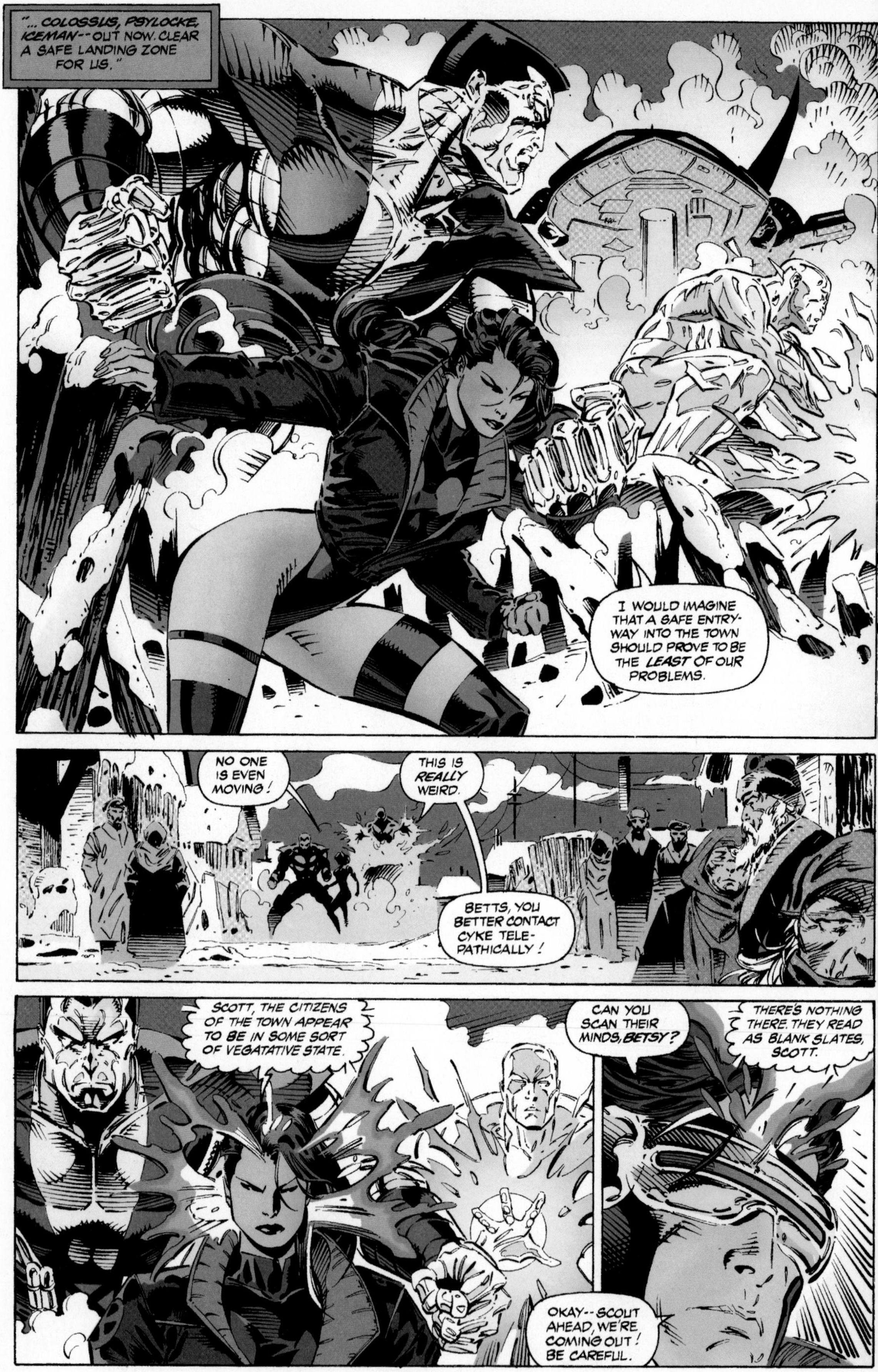
"... COLOSSUS, PSYLOCKE, ICEMAN-- OUT NOW. CLEAR A SAFE LANDING ZONE FOR US."
I WOULD IMAGINE THAT A SAFE ENTRY-WAY INTO THE TOWN SHOULD PROVE TO BE THE LEAST OF OUR PROBLEMS.
NO ONE IS EVEN MOVING!
THIS IS REALLY WEIRD.
BETTS, YOU BETTER CONTACT CYKE TELE-PATHICALLY!
SCOTT, THE CITIZENS OF THE TOWN APPEAR TO BE IN SOME SORT OF VEGATATIVE STATE.
CAN YOU SCAN THEIR MINDS, BETSY?
THERE'S NOTHING THERE. THEY READ AS BLANK SLATES, SCOTT.
OKAY-- SCOUT AHEAD, WE'RE COMING OUT! BE CAREFUL.

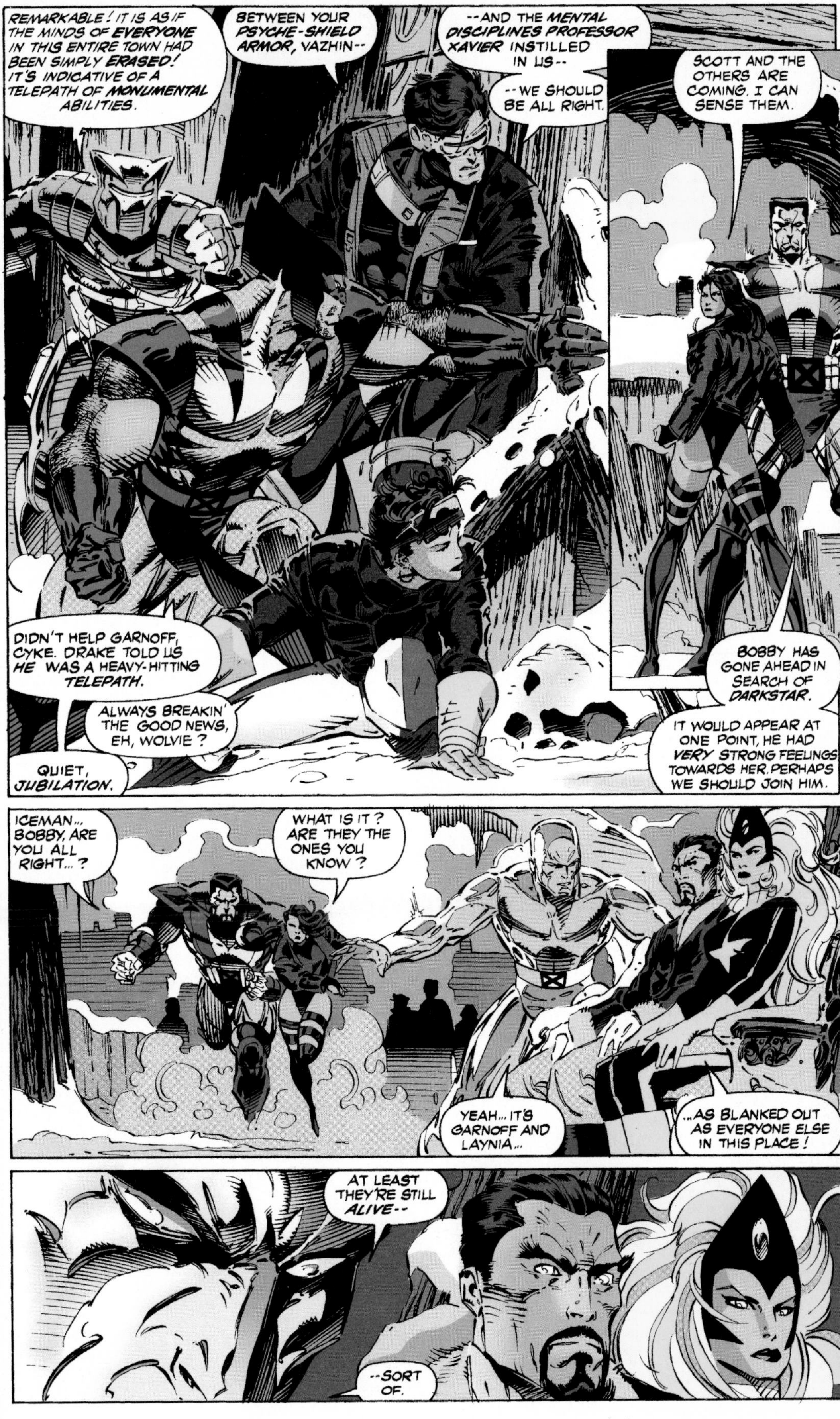
REMARKABLE! IT IS AS IF THE MINDS OF EVERYONE IN THIS ENTIRE TOWN HAD BEEN SIMPLY ERASED! IT'S INDICATIVE OF A TELEPATH OF MONUMENTAL ABILITIES.
BETWEEN YOUR PSYCHE-SHIELD ARMOR, VAZHIN--
--AND THE MENTAL DISCIPLINES PROFESSOR XAVIER INSTILLED IN US--
--WE SHOULD BE ALL RIGHT.
DIDN'T HELP GARNOFF, CYKE. DRAKE TOLD US HE WAS A HEAVY-HITTING TELEPATH.
ALWAYS BREAKIN' THE GOOD NEWS, EH, WOLVIE?
QUIET, JUBILATION.
SCOTT AND THE OTHERS ARE COMING. I CAN SENSE THEM.
BOBBY HAS GONE AHEAD IN SEARCH OF DARKSTAR.
IT WOULD APPEAR AT ONE POINT, HE HAD VERY STRONG FEELINGS TOWARDS HER. PERHAPS WE SHOULD JOIN HIM.
ICEMAN... BOBBY, ARE YOU ALL RIGHT...?
WHAT IS IT? ARE THEY THE ONES YOU KNOW?
YEAH... IT'S GARNOFF AND LAYNIA...
...AS BLANKED OUT AS EVERYONE ELSE IN THIS PLACE!
AT LEAST THEY'RE STILL ALIVE--
--SORT OF.

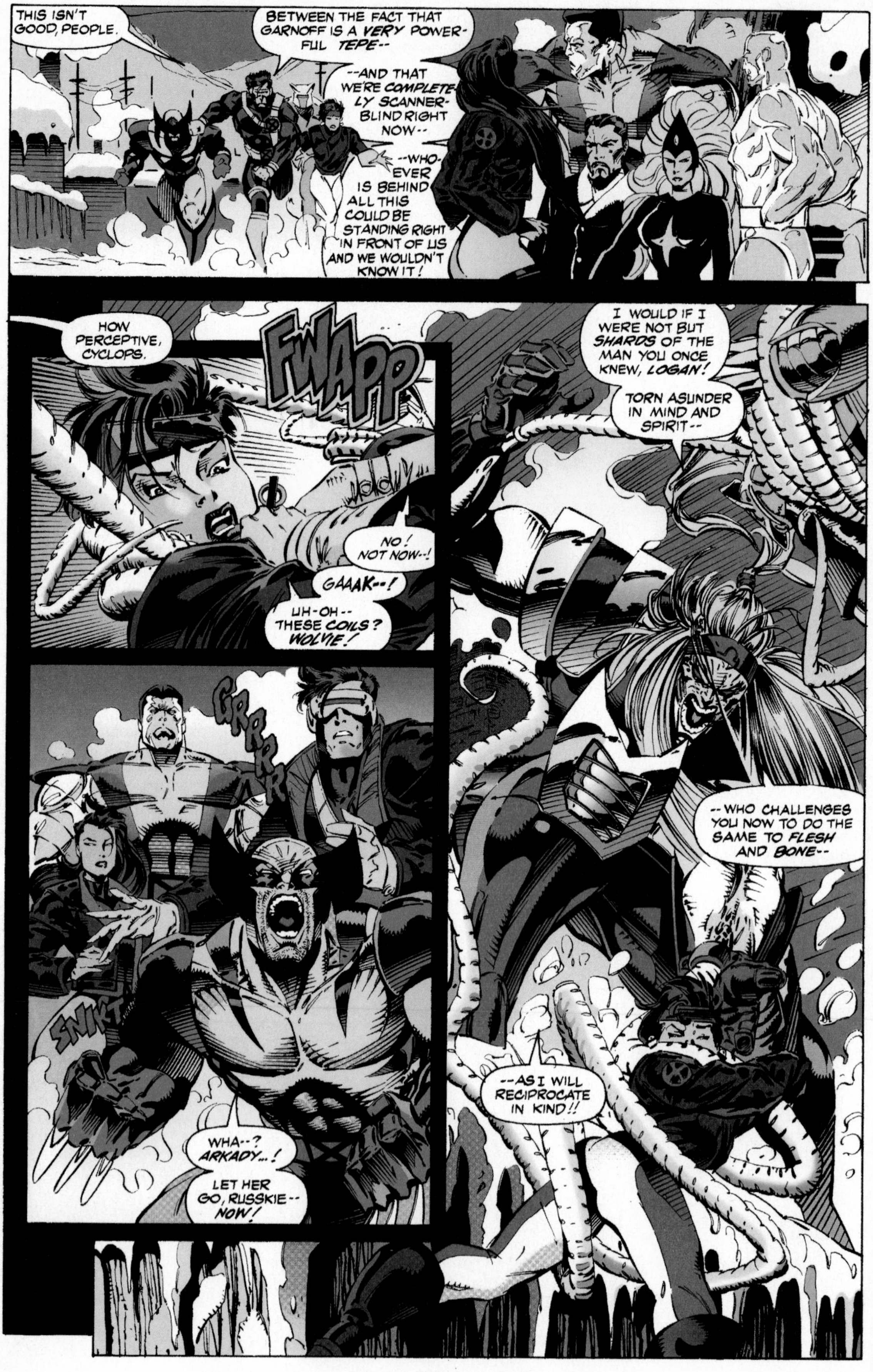
THIS ISN'T GOOD, PEOPLE.
BETWEEN THE FACT THAT GARNOFF IS A VERY POWERFUL TEPE--
--AND THAT WE'RE COMPLETELY SCANNER-BLIND RIGHT NOW--
--WHOEVER IS BEHIND ALL THIS COULD BE STANDING RIGHT IN FRONT OF US AND WE WOULDN'T KNOW IT!
HOW PERCEPTIVE, CYCLOPS.
FWAPP
NO! NOT NOW--!
GAAAK--!
UH-OH-- THESE COILS? WOLVIE!
I WOULD IF I WERE NOT BUT SHARDS OF THE MAN YOU ONCE KNEW, LOGAN!
TORN ASUNDER IN MIND AND SPIRIT--
GRRRR
SNIKT
--WHO CHALLENGES YOU NOW TO DO THE SAME TO FLESH AND BONE--
--AS I WILL RECIPROCATE IN KIND!!
WHA--? ARKADY...!
LET HER GO, RUSSKIE-- NOW!

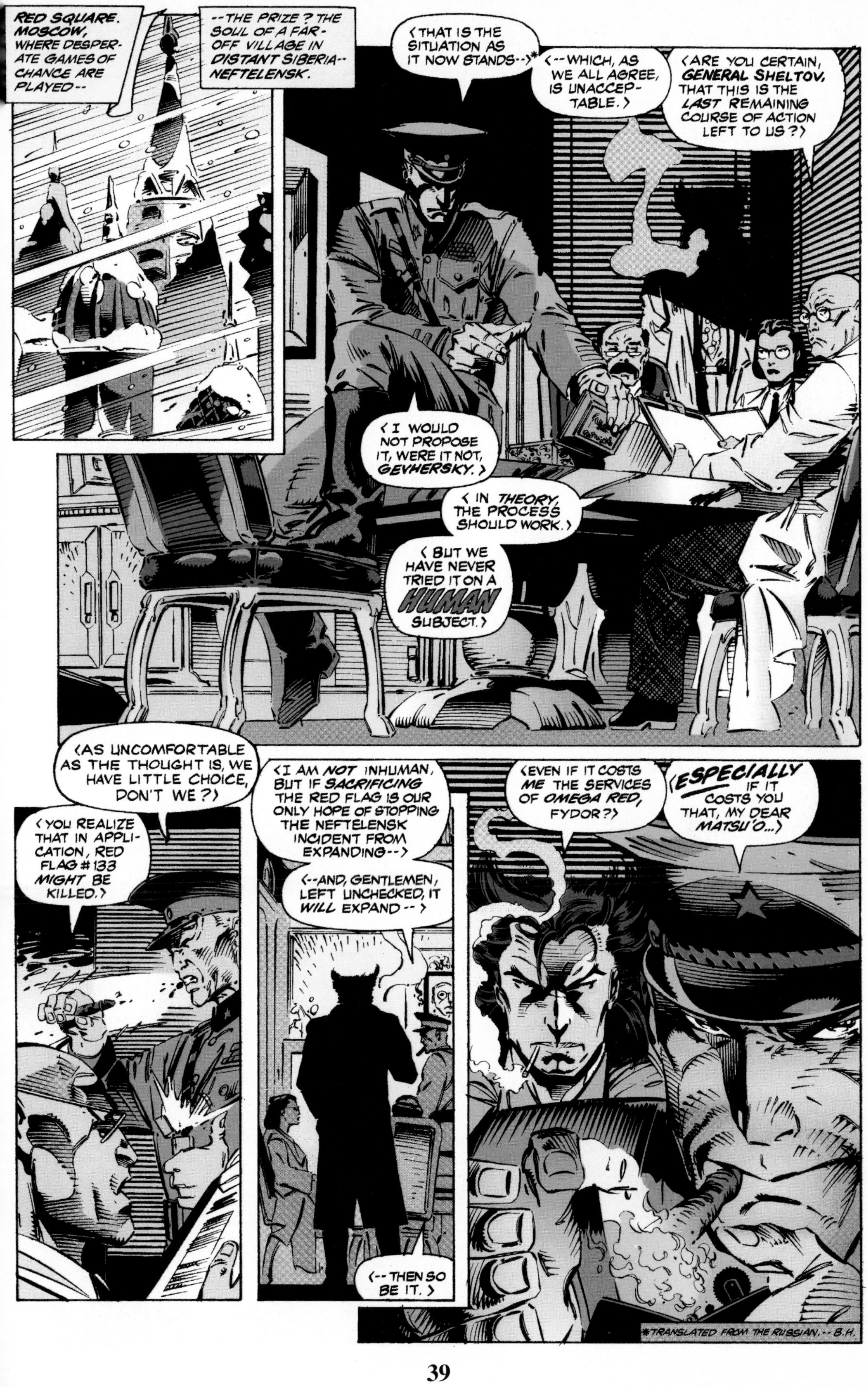
RED SQUARE. MOSCOW, WHERE DESPERATE GAMES OF CHANCE ARE PLAYED--
--THE PRIZE? THE SOUL OF A FAR-OFF VILLAGE IN DISTANT SIBERIA-- NEFTELENSK.
<THAT IS THE SITUATION AS IT NOW STANDS-->*
<--WHICH, AS WE ALL AGREE, IS UNACCEPTABLE.>
<ARE YOU CERTAIN, GENERAL SHELTOV, THAT THIS IS THE LAST REMAINING COURSE OF ACTION LEFT TO US?>
<I WOULD NOT PROPOSE IT, WERE IT NOT, GEVHERSKY.>
<IN THEORY, THE PROCESS SHOULD WORK.>
<BUT WE HAVE NEVER TRIED IT ON A HUMAN SUBJECT.>
<AS UNCOMFORTABLE AS THE THOUGHT IS, WE HAVE LITTLE CHOICE, DON'T WE?>
<YOU REALIZE THAT IN APPLICATION, RED FLAG #133 MIGHT BE KILLED.>
<I AM NOT INHUMAN, BUT IF SACRIFICING THE RED FLAG IS OUR ONLY HOPE OF STOPPING THE NEFTELENSK INCIDENT FROM EXPANDING-->
<--AND, GENTLEMEN, LEFT UNCHECKED, IT WILL EXPAND-->
<--THEN SO BE IT.>
<EVEN IF IT COSTS ME THE SERVICES OF OMEGA RED, FYDOR?>
<ESPECIALLY IF IT COSTS YOU THAT, MY DEAR MATSU'O...>
*TRANSLATED FROM THE RUSSIAN. -- B.H.

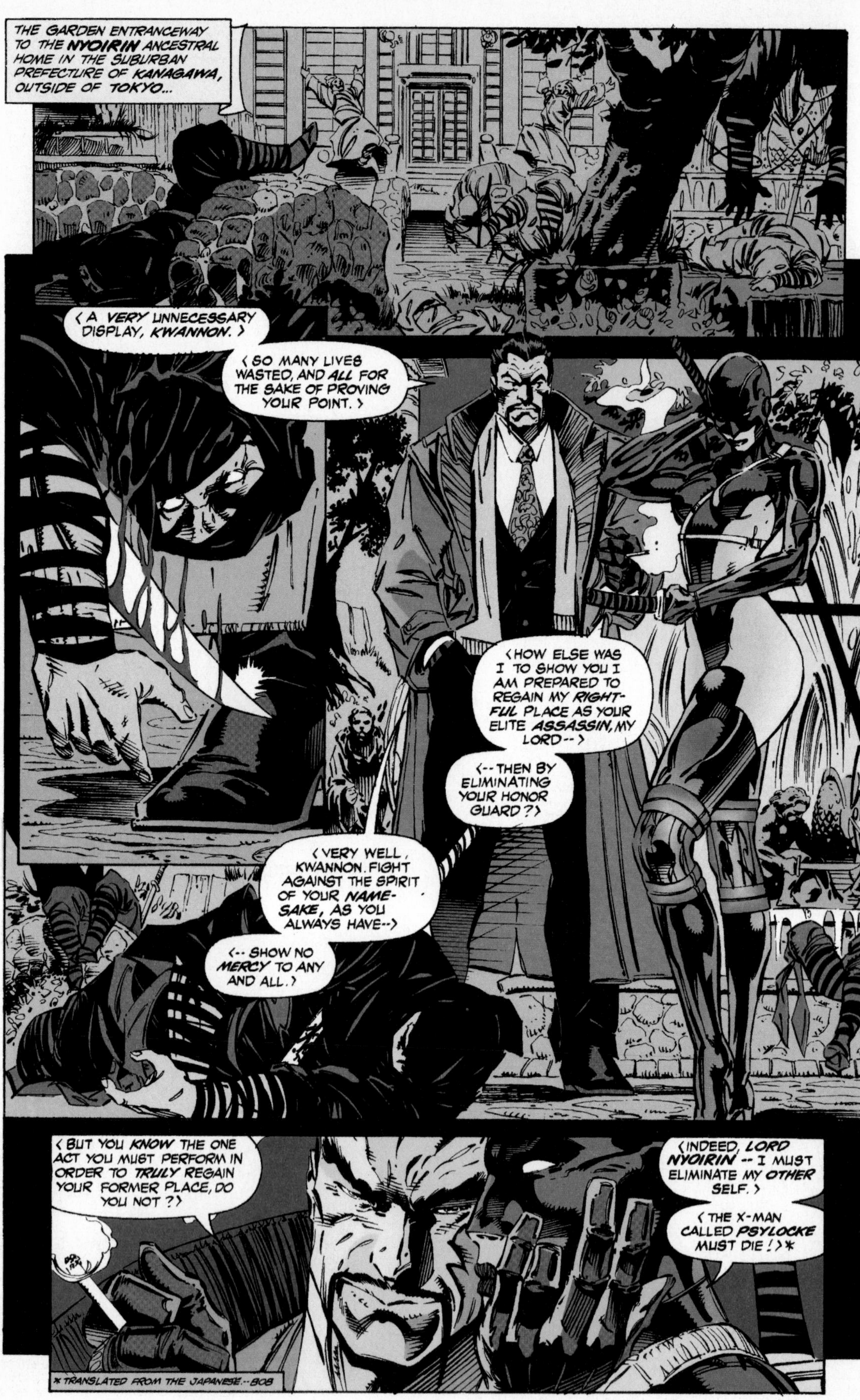
THE GARDEN ENTRANCEWAY TO THE NYOIRIN ANCESTRAL HOME IN THE SUBURBAN PREFECTURE OF KANAGAWA, OUTSIDE OF TOKYO...
‹ A VERY UNNECESSARY DISPLAY, KWANNON. ›
‹ SO MANY LIVES WASTED, AND ALL FOR THE SAKE OF PROVING YOUR POINT. ›
‹ HOW ELSE WAS I TO SHOW YOU I AM PREPARED TO REGAIN MY RIGHTFUL PLACE AS YOUR ELITE ASSASSIN, MY LORD-- ›
‹ --THEN BY ELIMINATING YOUR HONOR GUARD? ›
‹ VERY WELL, KWANNON. FIGHT AGAINST THE SPIRIT OF YOUR NAMESAKE, AS YOU ALWAYS HAVE-- ›
‹ --SHOW NO MERCY TO ANY AND ALL. ›
‹ BUT YOU KNOW THE ONE ACT YOU MUST PERFORM IN ORDER TO TRULY REGAIN YOUR FORMER PLACE, DO YOU NOT? ›
‹ INDEED, LORD NYOIRIN -- I MUST ELIMINATE MY OTHER SELF. ›
‹ THE X-MAN CALLED PSYLOCKE MUST DIE! ›*
*TRANSLATED FROM THE JAPANESE.--BOB

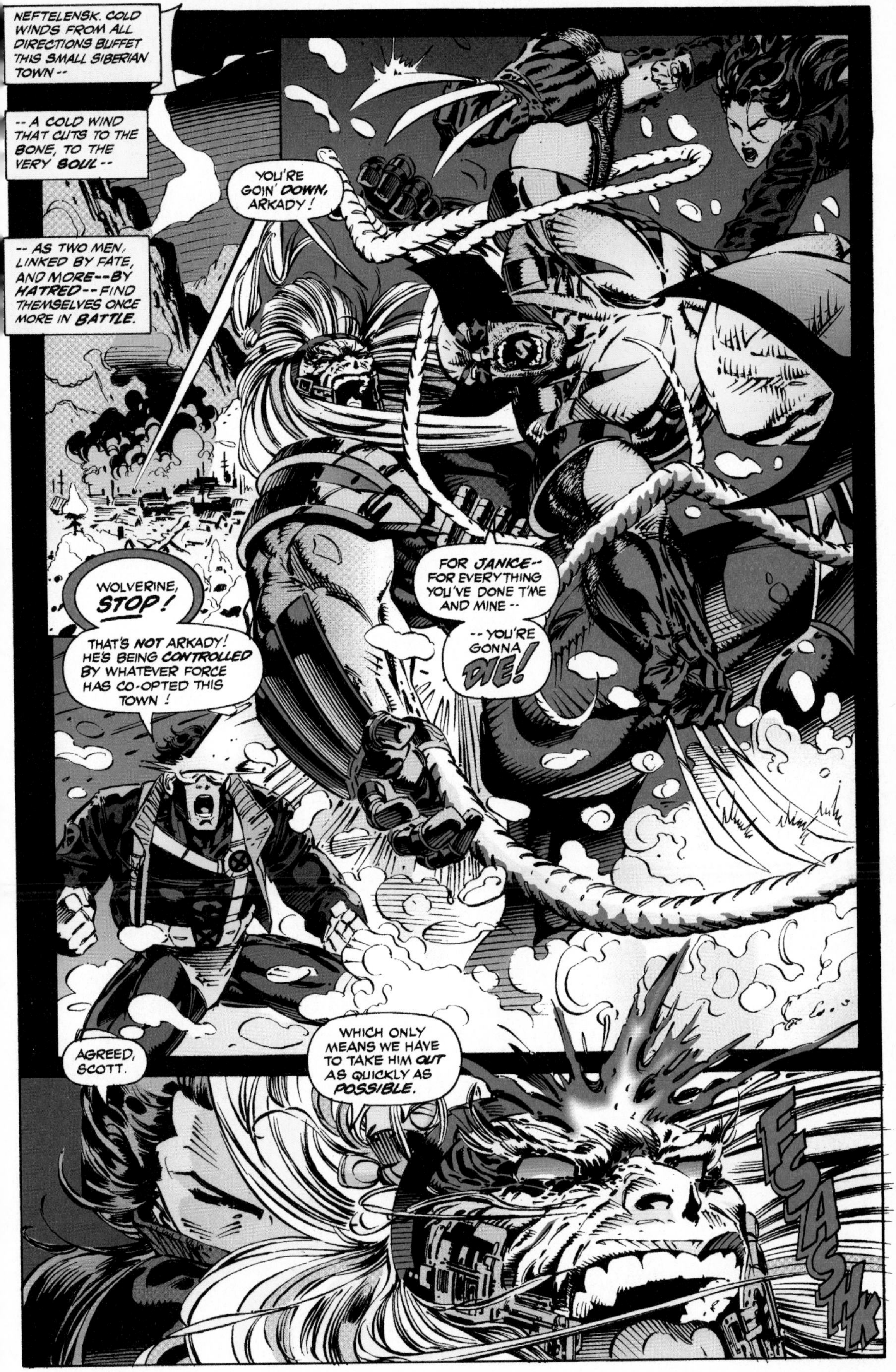
NEFTELENSK. COLD WINDS FROM ALL DIRECTIONS BUFFET THIS SMALL SIBERIAN TOWN --
-- A COLD WIND THAT CUTS TO THE BONE, TO THE VERY SOUL --
-- AS TWO MEN, LINKED BY FATE, AND MORE--BY HATRED--FIND THEMSELVES ONCE MORE IN BATTLE.
YOU'RE GOIN' DOWN, ARKADY!
FOR JANICE-- FOR EVERYTHING YOU'VE DONE T'ME AND MINE --
-- YOU'RE GONNA DIE!
WOLVERINE, STOP!
THAT'S NOT ARKADY! HE'S BEING CONTROLLED BY WHATEVER FORCE HAS CO-OPTED THIS TOWN!
AGREED, SCOTT.
WHICH ONLY MEANS WE HAVE TO TAKE HIM OUT AS QUICKLY AS POSSIBLE.
FSSASHK

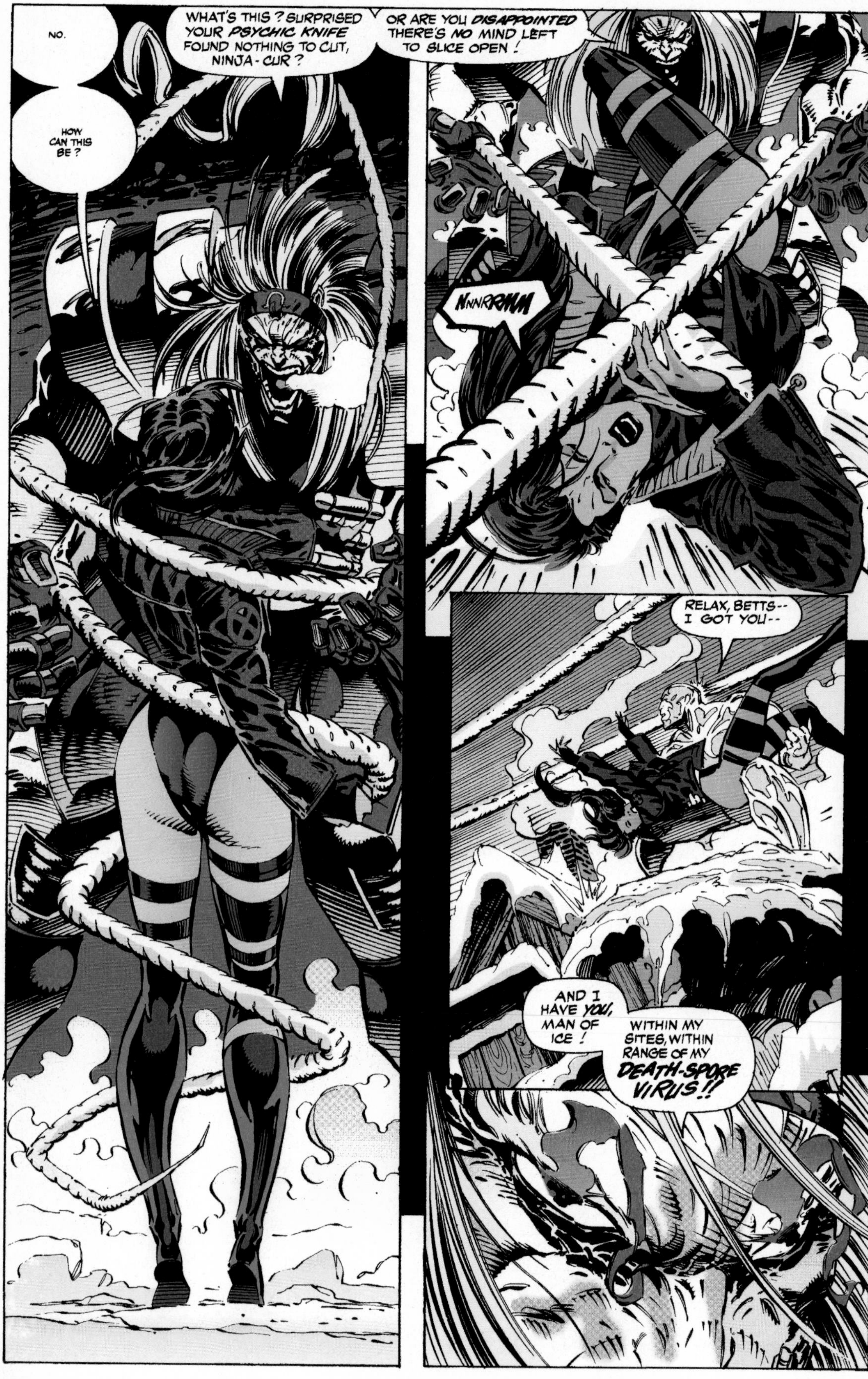
NO.
HOW CAN THIS BE?
WHAT'S THIS? SURPRISED YOUR PSYCHIC KNIFE FOUND NOTHING TO CUT, NINJA-CUR?
OR ARE YOU DISAPPOINTED THERE'S NO MIND LEFT TO SLICE OPEN!
NNNRRMM
RELAX, BETTS-- I GOT YOU--
AND I HAVE YOU, MAN OF ICE!
WITHIN MY SITES, WITHIN RANGE OF MY DEATH-SPORE VIRUS!!

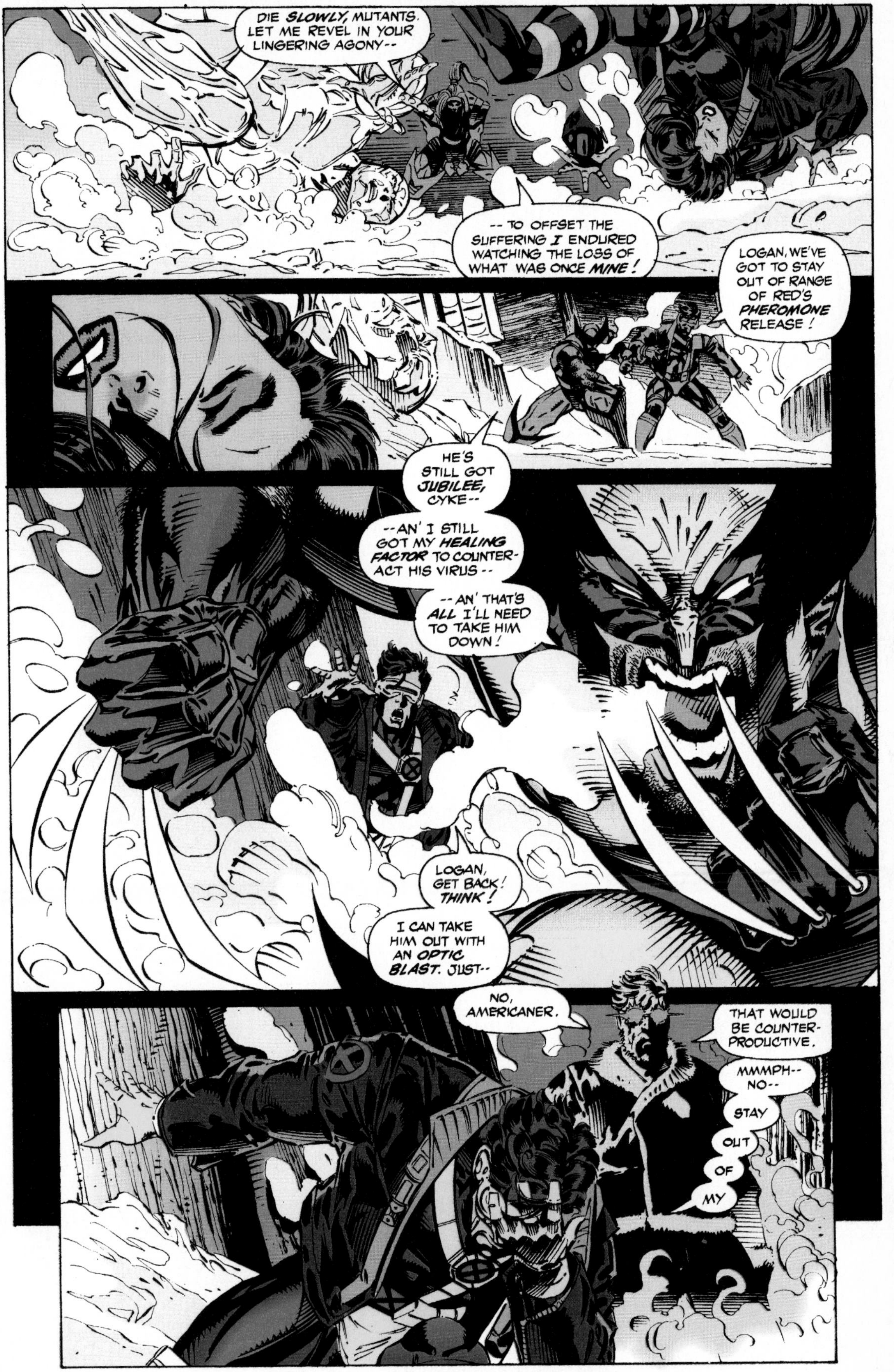
DIE SLOWLY, MUTANTS. LET ME REVEL IN YOUR LINGERING AGONY--
-- TO OFFSET THE SUFFERING I ENDURED WATCHING THE LOSS OF WHAT WAS ONCE MINE!
LOGAN, WE'VE GOT TO STAY OUT OF RANGE OF RED'S PHEROMONE RELEASE!
HE'S STILL GOT JUBILEE, CYKE--
--AN' I STILL GOT MY HEALING FACTOR TO COUNTERACT HIS VIRUS--
-- AN' THAT'S ALL I'LL NEED TO TAKE HIM DOWN!
LOGAN, GET BACK! THINK!
I CAN TAKE HIM OUT WITH AN OPTIC BLAST. JUST--
NO, AMERICANER.
THAT WOULD BE COUNTER-PRODUCTIVE.
MMMPH-- NO--
STAY
OUT
OF
MY

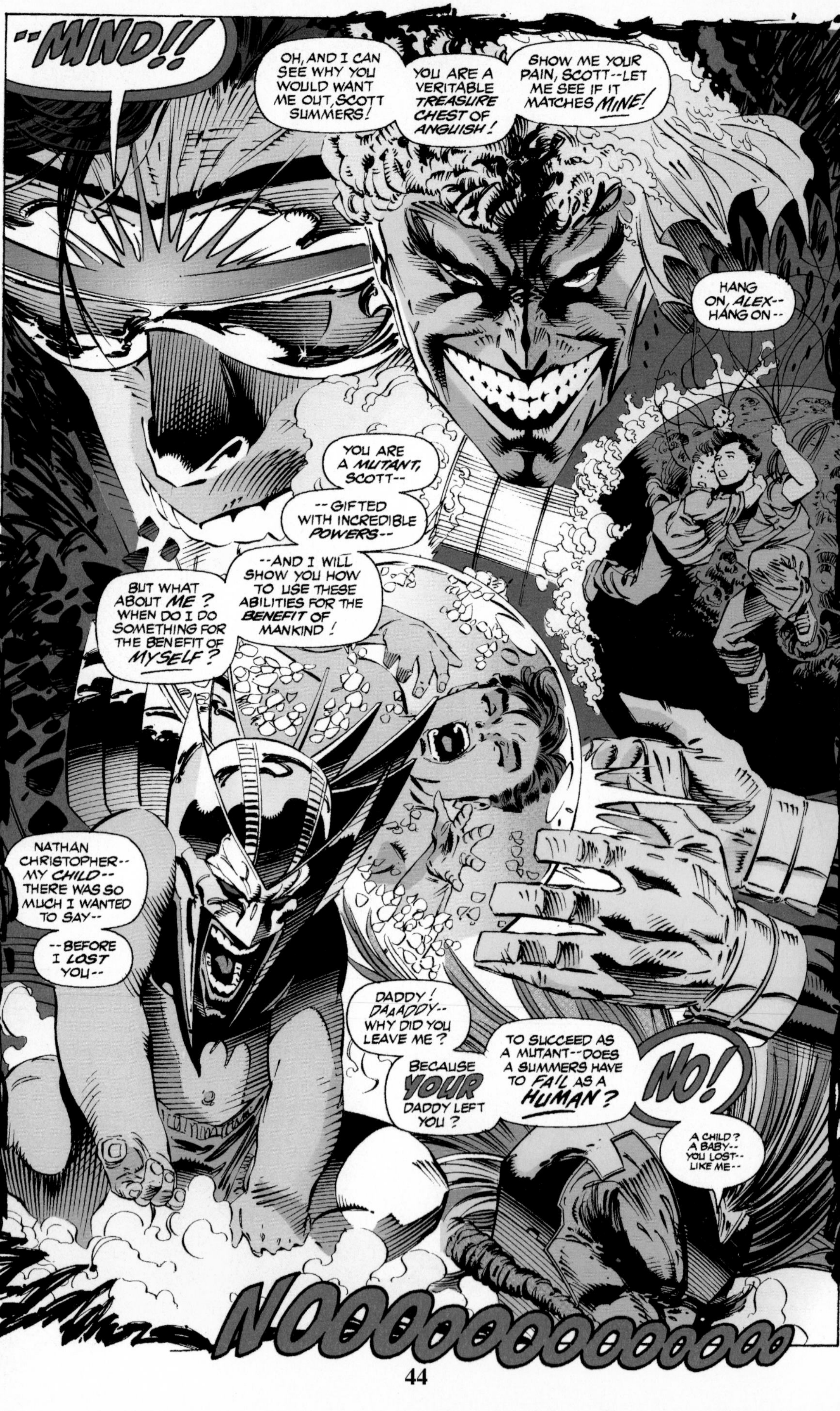
--MIND!!
OH, AND I CAN SEE WHY YOU WOULD WANT ME OUT, SCOTT SUMMERS!
YOU ARE A VERITABLE TREASURE CHEST OF ANGUISH!
SHOW ME YOUR PAIN, SCOTT--LET ME SEE IF IT MATCHES MINE!
HANG ON, ALEX-- HANG ON--
YOU ARE A MUTANT, SCOTT--
--GIFTED WITH INCREDIBLE POWERS--
--AND I WILL SHOW YOU HOW TO USE THESE ABILITIES FOR THE BENEFIT OF MANKIND!
BUT WHAT ABOUT ME? WHEN DO I DO SOMETHING FOR THE BENEFIT OF MYSELF?
NATHAN CHRISTOPHER-- MY CHILD-- THERE WAS SO MUCH I WANTED TO SAY--
--BEFORE I LOST YOU--
DADDY! DAAADDY-- WHY DID YOU LEAVE ME?
BECAUSE YOUR DADDY LEFT YOU?
TO SUCCEED AS A MUTANT--DOES A SUMMERS HAVE TO FAIL AS A HUMAN?
NO!
A CHILD? A BABY-- YOU LOST-- LIKE ME--
NOOOOOOOOOOOOO

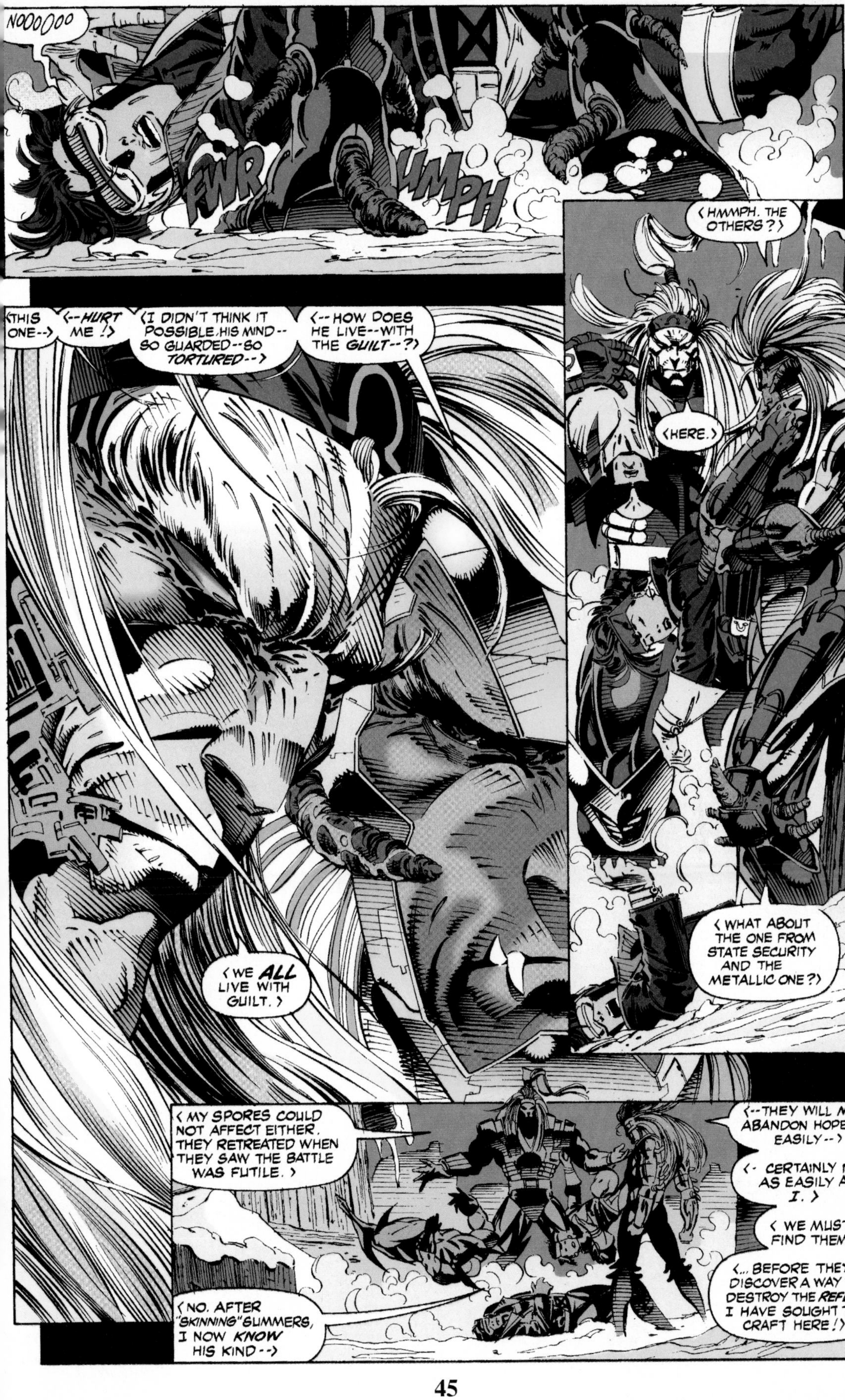

NOOOOOO
FWRUMPH
‹HMMPH. THE OTHERS?›
‹THIS ONE--›
‹--HURT ME!›
‹I DIDN'T THINK IT POSSIBLE. HIS MIND--SO GUARDED--SO TORTURED--›
‹--HOW DOES HE LIVE--WITH THE GUILT--?›
‹HERE.›
‹WE ALL LIVE WITH GUILT.›
‹WHAT ABOUT THE ONE FROM STATE SECURITY AND THE METALLIC ONE?›
‹MY SPORES COULD NOT AFFECT EITHER. THEY RETREATED WHEN THEY SAW THE BATTLE WAS FUTILE.›
‹NO. AFTER "SKINNING" SUMMERS, I NOW KNOW HIS KIND--›
‹--THEY WILL NOT ABANDON HOPE SO EASILY--›
‹- CERTAINLY NOT AS EASILY AS I.›
‹WE MUST FIND THEM...›
‹...BEFORE THEY DISCOVER A WAY TO DESTROY THE REFUGE I HAVE SOUGHT TO CRAFT HERE!›

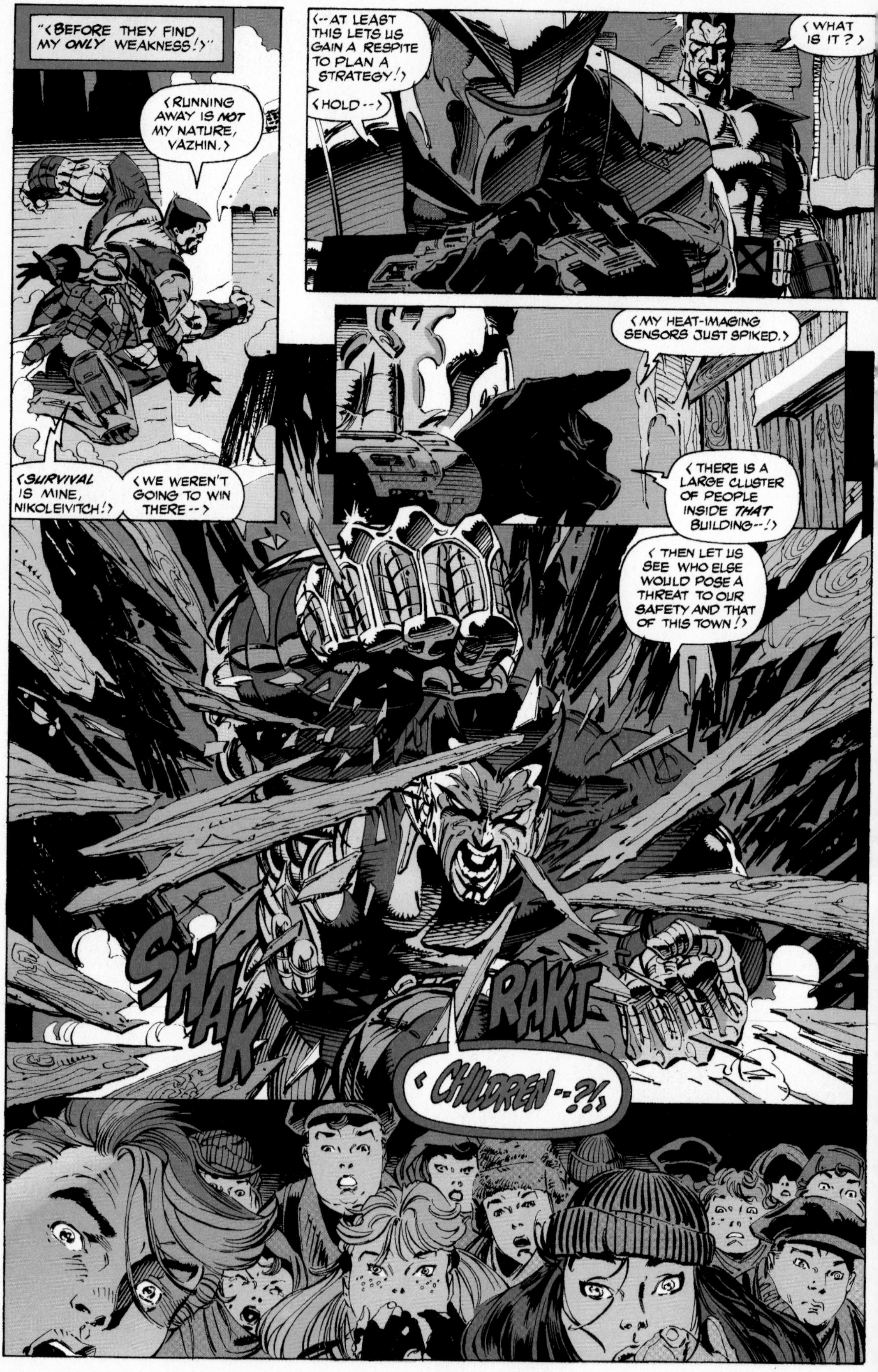
"‹BEFORE THEY FIND MY ONLY WEAKNESS!›"
‹RUNNING AWAY IS NOT MY NATURE, VAZHIN.›
‹SURVIVAL IS MINE, NIKOLEIVITCH!›
‹WE WEREN'T GOING TO WIN THERE--›
‹--AT LEAST THIS LETS US GAIN A RESPITE TO PLAN A STRATEGY!›
‹HOLD--›
‹WHAT IS IT?›
‹MY HEAT-IMAGING SENSORS JUST SPIKED.›
‹THERE IS A LARGE CLUSTER OF PEOPLE INSIDE THAT BUILDING--!›
‹THEN LET US SEE WHO ELSE WOULD POSE A THREAT TO OUR SAFETY AND THAT OF THIS TOWN!›
SHAK
RAKT
‹CHILDREN--?!›

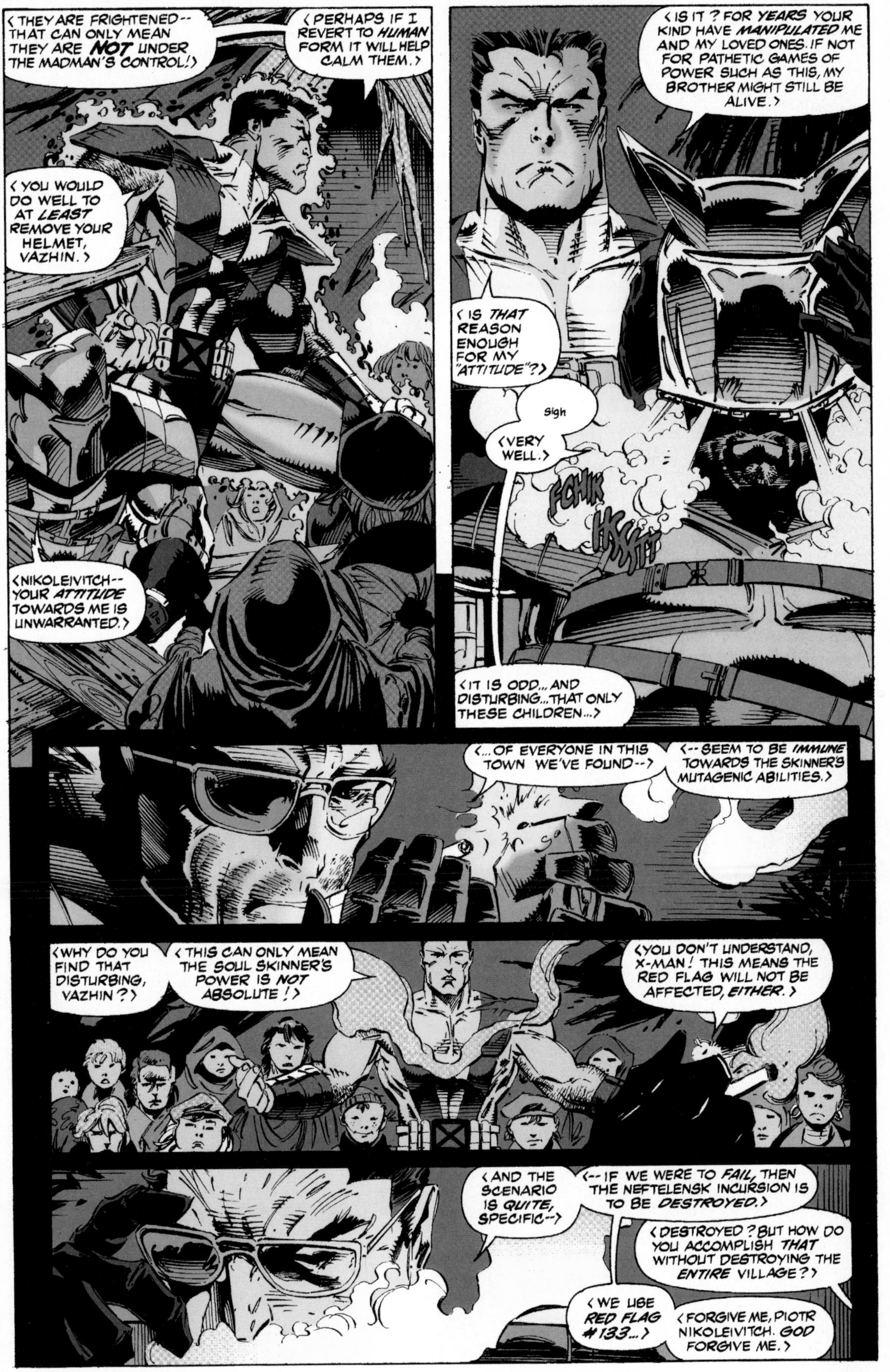
‹THEY ARE FRIGHTENED-- THAT CAN ONLY MEAN THEY ARE NOT UNDER THE MADMAN'S CONTROL!›
‹PERHAPS IF I REVERT TO HUMAN FORM IT WILL HELP CALM THEM.›
‹YOU WOULD DO WELL TO AT LEAST REMOVE YOUR HELMET, VAZHIN.›
‹NIKOLEIVITCH-- YOUR ATTITUDE TOWARDS ME IS UNWARRANTED.›
‹IS IT? FOR YEARS YOUR KIND HAVE MANIPULATED ME AND MY LOVED ONES. IF NOT FOR PATHETIC GAMES OF POWER SUCH AS THIS, MY BROTHER MIGHT STILL BE ALIVE.›
‹IS THAT REASON ENOUGH FOR MY "ATTITUDE"?›
Sigh
‹VERY WELL.›
FCHIK
HKSSTT
‹IT IS ODD... AND DISTURBING... THAT ONLY THESE CHILDREN...›
‹...OF EVERYONE IN THIS TOWN WE'VE FOUND--›
‹--SEEM TO BE IMMUNE TOWARDS THE SKINNER'S MUTAGENIC ABILITIES.›
‹WHY DO YOU FIND THAT DISTURBING, VAZHIN?›
‹THIS CAN ONLY MEAN THE SOUL SKINNER'S POWER IS NOT ABSOLUTE!›
‹YOU DON'T UNDERSTAND, X-MAN! THIS MEANS THE RED FLAG WILL NOT BE AFFECTED, EITHER.›
‹AND THE SCENARIO IS QUITE, SPECIFIC--›
‹--IF WE WERE TO FAIL, THEN THE NEFTELENSK INCURSION IS TO BE DESTROYED.›
‹DESTROYED? BUT HOW DO YOU ACCOMPLISH THAT WITHOUT DESTROYING THE ENTIRE VILLAGE?›
‹WE USE RED FLAG #133...›
‹FORGIVE ME, PIOTR NIKOLEIVITCH. GOD FORGIVE ME.›

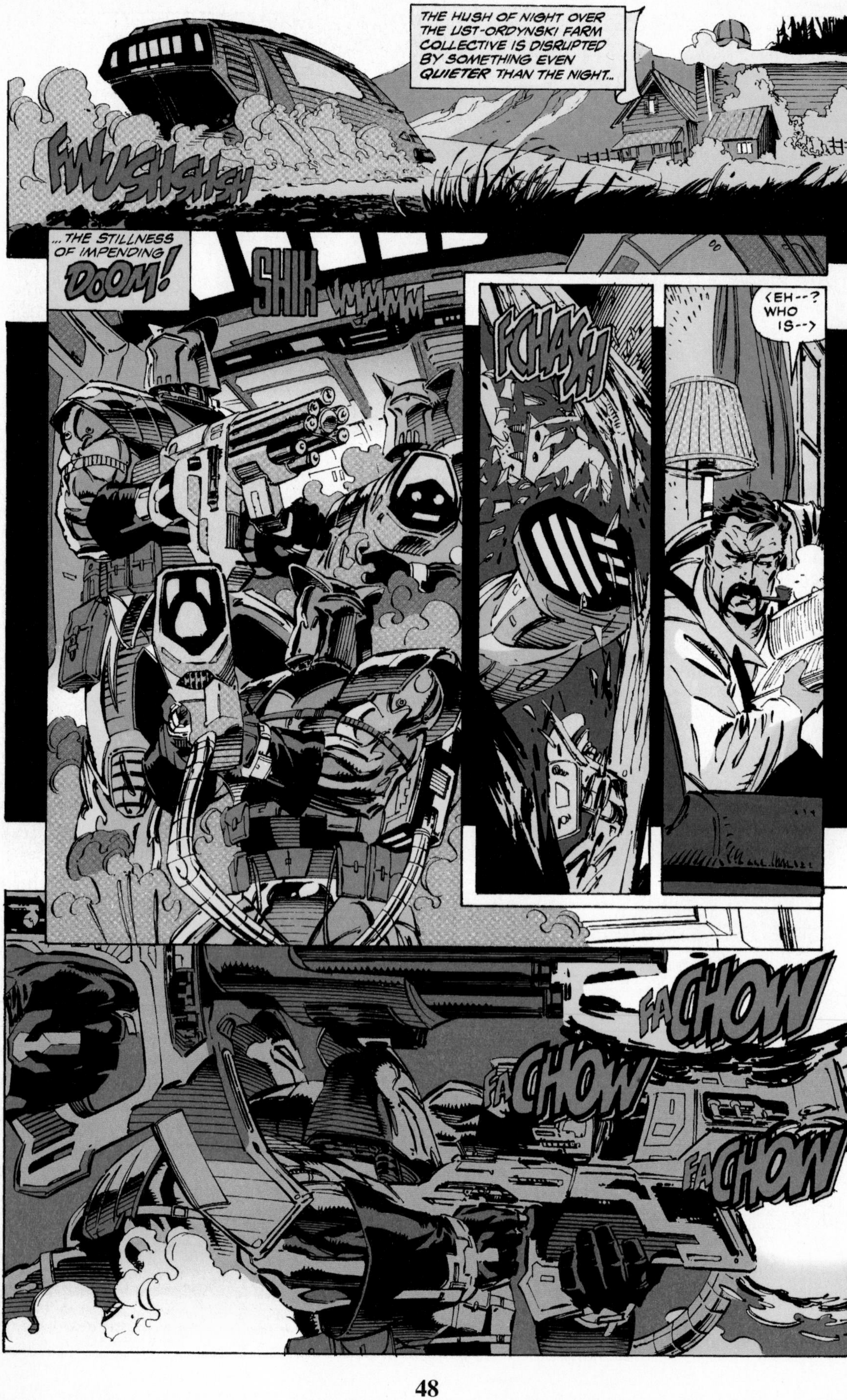
THE HUSH OF NIGHT OVER THE UST-ORDYNSKI FARM COLLECTIVE IS DISRUPTED BY SOMETHING EVEN QUIETER THAN THE NIGHT...
FWUSHSHSH
...THE STILLNESS OF IMPENDING DOOM!
SHIK
VMMMM
FCHASH
<EH--? WHO IS-->
FACHOW
FACHOW
FACHOW

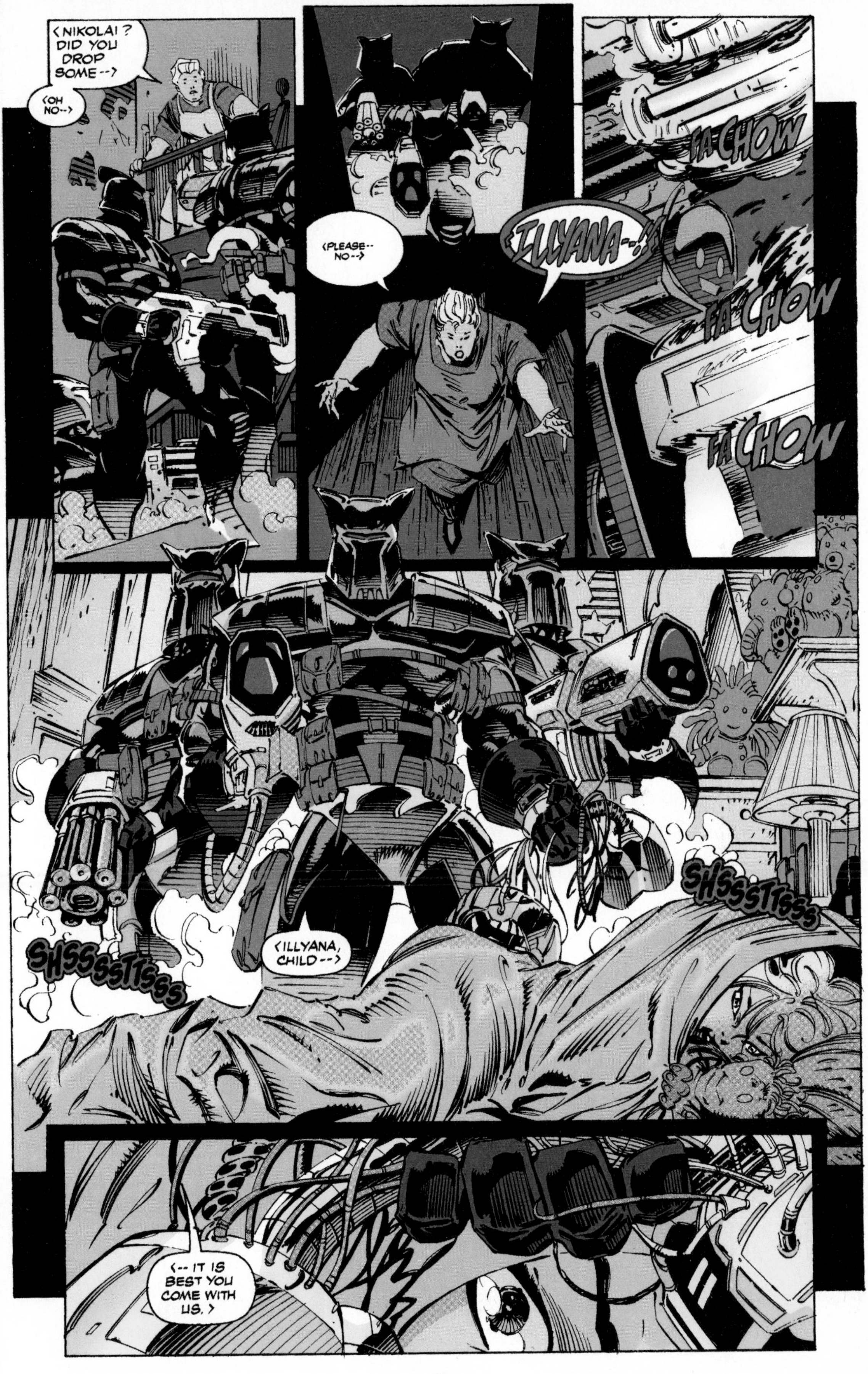

‹NIKOLAI? DID YOU DROP SOME--›
‹OH NO--›
‹PLEASE-- NO--›
‹ILLYANA--!›
FA CHOW
FA CHOW
FA CHOW
SHSSSTTSSS
‹ILLYANA, CHILD--›
SHSSSSTTSSS
‹-- IT IS BEST YOU COME WITH US.›

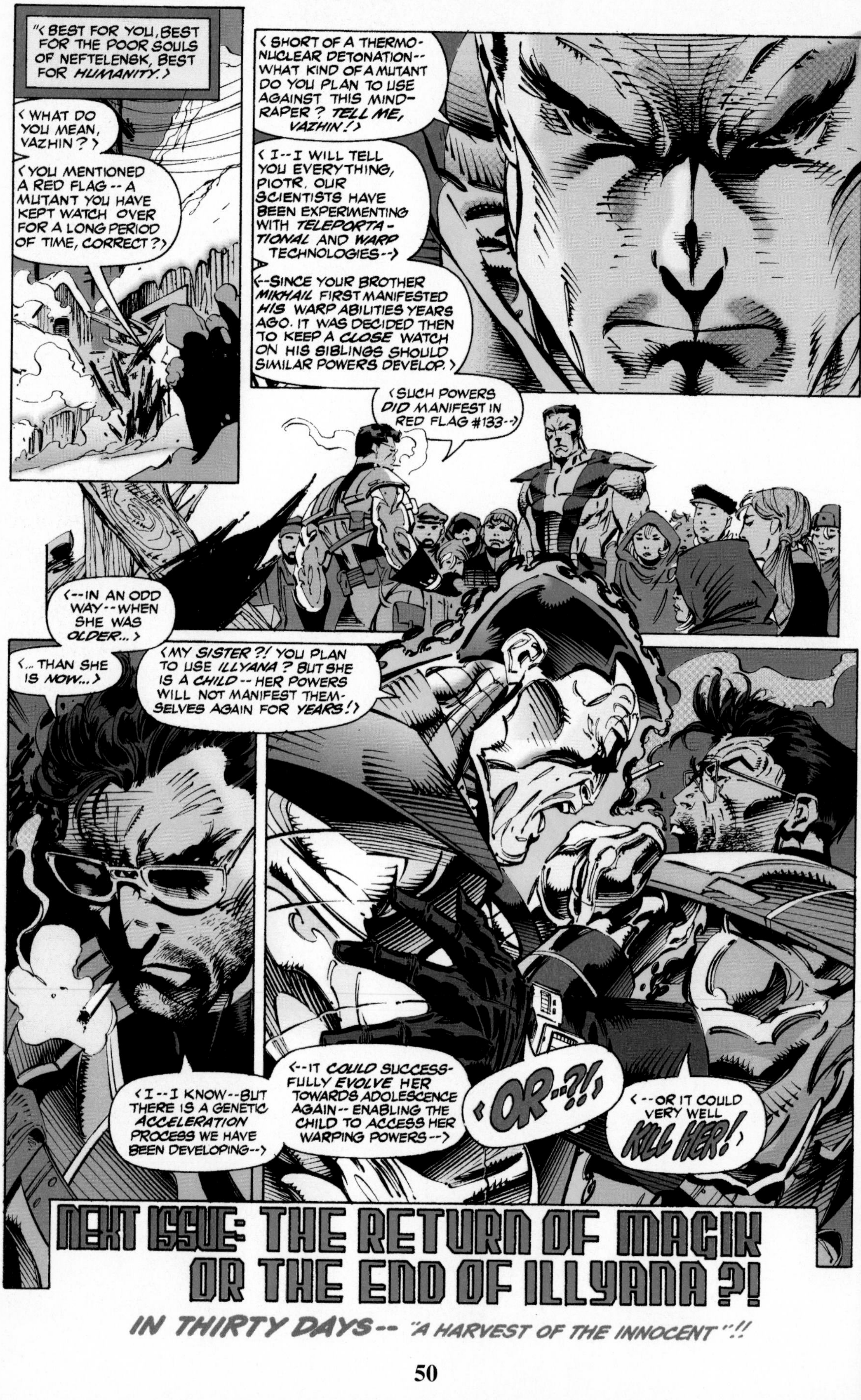
"< BEST FOR YOU, BEST FOR THE POOR SOULS OF NEFTELENSK, BEST FOR *HUMANITY*.>
< WHAT DO YOU MEAN, VAZHIN? >
< YOU MENTIONED A RED FLAG -- A MUTANT YOU HAVE KEPT WATCH OVER FOR A LONG PERIOD OF TIME, CORRECT? >
< SHORT OF A THERMO-NUCLEAR DETONATION -- WHAT KIND OF A MUTANT DO YOU PLAN TO USE AGAINST THIS MIND-RAPER? *TELL ME, VAZHIN!* >
< I -- I WILL TELL YOU EVERYTHING, PIOTR. OUR SCIENTISTS HAVE BEEN EXPERIMENTING WITH *TELEPORTATIONAL* AND *WARP* TECHNOLOGIES -- >
< -- SINCE YOUR BROTHER *MIKHAIL* FIRST MANIFESTED *HIS* WARP ABILITIES YEARS AGO. IT WAS DECIDED THEN TO KEEP A *CLOSE* WATCH ON HIS SIBLINGS SHOULD SIMILAR POWERS DEVELOP. >
< SUCH POWERS *DID* MANIFEST IN RED FLAG #133 -- >
< -- IN AN ODD WAY -- WHEN SHE WAS *OLDER*... >
< ... THAN SHE IS *NOW*... >
< MY *SISTER*?! YOU PLAN TO USE *ILLYANA*? BUT SHE IS A *CHILD* -- HER POWERS WILL NOT MANIFEST THEMSELVES AGAIN FOR *YEARS*! >
< I -- I KNOW -- BUT THERE IS A GENETIC *ACCELERATION* PROCESS WE HAVE BEEN DEVELOPING -- >
< -- IT *COULD* SUCCESSFULLY *EVOLVE* HER TOWARDS ADOLESCENCE AGAIN -- ENABLING THE CHILD TO ACCESS HER WARPING POWERS -- >
< OR --?! >
< -- OR IT COULD VERY WELL *KILL HER!* >
NEXT ISSUE: THE RETURN OF MAGIK OR THE END OF ILLYANA?!

IN THIRTY DAYS -- "A HARVEST OF THE INNOCENT"!!

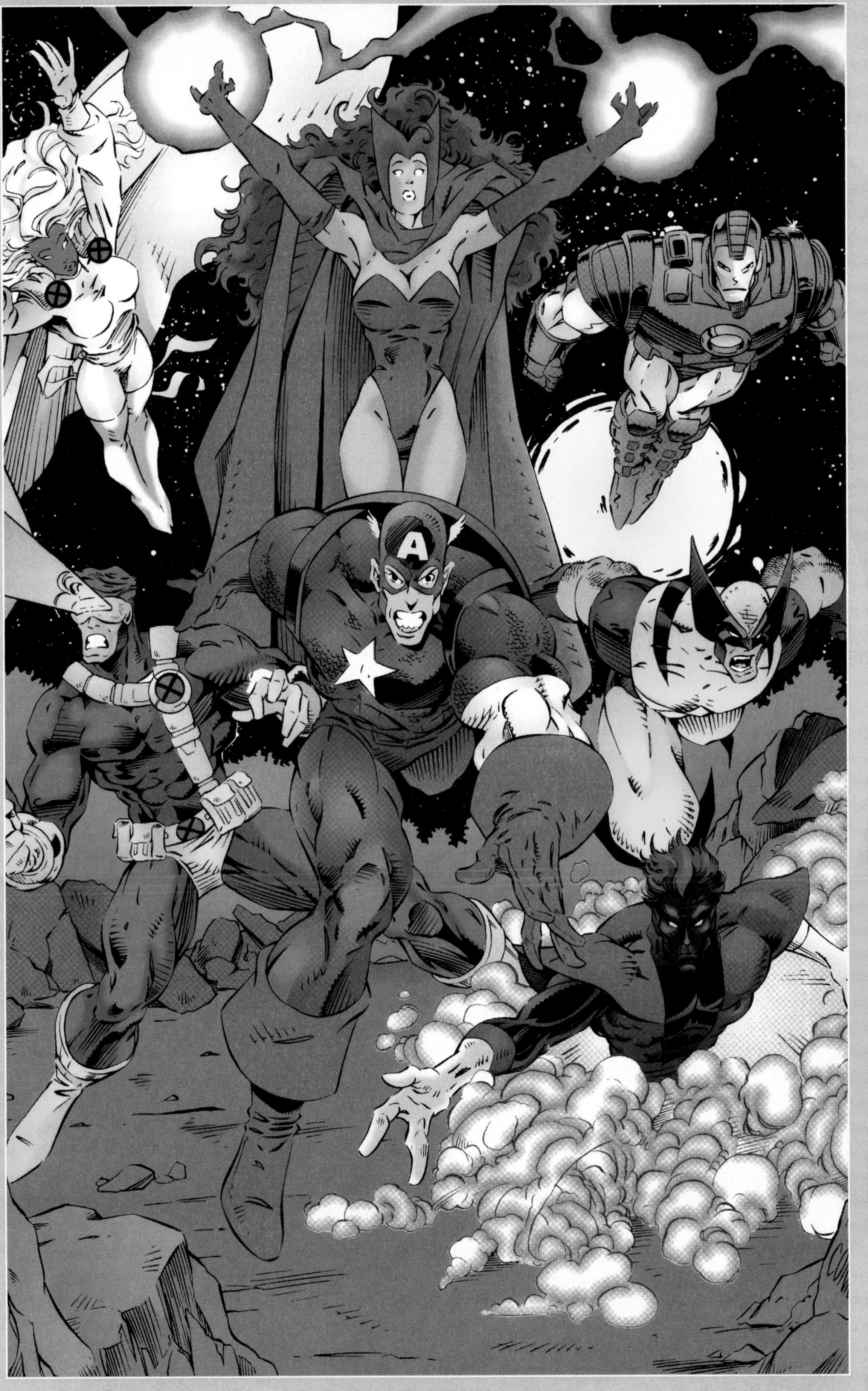

M.A.X. (Maximum Anniversary X-Perience) Yearbook pinup by Joe Madureira & Kevin Conrad

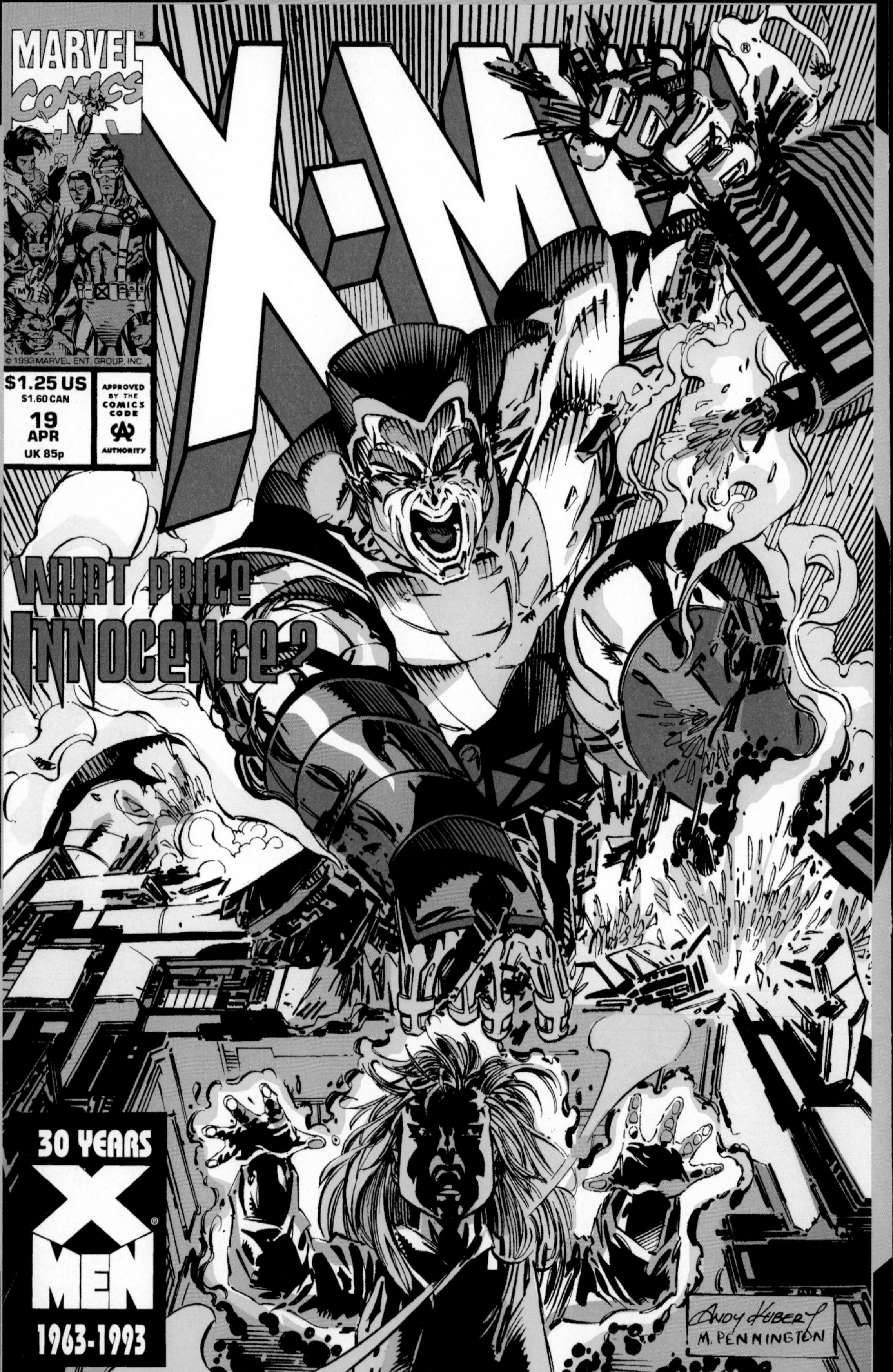
MARVEL COMICS
X-MEN
© 1993 MARVEL ENT. GROUP, INC.
$1.25 US
$1.60 CAN
19
APR
UK 85p
APPROVED BY THE COMICS CODE AUTHORITY
WHAT PRICE INNOCENCE?
30 YEARS
X MEN
1963-1993
ANDY KUBERT
M. PENNINGTON

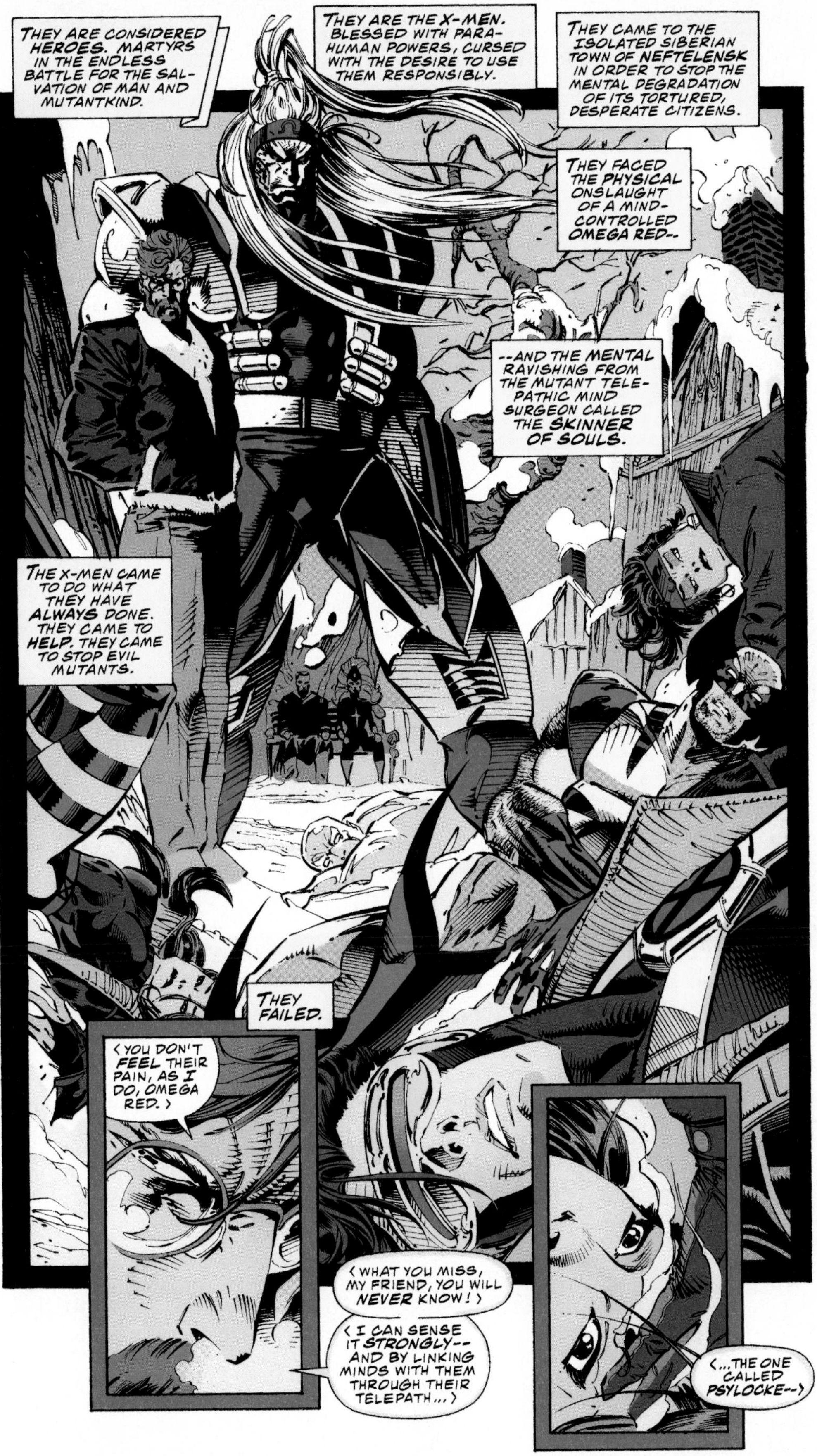
THEY ARE CONSIDERED HEROES. MARTYRS IN THE ENDLESS BATTLE FOR THE SALVATION OF MAN AND MUTANTKIND.
THEY ARE THE X-MEN. BLESSED WITH PARA-HUMAN POWERS, CURSED WITH THE DESIRE TO USE THEM RESPONSIBLY.
THEY CAME TO THE ISOLATED SIBERIAN TOWN OF NEFTELENSK IN ORDER TO STOP THE MENTAL DEGRADATION OF ITS TORTURED, DESPERATE CITIZENS.
THEY FACED THE PHYSICAL ONSLAUGHT OF A MIND-CONTROLLED OMEGA RED--
--AND THE MENTAL RAVISHING FROM THE MUTANT TELEPATHIC MIND SURGEON CALLED THE SKINNER OF SOULS.
THE X-MEN CAME TO DO WHAT THEY HAVE ALWAYS DONE. THEY CAME TO HELP. THEY CAME TO STOP EVIL MUTANTS.
THEY FAILED.
‹YOU DON'T FEEL THEIR PAIN, AS I DO, OMEGA RED.›
‹WHAT YOU MISS, MY FRIEND, YOU WILL NEVER KNOW!›
‹I CAN SENSE IT STRONGLY-- AND BY LINKING MINDS WITH THEM THROUGH THEIR TELEPATH...›
‹...THE ONE CALLED PSYLOCKE--›

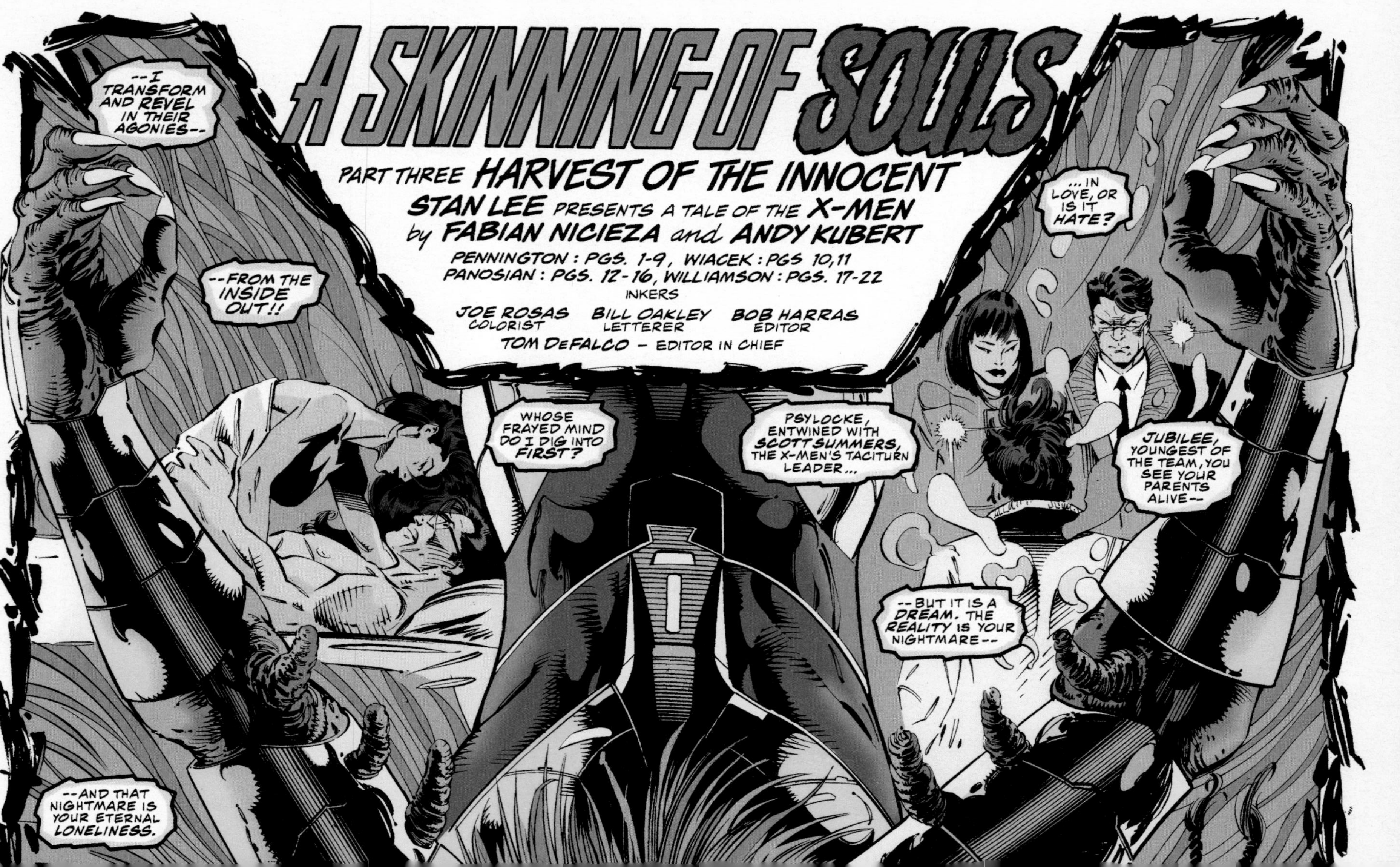

A SKINNING OF SOULS
PART THREE HARVEST OF THE INNOCENT
STAN LEE PRESENTS A TALE OF THE X-MEN
by FABIAN NICIEZA and ANDY KUBERT
PENNINGTON : PGS. 1-9, WIACEK : PGS 10,11
PANOSIAN : PGS. 12-16, WILLIAMSON : PGS. 17-22
INKERS
JOE ROSAS COLORIST
BILL OAKLEY LETTERER
BOB HARRAS EDITOR
TOM DEFALCO - EDITOR IN CHIEF
--I TRANSFORM AND REVEL IN THEIR AGONIES--
--FROM THE INSIDE OUT!!
WHOSE FRAYED MIND DO I DIG INTO FIRST?
PSYLOCKE, ENTWINED WITH SCOTT SUMMERS, THE X-MEN'S TACITURN LEADER...
...IN LOVE, OR IS IT HATE?
JUBILEE, YOUNGEST OF THE TEAM, YOU SEE YOUR PARENTS ALIVE--
--BUT IT IS A DREAM. THE REALITY IS YOUR NIGHTMARE--
--AND THAT NIGHTMARE IS YOUR ETERNAL LONELINESS.

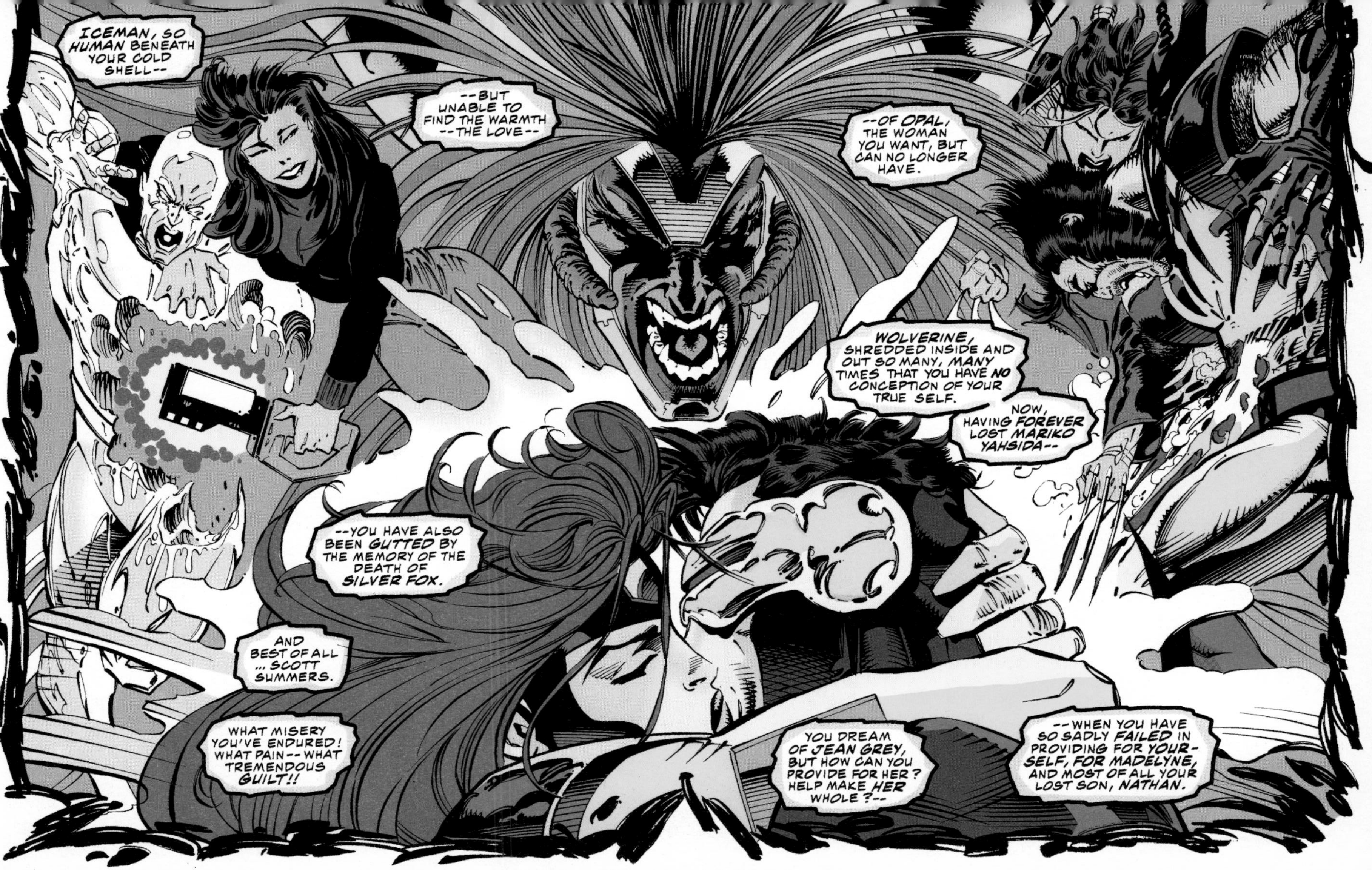
ICEMAN, SO HUMAN BENEATH YOUR COLD SHELL--
--BUT UNABLE TO FIND THE WARMTH --THE LOVE--
--OF OPAL, THE WOMAN YOU WANT, BUT CAN NO LONGER HAVE.
WOLVERINE, SHREDDED INSIDE AND OUT SO MANY, MANY TIMES THAT YOU HAVE NO CONCEPTION OF YOUR TRUE SELF.
NOW, HAVING FOREVER LOST MARIKO YAHSIDA--
--YOU HAVE ALSO BEEN GUTTED BY THE MEMORY OF THE DEATH OF SILVER FOX.
AND BEST OF ALL ...SCOTT SUMMERS.
WHAT MISERY YOU'VE ENDURED! WHAT PAIN--WHAT TREMENDOUS GUILT!!
YOU DREAM OF JEAN GREY, BUT HOW CAN YOU PROVIDE FOR HER? HELP MAKE HER WHOLE?--
--WHEN YOU HAVE SO SADLY FAILED IN PROVIDING FOR YOURSELF, FOR MADELYNE, AND MOST OF ALL YOUR LOST SON, NATHAN.

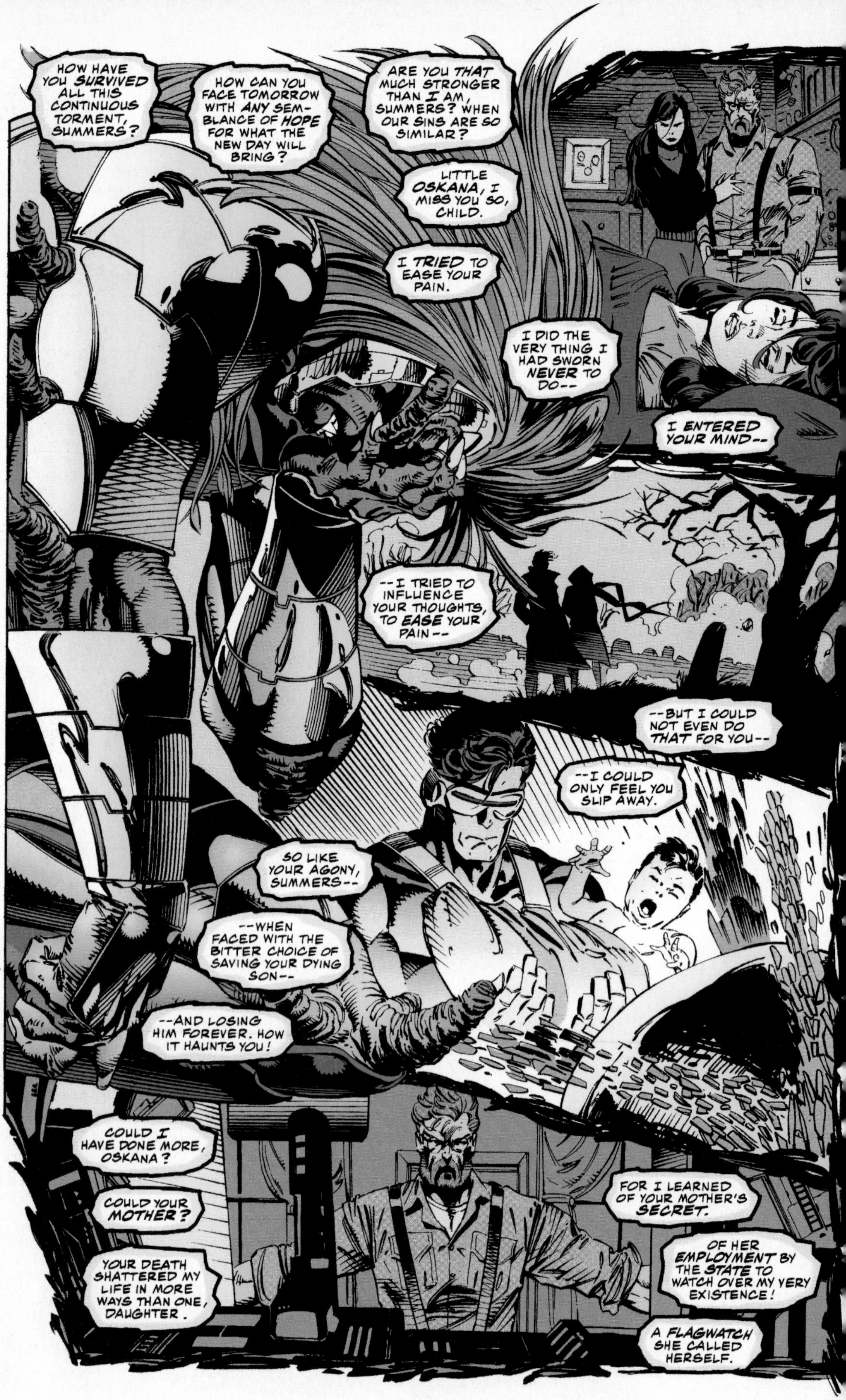
HOW HAVE YOU SURVIVED ALL THIS CONTINUOUS TORMENT, SUMMERS?
HOW CAN YOU FACE TOMORROW WITH ANY SEMBLANCE OF HOPE FOR WHAT THE NEW DAY WILL BRING?
ARE YOU THAT MUCH STRONGER THAN I AM, SUMMERS? WHEN OUR SINS ARE SO SIMILAR?
LITTLE OSKANA, I MISS YOU SO, CHILD.
I TRIED TO EASE YOUR PAIN.
I DID THE VERY THING I HAD SWORN NEVER TO DO--
I ENTERED YOUR MIND--
--I TRIED TO INFLUENCE YOUR THOUGHTS, TO EASE YOUR PAIN--
--BUT I COULD NOT EVEN DO THAT FOR YOU--
--I COULD ONLY FEEL YOU SLIP AWAY.
SO LIKE YOUR AGONY, SUMMERS--
--WHEN FACED WITH THE BITTER CHOICE OF SAVING YOUR DYING SON--
--AND LOSING HIM FOREVER. HOW IT HAUNTS YOU!
COULD I HAVE DONE MORE, OSKANA?
COULD YOUR MOTHER?
YOUR DEATH SHATTERED MY LIFE IN MORE WAYS THAN ONE, DAUGHTER.
FOR I LEARNED OF YOUR MOTHER'S SECRET.
OF HER EMPLOYMENT BY THE STATE TO WATCH OVER MY VERY EXISTENCE!
A FLAGWATCH SHE CALLED HERSELF.

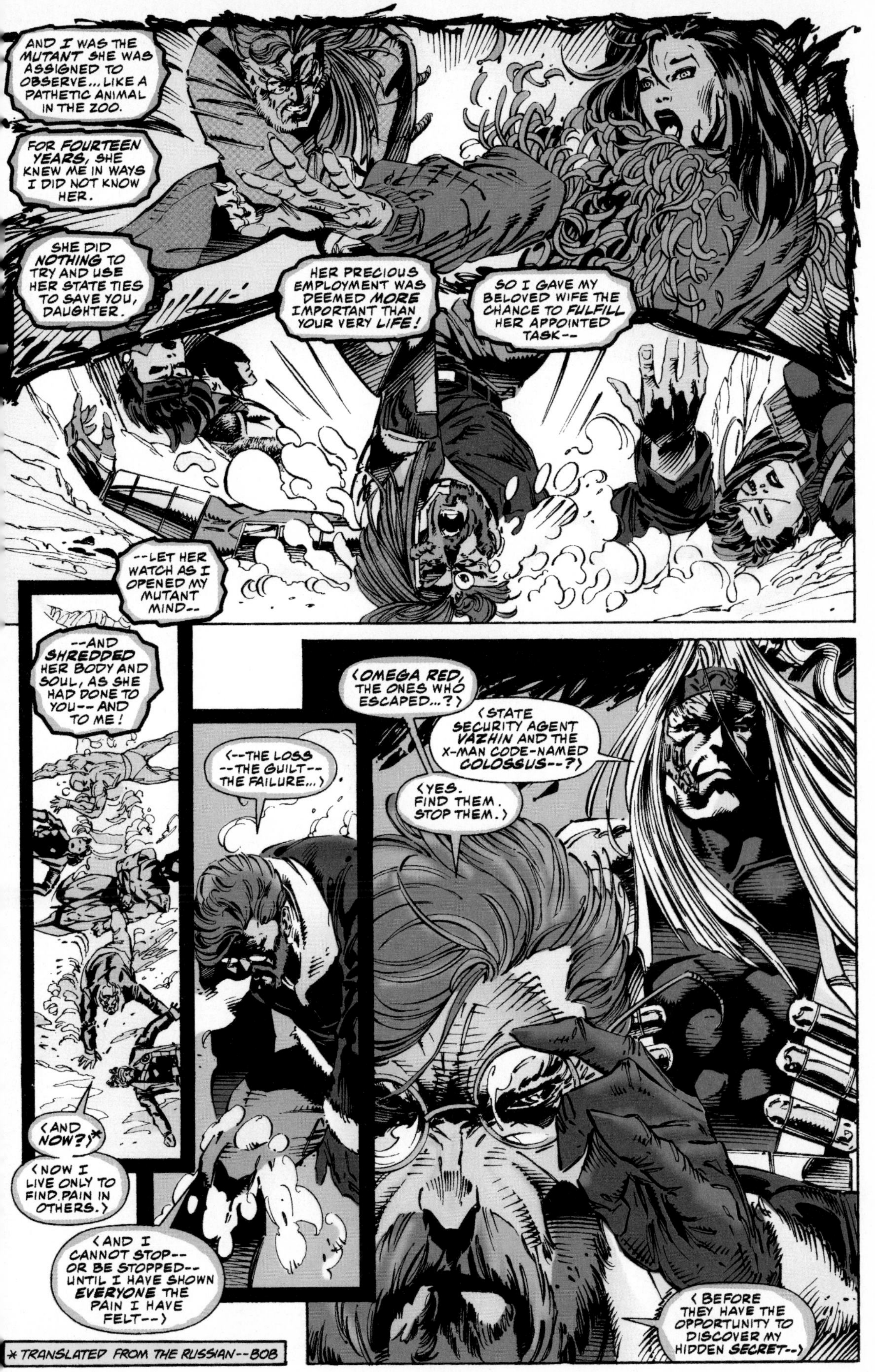

AND I WAS THE MUTANT SHE WAS ASSIGNED TO OBSERVE... LIKE A PATHETIC ANIMAL IN THE ZOO.
FOR FOURTEEN YEARS, SHE KNEW ME IN WAYS I DID NOT KNOW HER.
SHE DID NOTHING TO TRY AND USE HER STATE TIES TO SAVE YOU, DAUGHTER.
HER PRECIOUS EMPLOYMENT WAS DEEMED MORE IMPORTANT THAN YOUR VERY LIFE!
SO I GAVE MY BELOVED WIFE THE CHANCE TO FULFILL HER APPOINTED TASK--
--LET HER WATCH AS I OPENED MY MUTANT MIND--
--AND SHREDDED HER BODY AND SOUL, AS SHE HAD DONE TO YOU--AND TO ME!
‹AND NOW?›*
‹NOW I LIVE ONLY TO FIND PAIN IN OTHERS.›
‹AND I CANNOT STOP--OR BE STOPPED--UNTIL I HAVE SHOWN EVERYONE THE PAIN I HAVE FELT--›
‹--THE LOSS --THE GUILT--THE FAILURE...›
‹OMEGA RED, THE ONES WHO ESCAPED...?›
‹STATE SECURITY AGENT VAZHIN AND THE X-MAN CODE-NAMED COLOSSUS--?›
‹YES. FIND THEM. STOP THEM.›
‹BEFORE THEY HAVE THE OPPORTUNITY TO DISCOVER MY HIDDEN SECRET--›
*TRANSLATED FROM THE RUSSIAN--BOB

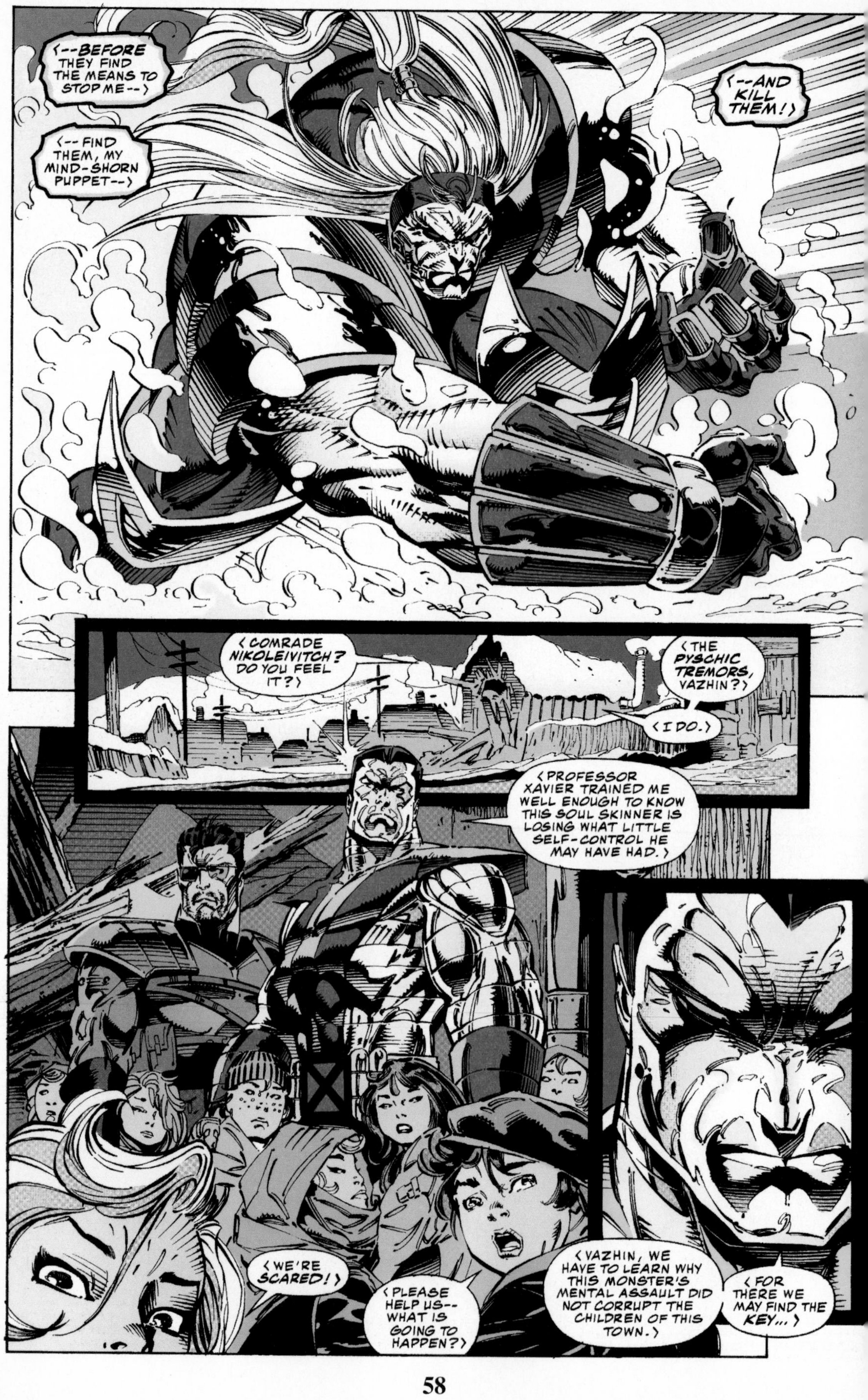
‹--BEFORE THEY FIND THE MEANS TO STOP ME--›
‹--FIND THEM, MY MIND-SHORN PUPPET--›
‹--AND KILL THEM!›
‹COMRADE NIKOLEIVITCH? DO YOU FEEL IT?›
‹THE PYSCHIC TREMORS, VAZHIN?›
‹I DO.›
‹PROFESSOR XAVIER TRAINED ME WELL ENOUGH TO KNOW THIS SOUL SKINNER IS LOSING WHAT LITTLE SELF-CONTROL HE MAY HAVE HAD.›
‹WE'RE SCARED!›
‹PLEASE HELP US-- WHAT IS GOING TO HAPPEN?›
‹VAZHIN, WE HAVE TO LEARN WHY THIS MONSTER'S MENTAL ASSAULT DID NOT CORRUPT THE CHILDREN OF THIS TOWN.›
‹FOR THERE WE MAY FIND THE KEY...›

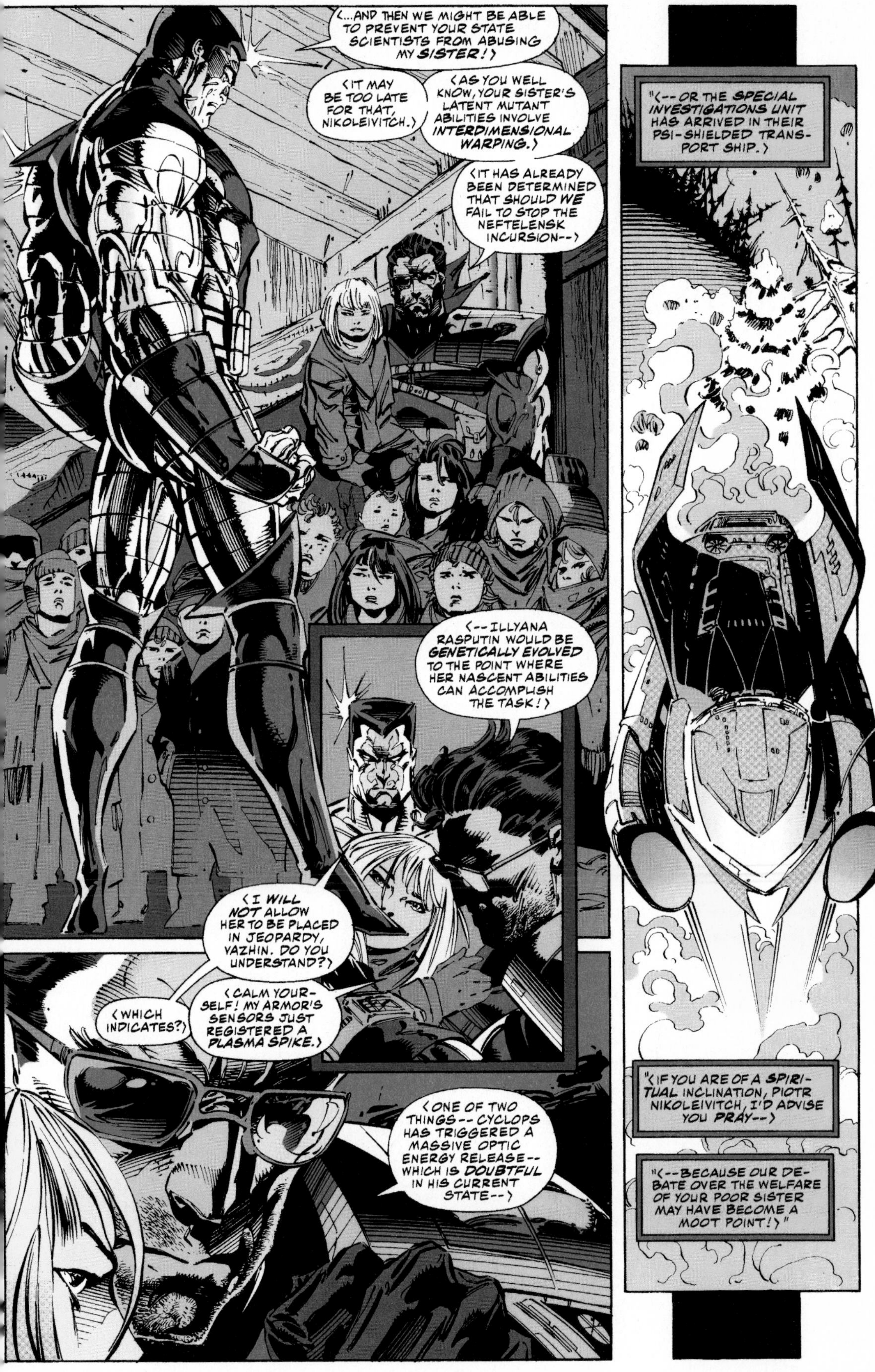
‹...AND THEN WE MIGHT BE ABLE TO PREVENT YOUR STATE SCIENTISTS FROM ABUSING MY SISTER!›
‹IT MAY BE TOO LATE FOR THAT, NIKOLEIVITCH.›
‹AS YOU WELL KNOW, YOUR SISTER'S LATENT MUTANT ABILITIES INVOLVE INTERDIMENSIONAL WARPING.›
‹IT HAS ALREADY BEEN DETERMINED THAT SHOULD WE FAIL TO STOP THE NEFTELENSK INCURSION--›
‹--ILLYANA RASPUTIN WOULD BE GENETICALLY EVOLVED TO THE POINT WHERE HER NASCENT ABILITIES CAN ACCOMPLISH THE TASK!›
‹I WILL NOT ALLOW HER TO BE PLACED IN JEOPARDY, VAZHIN. DO YOU UNDERSTAND?›
‹CALM YOURSELF! MY ARMOR'S SENSORS JUST REGISTERED A PLASMA SPIKE.›
‹WHICH INDICATES?›
‹ONE OF TWO THINGS--CYCLOPS HAS TRIGGERED A MASSIVE OPTIC ENERGY RELEASE--WHICH IS DOUBTFUL IN HIS CURRENT STATE--›
"‹--OR THE SPECIAL INVESTIGATIONS UNIT HAS ARRIVED IN THEIR PSI-SHIELDED TRANSPORT SHIP.›
"‹IF YOU ARE OF A SPIRITUAL INCLINATION, PIOTR NIKOLEIVITCH, I'D ADVISE YOU PRAY--›
"‹--BECAUSE OUR DEBATE OVER THE WELFARE OF YOUR POOR SISTER MAY HAVE BECOME A MOOT POINT!›"

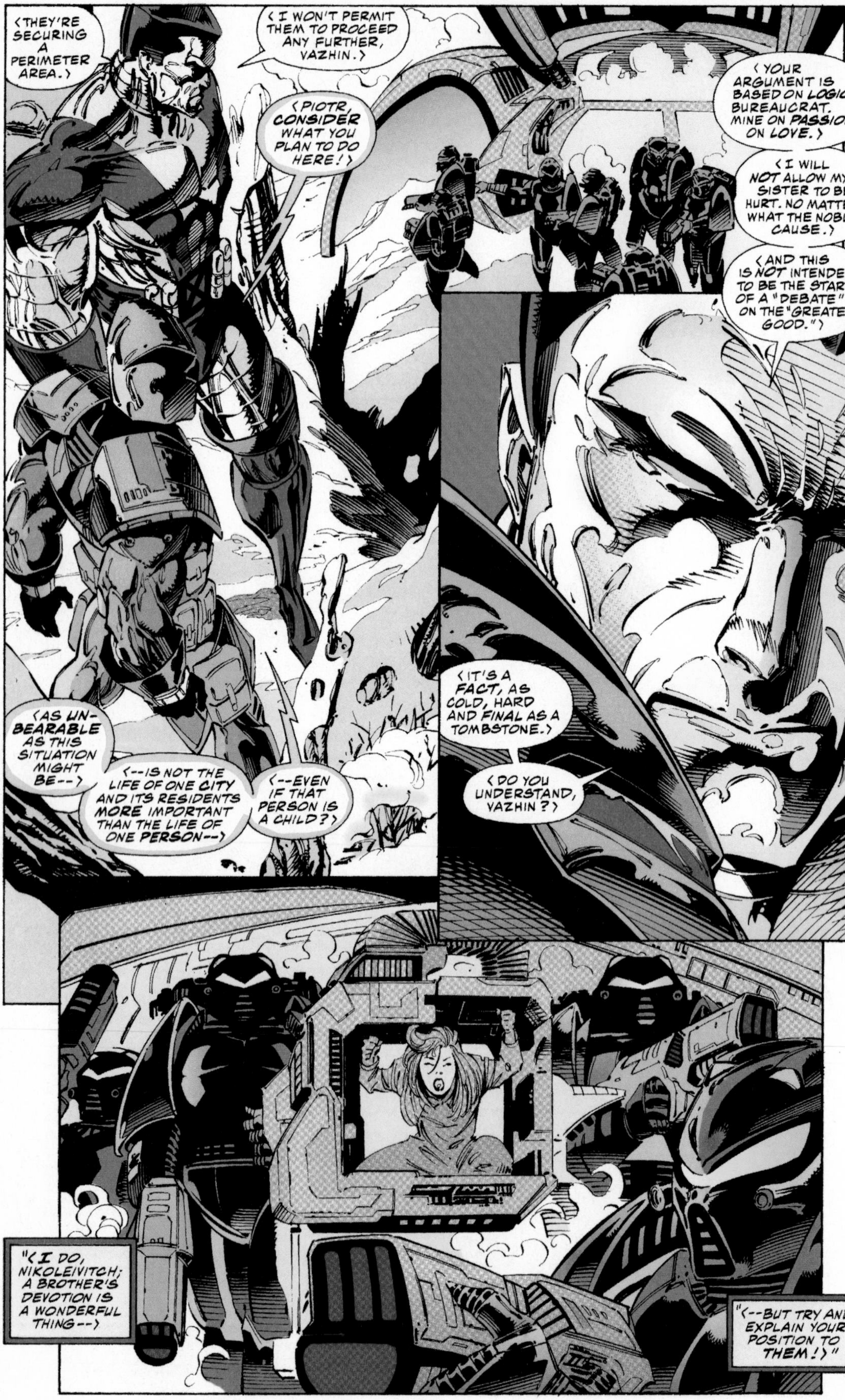
‹THEY'RE SECURING A PERIMETER AREA.›
‹I WON'T PERMIT THEM TO PROCEED ANY FURTHER, VAZHIN.›
‹PIOTR, CONSIDER WHAT YOU PLAN TO DO HERE!›
‹YOUR ARGUMENT IS BASED ON LOGIC, BUREAUCRAT. MINE ON PASSION. ON LOVE.›
‹I WILL NOT ALLOW MY SISTER TO BE HURT. NO MATTER WHAT THE NOBLE CAUSE.›
‹AND THIS IS NOT INTENDED TO BE THE START OF A "DEBATE" ON THE "GREATER GOOD."›
‹AS UN-BEARABLE AS THIS SITUATION MIGHT BE--›
‹--IS NOT THE LIFE OF ONE CITY AND ITS RESIDENTS MORE IMPORTANT THAN THE LIFE OF ONE PERSON--›
‹--EVEN IF THAT PERSON IS A CHILD?›
‹IT'S A FACT, AS COLD, HARD AND FINAL AS A TOMBSTONE.›
‹DO YOU UNDERSTAND, VAZHIN?›
"‹I DO, NIKOLEIVITCH; A BROTHER'S DEVOTION IS A WONDERFUL THING--›
"‹--BUT TRY AND EXPLAIN YOUR POSITION TO THEM!›"

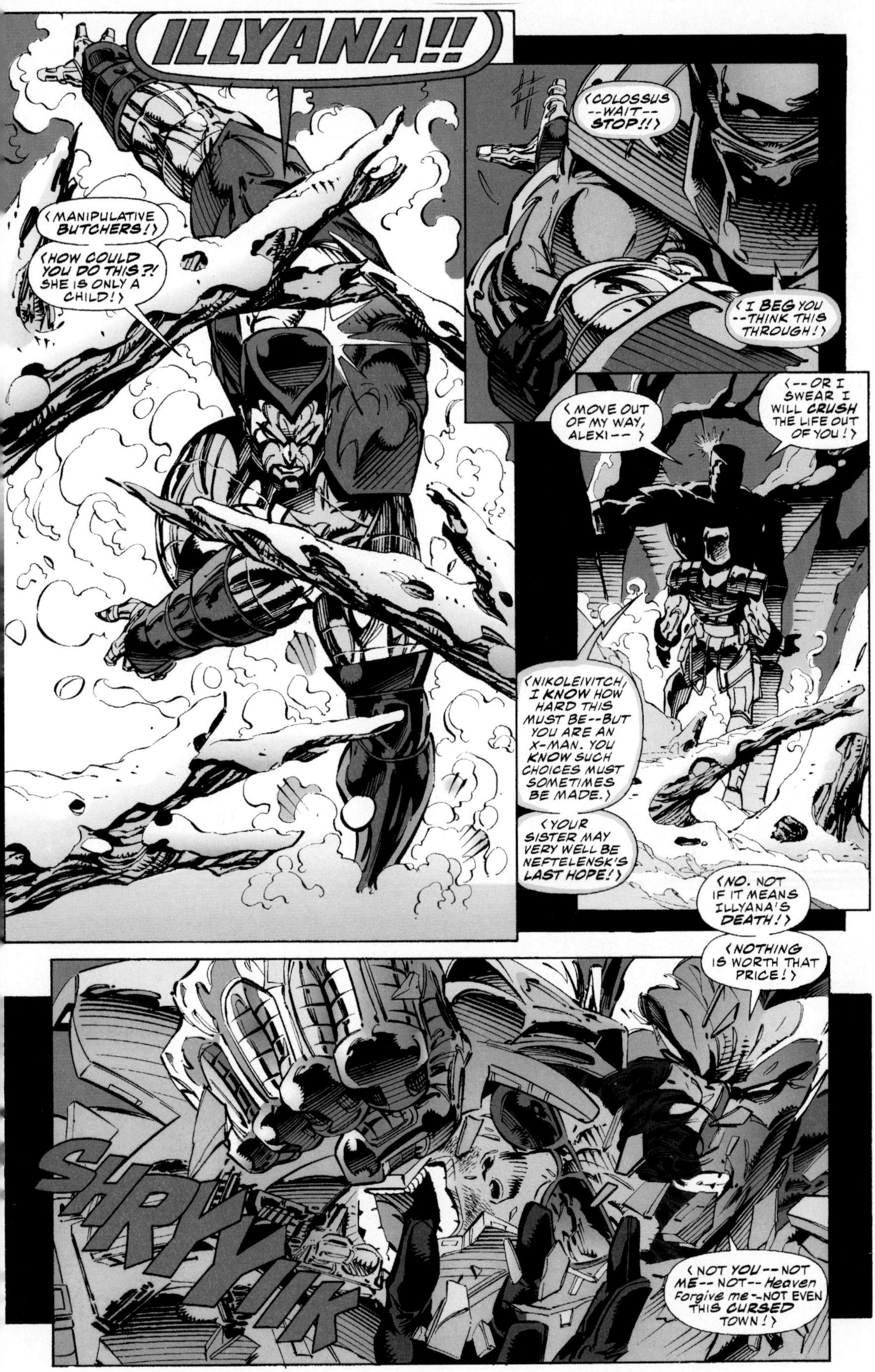
ILLYANA!!
‹MANIPULATIVE BUTCHERS!›
‹HOW COULD YOU DO THIS?! SHE IS ONLY A CHILD!›
‹COLOSSUS --WAIT-- STOP!!›
‹I BEG YOU --THINK THIS THROUGH!›
‹MOVE OUT OF MY WAY, ALEXI-- ›
‹--OR I SWEAR I WILL CRUSH THE LIFE OUT OF YOU!›
‹NIKOLEIVITCH, I KNOW HOW HARD THIS MUST BE--BUT YOU ARE AN X-MAN. YOU KNOW SUCH CHOICES MUST SOMETIMES BE MADE.›
‹YOUR SISTER MAY VERY WELL BE NEFTELENSK'S LAST HOPE!›
‹NO. NOT IF IT MEANS ILLYANA'S DEATH!›
‹NOTHING IS WORTH THAT PRICE!›
SHRYYIK
‹NOT YOU--NOT ME--NOT--Heaven forgive me--NOT EVEN THIS CURSED TOWN!›

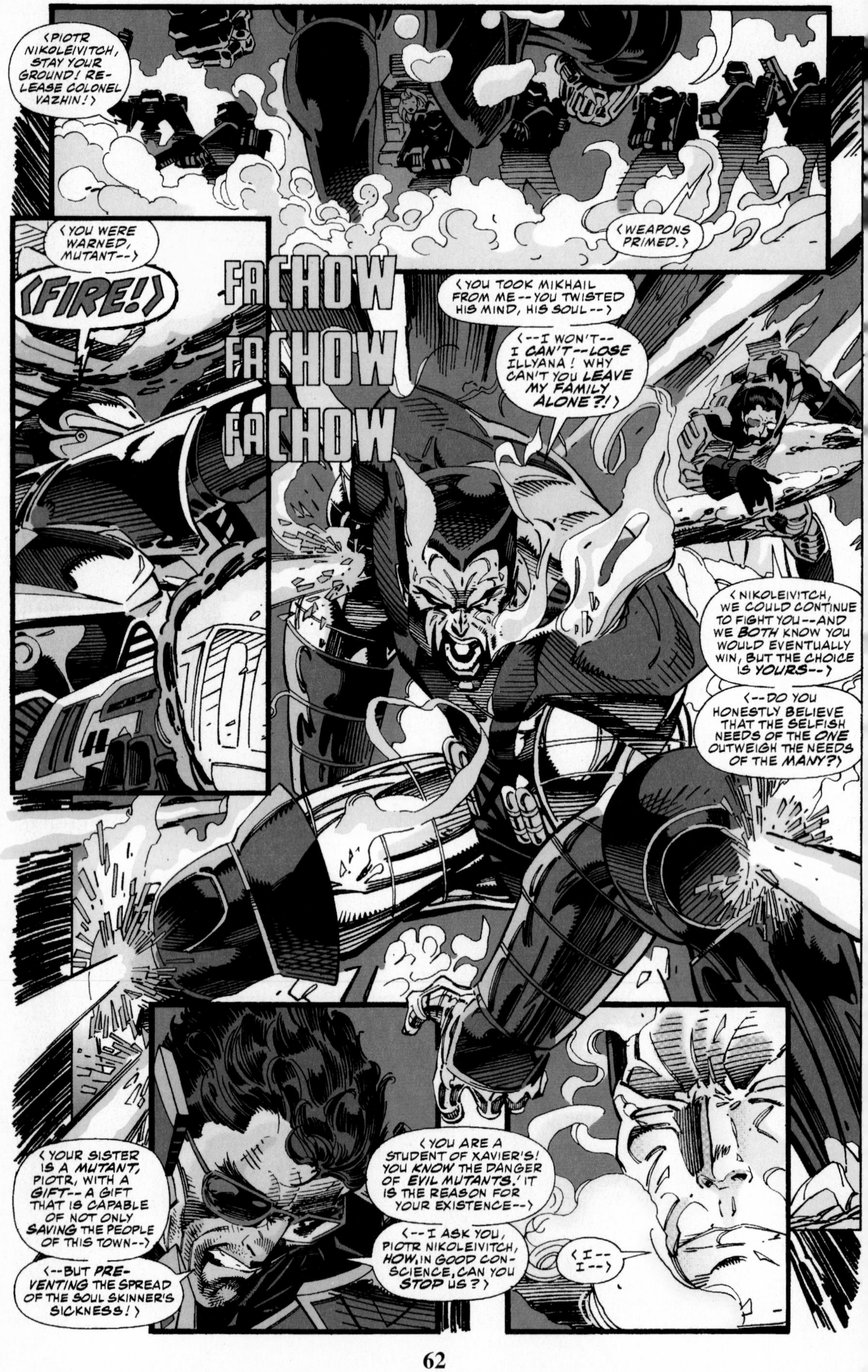

‹PIOTR NIKOLEIVITCH, STAY YOUR GROUND! RE-LEASE COLONEL VAZHIN!›
‹WEAPONS PRIMED.›
‹YOU WERE WARNED, MUTANT--›
‹FIRE!›
FACHOW
FACHOW
FACHOW
‹YOU TOOK MIKHAIL FROM ME--YOU TWISTED HIS MIND, HIS SOUL--›
‹--I WON'T--I CAN'T--LOSE ILLYANA! WHY CAN'T YOU LEAVE MY FAMILY ALONE?!›
‹NIKOLEIVITCH, WE COULD CONTINUE TO FIGHT YOU--AND WE BOTH KNOW YOU WOULD EVENTUALLY WIN, BUT THE CHOICE IS YOURS--›
‹--DO YOU HONESTLY BELIEVE THAT THE SELFISH NEEDS OF THE ONE OUTWEIGH THE NEEDS OF THE MANY?›
‹YOUR SISTER IS A MUTANT, PIOTR, WITH A GIFT--A GIFT THAT IS CAPABLE OF NOT ONLY SAVING THE PEOPLE OF THIS TOWN--›
‹--BUT PRE-VENTING THE SPREAD OF THE SOUL SKINNER'S SICKNESS!›
‹YOU ARE A STUDENT OF XAVIER'S! YOU KNOW THE DANGER OF EVIL MUTANTS! IT IS THE REASON FOR YOUR EXISTENCE--›
‹--I ASK YOU, PIOTR NIKOLEIVITCH, HOW, IN GOOD CON-SCIENCE, CAN YOU STOP US?›
‹I--I--›

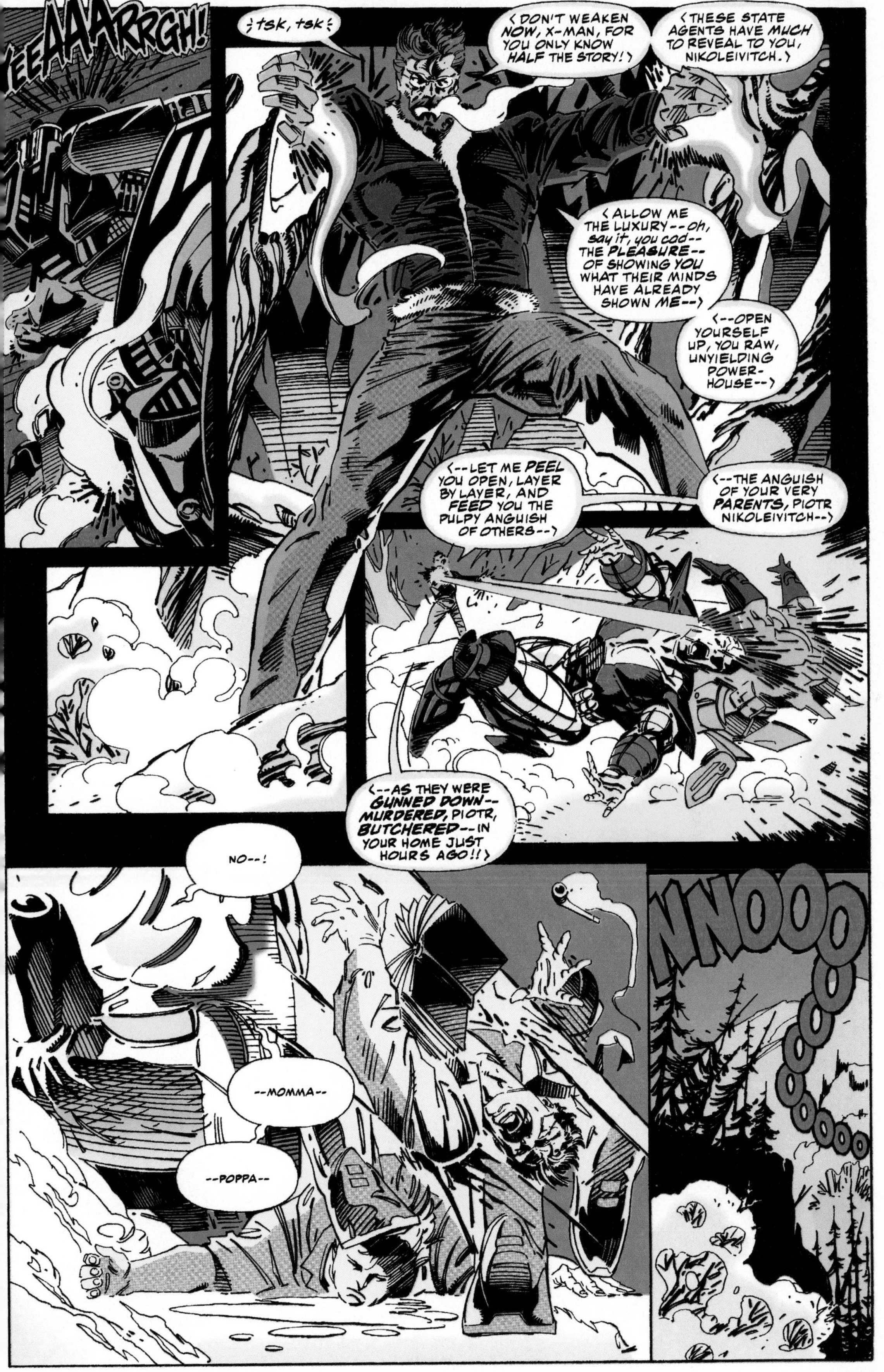
YEEAAARRGH!
;tsk, tsk;
<DON'T WEAKEN NOW, X-MAN, FOR YOU ONLY KNOW HALF THE STORY!>
<THESE STATE AGENTS HAVE MUCH TO REVEAL TO YOU, NIKOLEIVITCH.>
<ALLOW ME THE LUXURY--oh, say it, you cod--THE PLEASURE--OF SHOWING YOU WHAT THEIR MINDS HAVE ALREADY SHOWN ME-->
<--OPEN YOURSELF UP, YOU RAW, UNYIELDING POWER-HOUSE-->
<--LET ME PEEL YOU OPEN, LAYER BY LAYER, AND FEED YOU THE PULPY ANGUISH OF OTHERS-->
<--THE ANGUISH OF YOUR VERY PARENTS, PIOTR NIKOLEIVITCH-->
<--AS THEY WERE GUNNED DOWN--MURDERED, PIOTR, BUTCHERED--IN YOUR HOME JUST HOURS AGO!!>
NO--!
--MOMMA--
--POPPA--
NNOOOOOOOOOO

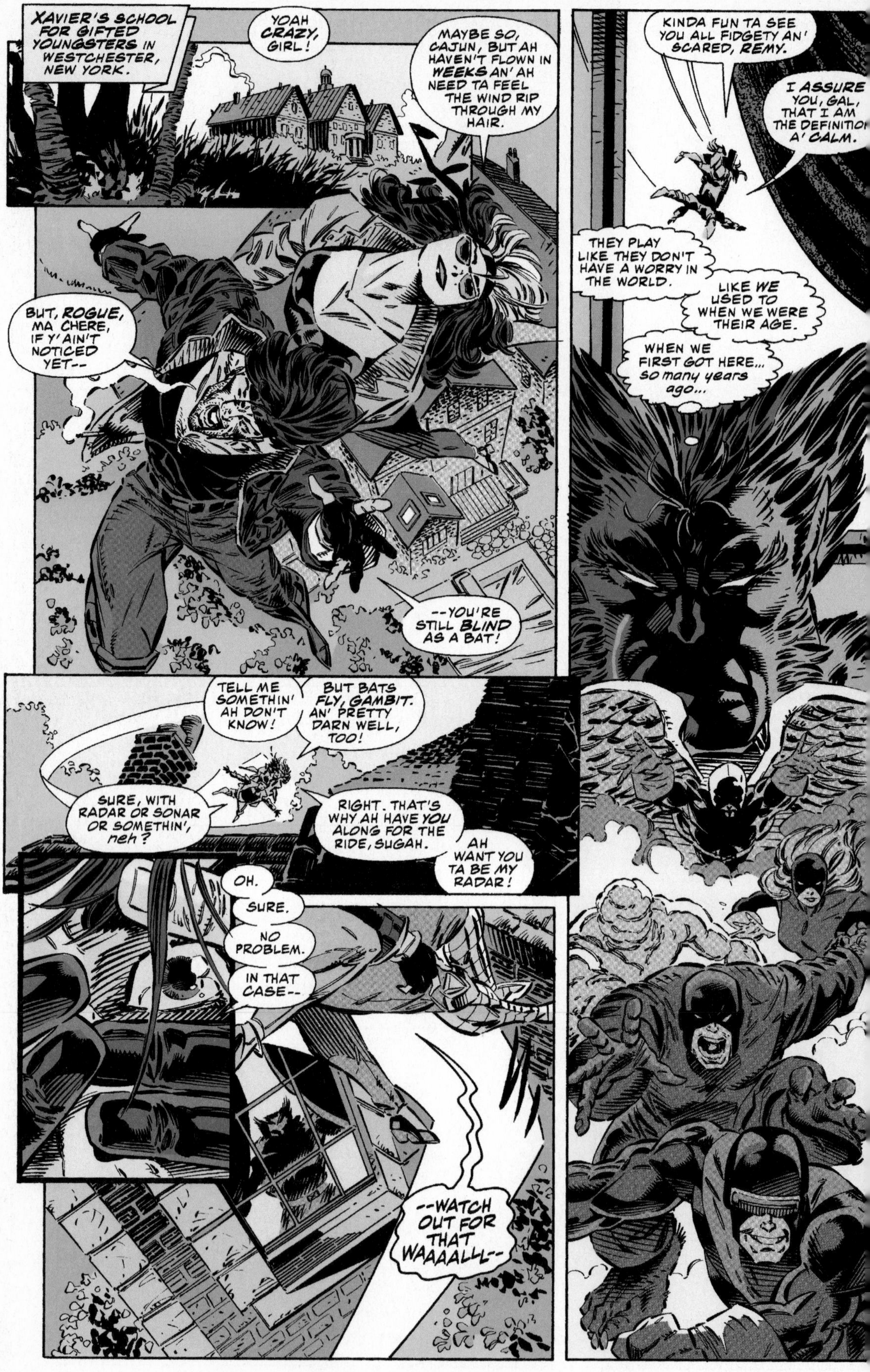

XAVIER'S SCHOOL FOR GIFTED YOUNGSTERS IN WESTCHESTER, NEW YORK.
YOAH CRAZY, GIRL!
MAYBE SO, CAJUN, BUT AH HAVEN'T FLOWN IN WEEKS AN' AH NEED TA FEEL THE WIND RIP THROUGH MY HAIR.
BUT, ROGUE, MA CHERE, IF Y'AIN'T NOTICED YET--
--YOU'RE STILL BLIND AS A BAT!
TELL ME SOMETHIN' AH DON'T KNOW!
BUT BATS FLY, GAMBIT. AN' PRETTY DARN WELL, TOO!
SURE, WITH RADAR OR SONAR OR SOMETHIN', neh?
RIGHT. THAT'S WHY AH HAVE YOU ALONG FOR THE RIDE, SUGAH.
AH WANT YOU TA BE MY RADAR!
OH.
SURE.
NO PROBLEM.
IN THAT CASE--
--WATCH OUT FOR THAT WAAAALLL--
KINDA FUN TA SEE YOU ALL FIDGETY AN' SCARED, REMY.
I ASSURE YOU, GAL, THAT I AM THE DEFINITIO A' CALM.
THEY PLAY LIKE THEY DON'T HAVE A WORRY IN THE WORLD.
LIKE WE USED TO WHEN WE WERE THEIR AGE.
WHEN WE FIRST GOT HERE... so many years ago...

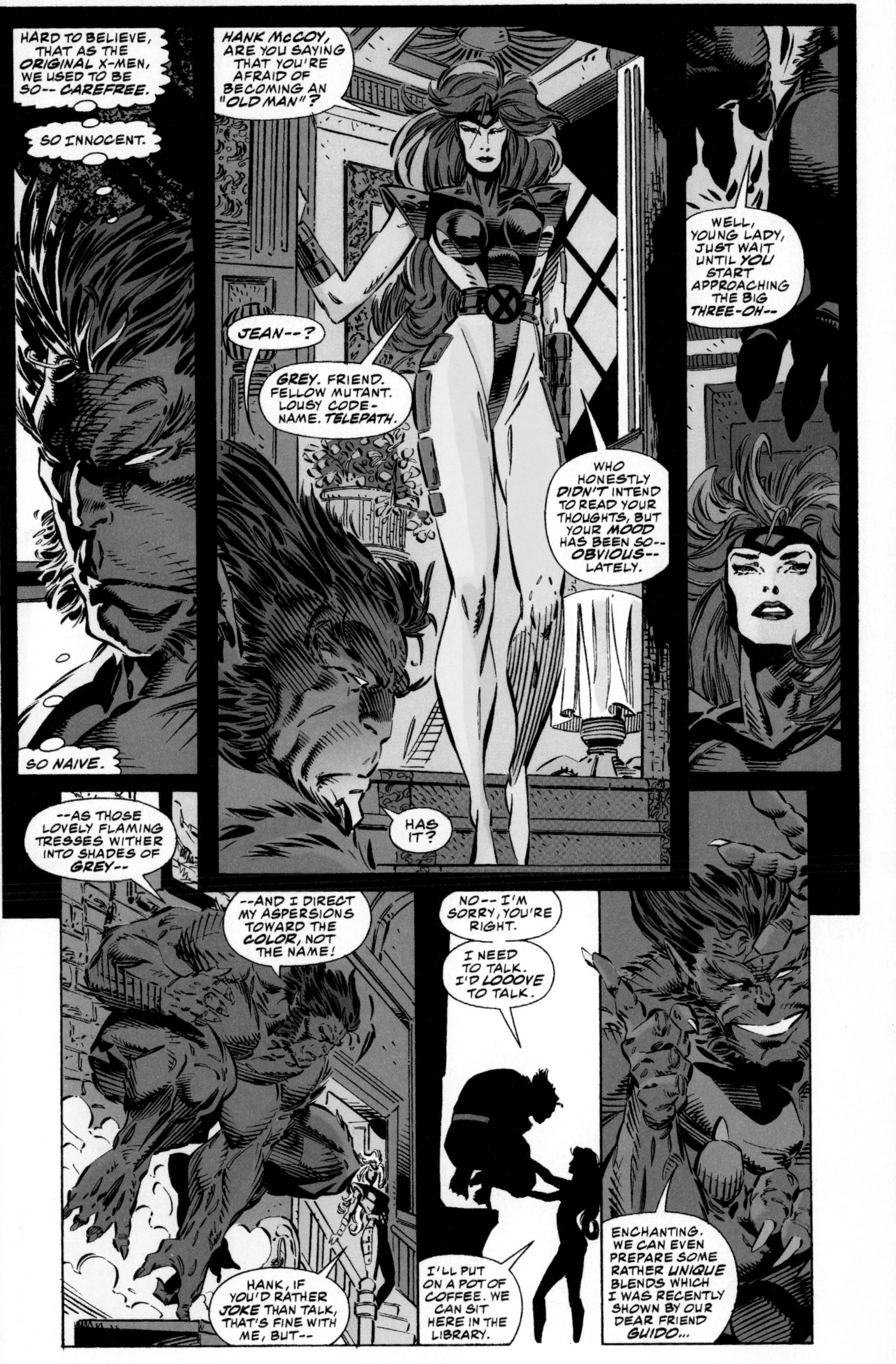
HARD TO BELIEVE, THAT AS THE ORIGINAL X-MEN, WE USED TO BE SO-- CAREFREE.
SO INNOCENT.
SO NAIVE.
HANK McCOY, ARE YOU SAYING THAT YOU'RE AFRAID OF BECOMING AN "OLD MAN"?
JEAN--?
GREY. FRIEND. FELLOW MUTANT. LOUSY CODE-NAME. TELEPATH.
WHO HONESTLY DIDN'T INTEND TO READ YOUR THOUGHTS, BUT YOUR MOOD HAS BEEN SO-- OBVIOUS-- LATELY.
HAS IT?
WELL, YOUNG LADY, JUST WAIT UNTIL YOU START APPROACHING THE BIG THREE-OH--
--AS THOSE LOVELY FLAMING TRESSES WITHER INTO SHADES OF GREY--
--AND I DIRECT MY ASPERSIONS TOWARD THE COLOR, NOT THE NAME!
HANK, IF YOU'D RATHER JOKE THAN TALK, THAT'S FINE WITH ME, BUT--
NO-- I'M SORRY, YOU'RE RIGHT.
I NEED TO TALK. I'D LOOOVE TO TALK.
I'LL PUT ON A POT OF COFFEE. WE CAN SIT HERE IN THE LIBRARY.
ENCHANTING. WE CAN EVEN PREPARE SOME RATHER UNIQUE BLENDS WHICH I WAS RECENTLY SHOWN BY OUR DEAR FRIEND GUIDO...

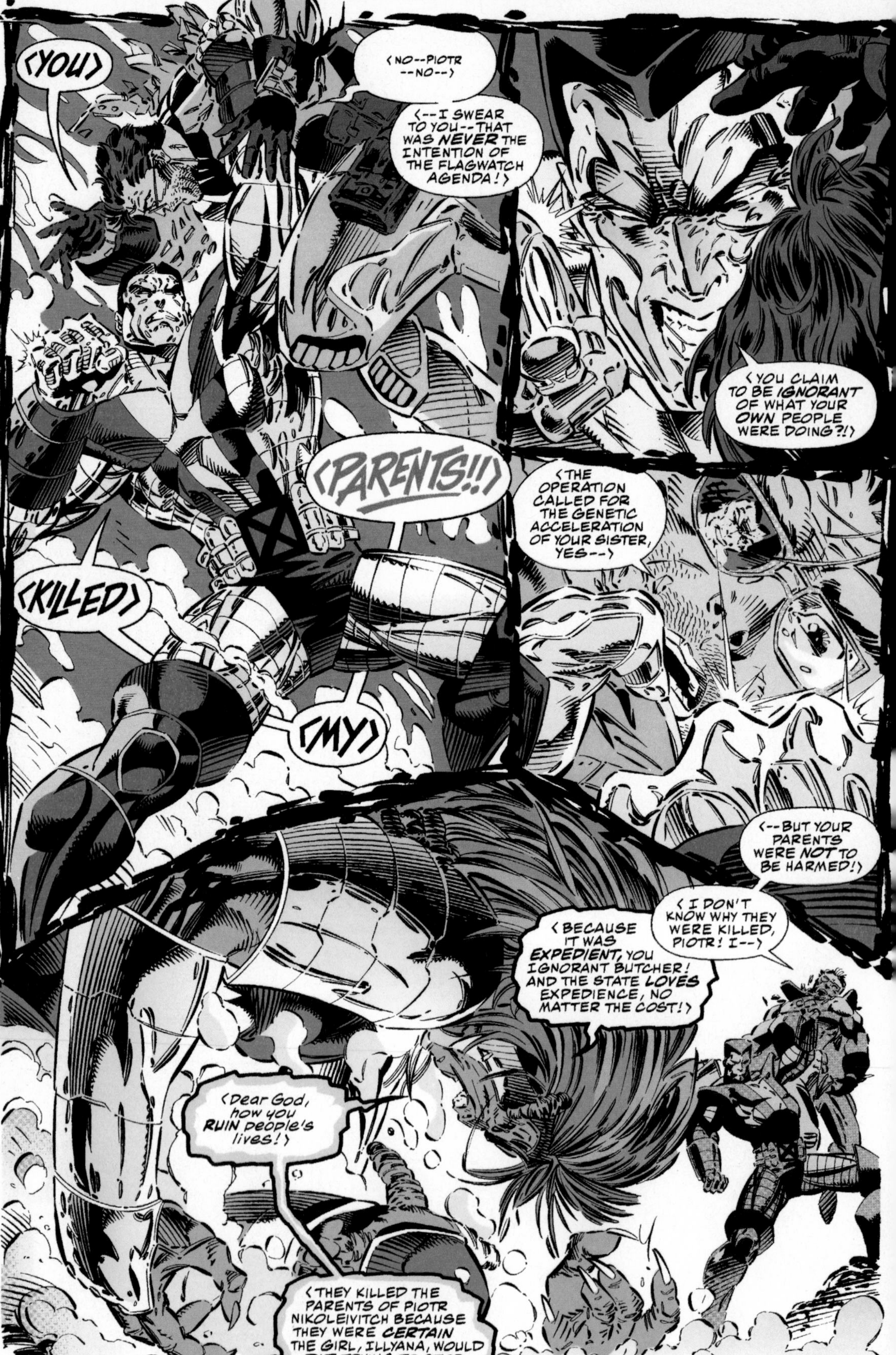
<YOU>
<NO--PIOTR --NO-->
<--I SWEAR TO YOU--THAT WAS NEVER THE INTENTION OF THE FLAGWATCH AGENDA!>
<YOU CLAIM TO BE IGNORANT OF WHAT YOUR OWN PEOPLE WERE DOING?!>
<KILLED>
<MY>
<PARENTS!!>
<THE OPERATION CALLED FOR THE GENETIC ACCELERATION OF YOUR SISTER, YES-->
<--BUT YOUR PARENTS WERE NOT TO BE HARMED!>
<I DON'T KNOW WHY THEY WERE KILLED, PIOTR! I-->
<BECAUSE IT WAS EXPEDIENT, YOU IGNORANT BUTCHER! AND THE STATE LOVES EXPEDIENCE, NO MATTER THE COST!>
<Dear God, how you RUIN people's lives!>
<THEY KILLED THE PARENTS OF PIOTR NIKOLEIVITCH BECAUSE THEY WERE CERTAIN THE GIRL, ILLYANA, WOULD DIE TRYING TO STOP ME!!>

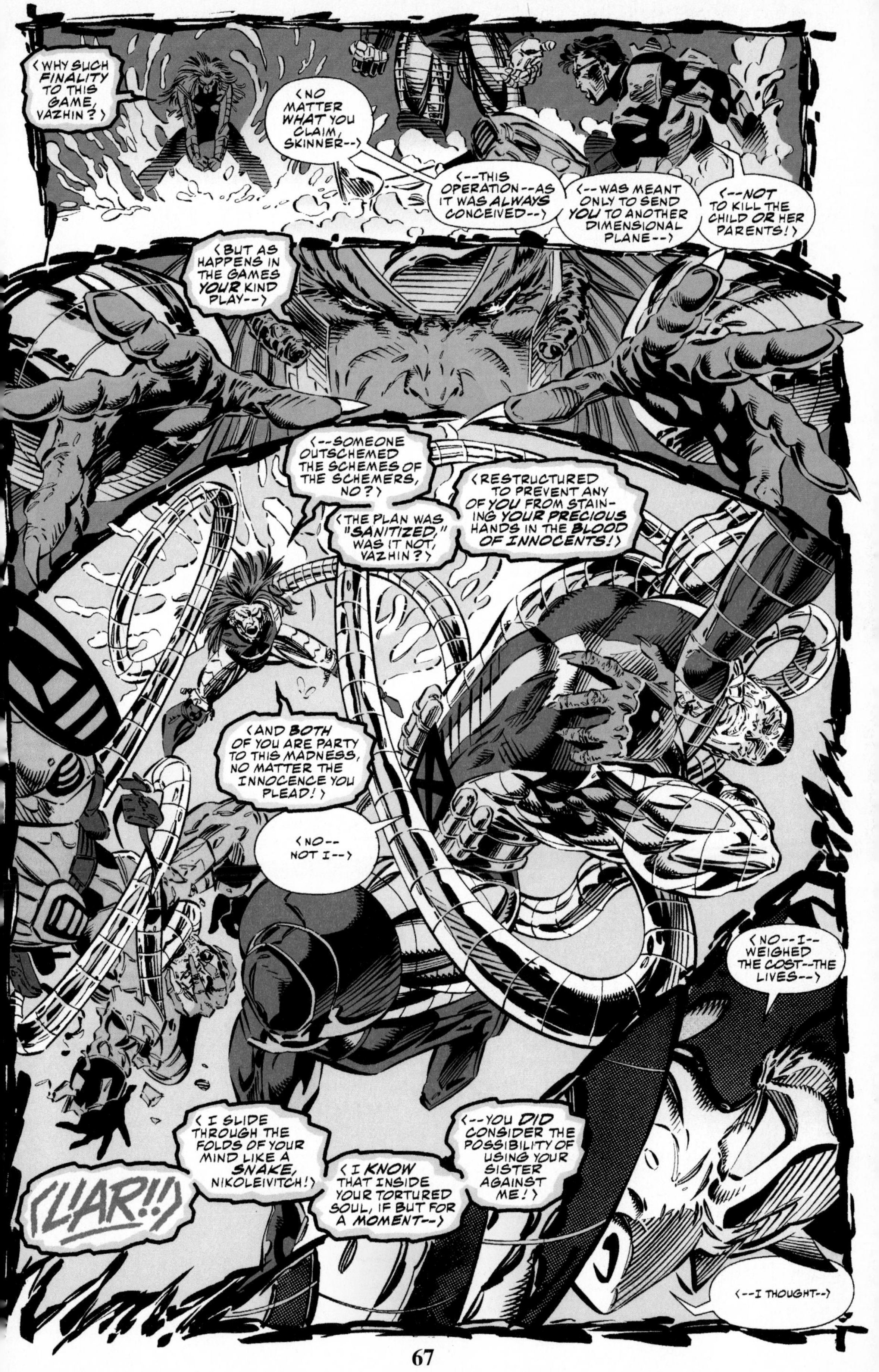

‹WHY SUCH FINALITY TO THIS GAME, VAZHIN?›
‹NO MATTER WHAT YOU CLAIM, SKINNER--›
‹--THIS OPERATION--AS IT WAS ALWAYS CONCEIVED--›
‹--WAS MEANT ONLY TO SEND YOU TO ANOTHER DIMENSIONAL PLANE--›
‹--NOT TO KILL THE CHILD OR HER PARENTS!›
‹BUT AS HAPPENS IN THE GAMES YOUR KIND PLAY--›
‹--SOMEONE OUTSCHEMED THE SCHEMES OF THE SCHEMERS, NO?›
‹THE PLAN WAS "SANITIZED," WAS IT NOT, VAZHIN?›
‹RESTRUCTURED TO PREVENT ANY OF YOU FROM STAINING YOUR PRECIOUS HANDS IN THE BLOOD OF INNOCENTS!›
‹AND BOTH OF YOU ARE PARTY TO THIS MADNESS, NO MATTER THE INNOCENCE YOU PLEAD!›
‹NO--NOT I--›
‹NO--I--WEIGHED THE COST--THE LIVES--›
‹LIAR!!›
‹I SLIDE THROUGH THE FOLDS OF YOUR MIND LIKE A SNAKE, NIKOLEIVITCH!›
‹I KNOW THAT INSIDE YOUR TORTURED SOUL, IF BUT FOR A MOMENT--›
‹--YOU DID CONSIDER THE POSSIBILITY OF USING YOUR SISTER AGAINST ME!›
‹--I THOUGHT--›

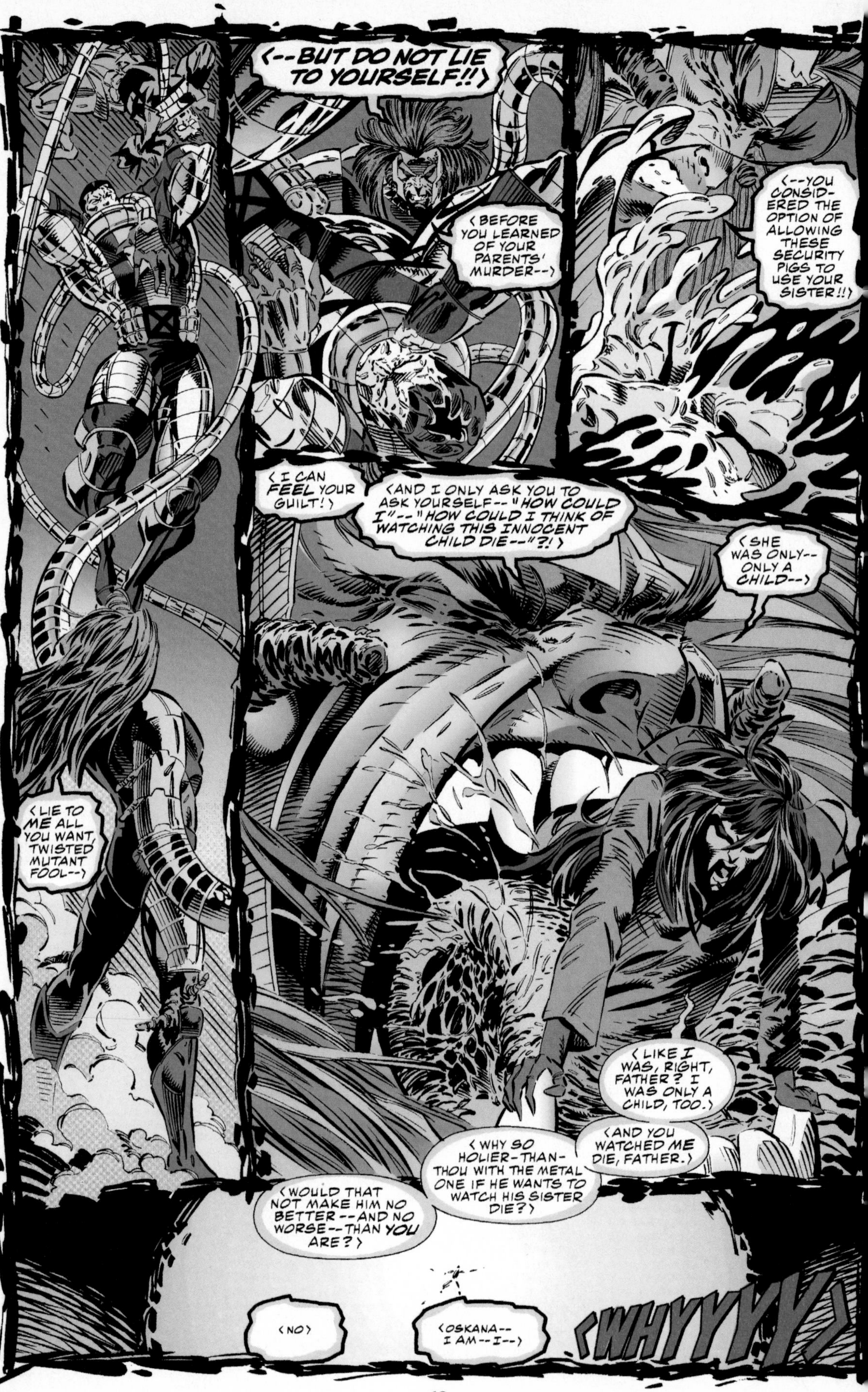

<--BUT DO NOT LIE TO YOURSELF!!>
<BEFORE YOU LEARNED OF YOUR PARENTS' MURDER-->
<--YOU CONSIDERED THE OPTION OF ALLOWING THESE SECURITY PIGS TO USE YOUR SISTER!!>
<I CAN FEEL YOUR GUILT!>
<AND I ONLY ASK YOU TO ASK YOURSELF--"HOW COULD I"--"HOW COULD I THINK OF WATCHING THIS INNOCENT CHILD DIE--"?!>
<SHE WAS ONLY--ONLY A CHILD-->
<LIE TO ME ALL YOU WANT, TWISTED MUTANT FOOL-->
<LIKE I WAS, RIGHT, FATHER? I WAS ONLY A CHILD, TOO.>
<AND YOU WATCHED ME DIE, FATHER.>
<WHY SO HOLIER-THAN-THOU WITH THE METAL ONE IF HE WANTS TO WATCH HIS SISTER DIE?>
<WOULD THAT NOT MAKE HIM NO BETTER--AND NO WORSE--THAN YOU ARE?>
<NO>
<OSKANA--I AM--I-->
<WHYYYY>

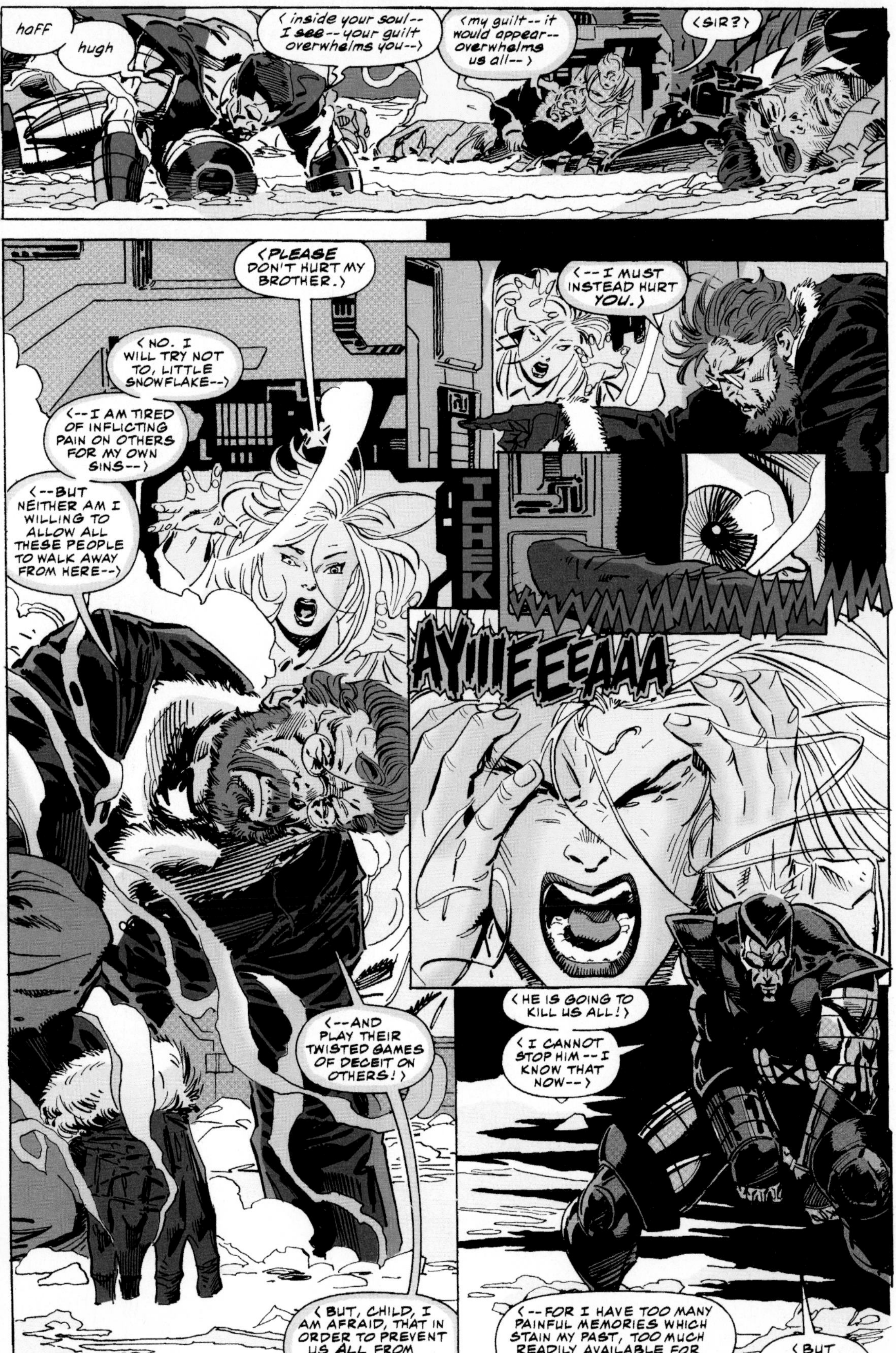

haff
hugh
< inside your soul-- I see--your guilt overwhelms you-- >
< my guilt-- it would appear-- overwhelms us all-- >
< SIR? >
< PLEASE DON'T HURT MY BROTHER. >
< NO. I WILL TRY NOT TO, LITTLE SNOWFLAKE-- >
< --I AM TIRED OF INFLICTING PAIN ON OTHERS FOR MY OWN SINS-- >
< --BUT NEITHER AM I WILLING TO ALLOW ALL THESE PEOPLE TO WALK AWAY FROM HERE-- >
< --AND PLAY THEIR TWISTED GAMES OF DECEIT ON OTHERS! >
< BUT, CHILD, I AM AFRAID, THAT IN ORDER TO PREVENT US ALL FROM HURTING EACH OTHER-- >
< --I MUST INSTEAD HURT YOU. >
TCHEK
AYIIIEEEAAA
< HE IS GOING TO KILL US ALL! >
< I CANNOT STOP HIM--I KNOW THAT NOW-- >
< --FOR I HAVE TOO MANY PAINFUL MEMORIES WHICH STAIN MY PAST, TOO MUCH READILY AVAILABLE FOR HIM TO MANIPULATE AND SLANDER! >
< BUT HE CAN BE STOPPED-- >

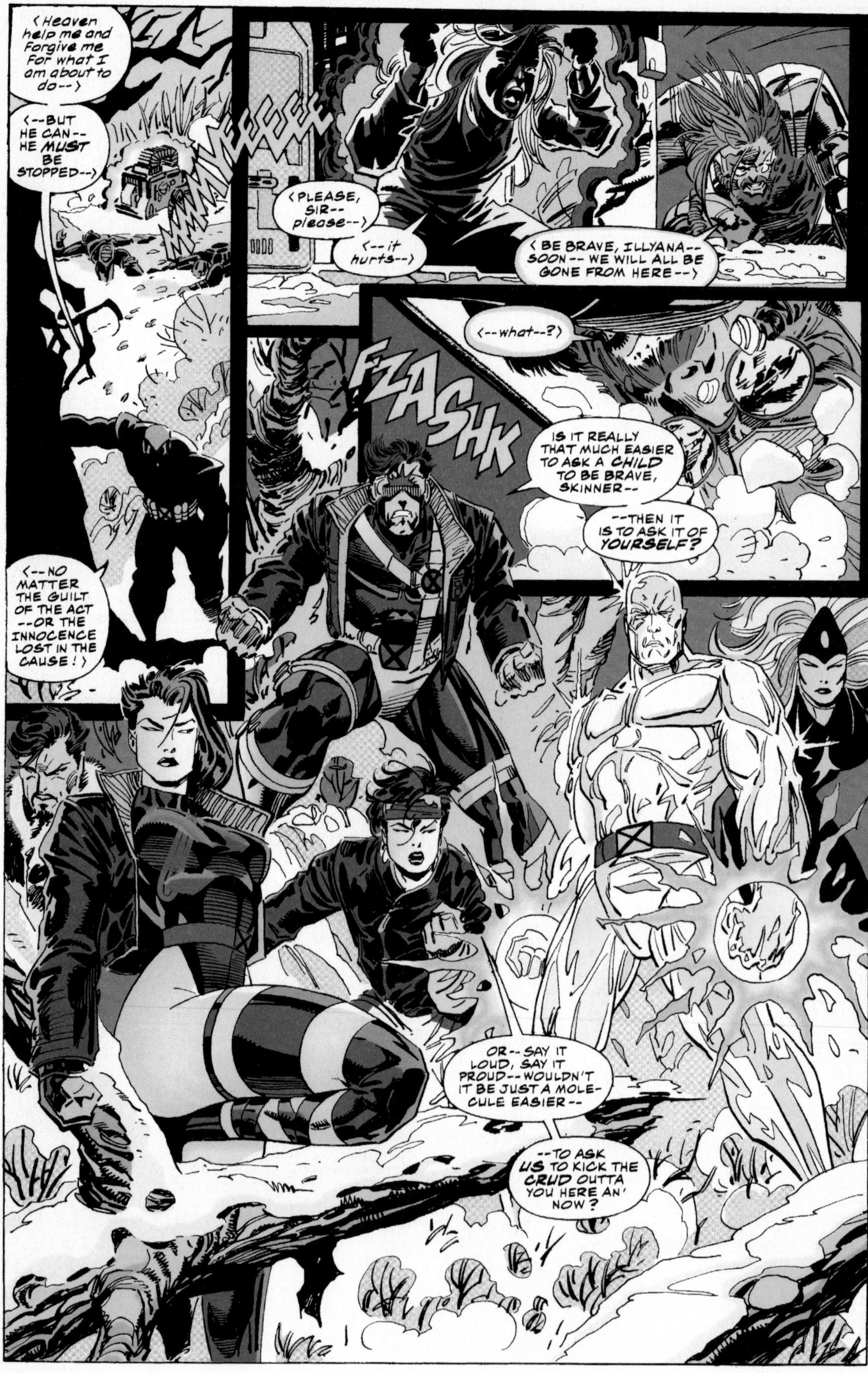

‹Heaven help me and forgive me for what I am about to do--›
‹--but he can-- he must be stopped--›
MMMWEEEEE
‹PLEASE, SIR-- please--›
‹--it hurts--›
‹BE BRAVE, ILLYANA-- SOON--WE WILL ALL BE GONE FROM HERE--›
‹--what--?›
FZASHK
IS IT REALLY THAT MUCH EASIER TO ASK A CHILD TO BE BRAVE, SKINNER--
--THEN IT IS TO ASK IT OF YOURSELF?
‹--NO MATTER THE GUILT OF THE ACT --OR THE INNOCENCE LOST IN THE CAUSE!›
OR--SAY IT LOUD, SAY IT PROUD--WOULDN'T IT BE JUST A MOLECULE EASIER--
--TO ASK US TO KICK THE CRUD OUTTA YOU HERE AN' NOW?

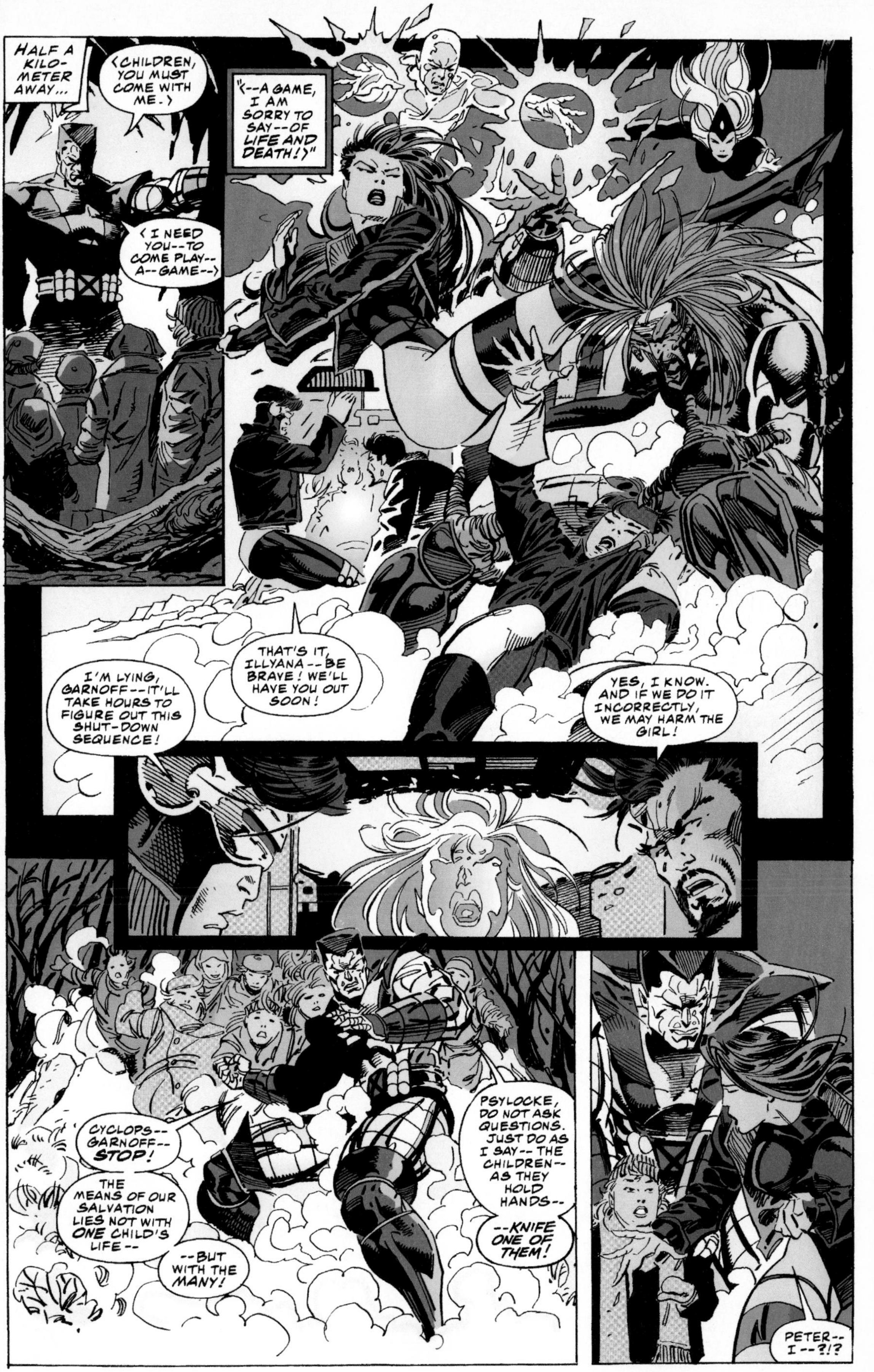
HALF A KILOMETER AWAY...
‹CHILDREN, YOU MUST COME WITH ME.›
‹I NEED YOU--TO COME PLAY--A--GAME--›
"‹--A GAME, I AM SORRY TO SAY--OF LIFE AND DEATH!›"
THAT'S IT, ILLYANA--BE BRAVE! WE'LL HAVE YOU OUT SOON!
I'M LYING, GARNOFF--IT'LL TAKE HOURS TO FIGURE OUT THIS SHUT-DOWN SEQUENCE!
YES, I KNOW. AND IF WE DO IT INCORRECTLY, WE MAY HARM THE GIRL!
CYCLOPS--GARNOFF--STOP!
THE MEANS OF OUR SALVATION LIES NOT WITH ONE CHILD'S LIFE--
--BUT WITH THE MANY!
PSYLOCKE, DO NOT ASK QUESTIONS. JUST DO AS I SAY--THE CHILDREN--AS THEY HOLD HANDS--
--KNIFE ONE OF THEM!
PETER--I--?!?

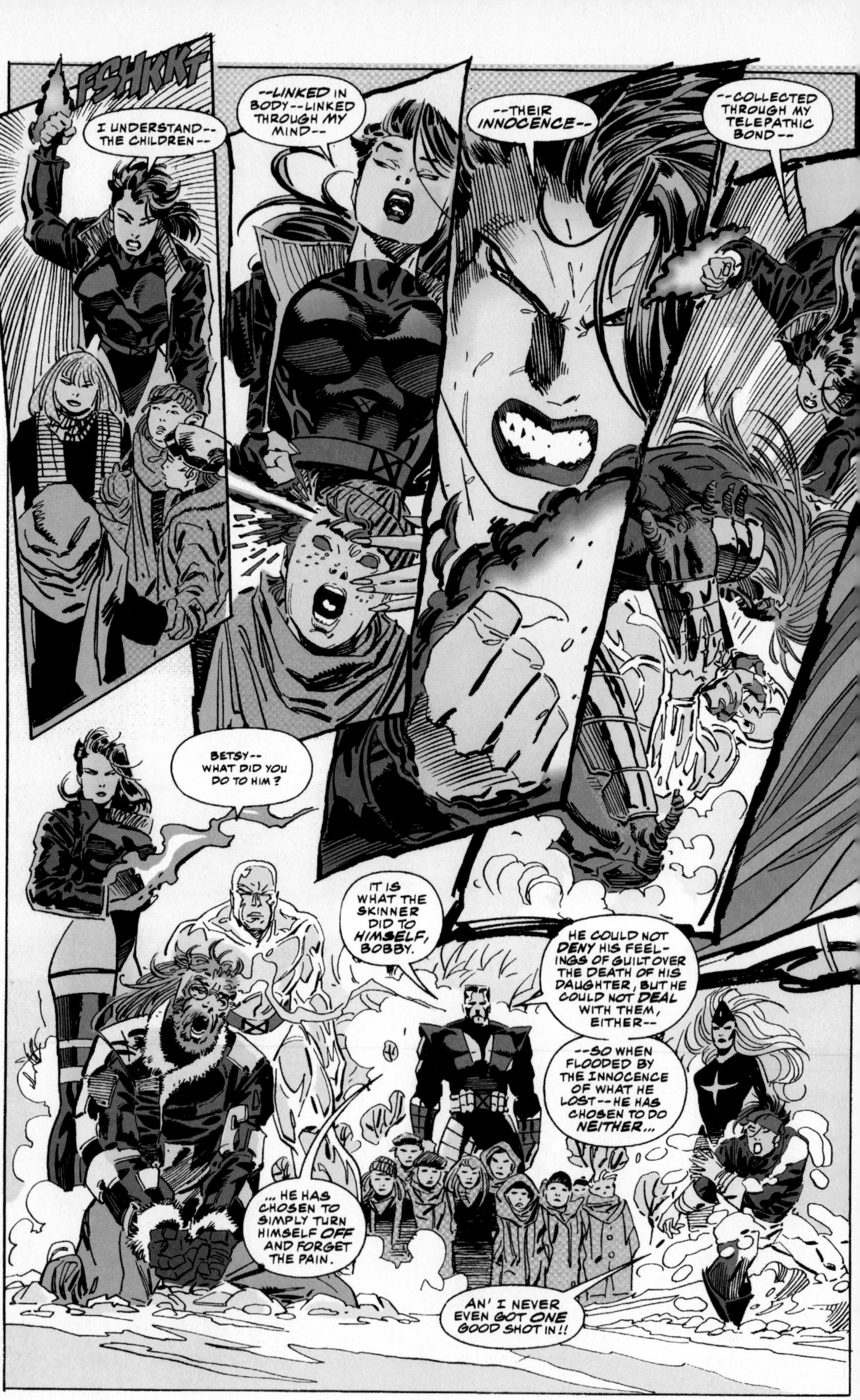
FSHKKT
I UNDERSTAND-- THE CHILDREN--
--LINKED IN BODY--LINKED THROUGH MY MIND--
--THEIR INNOCENCE--
--COLLECTED THROUGH MY TELEPATHIC BOND--
BETSY-- WHAT DID YOU DO TO HIM?
IT IS WHAT THE SKINNER DID TO HIMSELF, BOBBY.
HE COULD NOT DENY HIS FEELINGS OF GUILT OVER THE DEATH OF HIS DAUGHTER, BUT HE COULD NOT DEAL WITH THEM, EITHER--
--SO WHEN FLOODED BY THE INNOCENCE OF WHAT HE LOST--HE HAS CHOSEN TO DO NEITHER...
...HE HAS CHOSEN TO SIMPLY TURN HIMSELF OFF AND FORGET THE PAIN.
AN' I NEVER EVEN GOT ONE GOOD SHOT IN!!

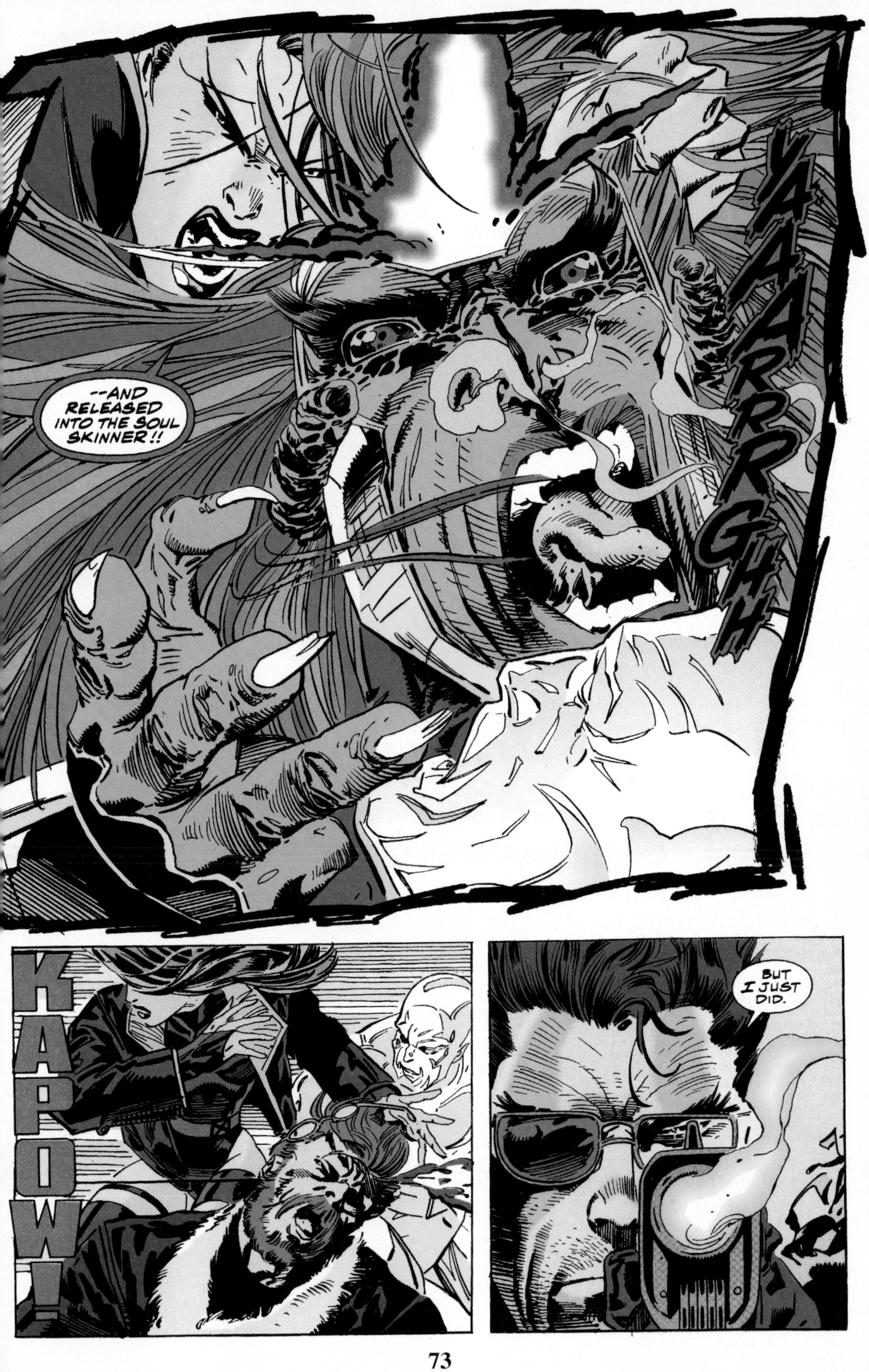
--AND RELEASED INTO THE SOUL SKINNER!!
AAARRRGHH
KAPOW!
BUT I JUST DID.

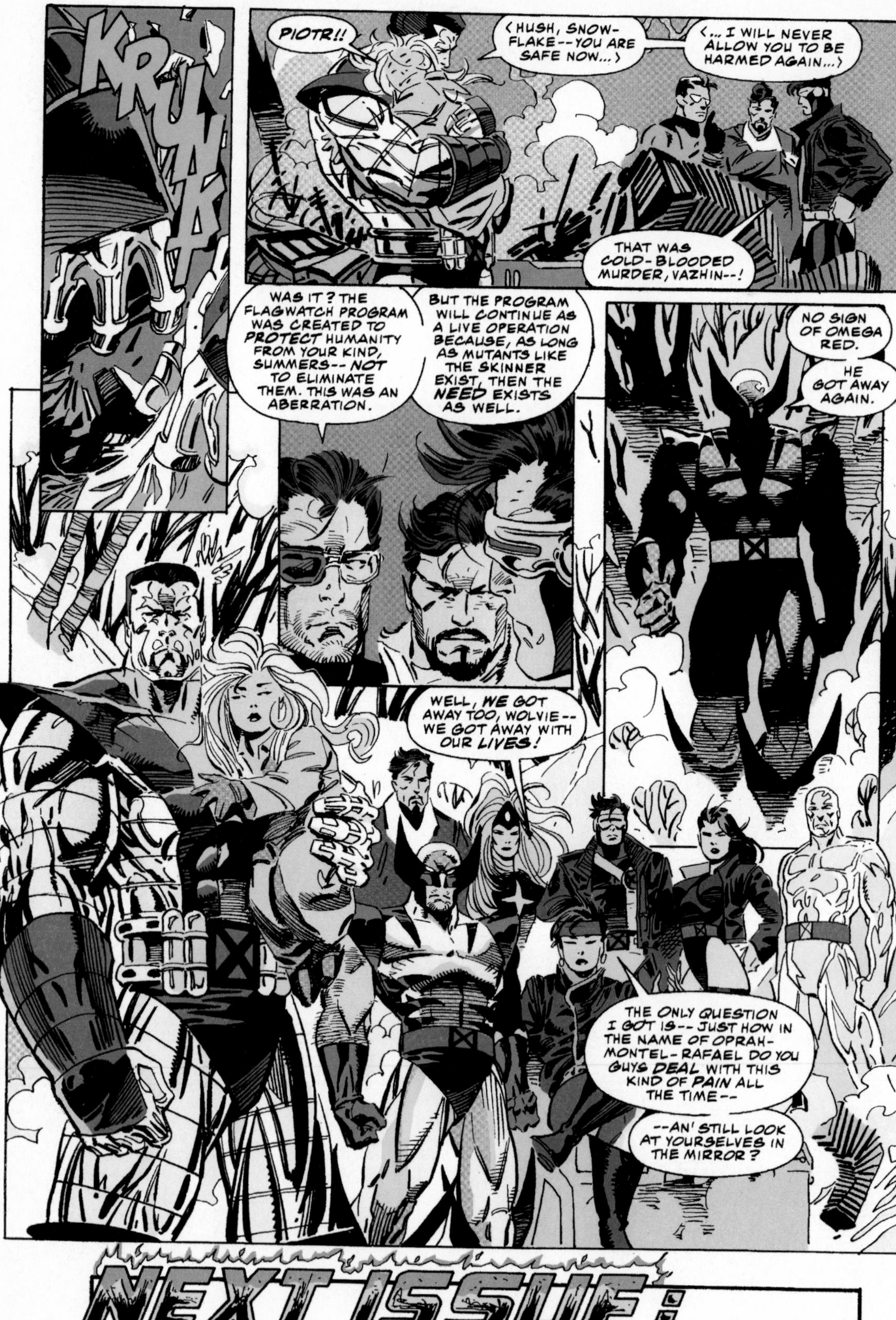
KRUNK
PIOTR!!
‹HUSH, SNOW-FLAKE--YOU ARE SAFE NOW...›
‹... I WILL NEVER ALLOW YOU TO BE HARMED AGAIN...›
THAT WAS COLD-BLOODED MURDER, VAZHIN--!
WAS IT? THE FLAGWATCH PROGRAM WAS CREATED TO PROTECT HUMANITY FROM YOUR KIND, SUMMERS-- NOT TO ELIMINATE THEM. THIS WAS AN ABERRATION.
BUT THE PROGRAM WILL CONTINUE AS A LIVE OPERATION BECAUSE, AS LONG AS MUTANTS LIKE THE SKINNER EXIST, THEN THE NEED EXISTS AS WELL.
NO SIGN OF OMEGA RED.
HE GOT AWAY AGAIN.
WELL, WE GOT AWAY TOO, WOLVIE-- WE GOT AWAY WITH OUR LIVES!
THE ONLY QUESTION I GOT IS-- JUST HOW IN THE NAME OF OPRAH-MONTEL-RAFAEL DO YOU GUYS DEAL WITH THIS KIND OF PAIN ALL THE TIME--
--AN' STILL LOOK AT YOURSELVES IN THE MIRROR?

NEXT ISSUE!

WE EXPLORE ***JUBILEE'S*** QUESTION AS SOME PERSONAL PROBLEMS DEVELOP AMONG THE ***X-MEN!*** (EVEN WHEN WE SLOW THINGS DOWN A BIT -- --WE STILL HEAT THINGS UP!)

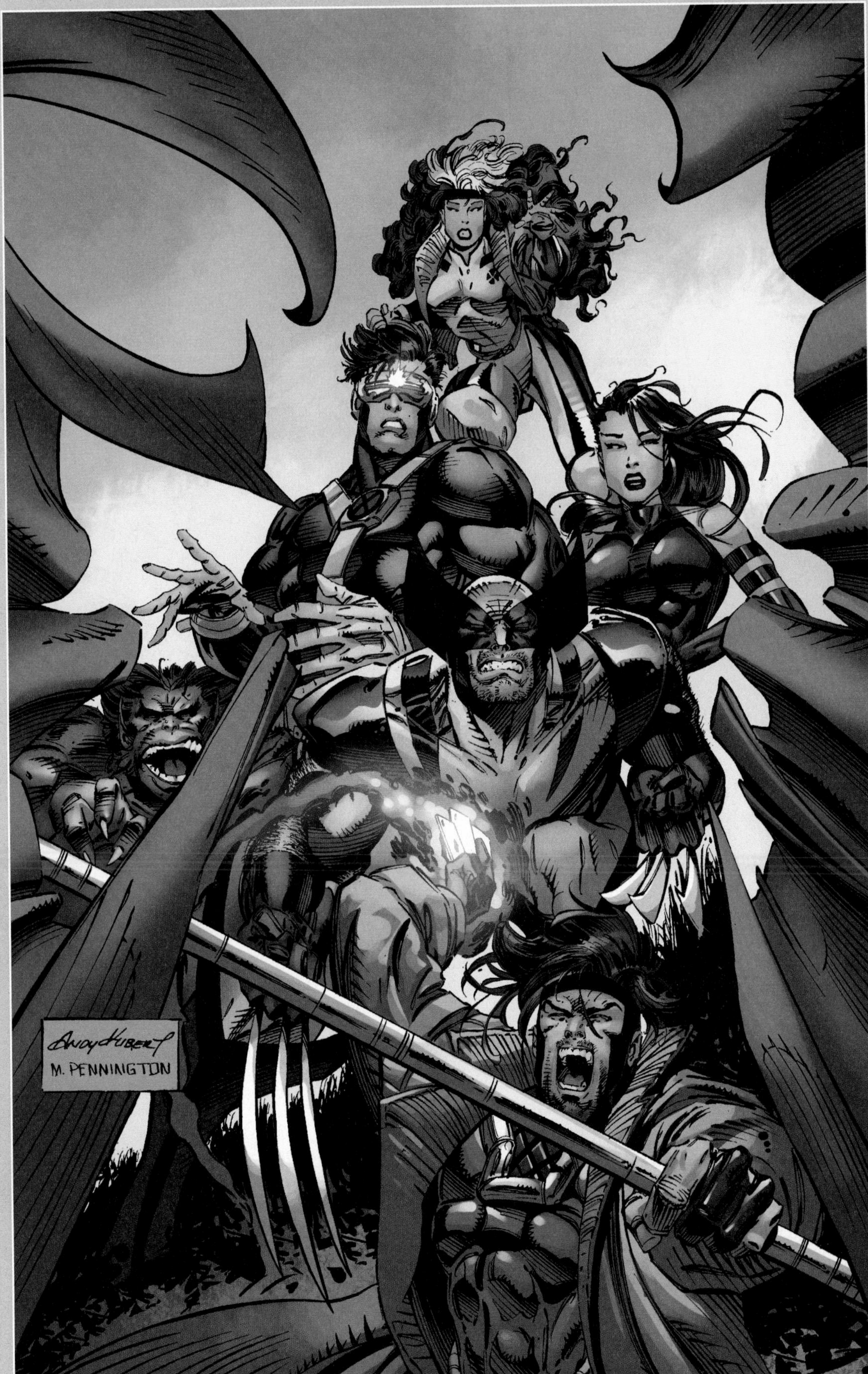
ANDY KUBERT
M. PENNINGTON

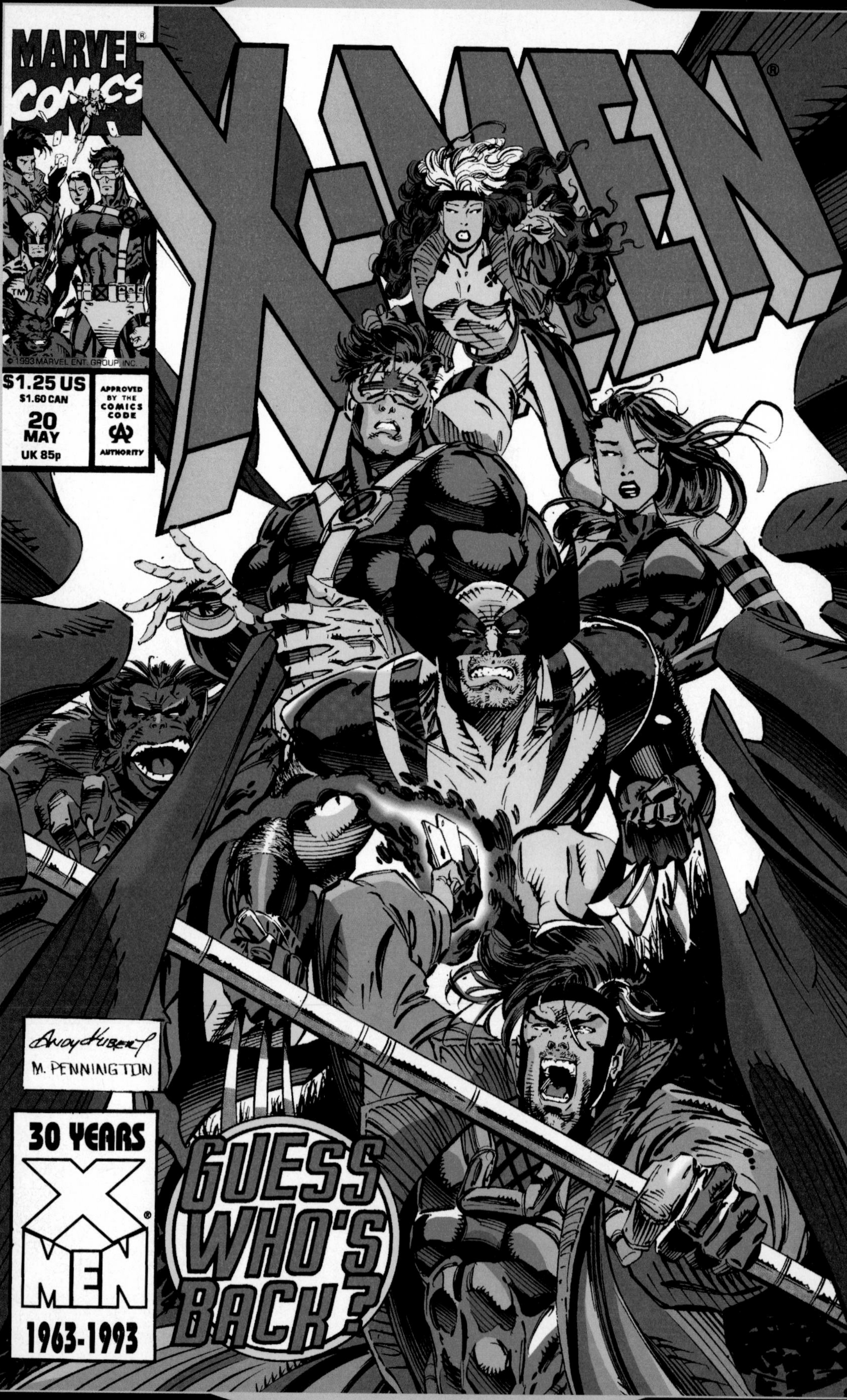
MARVEL COMICS
X-MEN
© 1993 MARVEL ENT. GROUP, INC.
$1.25 US
$1.60 CAN
20
MAY
UK 85p
APPROVED BY THE COMICS CODE AUTHORITY
Andy Kubert
M. PENNINGTON
30 YEARS
X MEN
1963-1993
GUESS WHO'S BACK?

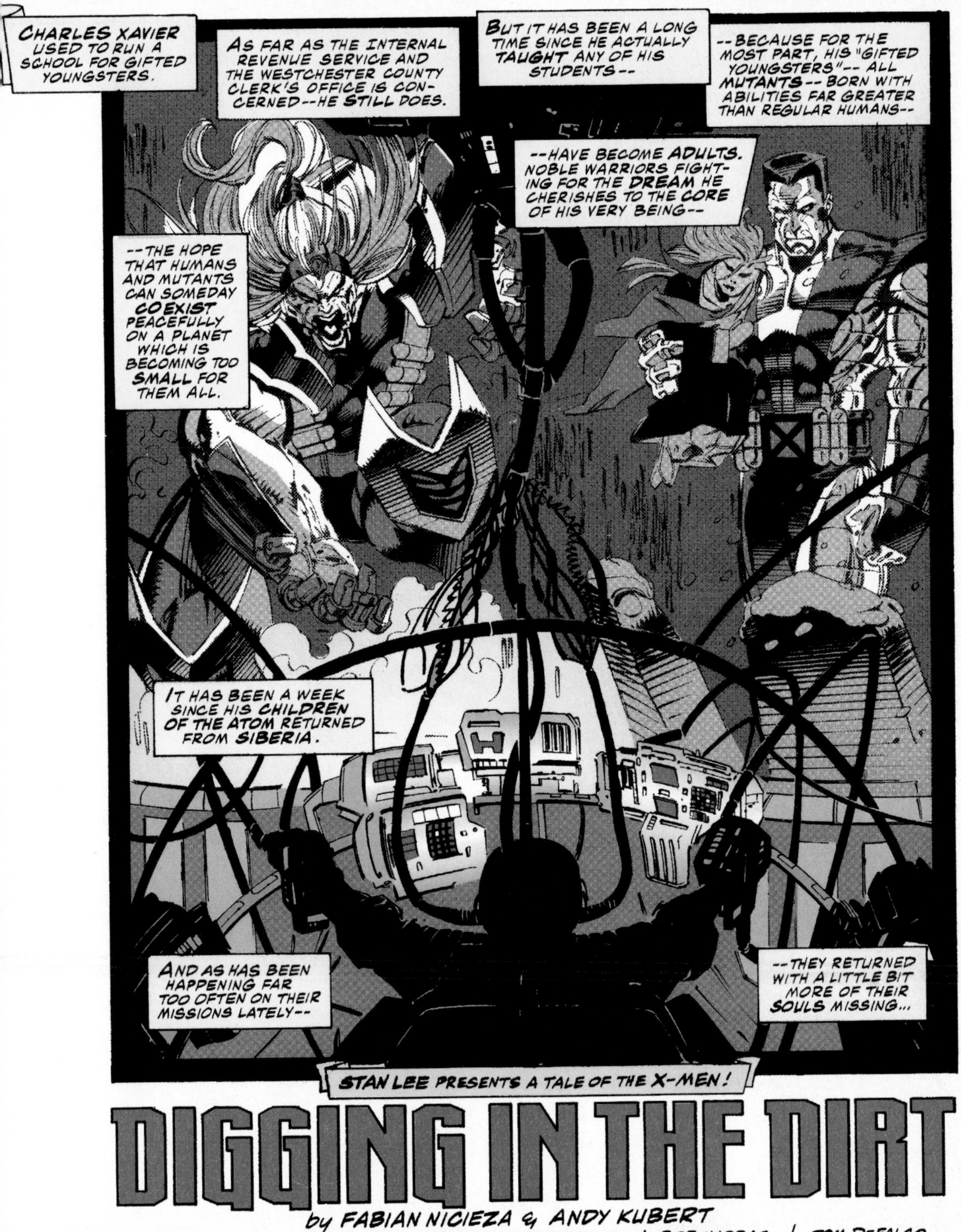
CHARLES XAVIER USED TO RUN A SCHOOL FOR GIFTED YOUNGSTERS.
AS FAR AS THE INTERNAL REVENUE SERVICE AND THE WESTCHESTER COUNTY CLERK'S OFFICE IS CONCERNED--HE STILL DOES.
BUT IT HAS BEEN A LONG TIME SINCE HE ACTUALLY TAUGHT ANY OF HIS STUDENTS--
--BECAUSE FOR THE MOST PART, HIS "GIFTED YOUNGSTERS"-- ALL MUTANTS-- BORN WITH ABILITIES FAR GREATER THAN REGULAR HUMANS--
--HAVE BECOME ADULTS. NOBLE WARRIORS FIGHTING FOR THE DREAM HE CHERISHES TO THE CORE OF HIS VERY BEING--
--THE HOPE THAT HUMANS AND MUTANTS CAN SOMEDAY COEXIST PEACEFULLY ON A PLANET WHICH IS BECOMING TOO SMALL FOR THEM ALL.
IT HAS BEEN A WEEK SINCE HIS CHILDREN OF THE ATOM RETURNED FROM SIBERIA.
AND AS HAS BEEN HAPPENING FAR TOO OFTEN ON THEIR MISSIONS LATELY--
--THEY RETURNED WITH A LITTLE BIT MORE OF THEIR SOULS MISSING...

STAN LEE PRESENTS A TALE OF THE X-MEN!

DIGGING IN THE DIRT

by FABIAN NICIEZA & ANDY KUBERT

MARK PENNINGTON / BOB WIACEK (PGS. 22,23) INKERS | BILL OAKLEY LETTERER | JOE ROSAS COLORIST | BOB HARRAS EDITOR | TOM DeFALCO EDITOR IN CHIEF

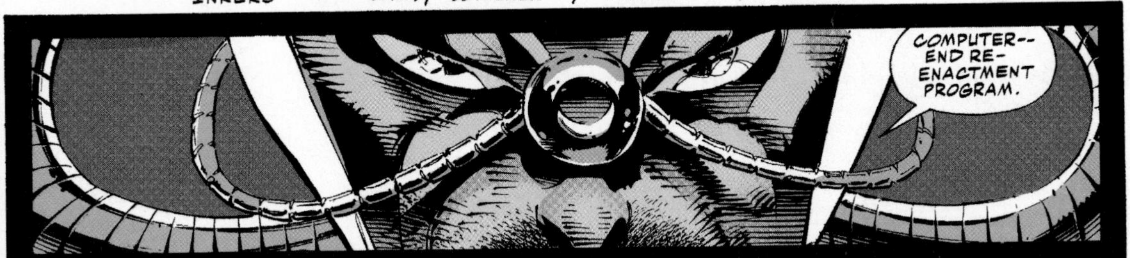
COMPUTER-- END RE-ENACTMENT PROGRAM.

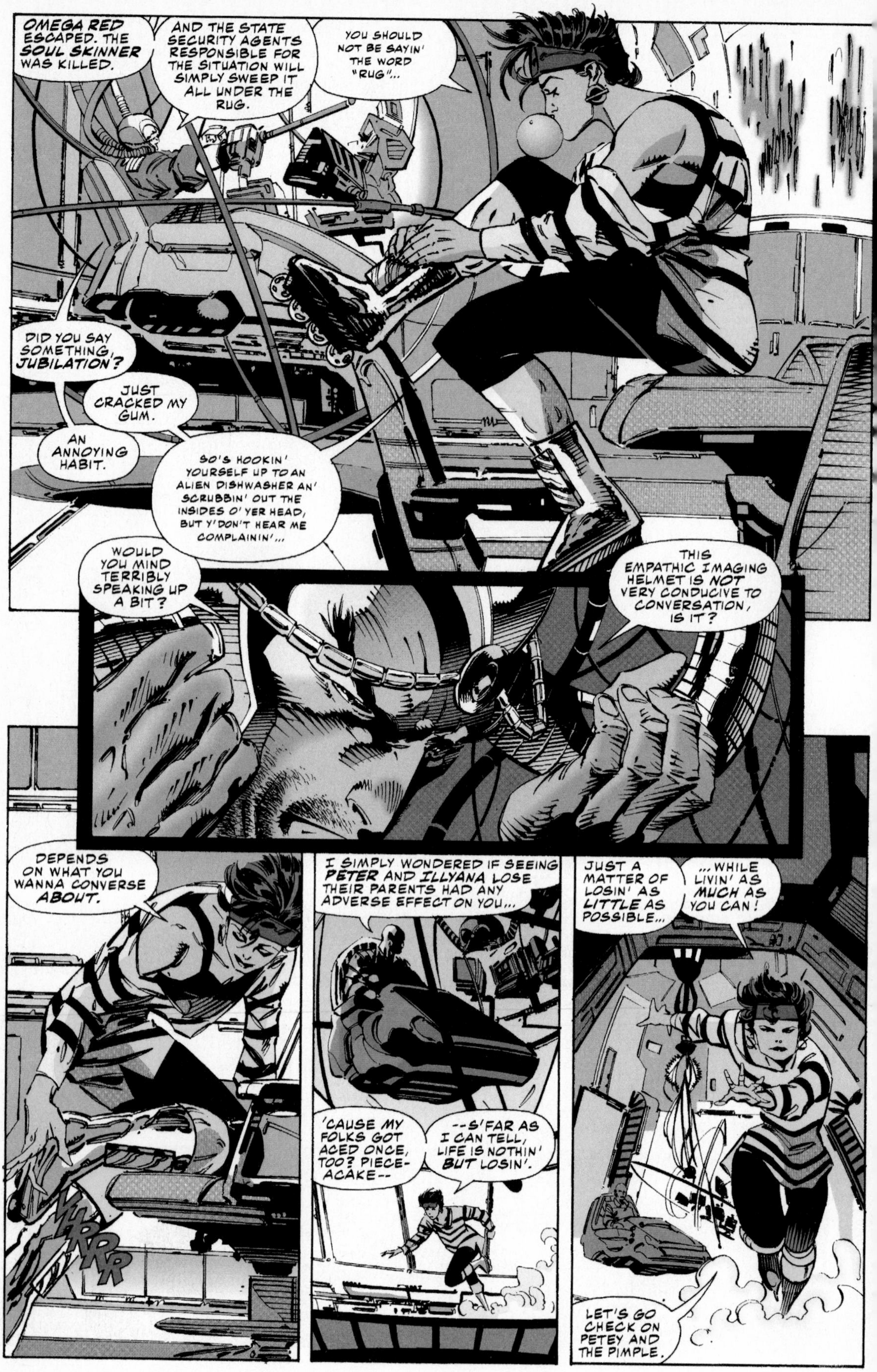
OMEGA RED ESCAPED. THE SOUL SKINNER WAS KILLED.
AND THE STATE SECURITY AGENTS RESPONSIBLE FOR THE SITUATION WILL SIMPLY SWEEP IT ALL UNDER THE RUG.
YOU SHOULD NOT BE SAYIN' THE WORD "RUG"...
DID YOU SAY SOMETHING, JUBILATION?
JUST CRACKED MY GUM.
AN ANNOYING HABIT.
SO'S HOOKIN' YOURSELF UP TO AN ALIEN DISHWASHER AN' SCRUBBIN' OUT THE INSIDES O' YER HEAD, BUT Y'DON'T HEAR ME COMPLAININ'...
WOULD YOU MIND TERRIBLY SPEAKING UP A BIT?
THIS EMPATHIC IMAGING HELMET IS NOT VERY CONDUCIVE TO CONVERSATION, IS IT?
DEPENDS ON WHAT YOU WANNA CONVERSE ABOUT.
VRRRR
I SIMPLY WONDERED IF SEEING PETER AND ILLYANA LOSE THEIR PARENTS HAD ANY ADVERSE EFFECT ON YOU...
'CAUSE MY FOLKS GOT ACED ONCE, TOO? PIECE-ACAKE--
--S'FAR AS I CAN TELL, LIFE IS NOTHIN' BUT LOSIN'.
JUST A MATTER OF LOSIN' AS LITTLE AS POSSIBLE...
...WHILE LIVIN' AS MUCH AS YOU CAN!
LET'S GO CHECK ON PETEY AND THE PIMPLE.

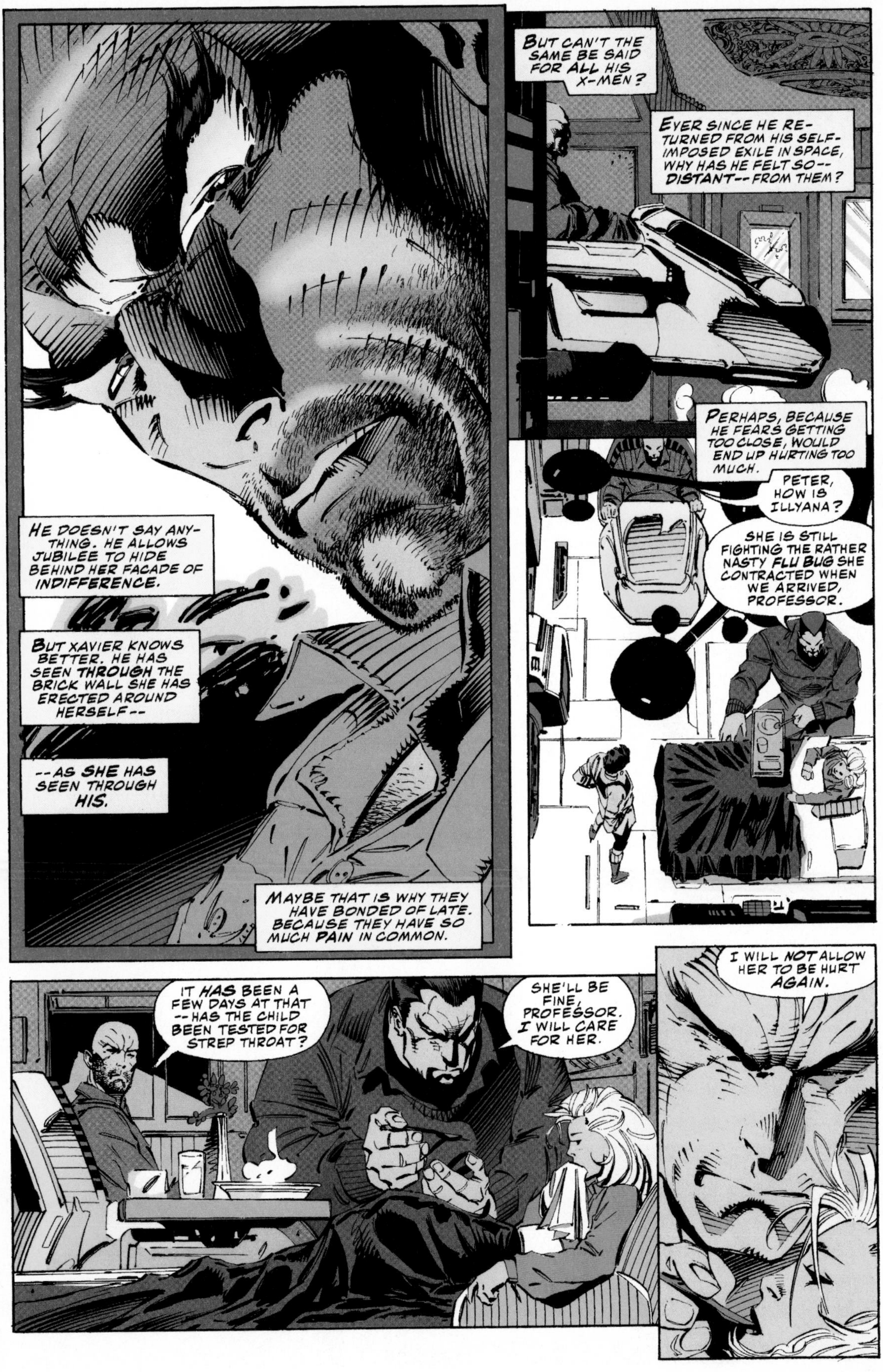
HE DOESN'T SAY ANYTHING. HE ALLOWS JUBILEE TO HIDE BEHIND HER FACADE OF INDIFFERENCE.
BUT XAVIER KNOWS BETTER. HE HAS SEEN THROUGH THE BRICK WALL SHE HAS ERECTED AROUND HERSELF--
--AS SHE HAS SEEN THROUGH HIS.
MAYBE THAT IS WHY THEY HAVE BONDED OF LATE. BECAUSE THEY HAVE SO MUCH PAIN IN COMMON.
BUT CAN'T THE SAME BE SAID FOR ALL HIS X-MEN?
EVER SINCE HE RETURNED FROM HIS SELF-IMPOSED EXILE IN SPACE, WHY HAS HE FELT SO--DISTANT--FROM THEM?
PERHAPS, BECAUSE HE FEARS GETTING TOO CLOSE, WOULD END UP HURTING TOO MUCH.
PETER, HOW IS ILLYANA?
SHE IS STILL FIGHTING THE RATHER NASTY FLU BUG SHE CONTRACTED WHEN WE ARRIVED, PROFESSOR.
IT HAS BEEN A FEW DAYS AT THAT --HAS THE CHILD BEEN TESTED FOR STREP THROAT?
SHE'LL BE FINE, PROFESSOR. I WILL CARE FOR HER.
I WILL NOT ALLOW HER TO BE HURT AGAIN.

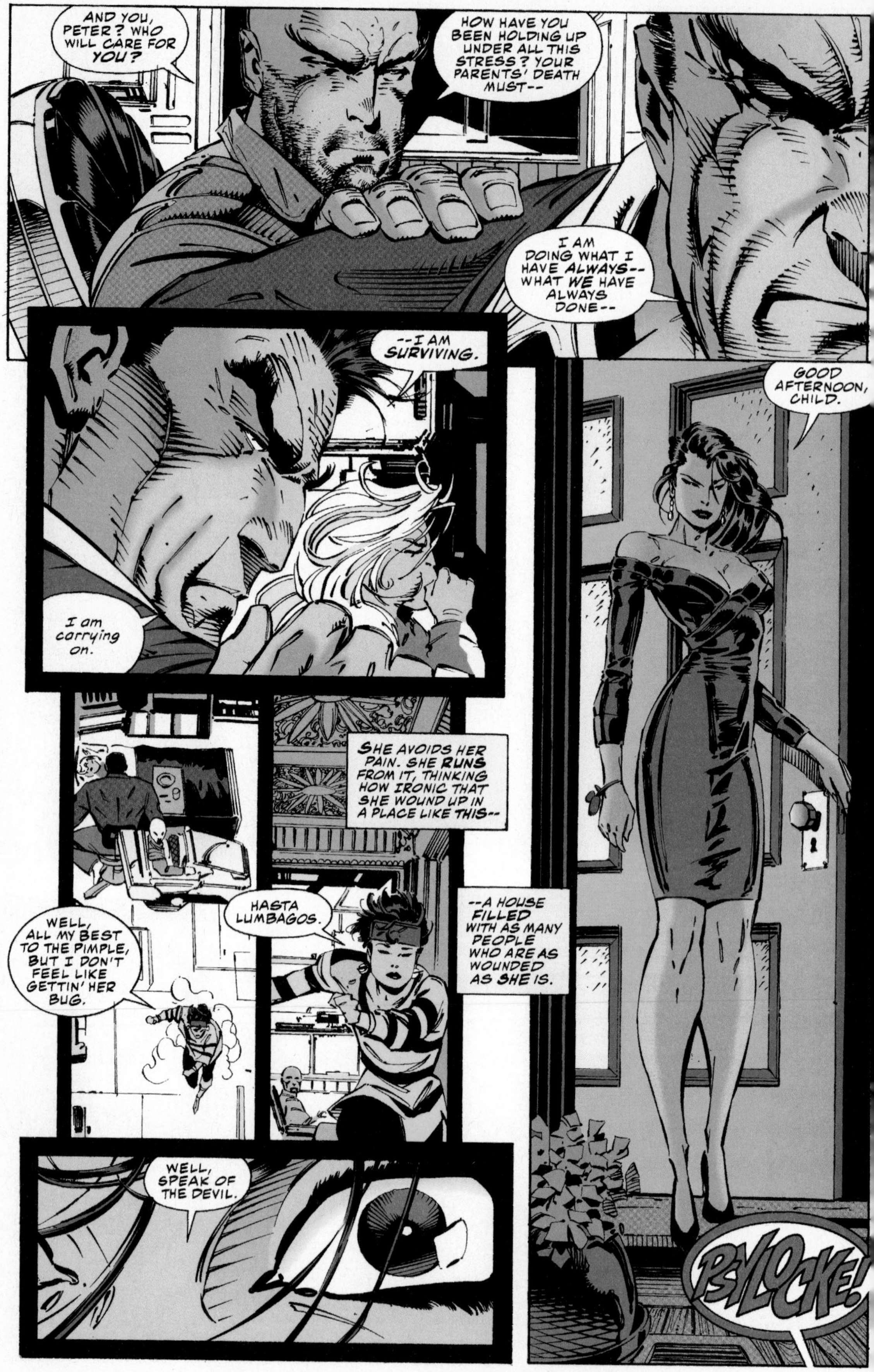
AND YOU, PETER? WHO WILL CARE FOR YOU?
HOW HAVE YOU BEEN HOLDING UP UNDER ALL THIS STRESS? YOUR PARENTS' DEATH MUST--
I AM DOING WHAT I HAVE ALWAYS-- WHAT WE HAVE ALWAYS DONE--
--I AM SURVIVING.
I am carrying on.
GOOD AFTERNOON, CHILD.
SHE AVOIDS HER PAIN. SHE RUNS FROM IT, THINKING HOW IRONIC THAT SHE WOUND UP IN A PLACE LIKE THIS--
HASTA LUMBAGOS.
--A HOUSE FILLED WITH AS MANY PEOPLE WHO ARE AS WOUNDED AS SHE IS.
WELL, ALL MY BEST TO THE PIMPLE, BUT I DON'T FEEL LIKE GETTIN' HER BUG.
WELL, SPEAK OF THE DEVIL.
PSYLOCKE!

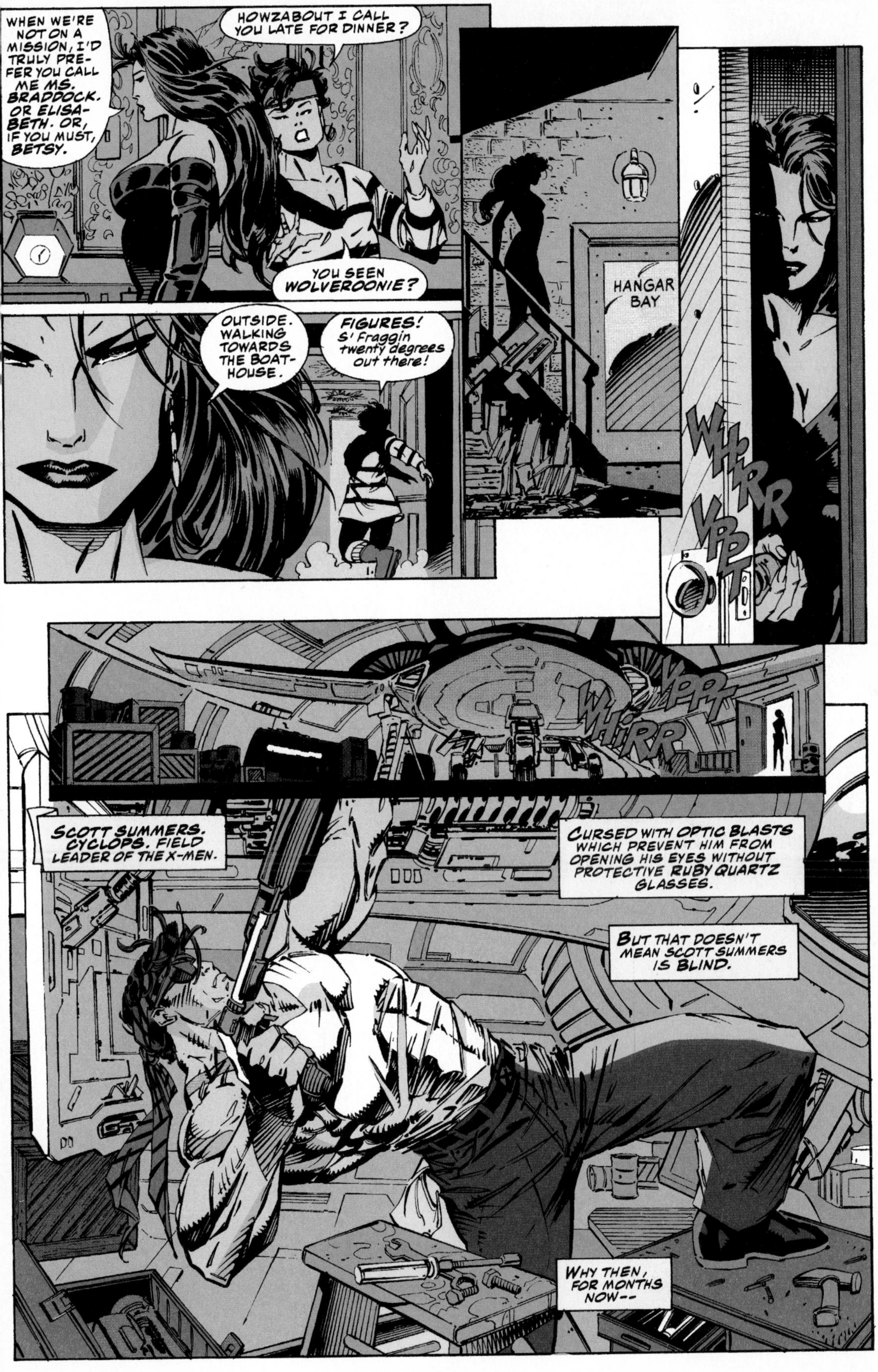

WHEN WE'RE NOT ON A MISSION, I'D TRULY PREFER YOU CALL ME MS. BRADDOCK. OR ELISABETH. OR, IF YOU MUST, BETSY.
HOWZABOUT I CALL YOU LATE FOR DINNER?
YOU SEEN WOLVEROONIE?
OUTSIDE. WALKING TOWARDS THE BOATHOUSE.
FIGURES! S' Fraggin twenty degrees out there!
HANGAR BAY
WHIRR
VPPT
VPPT
WHIRR
SCOTT SUMMERS. CYCLOPS. FIELD LEADER OF THE X-MEN.
CURSED WITH OPTIC BLASTS WHICH PREVENT HIM FROM OPENING HIS EYES WITHOUT PROTECTIVE RUBY QUARTZ GLASSES.
BUT THAT DOESN'T MEAN SCOTT SUMMERS IS BLIND.
WHY THEN, FOR MONTHS NOW--

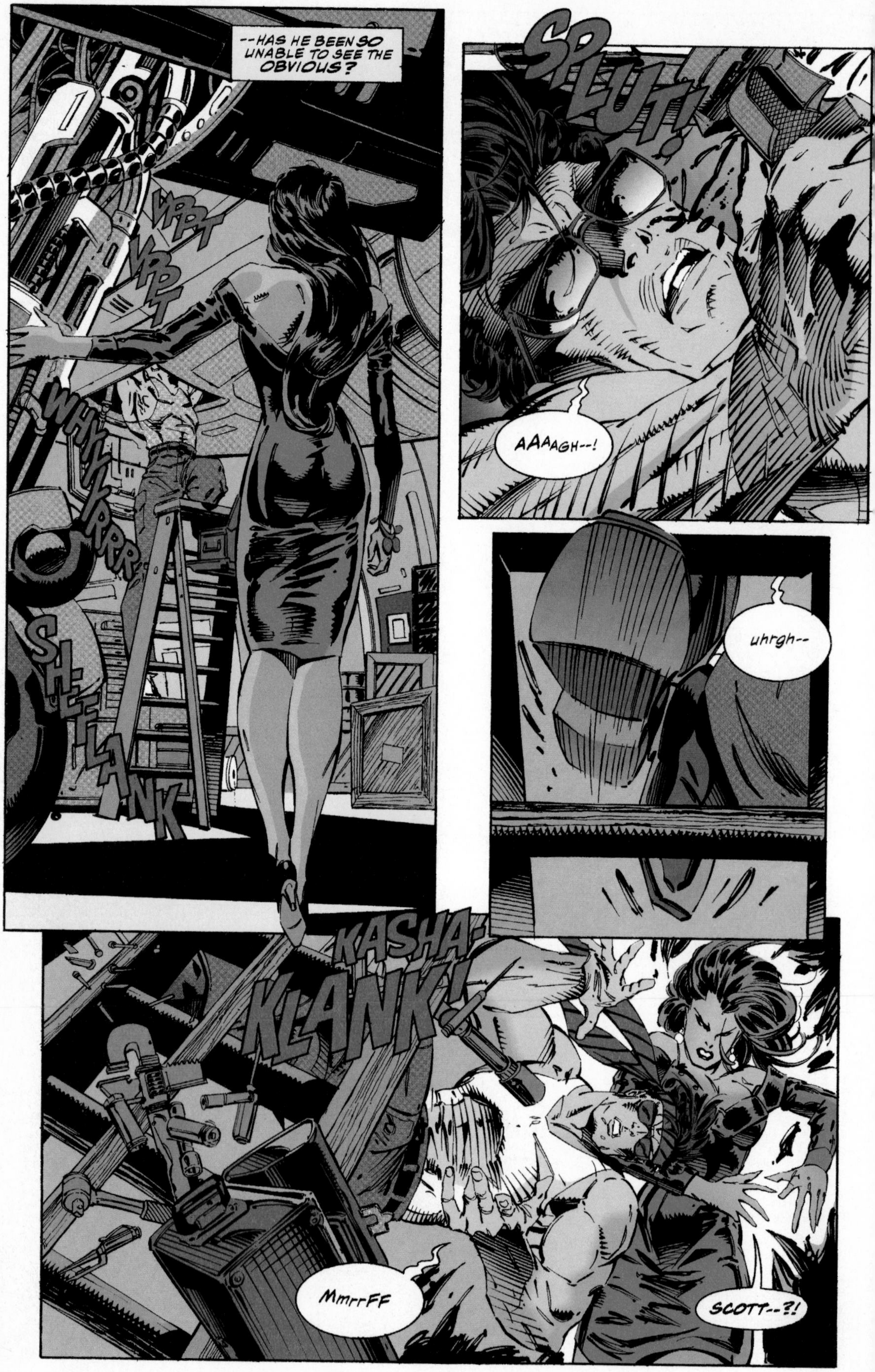
--HAS HE BEEN SO UNABLE TO SEE THE OBVIOUS?
VPPT VPPT
WHYYYRRR
SHEFLANK
SPLUT!
AAAAGH--!
uhrgh--
KASHA-KLANK!
MmrrFF
SCOTT--?!

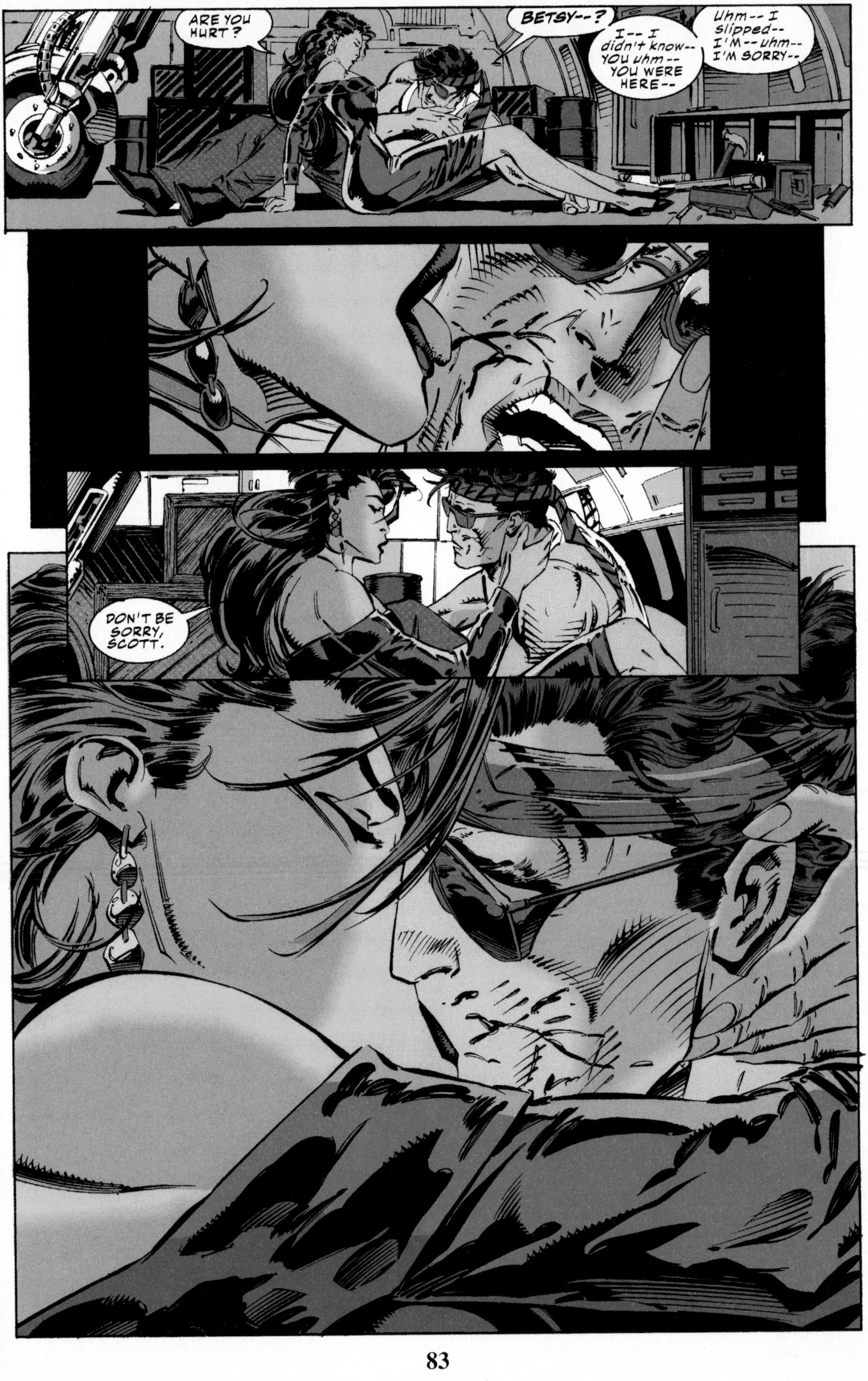
ARE YOU HURT?
BETSY--?
I-- I didn't know-- YOU uhm -- YOU WERE HERE--
Uhm-- I slipped-- I'M--uhm-- I'M SORRY--
DON'T BE SORRY, SCOTT.

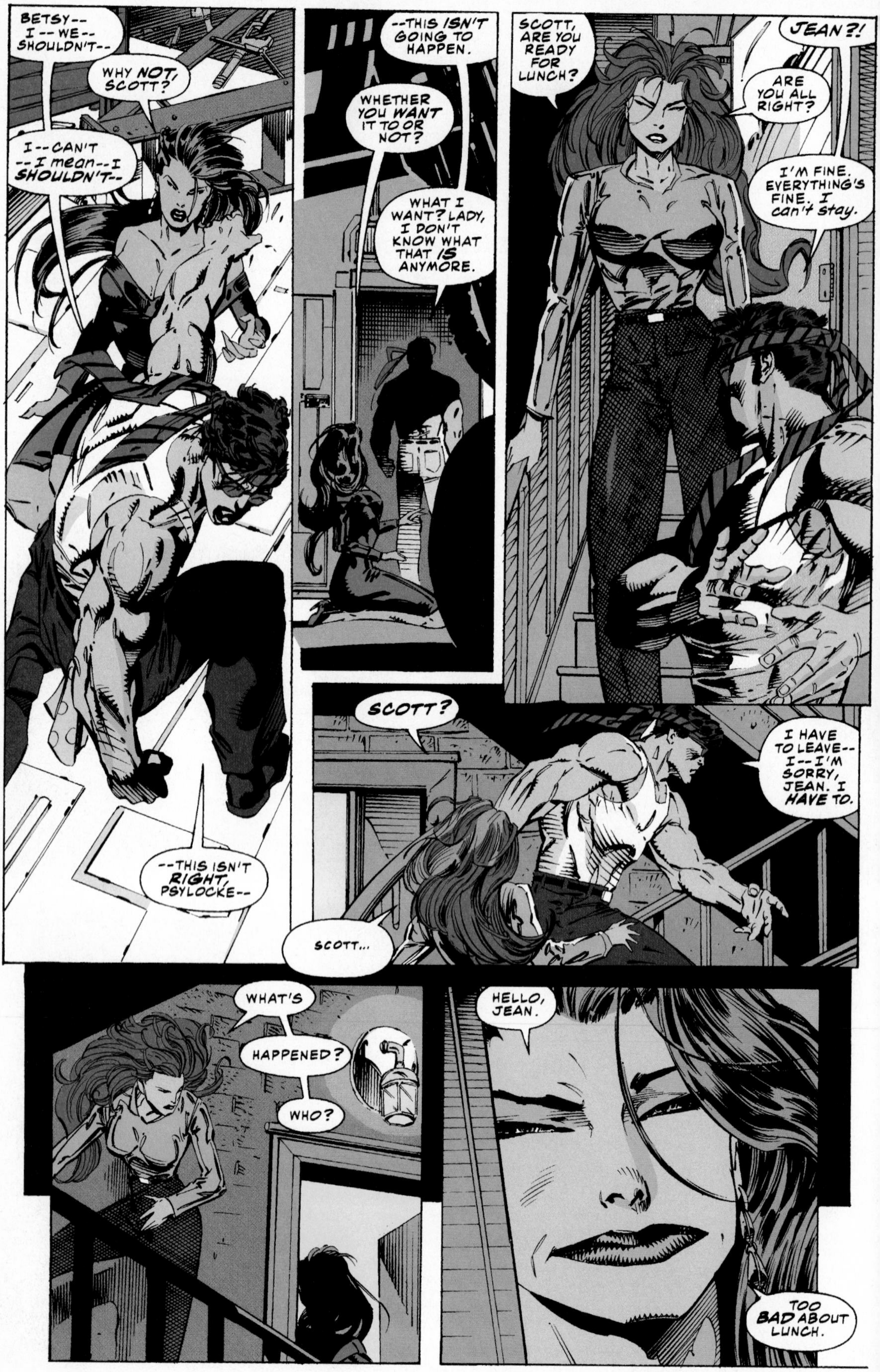
BETSY-- I--WE-- SHOULDN'T--
WHY NOT, SCOTT?
I--CAN'T --I mean--I SHOULDN'T--
--THIS ISN'T RIGHT, PSYLOCKE--
--THIS ISN'T GOING TO HAPPEN.
WHETHER YOU WANT IT TO OR NOT?
WHAT I WANT? LADY, I DON'T KNOW WHAT THAT IS ANYMORE.
SCOTT, ARE YOU READY FOR LUNCH?
JEAN?!
ARE YOU ALL RIGHT?
I'M FINE. EVERYTHING'S FINE. I can't stay.
SCOTT?
I HAVE TO LEAVE-- I--I'M SORRY, JEAN. I HAVE TO.
SCOTT...
WHAT'S
HAPPENED?
WHO?
HELLO, JEAN.
TOO BAD ABOUT LUNCH.

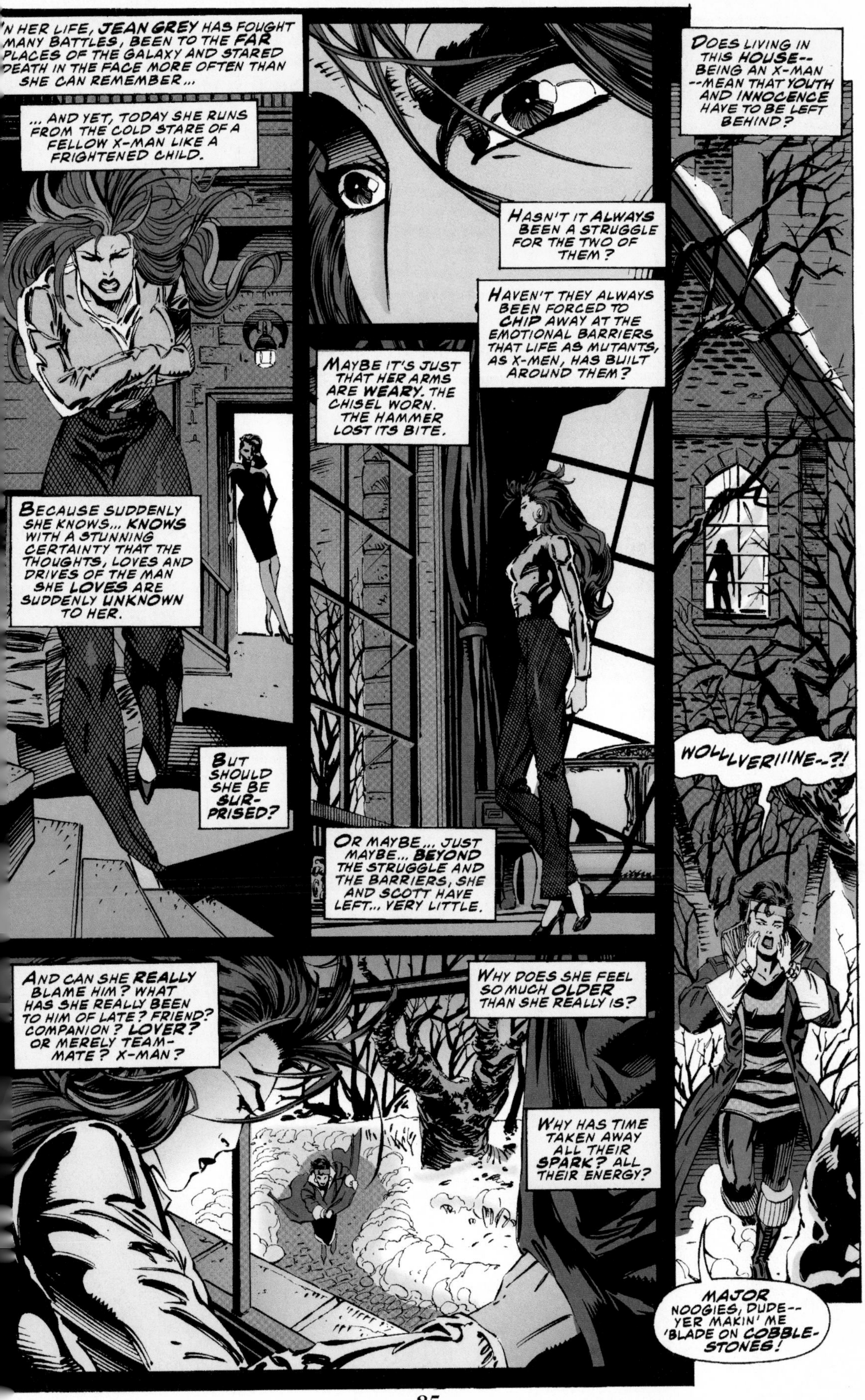
IN HER LIFE, JEAN GREY HAS FOUGHT MANY BATTLES, BEEN TO THE FAR PLACES OF THE GALAXY AND STARED DEATH IN THE FACE MORE OFTEN THAN SHE CAN REMEMBER...
...AND YET, TODAY SHE RUNS FROM THE COLD STARE OF A FELLOW X-MAN LIKE A FRIGHTENED CHILD.
BECAUSE SUDDENLY SHE KNOWS... KNOWS WITH A STUNNING CERTAINTY THAT THE THOUGHTS, LOVES AND DRIVES OF THE MAN SHE LOVES ARE SUDDENLY UNKNOWN TO HER.
BUT SHOULD SHE BE SUR-PRISED?
HASN'T IT ALWAYS BEEN A STRUGGLE FOR THE TWO OF THEM?
HAVEN'T THEY ALWAYS BEEN FORCED TO CHIP AWAY AT THE EMOTIONAL BARRIERS THAT LIFE AS MUTANTS, AS X-MEN, HAS BUILT AROUND THEM?
MAYBE IT'S JUST THAT HER ARMS ARE WEARY. THE CHISEL WORN. THE HAMMER LOST ITS BITE.
OR MAYBE... JUST MAYBE... BEYOND THE STRUGGLE AND THE BARRIERS, SHE AND SCOTT HAVE LEFT... VERY LITTLE.
DOES LIVING IN THIS HOUSE-- BEING AN X-MAN --MEAN THAT YOUTH AND INNOCENCE HAVE TO BE LEFT BEHIND?
WOLLLVERIIINE--?!
AND CAN SHE REALLY BLAME HIM? WHAT HAS SHE REALLY BEEN TO HIM OF LATE? FRIEND? COMPANION? LOVER? OR MERELY TEAM-MATE? X-MAN?
WHY DOES SHE FEEL SO MUCH OLDER THAN SHE REALLY IS?
WHY HAS TIME TAKEN AWAY ALL THEIR SPARK? ALL THEIR ENERGY?
MAJOR NOOGIES, DUDE-- YER MAKIN' ME 'BLADE ON COBBLE-STONES!

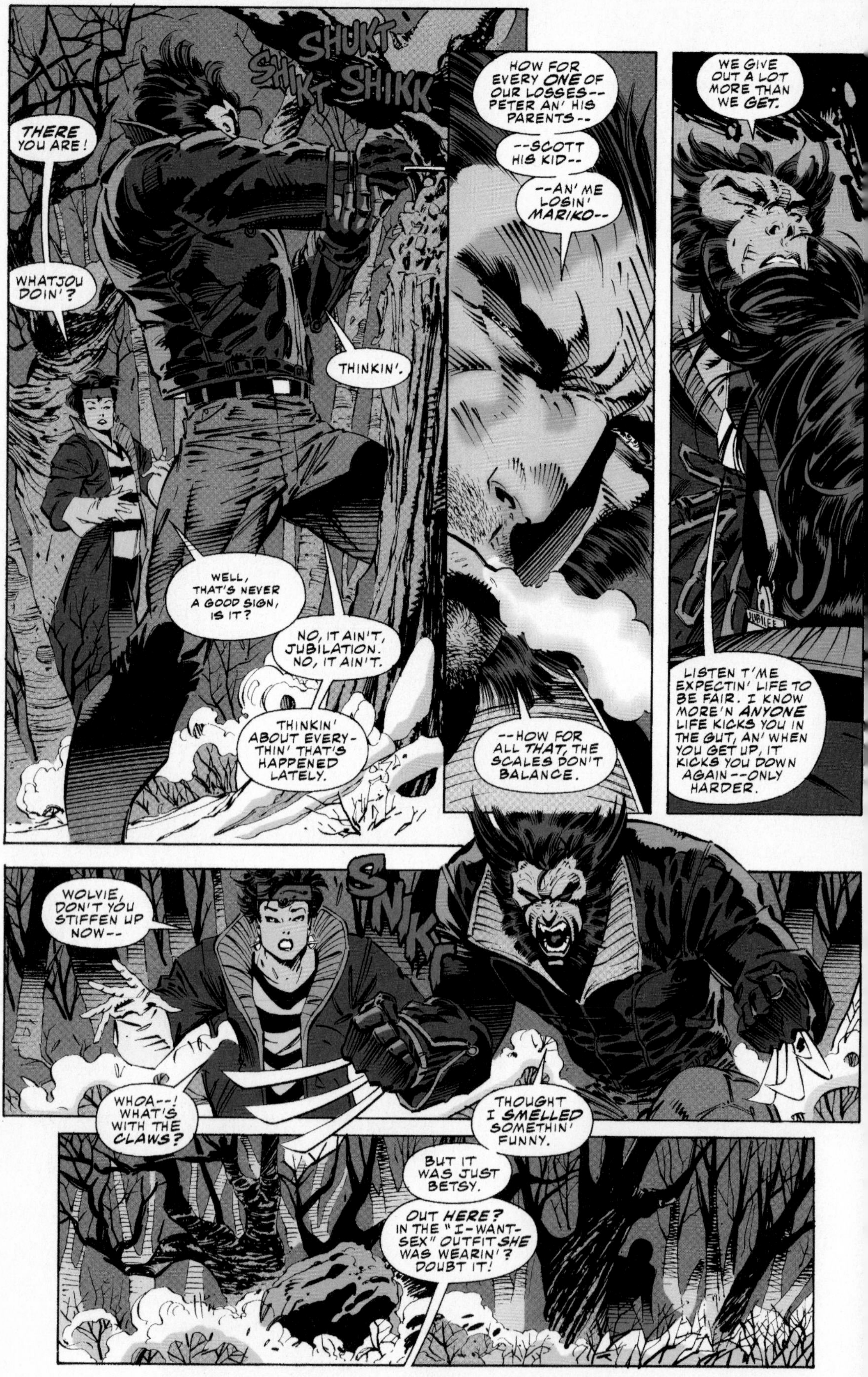

SHUKT SHIKT SHIKK
THERE YOU ARE!
WHATJOU DOIN'?
THINKIN'.
WELL, THAT'S NEVER A GOOD SIGN, IS IT?
NO, IT AIN'T, JUBILATION. NO, IT AIN'T.
THINKIN' ABOUT EVERYTHIN' THAT'S HAPPENED LATELY.
HOW FOR EVERY ONE OF OUR LOSSES-- PETER AN' HIS PARENTS--
--SCOTT HIS KID--
--AN' ME LOSIN' MARIKO--
--HOW FOR ALL THAT, THE SCALES DON'T BALANCE.
WE GIVE OUT A LOT MORE THAN WE GET.
LISTEN T'ME EXPECTIN' LIFE TO BE FAIR. I KNOW MORE'N ANYONE LIFE KICKS YOU IN THE GUT, AN' WHEN YOU GET UP, IT KICKS YOU DOWN AGAIN--ONLY HARDER.
SNIKT
WOLVIE, DON'T YOU STIFFEN UP NOW--
WHOA--! WHAT'S WITH THE CLAWS?
THOUGHT I SMELLED SOMETHIN' FUNNY.
BUT IT WAS JUST BETSY.
OUT HERE? IN THE "I-WANT-SEX" OUTFIT SHE WAS WEARIN'? DOUBT IT!

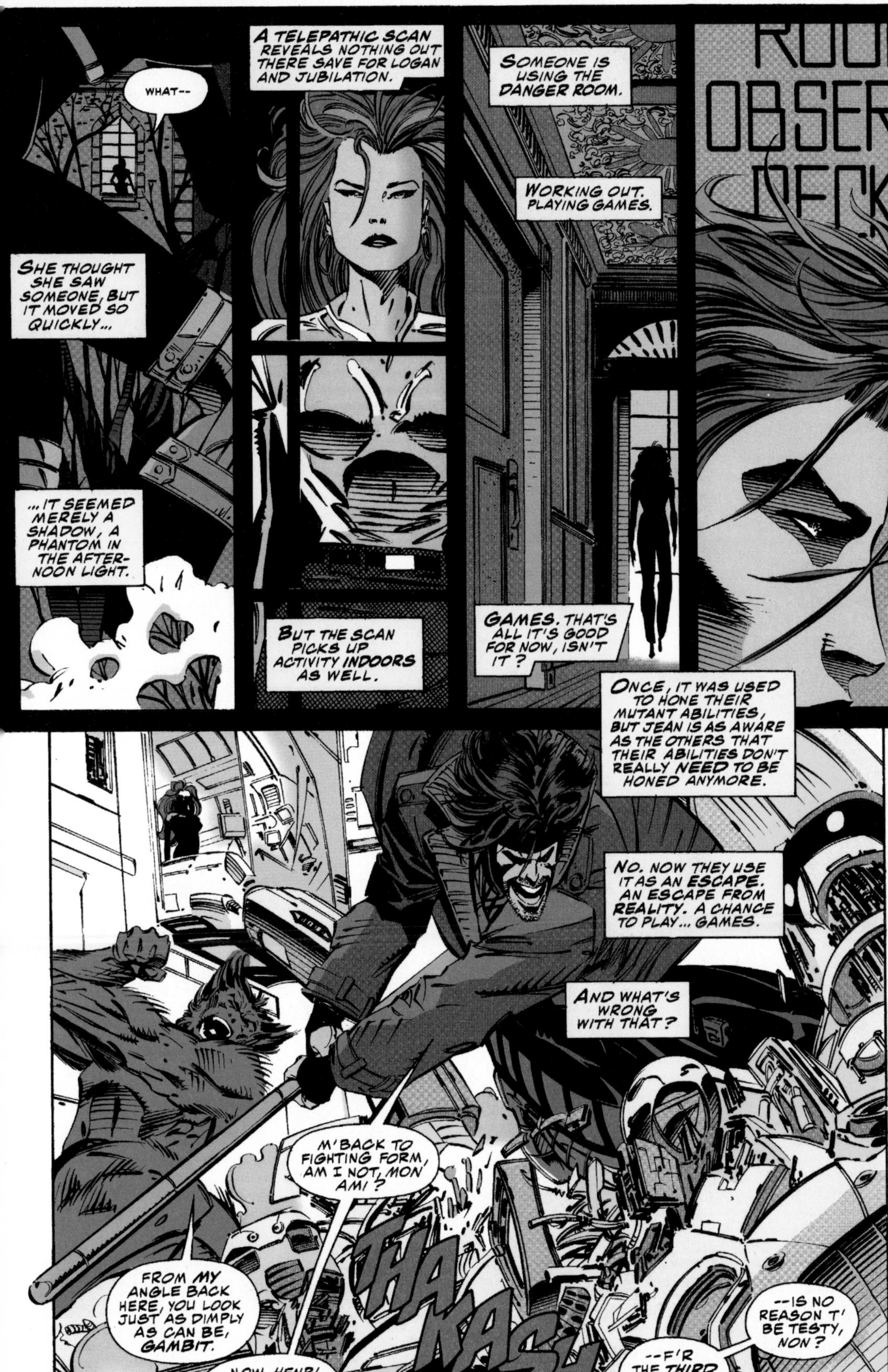

WHAT--
SHE THOUGHT SHE SAW SOMEONE, BUT IT MOVED SO QUICKLY...
...IT SEEMED MERELY A SHADOW, A PHANTOM IN THE AFTER-NOON LIGHT.
A TELEPATHIC SCAN REVEALS NOTHING OUT THERE SAVE FOR LOGAN AND JUBILATION.
BUT THE SCAN PICKS UP ACTIVITY INDOORS AS WELL.
SOMEONE IS USING THE DANGER ROOM.
WORKING OUT. PLAYING GAMES.
GAMES. THAT'S ALL IT'S GOOD FOR NOW, ISN'T IT?
ROOM OBSER DECK
ONCE, IT WAS USED TO HONE THEIR MUTANT ABILITIES, BUT JEAN IS AS AWARE AS THE OTHERS THAT THEIR ABILITIES DON'T REALLY NEED TO BE HONED ANYMORE.
NO. NOW THEY USE IT AS AN ESCAPE. AN ESCAPE FROM REALITY. A CHANCE TO PLAY... GAMES.
AND WHAT'S WRONG WITH THAT?
M' BACK TO FIGHTING FORM, AM I NOT, MON AMI?
FROM MY ANGLE BACK HERE, YOU LOOK JUST AS DIMPLY AS CAN BE, GAMBIT.
THA KASH
NOW, HENRI --JUS' 'CAUSE I'M AS LIKELY T' WIN THIS SCENARIO--
--F'R THE THIRD STRAIGHT TIME--
--IS NO REASON T' BE TESTY, NON?

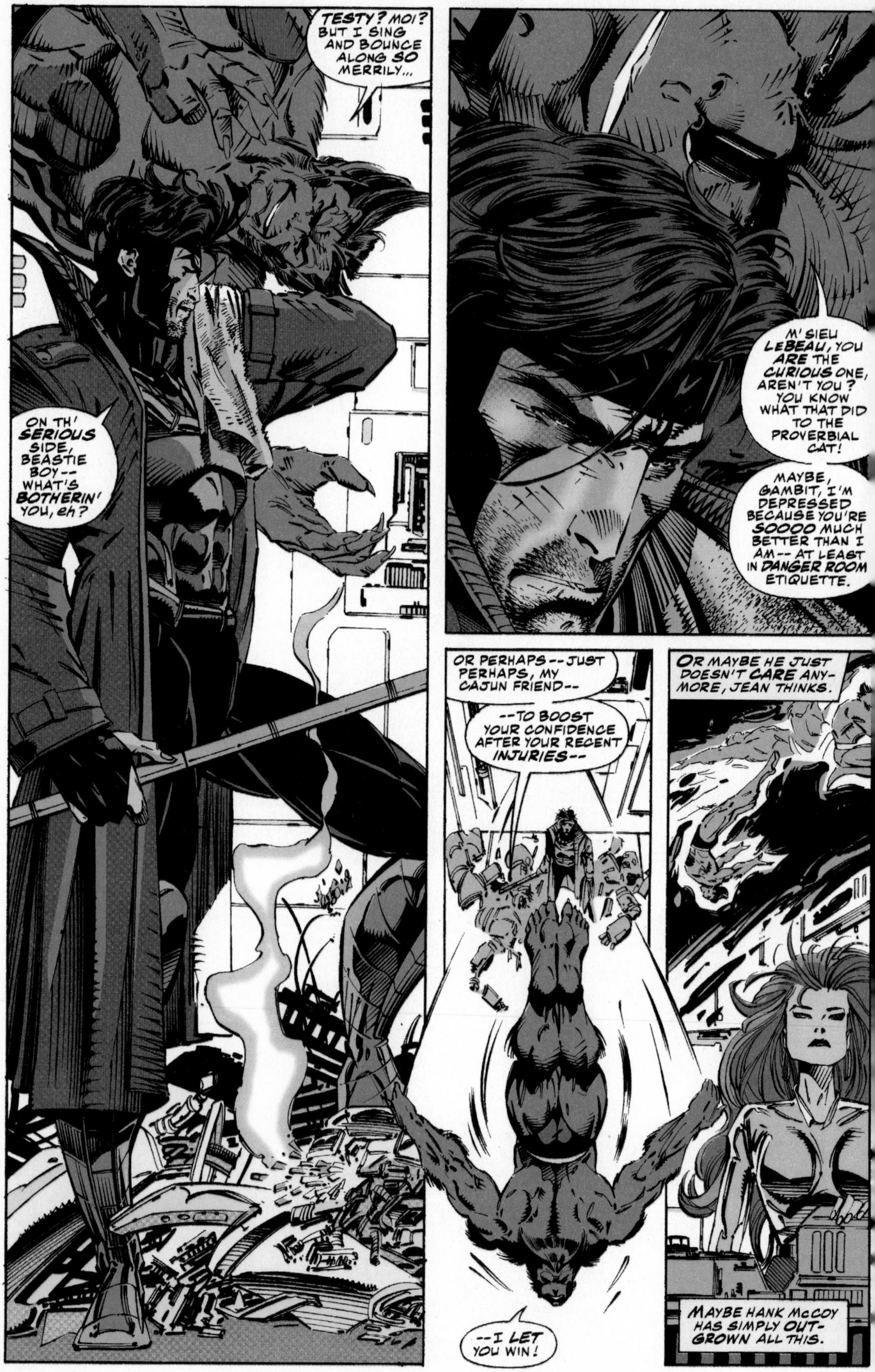
TESTY? MOI? BUT I SING AND BOUNCE ALONG SO MERRILY...
ON TH' SERIOUS SIDE, BEASTIE BOY-- WHAT'S BOTHERIN' YOU, eh?
M'SIEU LEBEAU, YOU ARE THE CURIOUS ONE, AREN'T YOU? YOU KNOW WHAT THAT DID TO THE PROVERBIAL CAT!
MAYBE, GAMBIT, I'M DEPRESSED BECAUSE YOU'RE SOOOO MUCH BETTER THAN I AM -- AT LEAST IN DANGER ROOM ETIQUETTE.
OR PERHAPS -- JUST PERHAPS, MY CAJUN FRIEND--
--TO BOOST YOUR CONFIDENCE AFTER YOUR RECENT INJURIES--
--I LET YOU WIN!
OR MAYBE HE JUST DOESN'T CARE ANYMORE, JEAN THINKS.
MAYBE HANK McCOY HAS SIMPLY OUTGROWN ALL THIS.

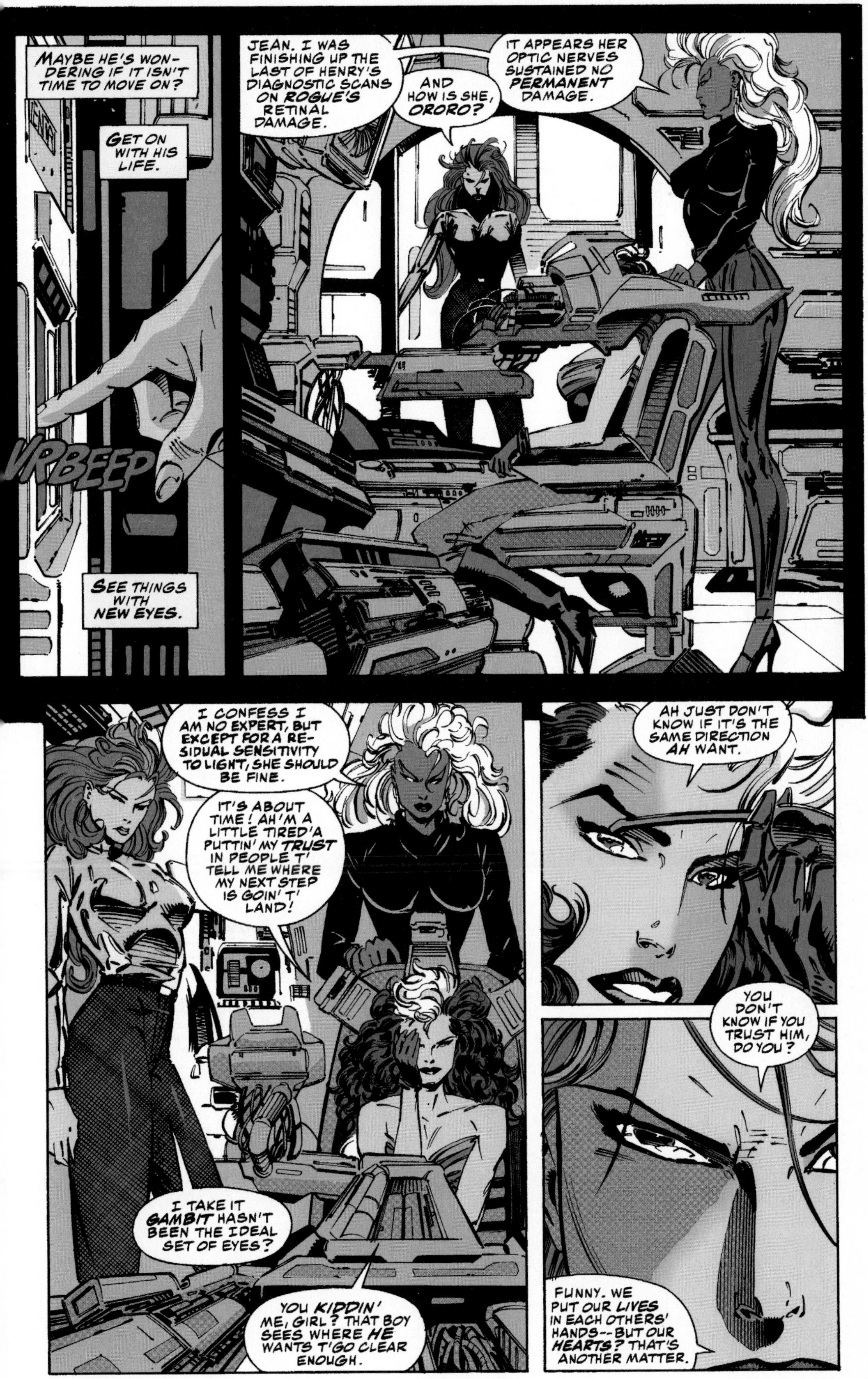

MAYBE HE'S WONDERING IF IT ISN'T TIME TO MOVE ON?
GET ON WITH HIS LIFE.
VRBEEP
SEE THINGS WITH NEW EYES.
JEAN. I WAS FINISHING UP THE LAST OF HENRY'S DIAGNOSTIC SCANS ON ROGUE'S RETINAL DAMAGE.
AND HOW IS SHE, ORORO?
IT APPEARS HER OPTIC NERVES SUSTAINED NO PERMANENT DAMAGE.
I CONFESS I AM NO EXPERT, BUT EXCEPT FOR A RESIDUAL SENSITIVITY TO LIGHT, SHE SHOULD BE FINE.
IT'S ABOUT TIME! AH'M A LITTLE TIRED'A PUTTIN' MY TRUST IN PEOPLE T' TELL ME WHERE MY NEXT STEP IS GOIN' T' LAND!
I TAKE IT GAMBIT HASN'T BEEN THE IDEAL SET OF EYES?
YOU KIDDIN' ME, GIRL? THAT BOY SEES WHERE HE WANTS T'GO CLEAR ENOUGH.
AH JUST DON'T KNOW IF IT'S THE SAME DIRECTION AH WANT.
YOU DON'T KNOW IF YOU TRUST HIM, DO YOU?
FUNNY. WE PUT OUR LIVES IN EACH OTHERS' HANDS-- BUT OUR HEARTS? THAT'S ANOTHER MATTER.

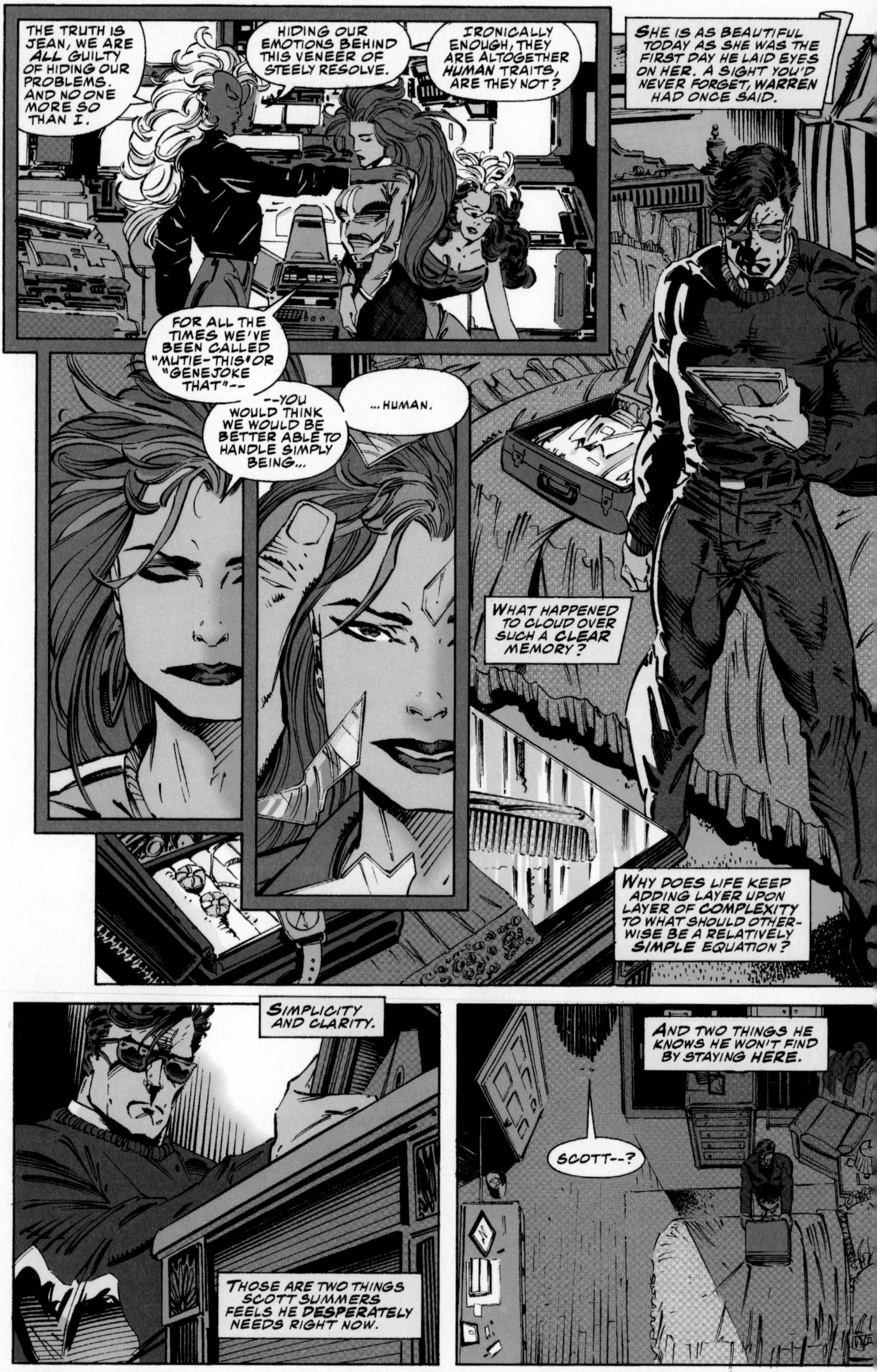
THE TRUTH IS JEAN, WE ARE ALL GUILTY OF HIDING OUR PROBLEMS. AND NO ONE MORE SO THAN I.
HIDING OUR EMOTIONS BEHIND THIS VENEER OF STEELY RESOLVE.
IRONICALLY ENOUGH, THEY ARE ALTOGETHER HUMAN TRAITS, ARE THEY NOT?
SHE IS AS BEAUTIFUL TODAY AS SHE WAS THE FIRST DAY HE LAID EYES ON HER. A SIGHT YOU'D NEVER FORGET, WARREN HAD ONCE SAID.
FOR ALL THE TIMES WE'VE BEEN CALLED "MUTIE-THIS" OR "GENEJOKE THAT"--
--YOU WOULD THINK WE WOULD BE BETTER ABLE TO HANDLE SIMPLY BEING...
...HUMAN.
WHAT HAPPENED TO CLOUD OVER SUCH A CLEAR MEMORY?
WHY DOES LIFE KEEP ADDING LAYER UPON LAYER OF COMPLEXITY TO WHAT SHOULD OTHERWISE BE A RELATIVELY SIMPLE EQUATION?
SIMPLICITY AND CLARITY.
THOSE ARE TWO THINGS SCOTT SUMMERS FEELS HE DESPERATELY NEEDS RIGHT NOW.
AND TWO THINGS HE KNOWS HE WON'T FIND BY STAYING HERE.
SCOTT--?

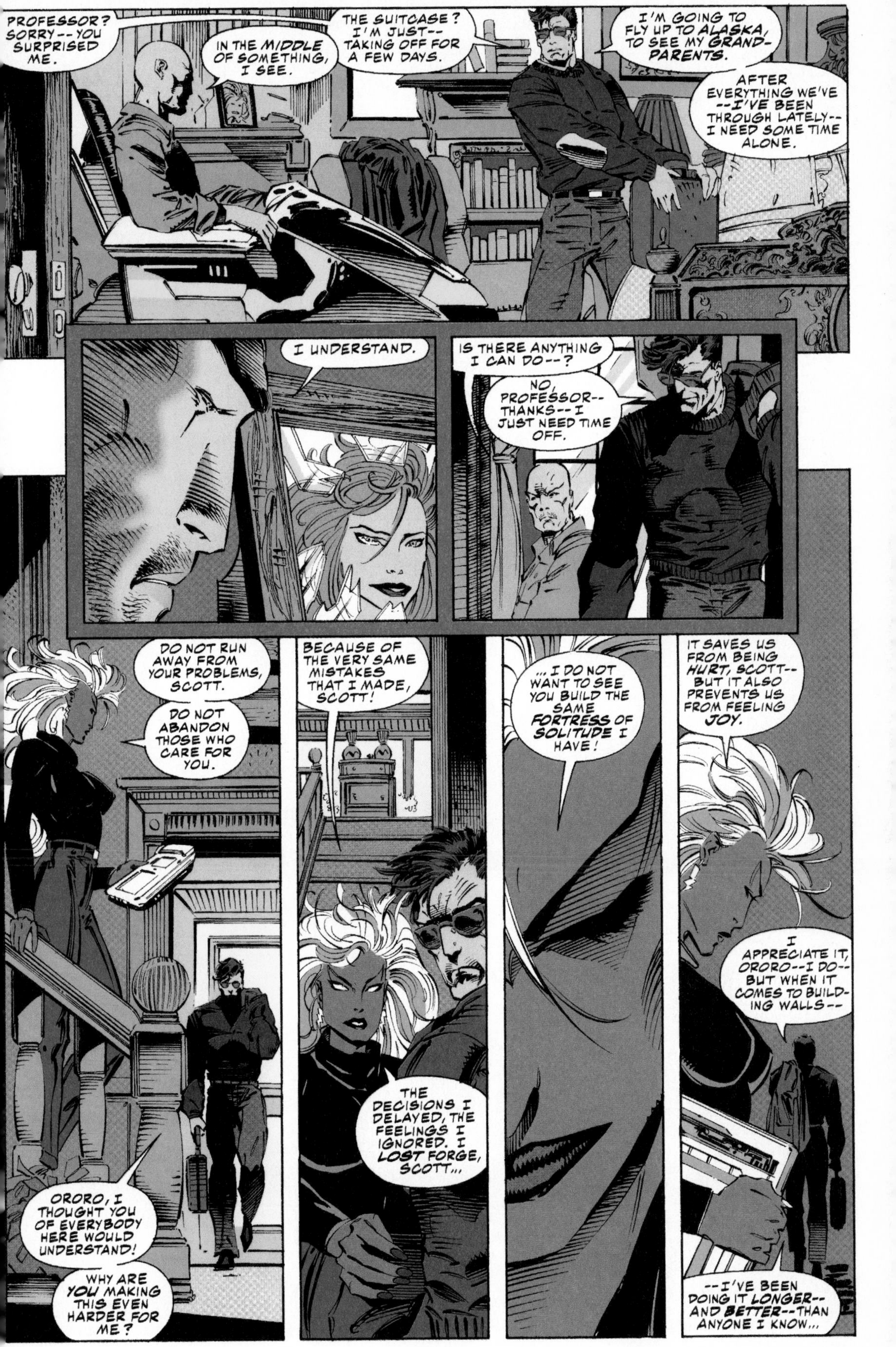
PROFESSOR? SORRY--YOU SURPRISED ME.
IN THE MIDDLE OF SOMETHING, I SEE.
THE SUITCASE? I'M JUST-- TAKING OFF FOR A FEW DAYS.
I'M GOING TO FLY UP TO ALASKA, TO SEE MY GRAND-PARENTS.
AFTER EVERYTHING WE'VE --I'VE BEEN THROUGH LATELY-- I NEED SOME TIME ALONE.
I UNDERSTAND.
IS THERE ANYTHING I CAN DO--?
NO, PROFESSOR-- THANKS--I JUST NEED TIME OFF.
DO NOT RUN AWAY FROM YOUR PROBLEMS, SCOTT.
DO NOT ABANDON THOSE WHO CARE FOR YOU.
ORORO, I THOUGHT YOU OF EVERYBODY HERE WOULD UNDERSTAND!
WHY ARE YOU MAKING THIS EVEN HARDER FOR ME?
BECAUSE OF THE VERY SAME MISTAKES THAT I MADE, SCOTT!
THE DECISIONS I DELAYED, THE FEELINGS I IGNORED. I LOST FORGE, SCOTT...
...I DO NOT WANT TO SEE YOU BUILD THE SAME FORTRESS OF SOLITUDE I HAVE!
IT SAVES US FROM BEING HURT, SCOTT-- BUT IT ALSO PREVENTS US FROM FEELING JOY.
I APPRECIATE IT, ORORO--I DO-- BUT WHEN IT COMES TO BUILDING WALLS--
--I'VE BEEN DOING IT LONGER-- AND BETTER--THAN ANYONE I KNOW...

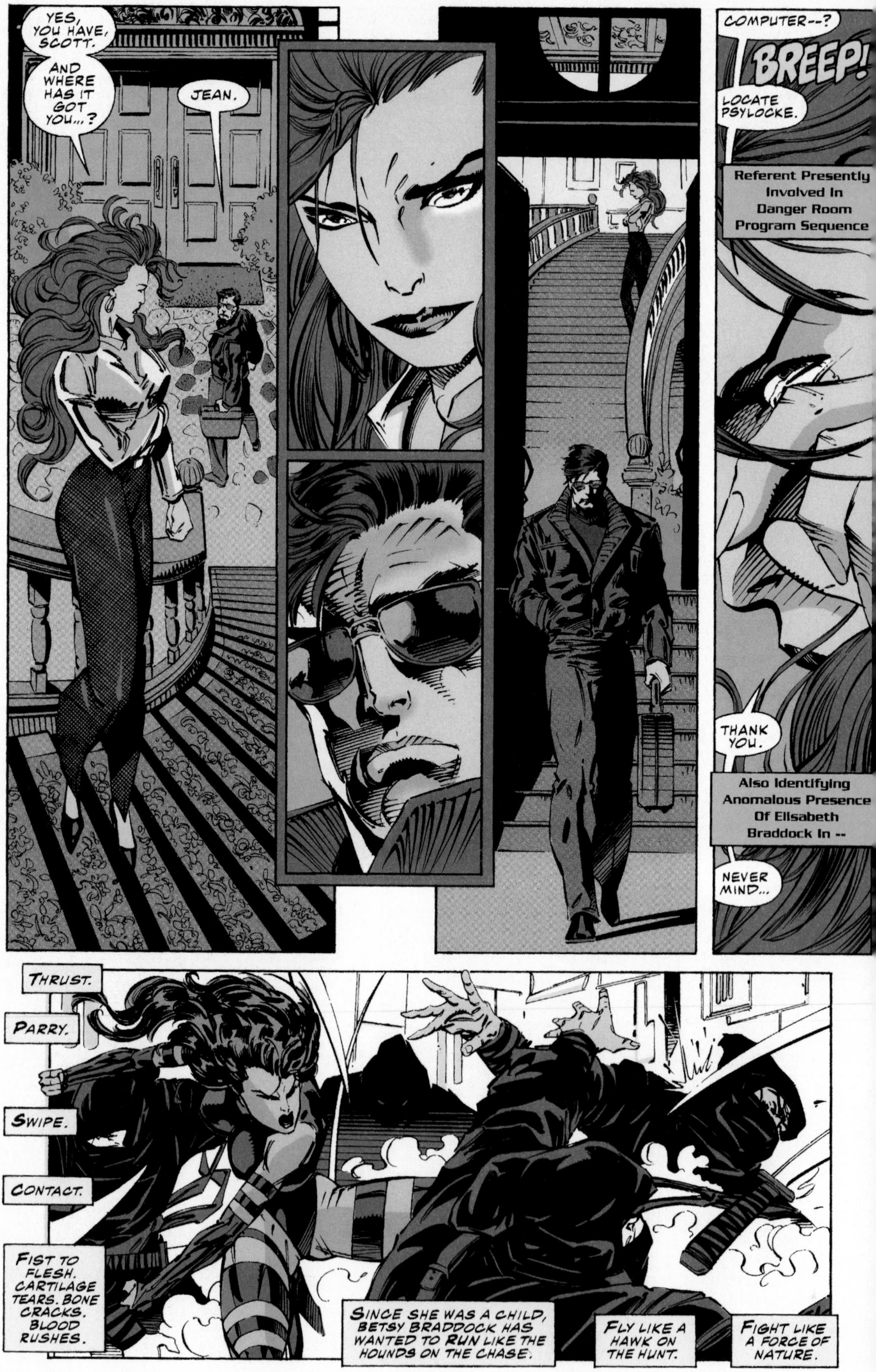
YES, YOU HAVE, SCOTT.
AND WHERE HAS IT GOT YOU...?
JEAN.
COMPUTER--?
BREEP!
LOCATE PSYLOCKE.
Referent Presently Involved In Danger Room Program Sequence
THANK YOU.
Also Identifying Anomalous Presence Of Elisabeth Braddock In --
NEVER MIND...
THRUST.
PARRY.
SWIPE.
CONTACT.
FIST TO FLESH. CARTILAGE TEARS. BONE CRACKS. BLOOD RUSHES.
SINCE SHE WAS A CHILD, BETSY BRADDOCK HAS WANTED TO RUN LIKE THE HOUNDS ON THE CHASE.
FLY LIKE A HAWK ON THE HUNT.
FIGHT LIKE A FORCE OF NATURE.

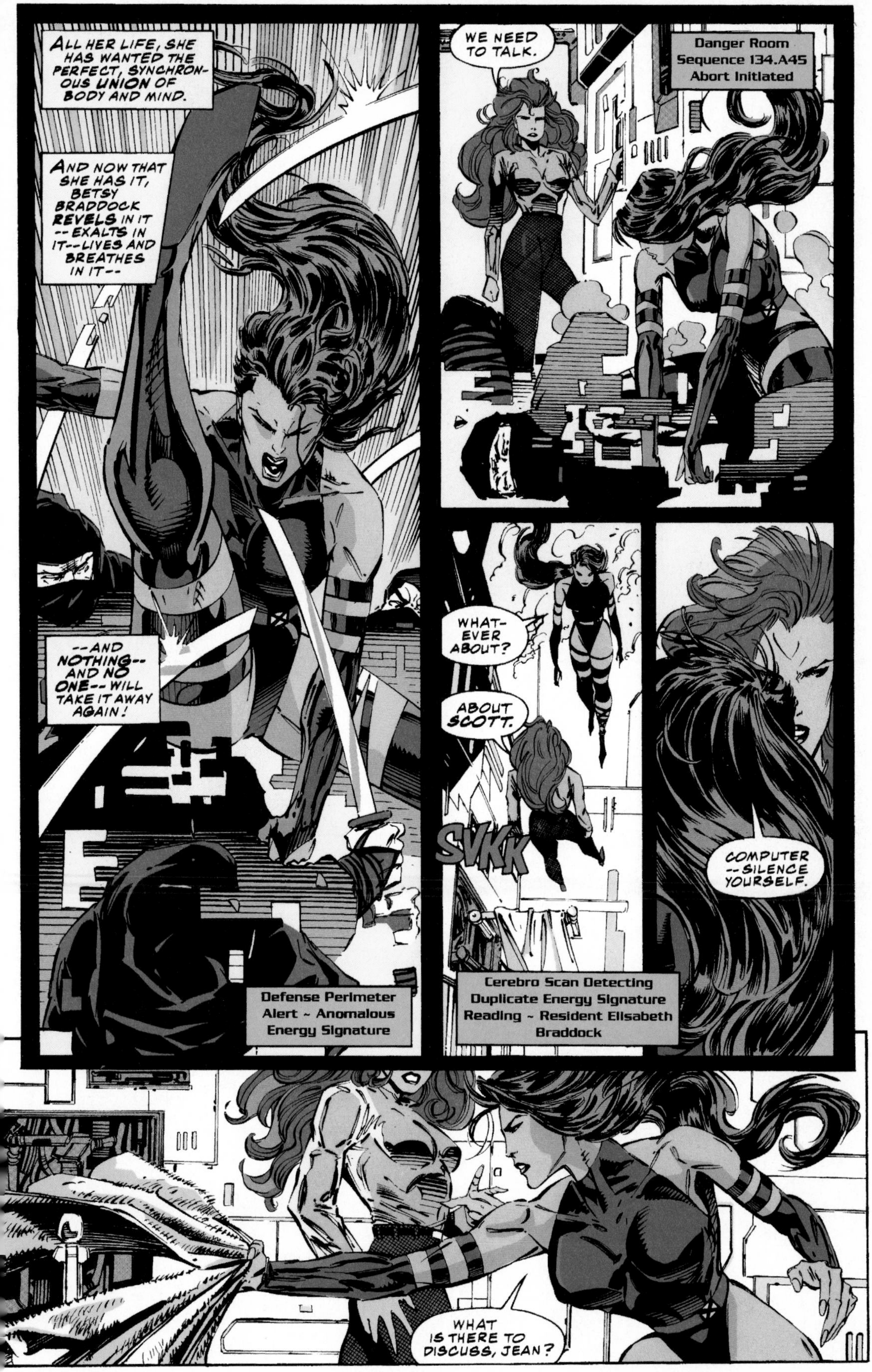
ALL HER LIFE, SHE HAS WANTED THE PERFECT, SYNCHRONOUS UNION OF BODY AND MIND.
AND NOW THAT SHE HAS IT, BETSY BRADDOCK REVELS IN IT -- EXALTS IN IT -- LIVES AND BREATHES IN IT --
--AND NOTHING-- AND NO ONE-- WILL TAKE IT AWAY AGAIN!
Defense Perimeter Alert ~ Anomalous Energy Signature
WE NEED TO TALK.
Danger Room Sequence 134.A45 Abort Initiated
WHAT-EVER ABOUT?
ABOUT SCOTT.
SVKK
Cerebro Scan Detecting Duplicate Energy Signature Reading ~ Resident Elisabeth Braddock
COMPUTER --SILENCE YOURSELF.
WHAT IS THERE TO DISCUSS, JEAN?

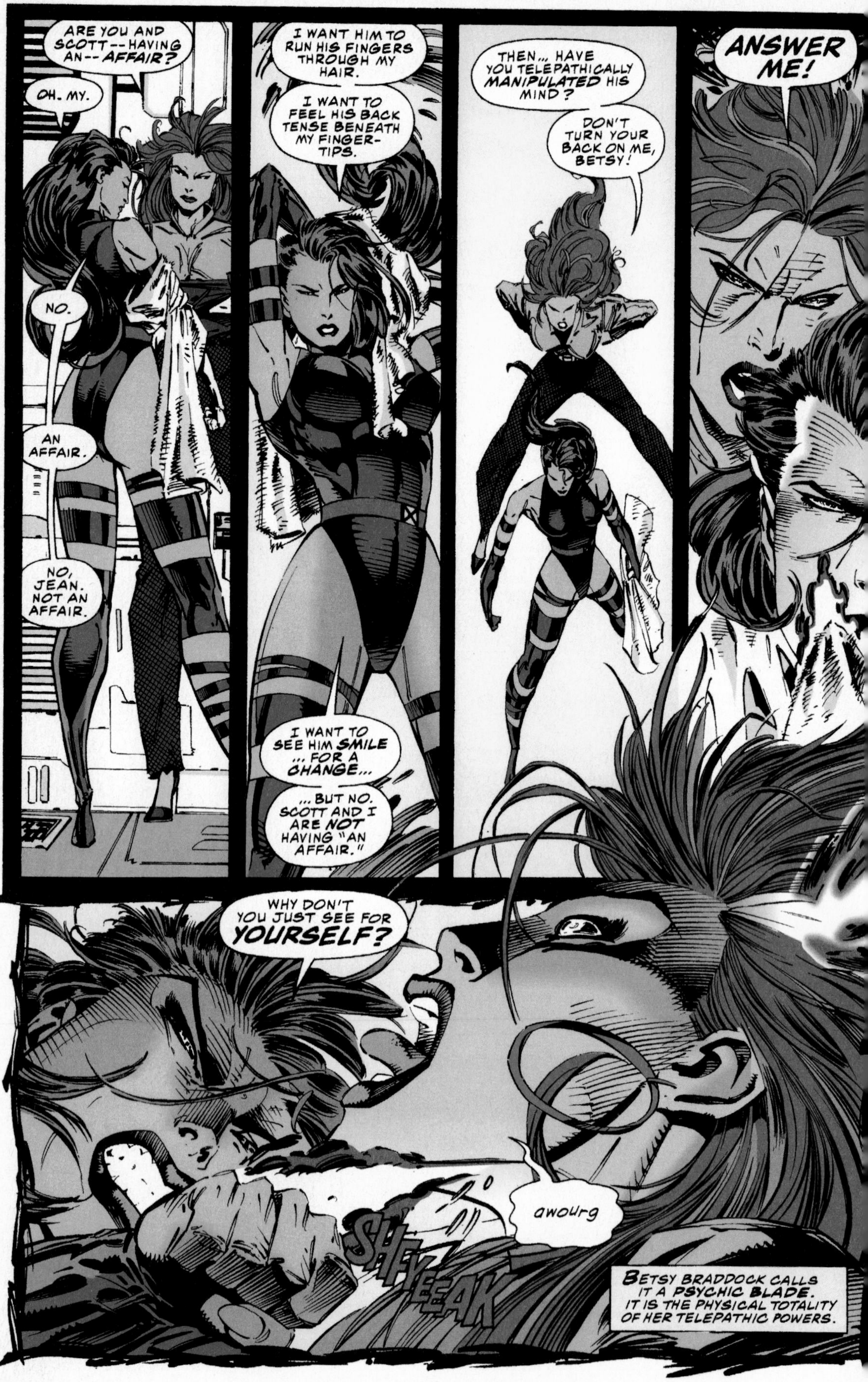
ARE YOU AND SCOTT--HAVING AN--AFFAIR?
OH. MY.
NO.
AN AFFAIR.
NO, JEAN. NOT AN AFFAIR.
I WANT HIM TO RUN HIS FINGERS THROUGH MY HAIR.
I WANT TO FEEL HIS BACK TENSE BENEATH MY FINGER-TIPS.
I WANT TO SEE HIM SMILE ...FOR A CHANGE...
...BUT NO. SCOTT AND I ARE NOT HAVING "AN AFFAIR."
THEN... HAVE YOU TELEPATHICALLY MANIPULATED HIS MIND?
DON'T TURN YOUR BACK ON ME, BETSY!
ANSWER ME!
WHY DON'T YOU JUST SEE FOR YOURSELF?
SHFYEEAK
awourg
BETSY BRADDOCK CALLS IT A PSYCHIC BLADE. IT IS THE PHYSICAL TOTALITY OF HER TELEPATHIC POWERS.

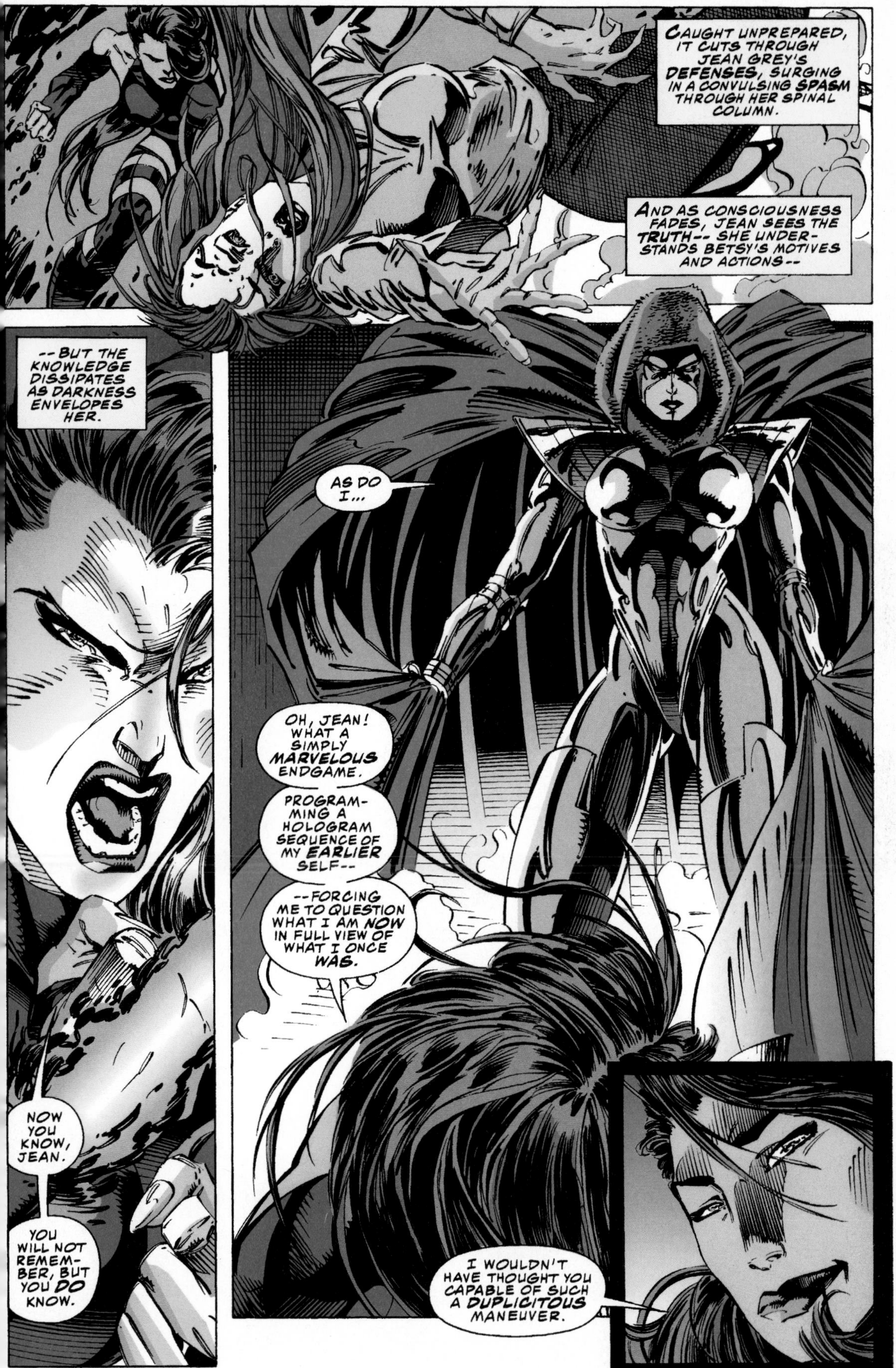
CAUGHT UNPREPARED, IT CUTS THROUGH JEAN GREY'S DEFENSES, SURGING IN A CONVULSING SPASM THROUGH HER SPINAL COLUMN.
AND AS CONSCIOUSNESS FADES, JEAN SEES THE TRUTH-- SHE UNDERSTANDS BETSY'S MOTIVES AND ACTIONS--
--BUT THE KNOWLEDGE DISSIPATES AS DARKNESS ENVELOPES HER.
AS DO I...
OH, JEAN! WHAT A SIMPLY MARVELOUS ENDGAME.
PROGRAMMING A HOLOGRAM SEQUENCE OF MY EARLIER SELF--
--FORCING ME TO QUESTION WHAT I AM NOW IN FULL VIEW OF WHAT I ONCE WAS.
NOW YOU KNOW, JEAN.
YOU WILL NOT REMEMBER, BUT YOU DO KNOW.
I WOULDN'T HAVE THOUGHT YOU CAPABLE OF SUCH A DUPLICITOUS MANEUVER.

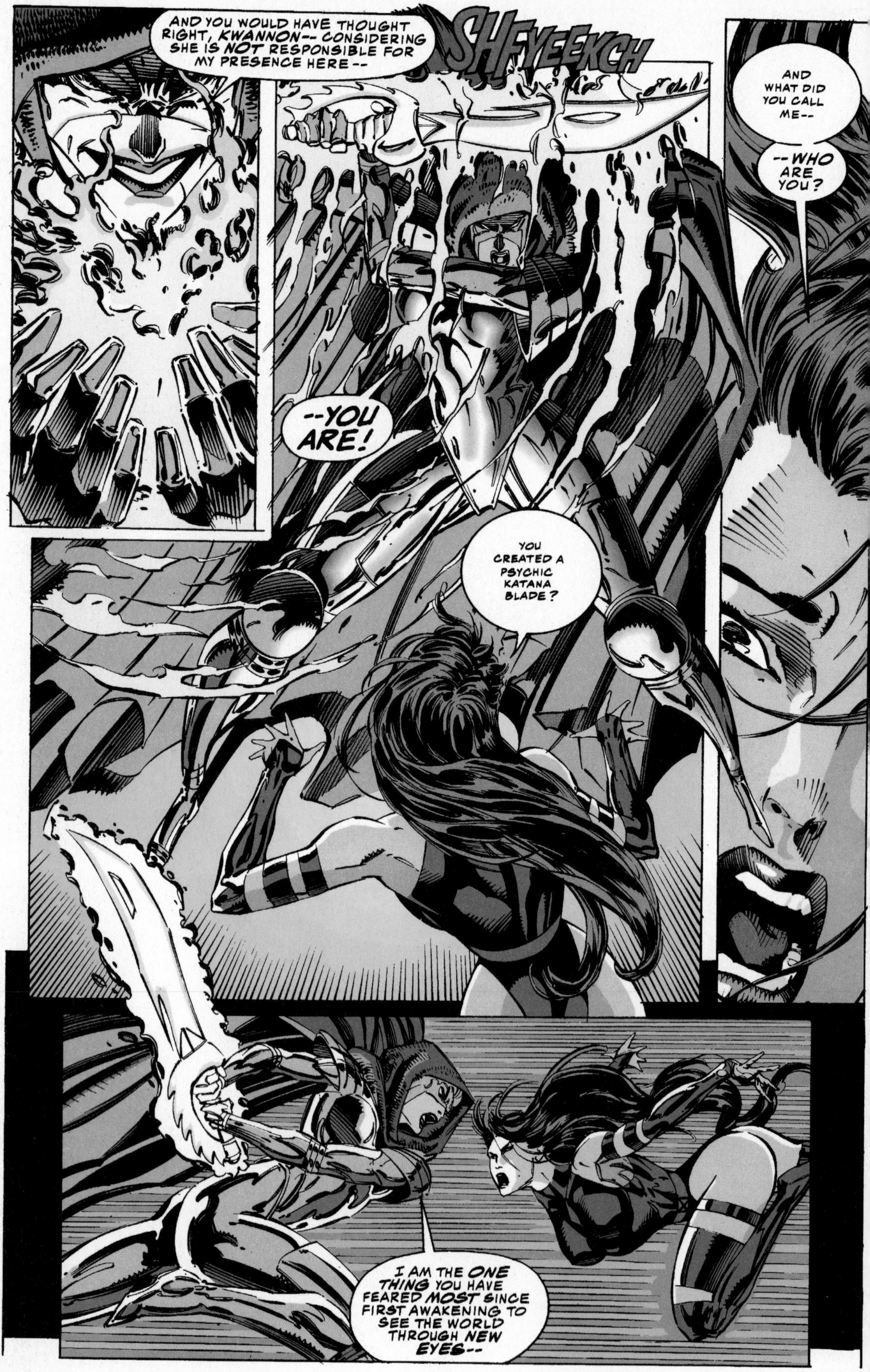
AND YOU WOULD HAVE THOUGHT RIGHT, KWANNON-- CONSIDERING SHE IS NOT RESPONSIBLE FOR MY PRESENCE HERE--
SHFYEEKCH
--YOU ARE!
AND WHAT DID YOU CALL ME--
--WHO ARE YOU?
YOU CREATED A PSYCHIC KATANA BLADE?
I AM THE ONE THING YOU HAVE FEARED MOST SINCE FIRST AWAKENING TO SEE THE WORLD THROUGH NEW EYES--

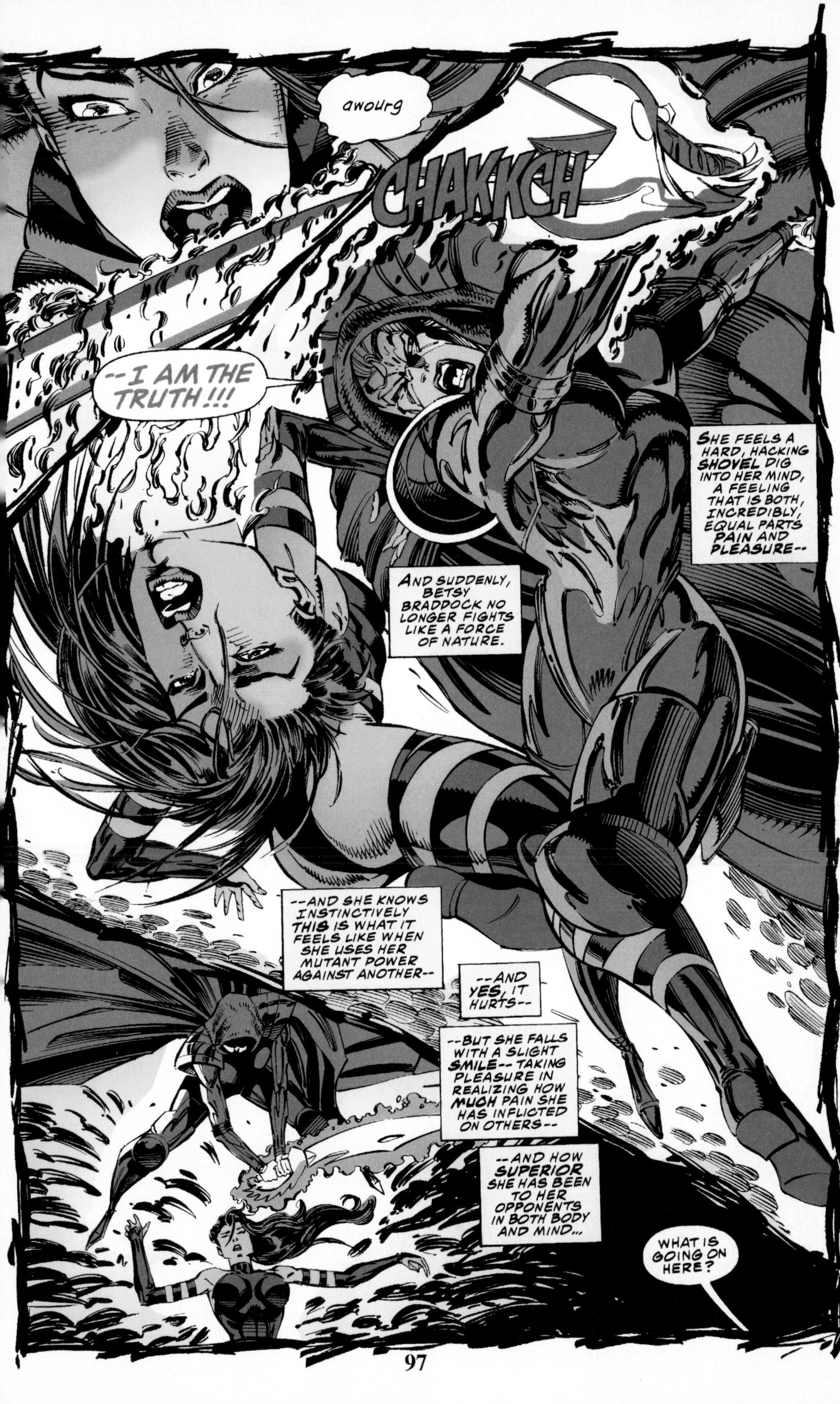
awourg
CHAKKCH
--I AM THE TRUTH!!!
SHE FEELS A HARD, HACKING SHOVEL DIG INTO HER MIND, A FEELING THAT IS BOTH, INCREDIBLY, EQUAL PARTS PAIN AND PLEASURE--
AND SUDDENLY, BETSY BRADDOCK NO LONGER FIGHTS LIKE A FORCE OF NATURE.
--AND SHE KNOWS INSTINCTIVELY THIS IS WHAT IT FEELS LIKE WHEN SHE USES HER MUTANT POWER AGAINST ANOTHER--
--AND YES, IT HURTS--
--BUT SHE FALLS WITH A SLIGHT SMILE-- TAKING PLEASURE IN REALIZING HOW MUCH PAIN SHE HAS INFLICTED ON OTHERS--
--AND HOW SUPERIOR SHE HAS BEEN TO HER OPPONENTS IN BOTH BODY AND MIND...
WHAT IS GOING ON HERE?

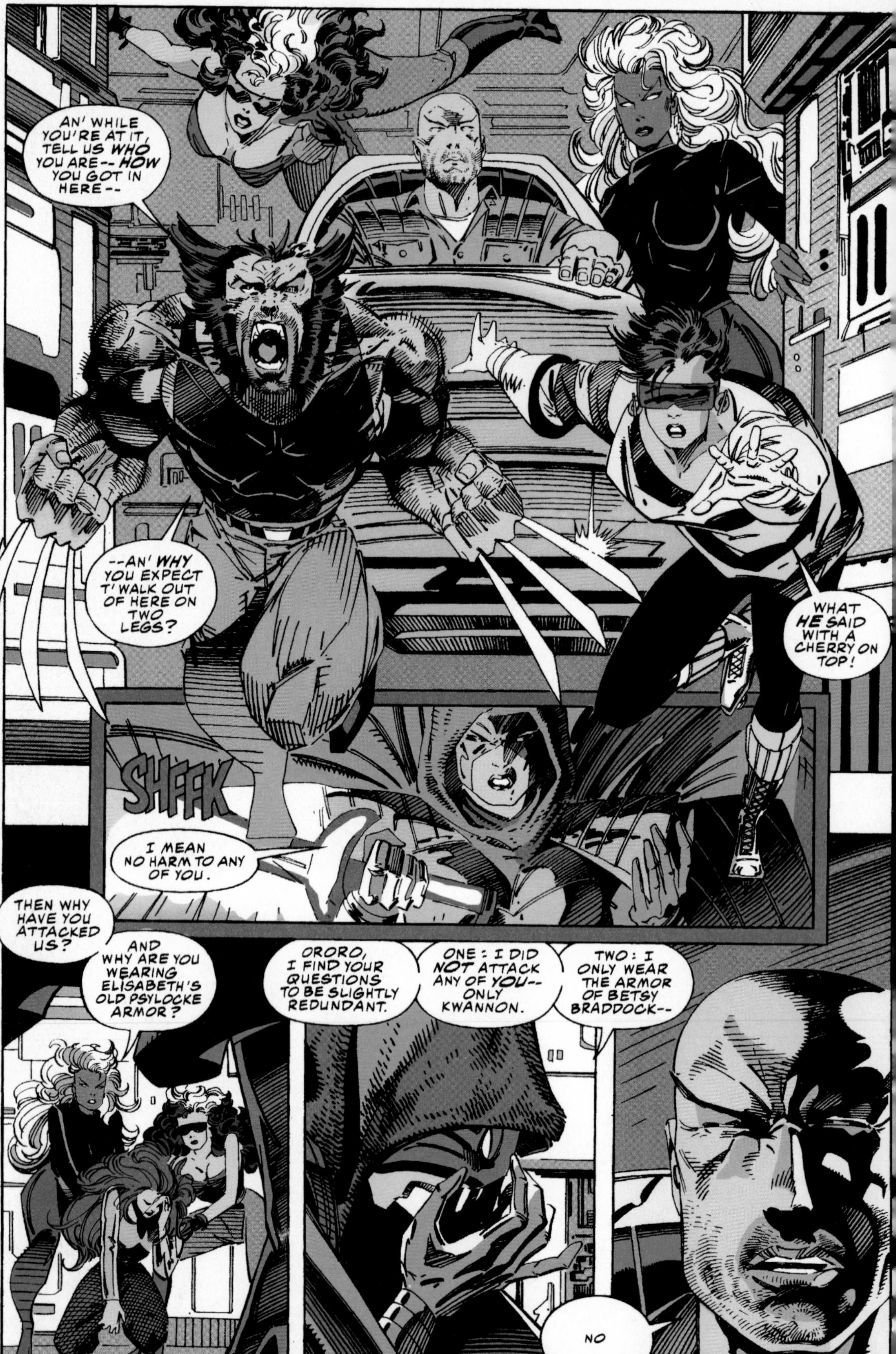
AN' WHILE YOU'RE AT IT, TELL US WHO YOU ARE-- HOW YOU GOT IN HERE--
--AN' WHY YOU EXPECT T' WALK OUT OF HERE ON TWO LEGS?
WHAT HE SAID WITH A CHERRY ON TOP!
SHFFK
I MEAN NO HARM TO ANY OF YOU.
THEN WHY HAVE YOU ATTACKED US?
AND WHY ARE YOU WEARING ELISABETH'S OLD PSYLOCKE ARMOR?
ORORO, I FIND YOUR QUESTIONS TO BE SLIGHTLY REDUNDANT.
ONE: I DID NOT ATTACK ANY OF YOU-- ONLY KWANNON.
TWO: I ONLY WEAR THE ARMOR OF BETSY BRADDOCK--
NO

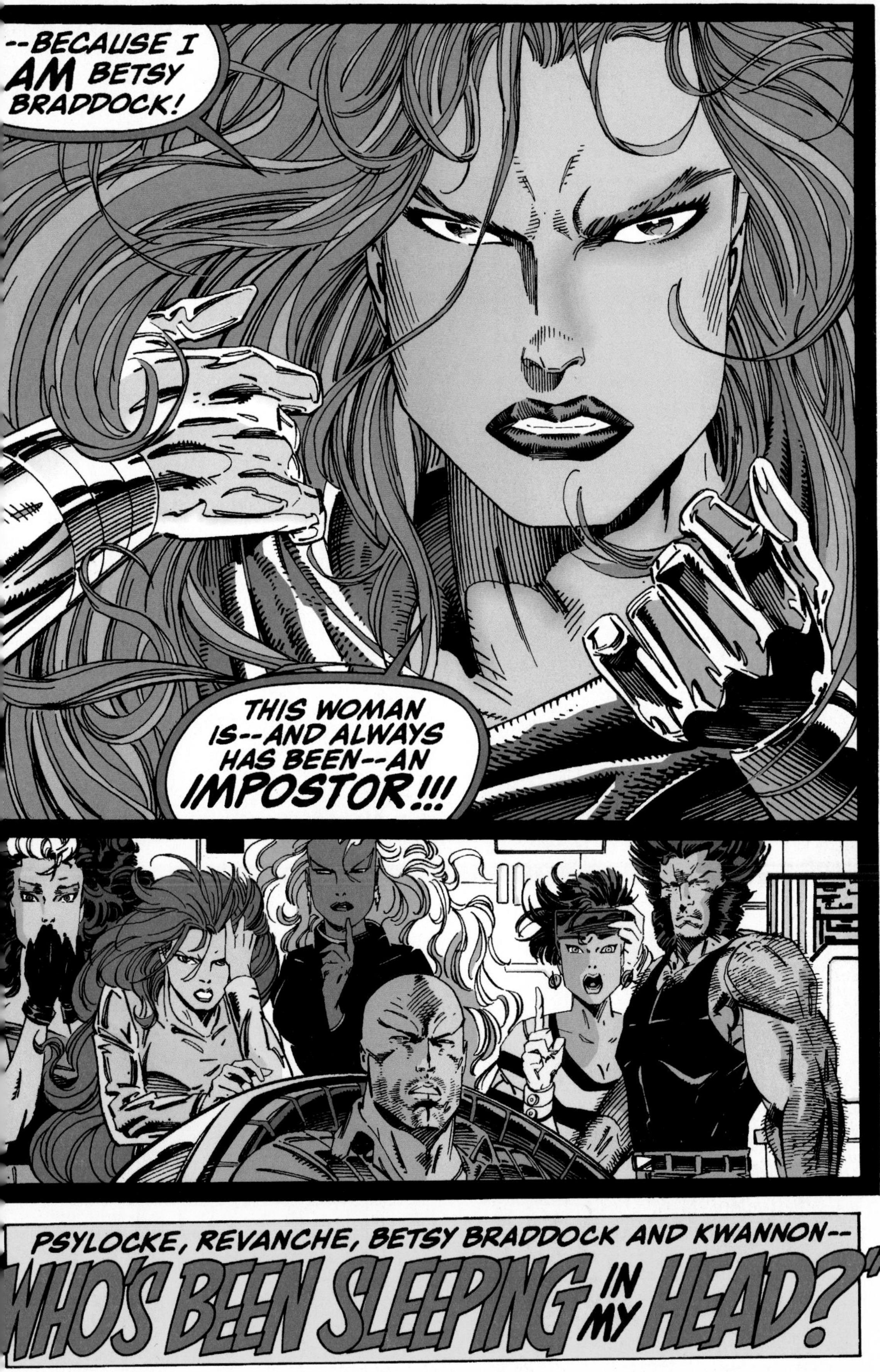

--BECAUSE I AM BETSY BRADDOCK!
THIS WOMAN IS--AND ALWAYS HAS BEEN--AN IMPOSTOR!!!
PSYLOCKE, REVANCHE, BETSY BRADDOCK AND KWANNON--
"WHO'S BEEN SLEEPING IN MY HEAD?"

MARVEL COMICS
X-MEN
© 1993 MARVEL ENT. GROUP, INC.
$1.25 US
$1.60 CAN
21
JUN
UK 95p
APPROVED BY THE COMICS CODE AUTHORITY
featuring
GAMBIT!
PSYLOCKE!
REVANCHE!
PETERSON '93
PANOSIAN
30 YEARS
X-MEN
1963-1993
the PUZZLE QUEST

THE PUZZLE BOX

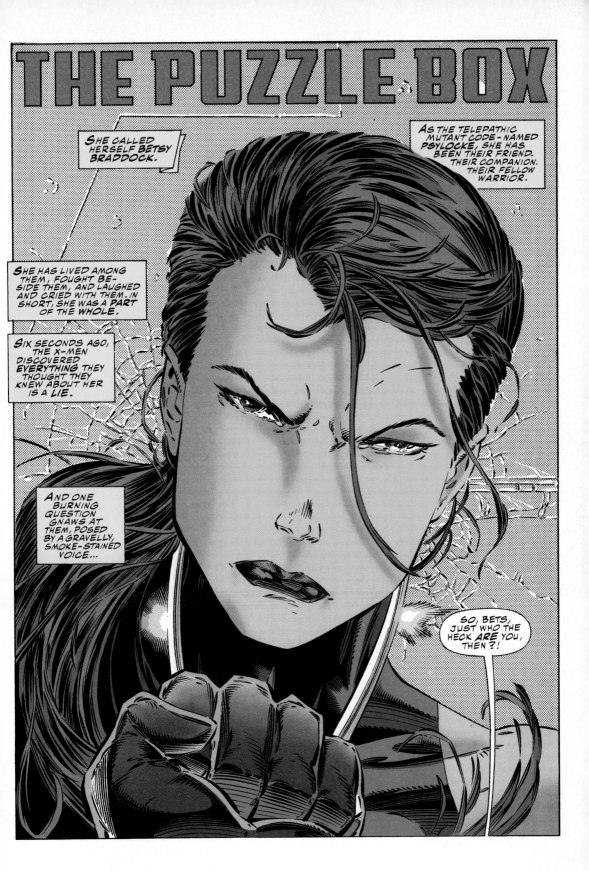

SHE CALLED HERSELF BETSY BRADDOCK.

AS THE TELEPATHIC MUTANT CODE-NAMED PSYLOCKE, SHE HAS BEEN THEIR FRIEND. THEIR COMPANION. THEIR FELLOW WARRIOR.

SHE HAS LIVED AMONG THEM, FOUGHT BESIDE THEM, AND LAUGHED AND CRIED WITH THEM. IN SHORT, SHE WAS A PART OF THE WHOLE.

SIX SECONDS AGO, THE X-MEN DISCOVERED EVERYTHING THEY THOUGHT THEY KNEW ABOUT HER IS A LIE.

AND ONE BURNING QUESTION GNAWS AT THEM, POSED BY A GRAVELLY, SMOKE-STAINED VOICE...

SO, BETS, JUST WHO THE HECK *ARE* YOU, THEN?!

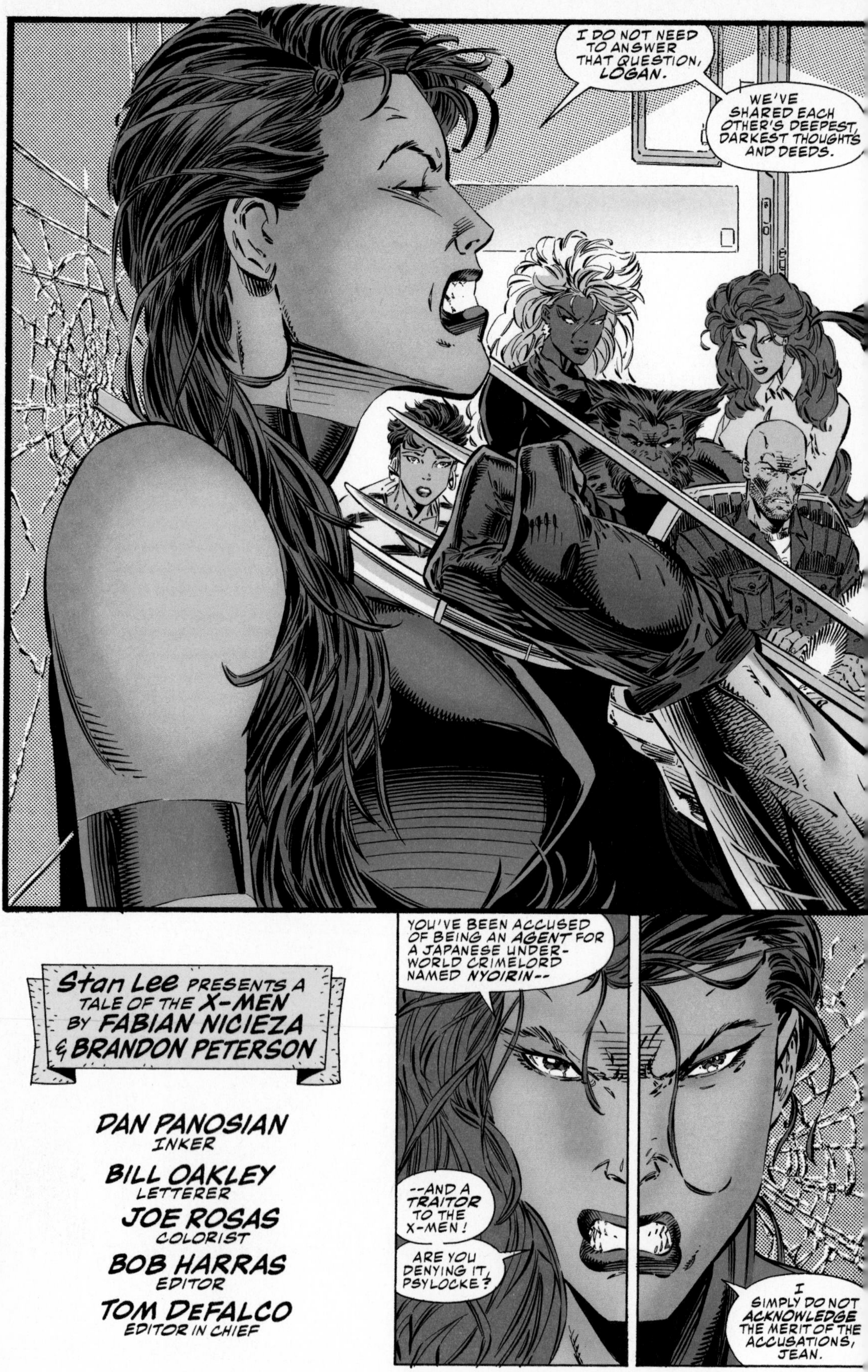

I DO NOT NEED TO ANSWER THAT QUESTION, LOGAN.
WE'VE SHARED EACH OTHER'S DEEPEST, DARKEST THOUGHTS AND DEEDS.
Stan Lee PRESENTS A TALE OF THE X-MEN BY FABIAN NICIEZA & BRANDON PETERSON
DAN PANOSIAN INKER
BILL OAKLEY LETTERER
JOE ROSAS COLORIST
BOB HARRAS EDITOR
TOM DeFALCO EDITOR IN CHIEF
YOU'VE BEEN ACCUSED OF BEING AN AGENT FOR A JAPANESE UNDER-WORLD CRIMELORD NAMED NYOIRIN--
--AND A TRAITOR TO THE X-MEN!
ARE YOU DENYING IT, PSYLOCKE?
I SIMPLY DO NOT ACKNOWLEDGE THE MERIT OF THE ACCUSATIONS, JEAN.

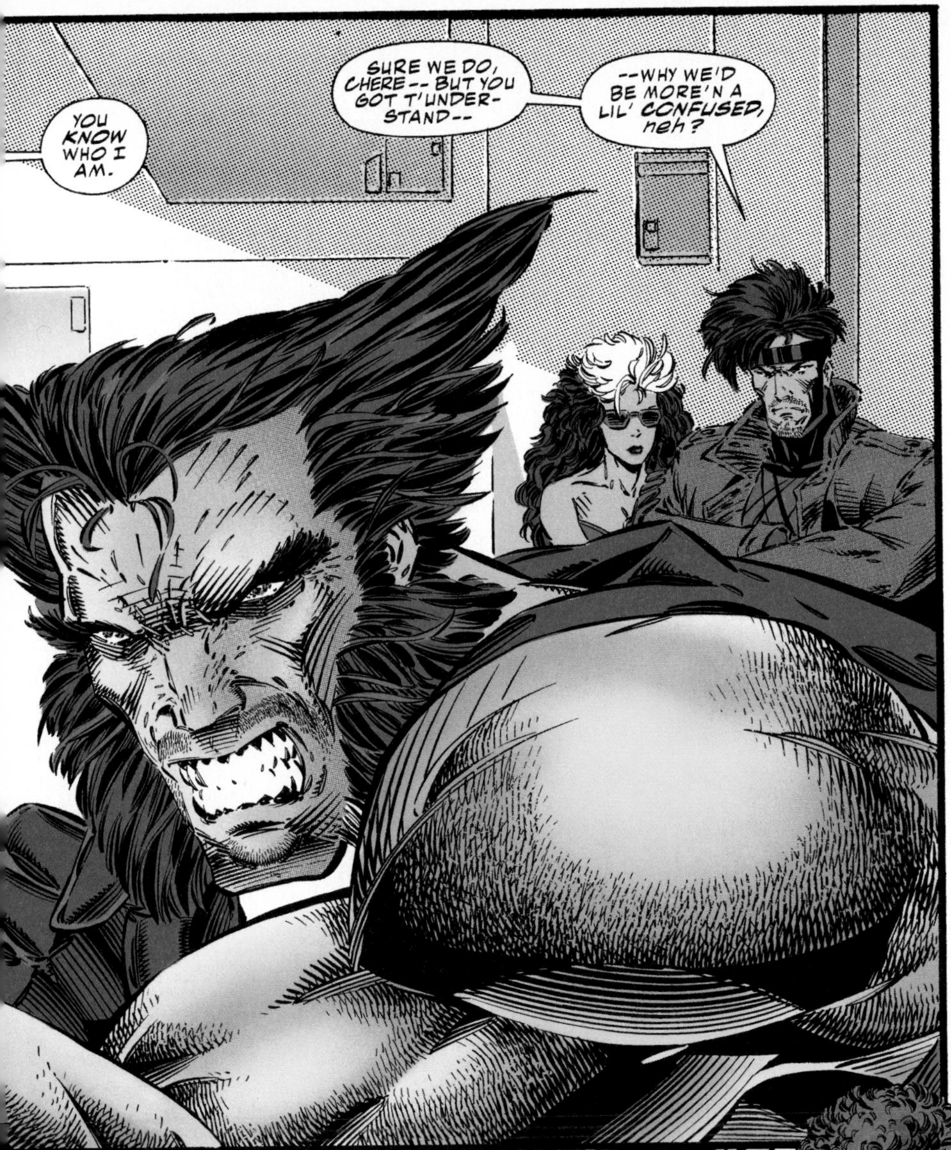
YOU KNOW WHO I AM.
SURE WE DO, CHERE-- BUT YOU GOT T'UNDER-STAND--
--WHY WE'D BE MORE'N A LIL' CONFUSED, neh?

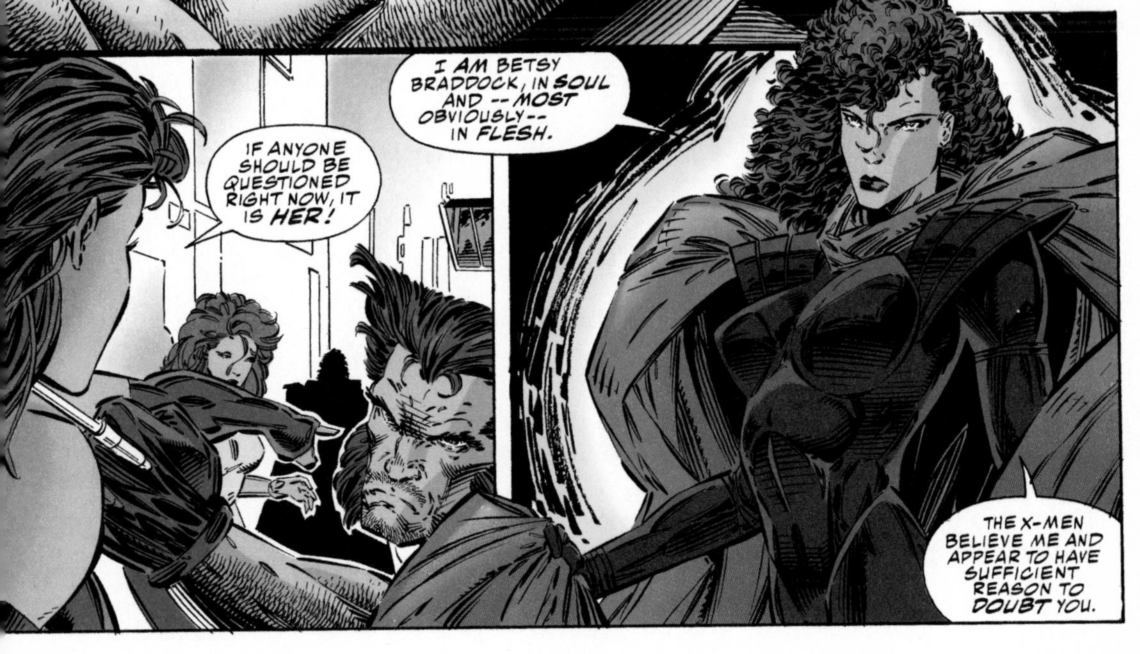
IF ANYONE SHOULD BE QUESTIONED RIGHT NOW, IT IS HER!
I AM BETSY BRADDOCK, IN SOUL AND --MOST OBVIOUSLY-- IN FLESH.
THE X-MEN BELIEVE ME AND APPEAR TO HAVE SUFFICIENT REASON TO DOUBT YOU.

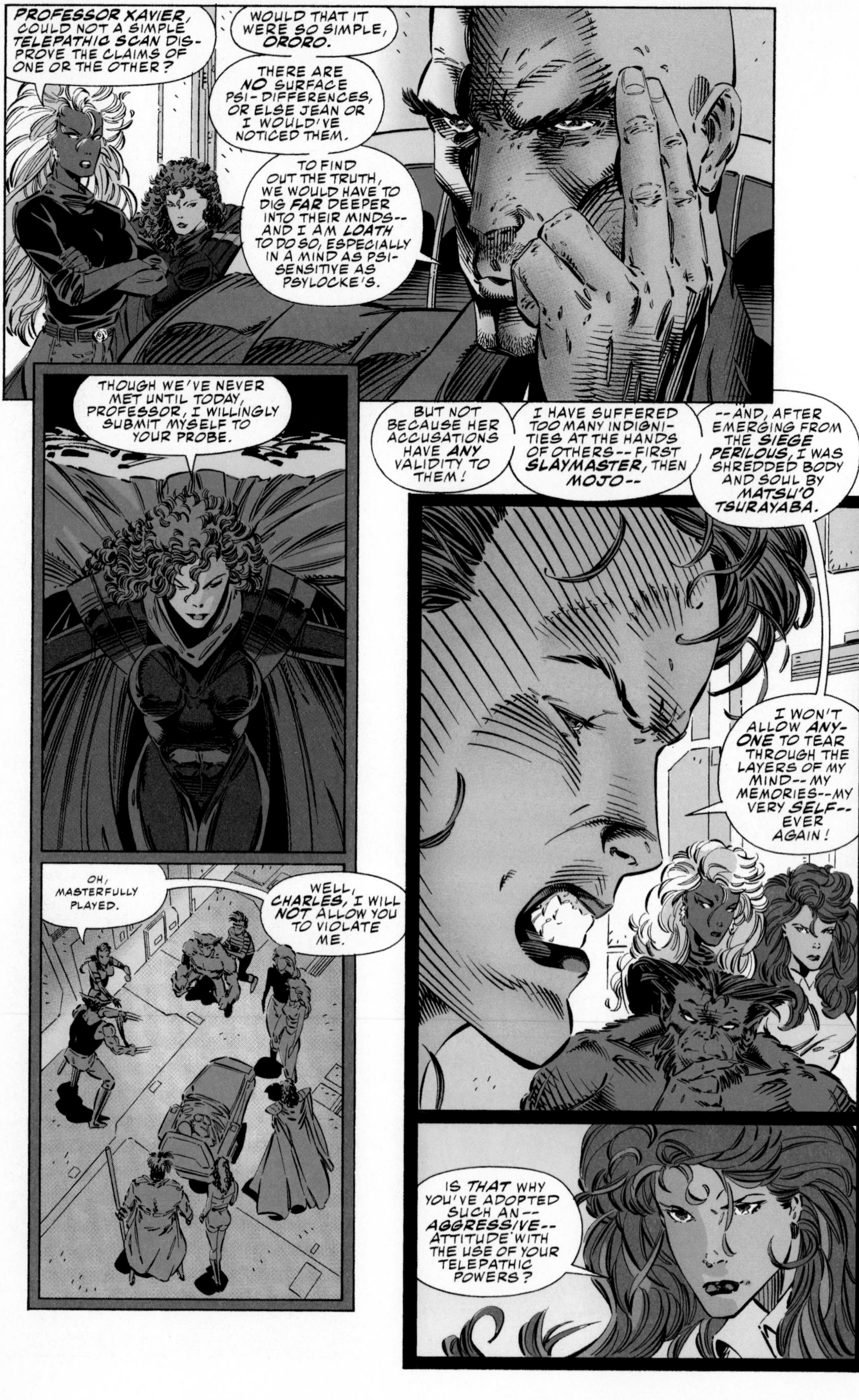
PROFESSOR XAVIER, COULD NOT A SIMPLE TELEPATHIC SCAN DISPROVE THE CLAIMS OF ONE OR THE OTHER?
WOULD THAT IT WERE SO SIMPLE, ORORO.
THERE ARE NO SURFACE PSI-DIFFERENCES, OR ELSE JEAN OR I WOULD'VE NOTICED THEM.
TO FIND OUT THE TRUTH, WE WOULD HAVE TO DIG FAR DEEPER INTO THEIR MINDS-- AND I AM LOATH TO DO SO, ESPECIALLY IN A MIND AS PSI-SENSITIVE AS PSYLOCKE'S.
THOUGH WE'VE NEVER MET UNTIL TODAY, PROFESSOR, I WILLINGLY SUBMIT MYSELF TO YOUR PROBE.
OH, MASTERFULLY PLAYED.
WELL, CHARLES, I WILL NOT ALLOW YOU TO VIOLATE ME.
BUT NOT BECAUSE HER ACCUSATIONS HAVE ANY VALIDITY TO THEM!
I HAVE SUFFERED TOO MANY INDIGNITIES AT THE HANDS OF OTHERS-- FIRST SLAYMASTER, THEN MOJO--
--AND, AFTER EMERGING FROM THE SIEGE PERILOUS, I WAS SHREDDED BODY AND SOUL BY MATSU'O TSURAYABA.
I WON'T ALLOW ANYONE TO TEAR THROUGH THE LAYERS OF MY MIND-- MY MEMORIES--MY VERY SELF-- EVER AGAIN!
IS THAT WHY YOU'VE ADOPTED SUCH AN-- AGGRESSIVE-- ATTITUDE WITH THE USE OF YOUR TELEPATHIC POWERS?

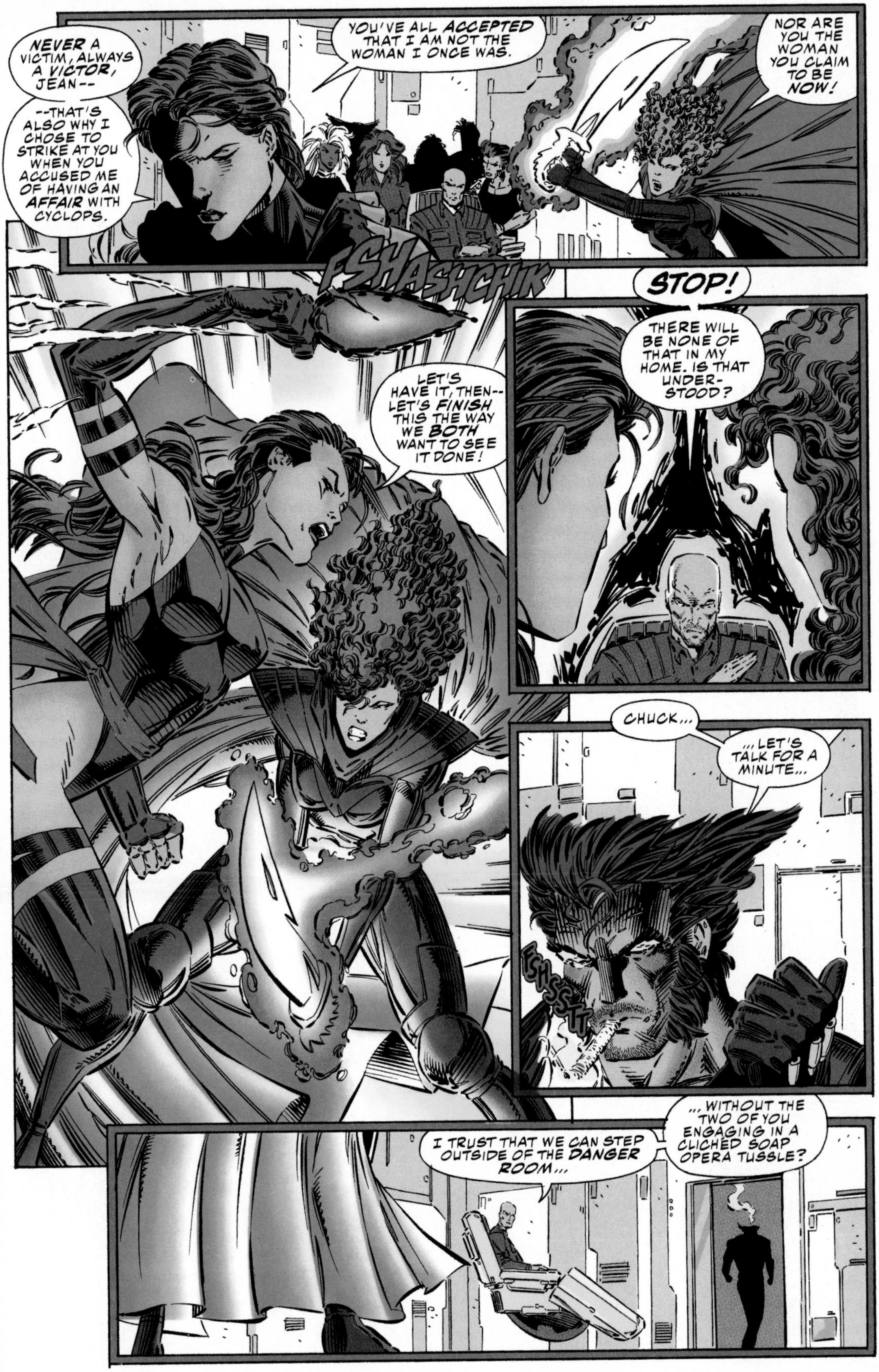
NEVER A VICTIM, ALWAYS A VICTOR, JEAN--
--THAT'S ALSO WHY I CHOSE TO STRIKE AT YOU WHEN YOU ACCUSED ME OF HAVING AN AFFAIR WITH CYCLOPS.
YOU'VE ALL ACCEPTED THAT I AM NOT THE WOMAN I ONCE WAS.
NOR ARE YOU THE WOMAN YOU CLAIM TO BE NOW!
FSHASHCHIK
LET'S HAVE IT, THEN-- LET'S FINISH THIS THE WAY WE BOTH WANT TO SEE IT DONE!
STOP!
THERE WILL BE NONE OF THAT IN MY HOME. IS THAT UNDER-STOOD?
CHUCK...
...LET'S TALK FOR A MINUTE...
FSHSSKT
I TRUST THAT WE CAN STEP OUTSIDE OF THE DANGER ROOM...
...WITHOUT THE TWO OF YOU ENGAGING IN A CLICHÉD SOAP OPERA TUSSLE?

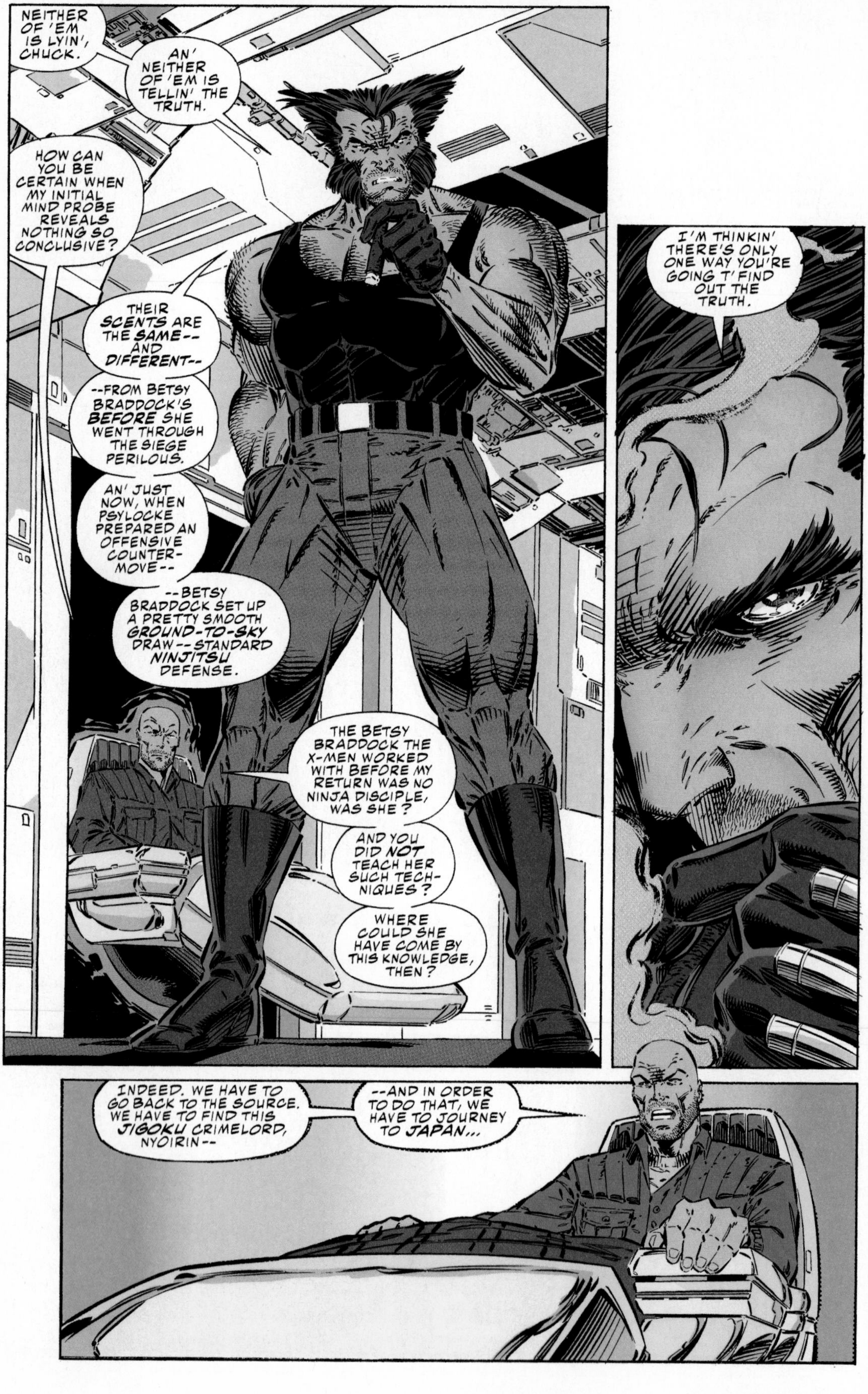
NEITHER OF 'EM IS LYIN', CHUCK.
AN' NEITHER OF 'EM IS TELLIN' THE TRUTH.
HOW CAN YOU BE CERTAIN WHEN MY INITIAL MIND PROBE REVEALS NOTHING SO CONCLUSIVE?
THEIR SCENTS ARE THE SAME-- AND DIFFERENT--
--FROM BETSY BRADDOCK'S BEFORE SHE WENT THROUGH THE SIEGE PERILOUS.
AN' JUST NOW, WHEN PSYLOCKE PREPARED AN OFFENSIVE COUNTER-MOVE--
--BETSY BRADDOCK SET UP A PRETTY SMOOTH GROUND-TO-SKY DRAW--STANDARD NINJITSU DEFENSE.
THE BETSY BRADDOCK THE X-MEN WORKED WITH BEFORE MY RETURN WAS NO NINJA DISCIPLE, WAS SHE?
AND YOU DID NOT TEACH HER SUCH TECH-NIQUES?
WHERE COULD SHE HAVE COME BY THIS KNOWLEDGE, THEN?
I'M THINKIN' THERE'S ONLY ONE WAY YOU'RE GOING T' FIND OUT THE TRUTH.
INDEED. WE HAVE TO GO BACK TO THE SOURCE. WE HAVE TO FIND THIS JIGOKU CRIMELORD, NYOIRIN--
--AND IN ORDER TO DO THAT, WE HAVE TO JOURNEY TO JAPAN...

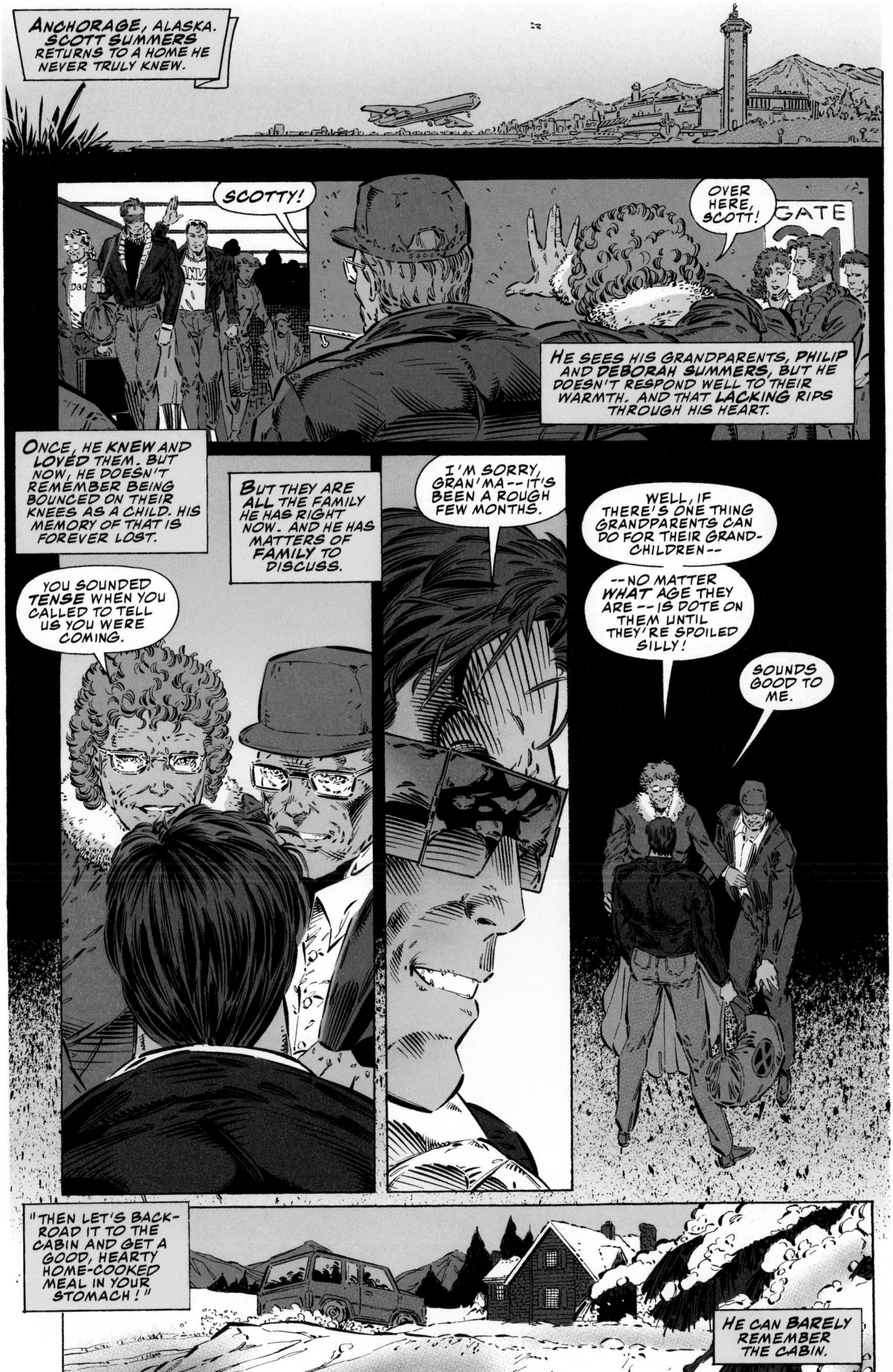

ANCHORAGE, ALASKA. SCOTT SUMMERS RETURNS TO A HOME HE NEVER TRULY KNEW.
SCOTTY!
OVER HERE, SCOTT!
GATE
HE SEES HIS GRANDPARENTS, PHILIP AND DEBORAH SUMMERS, BUT HE DOESN'T RESPOND WELL TO THEIR WARMTH. AND THAT LACKING RIPS THROUGH HIS HEART.
ONCE, HE KNEW AND LOVED THEM. BUT NOW, HE DOESN'T REMEMBER BEING BOUNCED ON THEIR KNEES AS A CHILD. HIS MEMORY OF THAT IS FOREVER LOST.
BUT THEY ARE ALL THE FAMILY HE HAS RIGHT NOW. AND HE HAS MATTERS OF FAMILY TO DISCUSS.
YOU SOUNDED TENSE WHEN YOU CALLED TO TELL US YOU WERE COMING.
I'M SORRY, GRAN'MA-- IT'S BEEN A ROUGH FEW MONTHS.
WELL, IF THERE'S ONE THING GRANDPARENTS CAN DO FOR THEIR GRAND-CHILDREN--
--NO MATTER WHAT AGE THEY ARE--IS DOTE ON THEM UNTIL THEY'RE SPOILED SILLY!
SOUNDS GOOD TO ME.
"THEN LET'S BACK-ROAD IT TO THE CABIN AND GET A GOOD, HEARTY HOME-COOKED MEAL IN YOUR STOMACH!"
HE CAN BARELY REMEMBER THE CABIN.

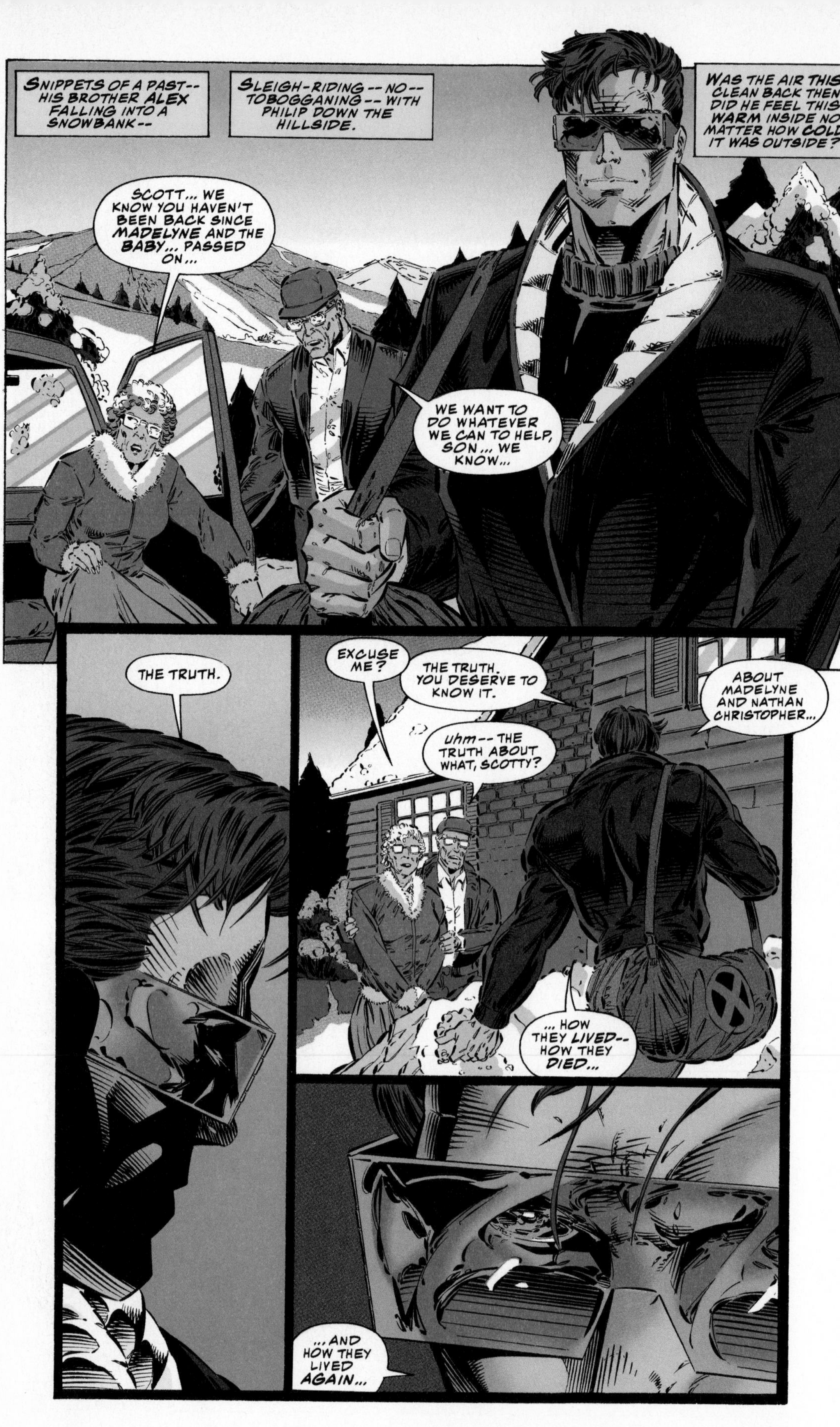

SNIPPETS OF A PAST-- HIS BROTHER ALEX FALLING INTO A SNOWBANK--
SLEIGH-RIDING -- NO -- TOBOGGANING -- WITH PHILIP DOWN THE HILLSIDE.
WAS THE AIR THIS CLEAN BACK THEN? DID HE FEEL THIS WARM INSIDE NO MATTER HOW COLD IT WAS OUTSIDE?
SCOTT... WE KNOW YOU HAVEN'T BEEN BACK SINCE MADELYNE AND THE BABY... PASSED ON...
WE WANT TO DO WHATEVER WE CAN TO HELP, SON... WE KNOW...
THE TRUTH.
EXCUSE ME?
THE TRUTH. YOU DESERVE TO KNOW IT.
ABOUT MADELYNE AND NATHAN CHRISTOPHER...
uhm-- THE TRUTH ABOUT WHAT, SCOTTY?
... HOW THEY LIVED-- HOW THEY DIED...
... AND HOW THEY LIVED AGAIN...

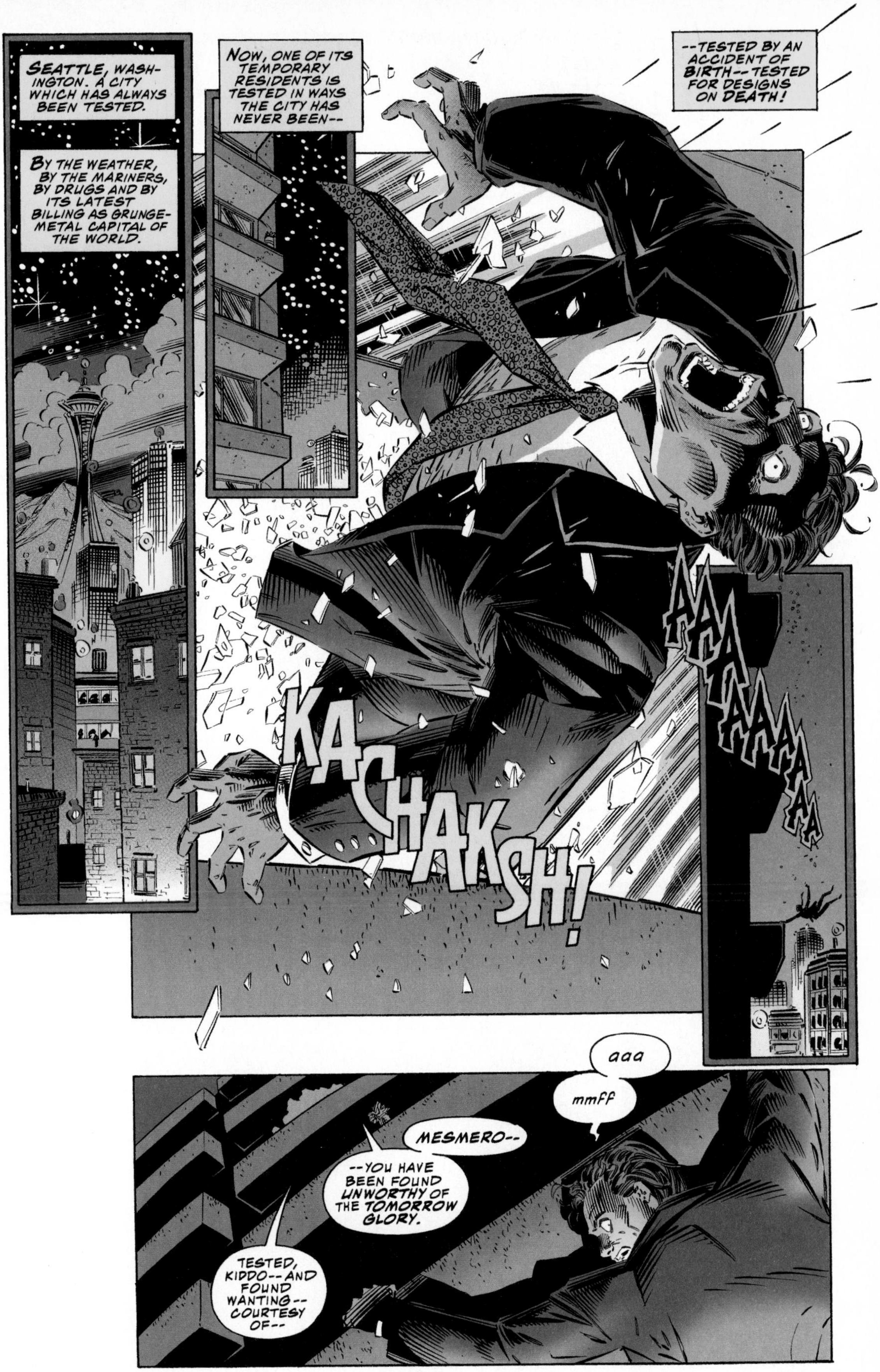
SEATTLE, WASHINGTON. A CITY WHICH HAS ALWAYS BEEN TESTED.
BY THE WEATHER, BY THE MARINERS, BY DRUGS AND BY ITS LATEST BILLING AS GRUNGE-METAL CAPITAL OF THE WORLD.
NOW, ONE OF ITS TEMPORARY RESIDENTS IS TESTED IN WAYS THE CITY HAS NEVER BEEN--
--TESTED BY AN ACCIDENT OF BIRTH--TESTED FOR DESIGNS ON DEATH!
KACHAKSH!
AAAAAAAAAAAA
aaa
mmff
MESMERO--
--YOU HAVE BEEN FOUND UNWORTHY OF THE TOMORROW GLORY.
TESTED, KIDDO--AND FOUND WANTING--COURTESY OF--

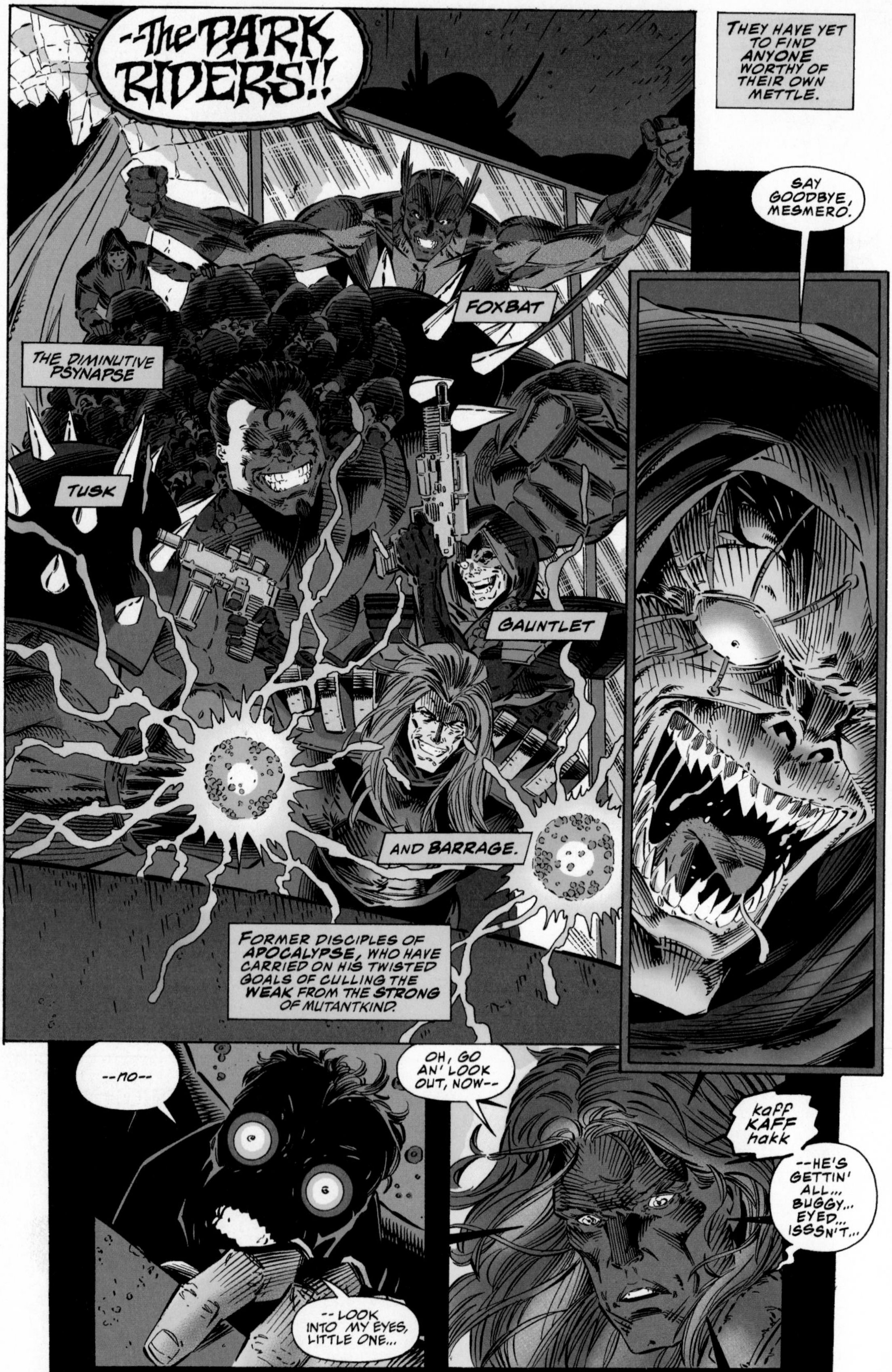
--The DARK RIDERS!!
THEY HAVE YET TO FIND ANYONE WORTHY OF THEIR OWN METTLE.
FOXBAT
THE DIMINUTIVE PSYNAPSE
TUSK
GAUNTLET
AND BARRAGE.
FORMER DISCIPLES OF APOCALYPSE, WHO HAVE CARRIED ON HIS TWISTED GOALS OF CULLING THE WEAK FROM THE STRONG OF MUTANTKIND.
SAY GOODBYE, MESMERO.
--no--
--LOOK INTO MY EYES, LITTLE ONE...
OH, GO AN' LOOK OUT, NOW--
kaff KAFF hakk
--HE'S GETTIN' ALL... BUGGY... EYED... ISSSN'T...

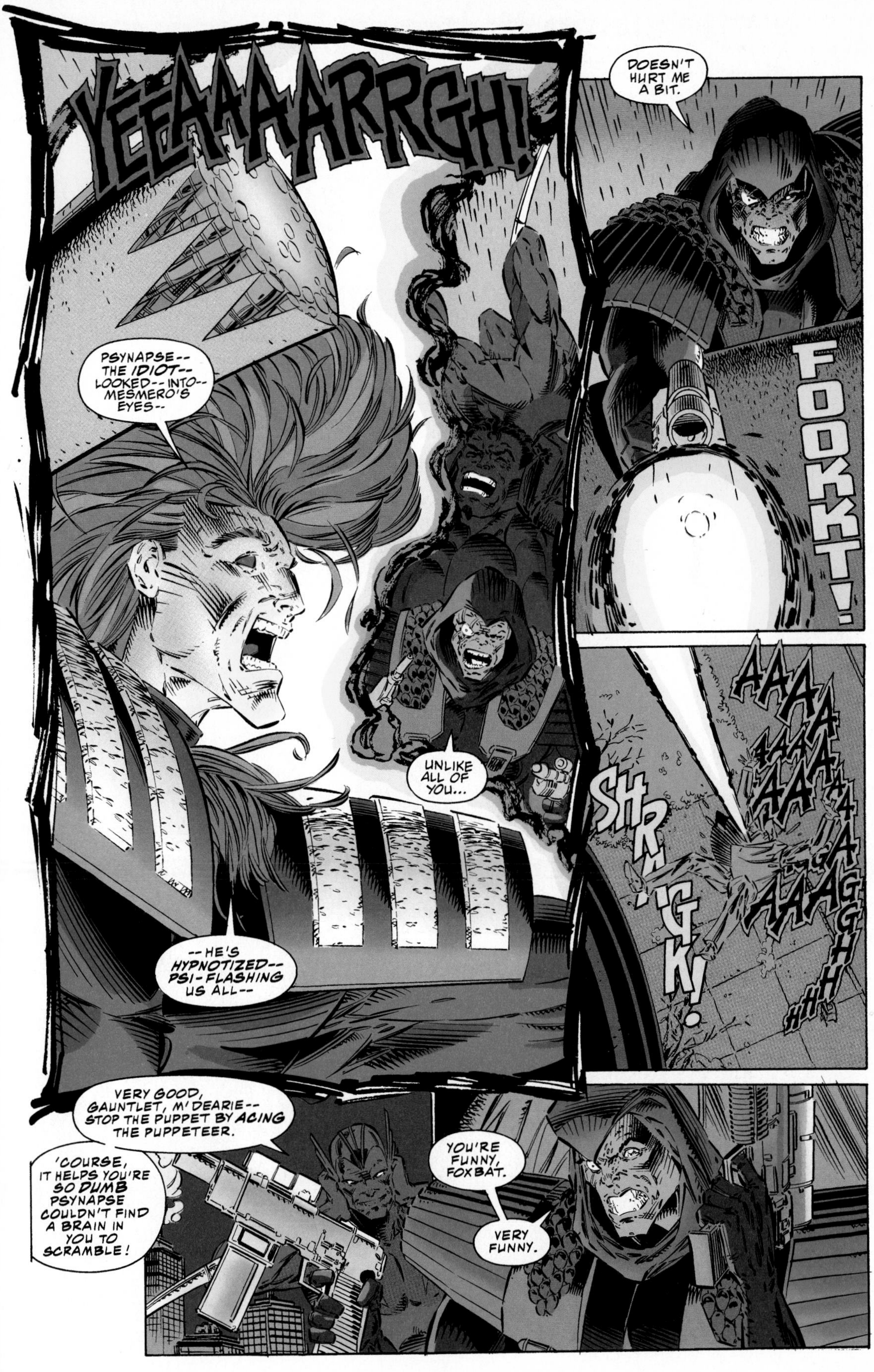
YEEAAAARRGH!
DOESN'T HURT ME A BIT.
PSYNAPSE--THE IDIOT--LOOKED--INTO--MESMERO'S EYES--
FOOKKT!
UNLIKE ALL OF YOU...
SHRAKK!
--HE'S HYPNOTIZED--PSI-FLASHING US ALL--
VERY GOOD, GAUNTLET, M'DEARIE--STOP THE PUPPET BY ACING THE PUPPETEER.
'COURSE, IT HELPS YOU'RE SO DUMB PSYNAPSE COULDN'T FIND A BRAIN IN YOU TO SCRAMBLE!
YOU'RE FUNNY, FOXBAT.
VERY FUNNY.

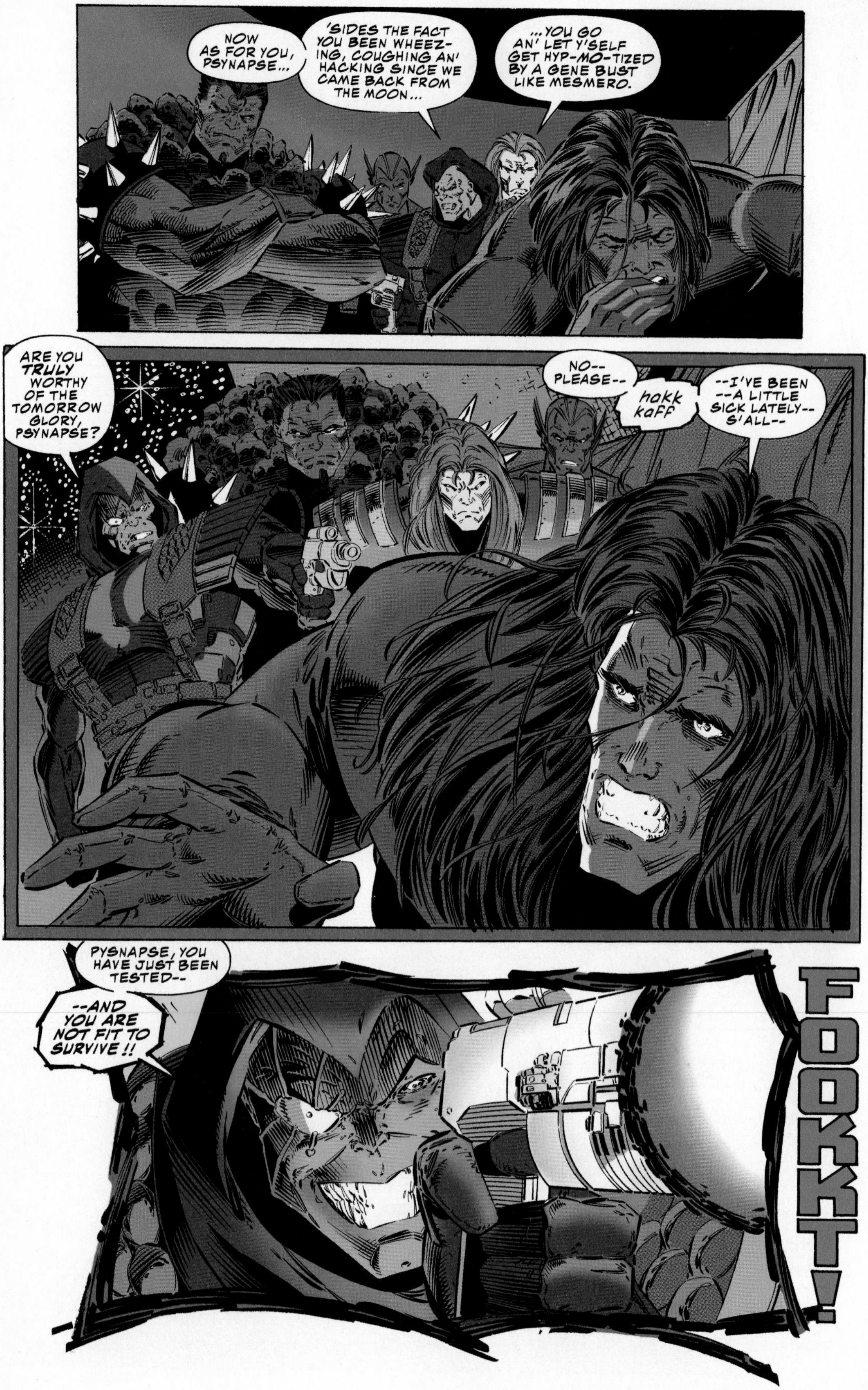
NOW AS FOR YOU, PSYNAPSE...
'SIDES THE FACT YOU BEEN WHEEZ-ING, COUGHING AN' HACKING SINCE WE CAME BACK FROM THE MOON...
...YOU GO AN' LET Y'SELF GET HYP-MO-TIZED BY A GENE BUST LIKE MESMERO.
ARE YOU TRULY WORTHY OF THE TOMORROW GLORY, PSYNAPSE?
NO-- PLEASE--
hokk kaff
--I'VE BEEN --A LITTLE SICK LATELY-- S'ALL--
PYSNAPSE, YOU HAVE JUST BEEN TESTED--
--AND YOU ARE NOT FIT TO SURVIVE!!
FOOKT!

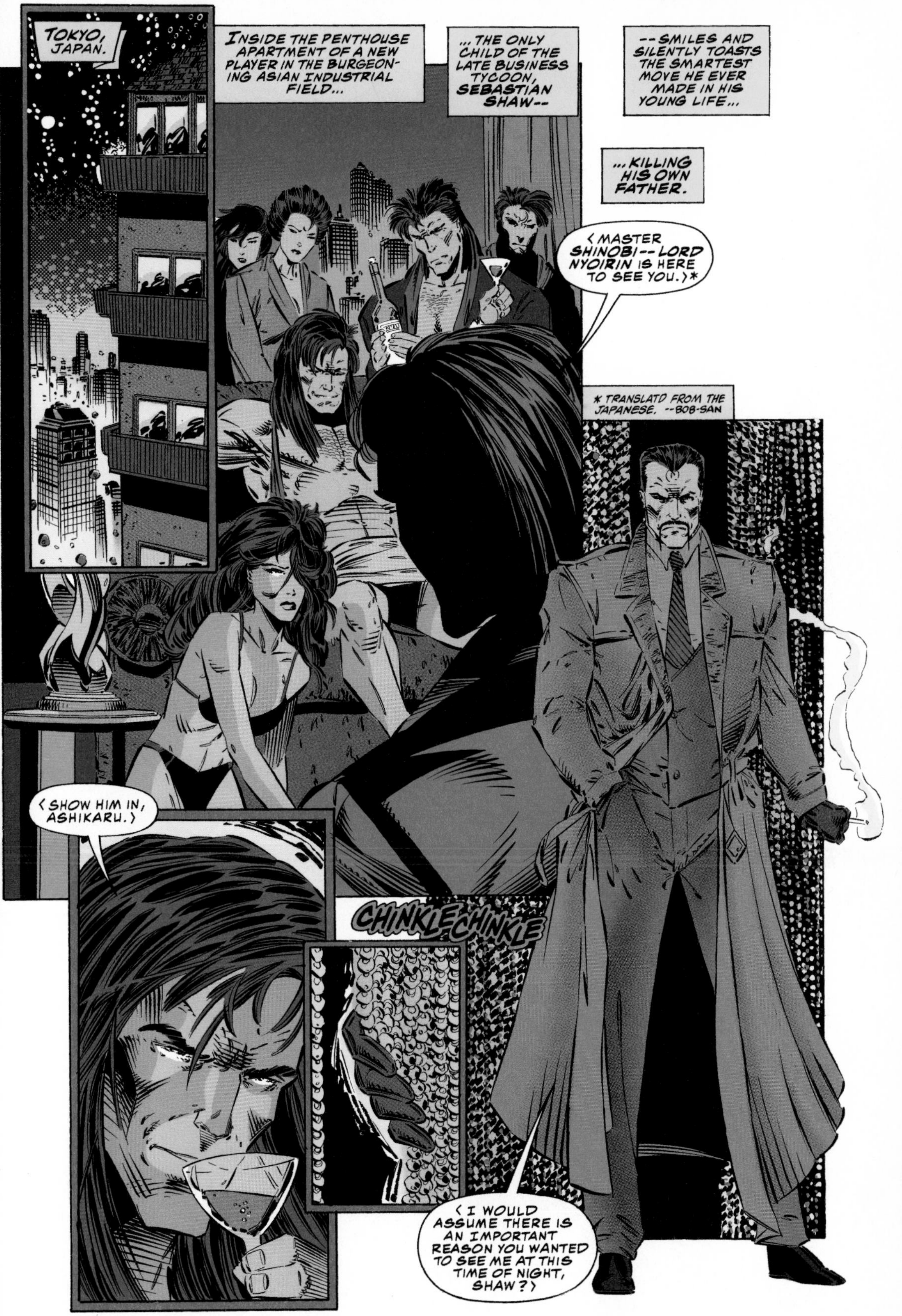
TOKYO, JAPAN.
INSIDE THE PENTHOUSE APARTMENT OF A NEW PLAYER IN THE BURGEONING ASIAN INDUSTRIAL FIELD...
...THE ONLY CHILD OF THE LATE BUSINESS TYCOON, SEBASTIAN SHAW--
--SMILES AND SILENTLY TOASTS THE SMARTEST MOVE HE EVER MADE IN HIS YOUNG LIFE...
...KILLING HIS OWN FATHER.
‹MASTER SHINOBI--LORD NYOIRIN IS HERE TO SEE YOU.›*
* TRANSLATD FROM THE JAPANESE. --BOB-SAN
‹SHOW HIM IN, ASHIKARU.›
CHINKLE CHINKLE
‹I WOULD ASSUME THERE IS AN IMPORTANT REASON YOU WANTED TO SEE ME AT THIS TIME OF NIGHT, SHAW?›

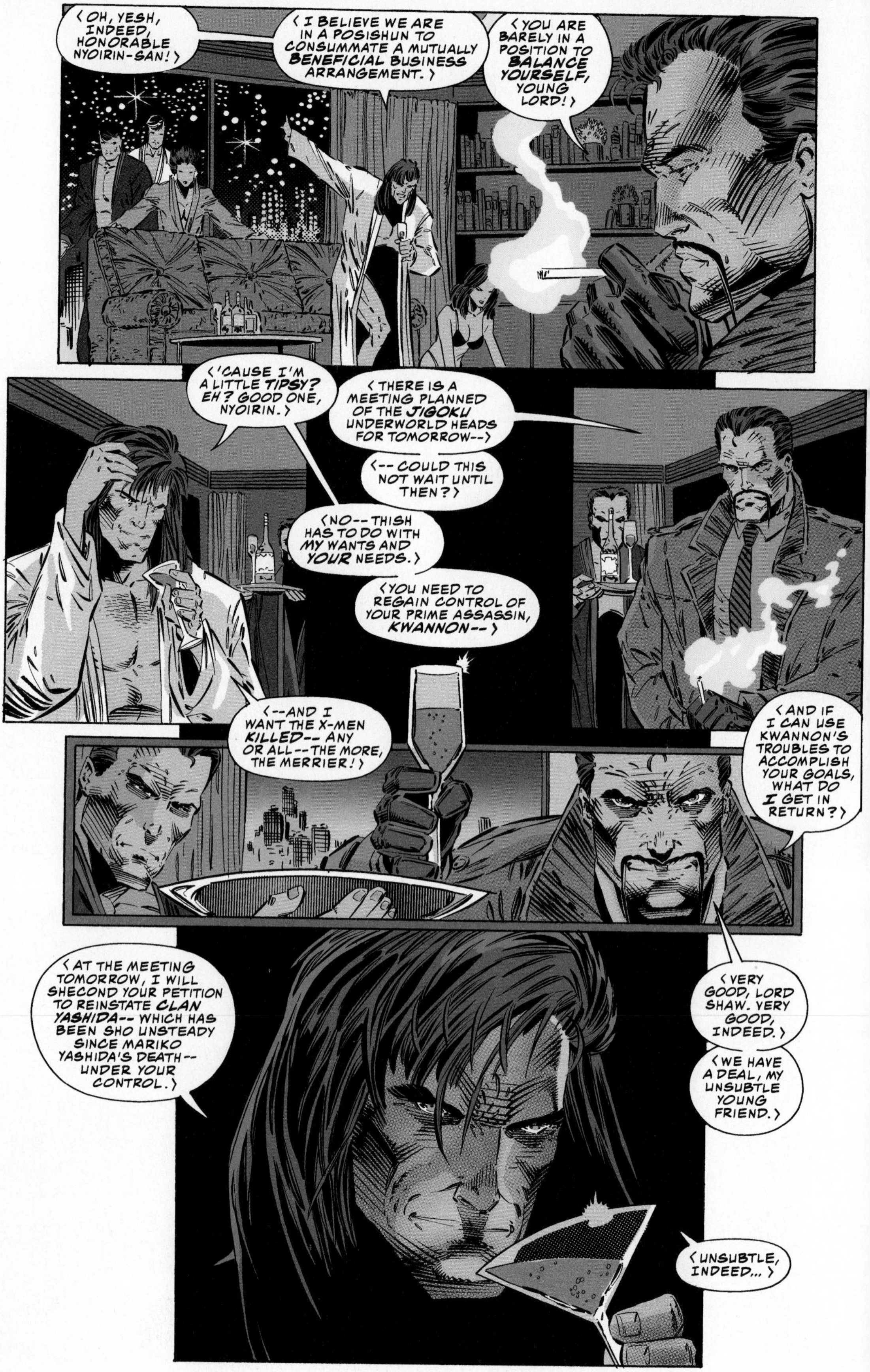
⟨OH, YESH, INDEED, HONORABLE NYOIRIN-SAN!⟩
⟨I BELIEVE WE ARE IN A POSISHUN TO CONSUMMATE A MUTUALLY BENEFICIAL BUSINESS ARRANGEMENT.⟩
⟨YOU ARE BARELY IN A POSITION TO BALANCE YOURSELF, YOUNG LORD!⟩
⟨'CAUSE I'M A LITTLE TIPSY? EH? GOOD ONE, NYOIRIN.⟩
⟨THERE IS A MEETING PLANNED OF THE JIGOKU UNDERWORLD HEADS FOR TOMORROW--⟩
⟨--COULD THIS NOT WAIT UNTIL THEN?⟩
⟨NO--THISH HAS TO DO WITH MY WANTS AND YOUR NEEDS.⟩
⟨YOU NEED TO REGAIN CONTROL OF YOUR PRIME ASSASSIN, KWANNON--⟩
⟨--AND I WANT THE X-MEN KILLED-- ANY OR ALL--THE MORE, THE MERRIER!⟩
⟨AND IF I CAN USE KWANNON'S TROUBLES TO ACCOMPLISH YOUR GOALS, WHAT DO I GET IN RETURN?⟩
⟨AT THE MEETING TOMORROW, I WILL SHECOND YOUR PETITION TO REINSTATE CLAN YASHIDA-- WHICH HAS BEEN SHO UNSTEADY SINCE MARIKO YASHIDA'S DEATH-- UNDER YOUR CONTROL.⟩
⟨VERY GOOD, LORD SHAW. VERY GOOD, INDEED.⟩
⟨WE HAVE A DEAL, MY UNSUBTLE YOUNG FRIEND.⟩
⟨UNSUBTLE, INDEED...⟩

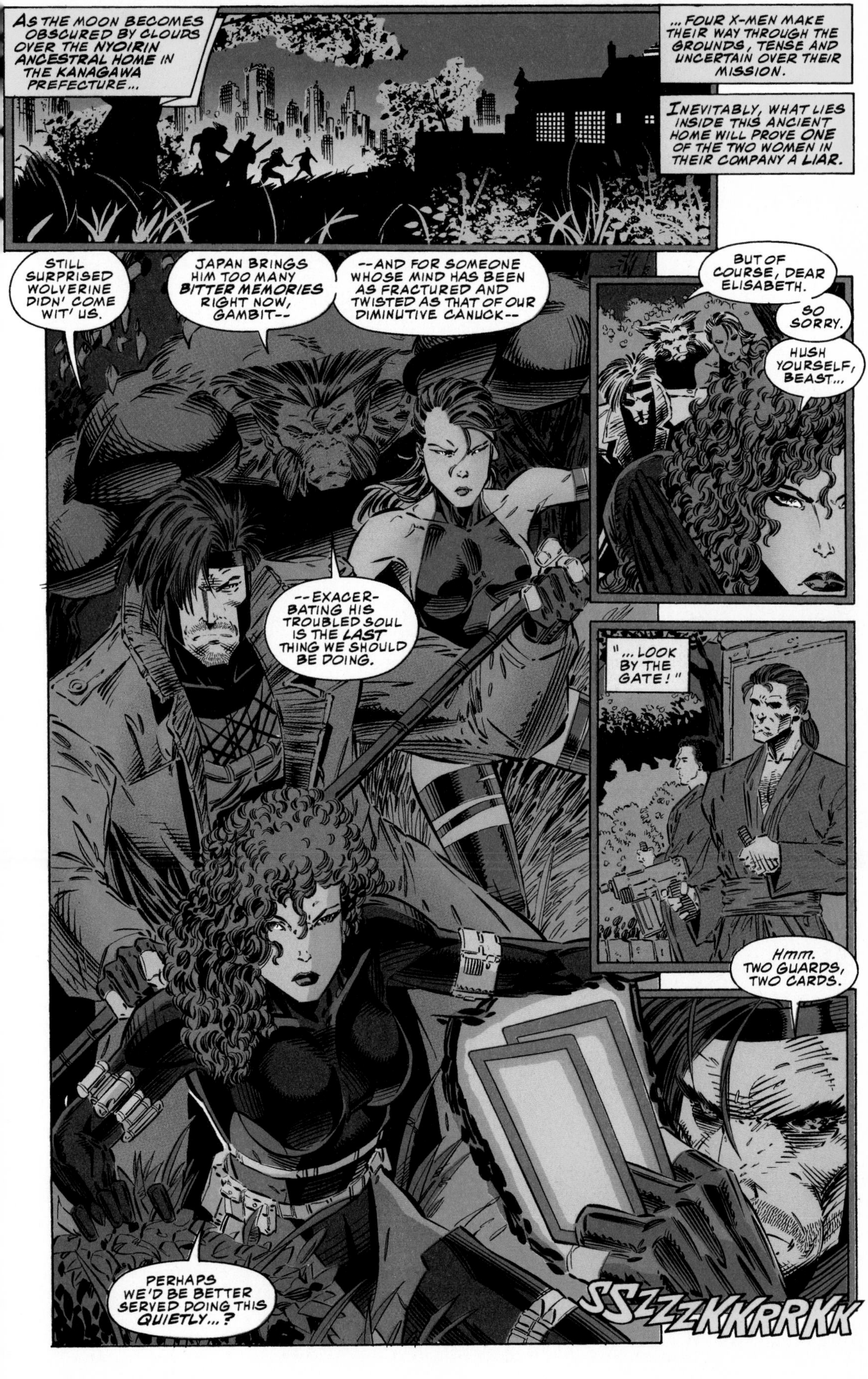
AS THE MOON BECOMES OBSCURED BY CLOUDS OVER THE NYOIRIN ANCESTRAL HOME IN THE KANAGAWA PREFECTURE...
...FOUR X-MEN MAKE THEIR WAY THROUGH THE GROUNDS, TENSE AND UNCERTAIN OVER THEIR MISSION.
INEVITABLY, WHAT LIES INSIDE THIS ANCIENT HOME WILL PROVE ONE OF THE TWO WOMEN IN THEIR COMPANY A LIAR.
STILL SURPRISED WOLVERINE DIDN' COME WIT' US.
JAPAN BRINGS HIM TOO MANY BITTER MEMORIES RIGHT NOW, GAMBIT--
--AND FOR SOMEONE WHOSE MIND HAS BEEN AS FRACTURED AND TWISTED AS THAT OF OUR DIMINUTIVE CANUCK--
--EXACER-BATING HIS TROUBLED SOUL IS THE LAST THING WE SHOULD BE DOING.
BUT OF COURSE, DEAR ELISABETH.
SO SORRY.
HUSH YOURSELF, BEAST...
PERHAPS WE'D BE BETTER SERVED DOING THIS QUIETLY...?
"...LOOK BY THE GATE!"
Hmm. TWO GUARDS, TWO CARDS.
SSZZZKKRRKK

TWO DOWN--

--THIS IS *TOO* EASY.

SHAFA ZZK

I WARN YOU, GAMBIT, DO NOT GET OVER CON- FIDENT.

ALL OF YOU, BE PRE- PARED--

--NYOIRIN'S ESTATE HAS *EYES* WE CAN- NOT SEE.

AND YOU KNOW THIS HOUSE *FAR* TOO WELL FOR SOME- ONE WHO CLAIMS TO BE *INNOCENT* OF ANY WRONG- DOING.

MY FAMILIARITY COMES ONLY FROM HAVING BEEN HELD *PRISONER* HERE FOR *MONTHS,* KWANNON!

LADIES, DO I HAVE TO ASK YOU AGAIN TO STOP THIS?

THEY NEED A *GOOD* SPANKIN'.

SUICIDAL, ARE YOU, MR. LEBEAU?

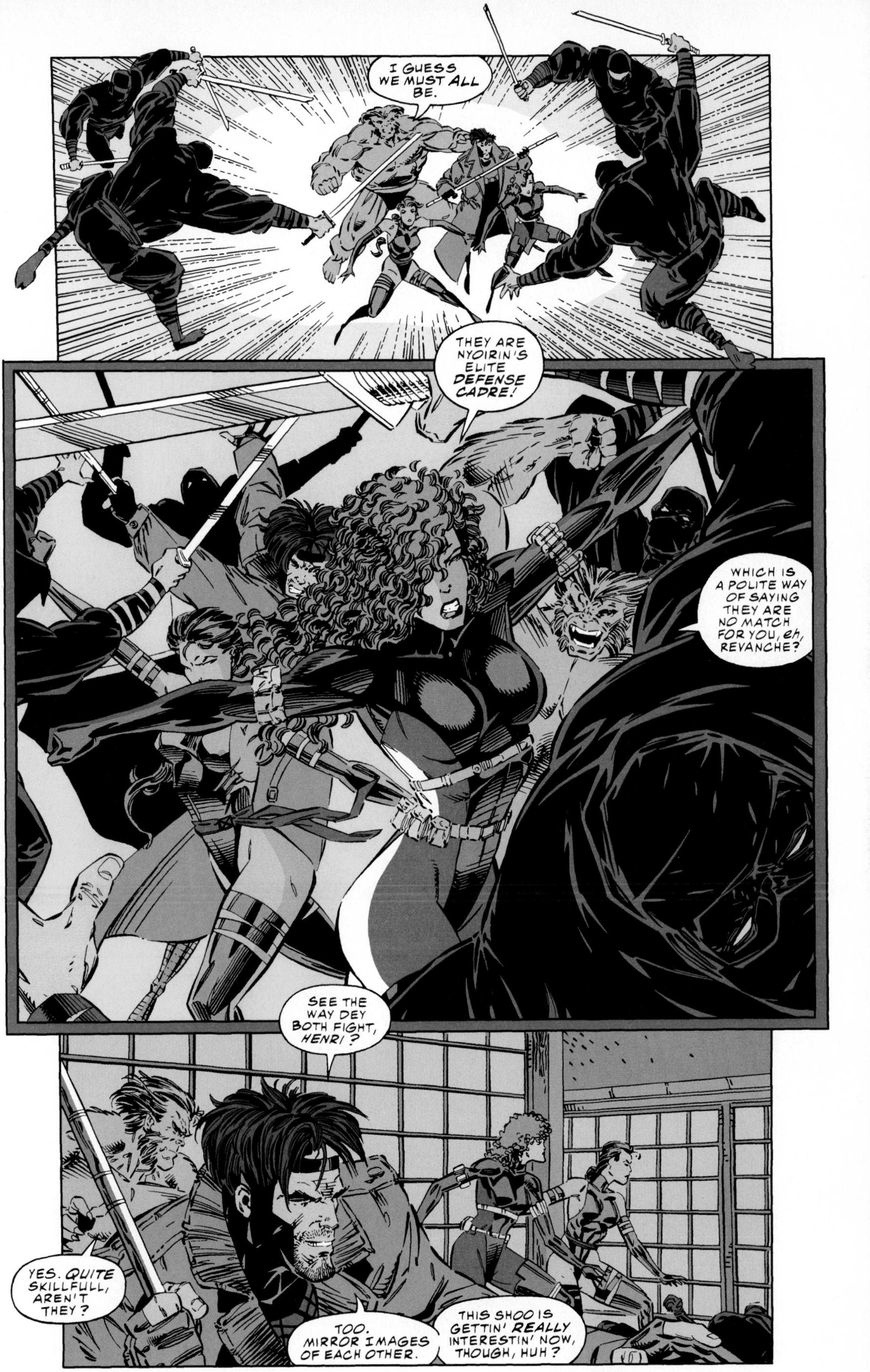
I GUESS WE MUST ALL BE.
THEY ARE NYOIRIN'S ELITE DEFENSE CADRE!
WHICH IS A POLITE WAY OF SAYING THEY ARE NO MATCH FOR YOU, eh, REVANCHE?
SEE THE WAY DEY BOTH FIGHT, HENRI?
YES. QUITE SKILLFULL, AREN'T THEY?
TOO. MIRROR IMAGES OF EACH OTHER.
THIS SHOO IS GETTIN' REALLY INTERESTIN' NOW, THOUGH, HUH?

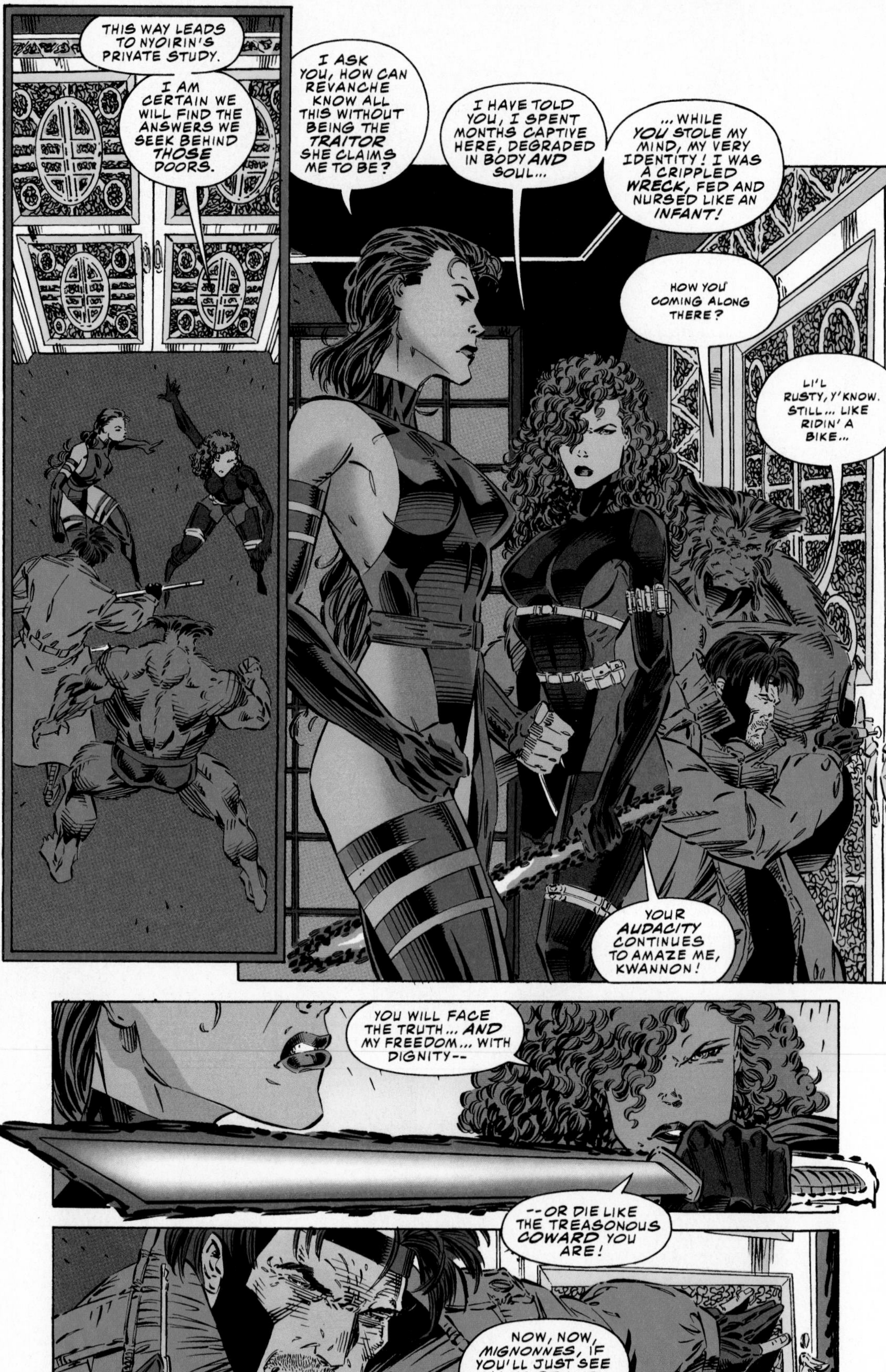
THIS WAY LEADS TO NYOIRIN'S PRIVATE STUDY.
I AM CERTAIN WE WILL FIND THE ANSWERS WE SEEK BEHIND THOSE DOORS.
I ASK YOU, HOW CAN REVANCHE KNOW ALL THIS WITHOUT BEING THE TRAITOR SHE CLAIMS ME TO BE?
I HAVE TOLD YOU, I SPENT MONTHS CAPTIVE HERE, DEGRADED IN BODY AND SOUL...
...WHILE YOU STOLE MY MIND, MY VERY IDENTITY! I WAS A CRIPPLED WRECK, FED AND NURSED LIKE AN INFANT!
HOW YOU COMING ALONG THERE?
LI'L RUSTY, Y'KNOW. STILL... LIKE RIDIN' A BIKE...
YOUR AUDACITY CONTINUES TO AMAZE ME, KWANNON!
YOU WILL FACE THE TRUTH... AND MY FREEDOM... WITH DIGNITY--
--OR DIE LIKE THE TREASONOUS COWARD YOU ARE!
NOW, NOW, MIGNONNES, IF YOU'LL JUST SEE WHAT'S BEHIND DOOR NUMBER ONE...?

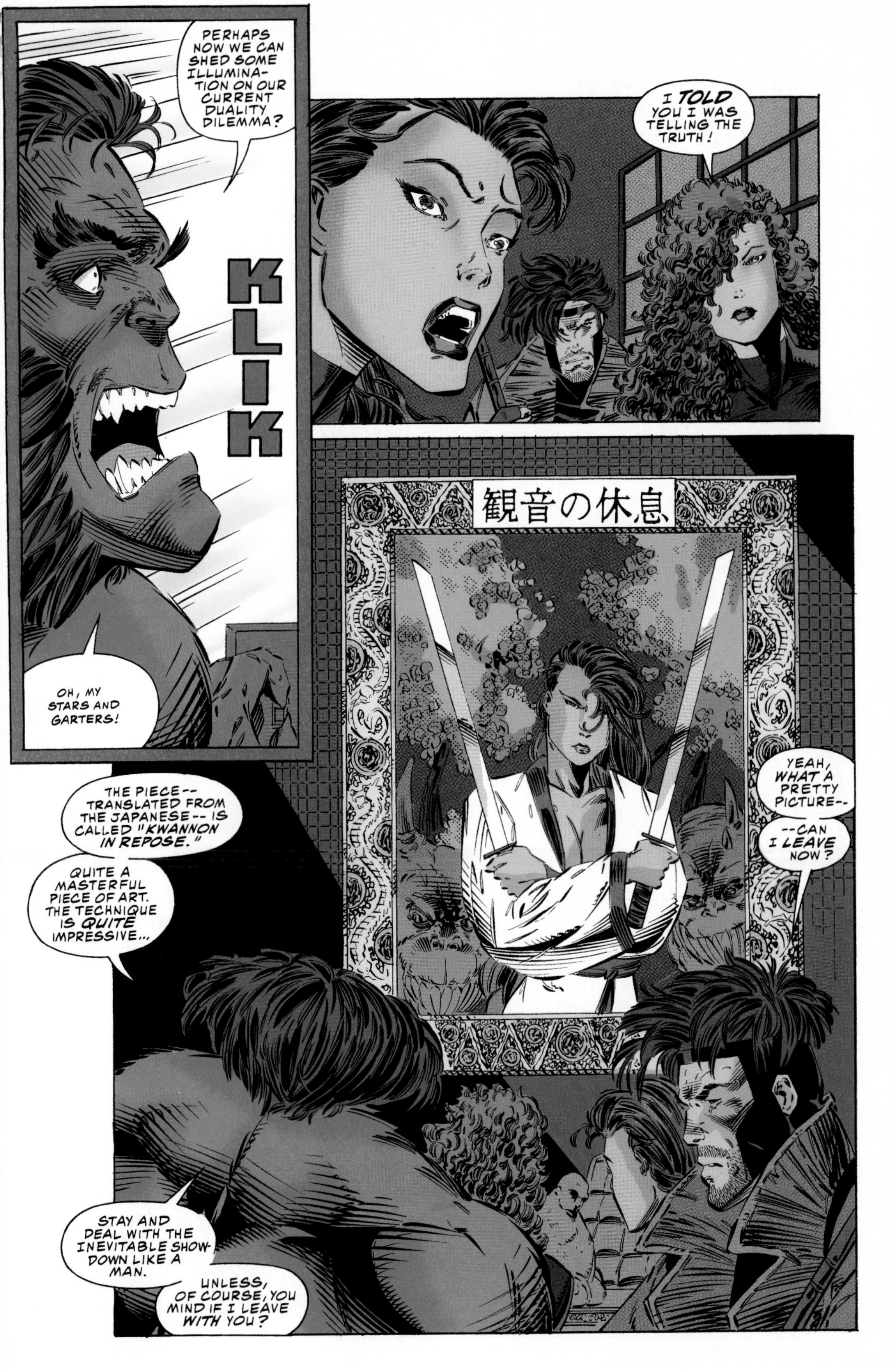
PERHAPS NOW WE CAN SHED SOME ILLUMINATION ON OUR CURRENT DUALITY DILEMMA?
KLIK
I TOLD YOU I WAS TELLING THE TRUTH!
OH, MY STARS AND GARTERS!
観音の休息
THE PIECE -- TRANSLATED FROM THE JAPANESE -- IS CALLED "KWANNON IN REPOSE."
QUITE A MASTERFUL PIECE OF ART. THE TECHNIQUE IS QUITE IMPRESSIVE...
YEAH, WHAT A PRETTY PICTURE--
--CAN I LEAVE NOW?
STAY AND DEAL WITH THE INEVITABLE SHOW-DOWN LIKE A MAN.
UNLESS, OF COURSE, YOU MIND IF I LEAVE WITH YOU?

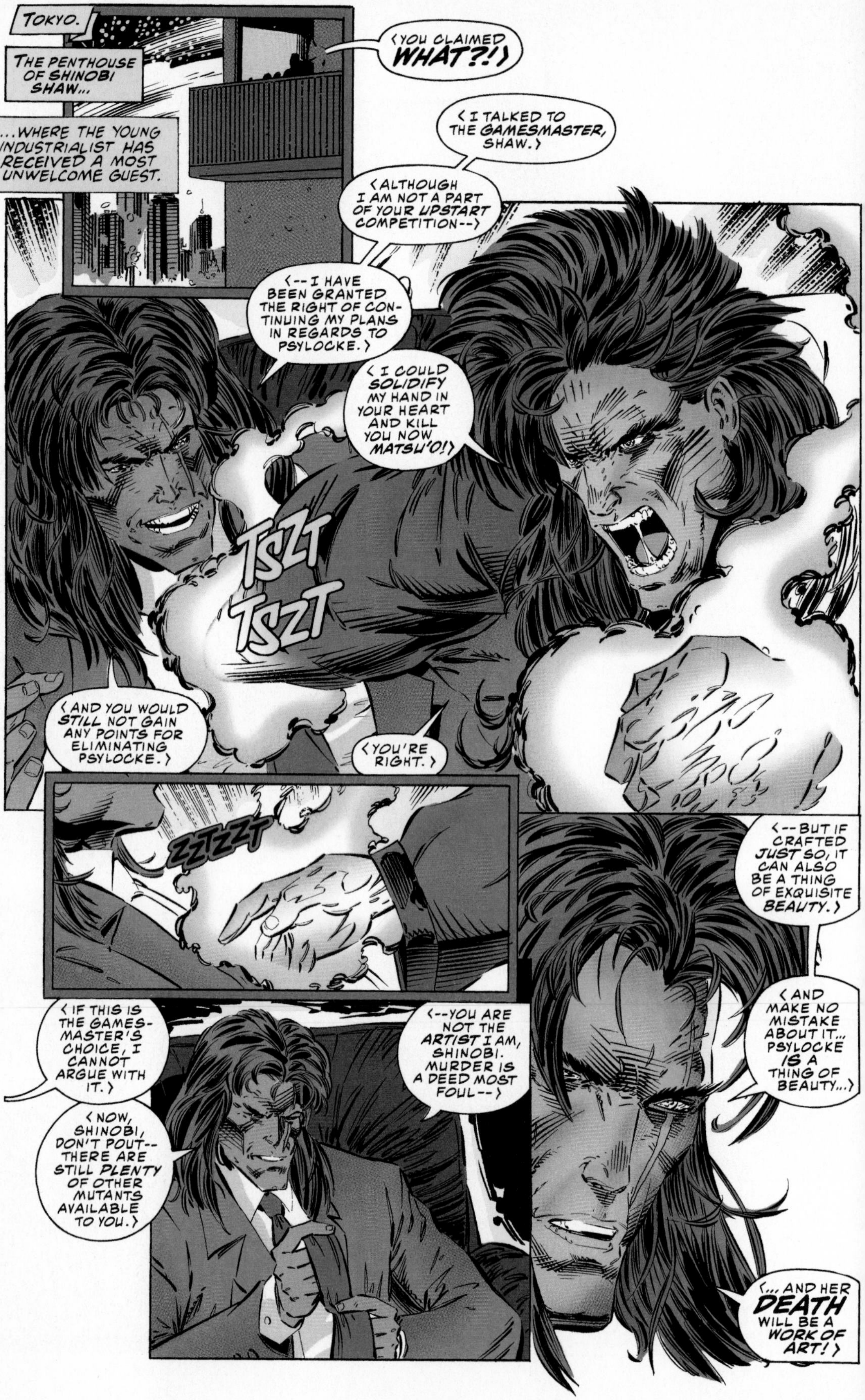
TOKYO.
THE PENTHOUSE OF SHINOBI SHAW...
...WHERE THE YOUNG INDUSTRIALIST HAS RECEIVED A MOST UNWELCOME GUEST.
‹YOU CLAIMED WHAT?!›
‹I TALKED TO THE GAMESMASTER, SHAW.›
‹ALTHOUGH I AM NOT A PART OF YOUR UPSTART COMPETITION--›
‹--I HAVE BEEN GRANTED THE RIGHT OF CONTINUING MY PLANS IN REGARDS TO PSYLOCKE.›
‹I COULD SOLIDIFY MY HAND IN YOUR HEART AND KILL YOU NOW MATSU'O!›
TSZT
TSZT
‹AND YOU WOULD STILL NOT GAIN ANY POINTS FOR ELIMINATING PSYLOCKE.›
‹YOU'RE RIGHT.›
ZZTZZT
‹IF THIS IS THE GAMESMASTER'S CHOICE, I CANNOT ARGUE WITH IT.›
‹NOW, SHINOBI, DON'T POUT-- THERE ARE STILL PLENTY OF OTHER MUTANTS AVAILABLE TO YOU.›
‹--YOU ARE NOT THE ARTIST I AM, SHINOBI. MURDER IS A DEED MOST FOUL--›
‹--BUT IF CRAFTED JUST SO, IT CAN ALSO BE A THING OF EXQUISITE BEAUTY.›
‹AND MAKE NO MISTAKE ABOUT IT... PSYLOCKE IS A THING OF BEAUTY...›
‹...AND HER DEATH WILL BE A WORK OF ART!›

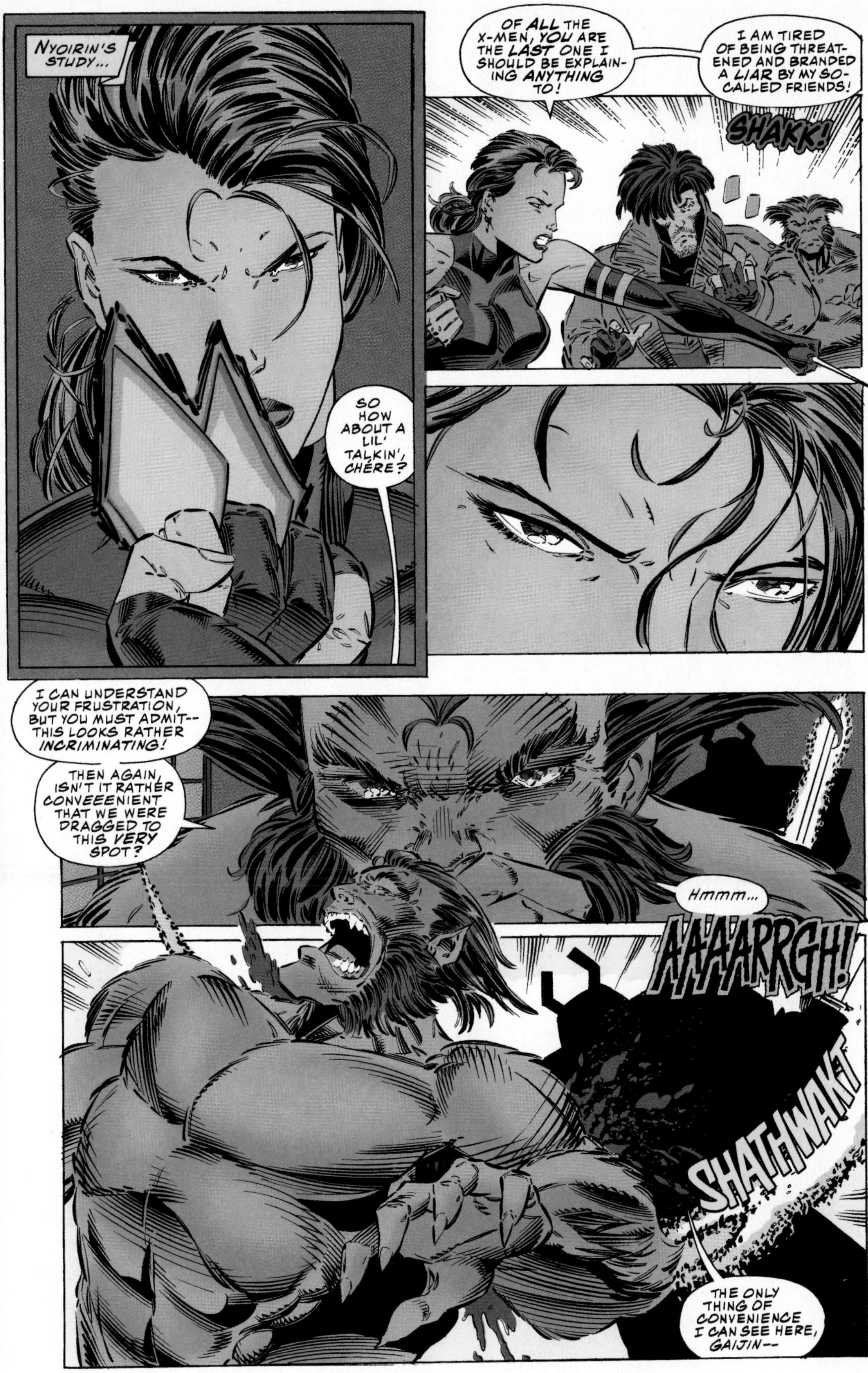
NYOIRIN'S STUDY...
SO HOW ABOUT A LIL' TALKIN', CHÉRE?
OF ALL THE X-MEN, YOU ARE THE LAST ONE I SHOULD BE EXPLAINING ANYTHING TO!
I AM TIRED OF BEING THREATENED AND BRANDED A LIAR BY MY SO-CALLED FRIENDS!
SHAKK!
I CAN UNDERSTAND YOUR FRUSTRATION, BUT YOU MUST ADMIT-- THIS LOOKS RATHER INCRIMINATING!
THEN AGAIN, ISN'T IT RATHER CONVEEEENIENT THAT WE WERE DRAGGED TO THIS VERY SPOT?
Hmmm...
AAAARRGH!
SHATHWAKT
THE ONLY THING OF CONVENIENCE I CAN SEE HERE, GAIJIN--

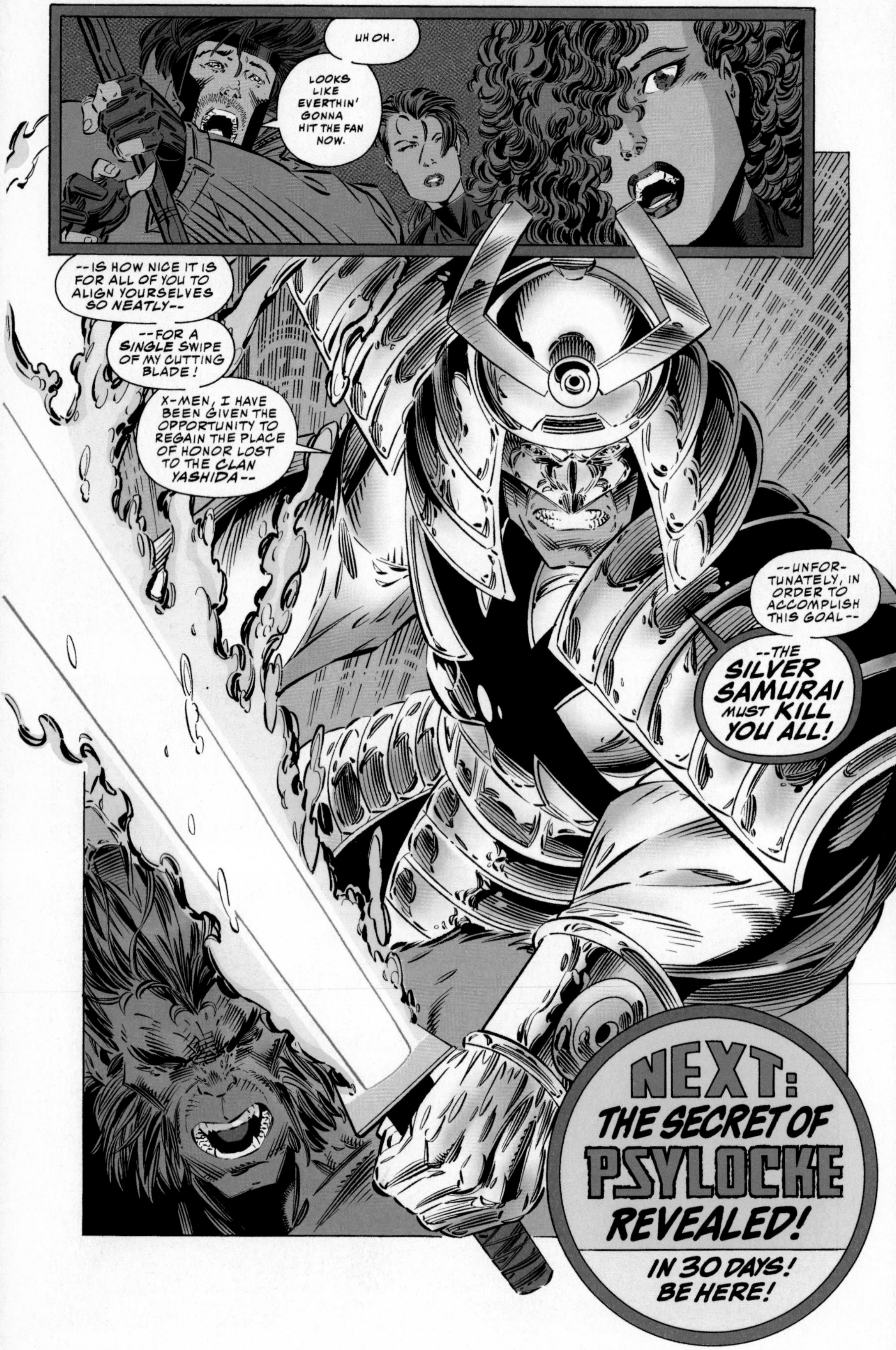
UH OH.
LOOKS LIKE EVERTHIN' GONNA HIT THE FAN NOW.
--IS HOW NICE IT IS FOR ALL OF YOU TO ALIGN YOURSELVES SO NEATLY--
--FOR A SINGLE SWIPE OF MY CUTTING BLADE!
X-MEN, I HAVE BEEN GIVEN THE OPPORTUNITY TO REGAIN THE PLACE OF HONOR LOST TO THE CLAN YASHIDA--
--UNFORTUNATELY, IN ORDER TO ACCOMPLISH THIS GOAL--
--THE SILVER SAMURAI MUST KILL YOU ALL!
NEXT: THE SECRET OF PSYLOCKE REVEALED!
IN 30 DAYS! BE HERE!

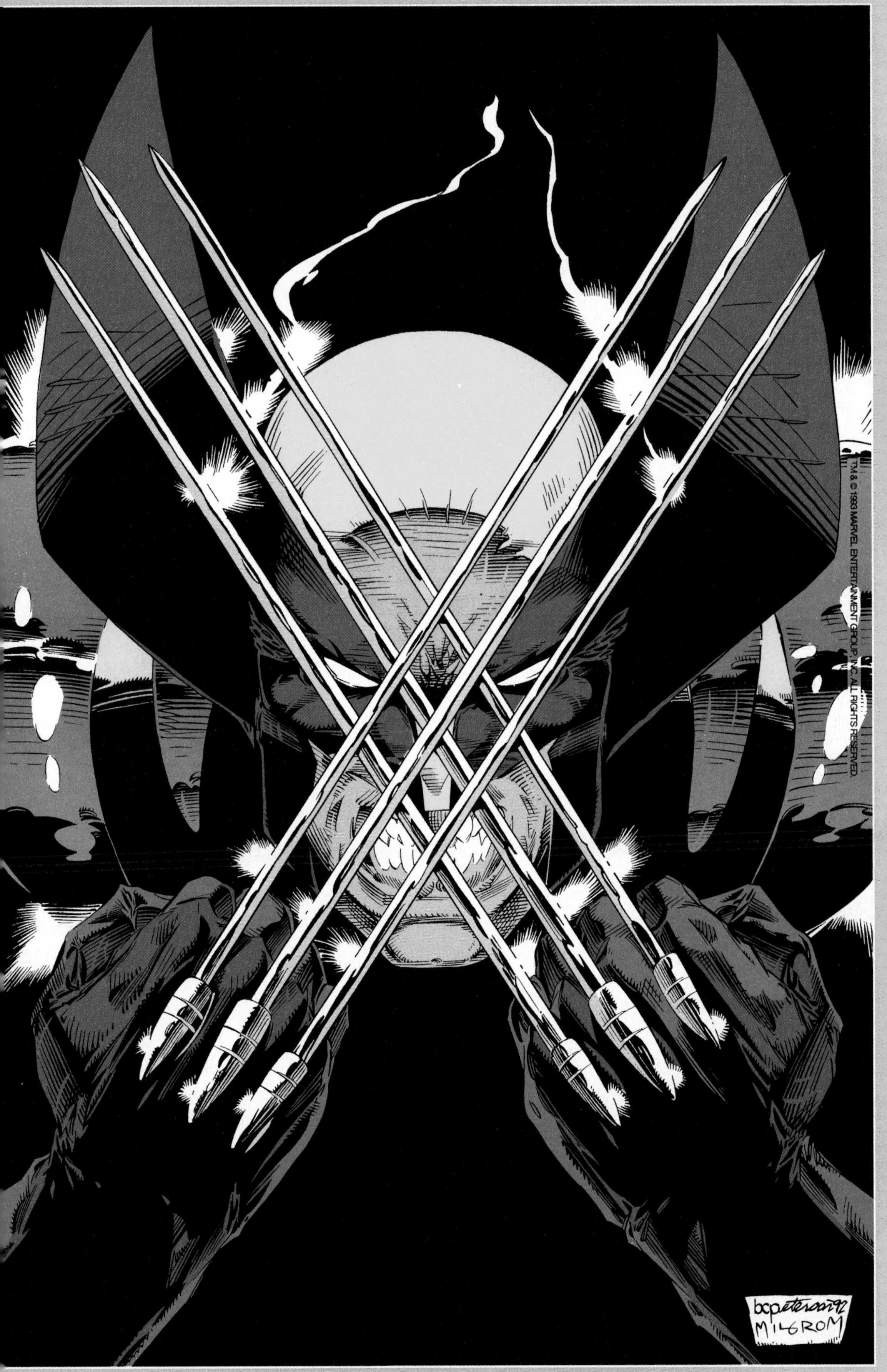
TM & © 1993 MARVEL ENTERTAINMENT GROUP, INC. ALL RIGHTS RESERVED.
bcpeterson'92
MILGROM

X-Men Poster Magazine #2 pinup by Brandon Peterson & Al Milgrom

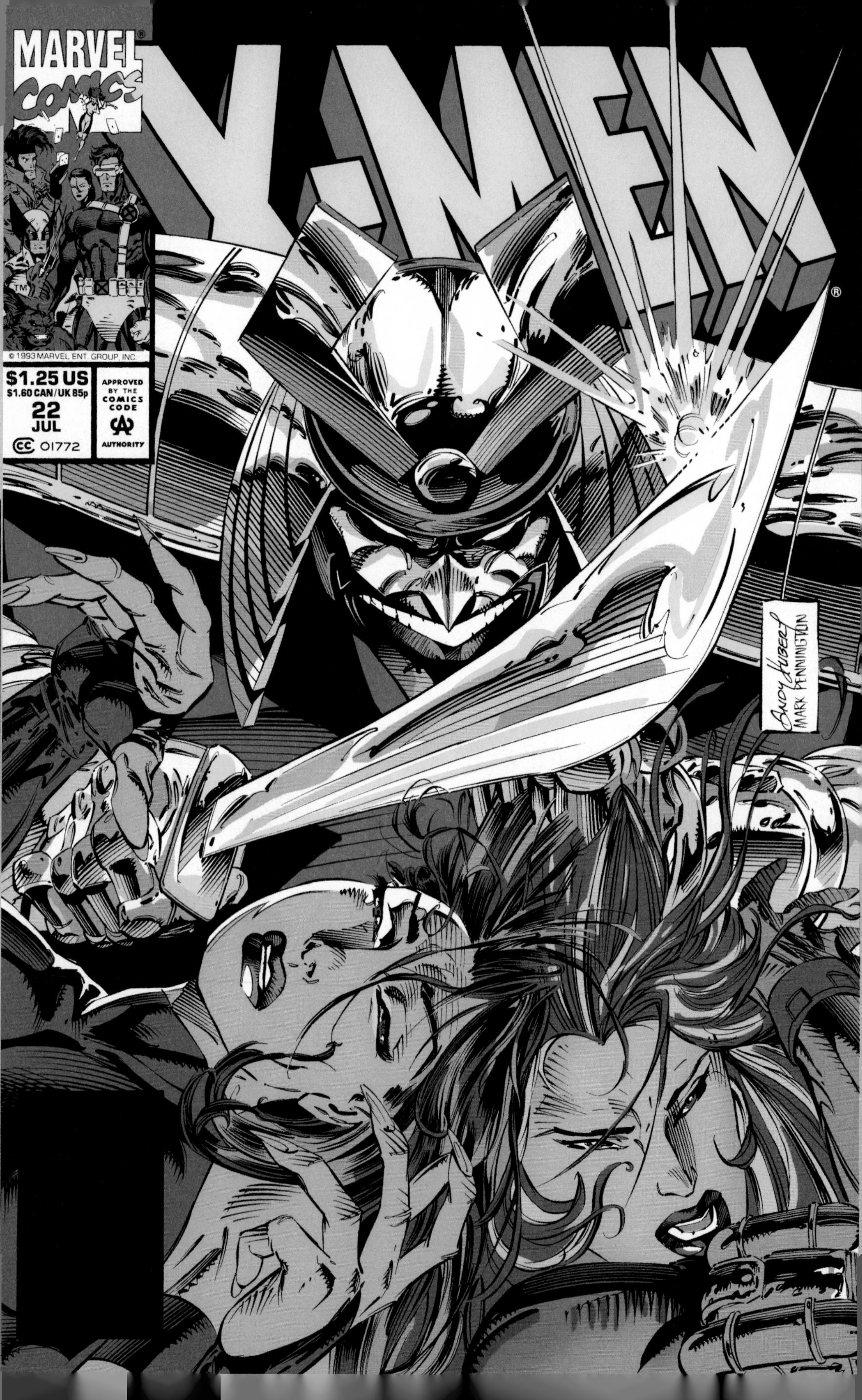
MARVEL COMICS
X-MEN
© 1993 MARVEL ENT. GROUP, INC.
$1.25 US
$1.60 CAN/UK 85p
22
JUL
01772
APPROVED BY THE COMICS CODE AUTHORITY
ANDY KUBERT
MARK PENNINGTON

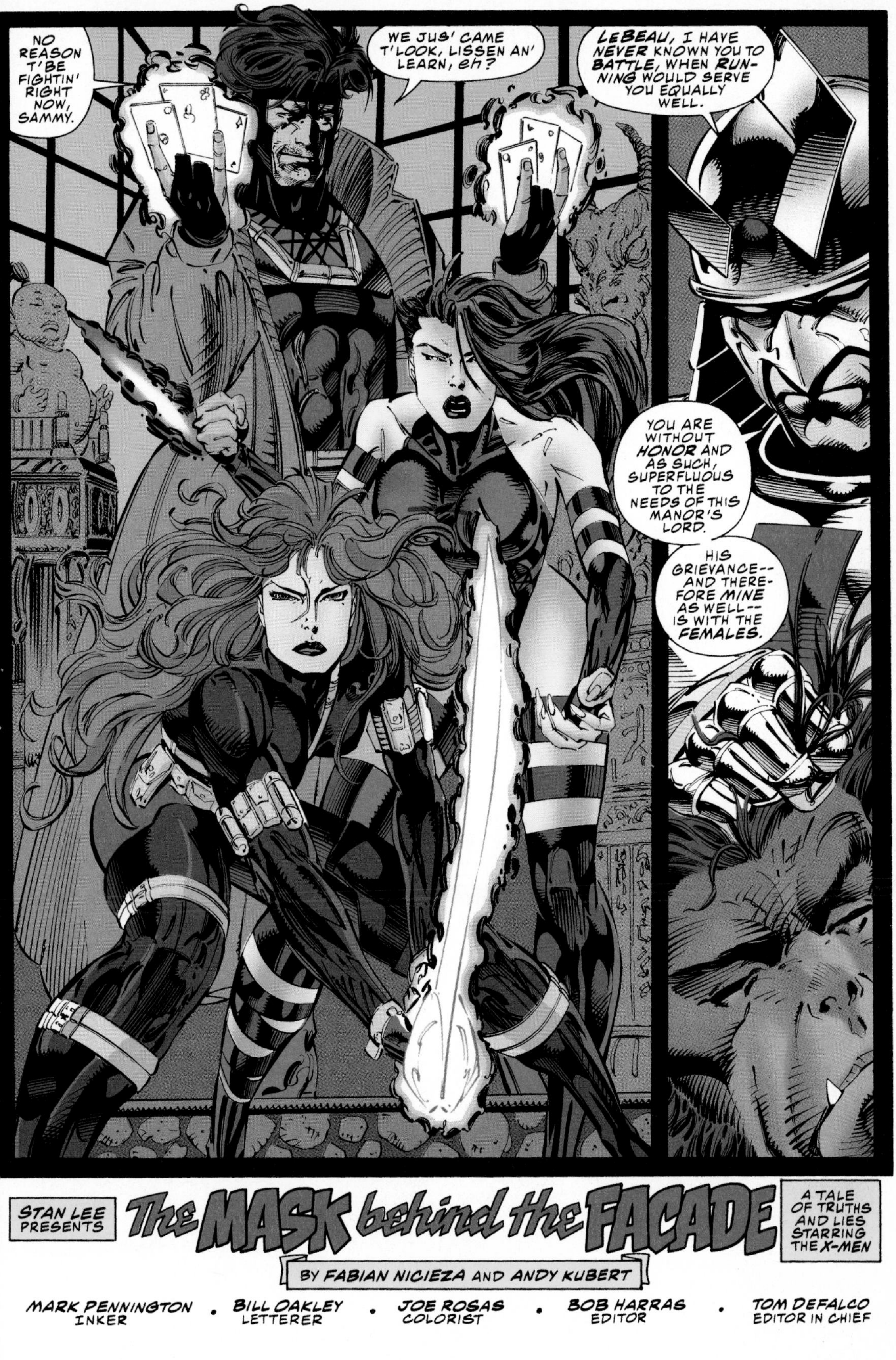

NO REASON T'BE FIGHTIN' RIGHT NOW, SAMMY.
WE JUS' CAME T'LOOK, LISSEN AN' LEARN, eh?
LEBEAU, I HAVE NEVER KNOWN YOU TO BATTLE, WHEN RUNNING WOULD SERVE YOU EQUALLY WELL.
YOU ARE WITHOUT HONOR AND AS SUCH, SUPERFLUOUS TO THE NEEDS OF THIS MANOR'S LORD.
HIS GRIEVANCE--AND THEREFORE MINE AS WELL--IS WITH THE FEMALES.
STAN LEE PRESENTS
The MASK behind the FACADE
A TALE OF TRUTHS AND LIES STARRING THE X-MEN
BY FABIAN NICIEZA AND ANDY KUBERT
MARK PENNINGTON INKER • BILL OAKLEY LETTERER • JOE ROSAS COLORIST • BOB HARRAS EDITOR • TOM DEFALCO EDITOR IN CHIEF

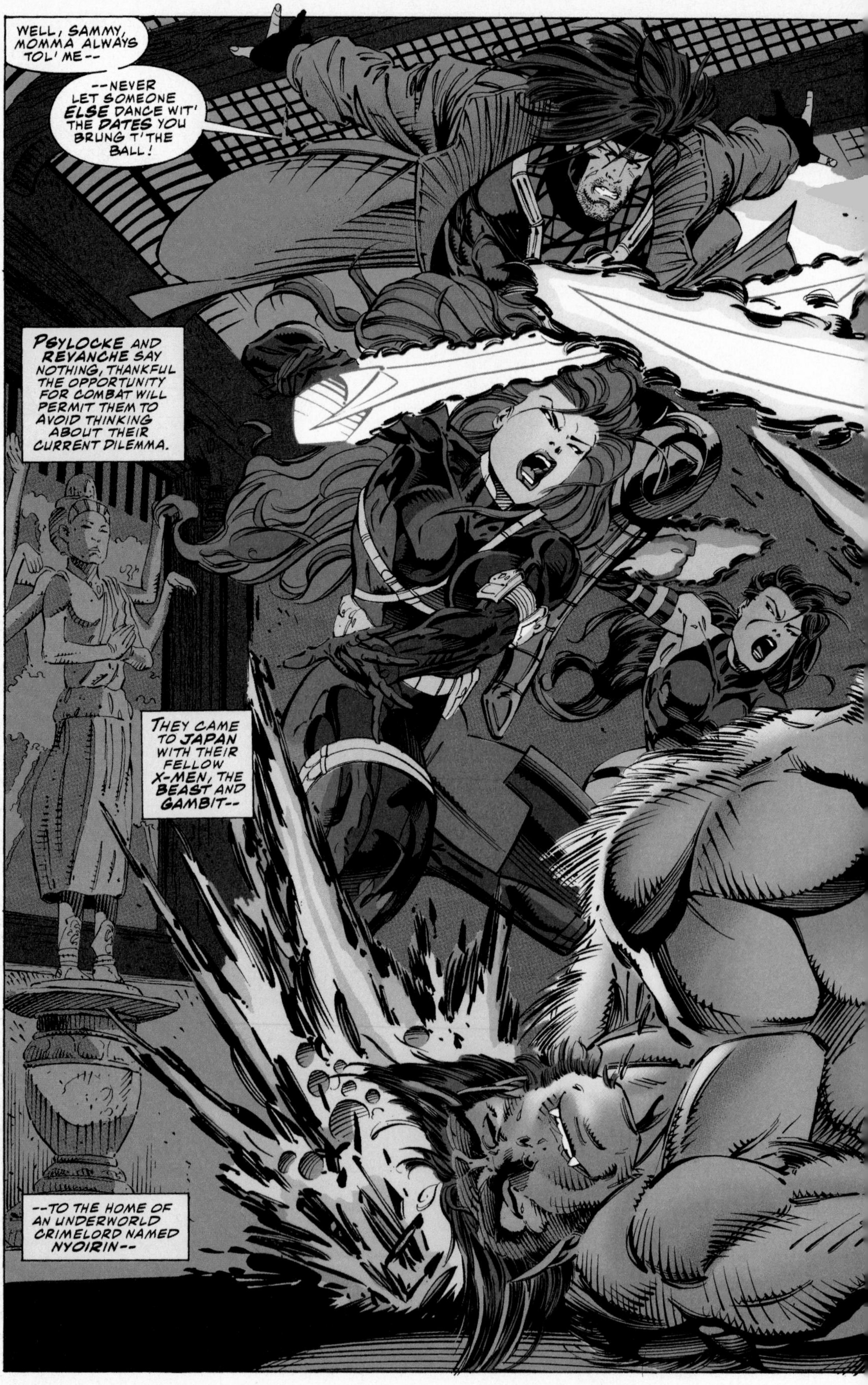
WELL, SAMMY, MOMMA ALWAYS TOL' ME--
--NEVER LET SOMEONE ELSE DANCE WIT' THE DATES YOU BRUNG T' THE BALL!
PSYLOCKE AND REVANCHE SAY NOTHING, THANKFUL THE OPPORTUNITY FOR COMBAT WILL PERMIT THEM TO AVOID THINKING ABOUT THEIR CURRENT DILEMMA.
THEY CAME TO JAPAN WITH THEIR FELLOW X-MEN, THE BEAST AND GAMBIT--
--TO THE HOME OF AN UNDERWORLD CRIMELORD NAMED NYOIRIN--

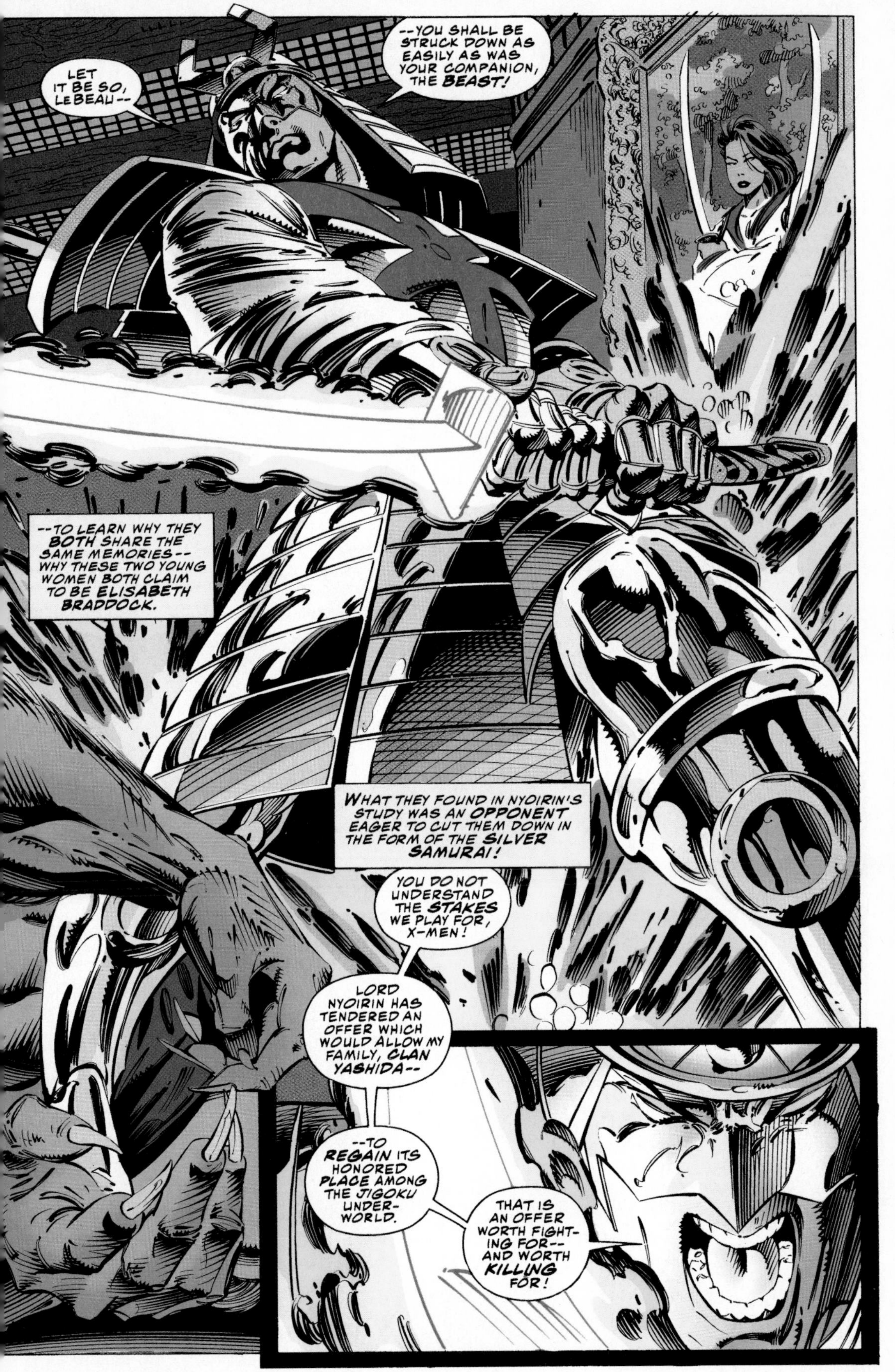
LET IT BE SO, LEBEAU--
--YOU SHALL BE STRUCK DOWN AS EASILY AS WAS YOUR COMPANION, THE BEAST!
--TO LEARN WHY THEY BOTH SHARE THE SAME MEMORIES--WHY THESE TWO YOUNG WOMEN BOTH CLAIM TO BE ELISABETH BRADDOCK.
WHAT THEY FOUND IN NYOIRIN'S STUDY WAS AN OPPONENT EAGER TO CUT THEM DOWN IN THE FORM OF THE SILVER SAMURAI!
YOU DO NOT UNDERSTAND THE STAKES WE PLAY FOR, X-MEN!
LORD NYOIRIN HAS TENDERED AN OFFER WHICH WOULD ALLOW MY FAMILY, CLAN YASHIDA--
--TO REGAIN ITS HONORED PLACE AMONG THE JIGOKU UNDER-WORLD.
THAT IS AN OFFER WORTH FIGHT-ING FOR--AND WORTH KILLING FOR!

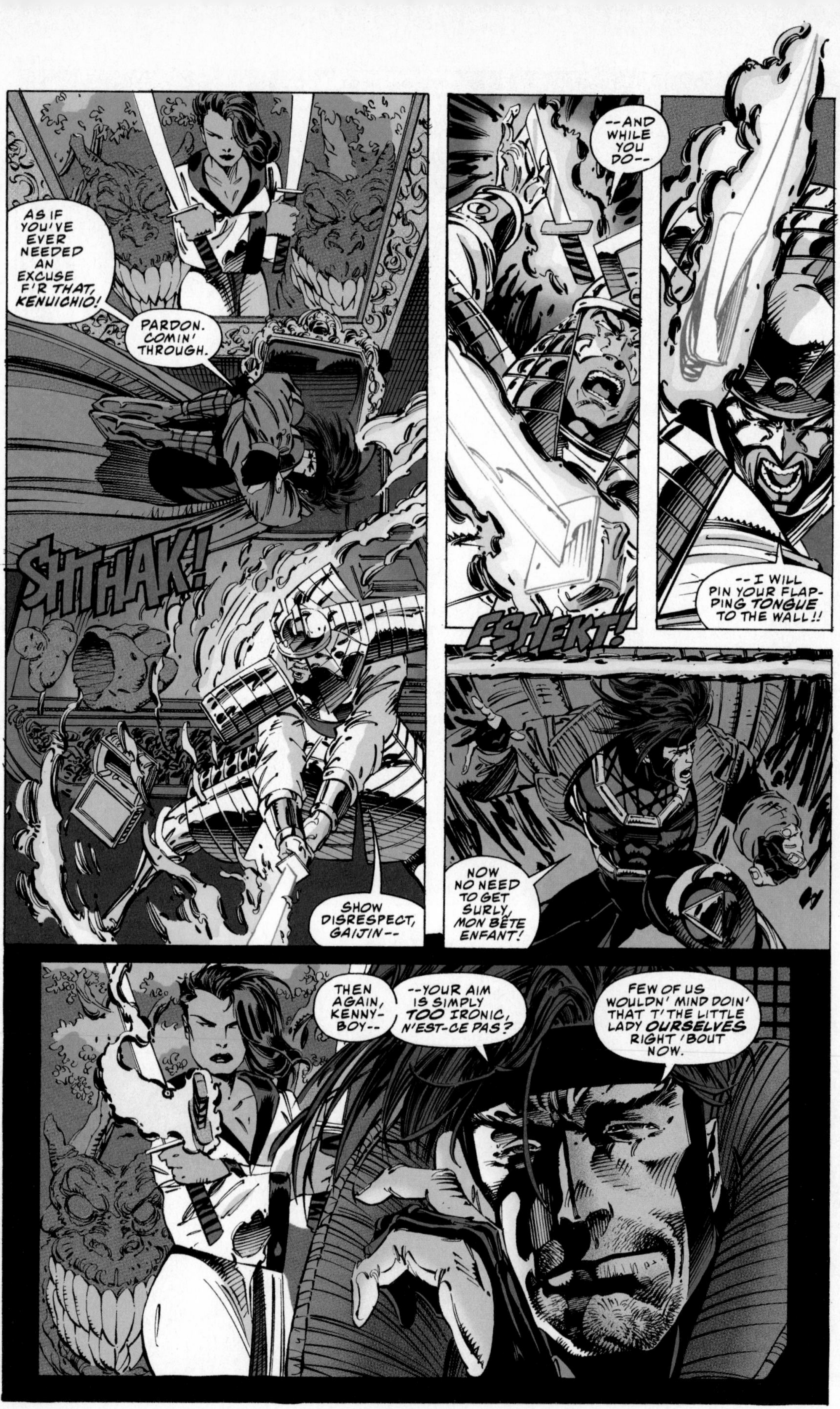

AS IF YOU'VE EVER NEEDED AN EXCUSE F'R THAT, KENUICHIO!
PARDON. COMIN' THROUGH.
$HTHAK!
SHOW DISRESPECT, GAIJIN--
--AND WHILE YOU DO--
--I WILL PIN YOUR FLAPPING TONGUE TO THE WALL!!
ESHEKT!
NOW NO NEED TO GET SURLY, MON BÊTE ENFANT!
THEN AGAIN, KENNY-BOY--
--YOUR AIM IS SIMPLY TOO IRONIC, N'EST-CE PAS?
FEW OF US WOULDN' MIND DOIN' THAT T' THE LITTLE LADY OURSELVES RIGHT 'BOUT NOW.

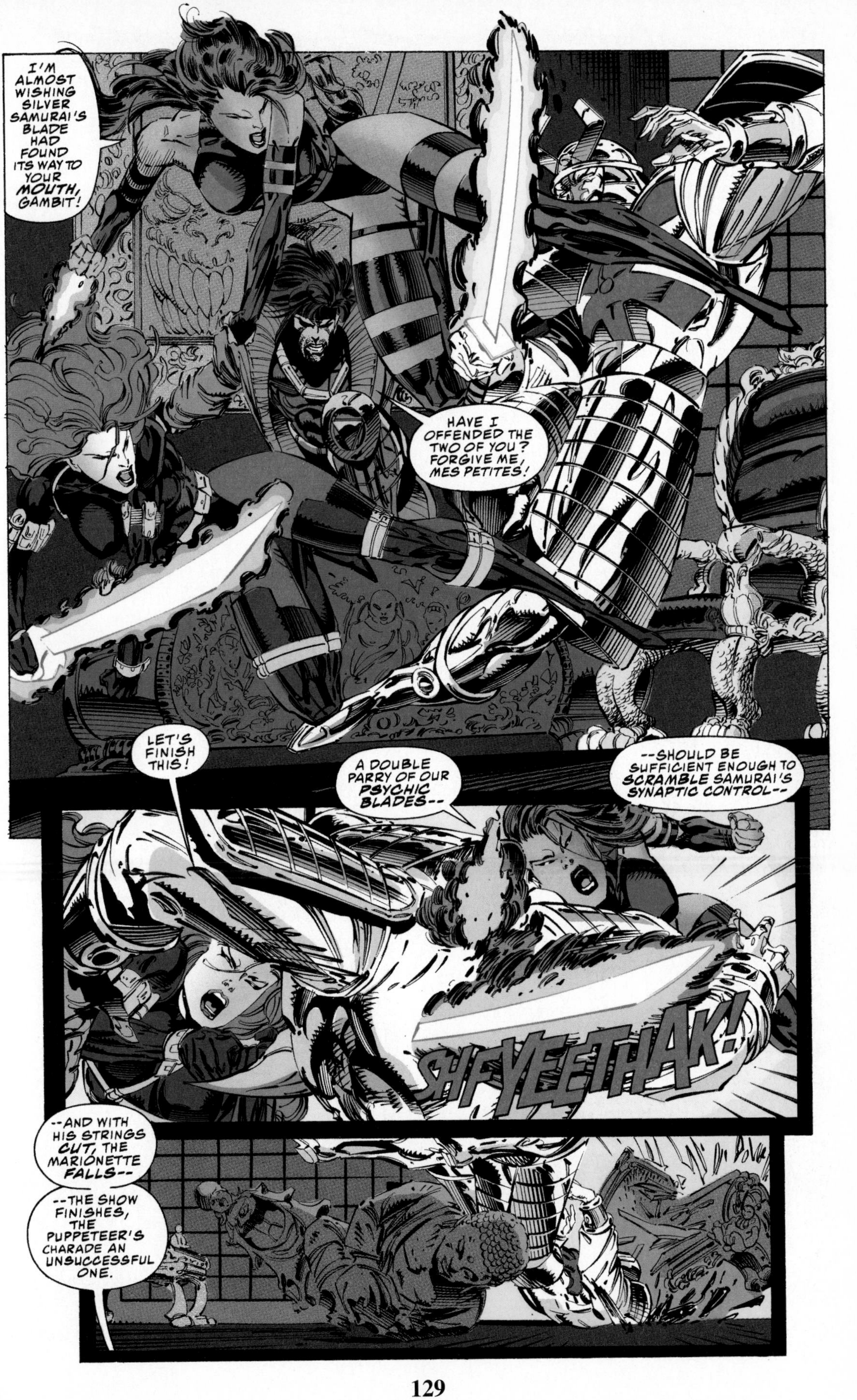
I'M ALMOST WISHING SILVER SAMURAI'S BLADE HAD FOUND ITS WAY TO YOUR MOUTH, GAMBIT!
HAVE I OFFENDED THE TWO OF YOU? FORGIVE ME, MES PETITES!
LET'S FINISH THIS!
A DOUBLE PARRY OF OUR PSYCHIC BLADES--
--SHOULD BE SUFFICIENT ENOUGH TO SCRAMBLE SAMURAI'S SYNAPTIC CONTROL--
SHFYEETHAK!
--AND WITH HIS STRINGS CUT, THE MARIONETTE FALLS--
--THE SHOW FINISHES, THE PUPPETEER'S CHARADE AN UNSUCCESSFUL ONE.

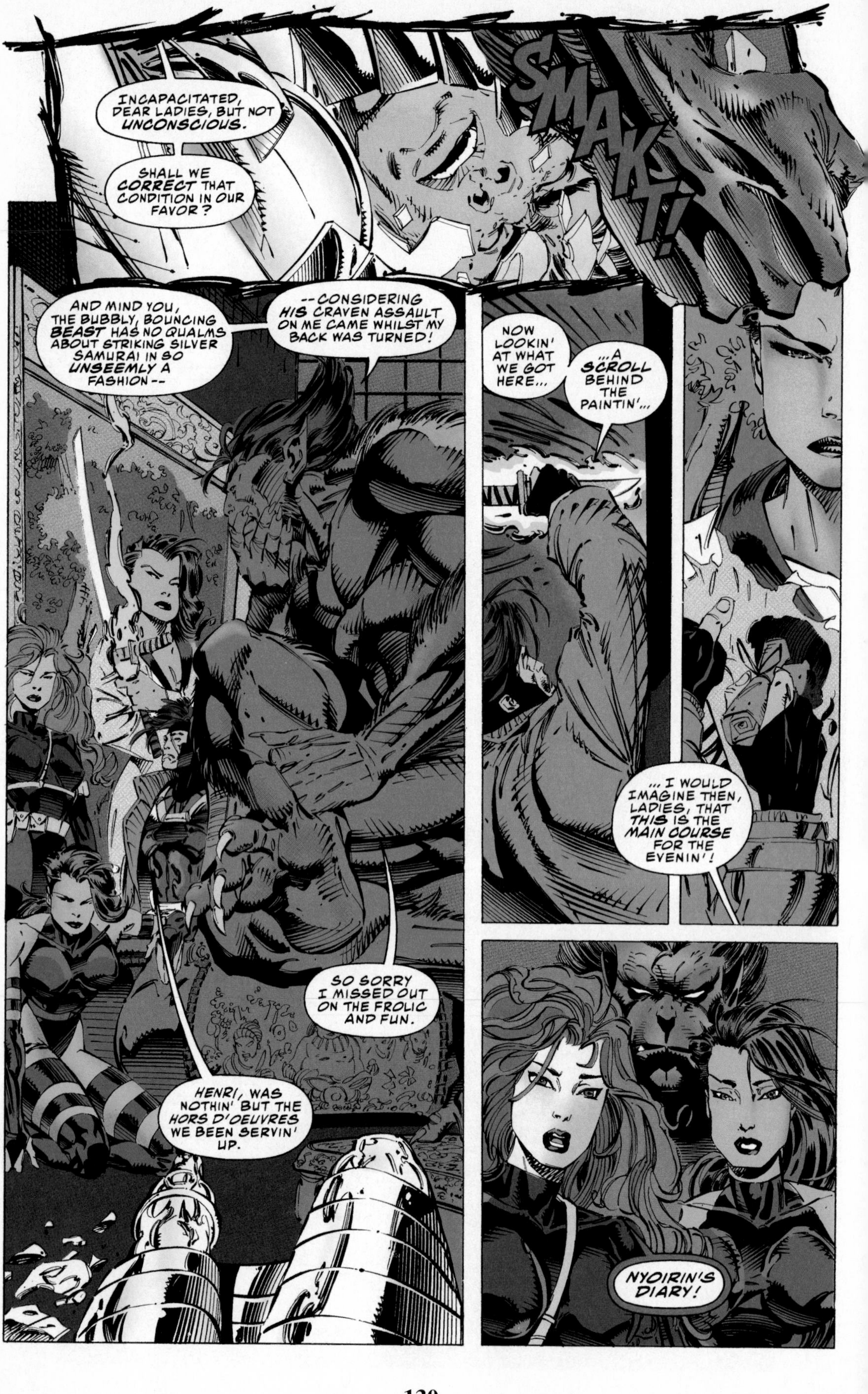

INCAPACITATED, DEAR LADIES, BUT NOT UNCONSCIOUS.
SHALL WE CORRECT THAT CONDITION IN OUR FAVOR?
SMAKT!
AND MIND YOU, THE BUBBLY, BOUNCING BEAST HAS NO QUALMS ABOUT STRIKING SILVER SAMURAI IN SO UNSEEMLY A FASHION --
-- CONSIDERING HIS CRAVEN ASSAULT ON ME CAME WHILST MY BACK WAS TURNED!
SO SORRY I MISSED OUT ON THE FROLIC AND FUN.
HENRI, WAS NOTHIN' BUT THE HORS D'OEUVRES WE BEEN SERVIN' UP.
NOW LOOKIN' AT WHAT WE GOT HERE...
...A SCROLL BEHIND THE PAINTIN'...
... I WOULD IMAGINE THEN, LADIES, THAT THIS IS THE MAIN COURSE FOR THE EVENIN'!
NYOIRIN'S DIARY!

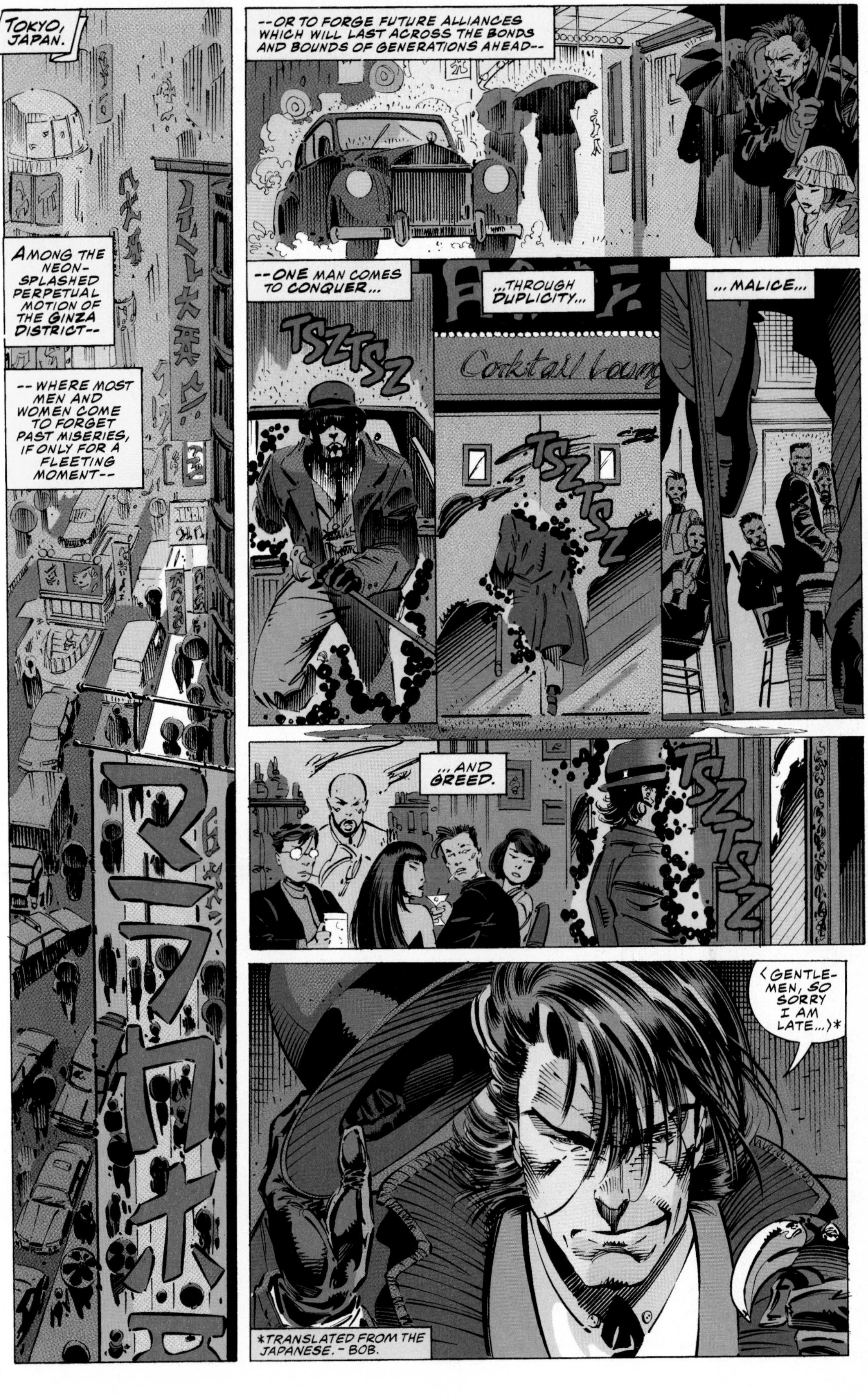

TOKYO, JAPAN.
AMONG THE NEON-SPLASHED PERPETUAL MOTION OF THE GINZA DISTRICT--
-- WHERE MOST MEN AND WOMEN COME TO FORGET PAST MISERIES, IF ONLY FOR A FLEETING MOMENT--
--OR TO FORGE FUTURE ALLIANCES WHICH WILL LAST ACROSS THE BONDS AND BOUNDS OF GENERATIONS AHEAD--
--ONE MAN COMES TO CONQUER...
TSZTSZ
...THROUGH DUPLICITY...
Cocktail Lounge
TSZTSZ
...MALICE...
...AND GREED.
TSZTSZ
<GENTLEMEN, SO SORRY I AM LATE...>*
*TRANSLATED FROM THE JAPANESE. - BOB.

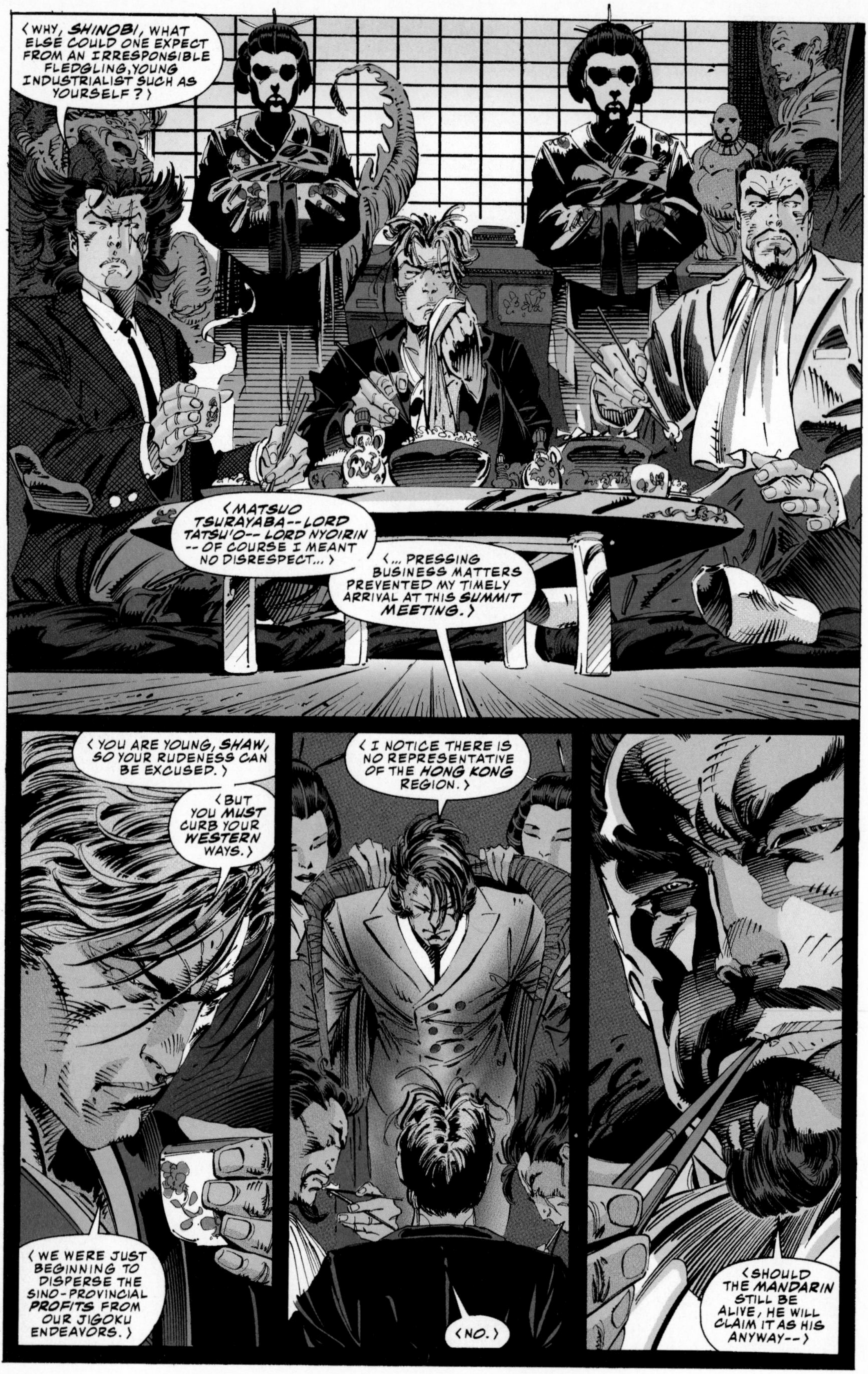
‹WHY, SHINOBI, WHAT ELSE COULD ONE EXPECT FROM AN IRRESPONSIBLE FLEDGLING, YOUNG INDUSTRIALIST SUCH AS YOURSELF?›
‹MATSUO TSURAYABA--LORD TATSU'O-- LORD NYOIRIN -- OF COURSE I MEANT NO DISRESPECT...›
‹... PRESSING BUSINESS MATTERS PREVENTED MY TIMELY ARRIVAL AT THIS SUMMIT MEETING.›
‹YOU ARE YOUNG, SHAW, SO YOUR RUDENESS CAN BE EXCUSED.›
‹BUT YOU MUST CURB YOUR WESTERN WAYS.›
‹WE WERE JUST BEGINNING TO DISPERSE THE SINO-PROVINCIAL PROFITS FROM OUR JIGOKU ENDEAVORS.›
‹I NOTICE THERE IS NO REPRESENTATIVE OF THE HONG KONG REGION.›
‹NO.›
‹SHOULD THE MANDARIN STILL BE ALIVE, HE WILL CLAIM IT AS HIS ANYWAY--›

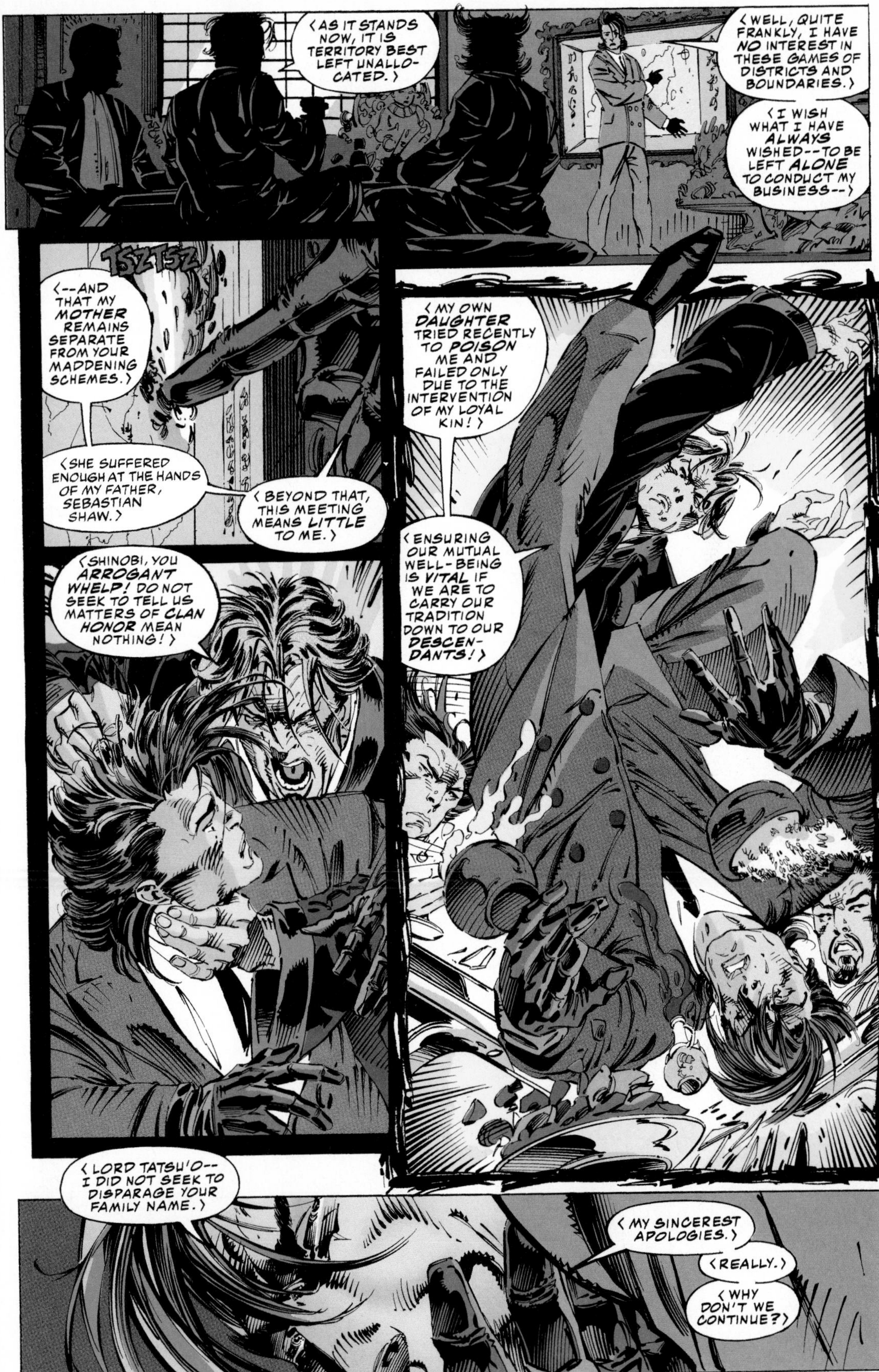

‹AS IT STANDS NOW, IT IS TERRITORY BEST LEFT UNALLOCATED.›
‹WELL, QUITE FRANKLY, I HAVE NO INTEREST IN THESE GAMES OF DISTRICTS AND BOUNDARIES.›
‹I WISH WHAT I HAVE ALWAYS WISHED--TO BE LEFT ALONE TO CONDUCT MY BUSINESS--›
TSZTSZ
‹--AND THAT MY MOTHER REMAINS SEPARATE FROM YOUR MADDENING SCHEMES.›
‹SHE SUFFERED ENOUGH AT THE HANDS OF MY FATHER, SEBASTIAN SHAW.›
‹BEYOND THAT, THIS MEETING MEANS LITTLE TO ME.›
‹MY OWN DAUGHTER TRIED RECENTLY TO POISON ME AND FAILED ONLY DUE TO THE INTERVENTION OF MY LOYAL KIN!›
‹ENSURING OUR MUTUAL WELL-BEING IS VITAL IF WE ARE TO CARRY OUR TRADITION DOWN TO OUR DESCENDANTS!›
‹SHINOBI, YOU ARROGANT WHELP! DO NOT SEEK TO TELL US MATTERS OF CLAN HONOR MEAN NOTHING!›
‹LORD TATSU'O-- I DID NOT SEEK TO DISPARAGE YOUR FAMILY NAME.›
‹MY SINCEREST APOLOGIES.›
‹REALLY.›
‹WHY DON'T WE CONTINUE?›

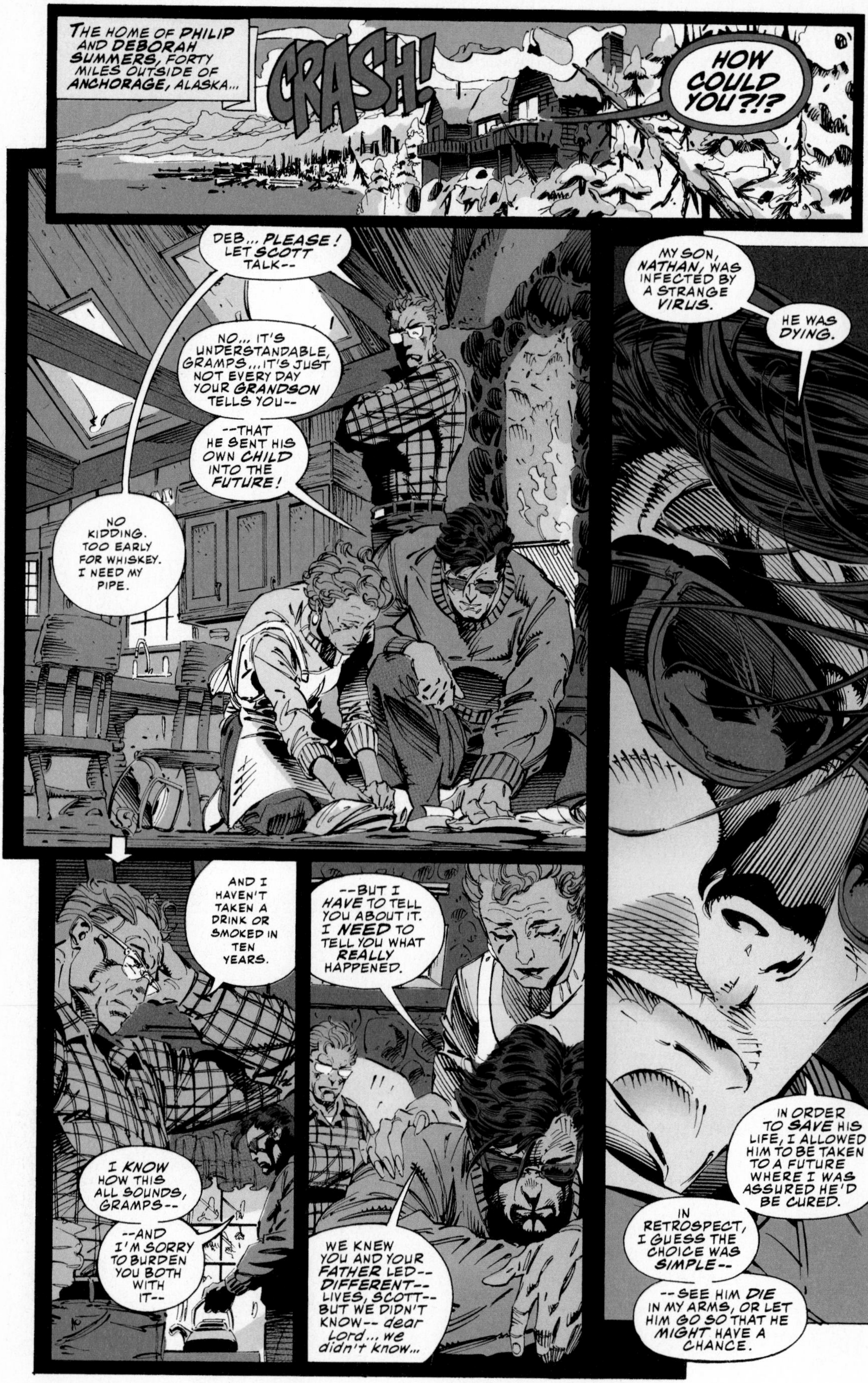
THE HOME OF PHILIP AND DEBORAH SUMMERS, FORTY MILES OUTSIDE OF ANCHORAGE, ALASKA...
CRASH!
HOW COULD YOU?!?
DEB... PLEASE! LET SCOTT TALK--
NO... IT'S UNDERSTANDABLE, GRAMPS... IT'S JUST NOT EVERY DAY YOUR GRANDSON TELLS YOU--
--THAT HE SENT HIS OWN CHILD INTO THE FUTURE!
NO KIDDING. TOO EARLY FOR WHISKEY. I NEED MY PIPE.
MY SON, NATHAN, WAS INFECTED BY A STRANGE VIRUS.
HE WAS DYING.
AND I HAVEN'T TAKEN A DRINK OR SMOKED IN TEN YEARS.
I KNOW HOW THIS ALL SOUNDS, GRAMPS--
--AND I'M SORRY TO BURDEN YOU BOTH WITH IT--
--BUT I HAVE TO TELL YOU ABOUT IT. I NEED TO TELL YOU WHAT REALLY HAPPENED.
WE KNEW YOU AND YOUR FATHER LED-- DIFFERENT-- LIVES, SCOTT-- BUT WE DIDN'T KNOW-- dear Lord... we didn't know...
IN ORDER TO SAVE HIS LIFE, I ALLOWED HIM TO BE TAKEN TO A FUTURE WHERE I WAS ASSURED HE'D BE CURED.
IN RETROSPECT, I GUESS THE CHOICE WAS SIMPLE--
--SEE HIM DIE IN MY ARMS, OR LET HIM GO SO THAT HE MIGHT HAVE A CHANCE.

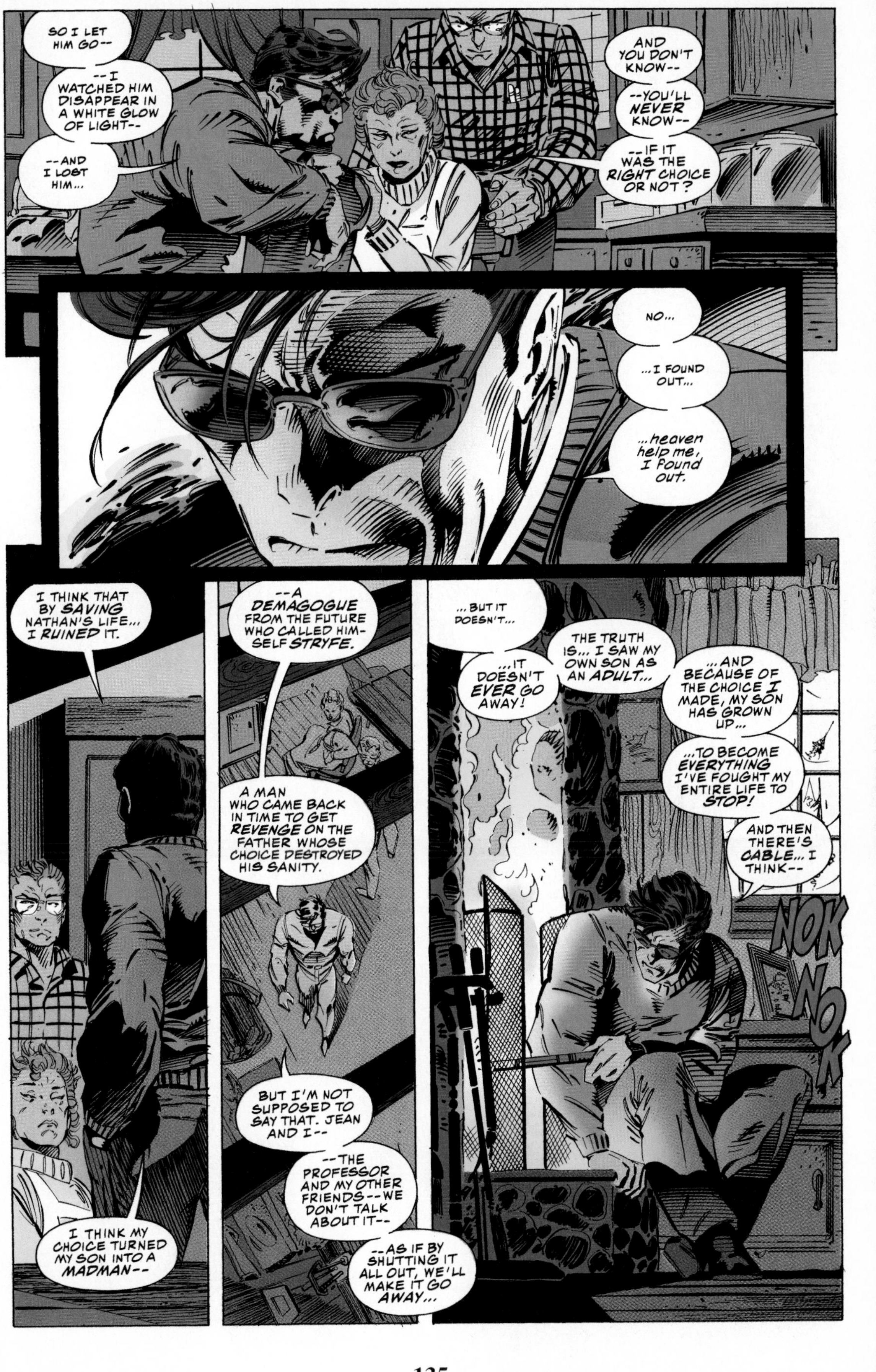
SO I LET HIM GO--
--I WATCHED HIM DISAPPEAR IN A WHITE GLOW OF LIGHT--
--AND I LOST HIM...
AND YOU DON'T KNOW--
--YOU'LL NEVER KNOW--
--IF IT WAS THE RIGHT CHOICE OR NOT?
NO...
...I FOUND OUT...
...heaven help me, I found out.
I THINK THAT BY SAVING NATHAN'S LIFE... I RUINED IT.
I THINK MY CHOICE TURNED MY SON INTO A MADMAN--
--A DEMAGOGUE FROM THE FUTURE WHO CALLED HIMSELF STRYFE.
A MAN WHO CAME BACK IN TIME TO GET REVENGE ON THE FATHER WHOSE CHOICE DESTROYED HIS SANITY.
BUT I'M NOT SUPPOSED TO SAY THAT. JEAN AND I--
--THE PROFESSOR AND MY OTHER FRIENDS--WE DON'T TALK ABOUT IT--
--AS IF BY SHUTTING IT ALL OUT, WE'LL MAKE IT GO AWAY...
...BUT IT DOESN'T...
...IT DOESN'T EVER GO AWAY!
THE TRUTH IS... I SAW MY OWN SON AS AN ADULT...
...AND BECAUSE OF THE CHOICE I MADE, MY SON HAS GROWN UP...
...TO BECOME EVERYTHING I'VE FOUGHT MY ENTIRE LIFE TO STOP!
AND THEN THERE'S CABLE... I THINK--
NOK
NOK
NOK

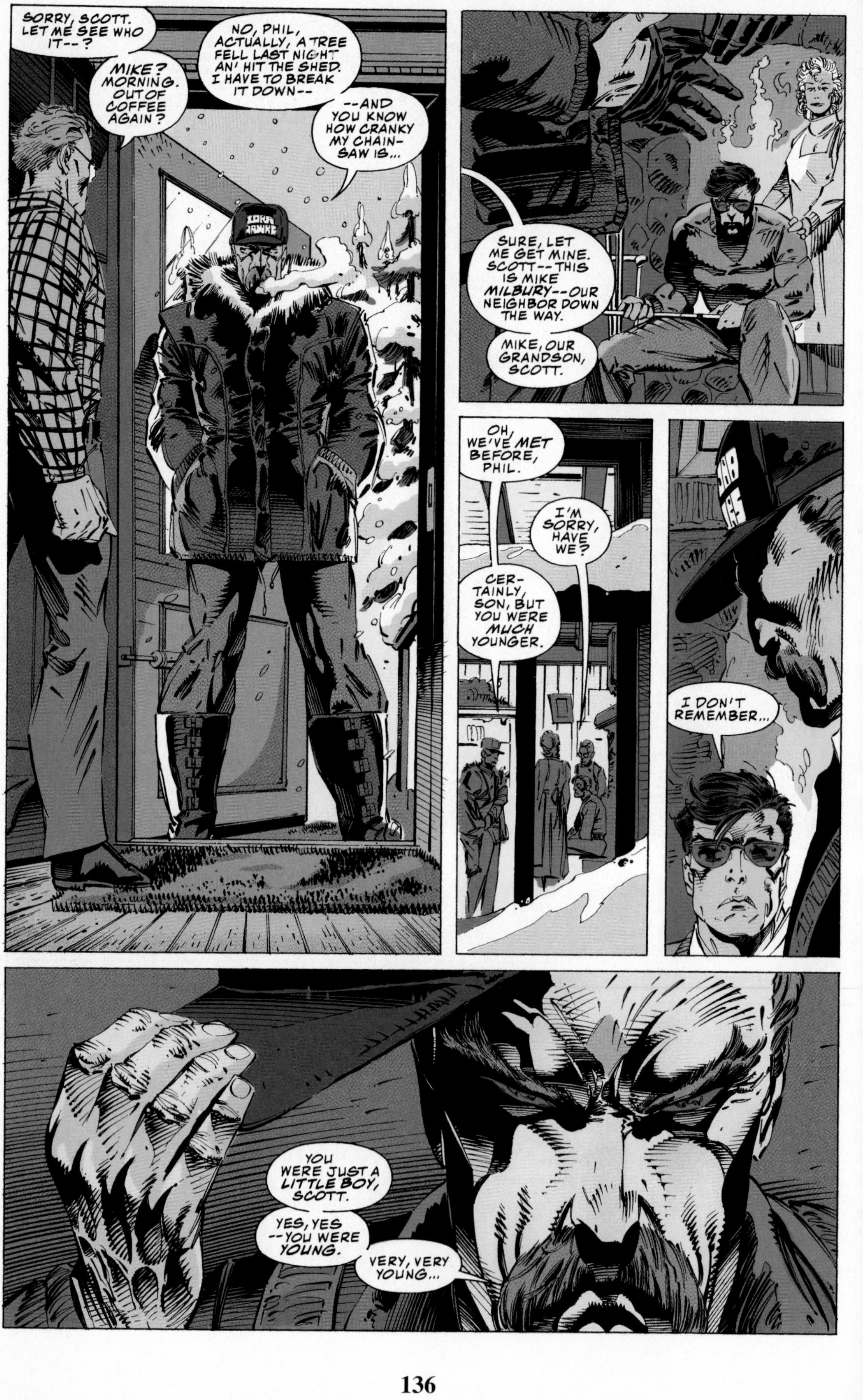
SORRY, SCOTT. LET ME SEE WHO IT--?
MIKE? MORNING. OUT OF COFFEE AGAIN?
NO, PHIL, ACTUALLY, A TREE FELL LAST NIGHT AN' HIT THE SHED. I HAVE TO BREAK IT DOWN--
--AND YOU KNOW HOW CRANKY MY CHAIN-SAW IS...
SURE, LET ME GET MINE. SCOTT--THIS IS MIKE MILBURY--OUR NEIGHBOR DOWN THE WAY.
MIKE, OUR GRANDSON, SCOTT.
OH, WE'VE MET BEFORE, PHIL.
I'M SORRY, HAVE WE?
CER-TAINLY, SON, BUT YOU WERE MUCH YOUNGER.
I DON'T REMEMBER...
YOU WERE JUST A LITTLE BOY, SCOTT.
YES, YES --YOU WERE YOUNG.
VERY, VERY YOUNG...

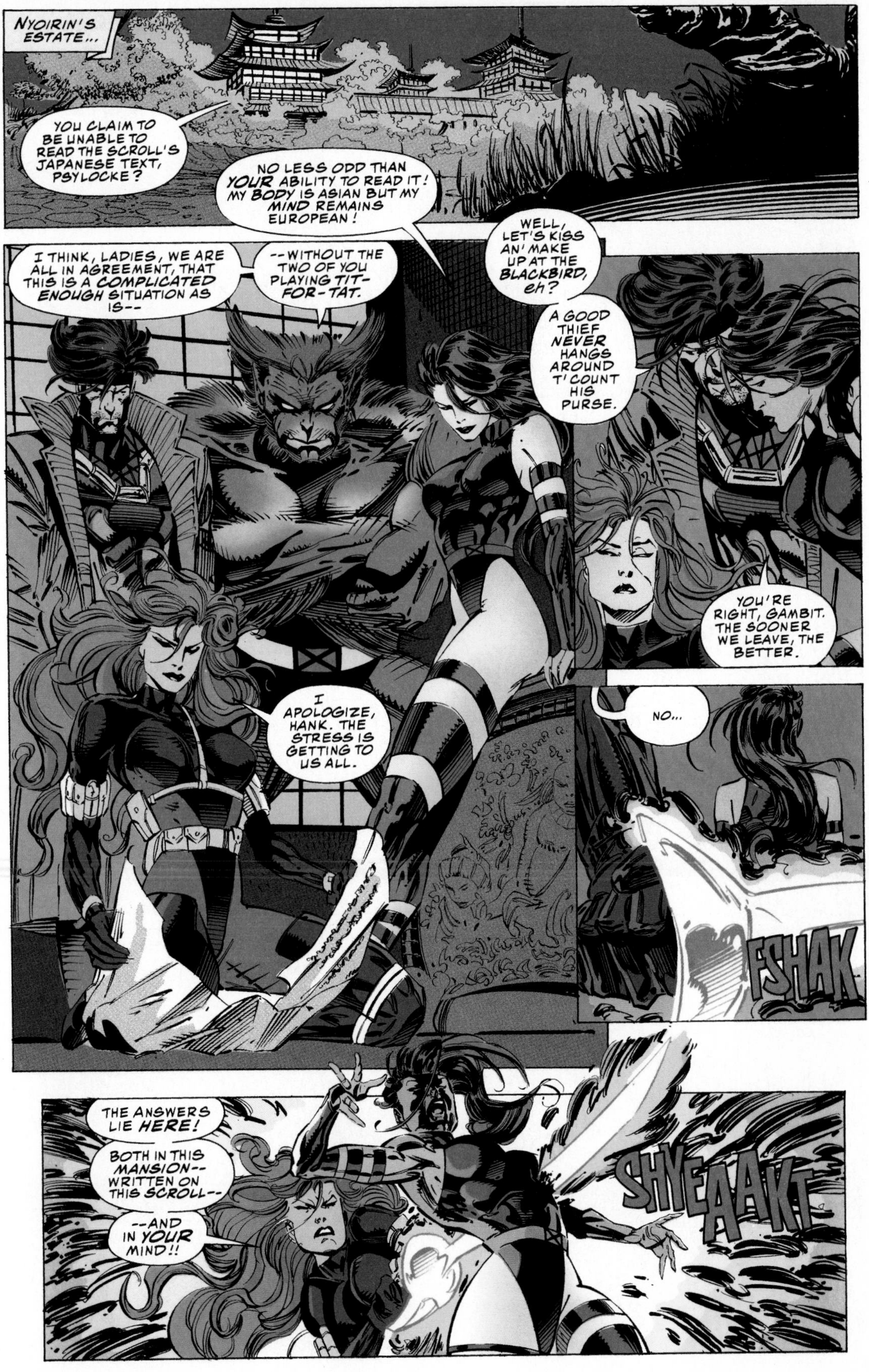
NYOIRIN'S ESTATE...
YOU CLAIM TO BE UNABLE TO READ THE SCROLL'S JAPANESE TEXT, PSYLOCKE?
NO LESS ODD THAN YOUR ABILITY TO READ IT! MY BODY IS ASIAN BUT MY MIND REMAINS EUROPEAN!
I THINK, LADIES, WE ARE ALL IN AGREEMENT, THAT THIS IS A COMPLICATED ENOUGH SITUATION AS IS--
--WITHOUT THE TWO OF YOU PLAYING TIT-FOR-TAT.
WELL, LET'S KISS AN' MAKE UP AT THE BLACKBIRD, eh?
A GOOD THIEF NEVER HANGS AROUND T' COUNT HIS PURSE.
I APOLOGIZE, HANK. THE STRESS IS GETTING TO US ALL.
YOU'RE RIGHT, GAMBIT. THE SOONER WE LEAVE, THE BETTER.
NO...
FSHAK
THE ANSWERS LIE HERE!
BOTH IN THIS MANSION-- WRITTEN ON THIS SCROLL--
--AND IN YOUR MIND!!
SHYEAAKT

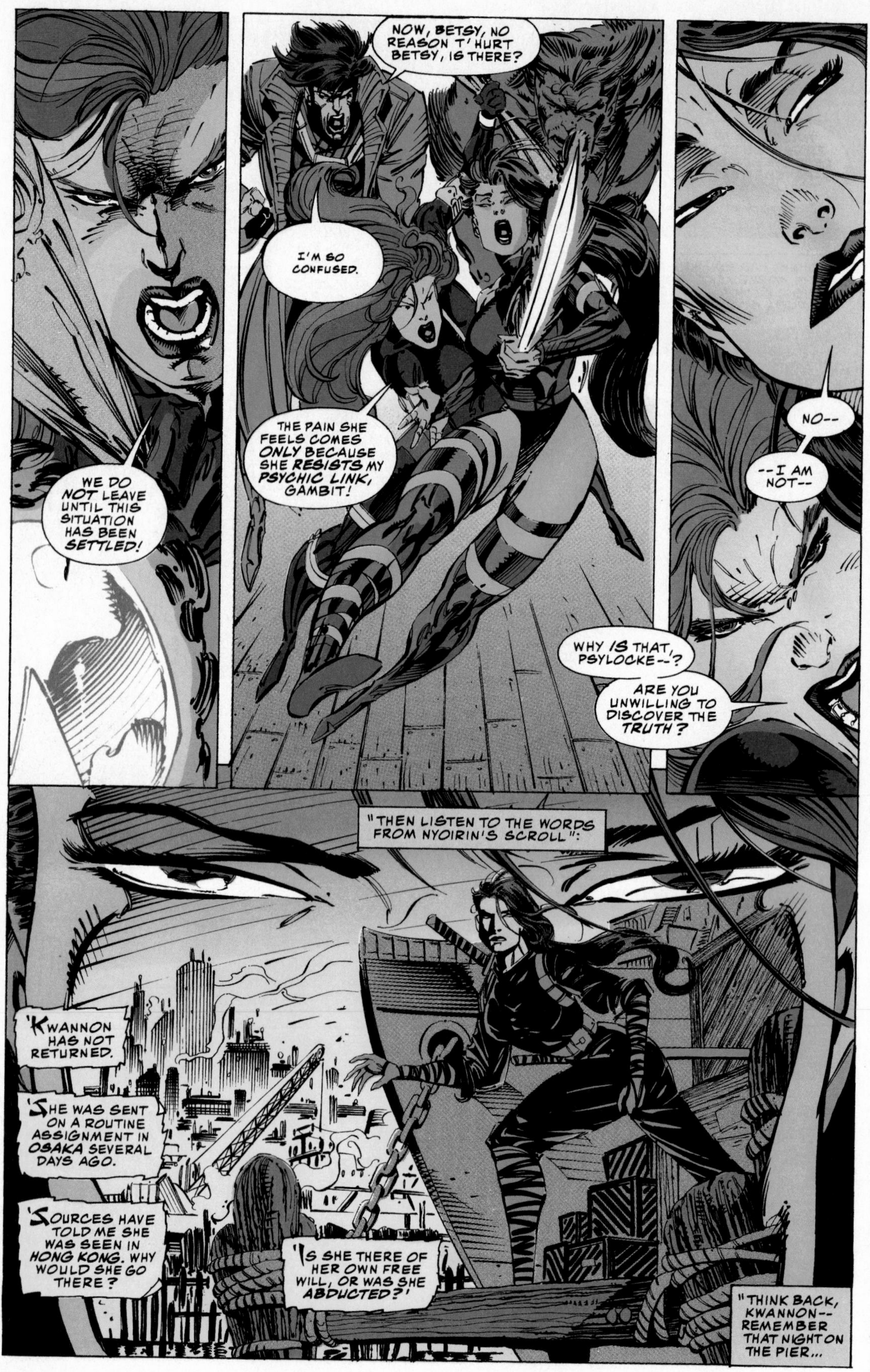

WE DO NOT LEAVE UNTIL THIS SITUATION HAS BEEN SETTLED!
NOW, BETSY, NO REASON T' HURT BETSY, IS THERE?
I'M SO CONFUSED.
THE PAIN SHE FEELS COMES ONLY BECAUSE SHE RESISTS MY PSYCHIC LINK, GAMBIT!
NO--
--I AM NOT--
WHY IS THAT, PSYLOCKE--?
ARE YOU UNWILLING TO DISCOVER THE TRUTH?
"THEN LISTEN TO THE WORDS FROM NYOIRIN'S SCROLL":
'KWANNON HAS NOT RETURNED.
'SHE WAS SENT ON A ROUTINE ASSIGNMENT IN OSAKA SEVERAL DAYS AGO.
'SOURCES HAVE TOLD ME SHE WAS SEEN IN HONG KONG. WHY WOULD SHE GO THERE?
'IS SHE THERE OF HER OWN FREE WILL, OR WAS SHE ABDUCTED?'
"THINK BACK, KWANNON--REMEMBER THAT NIGHT ON THE PIER...

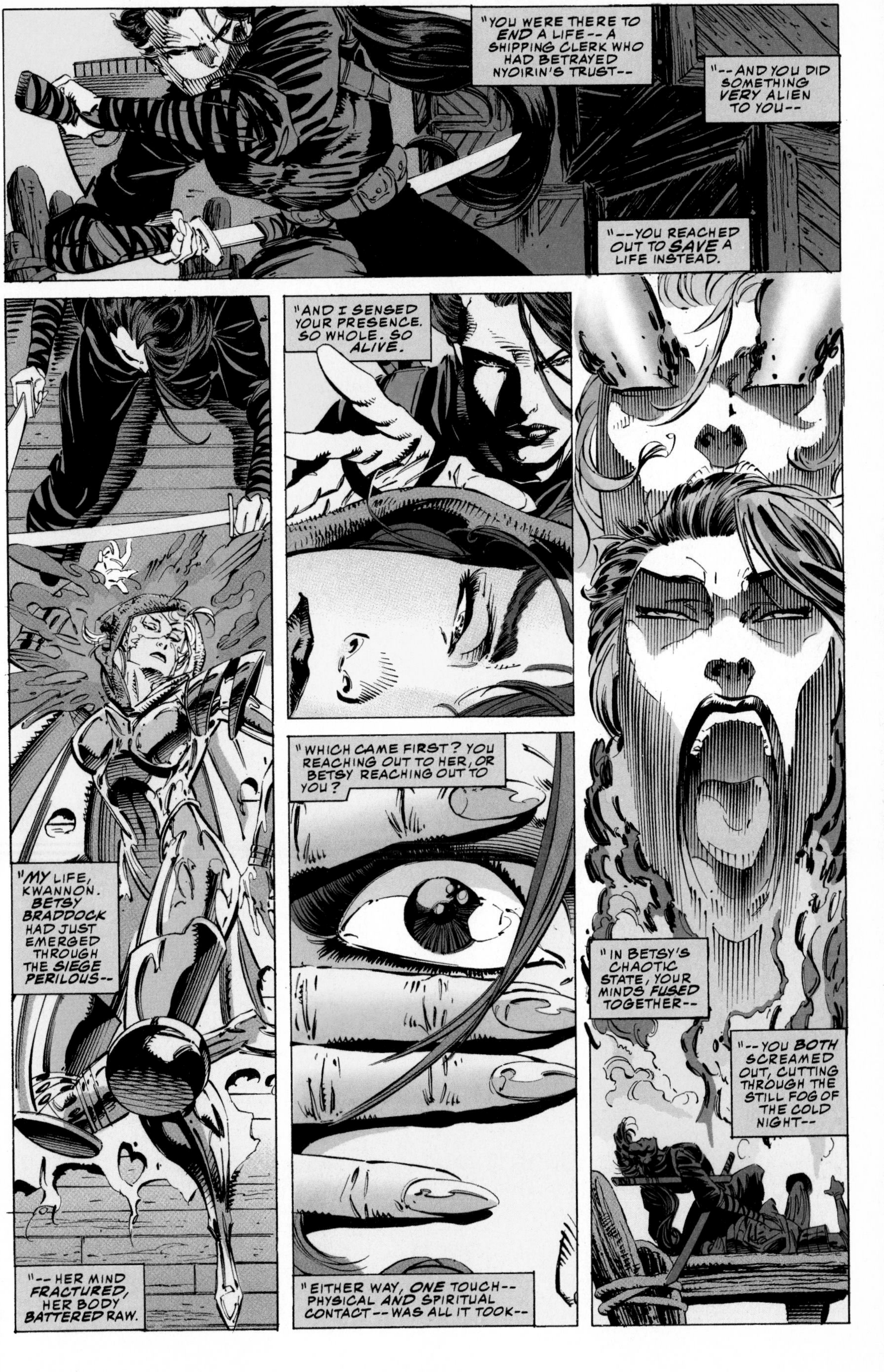
"YOU WERE THERE TO END A LIFE -- A SHIPPING CLERK WHO HAD BETRAYED NYOIRIN'S TRUST--
"--AND YOU DID SOMETHING VERY ALIEN TO YOU--
"--YOU REACHED OUT TO SAVE A LIFE INSTEAD.
"AND I SENSED YOUR PRESENCE. SO WHOLE. SO ALIVE.
"MY LIFE, KWANNON. BETSY BRADDOCK HAD JUST EMERGED THROUGH THE SIEGE PERILOUS--
"-- HER MIND FRACTURED, HER BODY BATTERED RAW.
"WHICH CAME FIRST? YOU REACHING OUT TO HER, OR BETSY REACHING OUT TO YOU?
"EITHER WAY, ONE TOUCH-- PHYSICAL AND SPIRITUAL CONTACT--WAS ALL IT TOOK--
"IN BETSY'S CHAOTIC STATE, YOUR MINDS FUSED TOGETHER--
"--YOU BOTH SCREAMED OUT, CUTTING THROUGH THE STILL FOG OF THE COLD NIGHT--

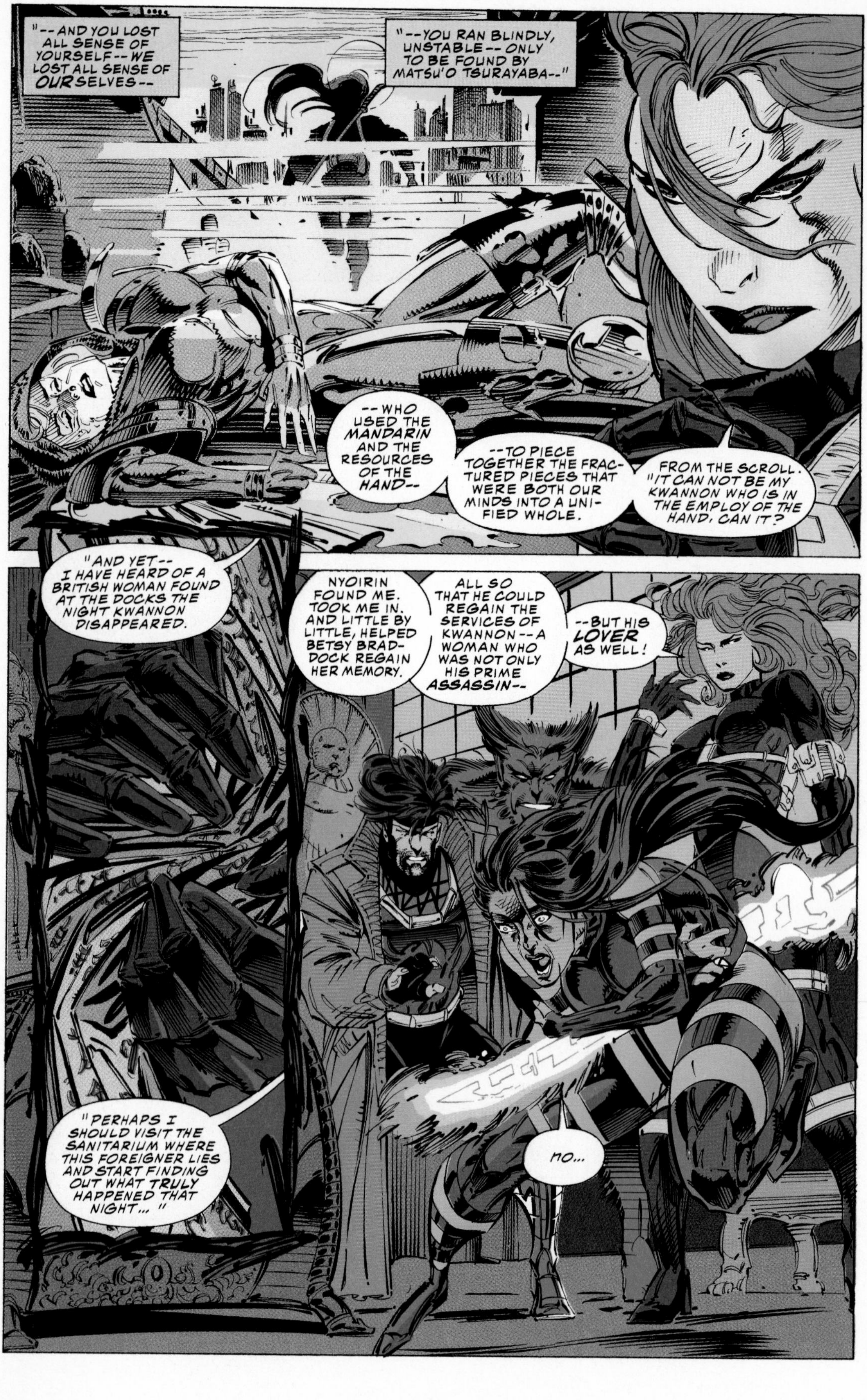
"--AND YOU LOST ALL SENSE OF YOURSELF--WE LOST ALL SENSE OF OURSELVES--
"--YOU RAN BLINDLY, UNSTABLE--ONLY TO BE FOUND BY MATSU'O TSURAYABA--"
--WHO USED THE MANDARIN AND THE RESOURCES OF THE HAND--
--TO PIECE TOGETHER THE FRACTURED PIECES THAT WERE BOTH OUR MINDS INTO A UNIFIED WHOLE.
FROM THE SCROLL. "IT CAN NOT BE MY KWANNON WHO IS IN THE EMPLOY OF THE HAND, CAN IT?
"AND YET-- I HAVE HEARD OF A BRITISH WOMAN FOUND AT THE DOCKS THE NIGHT KWANNON DISAPPEARED.
NYOIRIN FOUND ME. TOOK ME IN. AND LITTLE BY LITTLE, HELPED BETSY BRADDOCK REGAIN HER MEMORY.
ALL SO THAT HE COULD REGAIN THE SERVICES OF KWANNON--A WOMAN WHO WAS NOT ONLY HIS PRIME ASSASSIN--
--BUT HIS LOVER AS WELL!
"PERHAPS I SHOULD VISIT THE SANITARIUM WHERE THIS FOREIGNER LIES AND START FINDING OUT WHAT TRULY HAPPENED THAT NIGHT..."
NO...

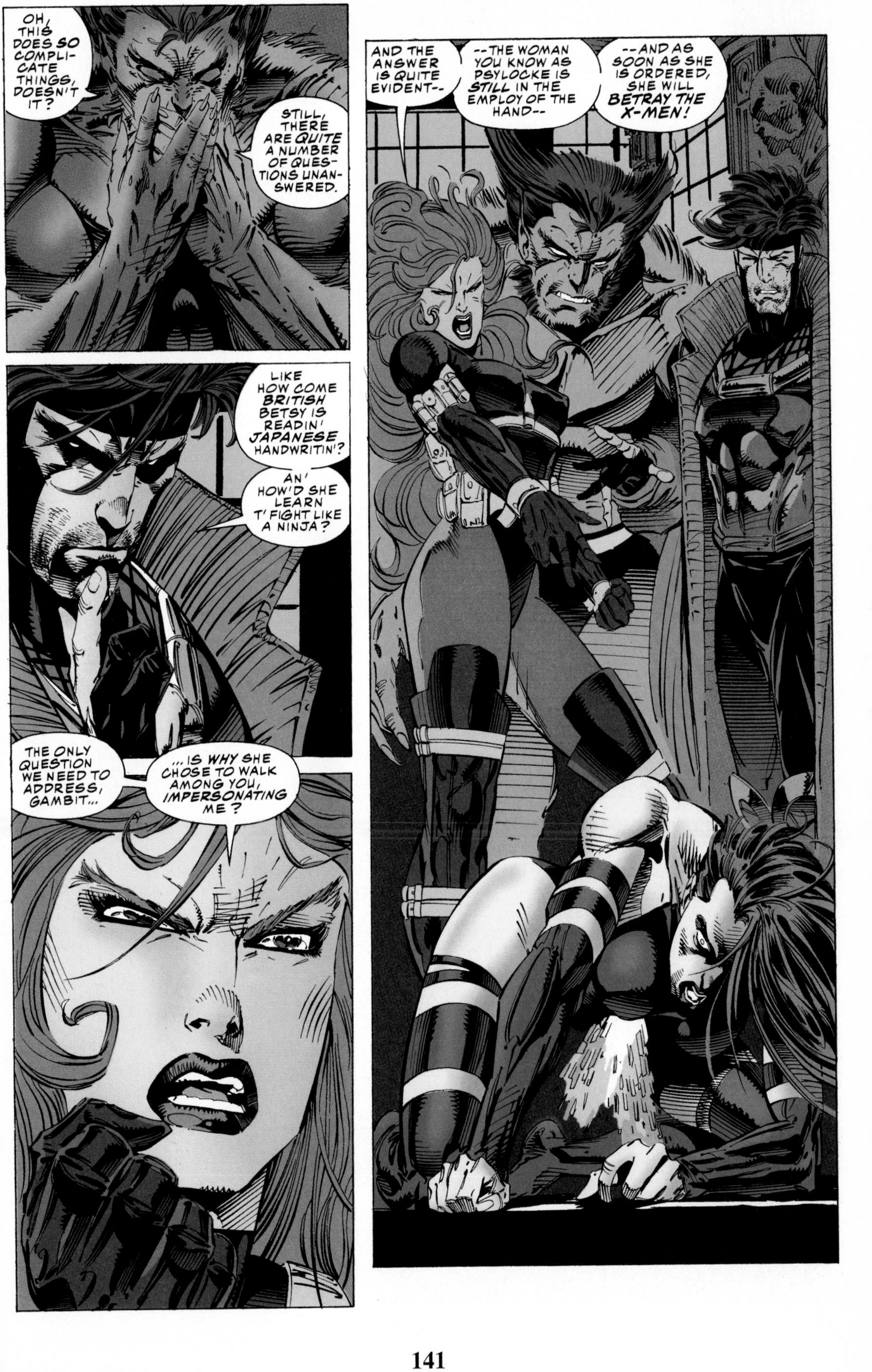
OH, THIS DOES SO COMPLICATE THINGS, DOESN'T IT?
STILL, THERE ARE QUITE A NUMBER OF QUESTIONS UNANSWERED.
LIKE HOW COME BRITISH BETSY IS READIN' JAPANESE HANDWRITIN'?
AN' HOW'D SHE LEARN T' FIGHT LIKE A NINJA?
THE ONLY QUESTION WE NEED TO ADDRESS, GAMBIT...
...IS WHY SHE CHOSE TO WALK AMONG YOU, IMPERSONATING ME?
AND THE ANSWER IS QUITE EVIDENT--
--THE WOMAN YOU KNOW AS PSYLOCKE IS STILL IN THE EMPLOY OF THE HAND--
--AND AS SOON AS SHE IS ORDERED, SHE WILL BETRAY THE X-MEN!

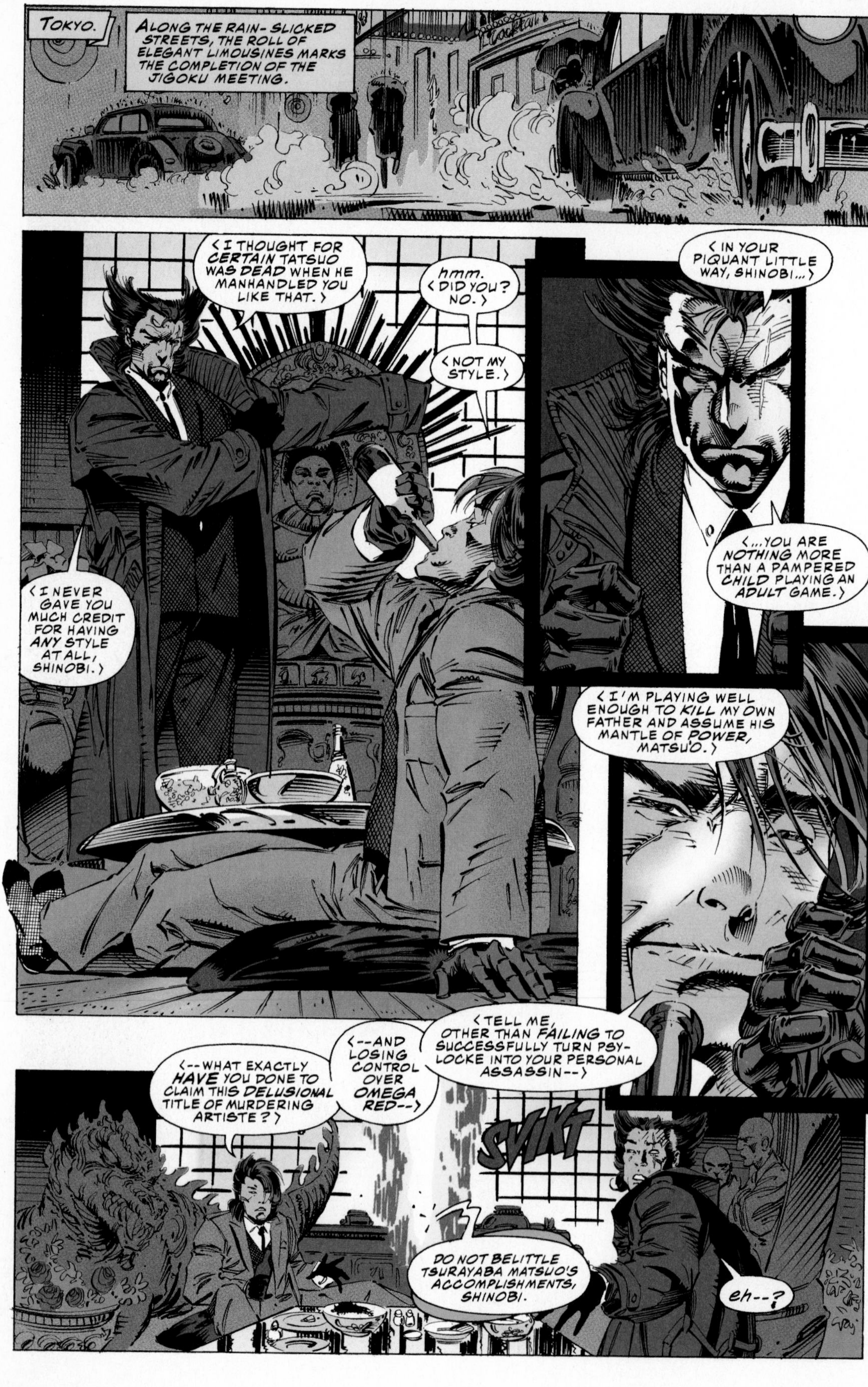
TOKYO.
ALONG THE RAIN-SLICKED STREETS, THE ROLL OF ELEGANT LIMOUSINES MARKS THE COMPLETION OF THE JIGOKU MEETING.
< I THOUGHT FOR CERTAIN TATSUO WAS DEAD WHEN HE MANHANDLED YOU LIKE THAT. >
hmm. < DID YOU? NO. >
< NOT MY STYLE. >
< I NEVER GAVE YOU MUCH CREDIT FOR HAVING ANY STYLE AT ALL, SHINOBI. >
< IN YOUR PIQUANT LITTLE WAY, SHINOBI... >
< ...YOU ARE NOTHING MORE THAN A PAMPERED CHILD PLAYING AN ADULT GAME. >
< I'M PLAYING WELL ENOUGH TO KILL MY OWN FATHER AND ASSUME HIS MANTLE OF POWER, MATSU'O. >
< TELL ME, OTHER THAN FAILING TO SUCCESSFULLY TURN PSY-LOCKE INTO YOUR PERSONAL ASSASSIN-- >
< --AND LOSING CONTROL OVER OMEGA RED-- >
< --WHAT EXACTLY HAVE YOU DONE TO CLAIM THIS DELUSIONAL TITLE OF MURDERING ARTISTE? >
SVIKT
DO NOT BELITTLE TSURAYABA MATSUO'S ACCOMPLISHMENTS, SHINOBI.
eh--?

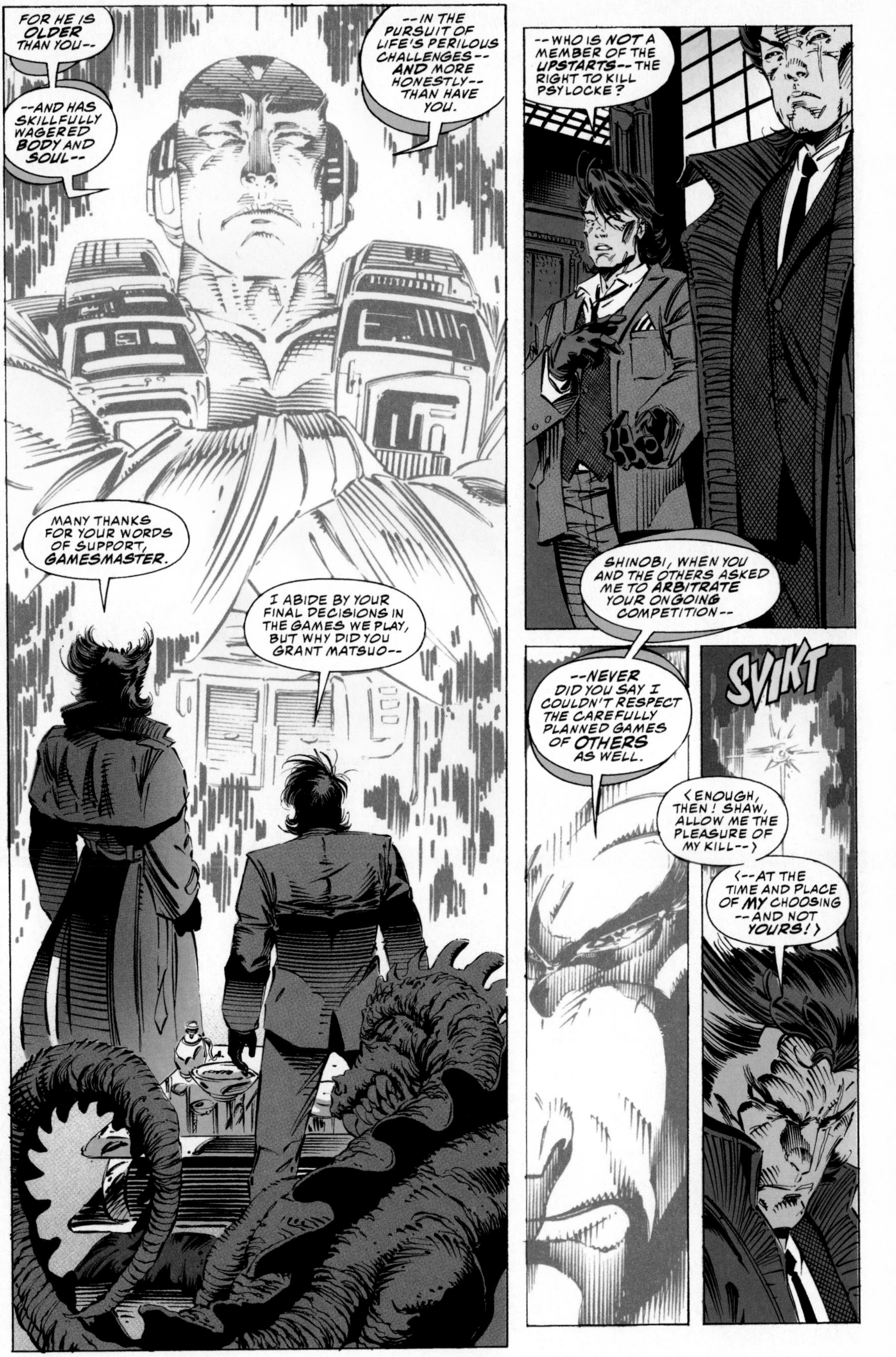
FOR HE IS OLDER THAN YOU--
--AND HAS SKILLFULLY WAGERED BODY AND SOUL--
--IN THE PURSUIT OF LIFE'S PERILOUS CHALLENGES--AND MORE HONESTLY--THAN HAVE YOU.
MANY THANKS FOR YOUR WORDS OF SUPPORT, GAMESMASTER.
I ABIDE BY YOUR FINAL DECISIONS IN THE GAMES WE PLAY, BUT WHY DID YOU GRANT MATSUO--
--WHO IS NOT A MEMBER OF THE UPSTARTS--THE RIGHT TO KILL PSYLOCKE?
SHINOBI, WHEN YOU AND THE OTHERS ASKED ME TO ARBITRATE YOUR ONGOING COMPETITION--
--NEVER DID YOU SAY I COULDN'T RESPECT THE CAREFULLY PLANNED GAMES OF OTHERS AS WELL.
SVIKT
<ENOUGH, THEN! SHAW, ALLOW ME THE PLEASURE OF MY KILL-->
<--AT THE TIME AND PLACE OF MY CHOOSING --AND NOT YOURS!>

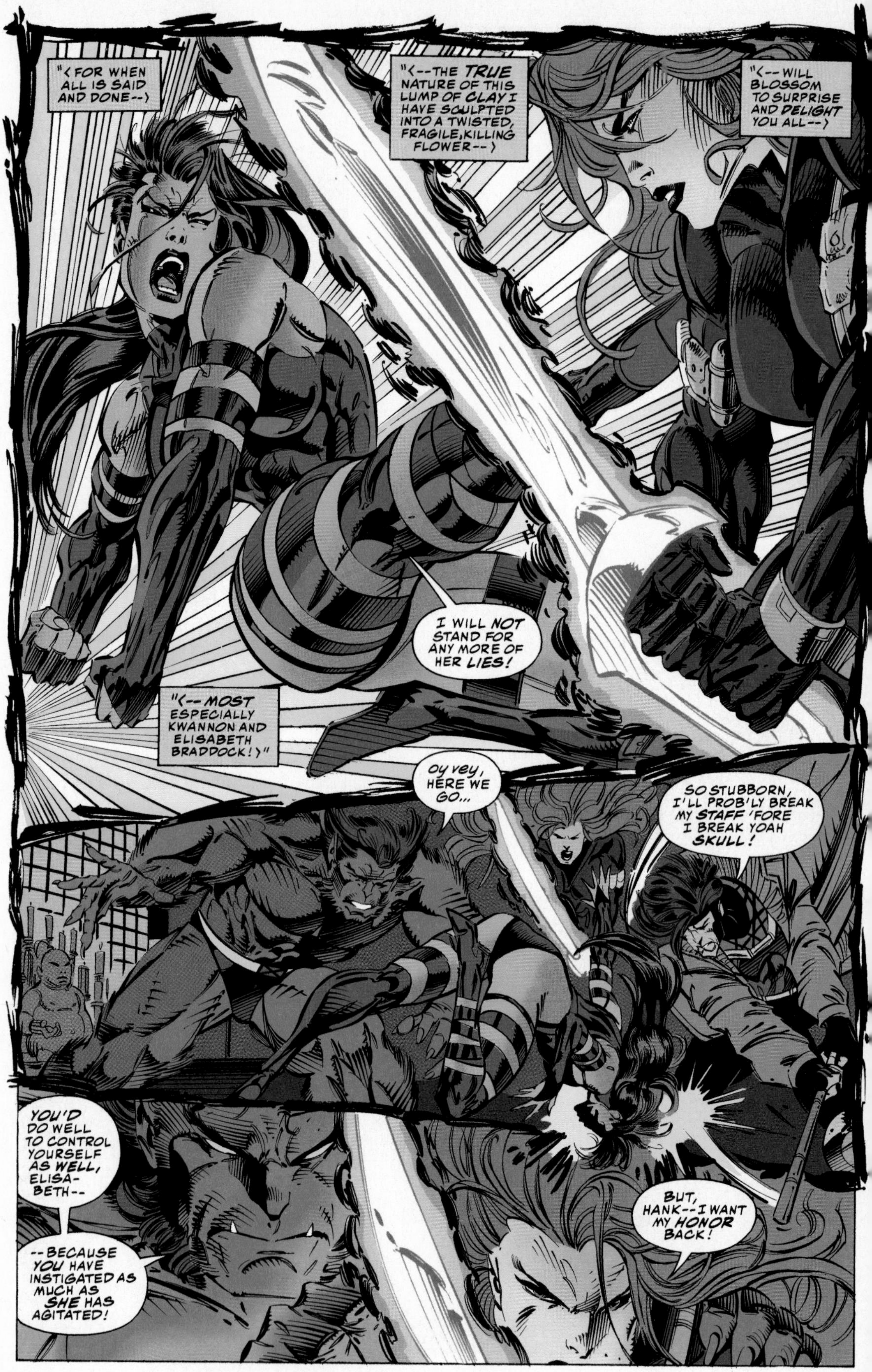
"< FOR WHEN ALL IS SAID AND DONE-->
"<--THE TRUE NATURE OF THIS LUMP OF CLAY I HAVE SCULPTED INTO A TWISTED, FRAGILE, KILLING FLOWER-->
"<--WILL BLOSSOM TO SURPRISE AND DELIGHT YOU ALL-->
I WILL NOT STAND FOR ANY MORE OF HER LIES!
"<--MOST ESPECIALLY KWANNON AND ELISABETH BRADDOCK!>"
OY VEY, HERE WE GO...
SO STUBBORN, I'LL PROB'LY BREAK MY STAFF 'FORE I BREAK YOAH SKULL!
YOU'D DO WELL TO CONTROL YOURSELF AS WELL, ELISA-BETH--
--BECAUSE YOU HAVE INSTIGATED AS MUCH AS SHE HAS AGITATED!
BUT, HANK--I WANT MY HONOR BACK!

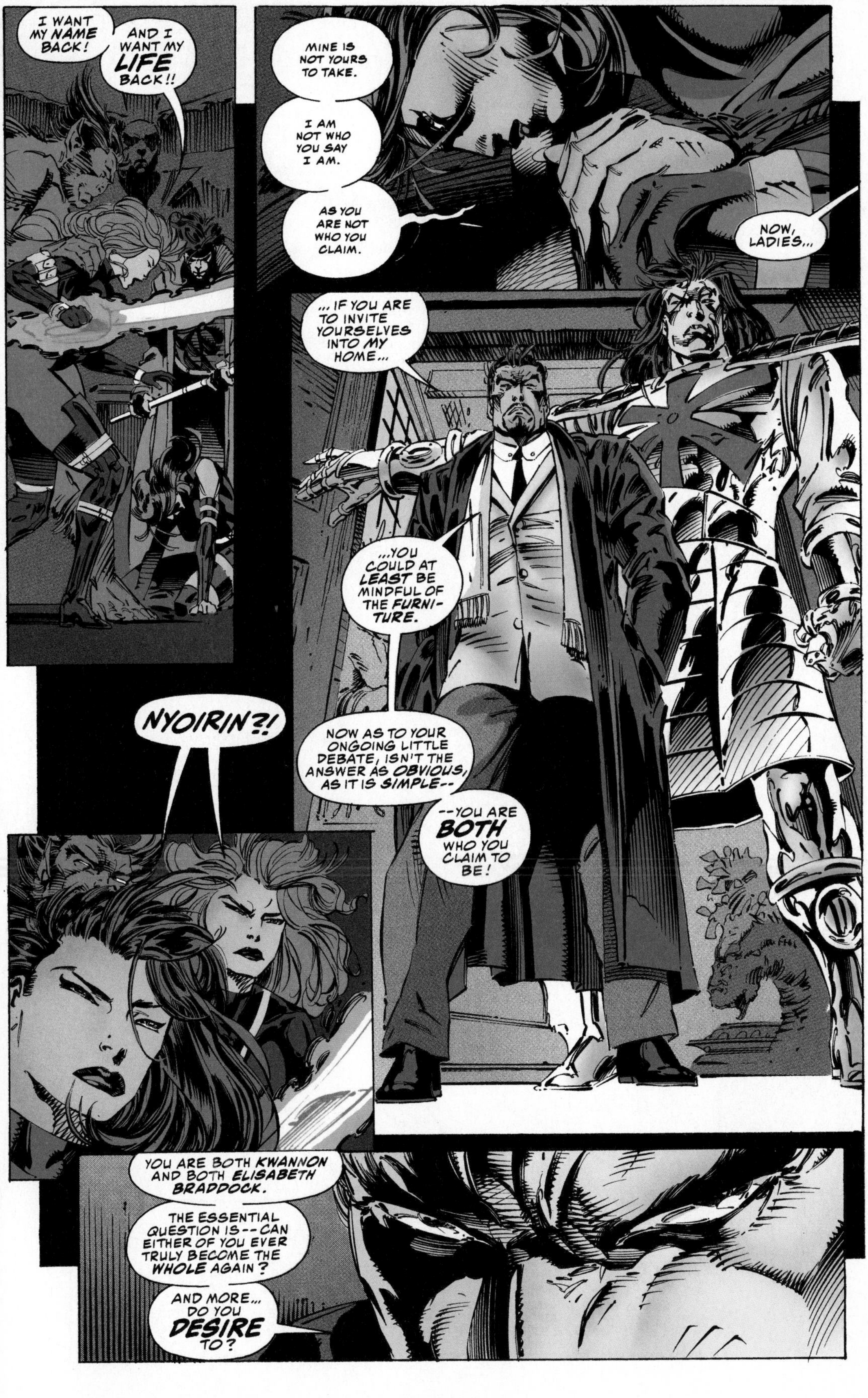
I WANT MY NAME BACK!
AND I WANT MY LIFE BACK!!
MINE IS NOT YOURS TO TAKE.
I AM NOT WHO YOU SAY I AM.
AS YOU ARE NOT WHO YOU CLAIM.
NOW, LADIES...
...IF YOU ARE TO INVITE YOURSELVES INTO MY HOME...
...YOU COULD AT LEAST BE MINDFUL OF THE FURNITURE.
NYOIRIN?!
NOW AS TO YOUR ONGOING LITTLE DEBATE, ISN'T THE ANSWER AS OBVIOUS, AS IT IS SIMPLE--
--YOU ARE BOTH WHO YOU CLAIM TO BE!
YOU ARE BOTH KWANNON AND BOTH ELISABETH BRADDOCK.
THE ESSENTIAL QUESTION IS--CAN EITHER OF YOU EVER TRULY BECOME THE WHOLE AGAIN?
AND MORE... DO YOU DESIRE TO?

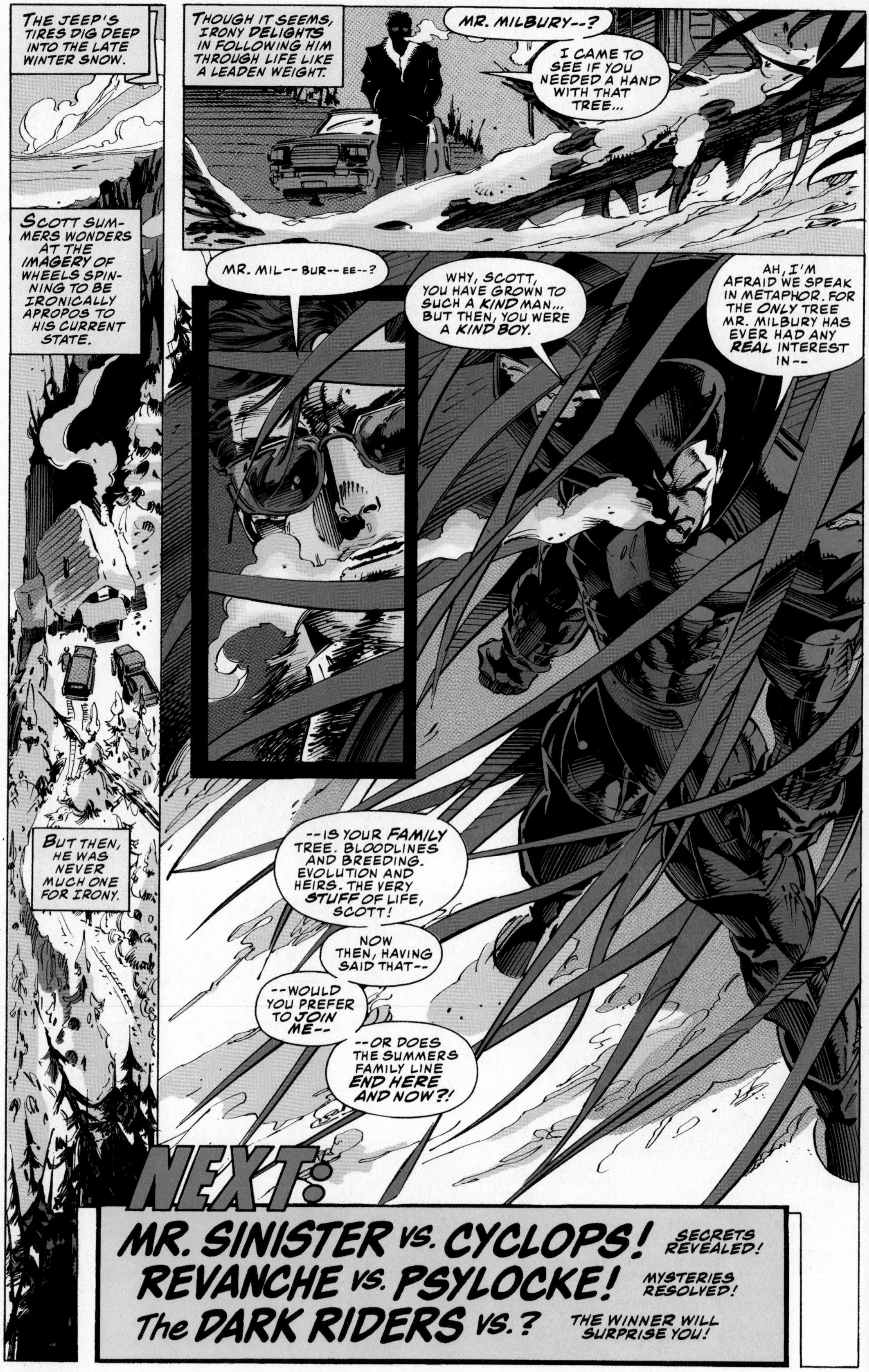
THE JEEP'S TIRES DIG DEEP INTO THE LATE WINTER SNOW.
THOUGH IT SEEMS, IRONY DELIGHTS IN FOLLOWING HIM THROUGH LIFE LIKE A LEADEN WEIGHT.
MR. MILBURY--?
I CAME TO SEE IF YOU NEEDED A HAND WITH THAT TREE...
SCOTT SUMMERS WONDERS AT THE IMAGERY OF WHEELS SPINNING TO BE IRONICALLY APROPOS TO HIS CURRENT STATE.
MR. MIL--BUR--EE--?
WHY, SCOTT, YOU HAVE GROWN TO SUCH A KIND MAN... BUT THEN, YOU WERE A KIND BOY.
AH, I'M AFRAID WE SPEAK IN METAPHOR. FOR THE ONLY TREE MR. MILBURY HAS EVER HAD ANY REAL INTEREST IN--
BUT THEN, HE WAS NEVER MUCH ONE FOR IRONY.
--IS YOUR FAMILY TREE. BLOODLINES AND BREEDING. EVOLUTION AND HEIRS. THE VERY STUFF OF LIFE, SCOTT!
NOW THEN, HAVING SAID THAT--
--WOULD YOU PREFER TO JOIN ME--
--OR DOES THE SUMMERS FAMILY LINE END HERE AND NOW?!
NEXT:
MR. SINISTER VS. CYCLOPS!
SECRETS REVEALED!
REVANCHE VS. PSYLOCKE!
MYSTERIES RESOLVED!
The DARK RIDERS VS.?
THE WINNER WILL SURPRISE YOU!

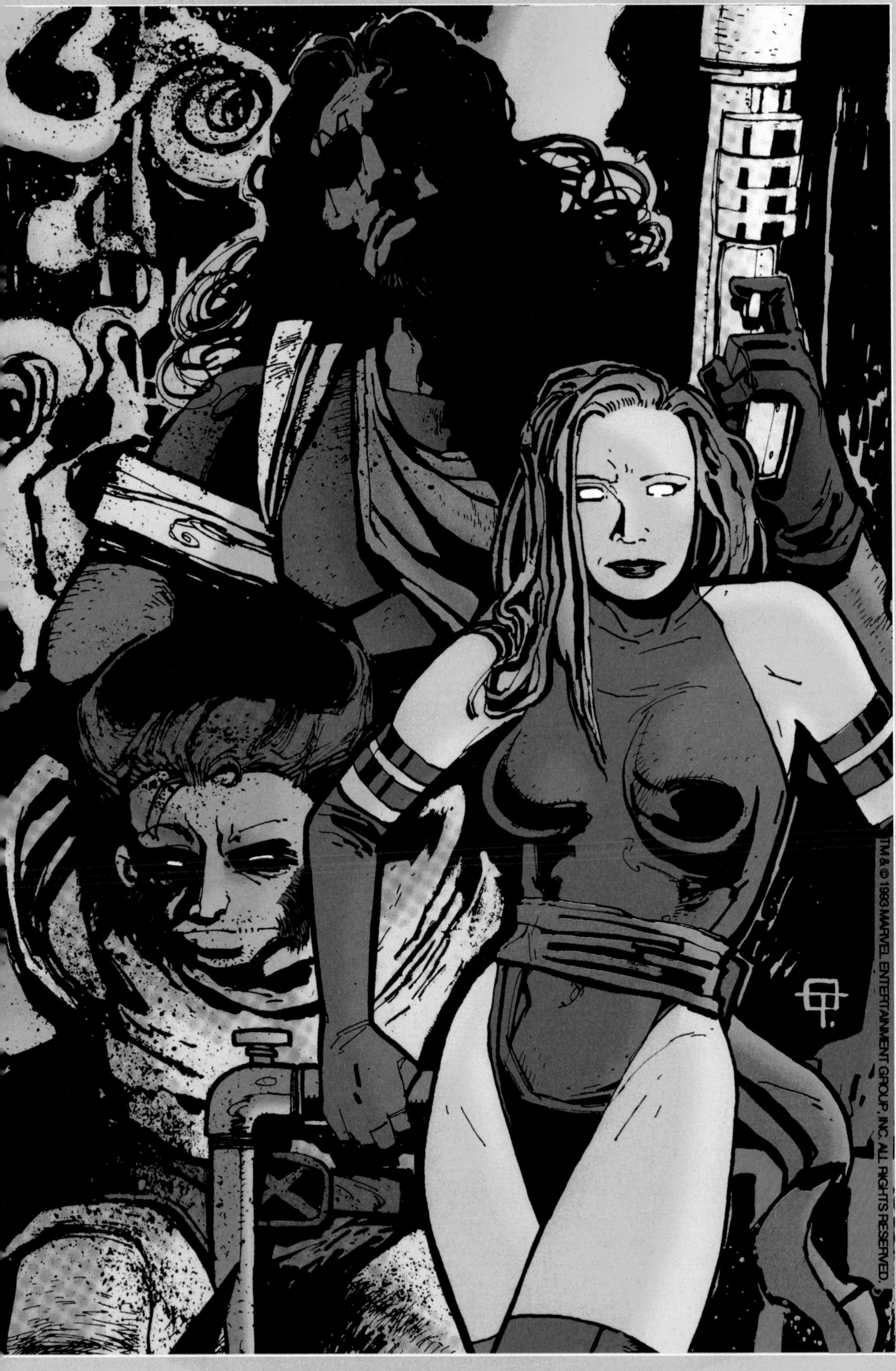

TM & © 1993 MARVEL ENTERTAINMENT GROUP, INC. ALL RIGHTS RESERVED.

X-Men Poster Magazine #2 pinup by Ted McKeever

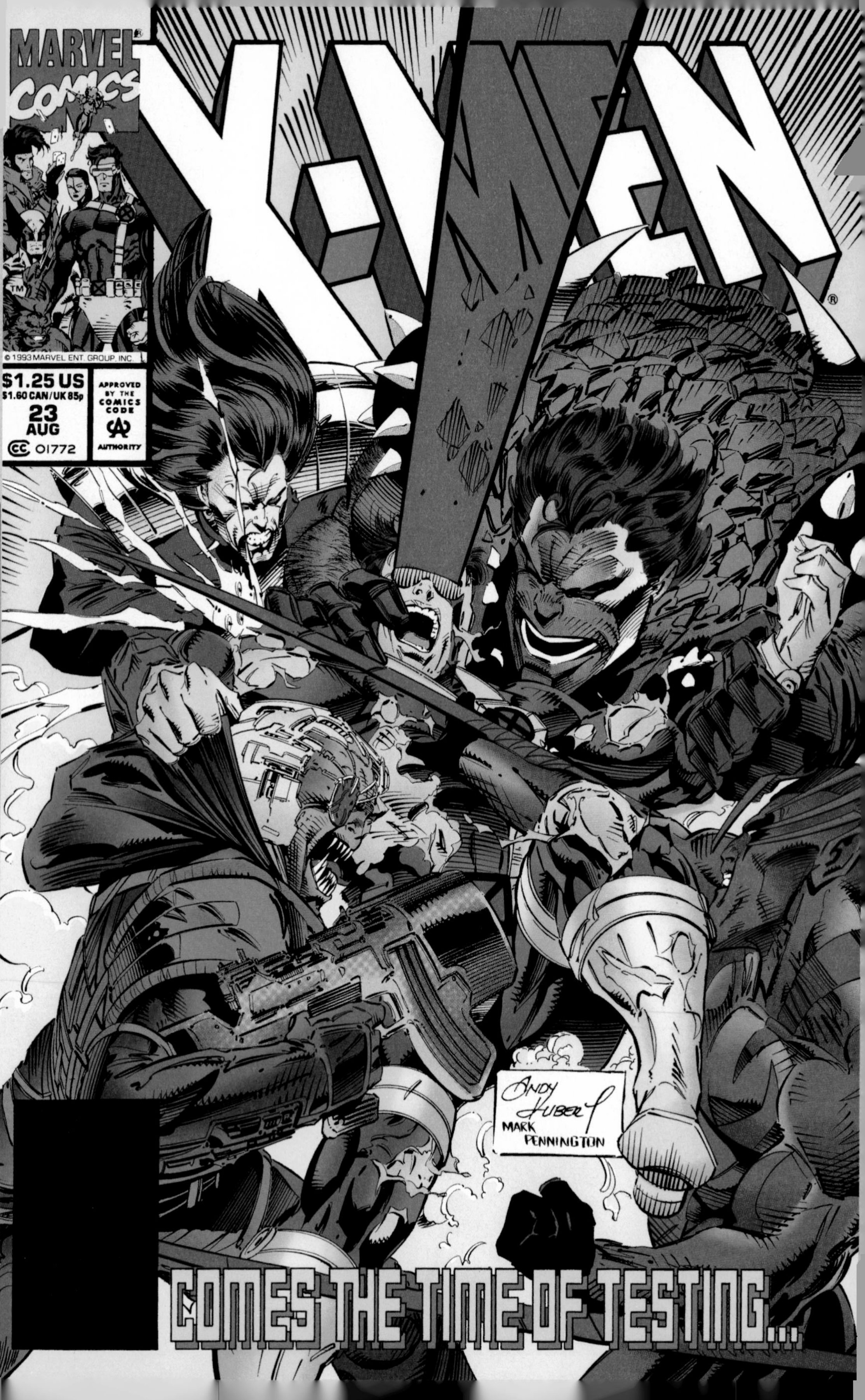
MARVEL COMICS
X-MEN
© 1993 MARVEL ENT. GROUP, INC.
$1.25 US
$1.60 CAN/UK 85p
23
AUG
01772
APPROVED BY THE COMICS CODE AUTHORITY
ANDY KUBERT
MARK PENNINGTON
COMES THE TIME OF TESTING...

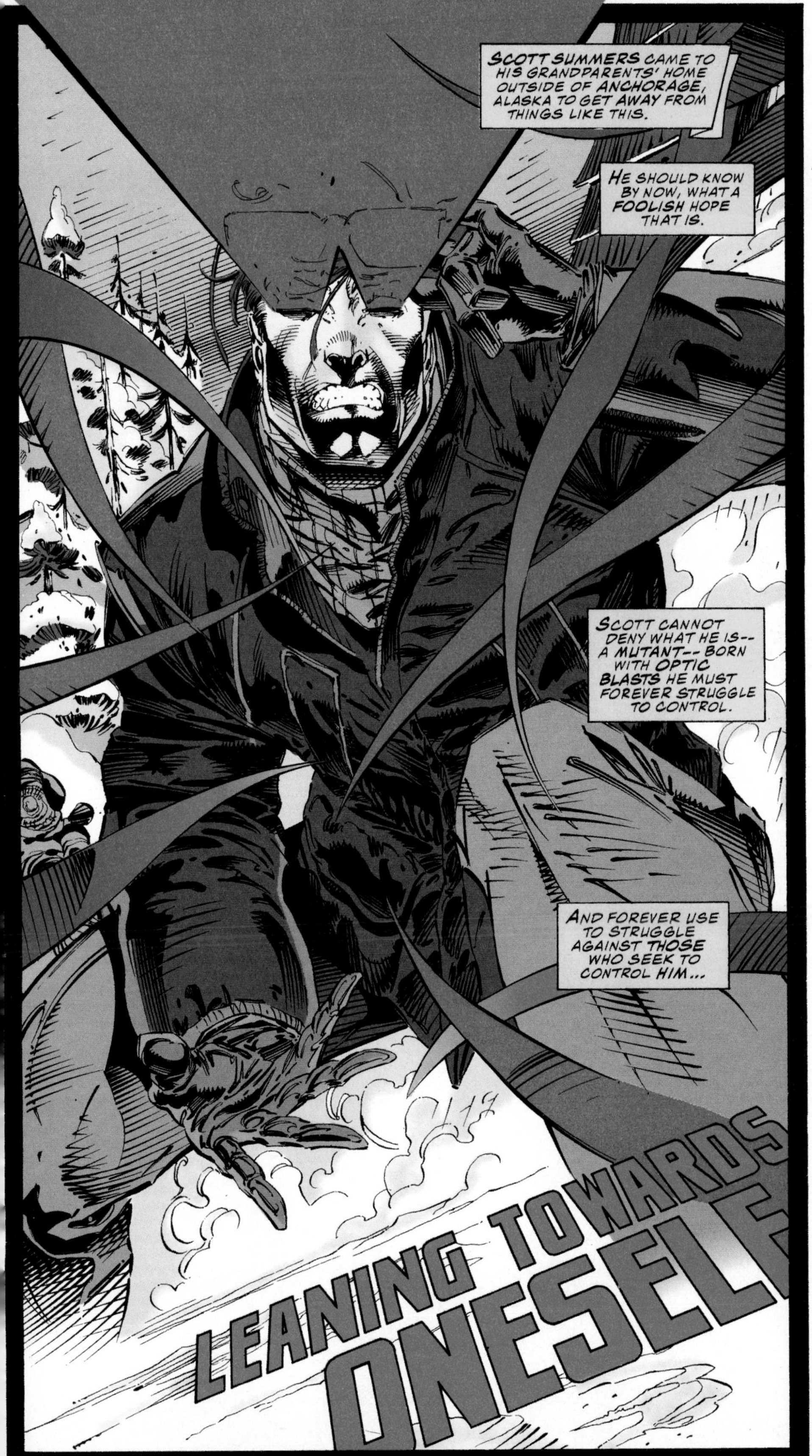
SCOTT SUMMERS CAME TO HIS GRANDPARENTS' HOME OUTSIDE OF ANCHORAGE, ALASKA TO GET AWAY FROM THINGS LIKE THIS.
HE SHOULD KNOW BY NOW, WHAT A FOOLISH HOPE THAT IS.
SCOTT CANNOT DENY WHAT HE IS-- A MUTANT-- BORN WITH OPTIC BLASTS HE MUST FOREVER STRUGGLE TO CONTROL.
AND FOREVER USE TO STRUGGLE AGAINST THOSE WHO SEEK TO CONTROL HIM...
LEANING TOWARDS ONESELF

A TALE OF THE

X MEN

BY FABIAN NICIEZA *AND* ANDY KUBERT

•

MARK PENNINGTON INKER

BILL OAKLEY LETTERER

JOE ROSAS COLORIST

BOB HARRAS EDITOR

TOM DEFALCO LEANING TOWER OF PIZZA

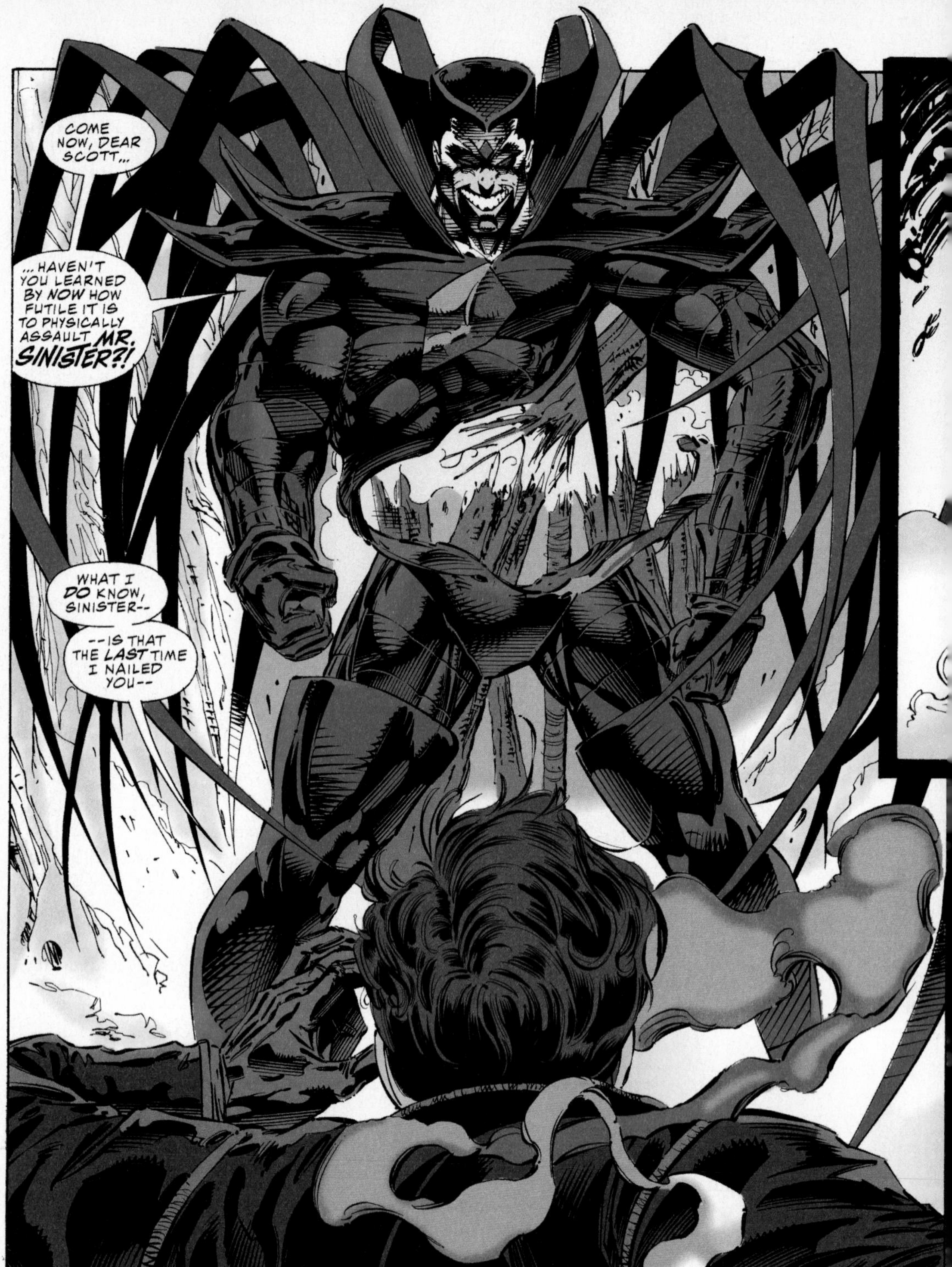
COME NOW, DEAR SCOTT...
...HAVEN'T YOU LEARNED BY NOW HOW FUTILE IT IS TO PHYSICALLY ASSAULT MR. SINISTER?!
WHAT I DO KNOW, SINISTER--
--IS THAT THE LAST TIME I NAILED YOU--

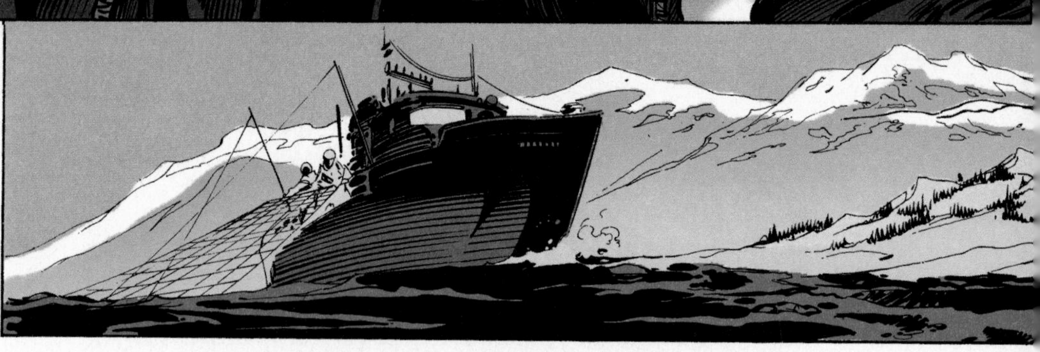

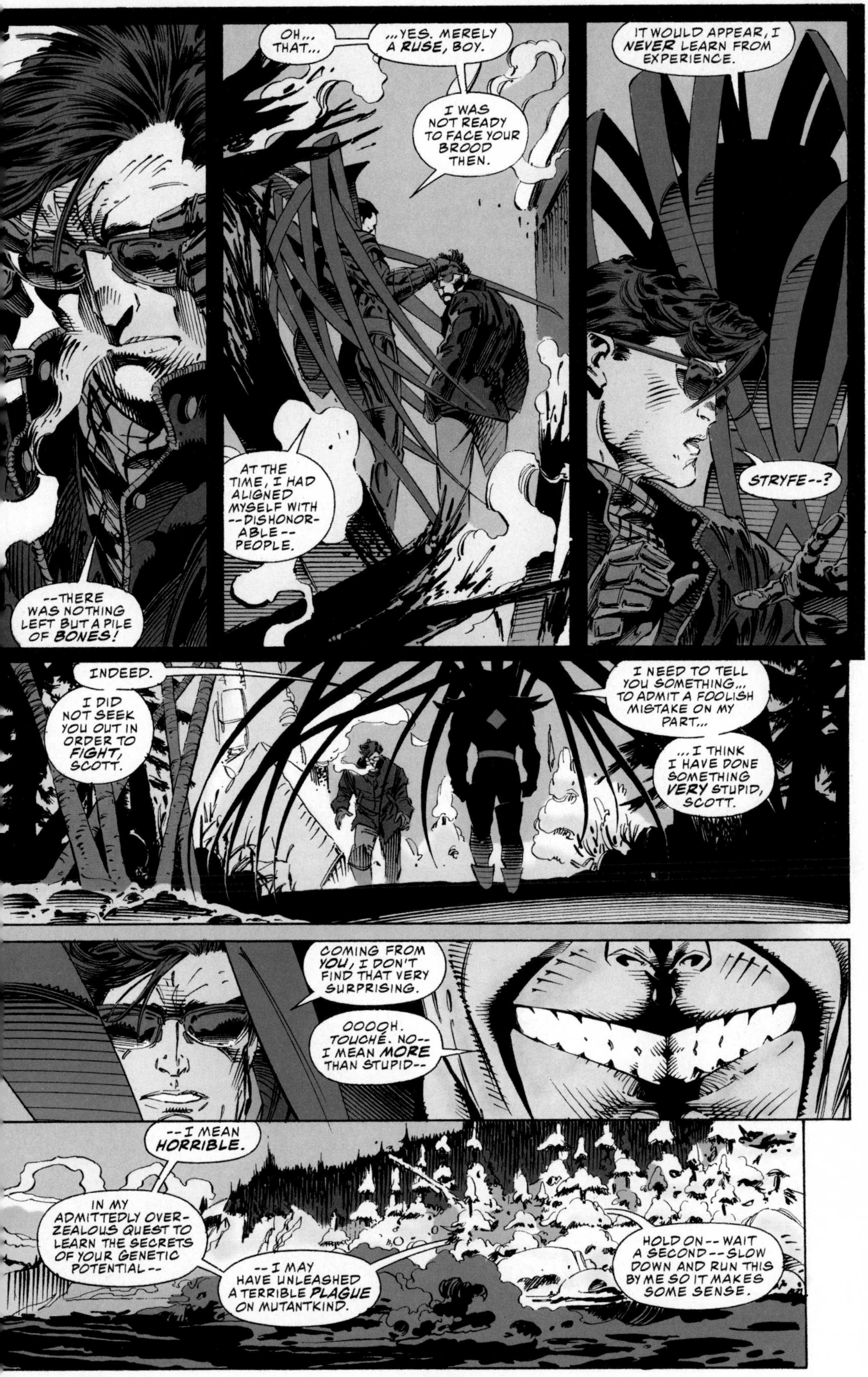
--THERE WAS NOTHING LEFT BUT A PILE OF BONES!
OH... THAT...
...YES. MERELY A RUSE, BOY.
I WAS NOT READY TO FACE YOUR BROOD THEN.
AT THE TIME, I HAD ALIGNED MYSELF WITH --DISHONORABLE-- PEOPLE.
IT WOULD APPEAR, I NEVER LEARN FROM EXPERIENCE.
STRYFE--?
INDEED.
I DID NOT SEEK YOU OUT IN ORDER TO FIGHT, SCOTT.
I NEED TO TELL YOU SOMETHING... TO ADMIT A FOOLISH MISTAKE ON MY PART...
...I THINK I HAVE DONE SOMETHING VERY STUPID, SCOTT.
COMING FROM YOU, I DON'T FIND THAT VERY SURPRISING.
OOOOH. TOUCHÉ. NO-- I MEAN MORE THAN STUPID--
--I MEAN HORRIBLE.
IN MY ADMITTEDLY OVER-ZEALOUS QUEST TO LEARN THE SECRETS OF YOUR GENETIC POTENTIAL--
--I MAY HAVE UNLEASHED A TERRIBLE PLAGUE ON MUTANTKIND.
HOLD ON--WAIT A SECOND--SLOW DOWN AND RUN THIS BY ME SO IT MAKES SOME SENSE.

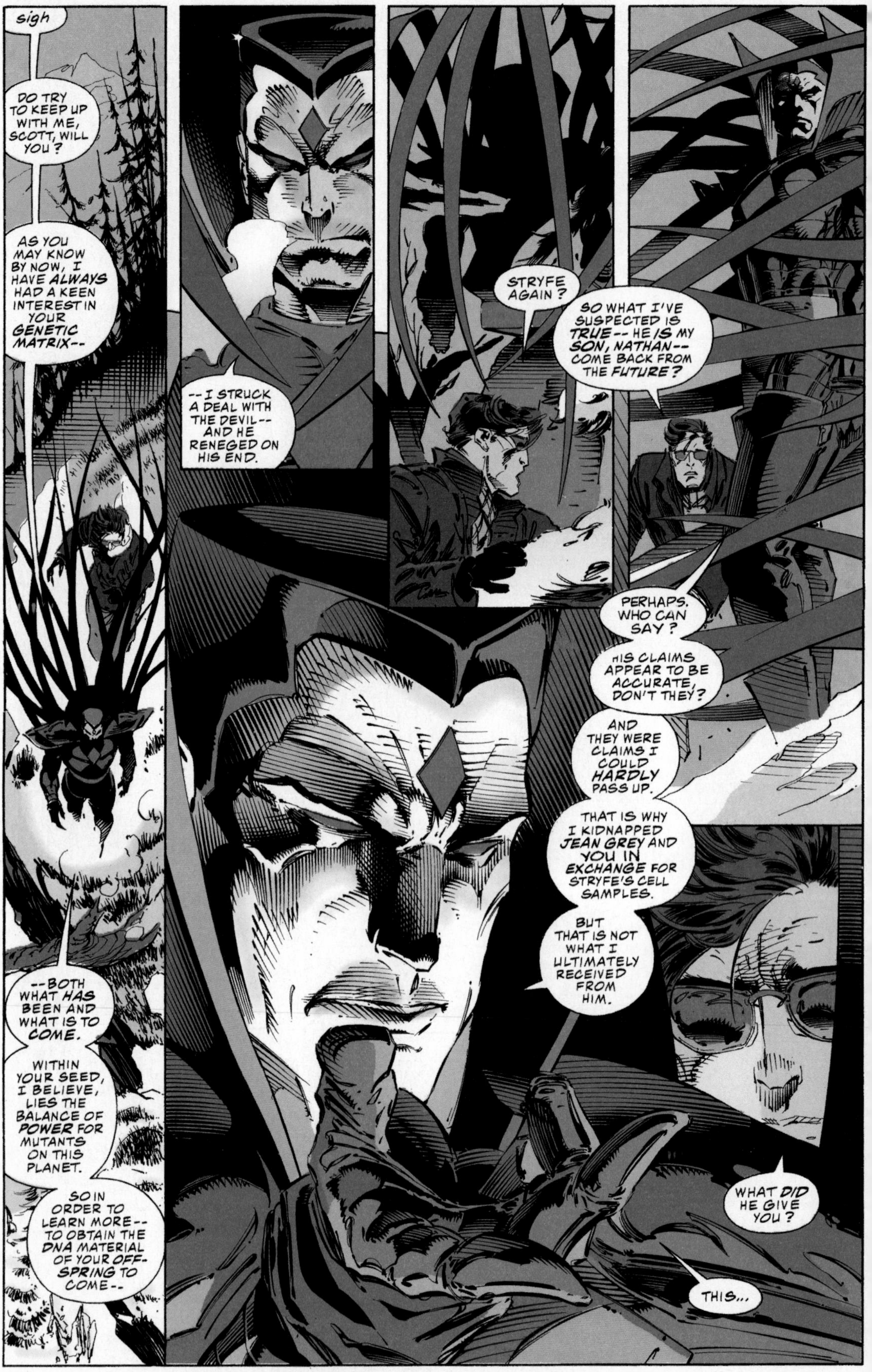
sigh
DO TRY TO KEEP UP WITH ME, SCOTT, WILL YOU?
AS YOU MAY KNOW BY NOW, I HAVE ALWAYS HAD A KEEN INTEREST IN YOUR GENETIC MATRIX--
--BOTH WHAT HAS BEEN AND WHAT IS TO COME.
WITHIN YOUR SEED, I BELIEVE, LIES THE BALANCE OF POWER FOR MUTANTS ON THIS PLANET.
SO IN ORDER TO LEARN MORE--TO OBTAIN THE DNA MATERIAL OF YOUR OFF-SPRING TO COME--
--I STRUCK A DEAL WITH THE DEVIL--AND HE RENEGED ON HIS END.
STRYFE AGAIN?
SO WHAT I'VE SUSPECTED IS TRUE--HE IS MY SON, NATHAN--COME BACK FROM THE FUTURE?
PERHAPS. WHO CAN SAY?
HIS CLAIMS APPEAR TO BE ACCURATE, DON'T THEY?
AND THEY WERE CLAIMS I COULD HARDLY PASS UP.
THAT IS WHY I KIDNAPPED JEAN GREY AND YOU IN EXCHANGE FOR STRYFE'S CELL SAMPLES.
BUT THAT IS NOT WHAT I ULTIMATELY RECEIVED FROM HIM.
WHAT DID HE GIVE YOU?
THIS...

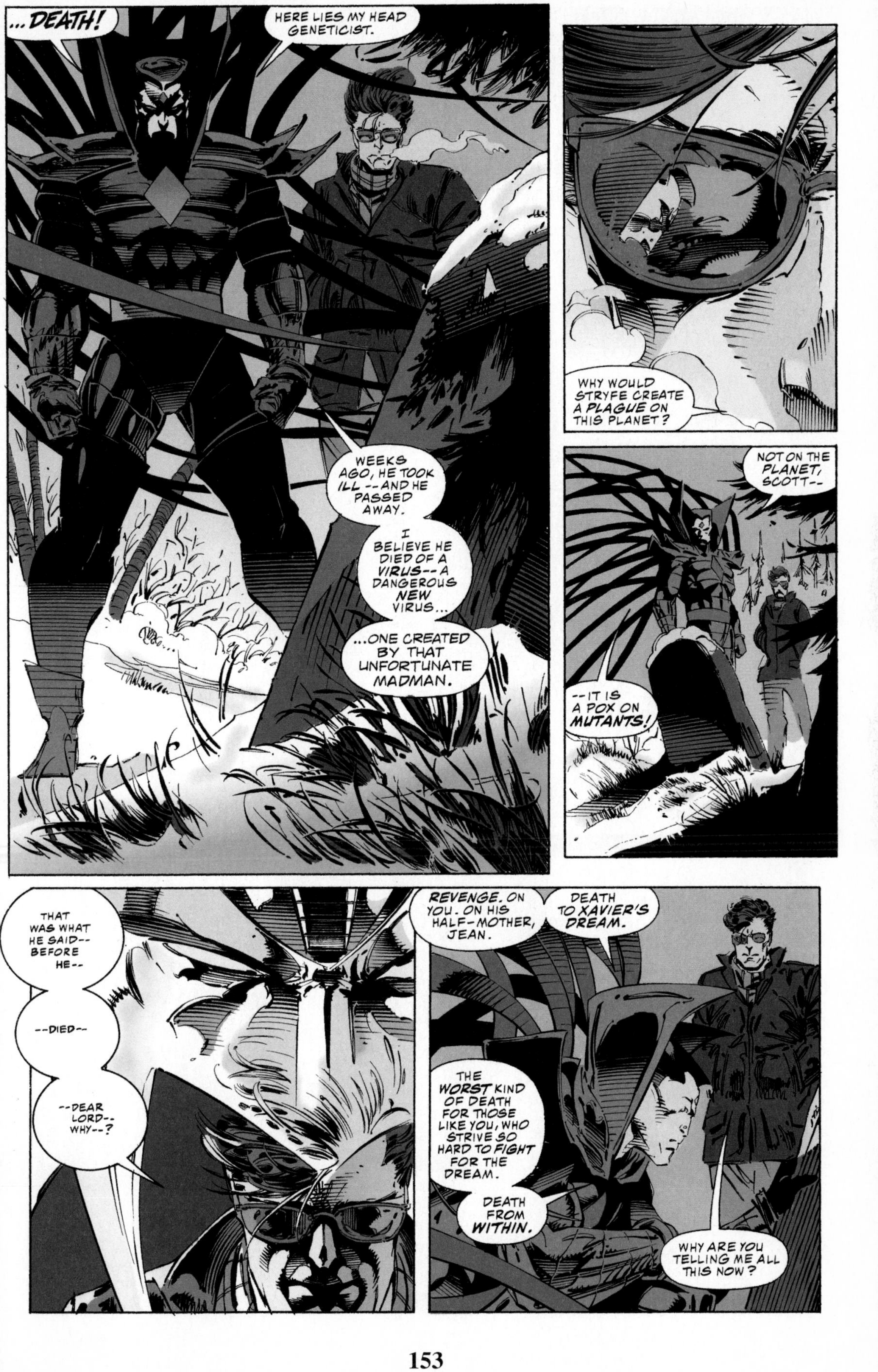
...DEATH!
HERE LIES MY HEAD GENETICIST.
WEEKS AGO, HE TOOK ILL --AND HE PASSED AWAY.
I BELIEVE HE DIED OF A VIRUS--A DANGEROUS NEW VIRUS...
...ONE CREATED BY THAT UNFORTUNATE MADMAN.
WHY WOULD STRYFE CREATE A PLAGUE ON THIS PLANET?
NOT ON THE PLANET, SCOTT--
--IT IS A POX ON MUTANTS!
THAT WAS WHAT HE SAID--BEFORE HE--
--DIED--
--DEAR LORD--WHY--?
REVENGE. ON YOU. ON HIS HALF-MOTHER, JEAN.
DEATH TO XAVIER'S DREAM.
THE WORST KIND OF DEATH FOR THOSE LIKE YOU, WHO STRIVE SO HARD TO FIGHT FOR THE DREAM.
DEATH FROM WITHIN.
WHY ARE YOU TELLING ME ALL THIS NOW?

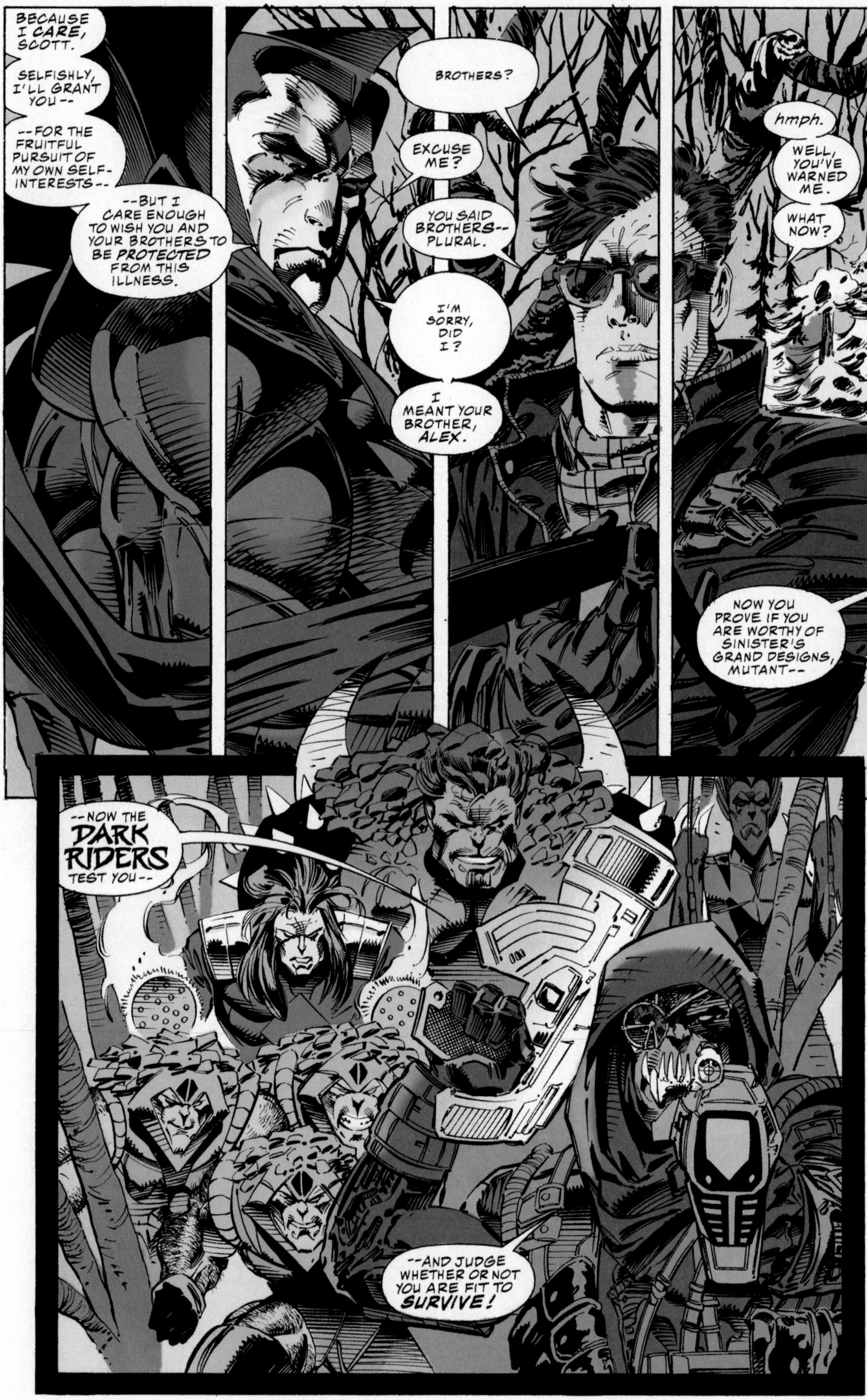

BECAUSE I CARE, SCOTT.
SELFISHLY, I'LL GRANT YOU--
--FOR THE FRUITFUL PURSUIT OF MY OWN SELF-INTERESTS--
--BUT I CARE ENOUGH TO WISH YOU AND YOUR BROTHERS TO BE PROTECTED FROM THIS ILLNESS.
BROTHERS?
EXCUSE ME?
YOU SAID BROTHERS-- PLURAL.
I'M SORRY, DID I?
I MEANT YOUR BROTHER, ALEX.
hmph.
WELL, YOU'VE WARNED ME.
WHAT NOW?
NOW YOU PROVE IF YOU ARE WORTHY OF SINISTER'S GRAND DESIGNS, MUTANT--
--NOW THE DARK RIDERS TEST YOU--
--AND JUDGE WHETHER OR NOT YOU ARE FIT TO SURVIVE!

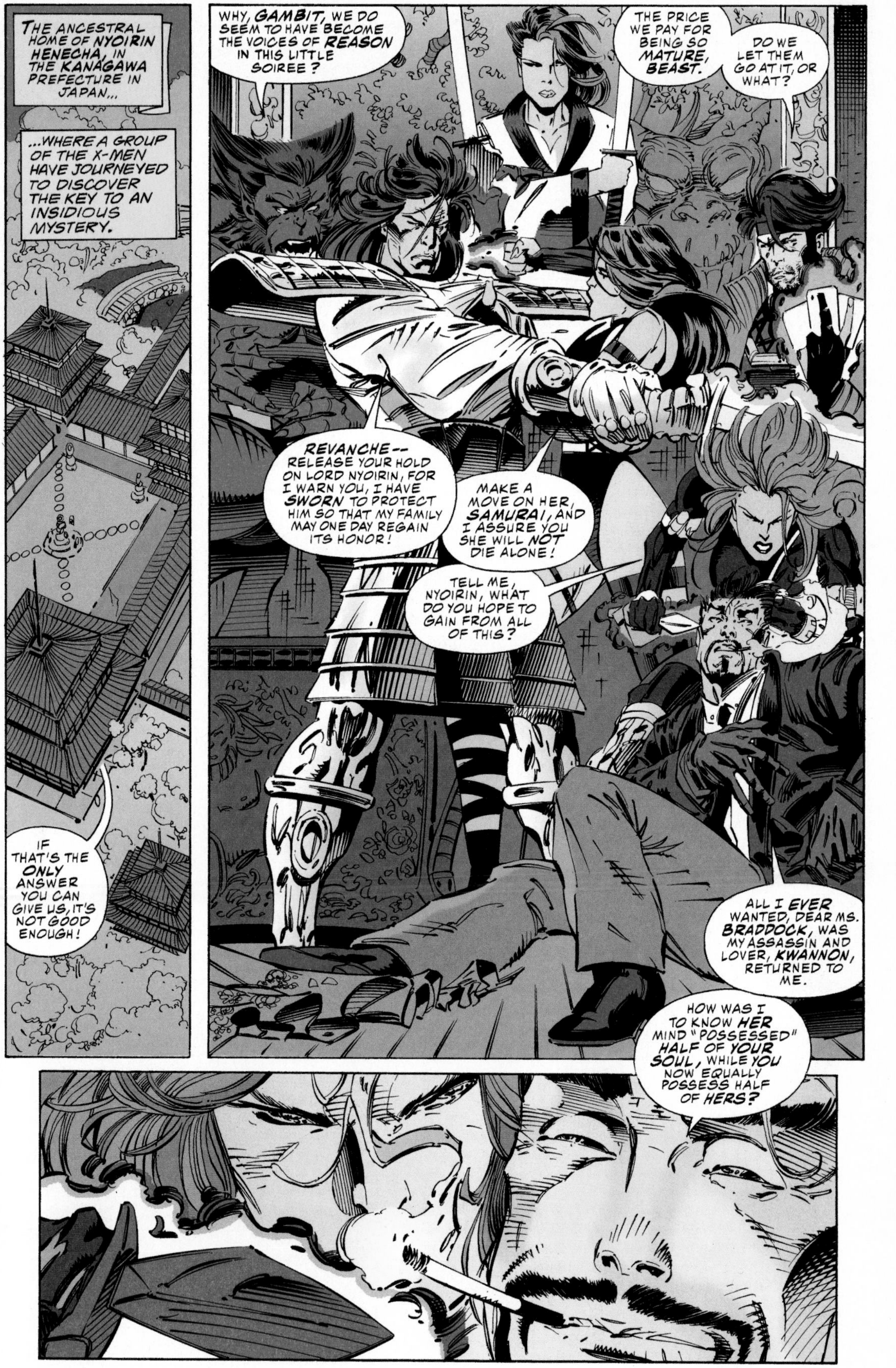
THE ANCESTRAL HOME OF NYOIRIN HENECHA, IN THE KANAGAWA PREFECTURE IN JAPAN...
...WHERE A GROUP OF THE X-MEN HAVE JOURNEYED TO DISCOVER THE KEY TO AN INSIDIOUS MYSTERY.
WHY, GAMBIT, WE DO SEEM TO HAVE BECOME THE VOICES OF REASON IN THIS LITTLE SOIREE?
THE PRICE WE PAY FOR BEING SO MATURE, BEAST.
DO WE LET THEM GO AT IT, OR WHAT?
REVANCHE-- RELEASE YOUR HOLD ON LORD NYOIRIN, FOR I WARN YOU, I HAVE SWORN TO PROTECT HIM SO THAT MY FAMILY MAY ONE DAY REGAIN ITS HONOR!
MAKE A MOVE ON HER, SAMURAI, AND I ASSURE YOU SHE WILL NOT DIE ALONE!
TELL ME, NYOIRIN, WHAT DO YOU HOPE TO GAIN FROM ALL OF THIS?
IF THAT'S THE ONLY ANSWER YOU CAN GIVE US, IT'S NOT GOOD ENOUGH!
ALL I EVER WANTED, DEAR MS. BRADDOCK, WAS MY ASSASSIN AND LOVER, KWANNON, RETURNED TO ME.
HOW WAS I TO KNOW HER MIND "POSSESSED" HALF OF YOUR SOUL, WHILE YOU NOW EQUALLY POSSESS HALF OF HERS?

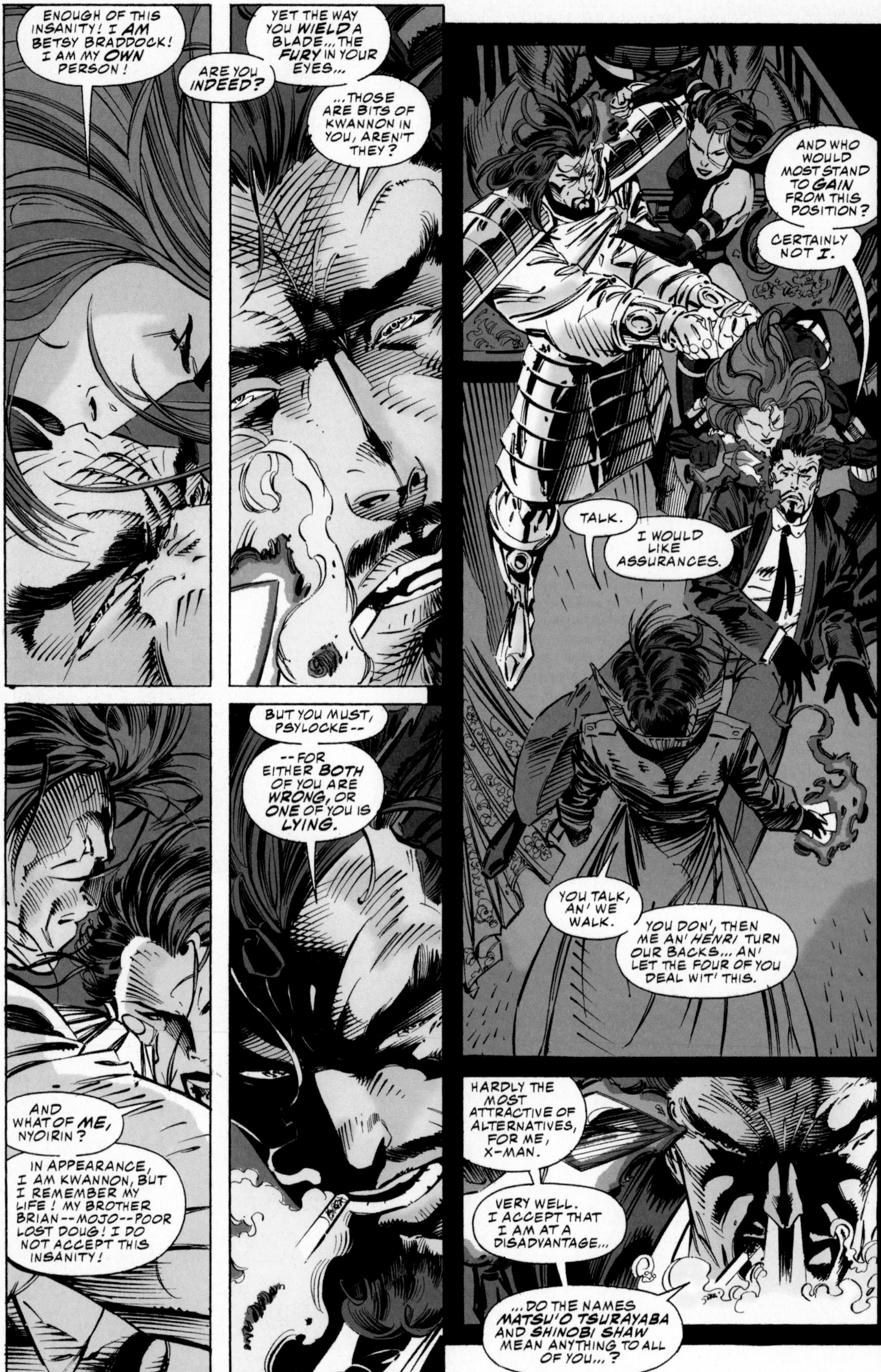

ENOUGH OF THIS INSANITY! I AM BETSY BRADDOCK! I AM MY OWN PERSON!
ARE YOU INDEED?
YET THE WAY YOU WIELD A BLADE... THE FURY IN YOUR EYES...
...THOSE ARE BITS OF KWANNON IN YOU, AREN'T THEY?
AND WHO WOULD MOST STAND TO GAIN FROM THIS POSITION?
CERTAINLY NOT I.
TALK.
I WOULD LIKE ASSURANCES.
YOU TALK, AN' WE WALK.
YOU DON', THEN ME AN' HENRI TURN OUR BACKS... AN' LET THE FOUR OF YOU DEAL WIT' THIS.
AND WHAT OF ME, NYOIRIN?
IN APPEARANCE, I AM KWANNON, BUT I REMEMBER MY LIFE! MY BROTHER BRIAN--MOJO--POOR LOST DOUG! I DO NOT ACCEPT THIS INSANITY!
BUT YOU MUST, PSYLOCKE--
--FOR EITHER BOTH OF YOU ARE WRONG, OR ONE OF YOU IS LYING.
HARDLY THE MOST ATTRACTIVE OF ALTERNATIVES, FOR ME, X-MAN.
VERY WELL. I ACCEPT THAT I AM AT A DISADVANTAGE...
...DO THE NAMES MATSU'O TSURAYABA AND SHINOBI SHAW MEAN ANYTHING TO ALL OF YOU...?

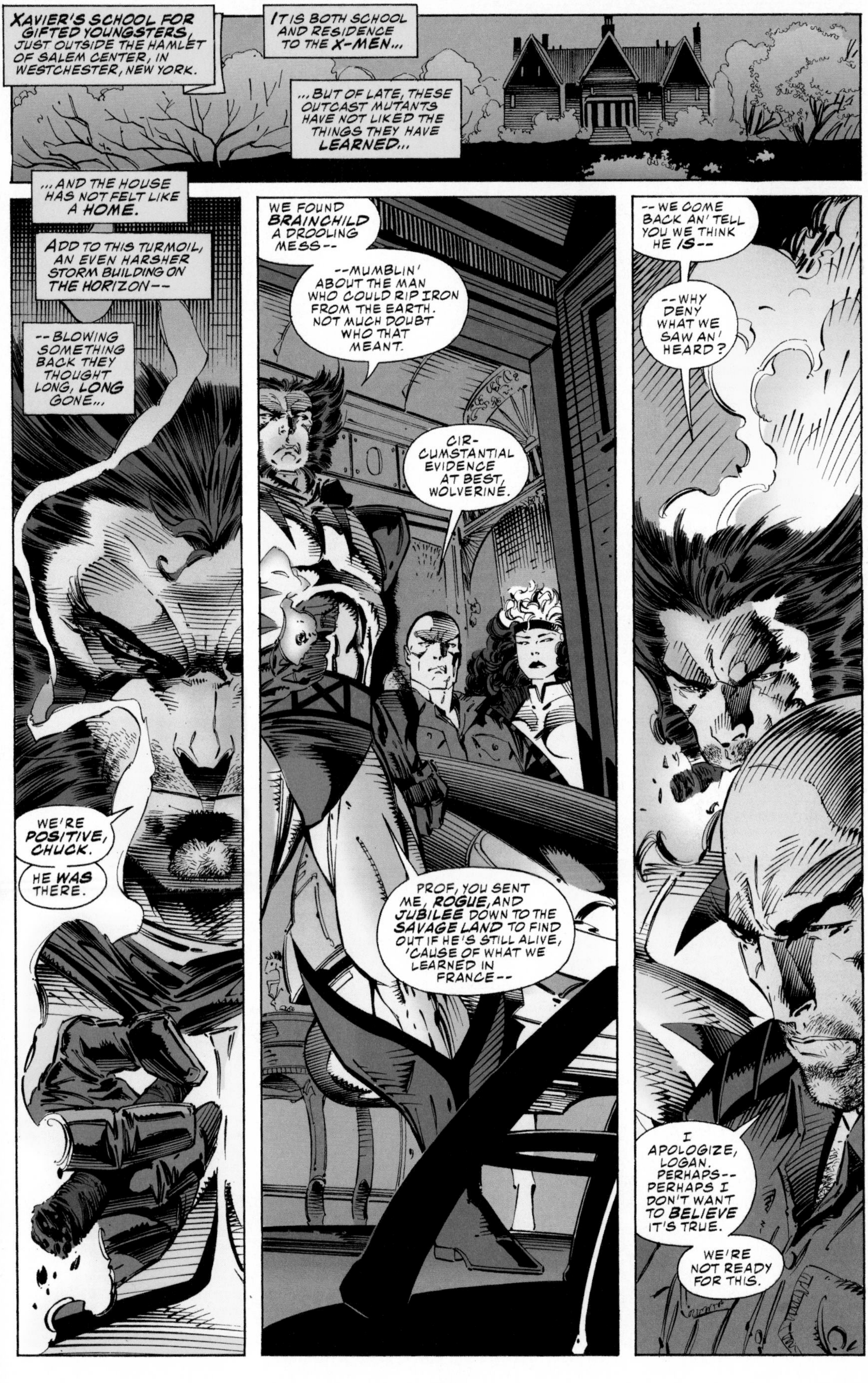
XAVIER'S SCHOOL FOR GIFTED YOUNGSTERS, JUST OUTSIDE THE HAMLET OF SALEM CENTER, IN WESTCHESTER, NEW YORK.
IT IS BOTH SCHOOL AND RESIDENCE TO THE X-MEN...
...BUT OF LATE, THESE OUTCAST MUTANTS HAVE NOT LIKED THE THINGS THEY HAVE LEARNED...
...AND THE HOUSE HAS NOT FELT LIKE A HOME.
ADD TO THIS TURMOIL, AN EVEN HARSHER STORM BUILDING ON THE HORIZON--
--BLOWING SOMETHING BACK THEY THOUGHT LONG, LONG GONE...
WE'RE POSITIVE, CHUCK.
HE WAS THERE.
WE FOUND BRAINCHILD A DROOLING MESS--
--MUMBLIN' ABOUT THE MAN WHO COULD RIP IRON FROM THE EARTH. NOT MUCH DOUBT WHO THAT MEANT.
CIR-CUMSTANTIAL EVIDENCE AT BEST, WOLVERINE.
PROF, YOU SENT ME, ROGUE, AND JUBILEE DOWN TO THE SAVAGE LAND TO FIND OUT IF HE'S STILL ALIVE, 'CAUSE OF WHAT WE LEARNED IN FRANCE--
--WE COME BACK AN' TELL YOU WE THINK HE IS--
--WHY DENY WHAT WE SAW AN' HEARD?
I APOLOGIZE, LOGAN. PERHAPS--PERHAPS I DON'T WANT TO BELIEVE IT'S TRUE.
WE'RE NOT READY FOR THIS.

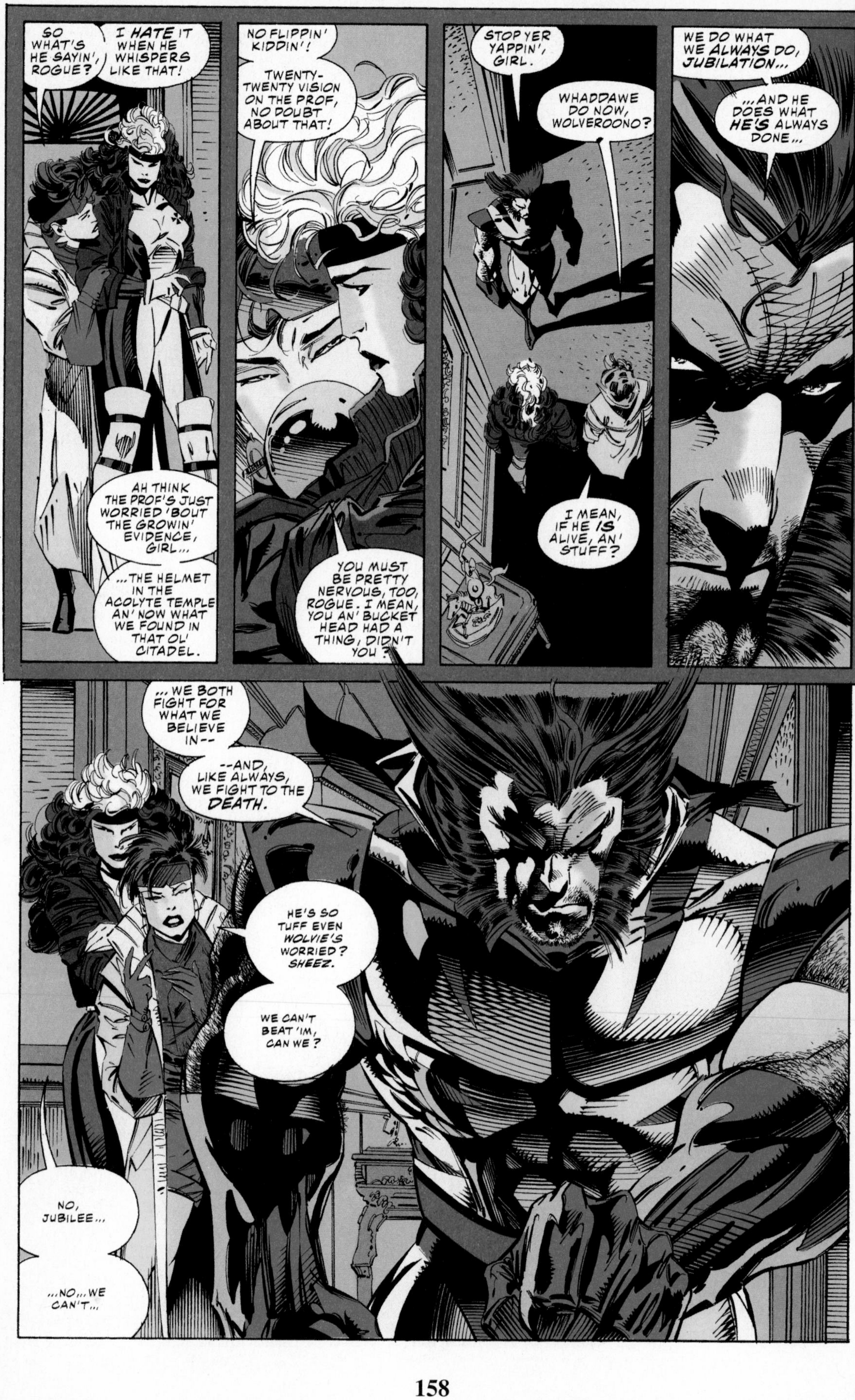
SO WHAT'S HE SAYIN', ROGUE?
I HATE IT WHEN HE WHISPERS LIKE THAT!
AH THINK THE PROF'S JUST WORRIED 'BOUT THE GROWIN' EVIDENCE, GIRL...
...THE HELMET IN THE ACOLYTE TEMPLE AN' NOW WHAT WE FOUND IN THAT OL' CITADEL.
NO FLIPPIN' KIDDIN'!
TWENTY-TWENTY VISION ON THE PROF, NO DOUBT ABOUT THAT!
YOU MUST BE PRETTY NERVOUS, TOO, ROGUE. I MEAN, YOU AN' BUCKET HEAD HAD A THING, DIDN'T YOU?
STOP YER YAPPIN', GIRL.
WHADDAWE DO NOW, WOLVEROONO?
I MEAN, IF HE IS ALIVE, AN' STUFF?
WE DO WHAT WE ALWAYS DO, JUBILATION...
...AND HE DOES WHAT HE'S ALWAYS DONE...
...WE BOTH FIGHT FOR WHAT WE BELIEVE IN--
--AND, LIKE ALWAYS, WE FIGHT TO THE DEATH.
HE'S SO TUFF EVEN WOLVIE'S WORRIED? SHEEZ.
WE CAN'T BEAT 'IM, CAN WE?
NO, JUBILEE...
...NO,...WE CAN'T...

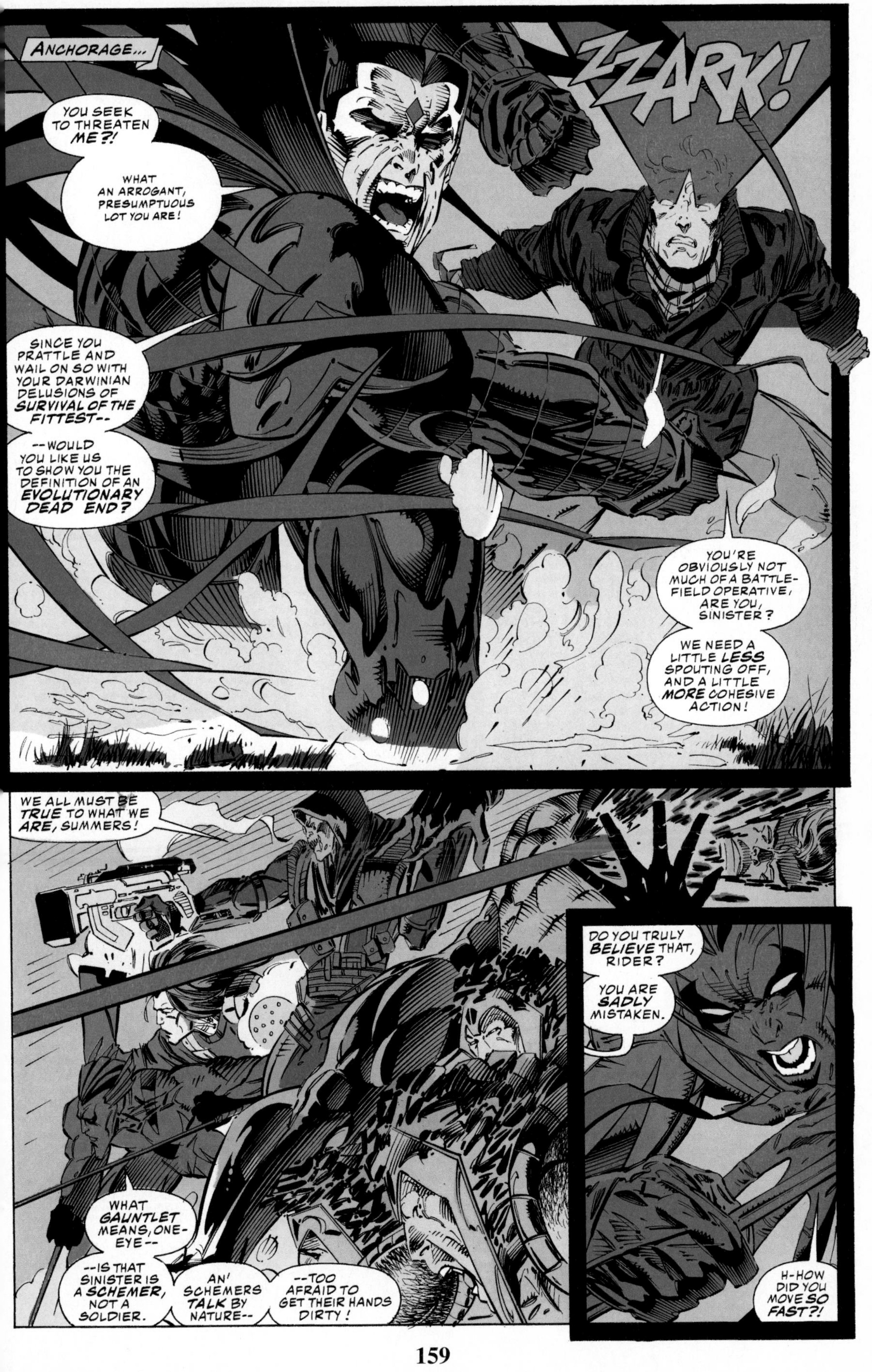

ANCHORAGE...
ZZARK!
YOU SEEK TO THREATEN ME?!
WHAT AN ARROGANT, PRESUMPTUOUS LOT YOU ARE!
SINCE YOU PRATTLE AND WAIL ON SO WITH YOUR DARWINIAN DELUSIONS OF SURVIVAL OF THE FITTEST--
--WOULD YOU LIKE US TO SHOW YOU THE DEFINITION OF AN EVOLUTIONARY DEAD END?
YOU'RE OBVIOUSLY NOT MUCH OF A BATTLE-FIELD OPERATIVE, ARE YOU, SINISTER?
WE NEED A LITTLE LESS SPOUTING OFF, AND A LITTLE MORE COHESIVE ACTION!
WE ALL MUST BE TRUE TO WHAT WE ARE, SUMMERS!
WHAT GAUNTLET MEANS, ONE-EYE--
--IS THAT SINISTER IS A SCHEMER, NOT A SOLDIER.
AN' SCHEMERS TALK BY NATURE--
--TOO AFRAID TO GET THEIR HANDS DIRTY!
DO YOU TRULY BELIEVE THAT, RIDER?
YOU ARE SADLY MISTAKEN.
H-HOW DID YOU MOVE SO FAST?!

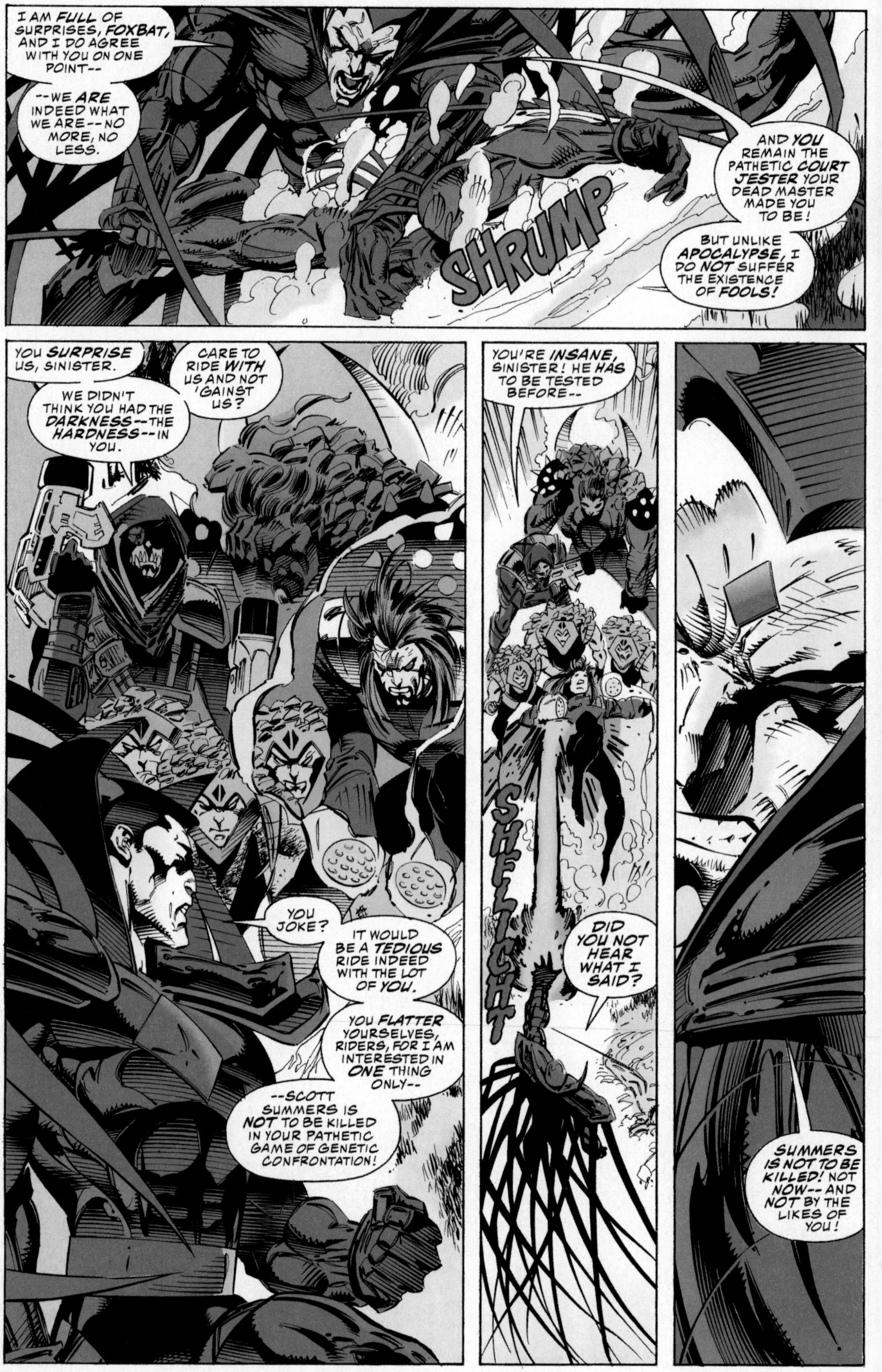

I AM FULL OF SURPRISES, FOXBAT, AND I DO AGREE WITH YOU ON ONE POINT--
--WE ARE INDEED WHAT WE ARE--NO MORE, NO LESS.
AND YOU REMAIN THE PATHETIC COURT JESTER YOUR DEAD MASTER MADE YOU TO BE!
BUT UNLIKE APOCALYPSE, I DO NOT SUFFER THE EXISTENCE OF FOOLS!
SHRUMP
YOU SURPRISE US, SINISTER.
WE DIDN'T THINK YOU HAD THE DARKNESS--THE HARDNESS--IN YOU.
CARE TO RIDE WITH US AND NOT 'GAINST US?
YOU JOKE?
IT WOULD BE A TEDIOUS RIDE INDEED WITH THE LOT OF YOU.
YOU FLATTER YOURSELVES, RIDERS, FOR I AM INTERESTED IN ONE THING ONLY--
--SCOTT SUMMERS IS NOT TO BE KILLED IN YOUR PATHETIC GAME OF GENETIC CONFRONTATION!
YOU'RE INSANE, SINISTER! HE HAS TO BE TESTED BEFORE--
SHFLICHT
DID YOU NOT HEAR WHAT I SAID?
SUMMERS IS NOT TO BE KILLED! NOT NOW--AND NOT BY THE LIKES OF YOU!

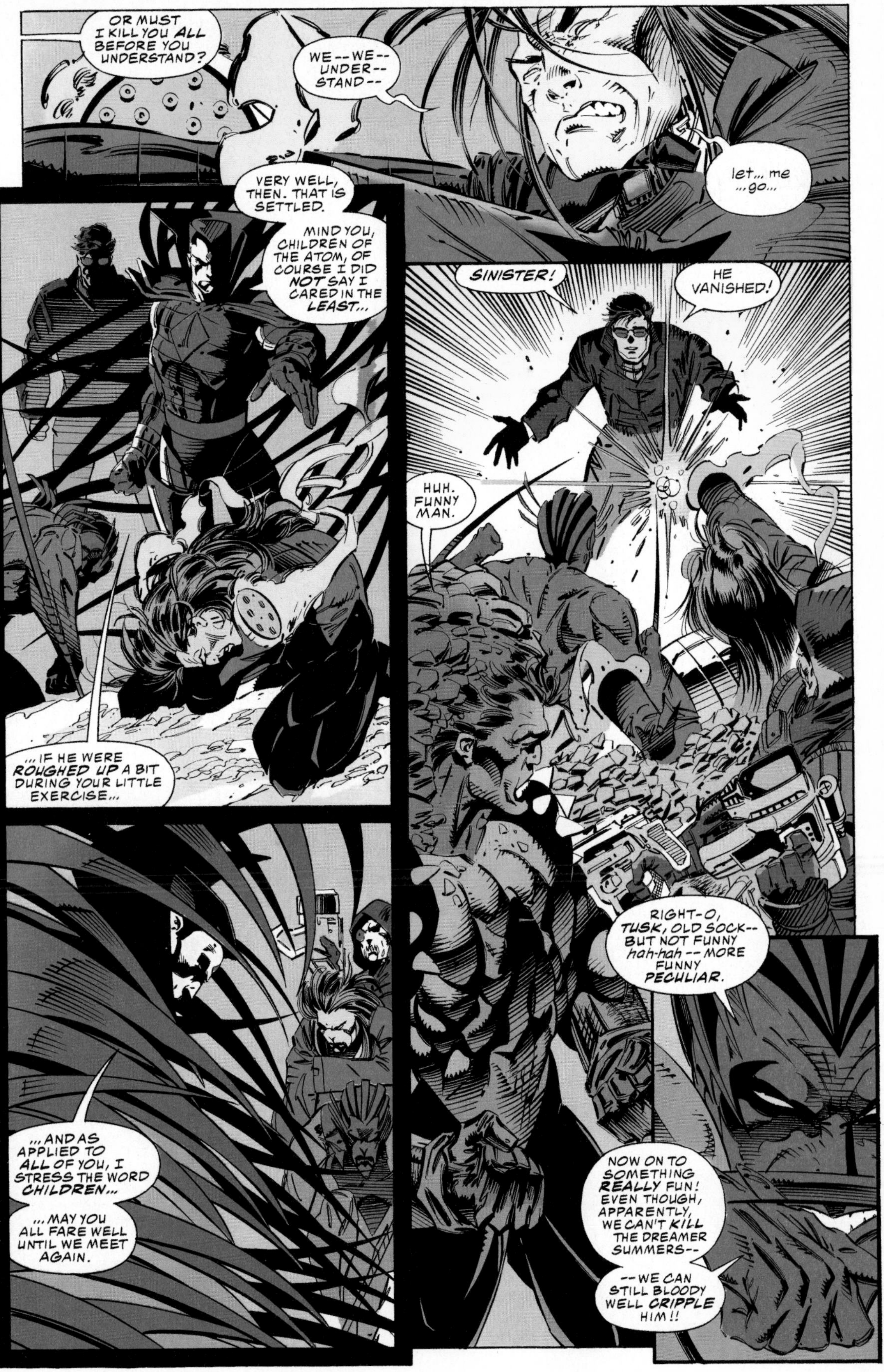
OR MUST I KILL YOU ALL BEFORE YOU UNDERSTAND?
WE--WE--UNDER-STAND--
let... me ...go...
VERY WELL, THEN. THAT IS SETTLED.
MIND YOU, CHILDREN OF THE ATOM, OF COURSE I DID NOT SAY I CARED IN THE LEAST...
...IF HE WERE ROUGHED UP A BIT DURING YOUR LITTLE EXERCISE...
SINISTER!
HE VANISHED!
HUH. FUNNY MAN.
RIGHT-O, TUSK, OLD SOCK--BUT NOT FUNNY hah-hah--MORE FUNNY PECULIAR.
...AND AS APPLIED TO ALL OF YOU, I STRESS THE WORD CHILDREN...
...MAY YOU ALL FARE WELL UNTIL WE MEET AGAIN.
NOW ON TO SOMETHING REALLY FUN! EVEN THOUGH, APPARENTLY, WE CAN'T KILL THE DREAMER SUMMERS--
--WE CAN STILL BLOODY WELL CRIPPLE HIM!!

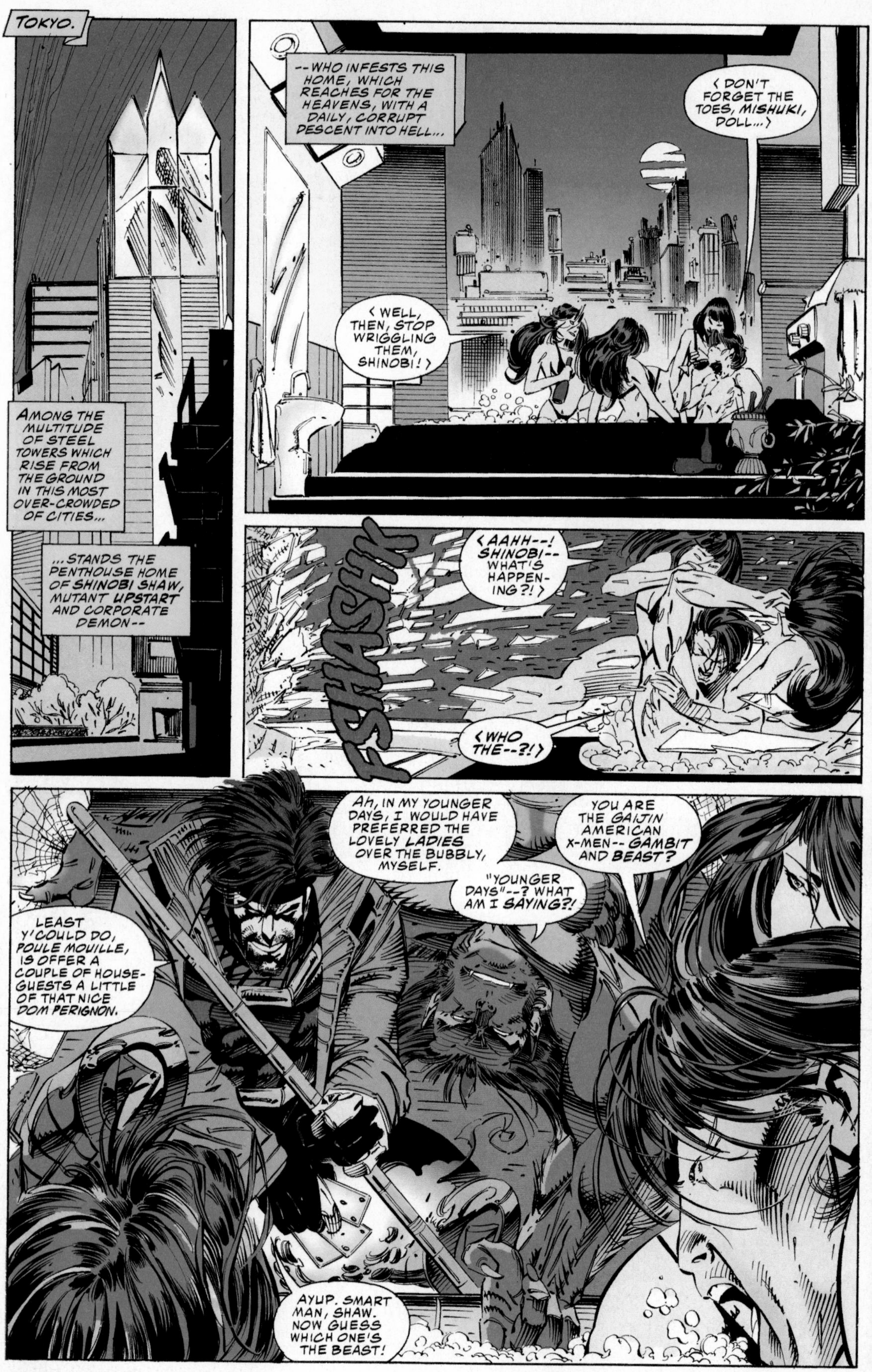
TOKYO.
AMONG THE MULTITUDE OF STEEL TOWERS WHICH RISE FROM THE GROUND IN THIS MOST OVER-CROWDED OF CITIES...
...STANDS THE PENTHOUSE HOME OF SHINOBI SHAW, MUTANT UPSTART AND CORPORATE DEMON--
--WHO INFESTS THIS HOME, WHICH REACHES FOR THE HEAVENS, WITH A DAILY, CORRUPT DESCENT INTO HELL...
< DON'T FORGET THE TOES, MISHUKI, DOLL... >
< WELL, THEN, STOP WRIGGLING THEM, SHINOBI! >
SHASHK
<AAHH--! SHINOBI-- WHAT'S HAPPEN-ING?! >
<WHO THE--?! >
AH, IN MY YOUNGER DAYS, I WOULD HAVE PREFERRED THE LOVELY LADIES OVER THE BUBBLY, MYSELF.
"YOUNGER DAYS"--? WHAT AM I SAYING?!
YOU ARE THE GAIJIN AMERICAN X-MEN-- GAMBIT AND BEAST?
LEAST Y'COULD DO, POULE MOUILLE, IS OFFER A COUPLE OF HOUSE-GUESTS A LITTLE OF THAT NICE DOM PERIGNON.
AYUP. SMART MAN, SHAW. NOW GUESS WHICH ONE'S THE BEAST!

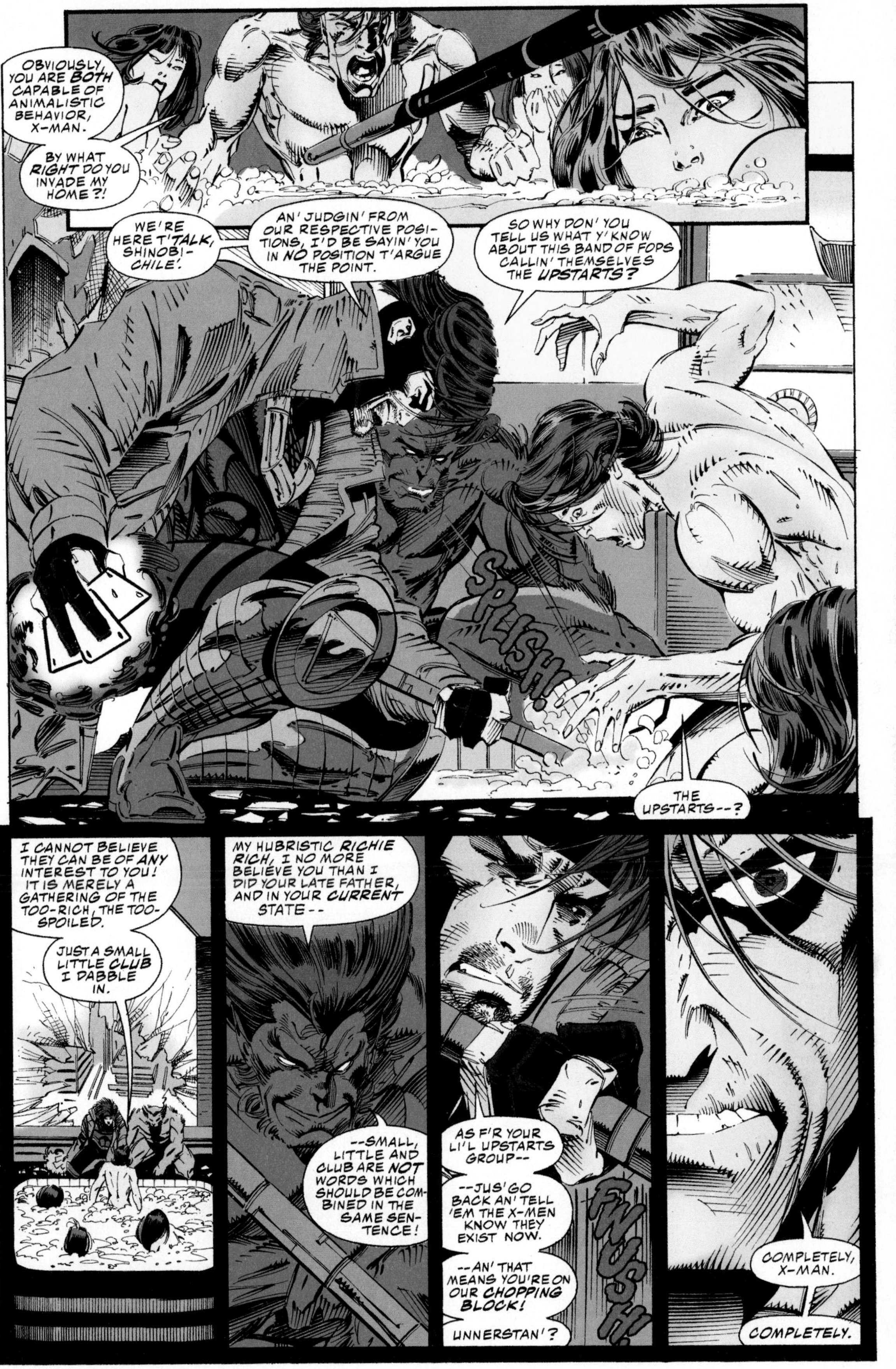
OBVIOUSLY, YOU ARE BOTH CAPABLE OF ANIMALISTIC BEHAVIOR, X-MAN.
BY WHAT RIGHT DO YOU INVADE MY HOME?!
WE'RE HERE T'TALK, SHINOBI-CHILE'.
AN' JUDGIN' FROM OUR RESPECTIVE POSITIONS, I'D BE SAYIN' YOU IN NO POSITION T'ARGUE THE POINT.
SO WHY DON' YOU TELL US WHAT Y' KNOW ABOUT THIS BAND OF FOPS CALLIN' THEMSELVES THE UPSTARTS?
SPLISH!
THE UPSTARTS--?
I CANNOT BELIEVE THEY CAN BE OF ANY INTEREST TO YOU! IT IS MERELY A GATHERING OF THE TOO-RICH, THE TOO-SPOILED.
JUST A SMALL LITTLE CLUB I DABBLE IN.
MY HUBRISTIC RICHIE RICH, I NO MORE BELIEVE YOU THAN I DID YOUR LATE FATHER, AND IN YOUR CURRENT STATE--
--SMALL, LITTLE AND CLUB ARE NOT WORDS WHICH SHOULD BE COMBINED IN THE SAME SENTENCE!
AS F'R YOUR LI'L UPSTARTS GROUP--
--JUS' GO BACK AN' TELL 'EM THE X-MEN KNOW THEY EXIST NOW.
--AN' THAT MEANS YOU'RE ON OUR CHOPPING BLOCK!
UNNERSTAN'?
FWUSH!
COMPLETELY, X-MAN.
COMPLETELY.

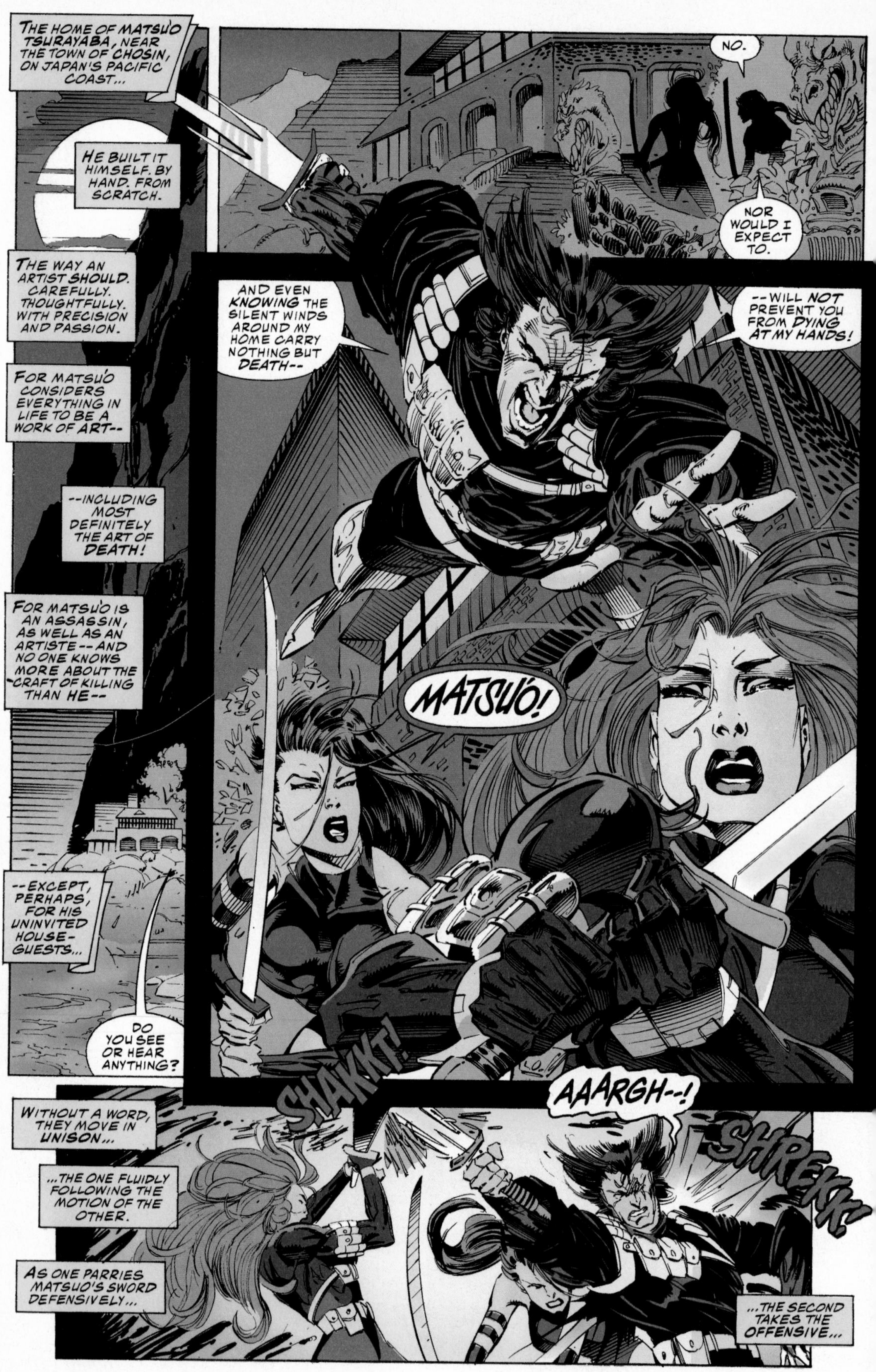
THE HOME OF MATSU'O TSURAYABA, NEAR THE TOWN OF CHOSIN, ON JAPAN'S PACIFIC COAST...
HE BUILT IT HIMSELF. BY HAND. FROM SCRATCH.
THE WAY AN ARTIST SHOULD. CAREFULLY. THOUGHTFULLY. WITH PRECISION AND PASSION.
FOR MATSU'O CONSIDERS EVERYTHING IN LIFE TO BE A WORK OF ART--
--INCLUDING MOST DEFINITELY THE ART OF DEATH!
FOR MATSU'O IS AN ASSASSIN, AS WELL AS AN ARTISTE--AND NO ONE KNOWS MORE ABOUT THE CRAFT OF KILLING THAN HE--
--EXCEPT, PERHAPS, FOR HIS UNINVITED HOUSE-GUESTS...
DO YOU SEE OR HEAR ANYTHING?
NO.
NOR WOULD I EXPECT TO.
AND EVEN KNOWING THE SILENT WINDS AROUND MY HOME CARRY NOTHING BUT DEATH--
--WILL NOT PREVENT YOU FROM DYING AT MY HANDS!
MATSU'O!
SHAKKT!
AAARGH--!
SHREKK!
WITHOUT A WORD, THEY MOVE IN UNISON...
...THE ONE FLUIDLY FOLLOWING THE MOTION OF THE OTHER.
AS ONE PARRIES MATSUO'S SWORD DEFENSIVELY...
...THE SECOND TAKES THE OFFENSIVE...

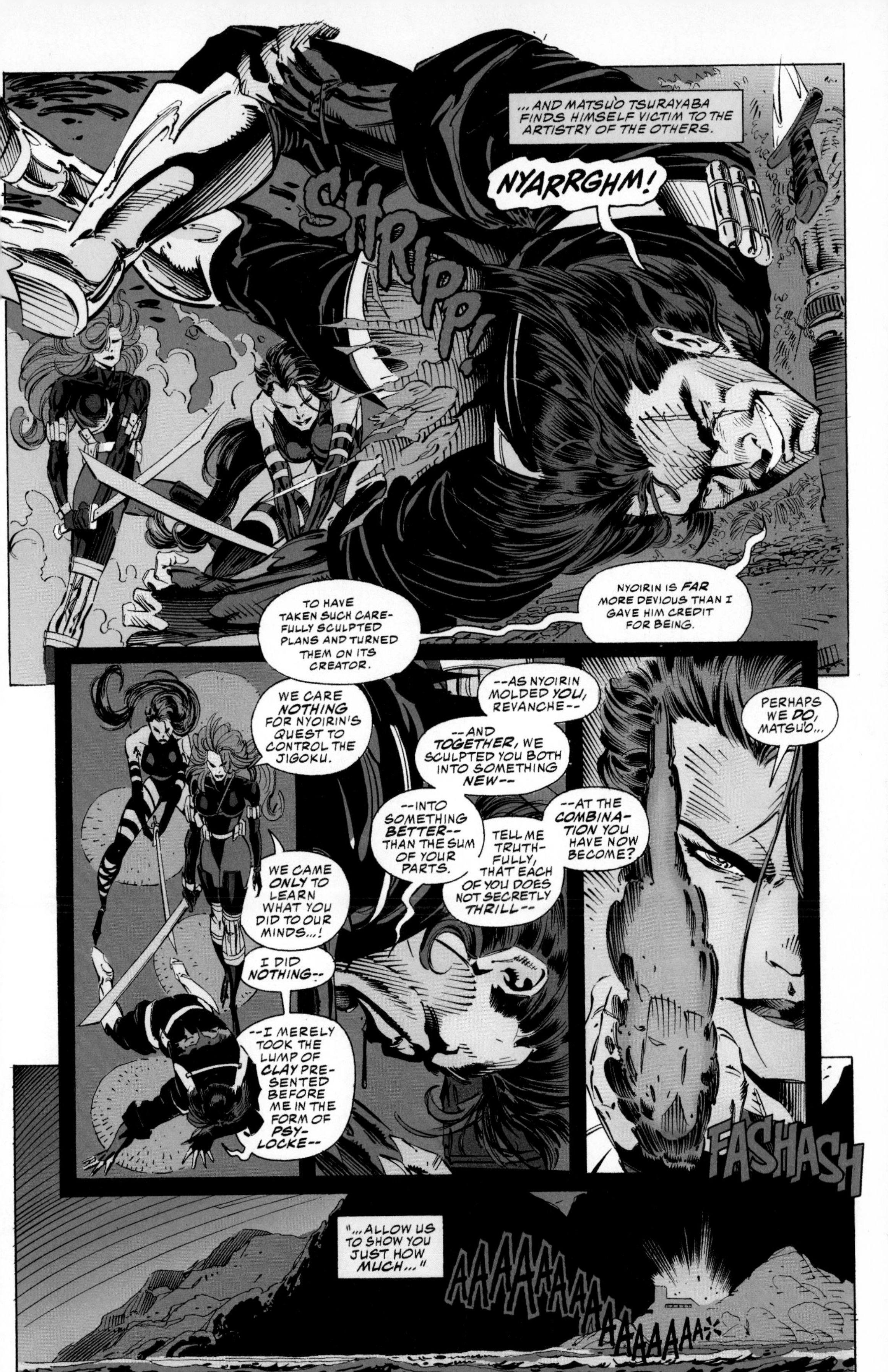
...AND MATSU'O TSURAYABA FINDS HIMSELF VICTIM TO THE ARTISTRY OF THE OTHERS.
SHRIPP!
NYARRGHM!
TO HAVE TAKEN SUCH CAREFULLY SCULPTED PLANS AND TURNED THEM ON ITS CREATOR.
NYOIRIN IS FAR MORE DEVIOUS THAN I GAVE HIM CREDIT FOR BEING.
WE CARE NOTHING FOR NYOIRIN'S QUEST TO CONTROL THE JIGOKU.
WE CAME ONLY TO LEARN WHAT YOU DID TO OUR MINDS...!
I DID NOTHING--
--I MERELY TOOK THE LUMP OF CLAY PRESENTED BEFORE ME IN THE FORM OF PSYLOCKE--
--AS NYOIRIN MOLDED YOU, REVANCHE--
--AND TOGETHER, WE SCULPTED YOU BOTH INTO SOMETHING NEW--
--INTO SOMETHING BETTER--THAN THE SUM OF YOUR PARTS.
TELL ME TRUTHFULLY, THAT EACH OF YOU DOES NOT SECRETLY THRILL--
--AT THE COMBINATION YOU HAVE NOW BECOME?
PERHAPS WE DO, MATSU'O...
FASHASH
"...ALLOW US TO SHOW YOU JUST HOW MUCH..."
AAAAAAAAAAAAAAAAAA*

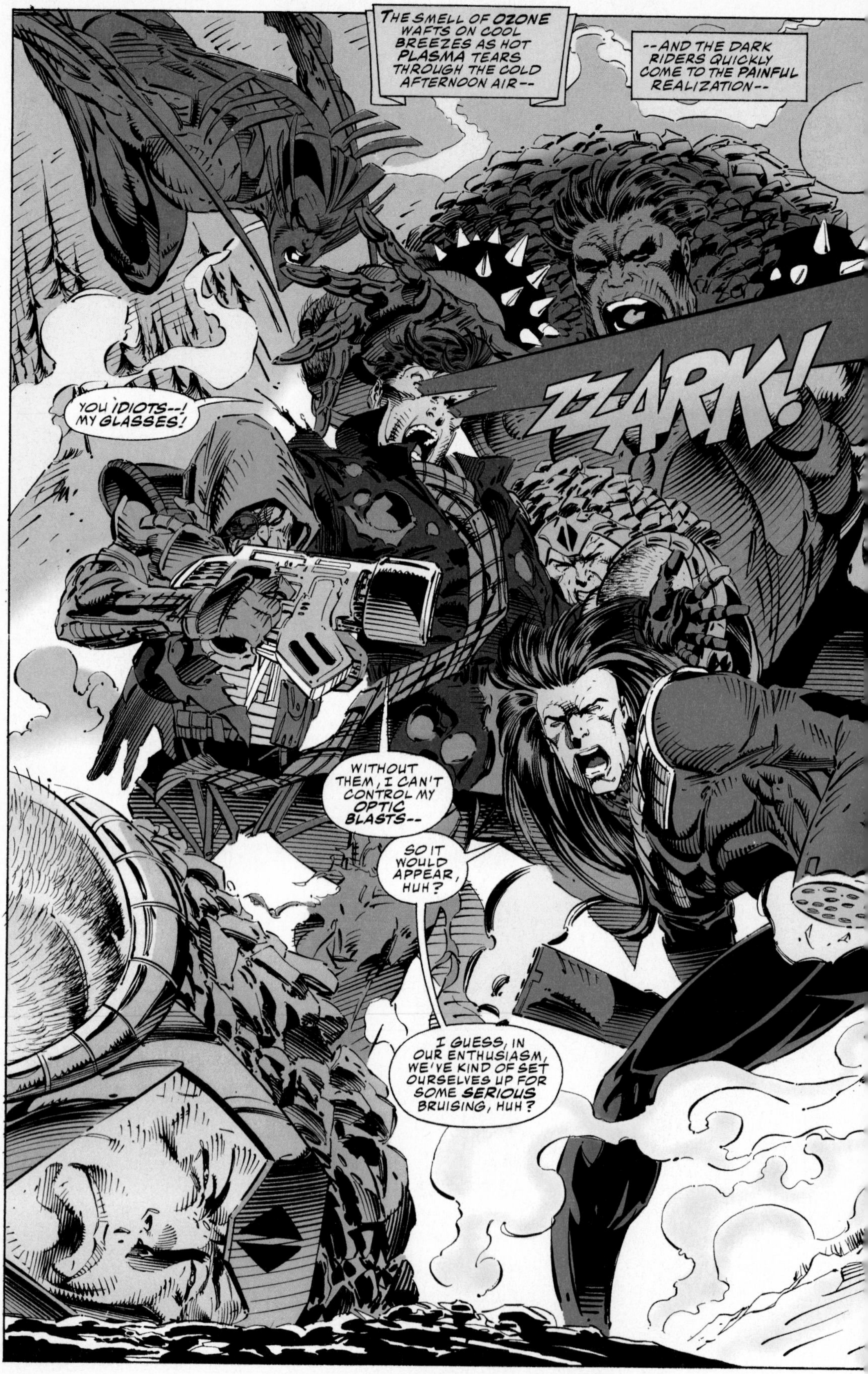
THE SMELL OF OZONE WAFTS ON COOL BREEZES AS HOT PLASMA TEARS THROUGH THE COLD AFTERNOON AIR--
--AND THE DARK RIDERS QUICKLY COME TO THE PAINFUL REALIZATION--
ZZARK!
YOU IDIOTS--! MY GLASSES!
WITHOUT THEM, I CAN'T CONTROL MY OPTIC BLASTS--
SO IT WOULD APPEAR, HUH?
I GUESS, IN OUR ENTHUSIASM, WE'VE KIND OF SET OURSELVES UP FOR SOME SERIOUS BRUISING, HUH?

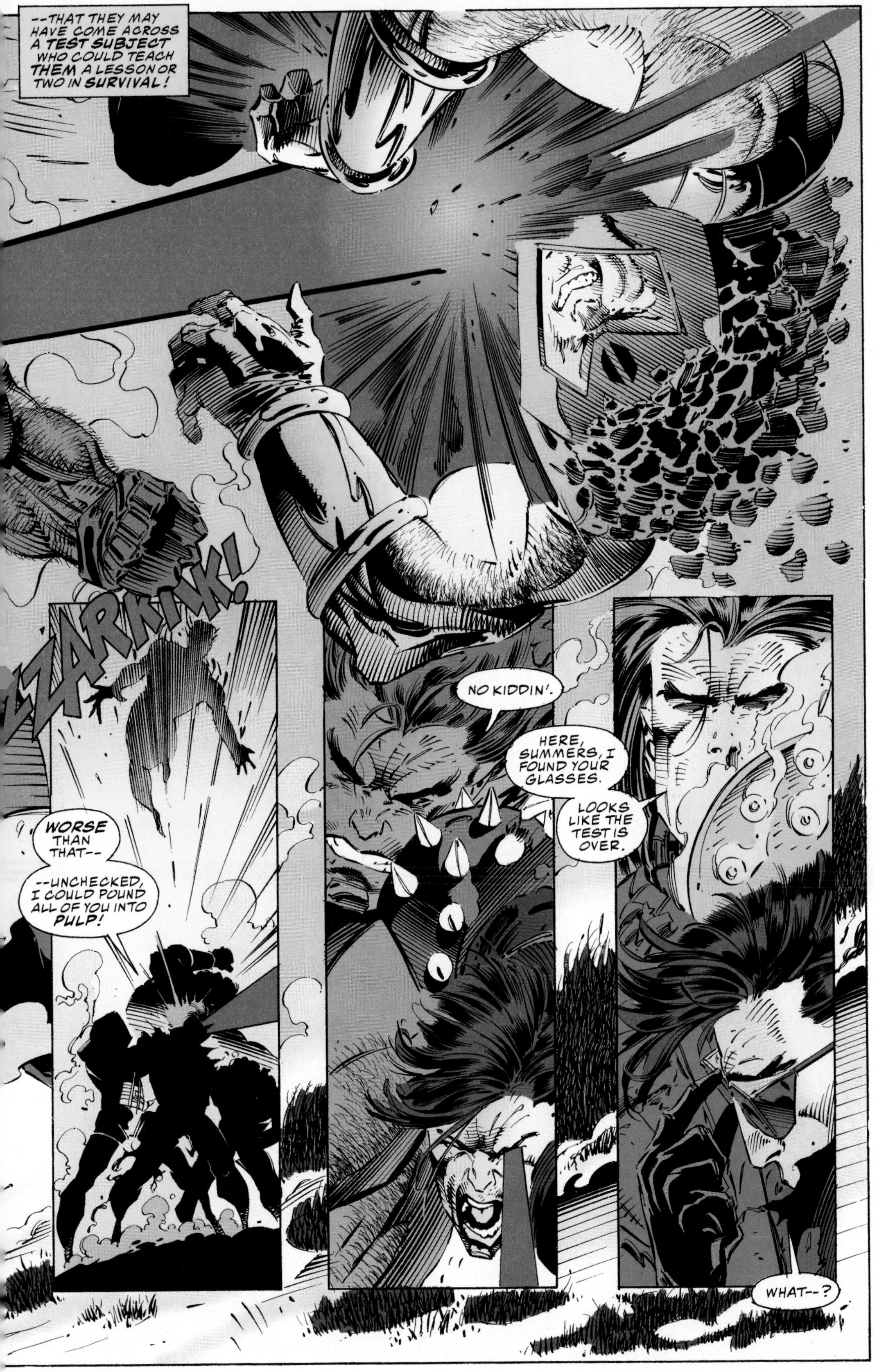

--THAT THEY MAY HAVE COME ACROSS A TEST SUBJECT WHO COULD TEACH THEM A LESSON OR TWO IN SURVIVAL!
ZZARKKK!
WORSE THAN THAT--
--UNCHECKED, I COULD POUND ALL OF YOU INTO PULP!
NO KIDDIN'.
HERE, SUMMERS, I FOUND YOUR GLASSES.
LOOKS LIKE THE TEST IS OVER.
WHAT--?

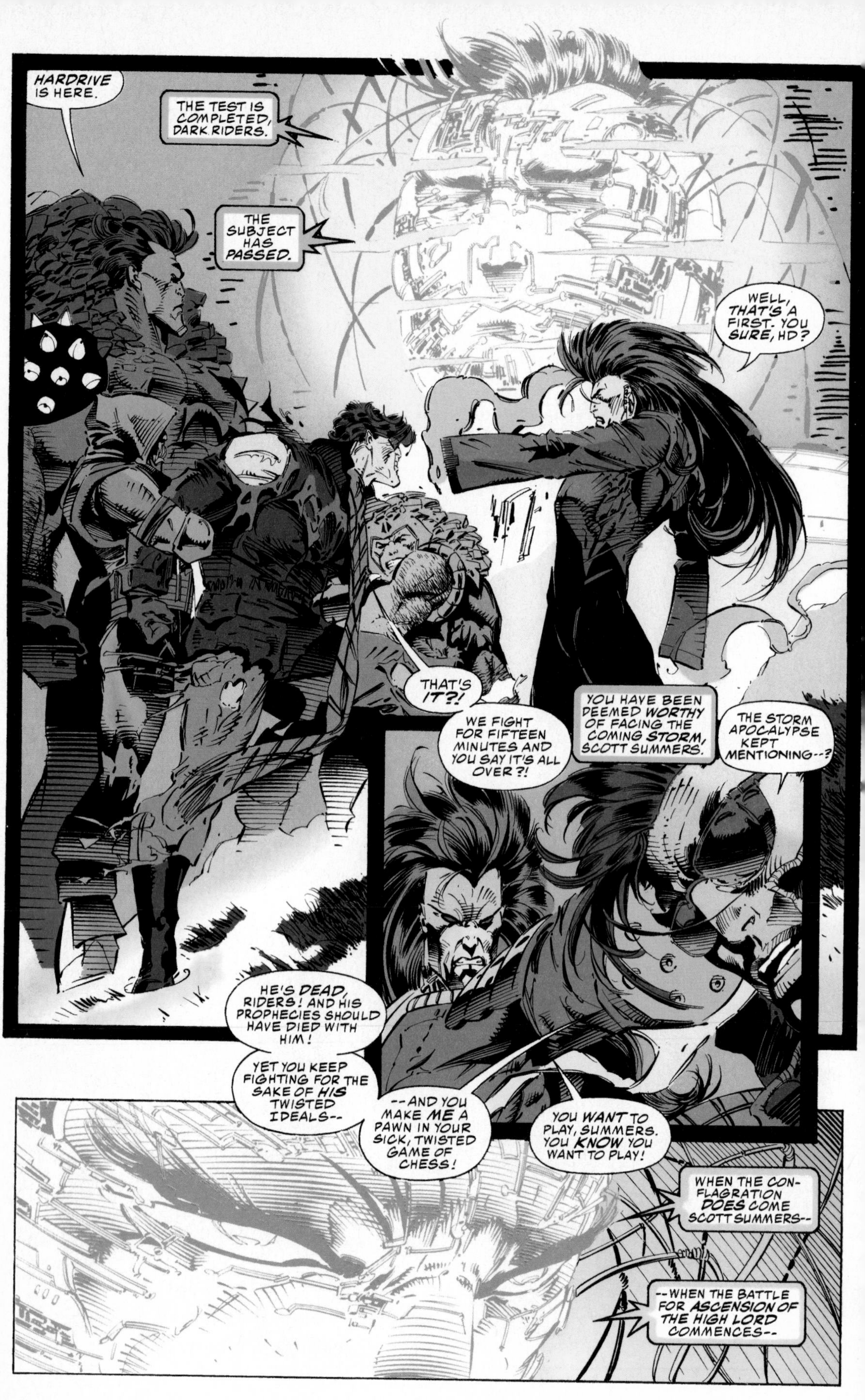
HARDRIVE IS HERE.
THE TEST IS COMPLETED, DARK RIDERS.
THE SUBJECT HAS PASSED.
WELL, THAT'S A FIRST. YOU SURE, HD?
THAT'S IT?!
WE FIGHT FOR FIFTEEN MINUTES AND YOU SAY IT'S ALL OVER?!
YOU HAVE BEEN DEEMED WORTHY OF FACING THE COMING STORM, SCOTT SUMMERS.
THE STORM APOCALYPSE KEPT MENTIONING--?
HE'S DEAD, RIDERS! AND HIS PROPHECIES SHOULD HAVE DIED WITH HIM!
YET YOU KEEP FIGHTING FOR THE SAKE OF HIS TWISTED IDEALS--
--AND YOU MAKE ME A PAWN IN YOUR SICK, TWISTED GAME OF CHESS!
YOU WANT TO PLAY, SUMMERS. YOU KNOW YOU WANT TO PLAY!
WHEN THE CON-FLAGRATION DOES COME SCOTT SUMMERS--
--WHEN THE BATTLE FOR ASCENSION OF THE HIGH LORD COMMENCES--

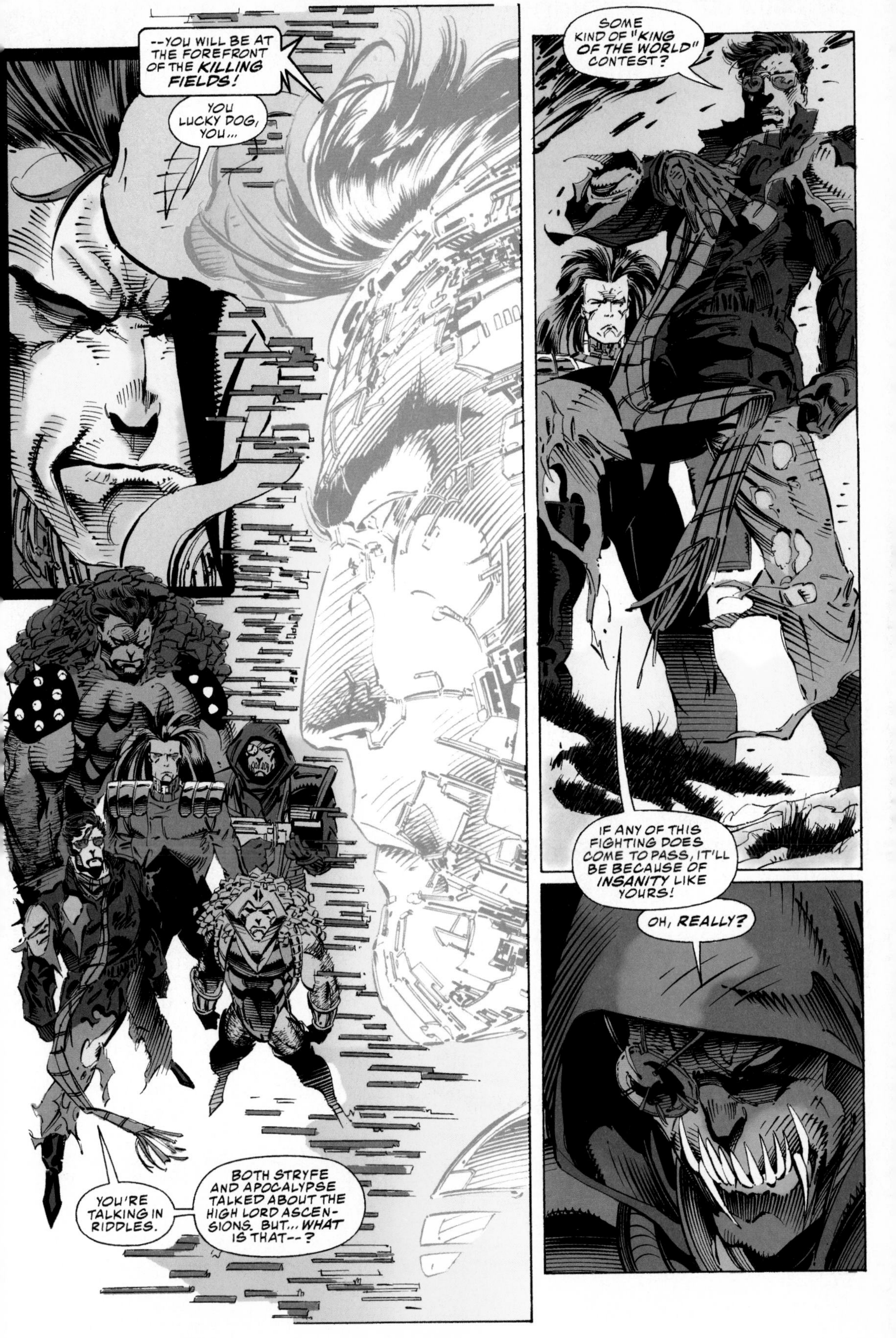
--YOU WILL BE AT THE FOREFRONT OF THE KILLING FIELDS!
YOU LUCKY DOG, YOU...
YOU'RE TALKING IN RIDDLES.
BOTH STRYFE AND APOCALYPSE TALKED ABOUT THE HIGH LORD ASCENSIONS. BUT... WHAT IS THAT--?
SOME KIND OF "KING OF THE WORLD" CONTEST?
IF ANY OF THIS FIGHTING DOES COME TO PASS, IT'LL BE BECAUSE OF INSANITY LIKE YOURS!
OH, REALLY?

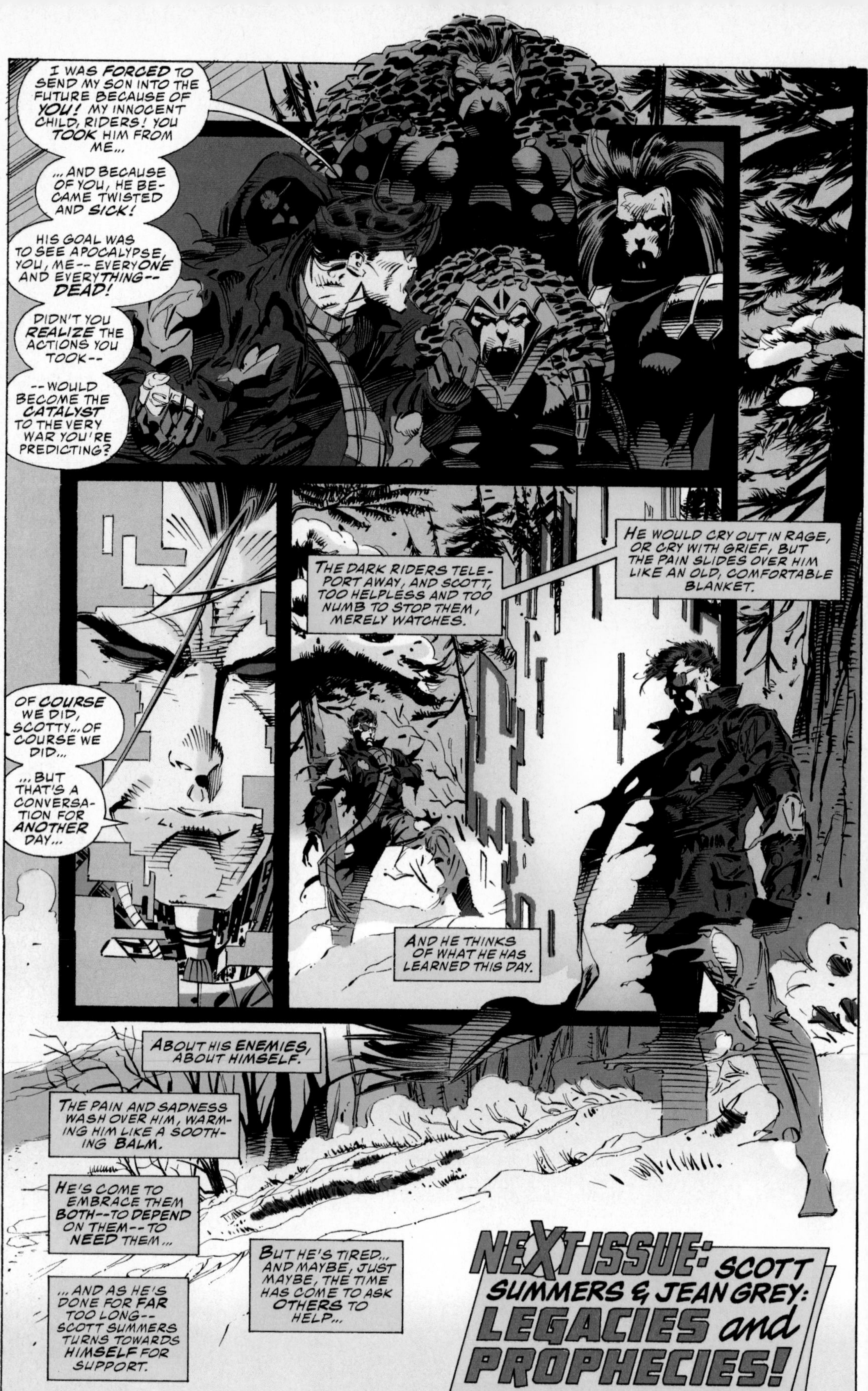
I WAS FORCED TO SEND MY SON INTO THE FUTURE BECAUSE OF YOU! MY INNOCENT CHILD, RIDERS! YOU TOOK HIM FROM ME...
...AND BECAUSE OF YOU, HE BECAME TWISTED AND SICK!
HIS GOAL WAS TO SEE APOCALYPSE, YOU, ME-- EVERYONE AND EVERYTHING-- DEAD!
DIDN'T YOU REALIZE THE ACTIONS YOU TOOK--
--WOULD BECOME THE CATALYST TO THE VERY WAR YOU'RE PREDICTING?
OF COURSE WE DID, SCOTTY... OF COURSE WE DID...
...BUT THAT'S A CONVERSATION FOR ANOTHER DAY...
THE DARK RIDERS TELEPORT AWAY, AND SCOTT, TOO HELPLESS AND TOO NUMB TO STOP THEM, MERELY WATCHES.
HE WOULD CRY OUT IN RAGE, OR CRY WITH GRIEF, BUT THE PAIN SLIDES OVER HIM LIKE AN OLD, COMFORTABLE BLANKET.
AND HE THINKS OF WHAT HE HAS LEARNED THIS DAY.
ABOUT HIS ENEMIES, ABOUT HIMSELF.
THE PAIN AND SADNESS WASH OVER HIM, WARMING HIM LIKE A SOOTHING BALM.
HE'S COME TO EMBRACE THEM BOTH--TO DEPEND ON THEM--TO NEED THEM...
...AND AS HE'S DONE FOR FAR TOO LONG--SCOTT SUMMERS TURNS TOWARDS HIMSELF FOR SUPPORT.
BUT HE'S TIRED... AND MAYBE, JUST MAYBE, THE TIME HAS COME TO ASK OTHERS TO HELP...
NEXT ISSUE: SCOTT SUMMERS & JEAN GREY: LEGACIES and PROPHECIES!

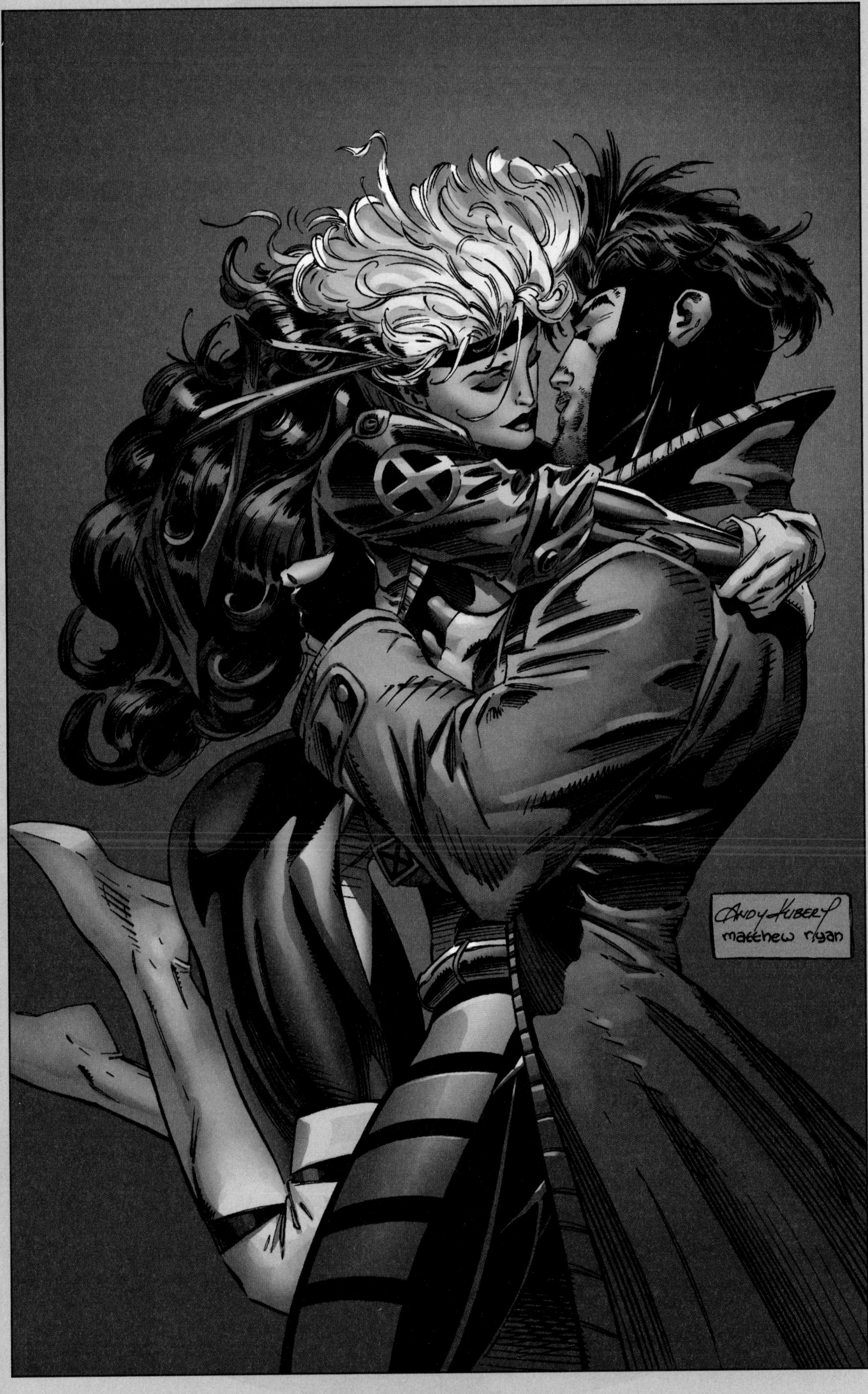

ANDY KUBERT
matthew ryan

As the X-Men continued finding evidence that Magneto was alive, Mr. Sinister's prediction abut Stryfe's virus proved true — and Illyana's "flu" soon transformed into a rapid, fatal disease. As Jubilee and Excalibur's Shadowcat tried to bolster Illyana's spirits, Professor X and Moira MacTaggert worked feverishly to find a cure — but to no avail. Tragically, Illyana died, sending Colossus and the X-Men into a deep depression...

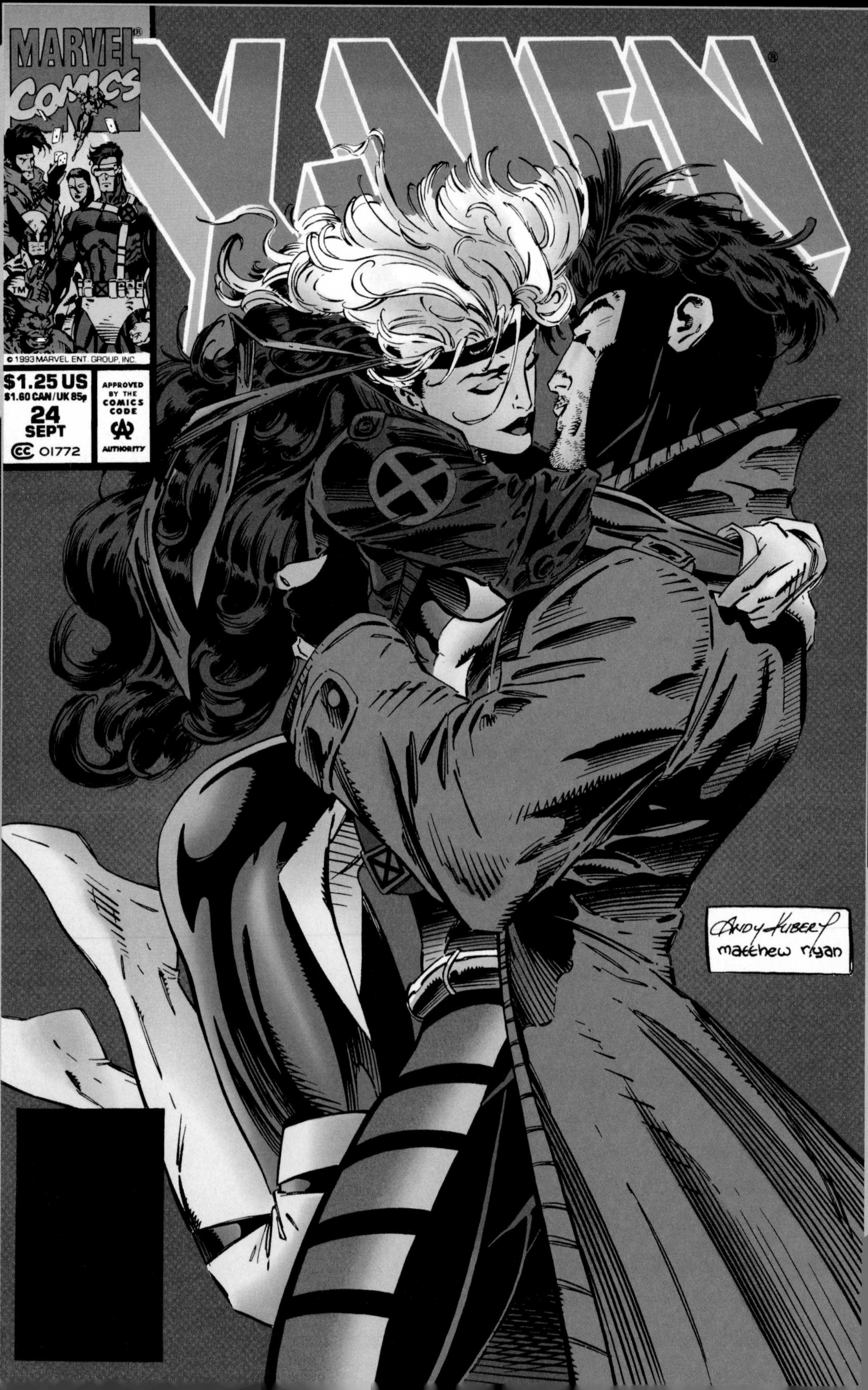

MARVEL COMICS
X-MEN
© 1993 MARVEL ENT. GROUP, INC.
$1.25 US
$1.60 CAN/UK 85p
24
SEPT
01772
APPROVED BY THE COMICS CODE AUTHORITY
ANDY KUBERT
matthew ryan

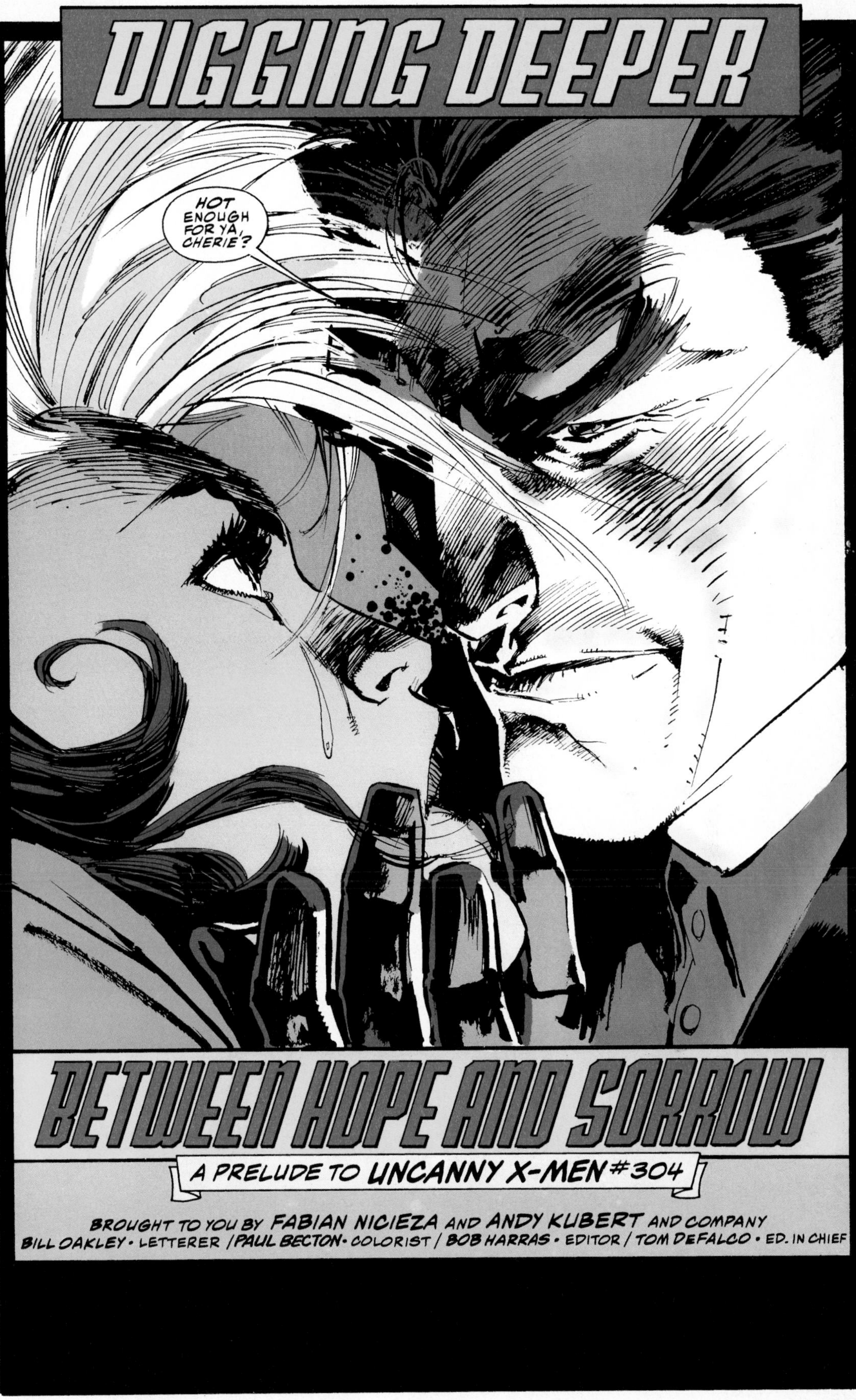
DIGGING DEEPER
HOT ENOUGH FOR YA, CHERIE?
BETWEEN HOPE AND SORROW
A PRELUDE TO UNCANNY X-MEN #304
BROUGHT TO YOU BY FABIAN NICIEZA AND ANDY KUBERT AND COMPANY
BILL OAKLEY • LETTERER / PAUL BECTON • COLORIST / BOB HARRAS • EDITOR / TOM DEFALCO • ED. IN CHIEF

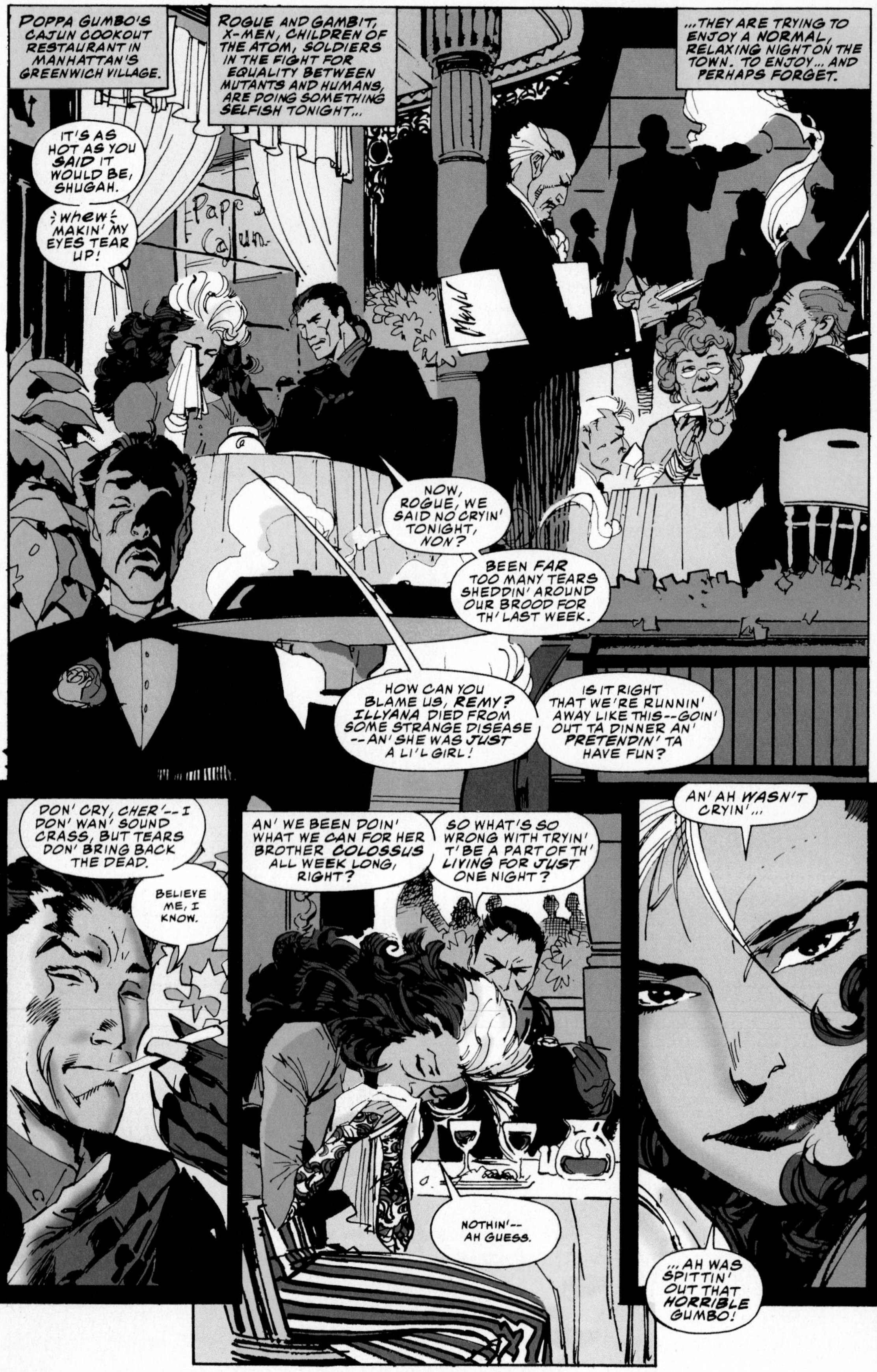

POPPA GUMBO'S CAJUN COOKOUT RESTAURANT IN MANHATTAN'S GREENWICH VILLAGE.
ROGUE AND GAMBIT, X-MEN, CHILDREN OF THE ATOM, SOLDIERS IN THE FIGHT FOR EQUALITY BETWEEN MUTANTS AND HUMANS, ARE DOING SOMETHING SELFISH TONIGHT...
...THEY ARE TRYING TO ENJOY A NORMAL, RELAXING NIGHT ON THE TOWN. TO ENJOY... AND PERHAPS FORGET.
IT'S AS HOT AS YOU SAID IT WOULD BE, SHUGAH.
whew MAKIN' MY EYES TEAR UP!
NOW, ROGUE, WE SAID NO CRYIN' TONIGHT, NON?
BEEN FAR TOO MANY TEARS SHEDDIN' AROUND OUR BROOD FOR TH' LAST WEEK.
HOW CAN YOU BLAME US, REMY? ILLYANA DIED FROM SOME STRANGE DISEASE --AN' SHE WAS JUST A LI'L GIRL!
IS IT RIGHT THAT WE'RE RUNNIN' AWAY LIKE THIS--GOIN' OUT TA DINNER AN' PRETENDIN' TA HAVE FUN?
DON' CRY, CHER'--I DON' WAN' SOUND CRASS, BUT TEARS DON' BRING BACK THE DEAD.
BELIEVE ME, I KNOW.
AN' WE BEEN DOIN' WHAT WE CAN FOR HER BROTHER COLOSSUS ALL WEEK LONG, RIGHT?
SO WHAT'S SO WRONG WITH TRYIN' T' BE A PART OF TH' LIVING FOR JUST ONE NIGHT?
NOTHIN'-- AH GUESS.
AN' AH WASN'T CRYIN'...
...AH WAS SPITTIN' OUT THAT HORRIBLE GUMBO!

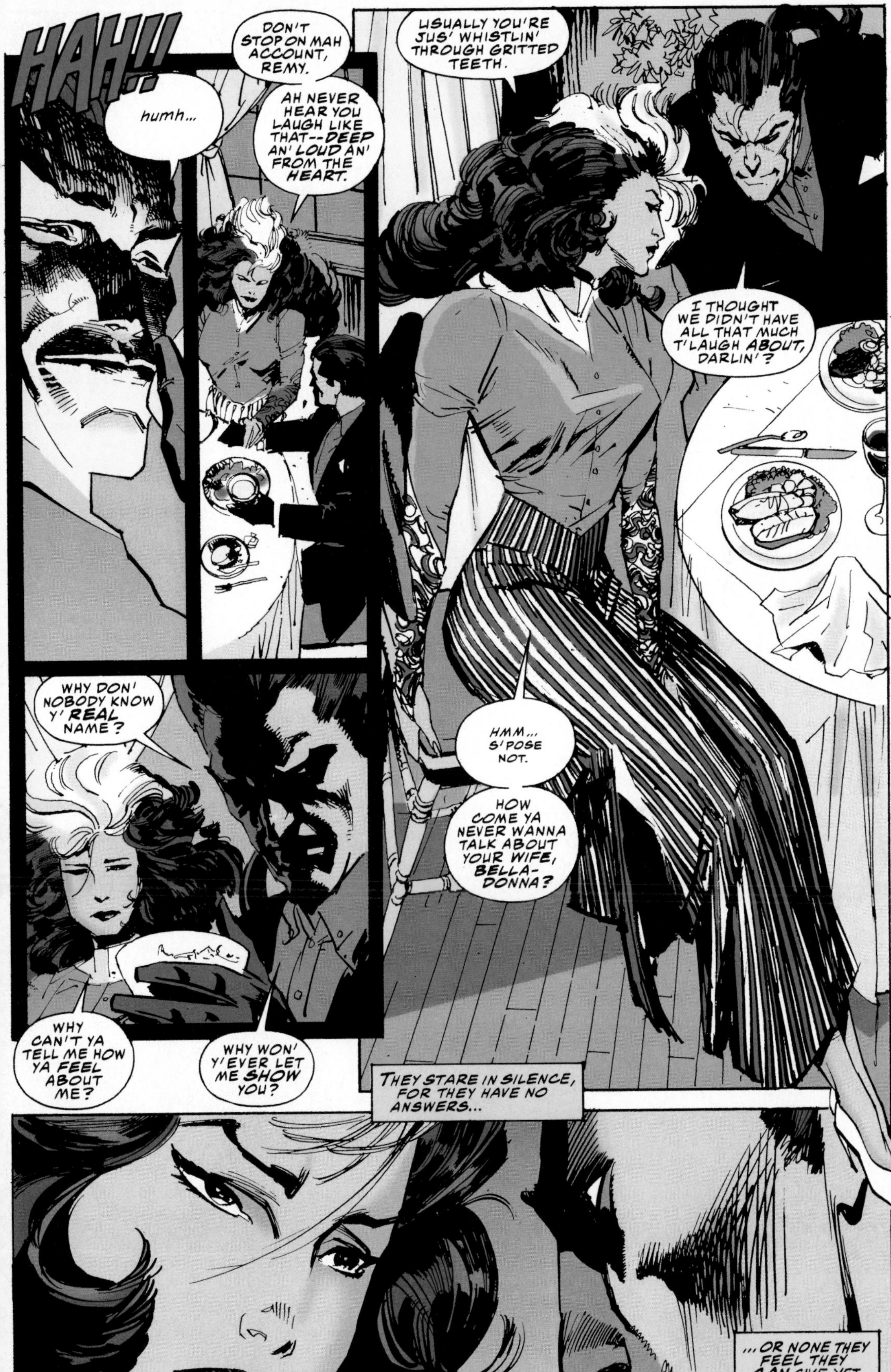
HAH!!
humh...
DON'T STOP ON MAH ACCOUNT, REMY.
AH NEVER HEAR YOU LAUGH LIKE THAT--DEEP AN' LOUD AN' FROM THE HEART.
USUALLY YOU'RE JUS' WHISTLIN' THROUGH GRITTED TEETH.
I THOUGHT WE DIDN'T HAVE ALL THAT MUCH T'LAUGH ABOUT, DARLIN'?
HMM... S'POSE NOT.
HOW COME YA NEVER WANNA TALK ABOUT YOUR WIFE, BELLA-DONNA?
WHY DON' NOBODY KNOW Y' REAL NAME?
WHY CAN'T YA TELL ME HOW YA FEEL ABOUT ME?
WHY WON' Y'EVER LET ME SHOW YOU?
THEY STARE IN SILENCE, FOR THEY HAVE NO ANSWERS...
...OR NONE THEY FEEL THEY CAN GIVE. YET...

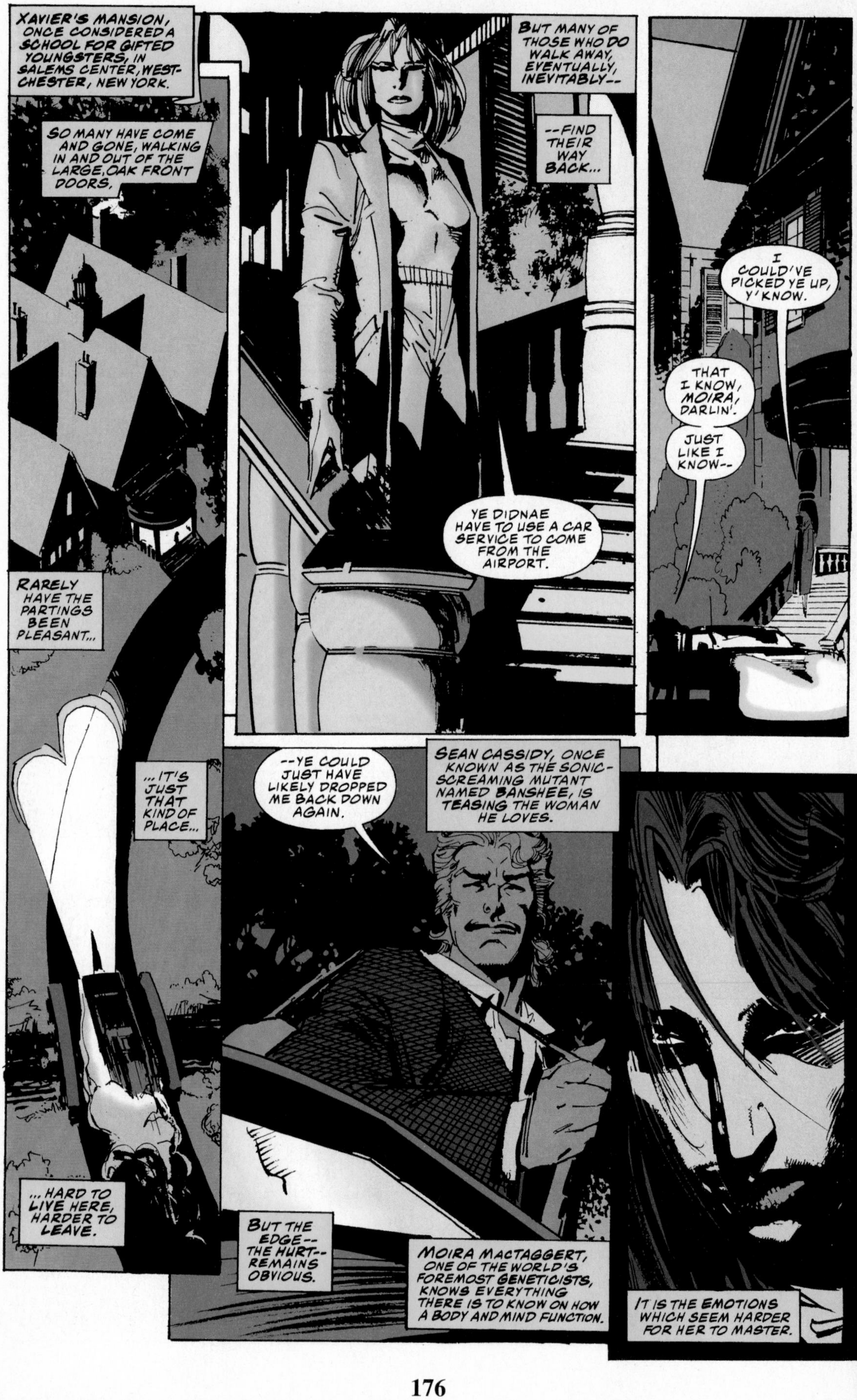
XAVIER'S MANSION, ONCE CONSIDERED A SCHOOL FOR GIFTED YOUNGSTERS, IN SALEMS CENTER, WEST-CHESTER, NEW YORK.
SO MANY HAVE COME AND GONE, WALKING IN AND OUT OF THE LARGE, OAK FRONT DOORS.
RARELY HAVE THE PARTINGS BEEN PLEASANT...
...IT'S JUST THAT KIND OF PLACE...
...HARD TO LIVE HERE, HARDER TO LEAVE.
BUT MANY OF THOSE WHO DO WALK AWAY, EVENTUALLY, INEVITABLY--
--FIND THEIR WAY BACK...
YE DIDNAE HAVE TO USE A CAR SERVICE TO COME FROM THE AIRPORT.
I COULD'VE PICKED YE UP, Y'KNOW.
THAT I KNOW, MOIRA, DARLIN'.
JUST LIKE I KNOW--
--YE COULD JUST HAVE LIKELY DROPPED ME BACK DOWN AGAIN.
SEAN CASSIDY, ONCE KNOWN AS THE SONIC-SCREAMING MUTANT NAMED BANSHEE, IS TEASING THE WOMAN HE LOVES.
BUT THE EDGE-- THE HURT-- REMAINS OBVIOUS.
MOIRA MACTAGGERT, ONE OF THE WORLD'S FOREMOST GENETICISTS, KNOWS EVERYTHING THERE IS TO KNOW ON HOW A BODY AND MIND FUNCTION.
IT IS THE EMOTIONS WHICH SEEM HARDER FOR HER TO MASTER.

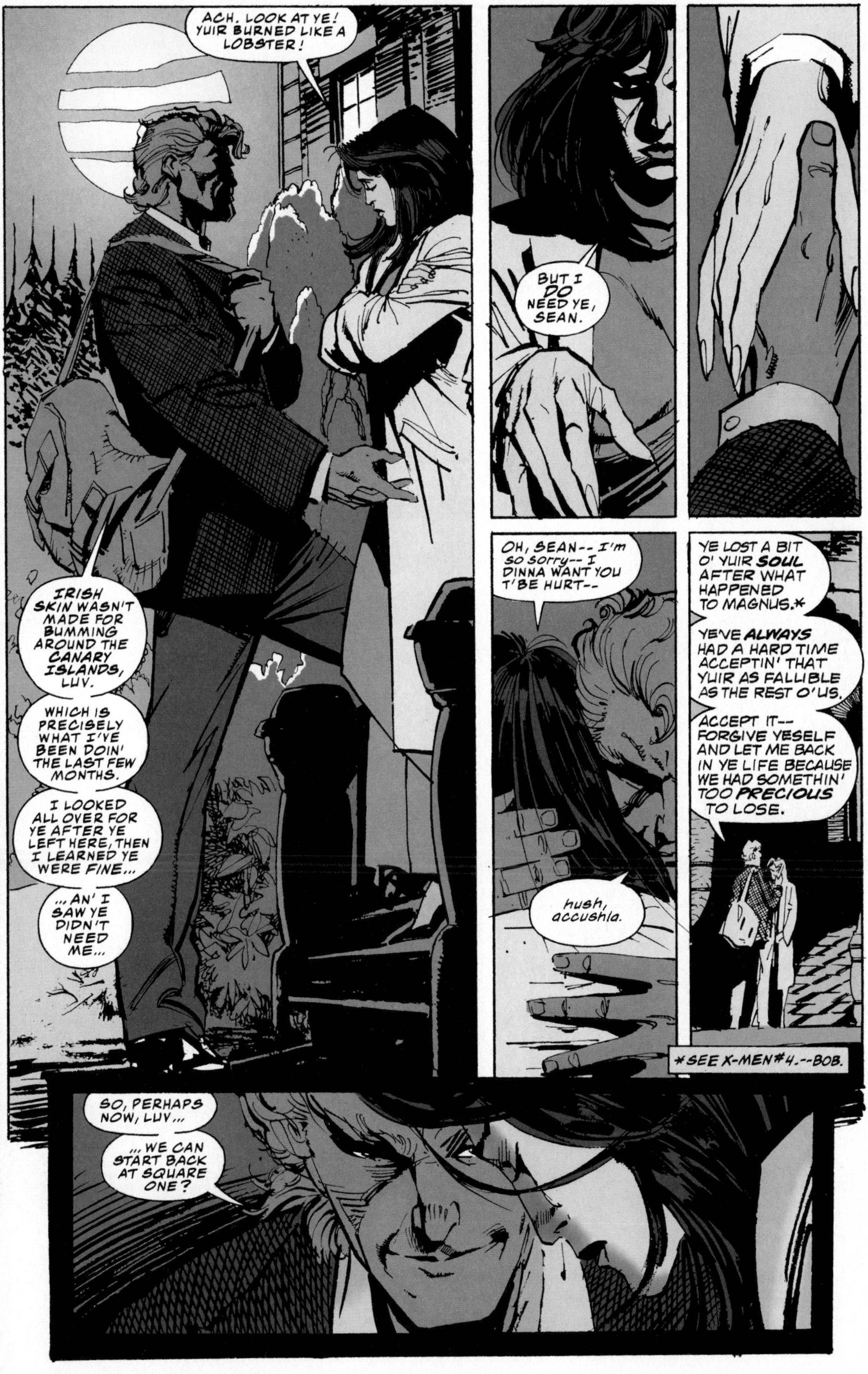
ACH. LOOK AT YE! YUIR BURNED LIKE A LOBSTER!
IRISH SKIN WASN'T MADE FOR BUMMING AROUND THE CANARY ISLANDS, LUV.
WHICH IS PRECISELY WHAT I'VE BEEN DOIN' THE LAST FEW MONTHS.
I LOOKED ALL OVER FOR YE AFTER YE LEFT HERE, THEN I LEARNED YE WERE FINE...
...AN' I SAW YE DIDN'T NEED ME...
BUT I DO NEED YE, SEAN.
OH, SEAN-- I'm so sorry-- I DINNA WANT YOU T'BE HURT--
hush, accushla.
YE LOST A BIT O' YUIR SOUL AFTER WHAT HAPPENED TO MAGNUS.*
YE'VE ALWAYS HAD A HARD TIME ACCEPTIN' THAT YUIR AS FALLIBLE AS THE REST O'US.
ACCEPT IT-- FORGIVE YESELF AND LET ME BACK IN YE LIFE BECAUSE WE HAD SOMETHIN' TOO PRECIOUS TO LOSE.
*SEE X-MEN #4.--BOB.
SO, PERHAPS NOW, LUV...
...WE CAN START BACK AT SQUARE ONE?

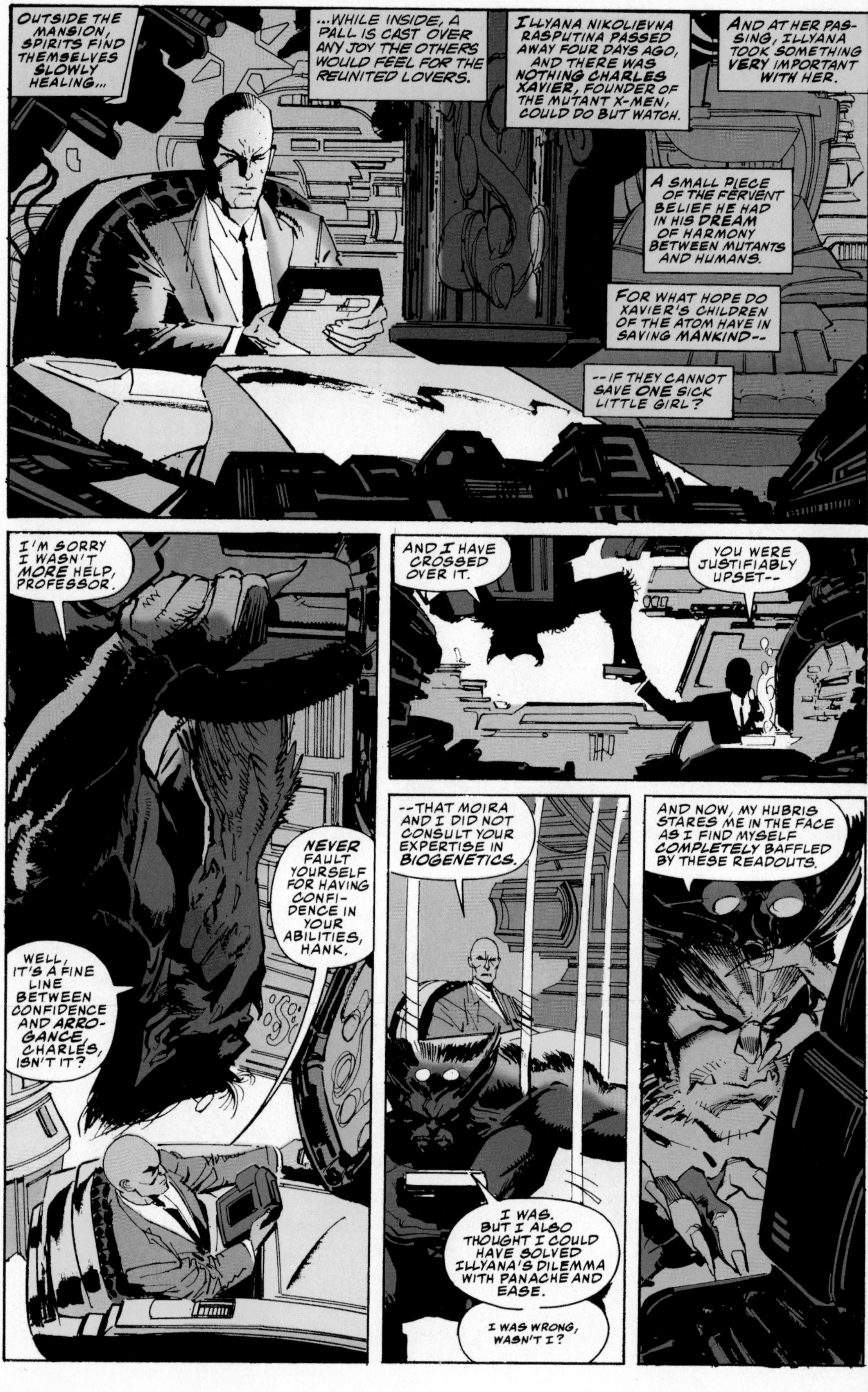
OUTSIDE THE MANSION, SPIRITS FIND THEMSELVES SLOWLY HEALING...
...WHILE INSIDE, A PALL IS CAST OVER ANY JOY THE OTHERS WOULD FEEL FOR THE REUNITED LOVERS.
ILLYANA NIKOLIEVNA RASPUTINA PASSED AWAY FOUR DAYS AGO, AND THERE WAS NOTHING CHARLES XAVIER, FOUNDER OF THE MUTANT X-MEN, COULD DO BUT WATCH.
AND AT HER PASSING, ILLYANA TOOK SOMETHING VERY IMPORTANT WITH HER.
A SMALL PIECE OF THE FERVENT BELIEF HE HAD IN HIS DREAM OF HARMONY BETWEEN MUTANTS AND HUMANS.
FOR WHAT HOPE DO XAVIER'S CHILDREN OF THE ATOM HAVE IN SAVING MANKIND--
--IF THEY CANNOT SAVE ONE SICK LITTLE GIRL?
I'M SORRY I WASN'T MORE HELP, PROFESSOR.
AND I HAVE CROSSED OVER IT.
YOU WERE JUSTIFIABLY UPSET--
--THAT MOIRA AND I DID NOT CONSULT YOUR EXPERTISE IN BIOGENETICS.
AND NOW, MY HUBRIS STARES ME IN THE FACE AS I FIND MYSELF COMPLETELY BAFFLED BY THESE READOUTS.
NEVER FAULT YOURSELF FOR HAVING CONFIDENCE IN YOUR ABILITIES, HANK.
WELL, IT'S A FINE LINE BETWEEN CONFIDENCE AND ARROGANCE, CHARLES, ISN'T IT?
I WAS. BUT I ALSO THOUGHT I COULD HAVE SOLVED ILLYANA'S DILEMMA WITH PANACHE AND EASE.
I WAS WRONG, WASN'T I?

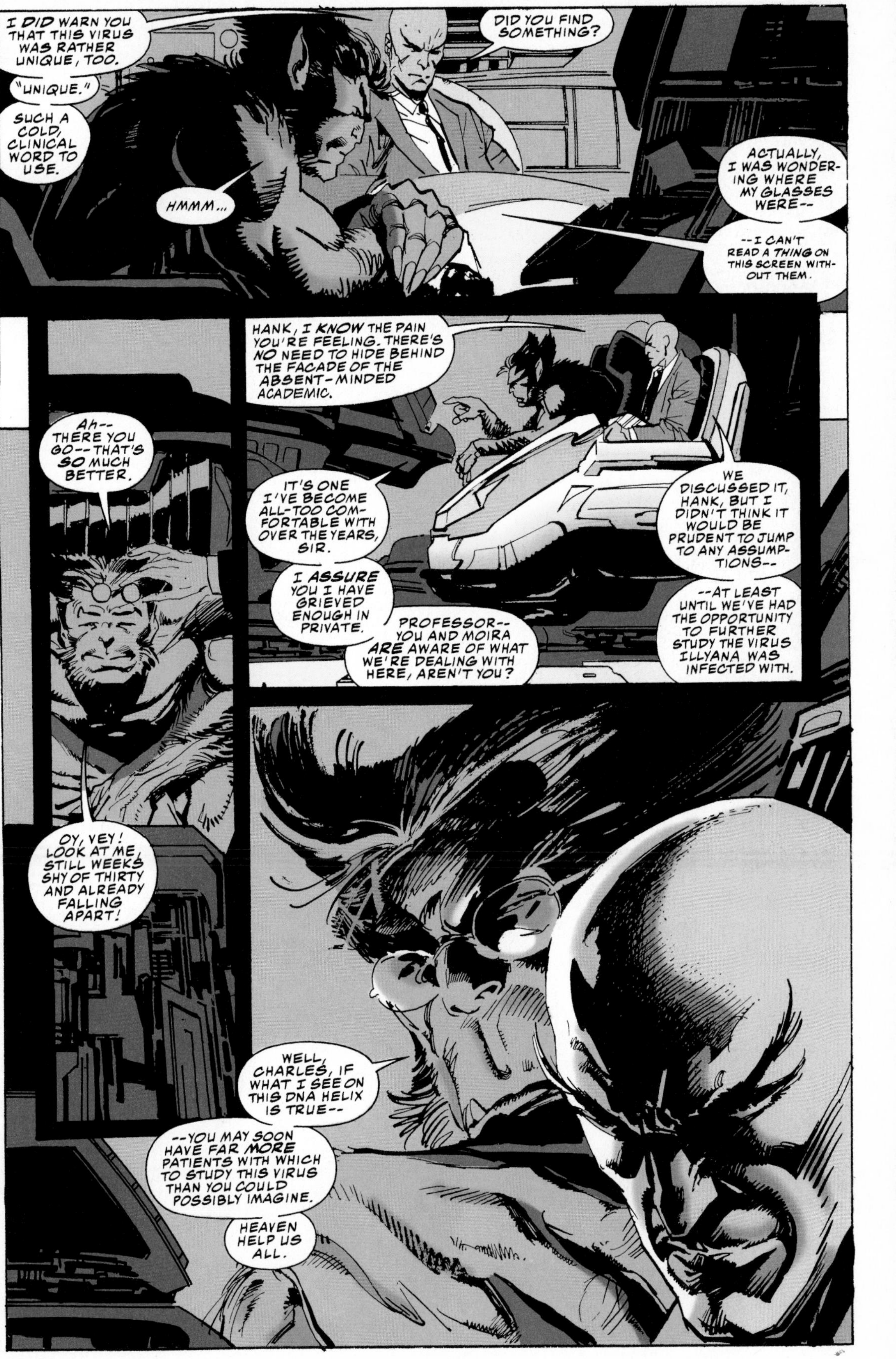

I DID WARN YOU THAT THIS VIRUS WAS RATHER UNIQUE, TOO.
DID YOU FIND SOMETHING?
"UNIQUE."
SUCH A COLD, CLINICAL WORD TO USE.
HMMM...
ACTUALLY, I WAS WONDERING WHERE MY GLASSES WERE--
--I CAN'T READ A THING ON THIS SCREEN WITHOUT THEM.
Ah-- THERE YOU GO--THAT'S SO MUCH BETTER.
HANK, I KNOW THE PAIN YOU'RE FEELING. THERE'S NO NEED TO HIDE BEHIND THE FACADE OF THE ABSENT-MINDED ACADEMIC.
IT'S ONE I'VE BECOME ALL-TOO COMFORTABLE WITH OVER THE YEARS, SIR.
I ASSURE YOU I HAVE GRIEVED ENOUGH IN PRIVATE.
PROFESSOR-- YOU AND MOIRA ARE AWARE OF WHAT WE'RE DEALING WITH HERE, AREN'T YOU?
WE DISCUSSED IT, HANK, BUT I DIDN'T THINK IT WOULD BE PRUDENT TO JUMP TO ANY ASSUMPTIONS--
--AT LEAST UNTIL WE'VE HAD THE OPPORTUNITY TO FURTHER STUDY THE VIRUS ILLYANA WAS INFECTED WITH.
OY, VEY! LOOK AT ME, STILL WEEKS SHY OF THIRTY AND ALREADY FALLING APART!
WELL, CHARLES, IF WHAT I SEE ON THIS DNA HELIX IS TRUE--
--YOU MAY SOON HAVE FAR MORE PATIENTS WITH WHICH TO STUDY THIS VIRUS THAN YOU COULD POSSIBLY IMAGINE.
HEAVEN HELP US ALL.

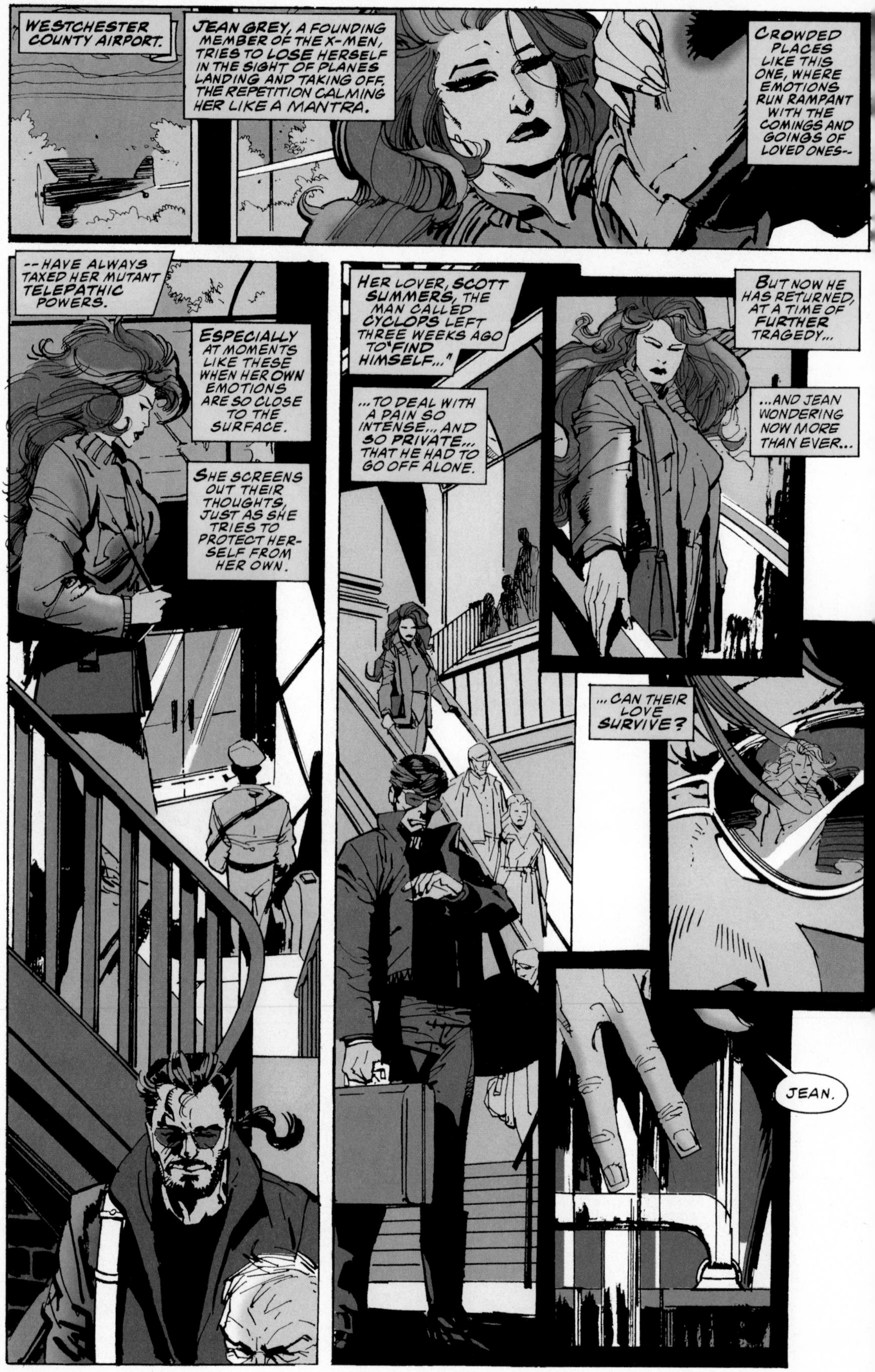

WESTCHESTER COUNTY AIRPORT.
JEAN GREY, A FOUNDING MEMBER OF THE X-MEN, TRIES TO LOSE HERSELF IN THE SIGHT OF PLANES LANDING AND TAKING OFF, THE REPETITION CALMING HER LIKE A MANTRA.
CROWDED PLACES LIKE THIS ONE, WHERE EMOTIONS RUN RAMPANT WITH THE COMINGS AND GOINGS OF LOVED ONES--
--HAVE ALWAYS TAXED HER MUTANT TELEPATHIC POWERS.
ESPECIALLY AT MOMENTS LIKE THESE WHEN HER OWN EMOTIONS ARE SO CLOSE TO THE SURFACE.
SHE SCREENS OUT THEIR THOUGHTS, JUST AS SHE TRIES TO PROTECT HER-SELF FROM HER OWN.
HER LOVER, SCOTT SUMMERS, THE MAN CALLED CYCLOPS LEFT THREE WEEKS AGO TO "FIND HIMSELF..."
...TO DEAL WITH A PAIN SO INTENSE... AND SO PRIVATE... THAT HE HAD TO GO OFF ALONE.
BUT NOW HE HAS RETURNED, AT A TIME OF FURTHER TRAGEDY...
...AND JEAN WONDERING NOW MORE THAN EVER...
...CAN THEIR LOVE SURVIVE?
JEAN.

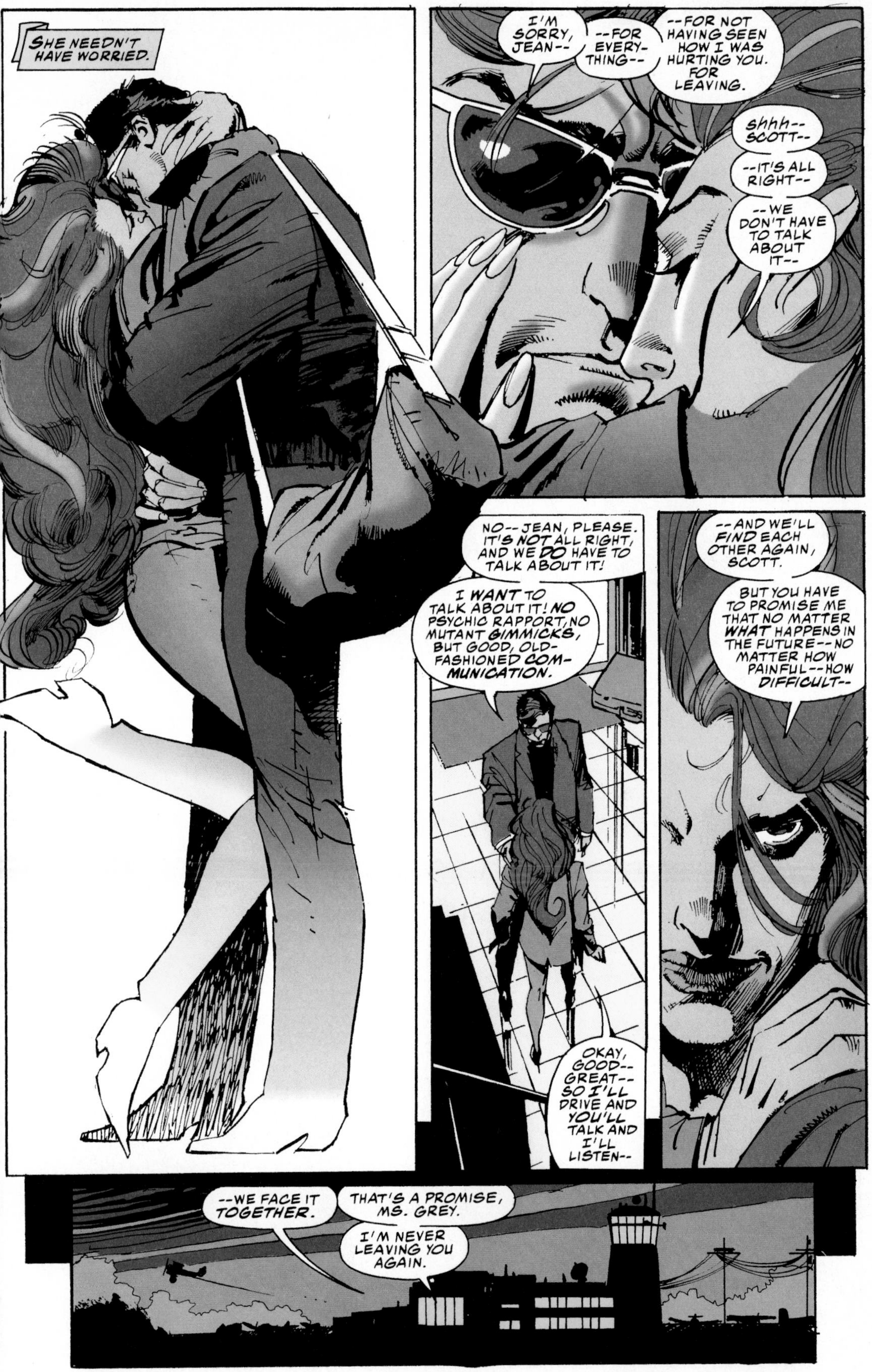

SHE NEEDN'T HAVE WORRIED.
I'M SORRY, JEAN--
--FOR EVERY-THING--
--FOR NOT HAVING SEEN HOW I WAS HURTING YOU. FOR LEAVING.
SHHH-- SCOTT--
--IT'S ALL RIGHT--
--WE DON'T HAVE TO TALK ABOUT IT--
NO-- JEAN, PLEASE. IT'S NOT ALL RIGHT, AND WE DO HAVE TO TALK ABOUT IT!
I WANT TO TALK ABOUT IT! NO PSYCHIC RAPPORT, NO MUTANT GIMMICKS, BUT GOOD, OLD-FASHIONED COMMUNICATION.
--AND WE'LL FIND EACH OTHER AGAIN, SCOTT.
BUT YOU HAVE TO PROMISE ME THAT NO MATTER WHAT HAPPENS IN THE FUTURE--NO MATTER HOW PAINFUL--HOW DIFFICULT--
OKAY, GOOD-- GREAT-- SO I'LL DRIVE AND YOU'LL TALK AND I'LL LISTEN--
--WE FACE IT TOGETHER.
THAT'S A PROMISE, MS. GREY.
I'M NEVER LEAVING YOU AGAIN.

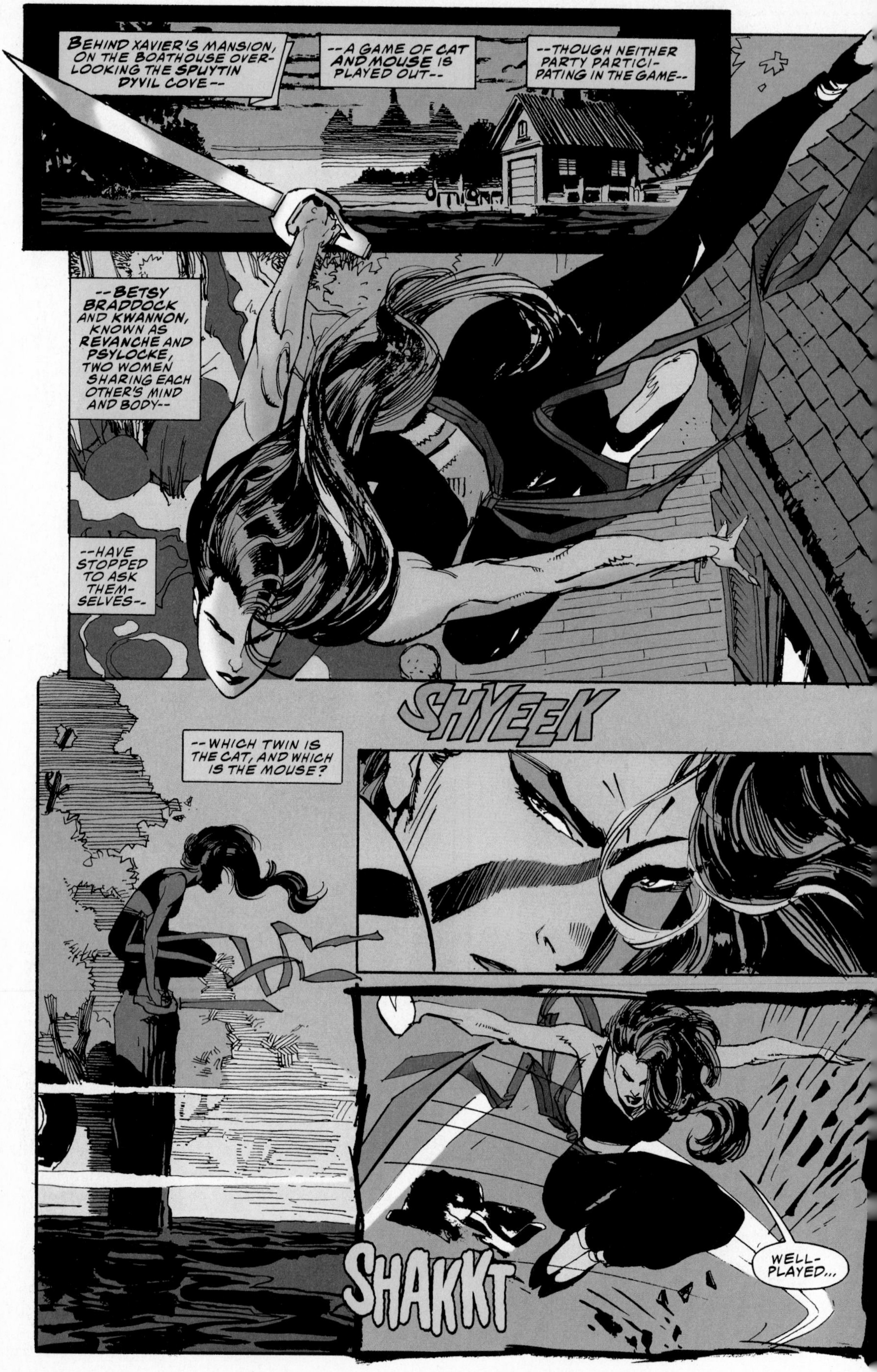
BEHIND XAVIER'S MANSION, ON THE BOATHOUSE OVER-LOOKING THE SPUYTIN DYVIL COVE--
--A GAME OF CAT AND MOUSE IS PLAYED OUT--
--THOUGH NEITHER PARTY PARTICI-PATING IN THE GAME--
--BETSY BRADDOCK AND KWANNON, KNOWN AS REVANCHE AND PSYLOCKE, TWO WOMEN SHARING EACH OTHER'S MIND AND BODY--
--HAVE STOPPED TO ASK THEM-SELVES--
SHYEEK
--WHICH TWIN IS THE CAT, AND WHICH IS THE MOUSE?
SHAKKT
WELL-PLAYED...

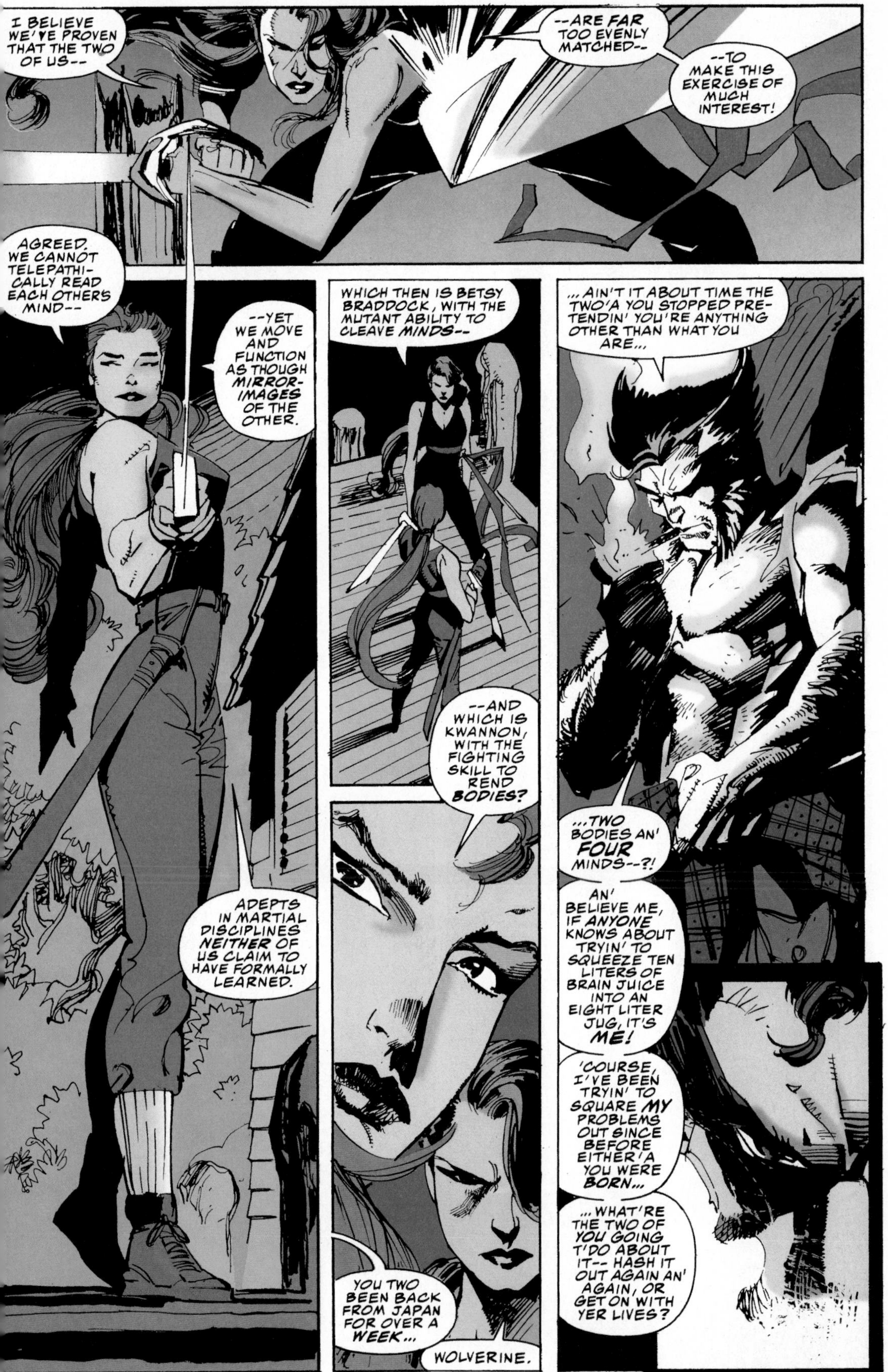

I BELIEVE WE'VE PROVEN THAT THE TWO OF US--
--ARE FAR TOO EVENLY MATCHED--
--TO MAKE THIS EXERCISE OF MUCH INTEREST!
AGREED. WE CANNOT TELEPATHI-CALLY READ EACH OTHER'S MIND--
--YET WE MOVE AND FUNCTION AS THOUGH MIRROR-IMAGES OF THE OTHER.
ADEPTS IN MARTIAL DISCIPLINES NEITHER OF US CLAIM TO HAVE FORMALLY LEARNED.
WHICH THEN IS BETSY BRADDOCK, WITH THE MUTANT ABILITY TO CLEAVE MINDS--
--AND WHICH IS KWANNON, WITH THE FIGHTING SKILL TO REND BODIES?
YOU TWO BEEN BACK FROM JAPAN FOR OVER A WEEK...
WOLVERINE.
...AIN'T IT ABOUT TIME THE TWO'A YOU STOPPED PRE-TENDIN' YOU'RE ANYTHING OTHER THAN WHAT YOU ARE...
...TWO BODIES AN' FOUR MINDS--?!
AN' BELIEVE ME, IF ANYONE KNOWS ABOUT TRYIN' TO SQUEEZE TEN LITERS OF BRAIN JUICE INTO AN EIGHT LITER JUG, IT'S ME!
'COURSE, I'VE BEEN TRYIN' TO SQUARE MY PROBLEMS OUT SINCE BEFORE EITHER'A YOU WERE BORN...
...WHAT'RE THE TWO OF YOU GOING T'DO ABOUT IT-- HASH IT OUT AGAIN AN' AGAIN, OR GET ON WITH YER LIVES?

JUBILATION LEE IS THE YOUNGEST MUTANT IN THE MANSION.

UNTIL THIS WEEK--THOUGH SHE WOULD ADMIT IT TO NO ONE-- LIVING HERE HAD BEEN THE GREATEST ADVENTURE OF HER TROUBLED, SAD LIFE.

BUT IT'S NOT A GAME NOW. IT'S NOT AN ADVENTURE ANYMORE.

EVEN LITTLE CHILDREN CAN DIE IF THEY LIVE IN THIS HOUSE.

THAT MAKES THINGS... SERIOUS...

...AND JUBILEE HAS FOUGHT LONG AND HARD TO PREVENT HER LIFE FROM GETTING SERIOUS...

...BECAUSE IF IT DOES, IF SHE LETS IT ALL IN, IT WOULD DROWN HER-- IT WOULD RIP HER APART--

--AND THEN WHAT WOULD HAPPEN TO HER?

JUBILEE...

--I GAVE ILLYANA THAT BAMF DOLL WHEN SHE WAS ABOUT YOUR AGE. IT IS KIND OF COMFORTING, ISN'T IT?

I THOUGHT MAYBE YOU'D LIKE TO HANG ON TO IT...

AT ONE TIME, KITTY PRYDE, NOW A MEMBER OF THE BRITISH MUTANT TEAM, EXCALIBUR, HAD BEEN IN JUBILEE'S PLACE.

SHE HAD BEEN THE YOUNGEST ONE IN THE HOUSE.

AND KITTY KNOWS FULL WELL HOW LONELY THAT CAN BE...

...ESPECIALLY IF YOU ALWAYS REFUSE TO ANSWER THE DOOR WHEN COMPANY COMES KNOCKING...

STUPID STUFFED RAG-- WHO CARES?

...IT'S IMPORTANT TO HANG ON TO THINGS IN LIFE, JUBILEE. THEY BECOME OUR TOUCHSTONES.

REMINDERS OF THOSE WE'VE ...LOST.

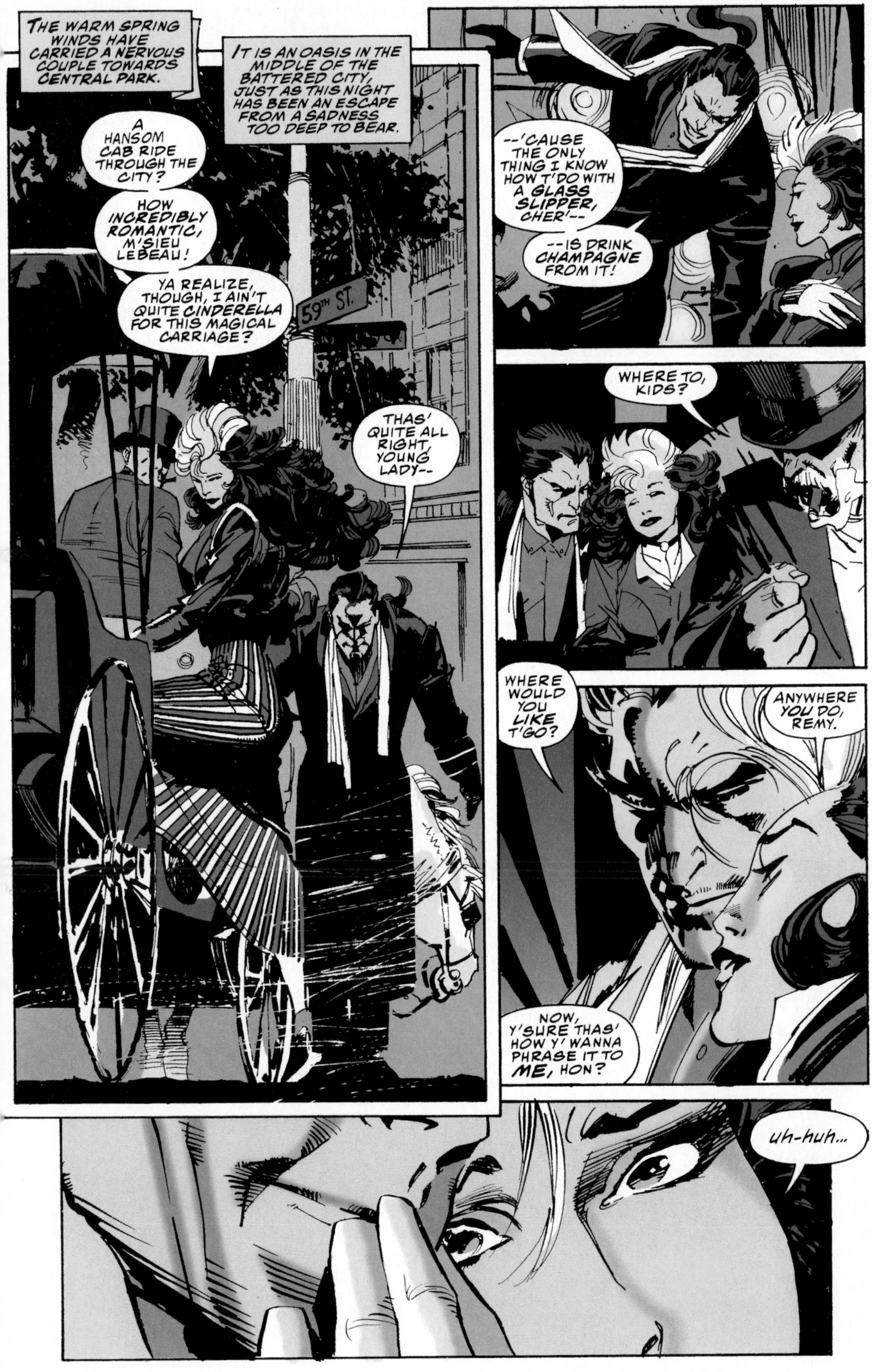
THE WARM SPRING WINDS HAVE CARRIED A NERVOUS COUPLE TOWARDS CENTRAL PARK.
IT IS AN OASIS IN THE MIDDLE OF THE BATTERED CITY, JUST AS THIS NIGHT HAS BEEN AN ESCAPE FROM A SADNESS TOO DEEP TO BEAR.
A HANSOM CAB RIDE THROUGH THE CITY?
HOW INCREDIBLY ROMANTIC, M'SIEU LEBEAU!
YA REALIZE, THOUGH, I AIN'T QUITE CINDERELLA FOR THIS MAGICAL CARRIAGE?
59TH ST.
THAS' QUITE ALL RIGHT, YOUNG LADY--
--'CAUSE THE ONLY THING I KNOW HOW T'DO WITH A GLASS SLIPPER, CHER'--
--IS DRINK CHAMPAGNE FROM IT!
WHERE TO, KIDS?
WHERE WOULD YOU LIKE T'GO?
ANYWHERE YOU DO, REMY.
NOW, Y'SURE THAS' HOW Y'WANNA PHRASE IT TO ME, HON?
uh-huh...

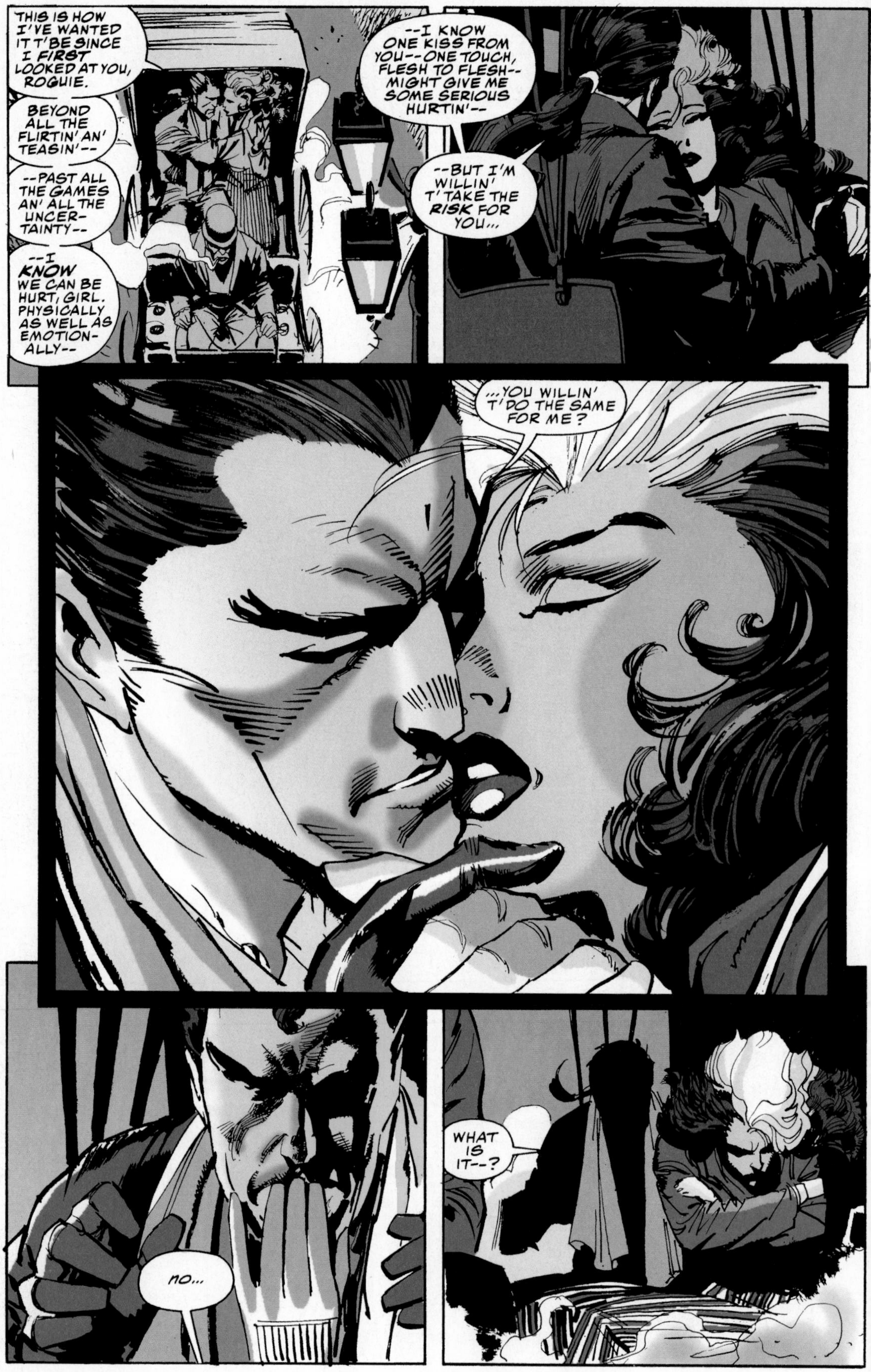
THIS IS HOW I'VE WANTED IT T'BE SINCE I FIRST LOOKED AT YOU, ROGUIE.
BEYOND ALL THE FLIRTIN' AN' TEASIN'--
--PAST ALL THE GAMES AN' ALL THE UNCER-TAINTY--
--I KNOW WE CAN BE HURT, GIRL. PHYSICALLY AS WELL AS EMOTION-ALLY--
--I KNOW ONE KISS FROM YOU--ONE TOUCH, FLESH TO FLESH--MIGHT GIVE ME SOME SERIOUS HURTIN'--
--BUT I'M WILLIN' T'TAKE THE RISK FOR YOU...
...YOU WILLIN' T'DO THE SAME FOR ME?
no...
WHAT IS IT--?

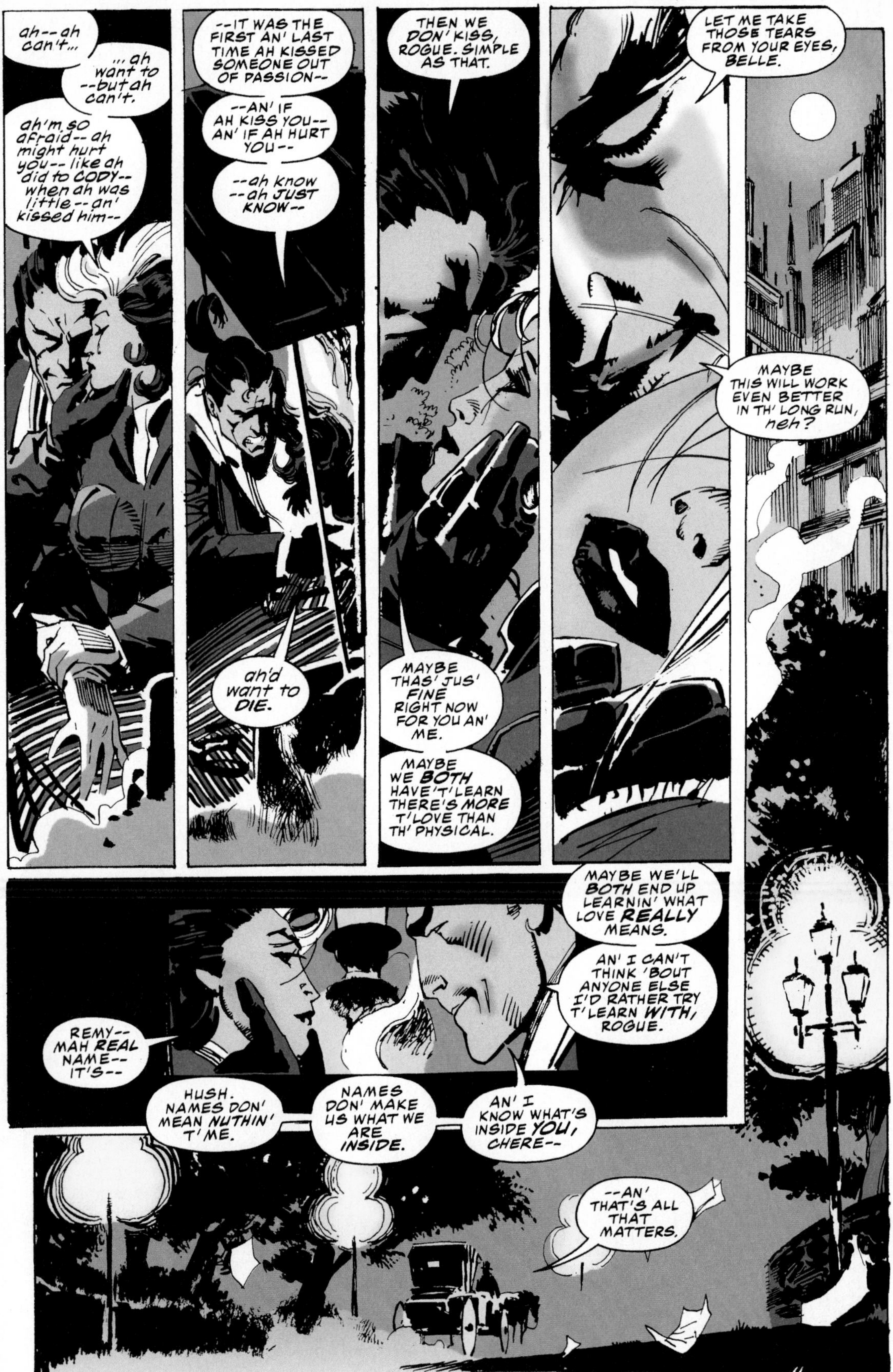

ah--ah can't...
...ah want to --but ah can't.
ah'm so afraid--ah might hurt you--like ah did to CODY--when ah was little--an' kissed him--
--IT WAS THE FIRST AN' LAST TIME AH KISSED SOMEONE OUT OF PASSION--
--AN' IF AH KISS YOU--AN' IF AH HURT YOU--
--ah know --ah JUST KNOW--
ah'd want to DIE.
THEN WE DON' KISS, ROGUE. SIMPLE AS THAT.
MAYBE THAS' JUS' FINE RIGHT NOW FOR YOU AN' ME.
MAYBE WE BOTH HAVE'T'LEARN THERE'S MORE T'LOVE THAN TH' PHYSICAL.
LET ME TAKE THOSE TEARS FROM YOUR EYES, BELLE.
MAYBE THIS WILL WORK EVEN BETTER IN TH' LONG RUN, neh?
MAYBE WE'LL BOTH END UP LEARNIN' WHAT LOVE REALLY MEANS.
AN' I CAN'T THINK 'BOUT ANYONE ELSE I'D RATHER TRY T'LEARN WITH, ROGUE.
REMY--MAH REAL NAME--IT'S--
HUSH. NAMES DON' MEAN NUTHIN' T'ME.
NAMES DON' MAKE US WHAT WE ARE INSIDE.
AN' I KNOW WHAT'S INSIDE YOU, CHERE--
--AN' THAT'S ALL THAT MATTERS.

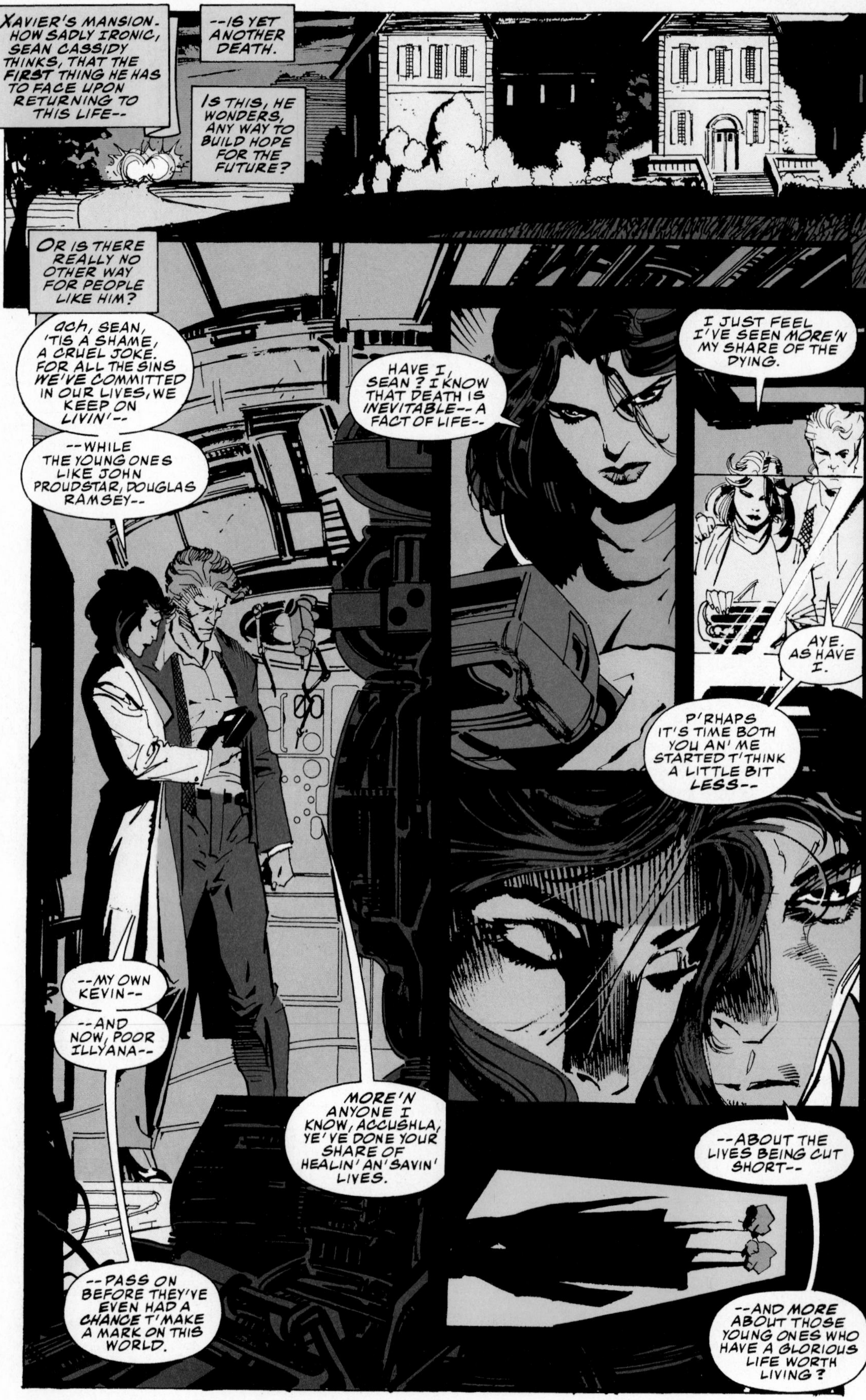
XAVIER'S MANSION. HOW SADLY IRONIC, SEAN CASSIDY THINKS, THAT THE FIRST THING HE HAS TO FACE UPON RETURNING TO THIS LIFE--
--IS YET ANOTHER DEATH.
IS THIS, HE WONDERS, ANY WAY TO BUILD HOPE FOR THE FUTURE?
OR IS THERE REALLY NO OTHER WAY FOR PEOPLE LIKE HIM?
ACH, SEAN, 'TIS A SHAME, A CRUEL JOKE. FOR ALL THE SINS WE'VE COMMITTED IN OUR LIVES, WE KEEP ON LIVIN'--
--WHILE THE YOUNG ONES LIKE JOHN PROUDSTAR, DOUGLAS RAMSEY--
--MY OWN KEVIN--
--AND NOW, POOR ILLYANA--
--PASS ON BEFORE THEY'VE EVEN HAD A CHANCE T'MAKE A MARK ON THIS WORLD.
MORE'N ANYONE I KNOW, ACCUSHLA, YE'VE DONE YOUR SHARE OF HEALIN' AN' SAVIN' LIVES.
HAVE I, SEAN? I KNOW THAT DEATH IS INEVITABLE-- A FACT OF LIFE--
I JUST FEEL I'VE SEEN MORE'N MY SHARE OF THE DYING.
AYE. AS HAVE I.
P'RHAPS IT'S TIME BOTH YOU AN' ME STARTED T'THINK A LITTLE BIT LESS--
--ABOUT THE LIVES BEING CUT SHORT--
--AND MORE ABOUT THOSE YOUNG ONES WHO HAVE A GLORIOUS LIFE WORTH LIVING?

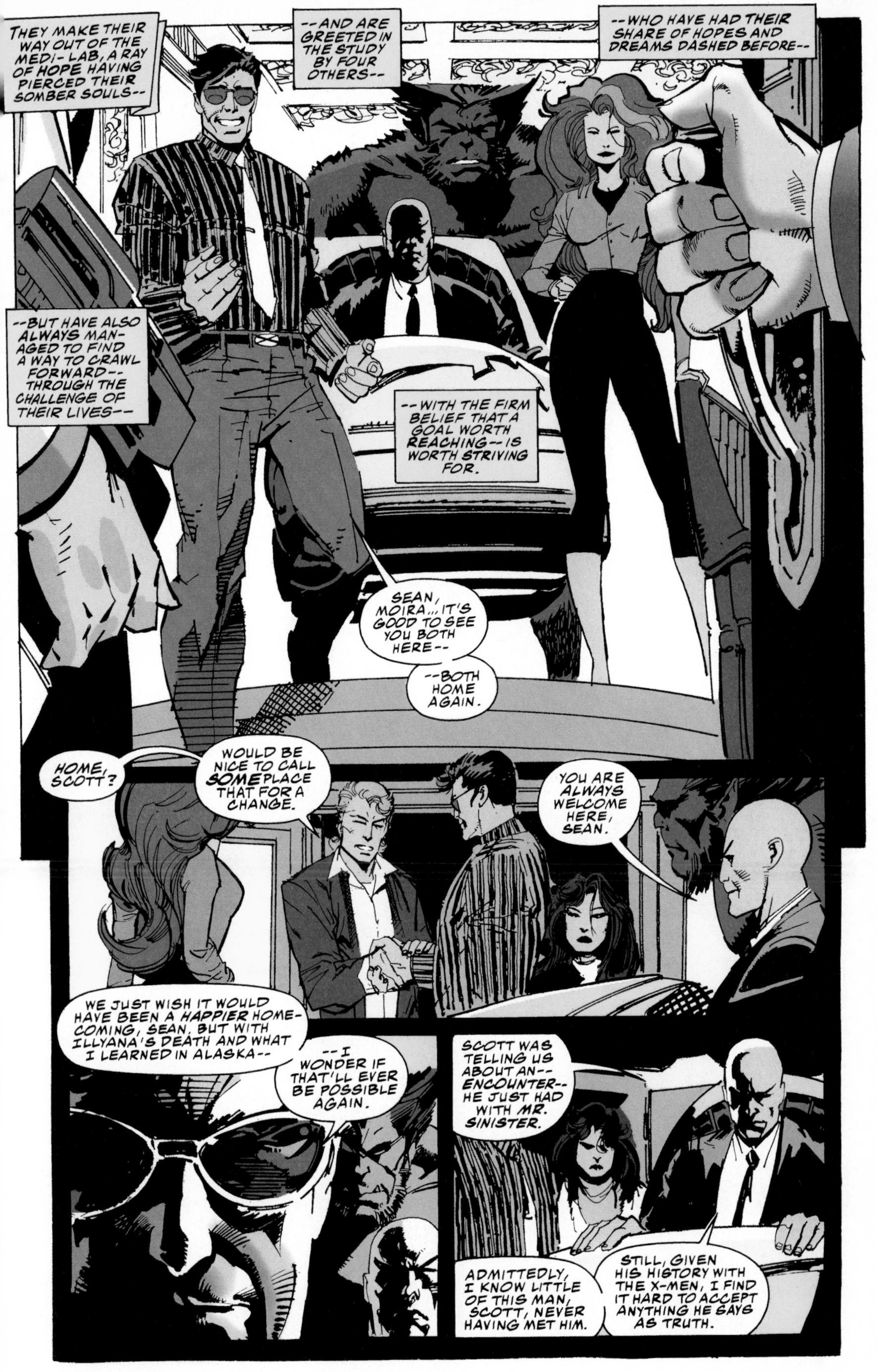
THEY MAKE THEIR WAY OUT OF THE MEDI-LAB, A RAY OF HOPE HAVING PIERCED THEIR SOMBER SOULS--
--AND ARE GREETED IN THE STUDY BY FOUR OTHERS--
--WHO HAVE HAD THEIR SHARE OF HOPES AND DREAMS DASHED BEFORE--
--BUT HAVE ALSO ALWAYS MANAGED TO FIND A WAY TO CRAWL FORWARD--THROUGH THE CHALLENGE OF THEIR LIVES--
--WITH THE FIRM BELIEF THAT A GOAL WORTH REACHING--IS WORTH STRIVING FOR.
SEAN, MOIRA... IT'S GOOD TO SEE YOU BOTH HERE--
--BOTH HOME AGAIN.
HOME, SCOTT?
WOULD BE NICE TO CALL SOMEPLACE THAT FOR A CHANGE.
YOU ARE ALWAYS WELCOME HERE, SEAN.
WE JUST WISH IT WOULD HAVE BEEN A HAPPIER HOMECOMING, SEAN. BUT WITH ILLYANA'S DEATH AND WHAT I LEARNED IN ALASKA--
--I WONDER IF THAT'LL EVER BE POSSIBLE AGAIN.
SCOTT WAS TELLING US ABOUT AN--ENCOUNTER--HE JUST HAD WITH MR. SINISTER.
ADMITTEDLY, I KNOW LITTLE OF THIS MAN, SCOTT, NEVER HAVING MET HIM.
STILL, GIVEN HIS HISTORY WITH THE X-MEN, I FIND IT HARD TO ACCEPT ANYTHING HE SAYS AS TRUTH.

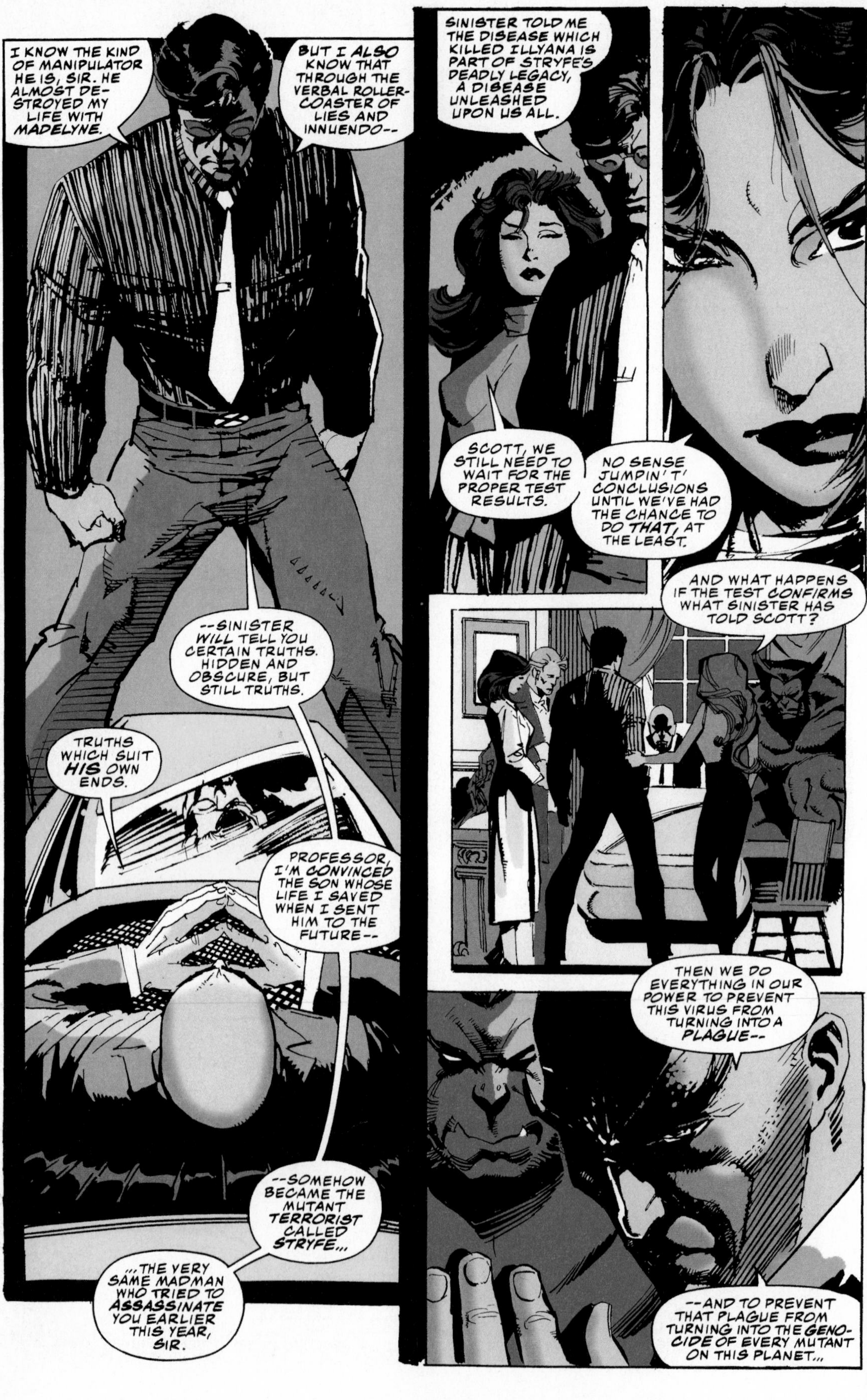
I KNOW THE KIND OF MANIPULATOR HE IS, SIR. HE ALMOST DESTROYED MY LIFE WITH MADELYNE.
BUT I ALSO KNOW THAT THROUGH THE VERBAL ROLLER-COASTER OF LIES AND INNUENDO--
--SINISTER WILL TELL YOU CERTAIN TRUTHS. HIDDEN AND OBSCURE, BUT STILL TRUTHS.
TRUTHS WHICH SUIT HIS OWN ENDS.
PROFESSOR, I'M CONVINCED THE SON WHOSE LIFE I SAVED WHEN I SENT HIM TO THE FUTURE--
--SOMEHOW BECAME THE MUTANT TERRORIST CALLED STRYFE...
...THE VERY SAME MADMAN WHO TRIED TO ASSASSINATE YOU EARLIER THIS YEAR, SIR.
SINISTER TOLD ME THE DISEASE WHICH KILLED ILLYANA IS PART OF STRYFE'S DEADLY LEGACY, A DISEASE UNLEASHED UPON US ALL.
SCOTT, WE STILL NEED TO WAIT FOR THE PROPER TEST RESULTS.
NO SENSE JUMPIN' T' CONCLUSIONS UNTIL WE'VE HAD THE CHANCE TO DO THAT, AT THE LEAST.
AND WHAT HAPPENS IF THE TEST CONFIRMS WHAT SINISTER HAS TOLD SCOTT?
THEN WE DO EVERYTHING IN OUR POWER TO PREVENT THIS VIRUS FROM TURNING INTO A PLAGUE--
--AND TO PREVENT THAT PLAGUE FROM TURNING INTO THE GENOCIDE OF EVERY MUTANT ON THIS PLANET...

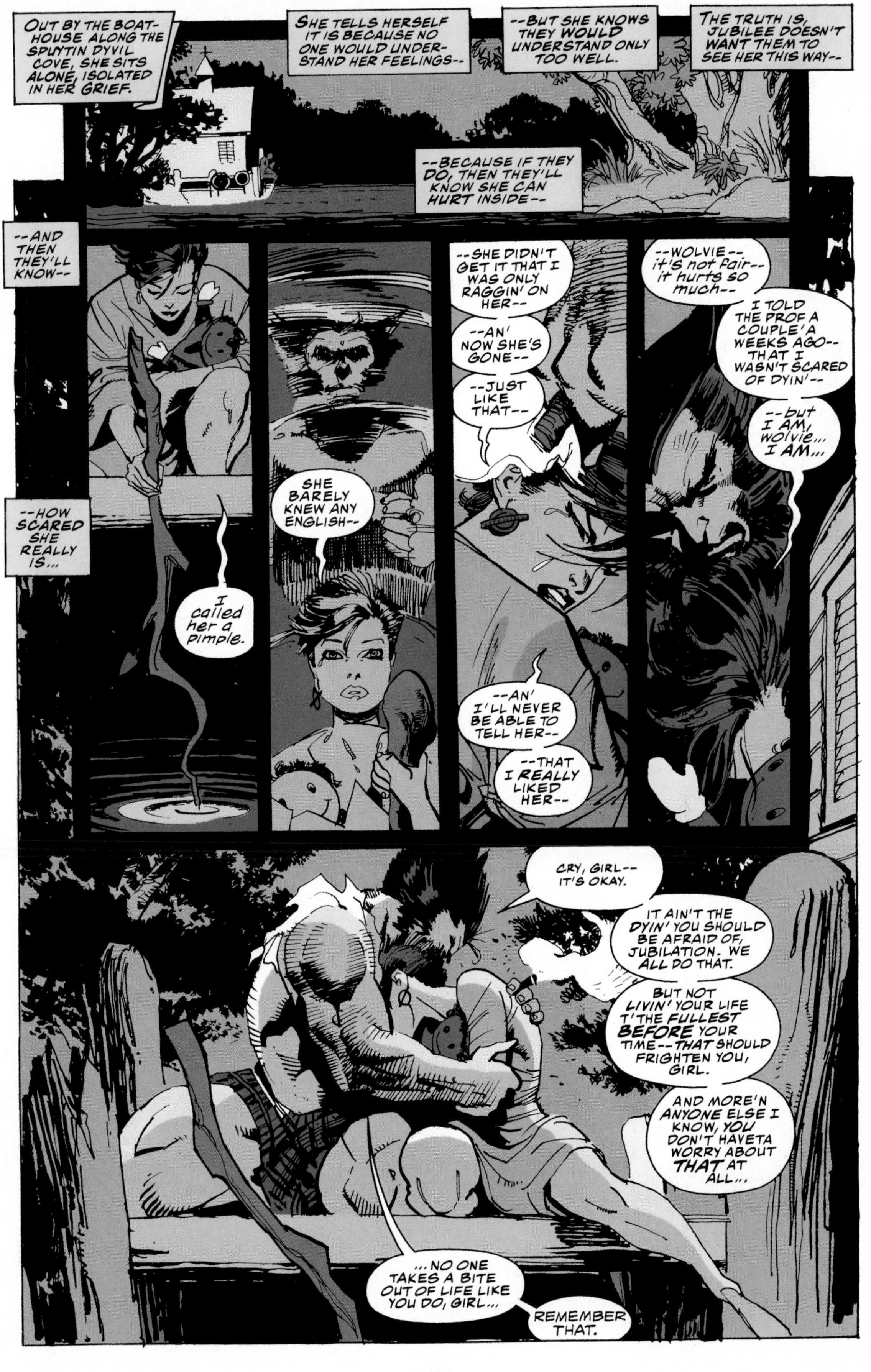
OUT BY THE BOATHOUSE ALONG THE SPUYTIN DYVIL COVE, SHE SITS ALONE, ISOLATED IN HER GRIEF.
SHE TELLS HERSELF IT IS BECAUSE NO ONE WOULD UNDERSTAND HER FEELINGS--
--BUT SHE KNOWS THEY WOULD UNDERSTAND ONLY TOO WELL.
THE TRUTH IS, JUBILEE DOESN'T WANT THEM TO SEE HER THIS WAY--
--BECAUSE IF THEY DO, THEN THEY'LL KNOW SHE CAN HURT INSIDE--
--AND THEN THEY'LL KNOW--
--HOW SCARED SHE REALLY IS...
I called her a pimple.
SHE BARELY KNEW ANY ENGLISH--
--SHE DIDN'T GET IT THAT I WAS ONLY RAGGIN' ON HER--
--AN' NOW SHE'S GONE--
--JUST LIKE THAT--
--AN' I'LL NEVER BE ABLE TO TELL HER--
--THAT I REALLY LIKED HER--
--WOLVIE-- it's not fair-- it hurts so much--
I TOLD THE PROF A COUPLE'A WEEKS AGO-- THAT I WASN'T SCARED OF DYIN'--
--but I AM, wolvie... I AM...
CRY, GIRL-- IT'S OKAY.
IT AIN'T THE DYIN' YOU SHOULD BE AFRAID OF, JUBILATION. WE ALL DO THAT.
BUT NOT LIVIN' YOUR LIFE T'THE FULLEST BEFORE YOUR TIME--THAT SHOULD FRIGHTEN YOU, GIRL.
AND MORE'N ANYONE ELSE I KNOW, YOU DON'T HAVETA WORRY ABOUT THAT AT ALL...
...NO ONE TAKES A BITE OUT OF LIFE LIKE YOU DO, GIRL...
REMEMBER THAT.

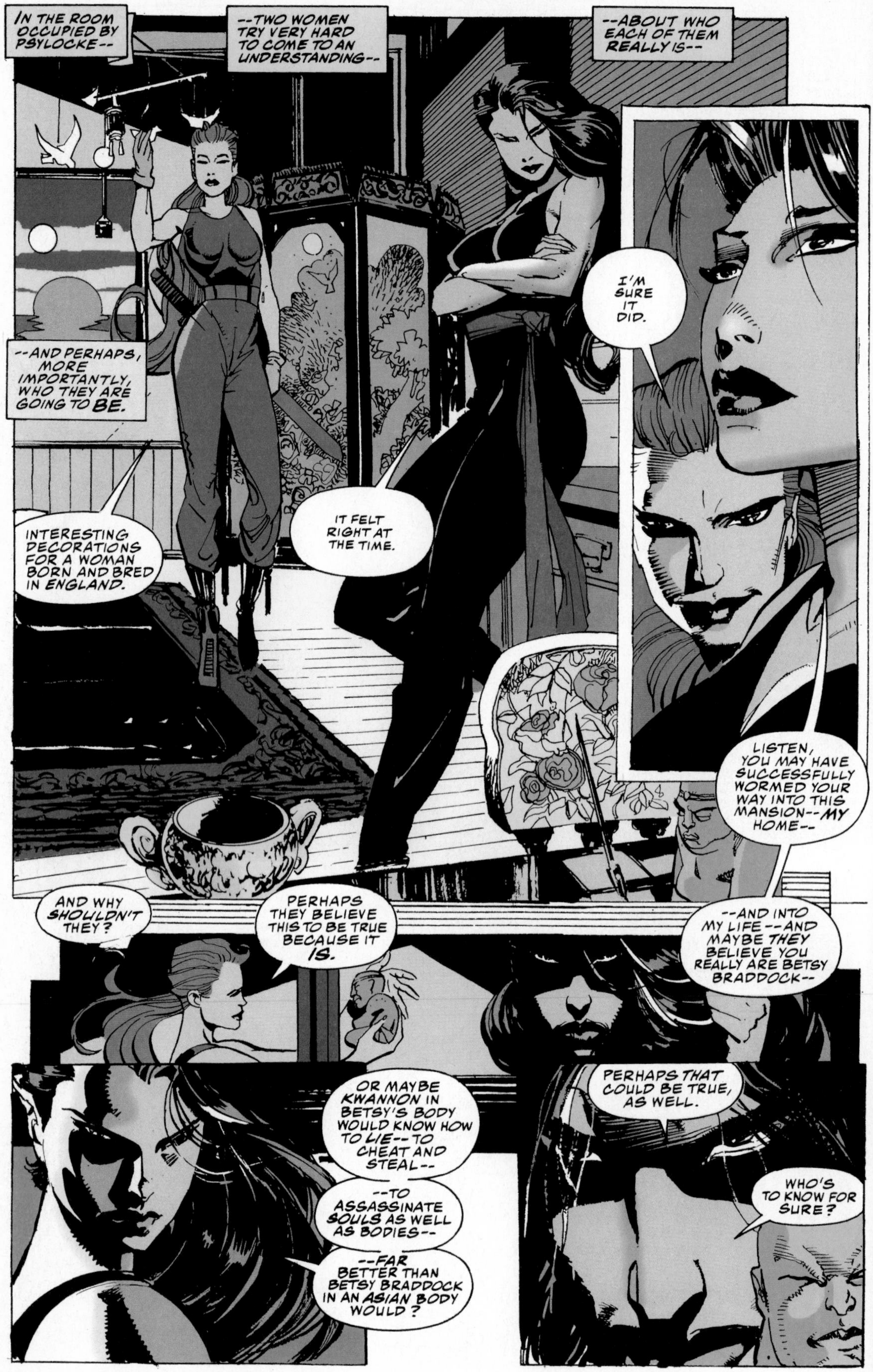
IN THE ROOM OCCUPIED BY PSYLOCKE--
--TWO WOMEN TRY VERY HARD TO COME TO AN UNDERSTANDING--
--ABOUT WHO EACH OF THEM REALLY IS--
--AND PERHAPS, MORE IMPORTANTLY, WHO THEY ARE GOING TO BE.
INTERESTING DECORATIONS FOR A WOMAN BORN AND BRED IN ENGLAND.
IT FELT RIGHT AT THE TIME.
I'M SURE IT DID.
LISTEN, YOU MAY HAVE SUCCESSFULLY WORMED YOUR WAY INTO THIS MANSION--MY HOME--
--AND INTO MY LIFE--AND MAYBE THEY BELIEVE YOU REALLY ARE BETSY BRADDOCK--
AND WHY SHOULDN'T THEY?
PERHAPS THEY BELIEVE THIS TO BE TRUE BECAUSE IT IS.
OR MAYBE KWANNON IN BETSY'S BODY WOULD KNOW HOW TO LIE--TO CHEAT AND STEAL--
--TO ASSASSINATE SOULS AS WELL AS BODIES--
--FAR BETTER THAN BETSY BRADDOCK IN AN ASIAN BODY WOULD?
PERHAPS THAT COULD BE TRUE, AS WELL.
WHO'S TO KNOW FOR SURE?

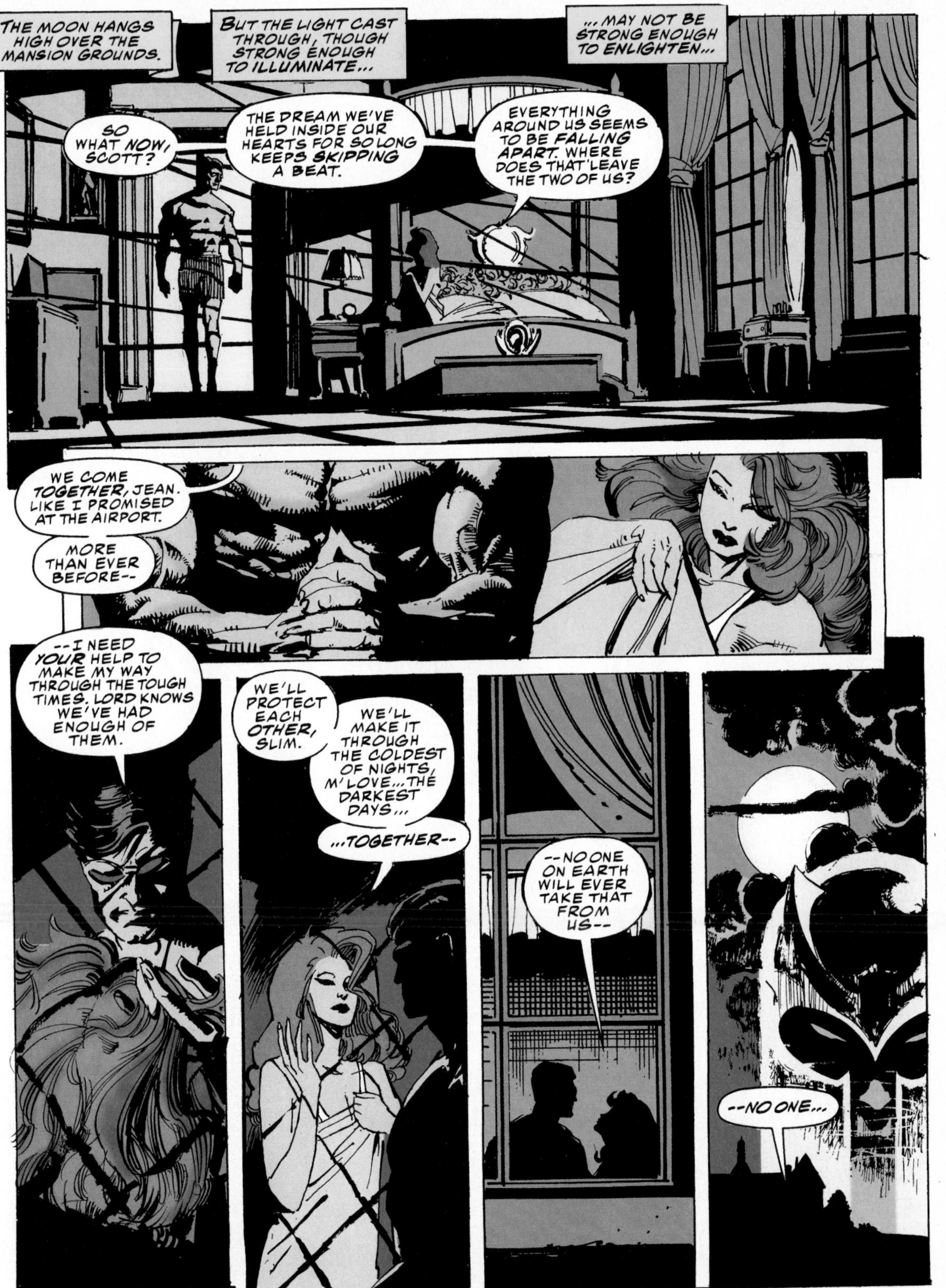
THE MOON HANGS HIGH OVER THE MANSION GROUNDS.
BUT THE LIGHT CAST THROUGH, THOUGH STRONG ENOUGH TO ILLUMINATE...
...MAY NOT BE STRONG ENOUGH TO ENLIGHTEN...
SO WHAT NOW, SCOTT?
THE DREAM WE'VE HELD INSIDE OUR HEARTS FOR SO LONG KEEPS SKIPPING A BEAT.
EVERYTHING AROUND US SEEMS TO BE FALLING APART. WHERE DOES THAT LEAVE THE TWO OF US?
WE COME TOGETHER, JEAN. LIKE I PROMISED AT THE AIRPORT.
MORE THAN EVER BEFORE--
--I NEED YOUR HELP TO MAKE MY WAY THROUGH THE TOUGH TIMES. LORD KNOWS WE'VE HAD ENOUGH OF THEM.
WE'LL PROTECT EACH OTHER, SLIM.
WE'LL MAKE IT THROUGH THE COLDEST OF NIGHTS, M'LOVE... THE DARKEST DAYS...
...TOGETHER--
--NO ONE ON EARTH WILL EVER TAKE THAT FROM US--
--NO ONE...

NEXT: OUR 25TH ISSUE SPECTACULAR! AN OVERLORD HOVERS ABOVE THE PLANET, AND HE CANNOT BE ALLOWED TO EXIST! THE WAR GETS TAKEN TO MAGNETO -- AN X-MAN FALLS -- AND THE DREAM WILL NEVER BE THE SAME AGAIN!!

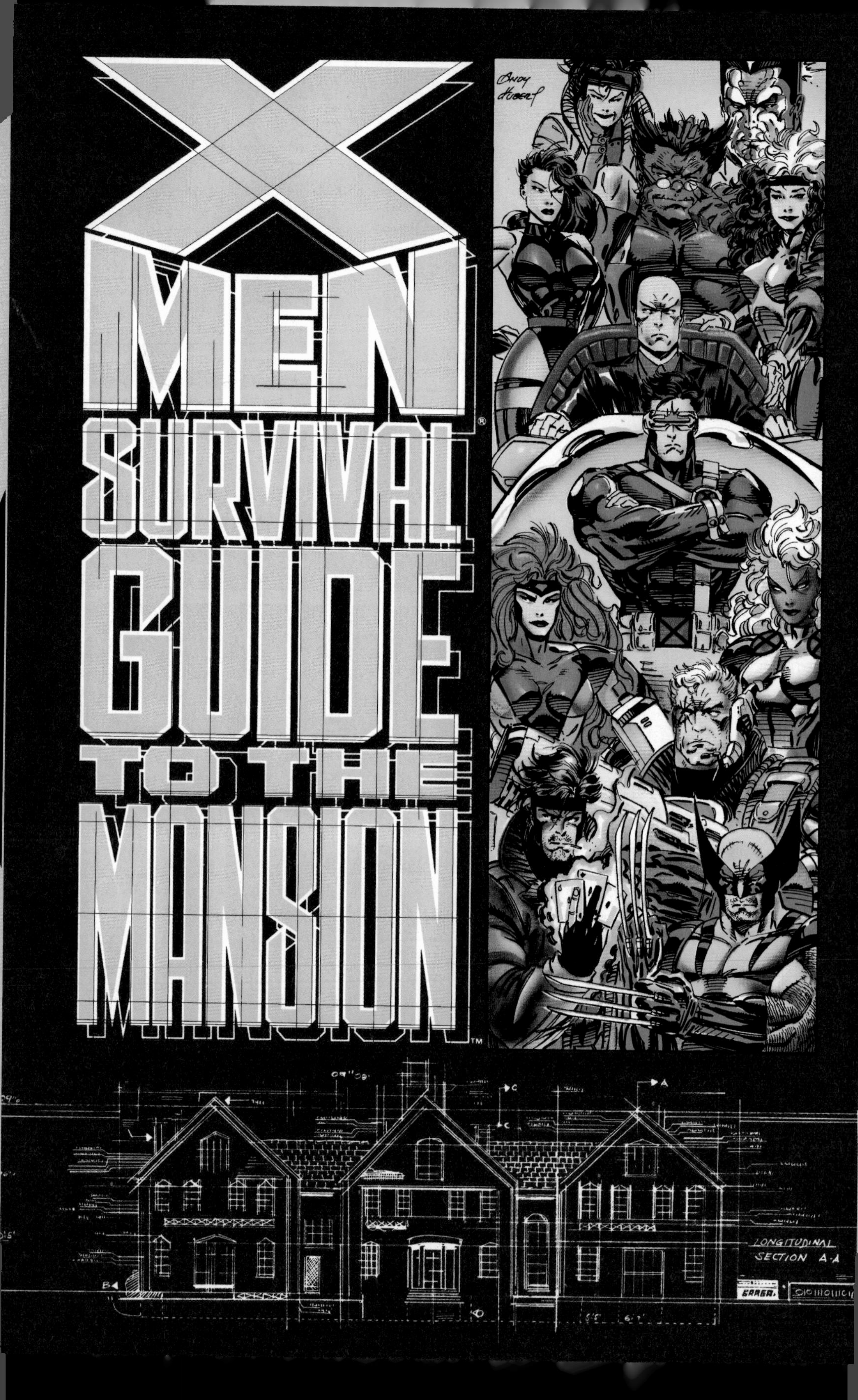

X-MEN
SURVIVAL GUIDE TO THE MANSION
LONGITUDINAL SECTION A-A

Dear Student,

Welcome to the Xavier Institute for Higher Learning. This is the home, the training center – the very foundation – of the X-Men.

In practice, we are a relative handful of mutants dedicated to fighting on the behalf of a world that often fears and hates us. It would be dishonest if I did not concede the truth that relations between humans and mutantkind have been deteriorating over the past decade. For every mutant who is accepted into this group or appointed to the United States government's X-Factor program, another makes the evening news with a campaign of terror designed to enslave humanity or – as is often the case – wipe the human race off the face of the Earth.

So why do we do it – why do we dare to dream a dream of a better world? Why are we willing to sacrifice any semblance of a "normal" life to make that dream a reality? Why do we seek, against seemingly impossible odds, to change a cold, often indifferent society into one that is a better place, a better more tolerant place?

Because underneath the uniforms, behind the code names, and despite the genetic anomalies the rest of the world would call our "powers," there is no fundamental difference between us and those we seek to protect. Because despite the divisive ethnic slurs designed to separate and belittle us, we are – each and every one of us – humans.

Gifted humans.

Misunderstood humans.

Hunted and persecuted humans.

But humans nonetheless. And as humans I believe we have a responsibility to shepherd the change. A change where all the branches of humanity live together as one.

Some would say this is a naive dream. Or even a fool's quest. Perhaps. But I say, it is our only hope if we are all to survive.

Apparently you believe it too.

So welcome, X-Men both old and new.

Welcome to the dream.

Charles Xavier, PHD

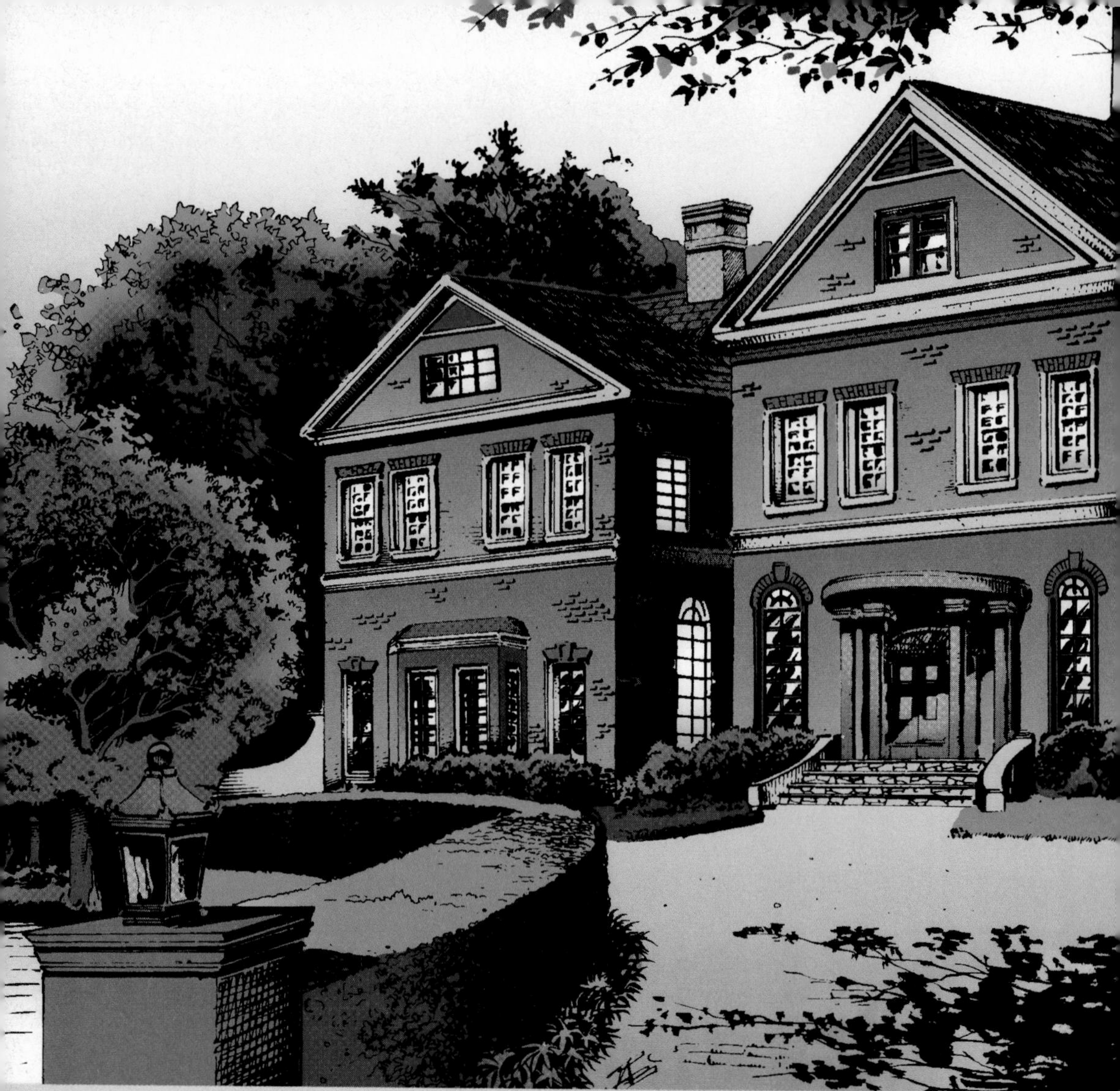

Table of Contents

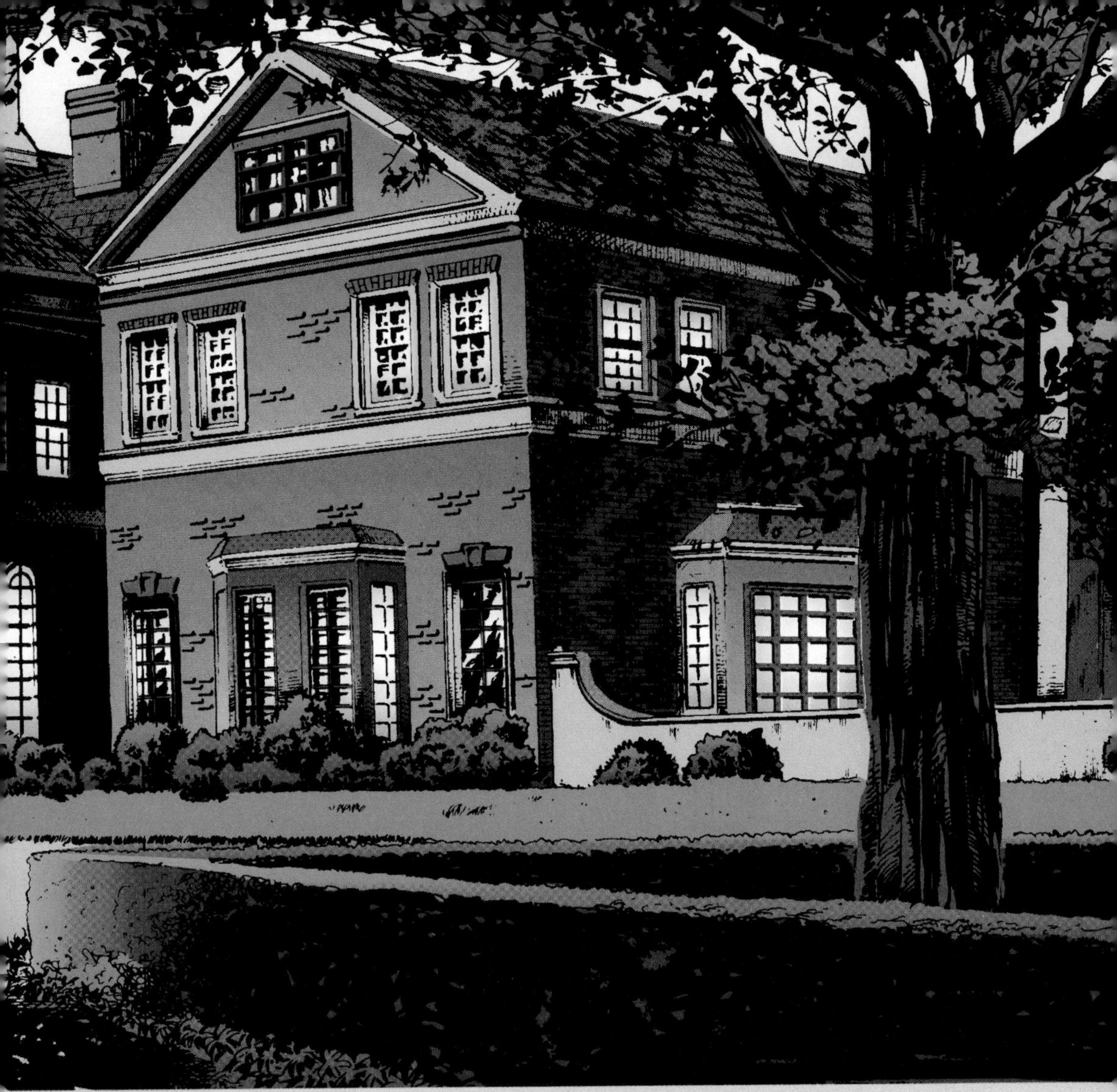

ARTISTS:
RICHARD BENNETT
(2-5,10-12,20,21,23,25,28-30,36-42,46,48-54)

ELIOT BROWN
(6,7,12-15,17-19,22,24,26,27,30-35,39,42-45,52)

KRIS RENKOWITZ/MICHAEL GOLDEN(8)
HENRY FLINT(40,41) WHILCE PORTACIO(9)
GREG CAPULLO/ HARRY CANDELARIO(9)
BRANDON PETERSON(47) STEVE ALEXANDROV(7)
ANDY KUBERT/MARK PENNINGTON/PAUL MOUNTS (COVER)
WRITER: **SCOTT LOBDELL**
COLORIST: **JOE ROSAS**

EDITOR/DESIGNER: SUZANNE GAFFNEY
GROUP EDITOR: BOB HARRAS
EDITOR IN CHIEF: TOM DEFALCO

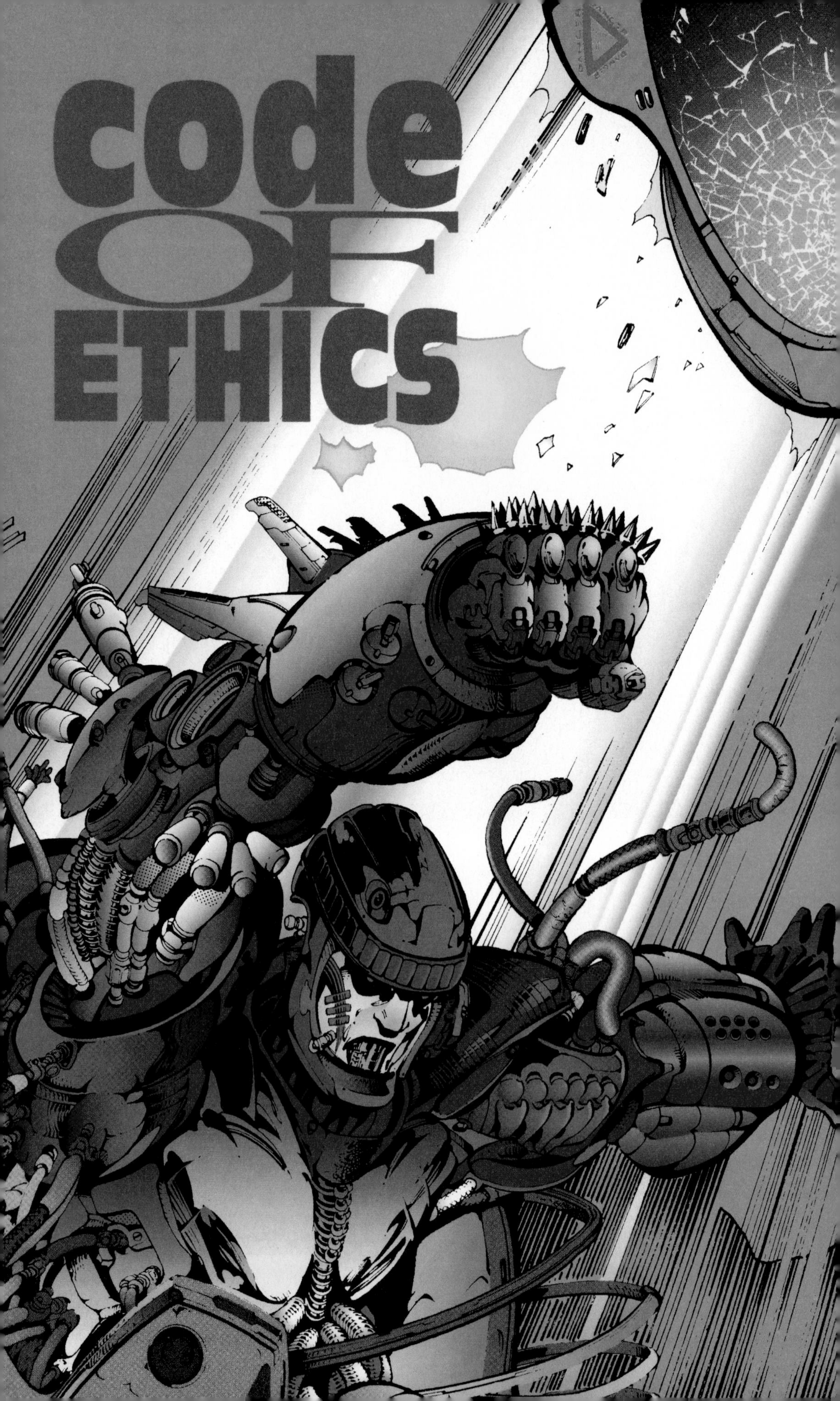
code OF ETHICS

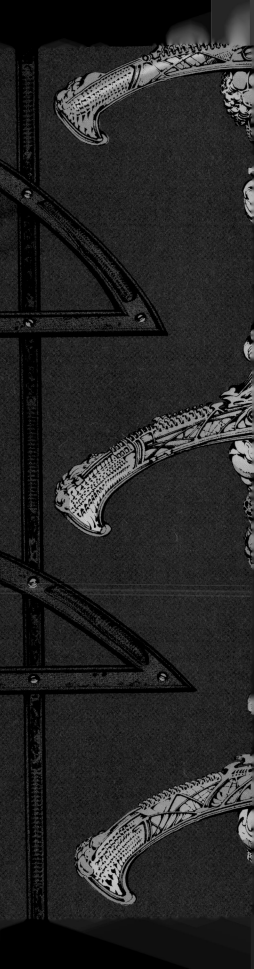

Before we, who assume the role of X-Men, can hope to reach our full potential, it is important to understand exactly who we are...what we hope to accomplish.

First and foremost we are mutants—a breed of individuals who have found themselves existing on humanity's next evolutionary plateau. Born with the genetic capacity for great power, we have chosen to assume the added burden of respons-bility, to defend those who have not the power or resources to protect themselves. At times this will mean coming to the aid of humans—providing a defense against those mutants who feel their powers allow them to dominate others. Just as often, we will be called on to safeguard mutants against the humans who fear and hate them simply because they are "different." All too often, we will defend mutants against their own kind—as the unfortunate quest for supremacy continues.

We are architects of the future—dedicated to constructing a bridge between the human and mutant population that shares this world. We are pathfinders—embarked on a journey to enlightenment and tolerance between two races that have more in common than either realizes. We are explorers—booking passage to a place where every living being co-exists in peace with every other.

Above all else, we believe every sentient entity is capable of change—indeed, mutants them-selves are the product of the ultimate change, evolution. To this end, we are compelled to open our doors—our very hearts—to all those who come to us for help.

FROM THE PAGES OF
FORGE'S NOTEBOOK

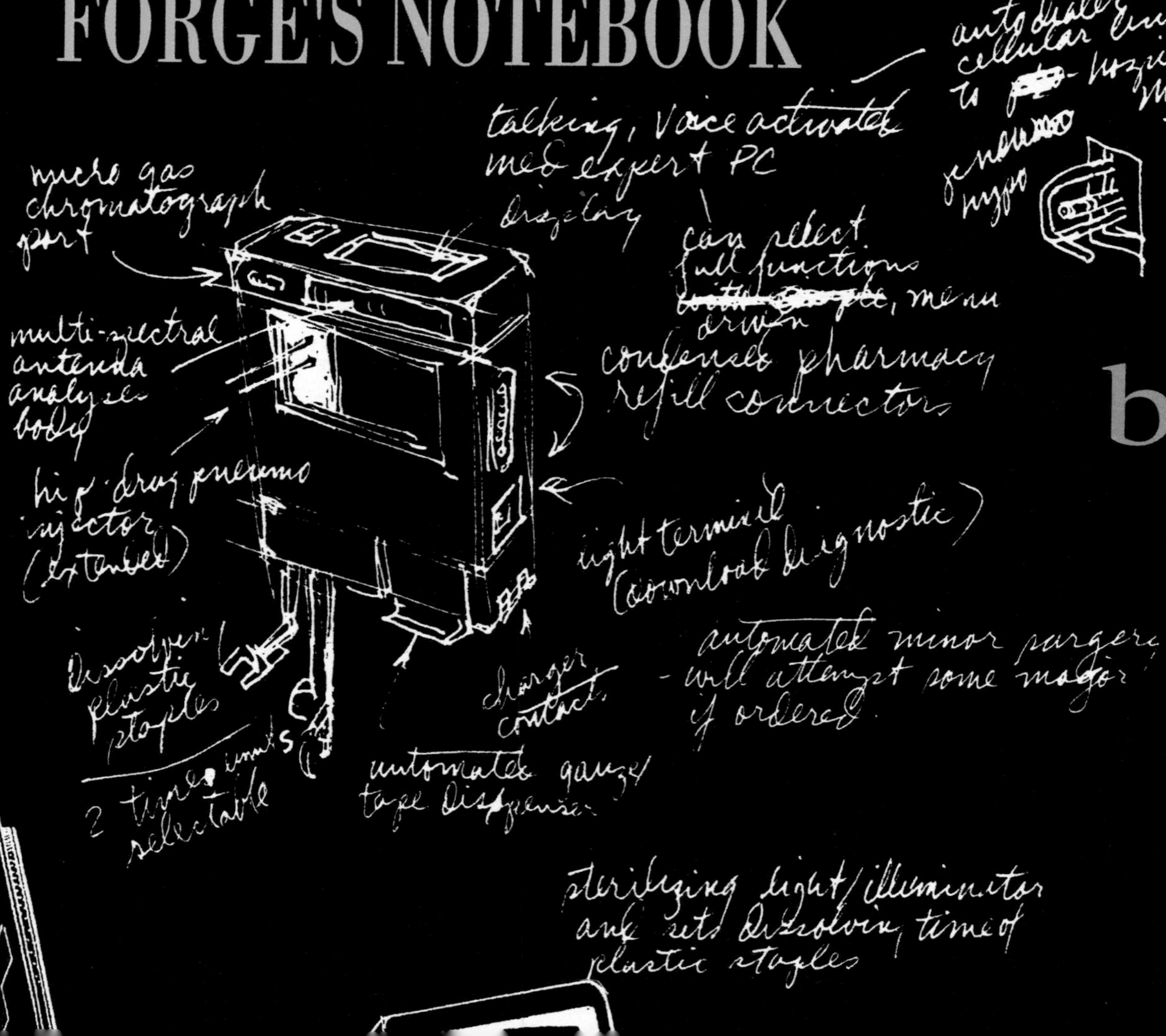

autodialer link
cellular to hospitals + mutant specialists +
tele-medical services
talking, voice activated
med expert PC
display
can select
full functions, menu
driven
condensed pharmacy
refill connectors
micro gas
chromatograph
port
multi-spectral
antenna
analyser
body
hi-g-drag pneumo
injector
(extended)
light terminal
(download diagnostic)
also: low
velocity
unguent +
eye dropper
automated minor surgery
- will attempt some major
if ordered
charger
contact
dissolving
plastic
staples
2 times units
selectable
automated gauze/
tape dispenser
sterilizing light/illuminator
and sets dissolving time of
plastic staples

beltpack EQUIPMENT

Equipment for the individual beltpacks is continually upgraded and monitored by Forge, the X-Men's techno-futurist. Pictured here are sketches and current designs for the portable triage unit and the Global Comm-Stat Unit. Additional equipment available includes biogen-trackers, Mini-Cerebros, 200 terabyte pc's, environmental oxygenators, and hydroponic ration units.

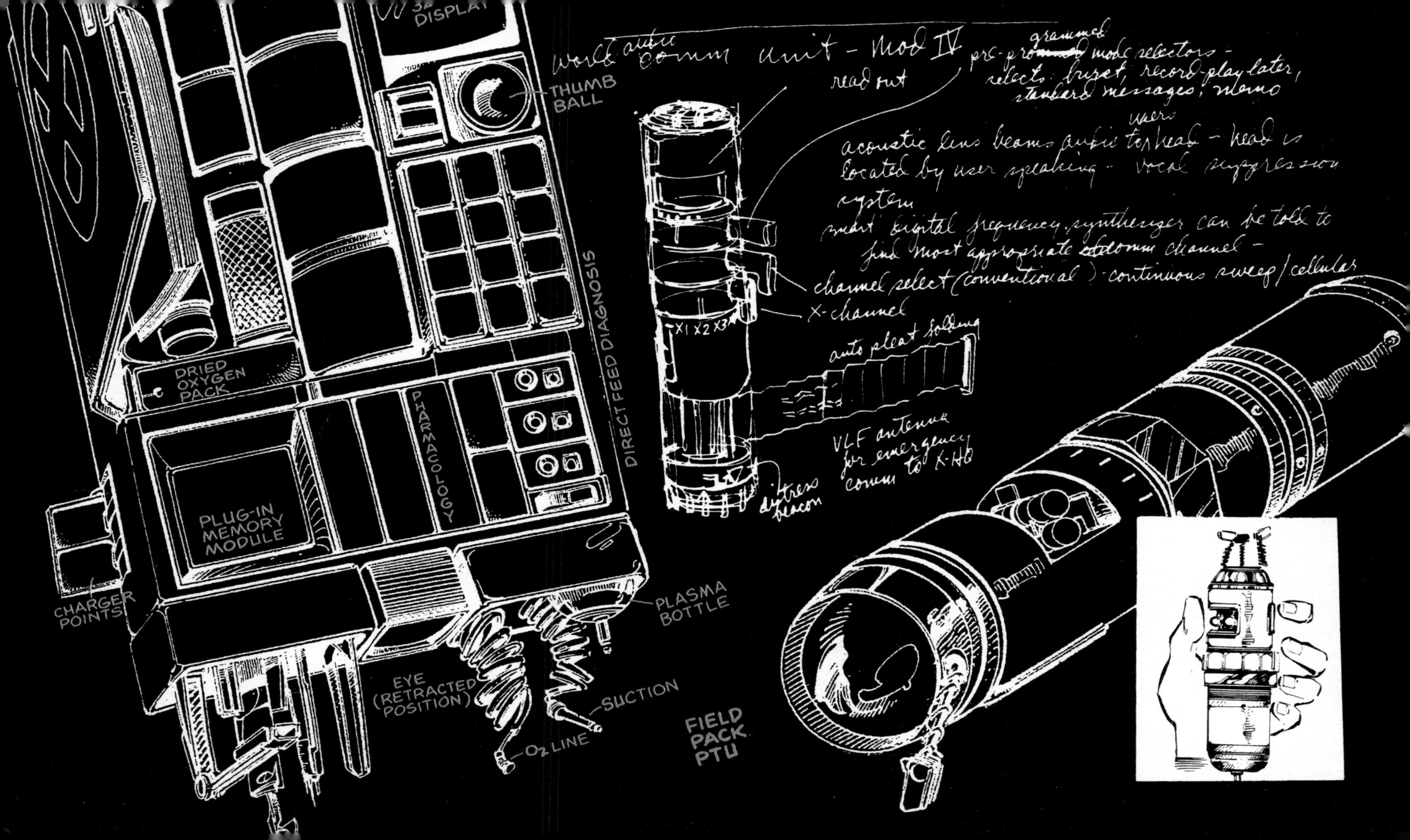
DISPLAY
THUMB BALL
DRIED OXYGEN PACK
PHARMACOLOGY
DIRECT FEED DIAGNOSIS
PLUG-IN MEMORY MODULE
CHARGER POINTS
PLASMA BOTTLE
EYE (RETRACTED POSITION)
SUCTION
O_2 LINE
FIELD PACK PTU
world audio comm unit - Mod IV
read out
pre-programmed mode selectors - select: buzzer, record-play later, standard messages, memo
acoustic lens beams audio to users head - head is located by user speaking - vocal suppression system
smart digital frequency synthesizer can be told to find most appropriate comm channel -
channel select (conventional) - continuous sweep/cellular
X-channel
X1 X2 X3
auto pleat folding
VLF antenna for emergency comm to X-HB
distress beacon

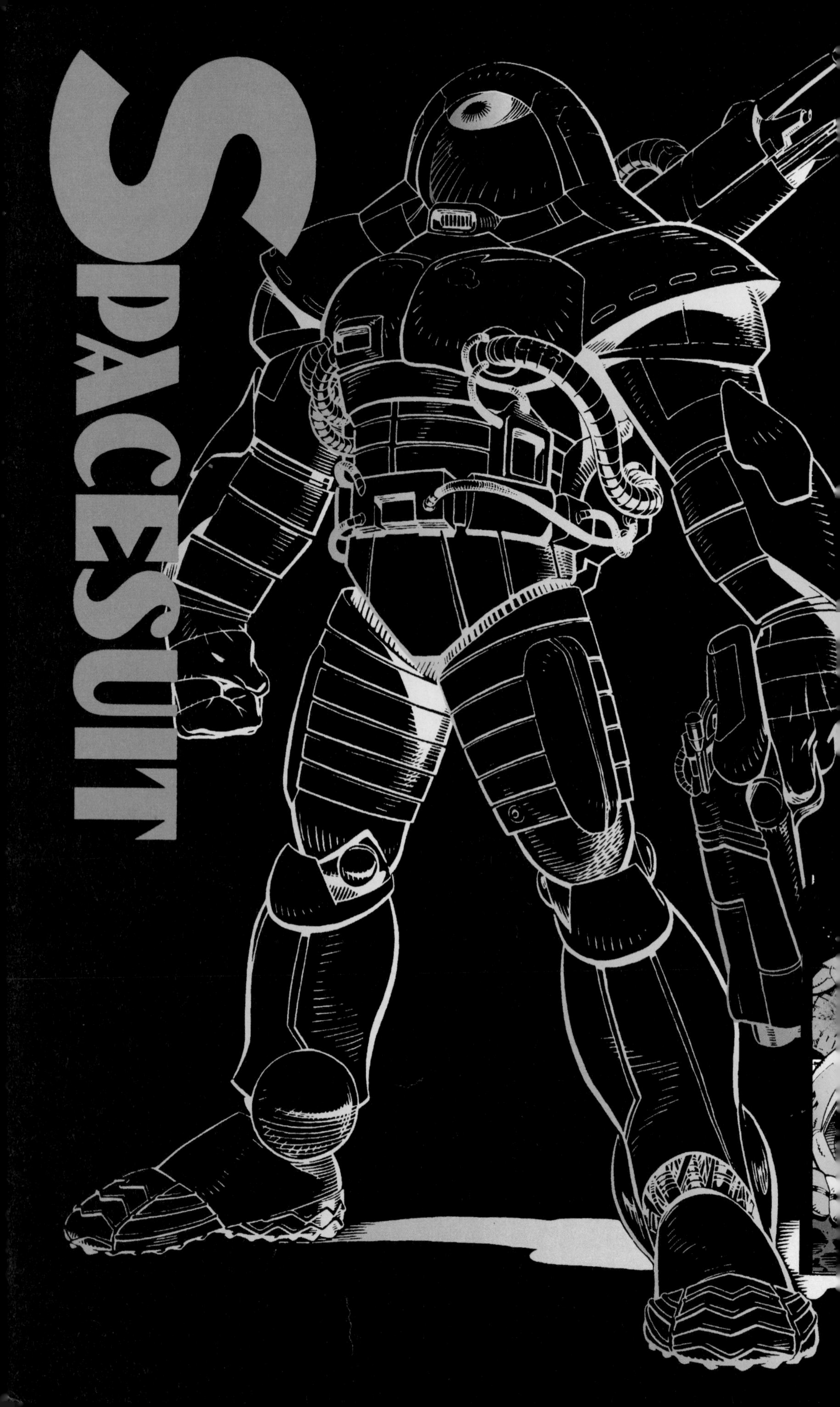
SPACESUIT

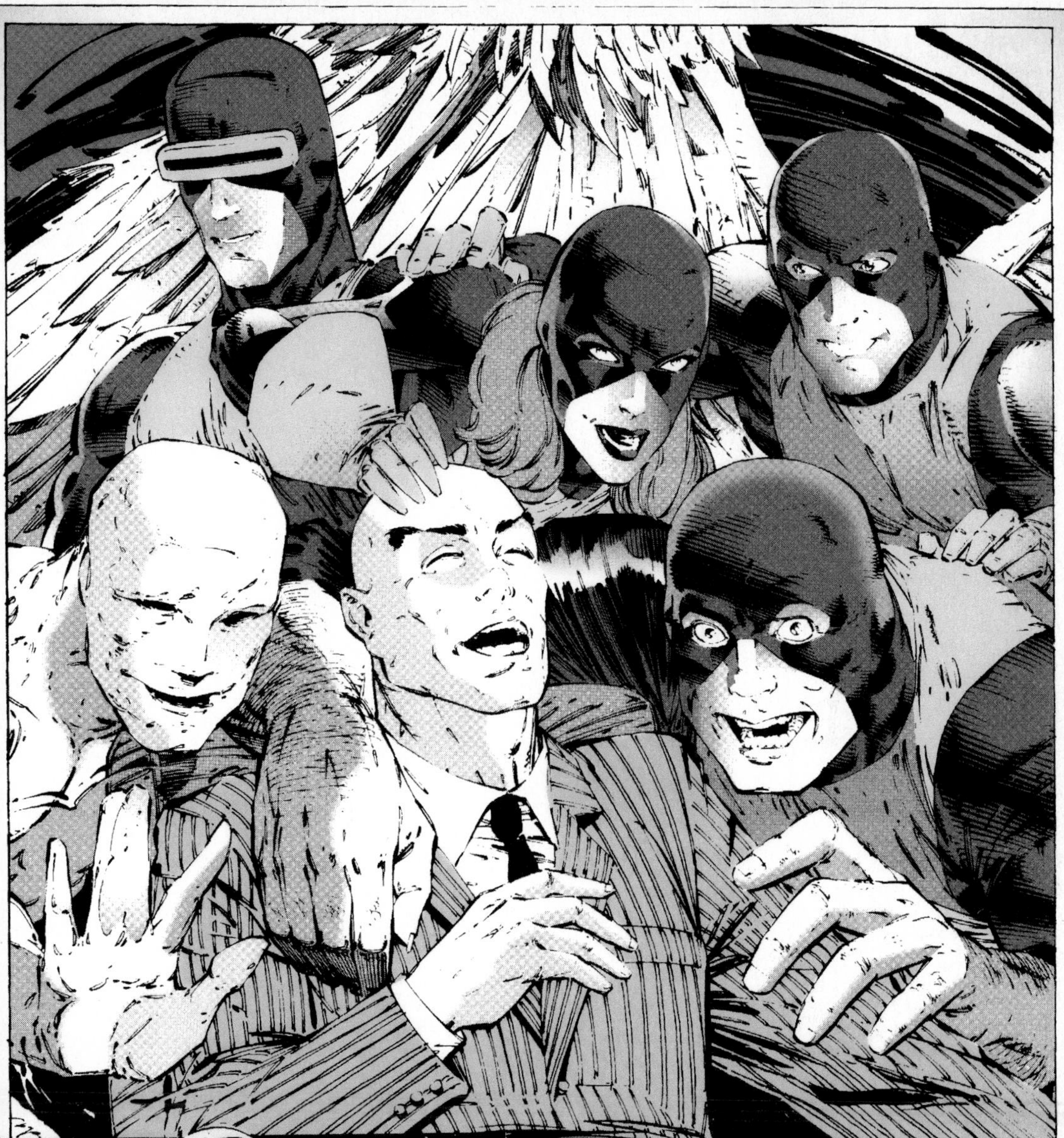

A candid shot of the founding members of the X-Men; Cyclops, Marvel Girl, Angel, Beast, Iceman, and myself, Professor Charles Xavier.

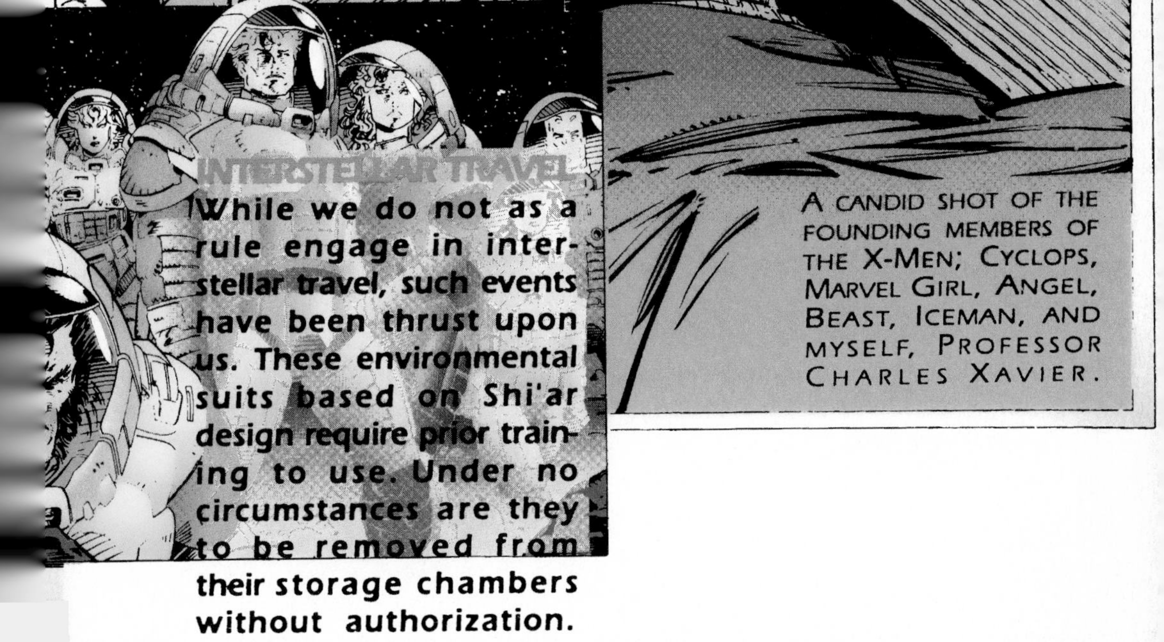

INTERSTELLAR TRAVEL

While we do not as a rule engage in interstellar travel, such events have been thrust upon us. These environmental suits based on Shi'ar design require prior training to use. Under no circumstances are they to be removed from their storage chambers without authorization.

There was a time when I placed much emphasis on the importance of a uniform look for all of the X-Men. In an effort to foster, nurture and define the role of the individual's contribution to the greater whole, however, personalized attire is now encouraged. (Standard blue and gold training gear available upon request.)

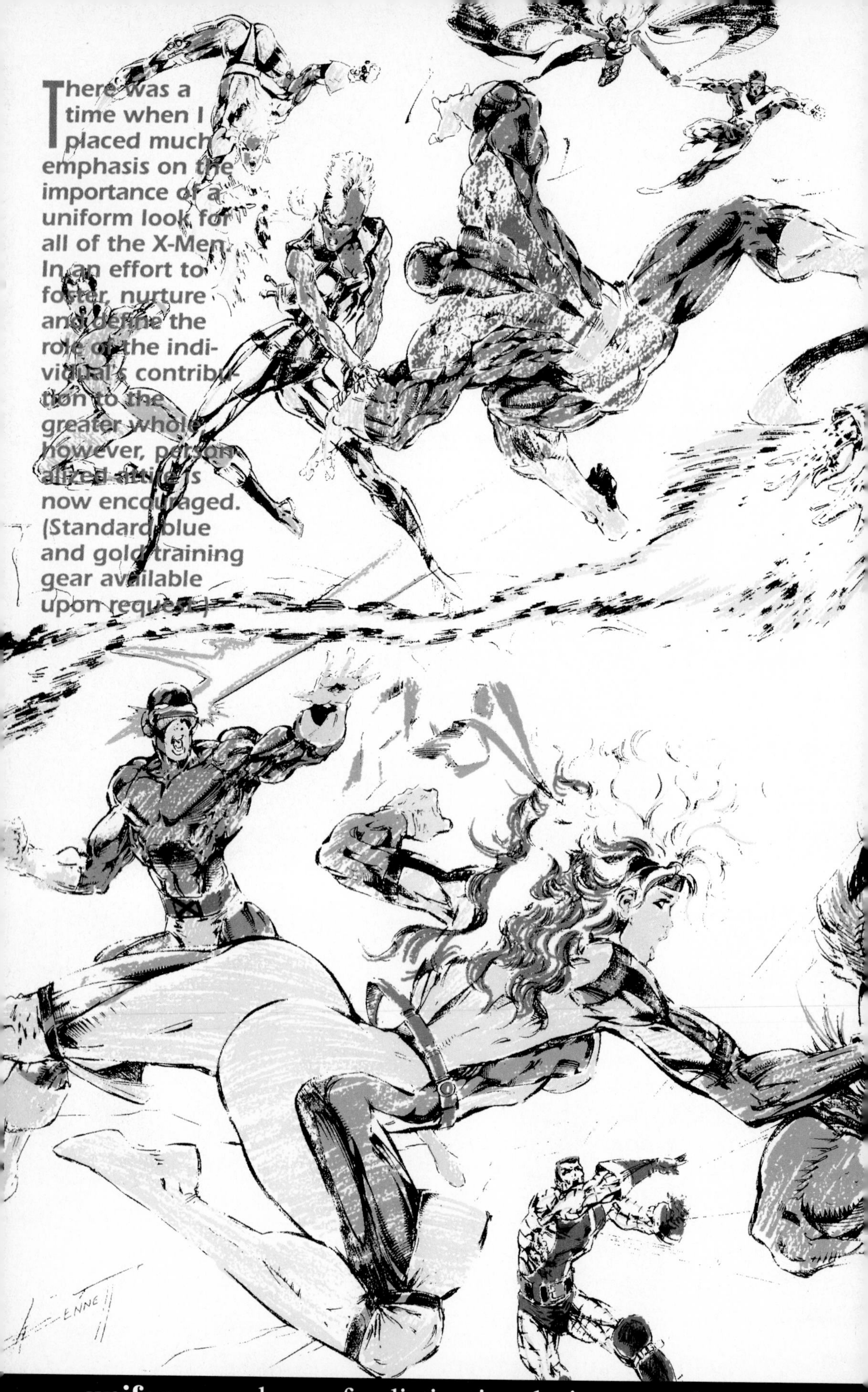

uniform *n.* **:** dress of a distinctive design worn by members

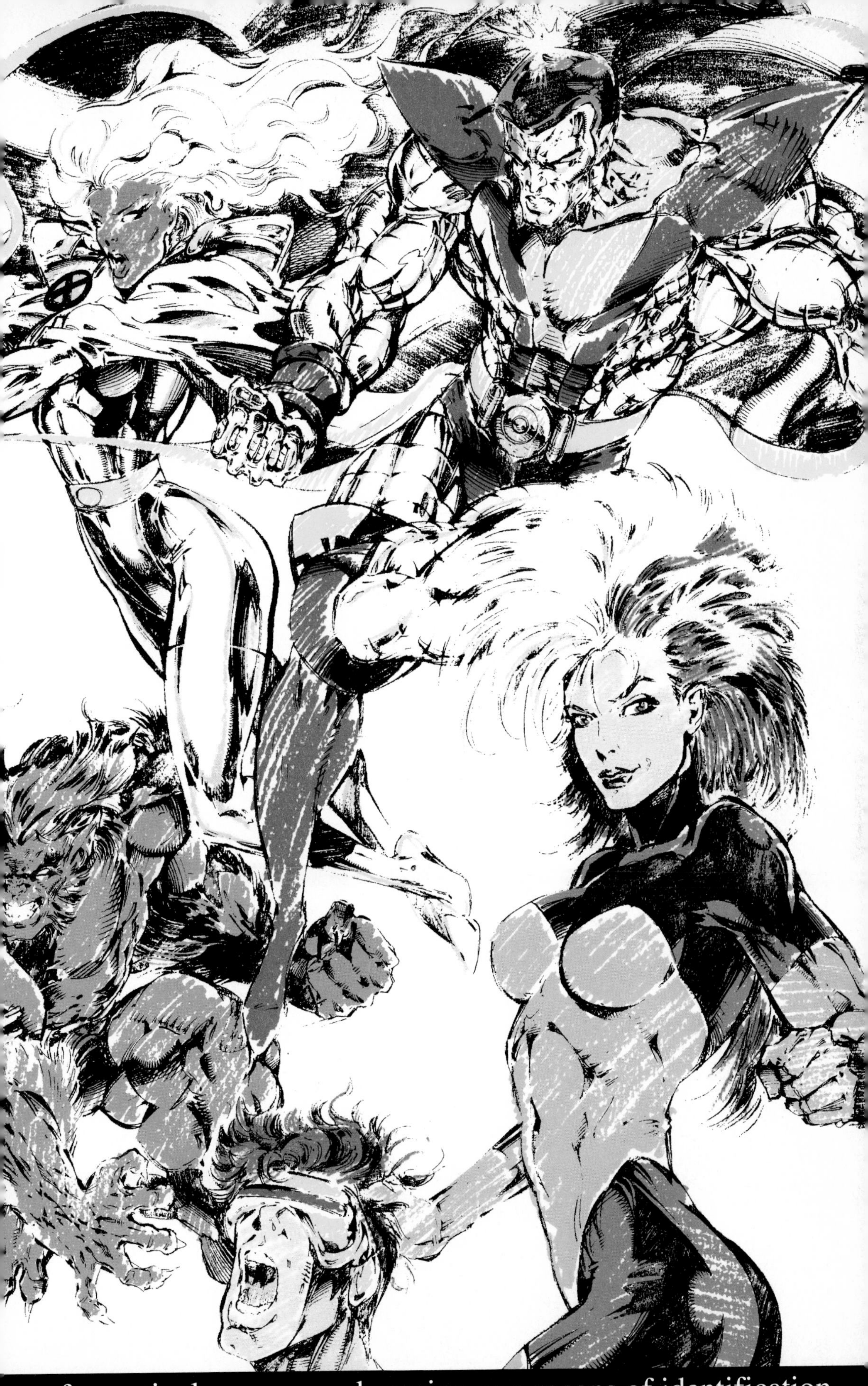

of a particular group and serving as a means of identification
(From *WEBSTER'S NINTH NEW COLLEGIATE DICTIONARY*)

SECURITY
on the estate grounds

Located as we are, approximately 5 kilometers outside of Salem Center, our relative seclusion is our first security. However, recent housing developments and the growing awareness by some of our foes of our location demands we be even more vigilant, even more cautious.

Authorized vehicles and personnel are detected by long range sensor scans. Visitors with appointments are issued a one-shot electro-pass at the gate which serves to identify and vocally guide them through the mansion. Access to other levels can only be gained with a team member or through an emergency computer decision.

The estate is equipped with state of the art environmental and individual protective technology. Prudence dictates that some of the Mansion's security parameters are not to be committed to hard copy. Complete security procedures are, however, psionically implanted in each student during orientation. As new threats to our safety become apparent, we will upgrade environmental and individual protective technology.

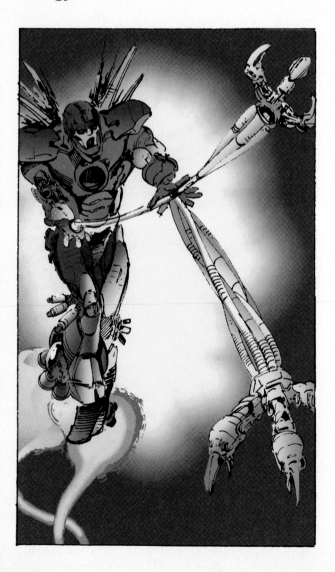

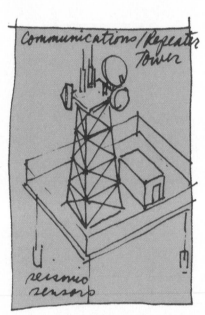

Communications/Repeater Tower

seismic sensors

This "radio shack" provides communication monitoring and equipment logs. The structure is explosion-proof and has standard battery backups. The tower provides seismic alarms below ground and motion detection alarms above.

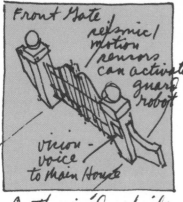

ypical guard obot–mainly sed for deternce but with mited offensive apability. Guard obots are part f in-ground nti-aircraft mplacements.

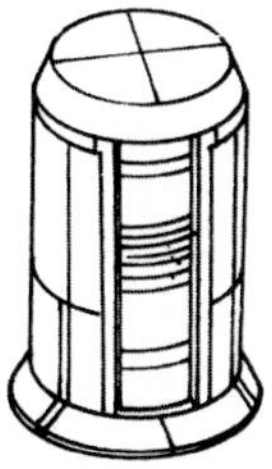

Front Gate

rejonic/motion sensors can activate guard robot

vision-voice to main House

Authorized vehicles and personnel are detected by long range sensor scan

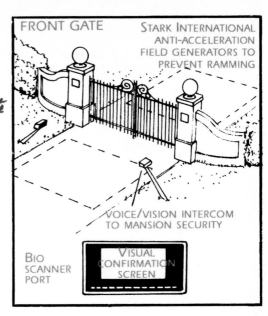

FRONT GATE — STARK INTERNATIONAL ANTI-ACCELERATION FIELD GENERATORS TO PREVENT RAMMING

VOICE/VISION INTERCOM TO MANSION SECURITY

BIO SCANNER PORT

VISUAL CONFIRMATION SCREEN

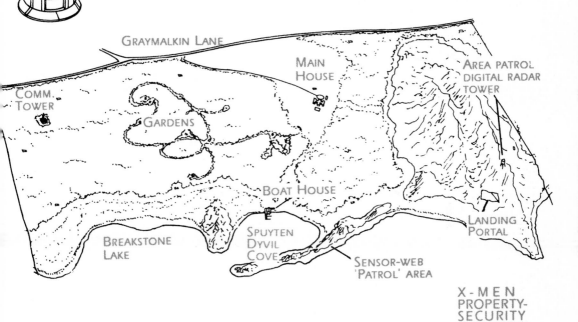

GRAYMALKIN LANE

MAIN HOUSE

AREA PATROL DIGITAL RADAR TOWER

COMM. TOWER

GARDENS

BOAT HOUSE

LANDING PORTAL

BREAKSTONE LAKE

SPUYTEN DYVIL COVE

SENSOR-WEB 'PATROL' AREA

X-MEN PROPERTY-SECURITY OVERVIEW

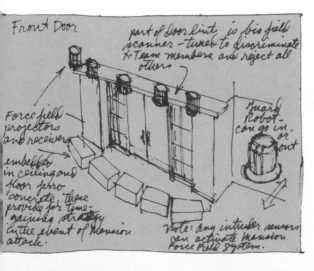

Front Door

part of Door lintl is bio field scanner – tuned to discriminate X-Team members and reject all others

Force field projectors and receivers

embedded in ceiling and floor ferro concrete these provide for time-gaining strategy in the event of Mansion attack.

Guard robot – can go in or out

Note: any intruder sensors can activate Mansion Force Field system.

Warning: Estate grounds are honey-combed with tunnels and underground passageways of great antiquity. Caution is advised. See page 22.

■Individuals are also advised to avoid the area containing Devil's Rock. Approach this stone with extreme caution for your own security.

■Also, as we are lakefront property, never go swimming alone. Follow standard water safety procedures around the lake and with boating equipment.

SECURITY
inside the mansion

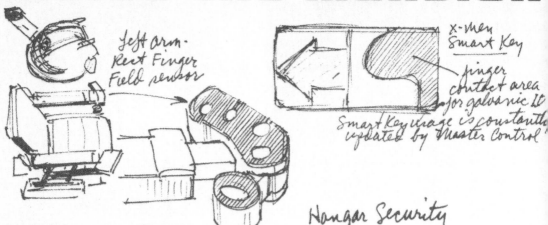

Left arm - Rest Finger Field sensor

X-men Smart Key

finger contact area for galvanic ID

Smart Key usage is constantly updated by Master Control

CEREBRO SECURITY

Finger pads (reconfigurable for other races) conduct expressive body-field measurements that identify individuals. The Lo-Res Antenna info plus the Finger Field sensor input is monitored throughout Cerebro use–any irregularities could be a sign of deception or psi intrusion.

The Cerebro User List is subject to periodic review and battlefield update.

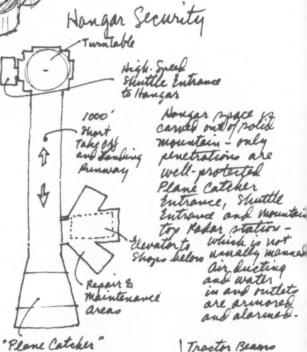

Hangar Security

Turntable

High-Speed Shuttle Entrance to Hangar

1000' short Take off and landing Runway

Hangar space is carved out of solid mountain - only penetrations are well-protected Plane Catcher Entrance, Shuttle Entrance and mountain top Radar station - which is not usually manned. Air ducting and water in and outlets are armored and alarmed.

Elevator to Shops below

Repair & Maintenance areas

"Plane Catcher" Tractor Beam array - guides invited guests without X-Men Instrument Landing System.

Tractor Beams also serve to repel casual visitors, either on foot or in aircraft

FROM THE PAGES OF
FORGE'S NOTEBOOK

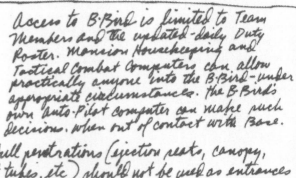

Access to B-Bird is limited to Team Members and the updated-daily Duty Roster. Mansion Housekeeping and Tactical Combat Computers can allow practically anyone into the B-Bird - under appropriate circumstances. The B-Bird's own Auto-Pilot computer can make such decisions when out of contact with Base.

All other Hull penetrations (ejection seats, canopy, bail-out tubes, etc) should not be used as entrances - but they can be, in emergency

BLACKBIRD -

SECURITY DOORS

Constructed of adamantium-melded steel to protect the most sensitive areas of the sub-basement complex, these specially designed doors with bio-molecular locking mechanisms respond only to authorized personnel (read: Professor Xavier and senior staff.)

WAR ROOM SECURITY

Security in this area is relatively tight because of the difficulty in reaching this area. Individual stations have constant monitoring for user integrity. Sensitive information sources such as The Mission Planning Globe and the Training Coordination Center are Key Switches." (See X-Men Smart Key")

DANGER ROOM SECURITY

Danger Room doors and walls are primarily constructed of a Nickel-titanium alloy. Layered within these walls are localized force fields triggered by Master Control Intruder Detection Systems. Similarly, dedicated electromechanical security devices regulate entry to the Ready Room Elevator and Control Room.

RESTRICTED AREAS

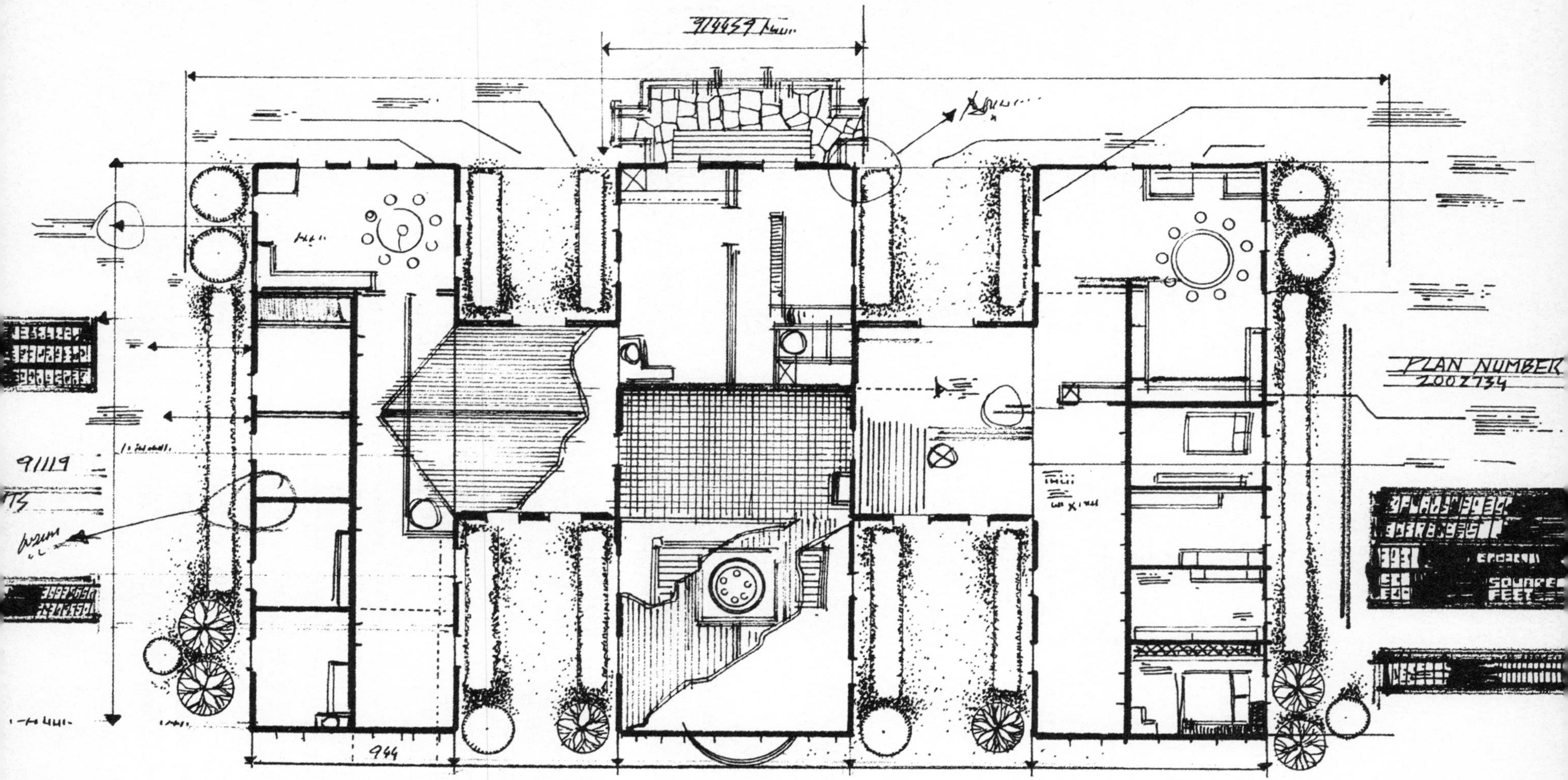

914459
PLAN NUMBER
2002734
SQUARE FEET
944
91119

OVERHEAD VIEW

This is an architect's cutaway overhead view of the mansion, executed during a recent renovation.

THE MANSION

Located at 1407 Graymalkin Lane in Salem Center, New York, the foundation of the mansion dates back to the 1700's and has always been in the Xavier family. Built on the edge of Breakstone Lake by Dutch ancestors, it is now publicly known as the Xavier Institute for Higher Learning, a respected private school with a highly limited enrollment.

In general, the mansion above ground is for public use and public observation. All attempts have been made to preserve the historical and architectural integrity of its above ground structure. All levels beginning at basement sub-level A are for X-Men use only and specially authorized non-X-Men personnel. This is, of course, for security reasons.

The mansion has been rebuilt and expanded several times in the last few years with a mind toward personal comfort, space and security. We have sought to provide our students ample living and study spaces, providing both privacy and comfort.

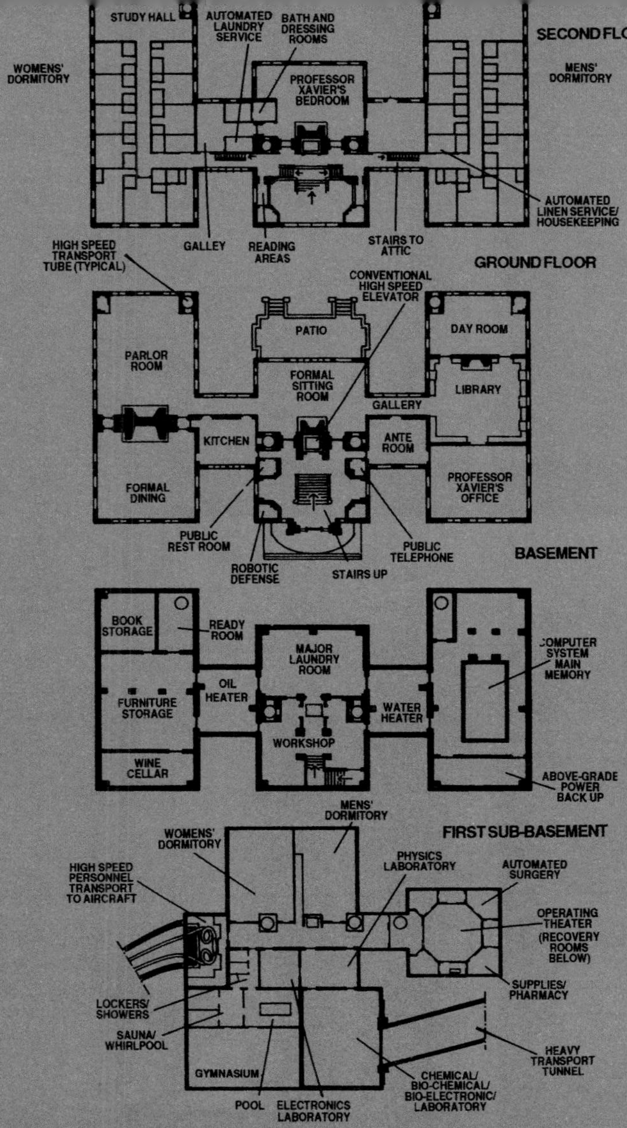
SECOND FLOOR
WOMENS' DORMITORY
STUDY HALL
AUTOMATED LAUNDRY SERVICE
BATH AND DRESSING ROOMS
PROFESSOR XAVIER'S BEDROOM
MENS' DORMITORY
AUTOMATED LINEN SERVICE/ HOUSEKEEPING
GALLEY
READING AREAS
STAIRS TO ATTIC
HIGH SPEED TRANSPORT TUBE (TYPICAL)
GROUND FLOOR
CONVENTIONAL HIGH SPEED ELEVATOR
PATIO
DAY ROOM
PARLOR ROOM
FORMAL SITTING ROOM
LIBRARY
GALLERY
KITCHEN
ANTE ROOM
FORMAL DINING
PROFESSOR XAVIER'S OFFICE
PUBLIC REST ROOM
PUBLIC TELEPHONE
ROBOTIC DEFENSE
STAIRS UP
BASEMENT
BOOK STORAGE
READY ROOM
MAJOR LAUNDRY ROOM
COMPUTER SYSTEM MAIN MEMORY
OIL HEATER
FURNITURE STORAGE
WATER HEATER
WORKSHOP
WINE CELLAR
ABOVE-GRADE POWER BACK UP
MENS' DORMITORY
FIRST SUB-BASEMENT
WOMENS' DORMITORY
PHYSICS LABORATORY
AUTOMATED SURGERY
HIGH SPEED PERSONNEL TRANSPORT TO AIRCRAFT
OPERATING THEATER (RECOVERY ROOMS BELOW)
SUPPLIES/ PHARMACY
LOCKERS/ SHOWERS
SAUNA/ WHIRLPOOL
HEAVY TRANSPORT TUNNEL
GYMNASIUM
CHEMICAL/ BIO-CHEMICAL/ BIO-ELECTRONIC/ LABORATORY
POOL
ELECTRONICS LABORATORY

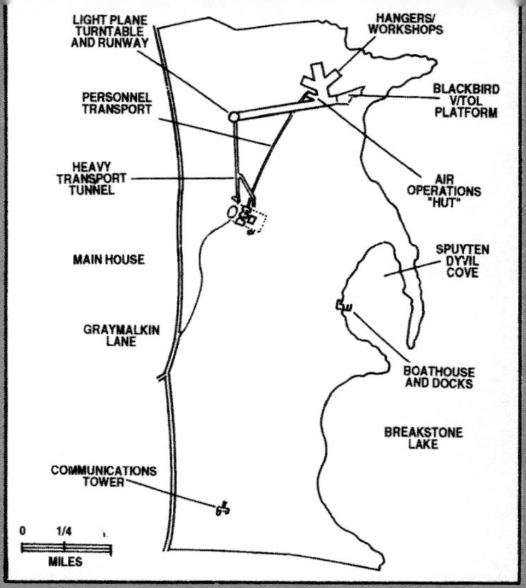
LIGHT PLANE TURNTABLE AND RUNWAY
HANGERS/ WORKSHOPS
PERSONNEL TRANSPORT
BLACKBIRD V/TOL PLATFORM
HEAVY TRANSPORT TUNNEL
AIR OPERATIONS "HUT"
MAIN HOUSE
SPUYTEN DYVIL COVE
GRAYMALKIN LANE
BOATHOUSE AND DOCKS
BREAKSTONE LAKE
COMMUNICATIONS TOWER
0
1/4
MILES

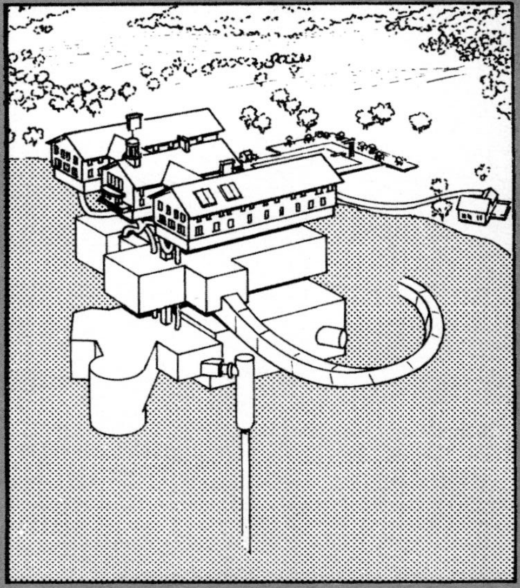

CUTAWAY OF GROUNDS

XAVIER
FOR HIGHE

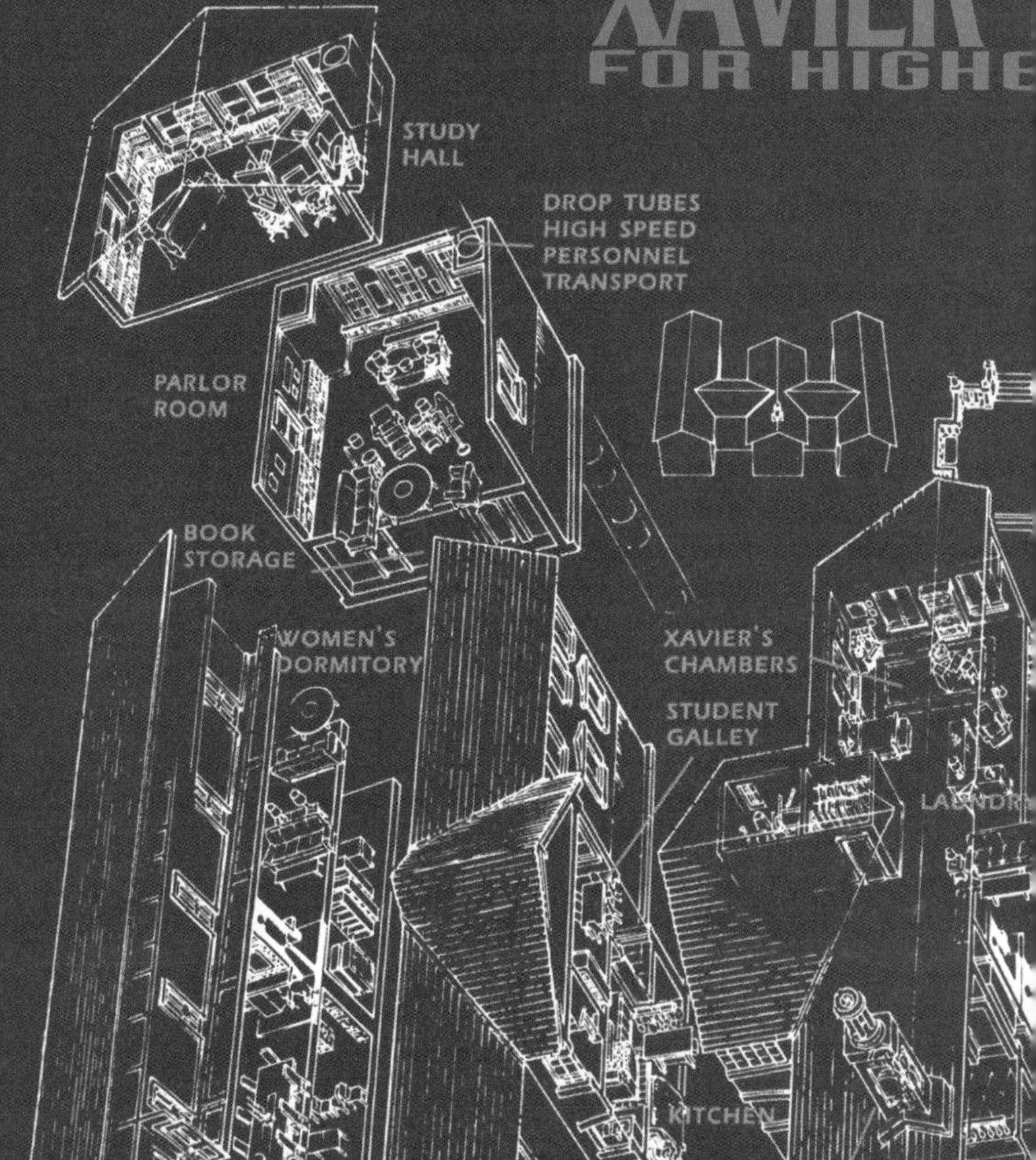
STUDY
HALL
DROP TUBES
HIGH SPEED
PERSONNEL
TRANSPORT
PARLOR
ROOM
BOOK
STORAGE
WOMEN'S
DORMITORY
XAVIER'S
CHAMBERS
STUDENT
GALLEY
KITCHEN
MANSION
THREAT
ASSESS RADAR/
COMMUNI-
CATIONS
MAST
WINE
CELLAR
FORMAL
DINING

STITUTE
LEARNING

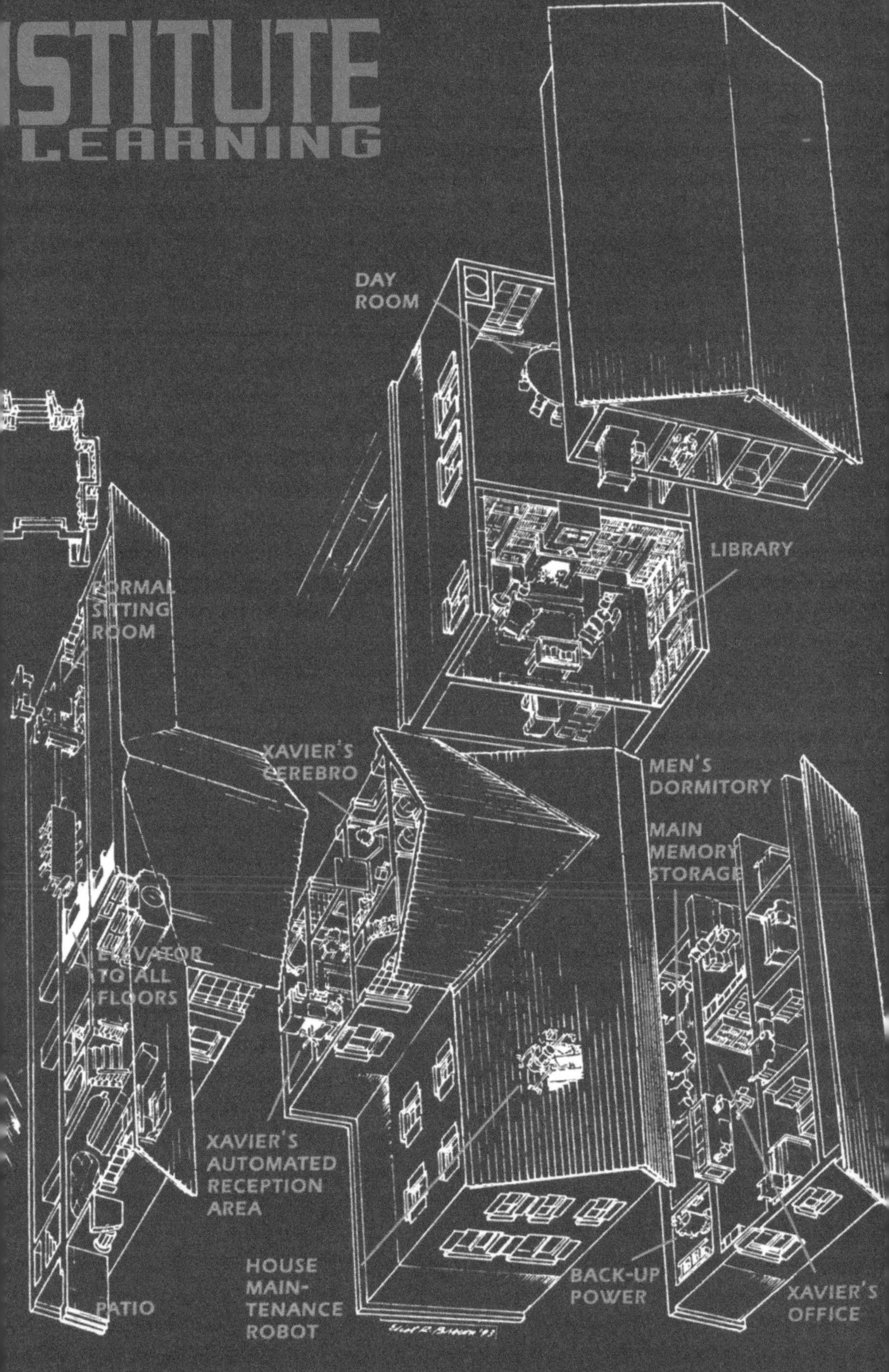

DAY ROOM
LIBRARY
FORMAL SITTING ROOM
XAVIER'S CEREBRO
MEN'S DORMITORY
MAIN MEMORY STORAGE
ELEVATOR TO ALL FLOORS
XAVIER'S AUTOMATED RECEPTION AREA
HOUSE MAIN-TENANCE ROBOT
BACK-UP POWER
XAVIER'S OFFICE
PATIO

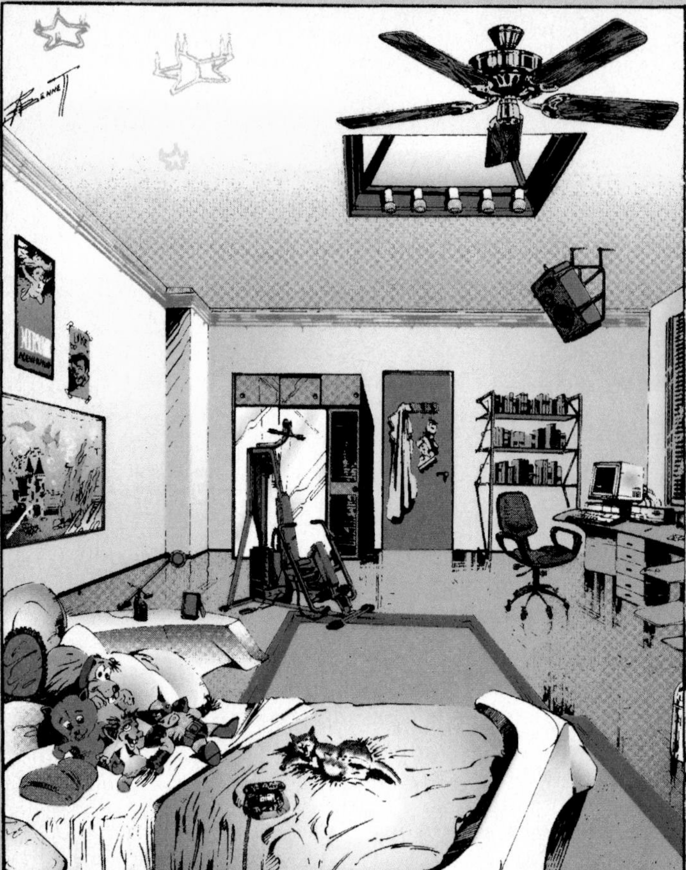

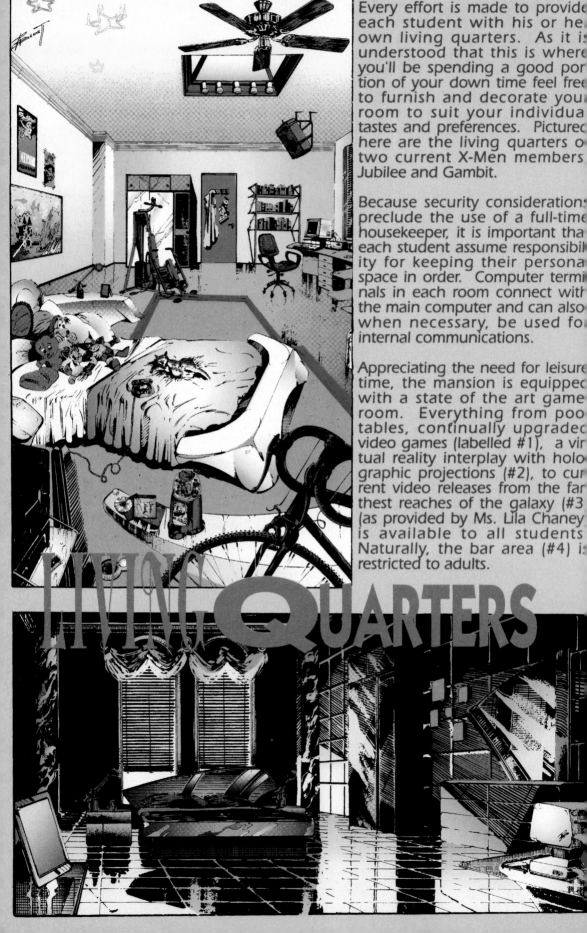

Every effort is made to provide each student with his or her own living quarters. As it is understood that this is where you'll be spending a good portion of your down time feel free to furnish and decorate your room to suit your individual tastes and preferences. Pictured here are the living quarters of two current X-Men members, Jubilee and Gambit.

Because security considerations preclude the use of a full-time housekeeper, it is important that each student assume responsibility for keeping their personal space in order. Computer terminals in each room connect with the main computer and can also, when necessary, be used for internal communications.

Appreciating the need for leisure time, the mansion is equipped with a state of the art game room. Everything from pool tables, continually upgraded video games (labelled #1), a virtual reality interplay with holographic projections (#2), to current video releases from the farthest reaches of the galaxy (#3) (as provided by Ms. Lila Cheney) is available to all students. Naturally, the bar area (#4) is restricted to adults.

LIVING QUARTERS

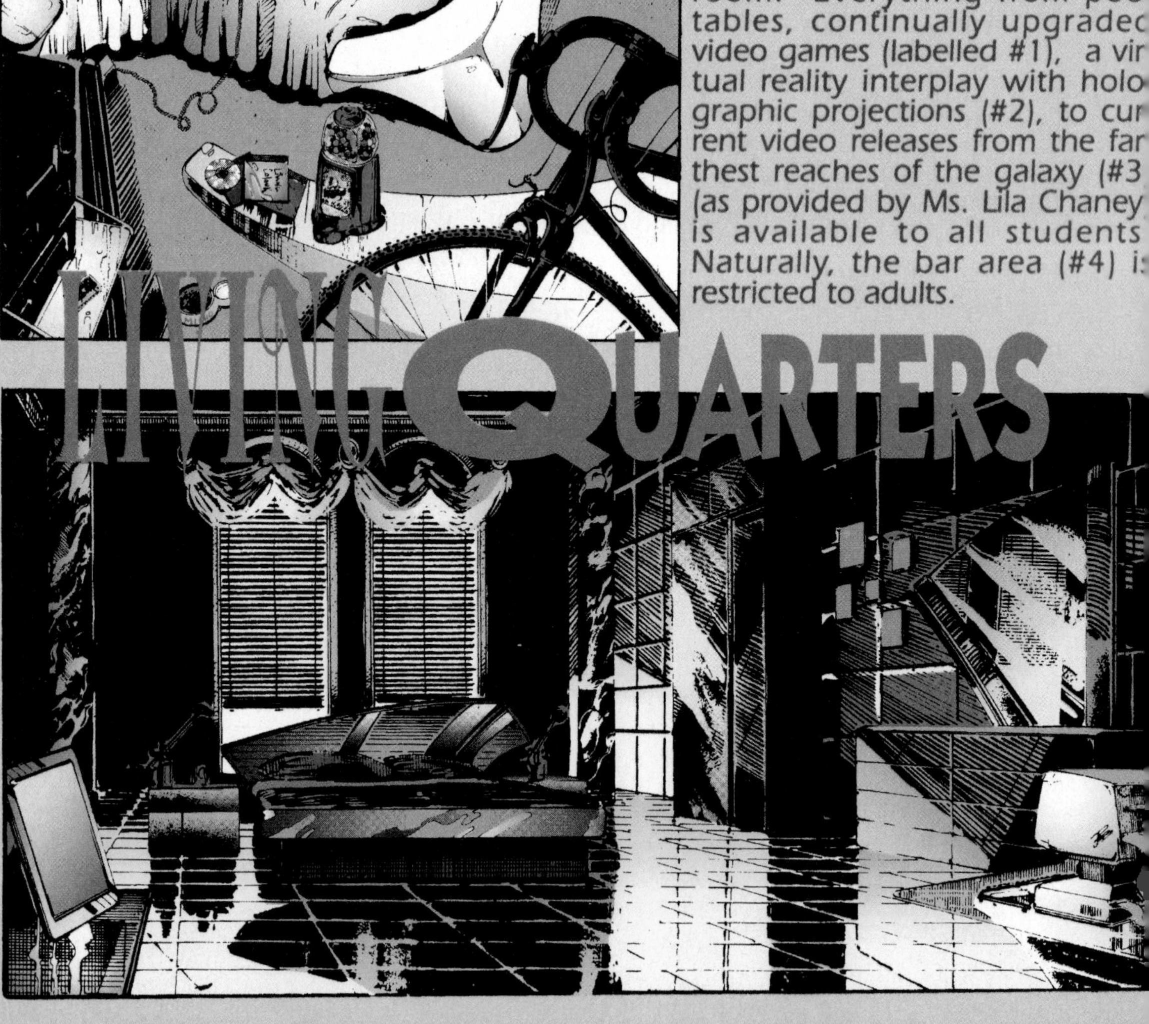

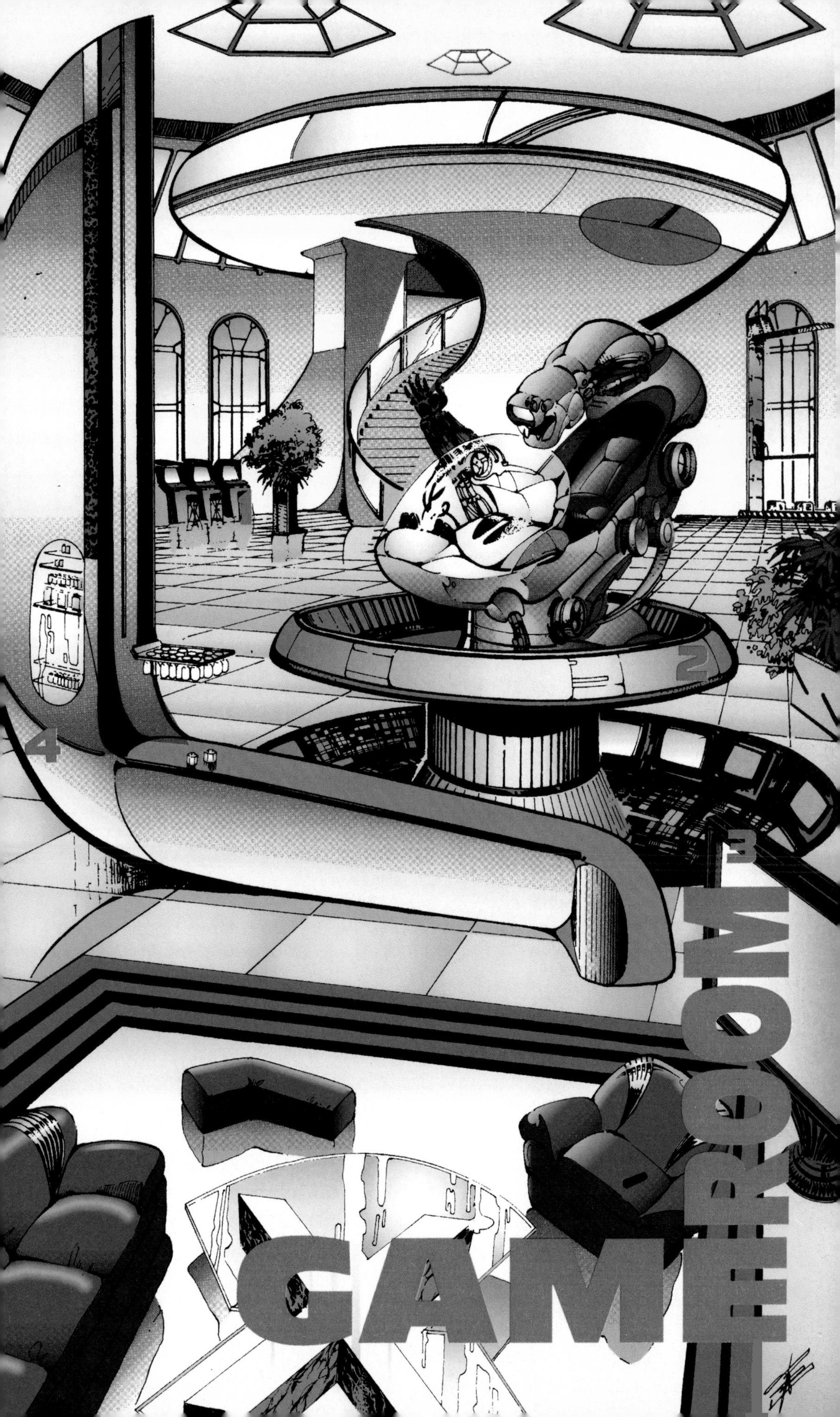
GAME ROOM
2
3
4

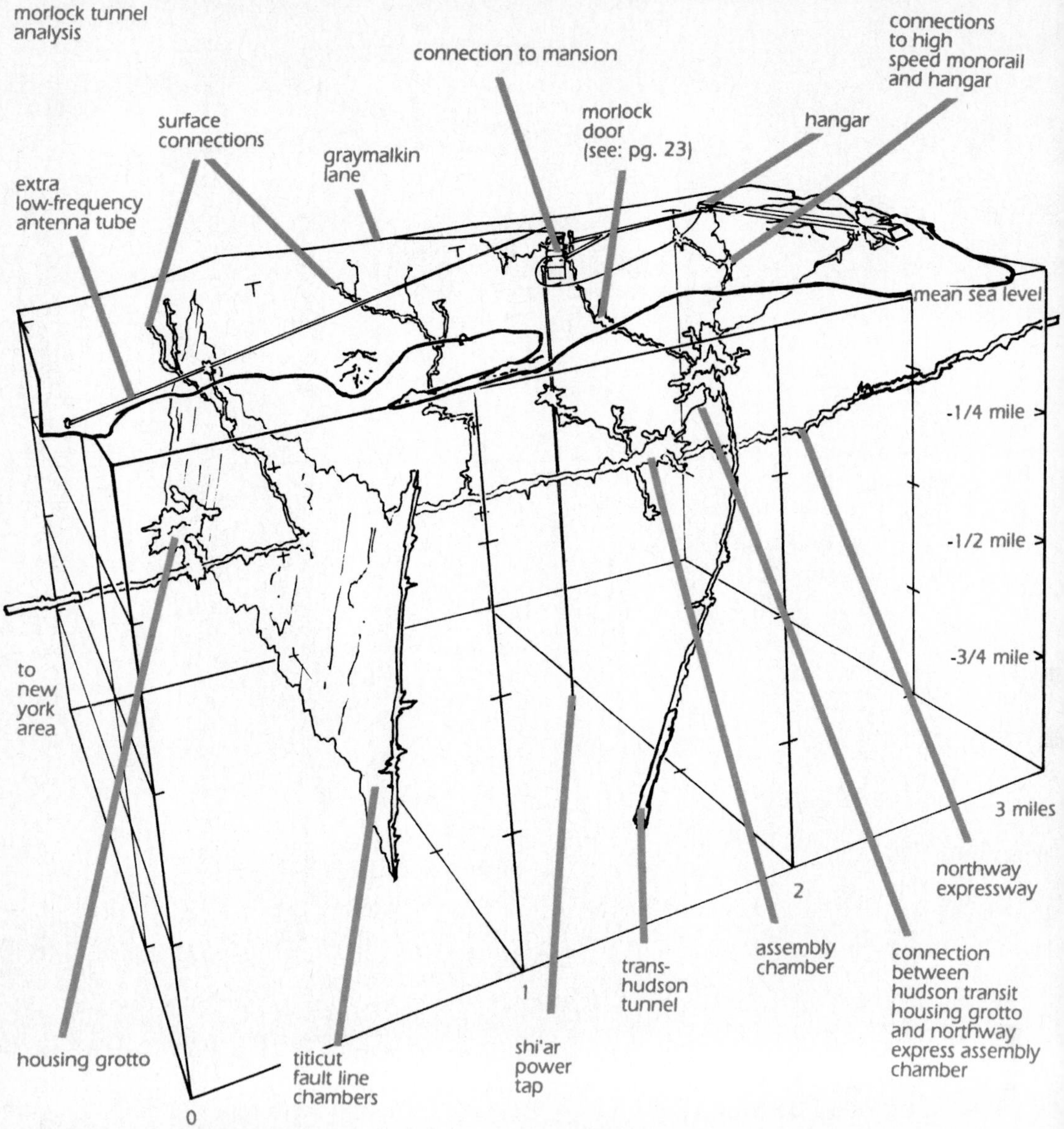
morlock tunnel analysis
connection to mansion
connections to high speed monorail and hangar
surface connections
morlock door (see: pg. 23)
hangar
graymalkin lane
extra low-frequency antenna tube
mean sea level
-1/4 mile
-1/2 mile
-3/4 mile
to new york area
3 miles
northway expressway
2
assembly chamber
connection between hudson transit housing grotto and northway express assembly chamber
trans-hudson tunnel
1
housing grotto
titicut fault line chambers
shi'ar power tap
0

Though the tunnels are no longer occupied by the often times hostile group of mutants known collectively as the Morlocks, this underground labyrinth remains our weakest area of defense. Little is known regarding the original construction of the tunnels which predates Morlock occupation. Because of the highly unstable and progressively deteriorating nature of these pathways, (further complicated by the presence of subterranean rivers with extremely dangerous currents) much of the tunnels remain uncharted—while that which is known to us is constantly monitored by computer surveillance, with defensive stun beams installed at crucial junctures to prevent attack from this quarter.

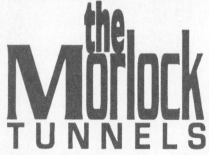

the Morlock TUNNELS

NOTE: Admittance to the tunnels is strictly prohibited except in the event of a full-scale assault on the mansion. If all other alternate routes have been cut off, the tunnels may become an egress of last resort. Subterranean evacuation drills are held in the Danger Room holo-grid once a month. Drill attendance is mandatory.

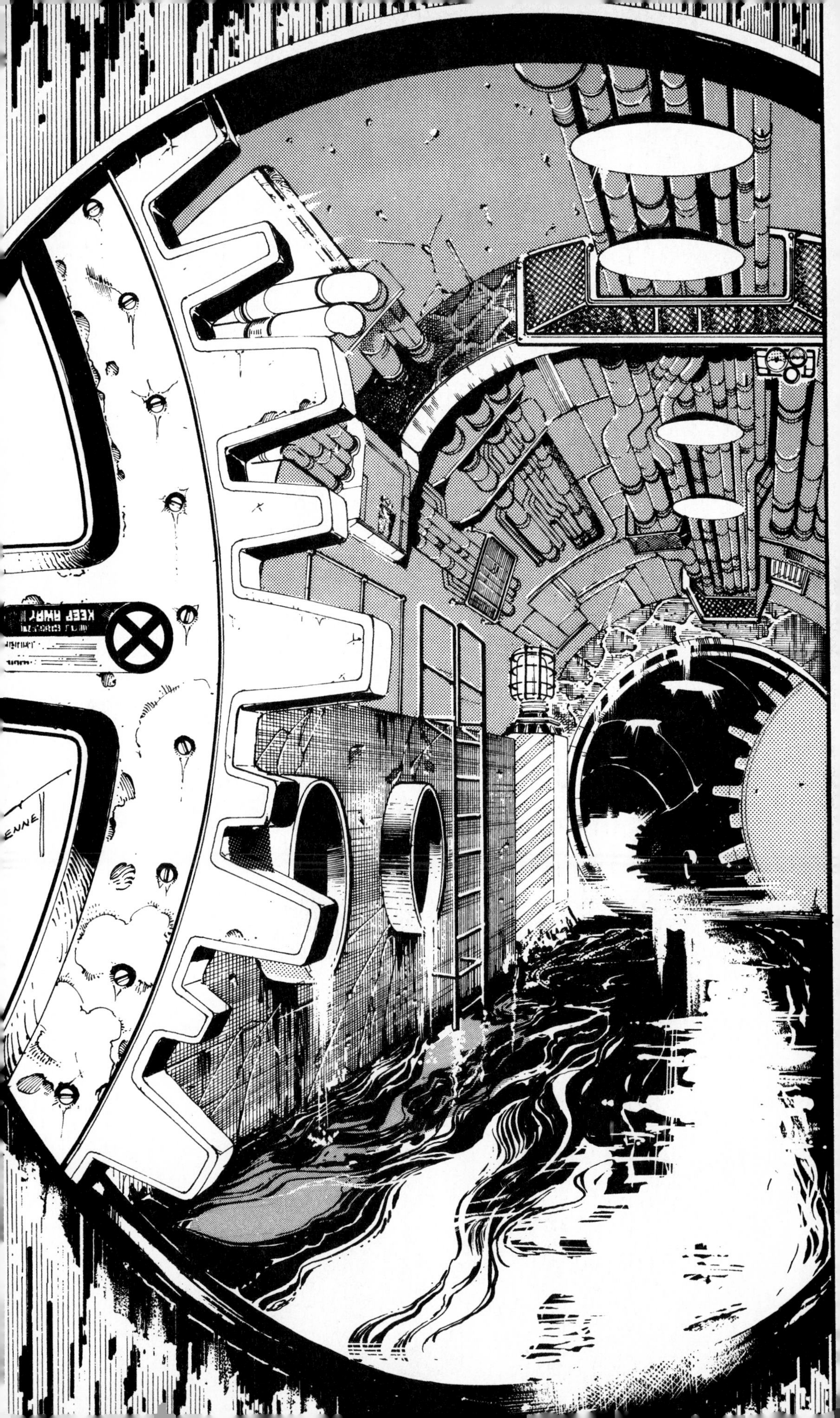
KEEP AWAY

THE HANGAR

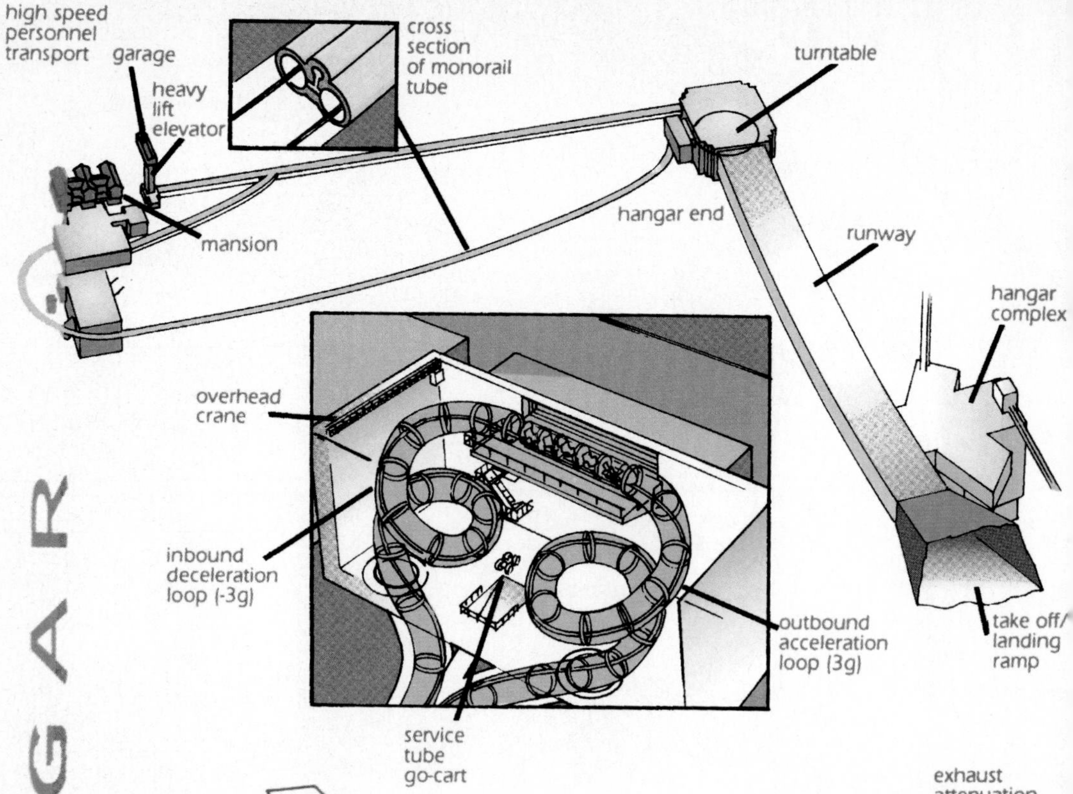
high speed personnel transport
garage
heavy lift elevator
cross section of monorail tube
turntable
mansion
hangar end
runway
hangar complex
overhead crane
inbound deceleration loop (-3g)
outbound acceleration loop (3g)
take off/ landing ramp
service tube go-cart

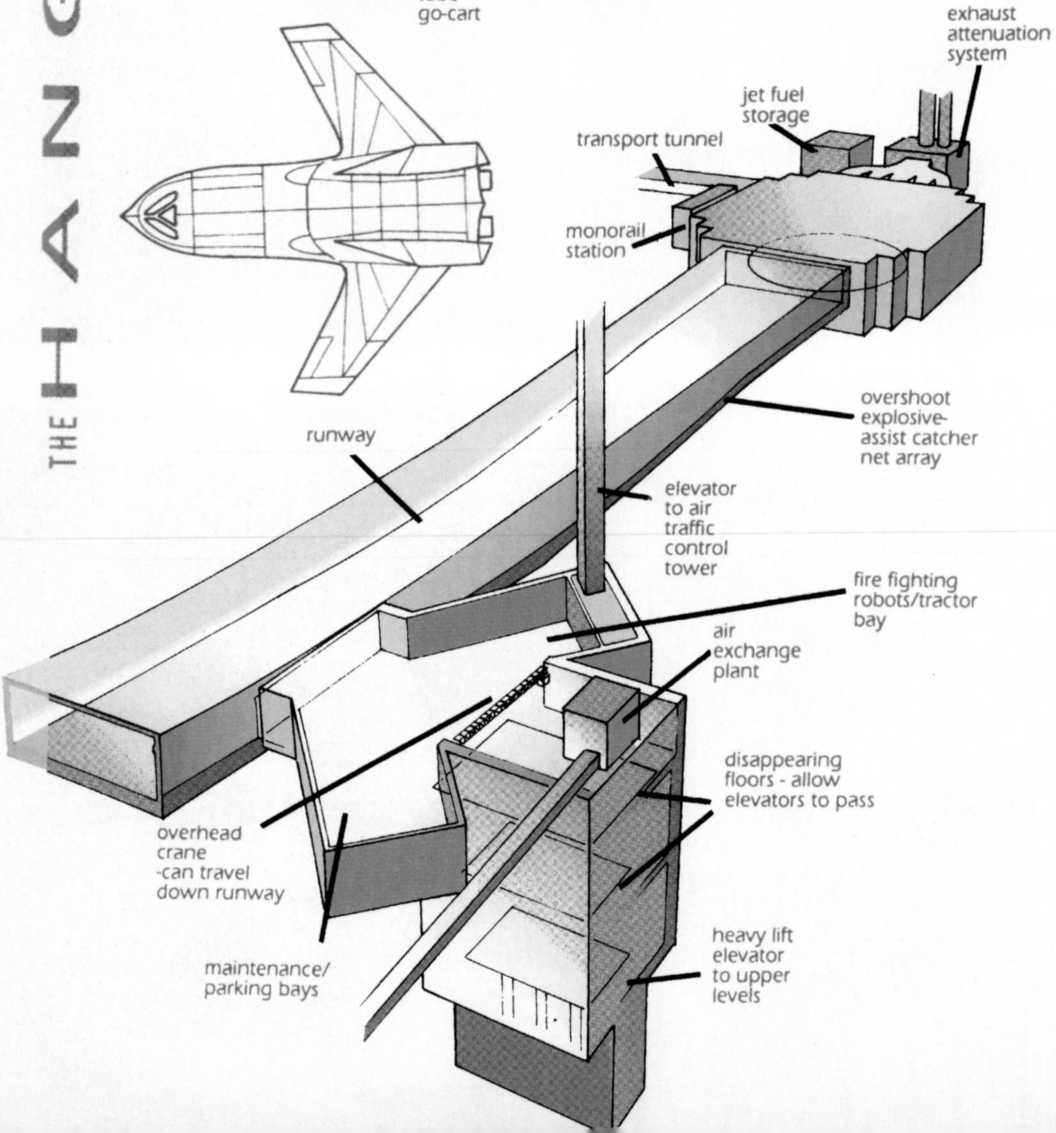
exhaust attenuation system
jet fuel storage
transport tunnel
monorail station
overshoot explosive-assist catcher net array
runway
elevator to air traffic control tower
fire fighting robots/tractor bay
air exchange plant
disappearing floors - allow elevators to pass
overhead crane -can travel down runway
maintenance/ parking bays
heavy lift elevator to upper levels

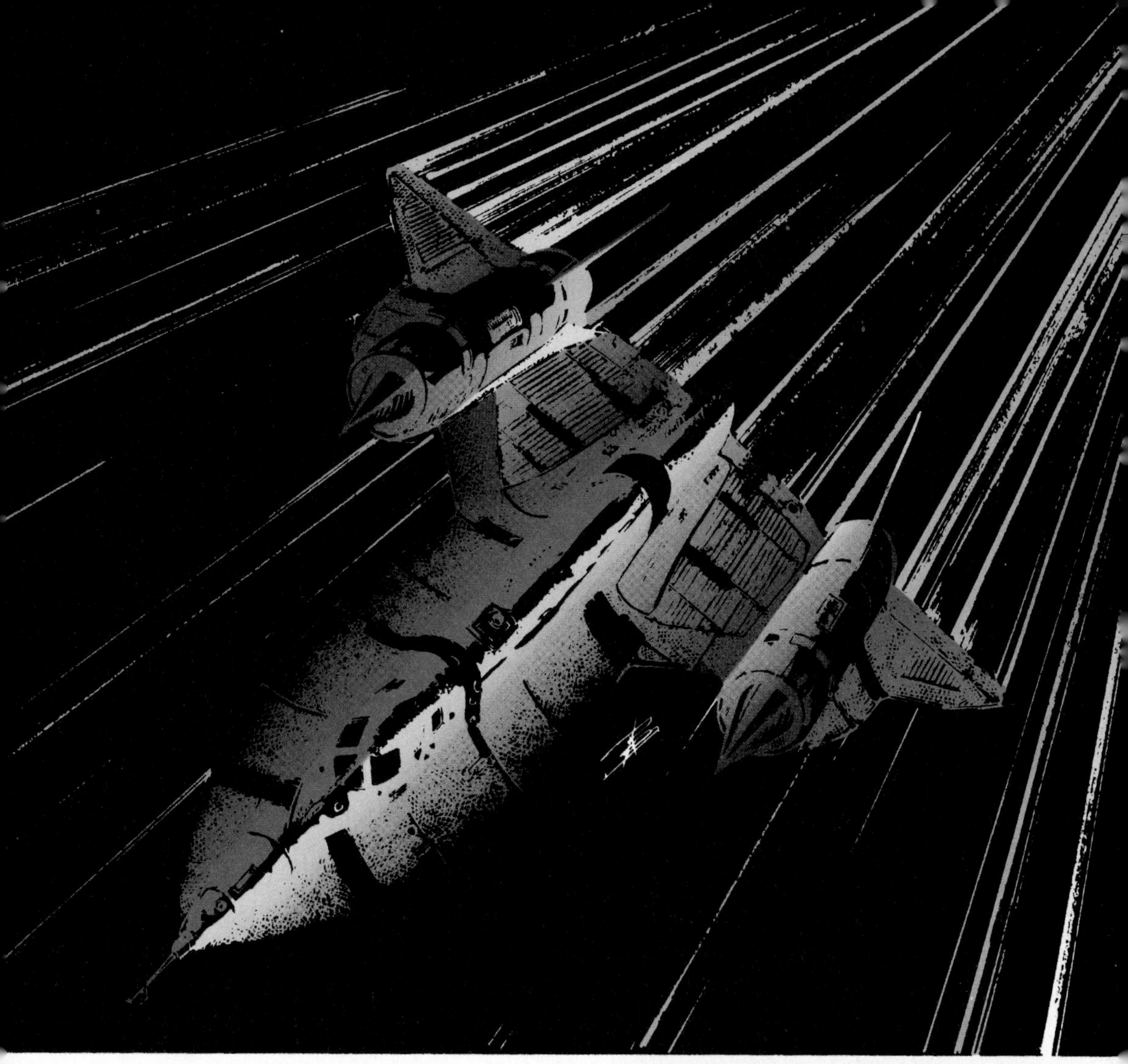

The Hangar bay, which is the storage port for the Blackbirds, can be reached by monorail leaving from sub level six. The distance of .62 miles can be covered in 20 seconds under emergency conditions. Practice drills are, again, mandatory to orient yourself with disembarking. At present the institute has 2 Blackbird jets—one designated for the X-Men's gold team and one for the blue team. Blackbird Blue is based on our original model and Blackbird Gold incorporates Forge's latest design features. Both are manufactured by Forge and are comparable in abilities, range and speed. Blackbird pilot training is available and strongly suggested, but not mandatory. Flight station simulators are located in Hangar Level 1A. Pilots are strictly required, whenever possible, to follow applicable FAA safety guidelines.

BLACKBIRD

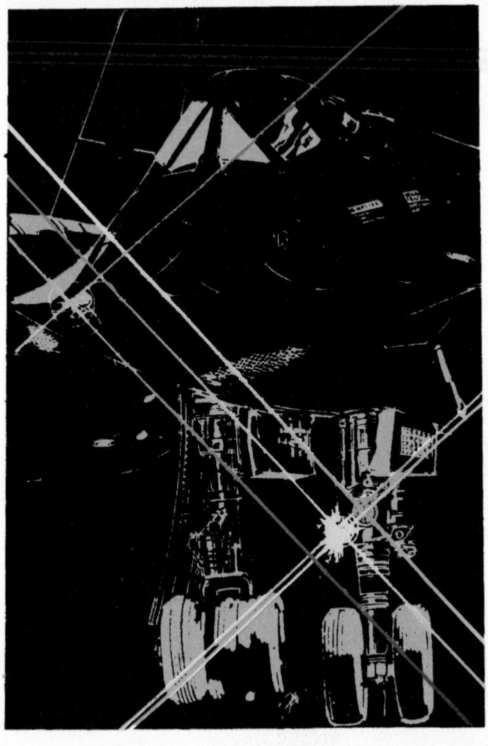

BLACKBIRD

THIS CRAFT IS INTENDED TO BE A TRANSSONIC TRANSPORTATION DEVICE THAT CAN CARRY ALL CURRENT MEMBERS OF THE X-MEN PLUS SEVERAL PASSENGERS. THE BLACKBIRD IS EQUIPPED TO FLY LONG-DURATION, HIGH-ALTITUDE RECONNAISSANCE MISSIONS AND SHORTER TRIPS, AS WELL AS TO ANY CLIMATE. A MISSION-SPECIFIC ADD-ON POD CAN BE EQUIPPED FOR SEVERAL PRE-PLANNED OR EXOTIC MISSION SCENARIOS.

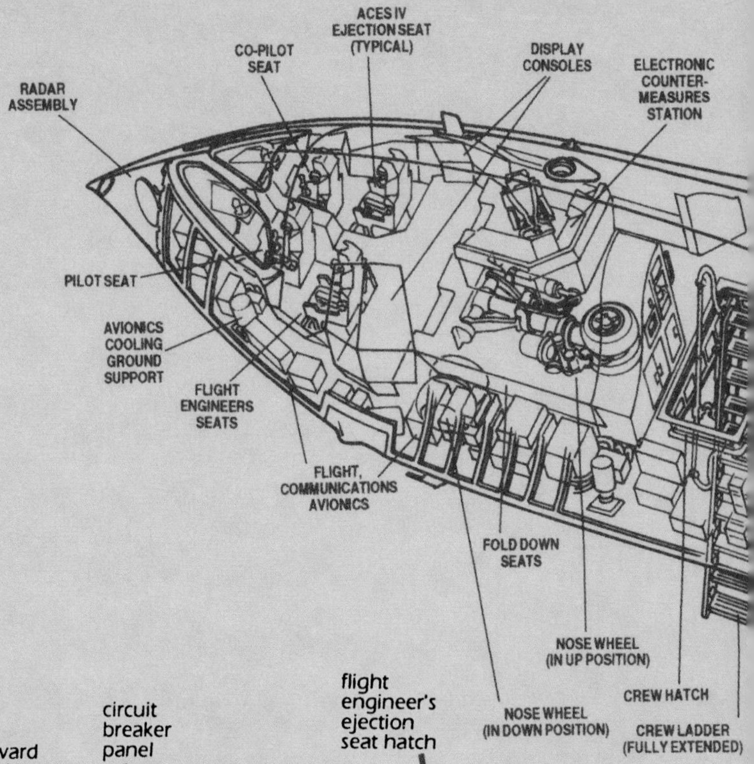
ACES IV EJECTION SEAT (TYPICAL)
CO-PILOT SEAT
DISPLAY CONSOLES
ELECTRONIC COUNTER-MEASURES STATION
RADAR ASSEMBLY
PILOT SEAT
AVIONICS COOLING GROUND SUPPORT
FLIGHT ENGINEERS SEATS
FLIGHT, COMMUNICATIONS AVIONICS
FOLD DOWN SEATS
NOSE WHEEL (IN UP POSITION)
CREW HATCH
NOSE WHEEL (IN DOWN POSITION)
CREW LADDER (FULLY EXTENDED)

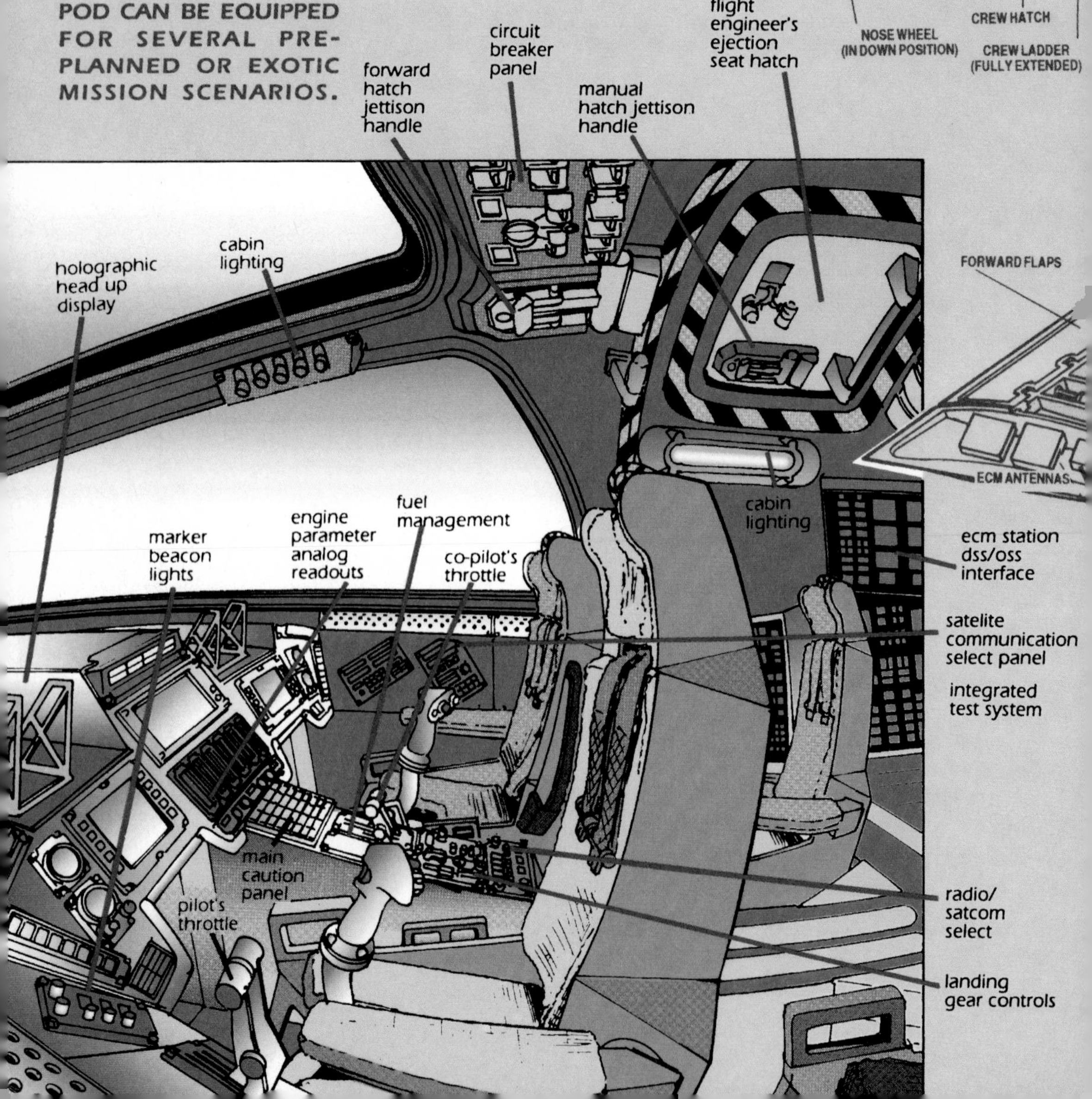
flight engineer's ejection seat hatch
circuit breaker panel
forward hatch jettison handle
manual hatch jettison handle
FORWARD FLAPS
cabin lighting
holographic head up display
ECM ANTENNAS
cabin lighting
fuel management
engine parameter analog readouts
marker beacon lights
co-pilot's throttle
ecm station dss/oss interface
satelite communication select panel
integrated test system
main caution panel
pilot's throttle
radio/ satcom select
landing gear controls

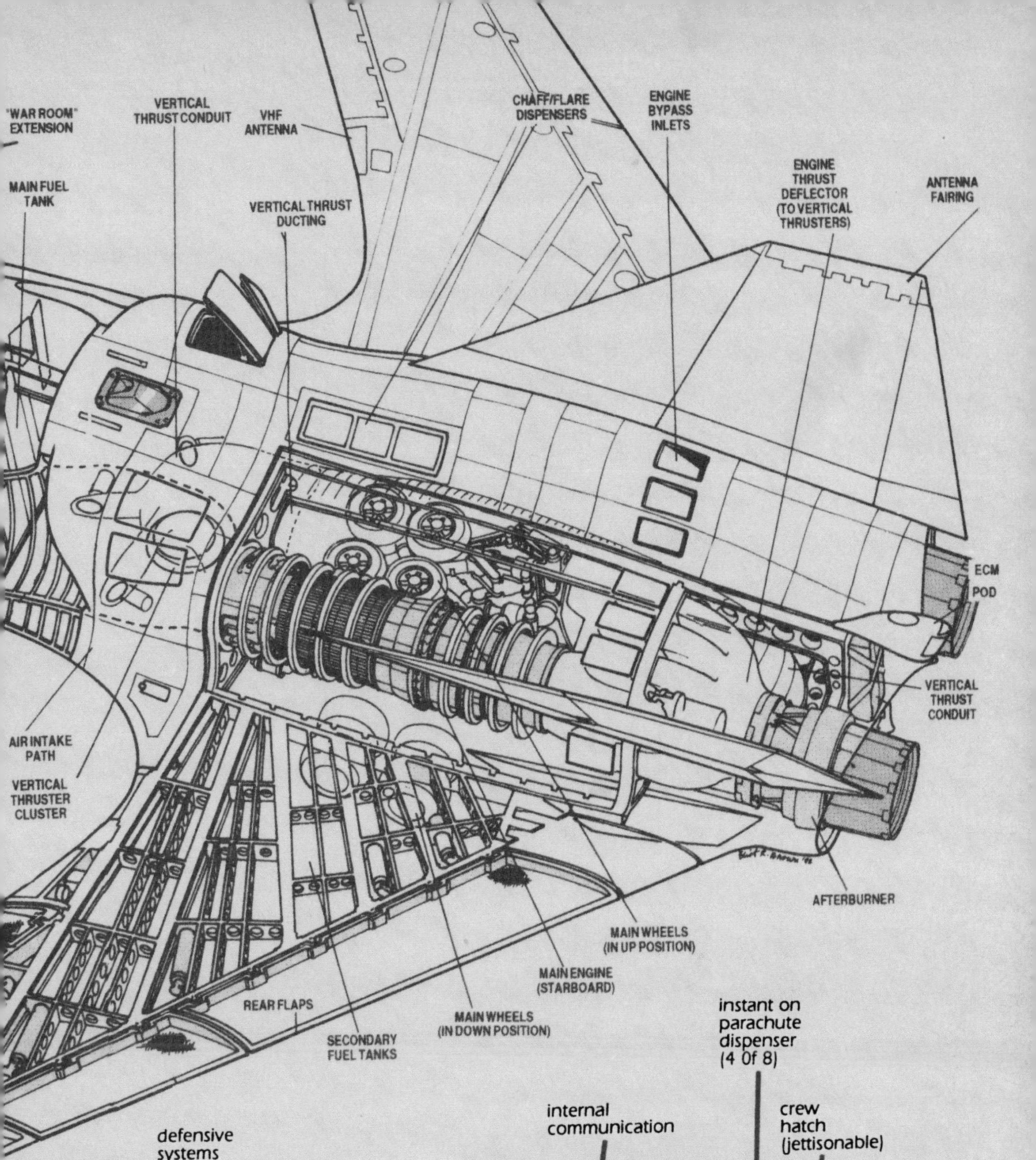

"WAR ROOM" EXTENSION
VERTICAL THRUST CONDUIT
VHF ANTENNA
CHAFF/FLARE DISPENSERS
ENGINE BYPASS INLETS
MAIN FUEL TANK
VERTICAL THRUST DUCTING
ENGINE THRUST DEFLECTOR (TO VERTICAL THRUSTERS)
ANTENNA FAIRING
ECM POD
VERTICAL THRUST CONDUIT
AIR INTAKE PATH
VERTICAL THRUSTER CLUSTER
AFTERBURNER
MAIN WHEELS (IN UP POSITION)
MAIN ENGINE (STARBOARD)
REAR FLAPS
MAIN WHEELS (IN DOWN POSITION)
SECONDARY FUEL TANKS

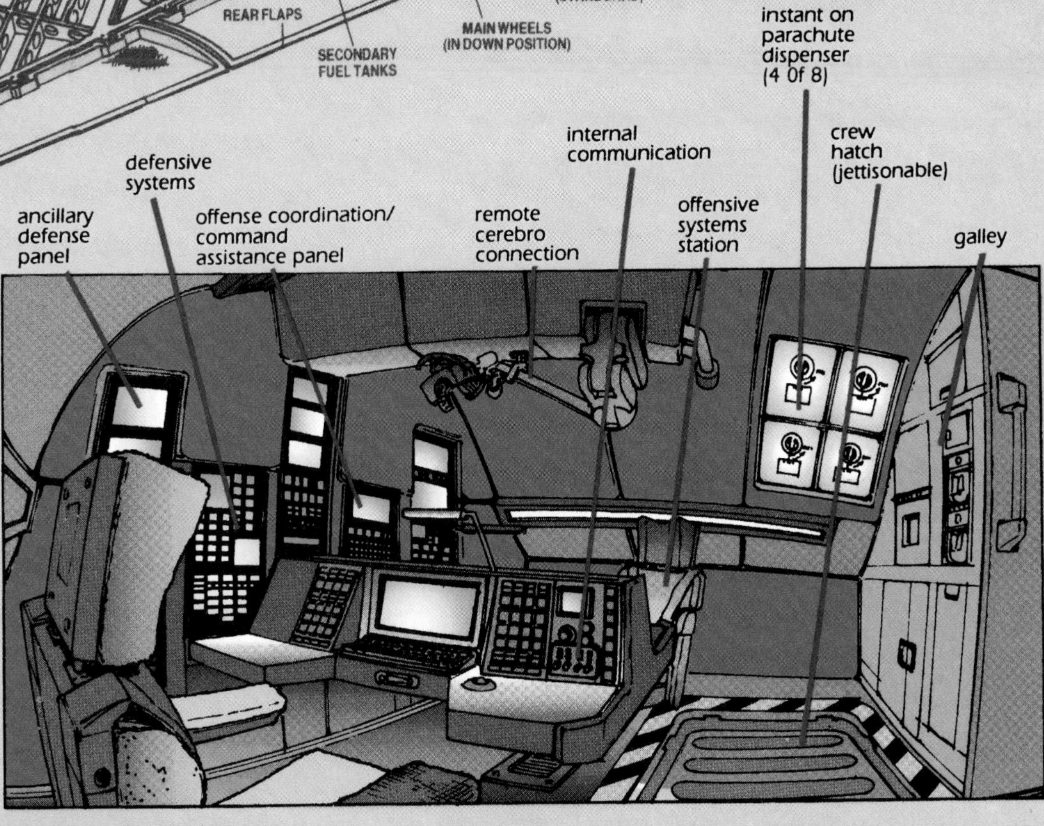

instant on parachute dispenser (4 0f 8)
internal communication
crew hatch (jettisonable)
defensive systems
ancillary defense panel
offense coordination/ command assistance panel
remote cerebro connection
offensive systems station
galley

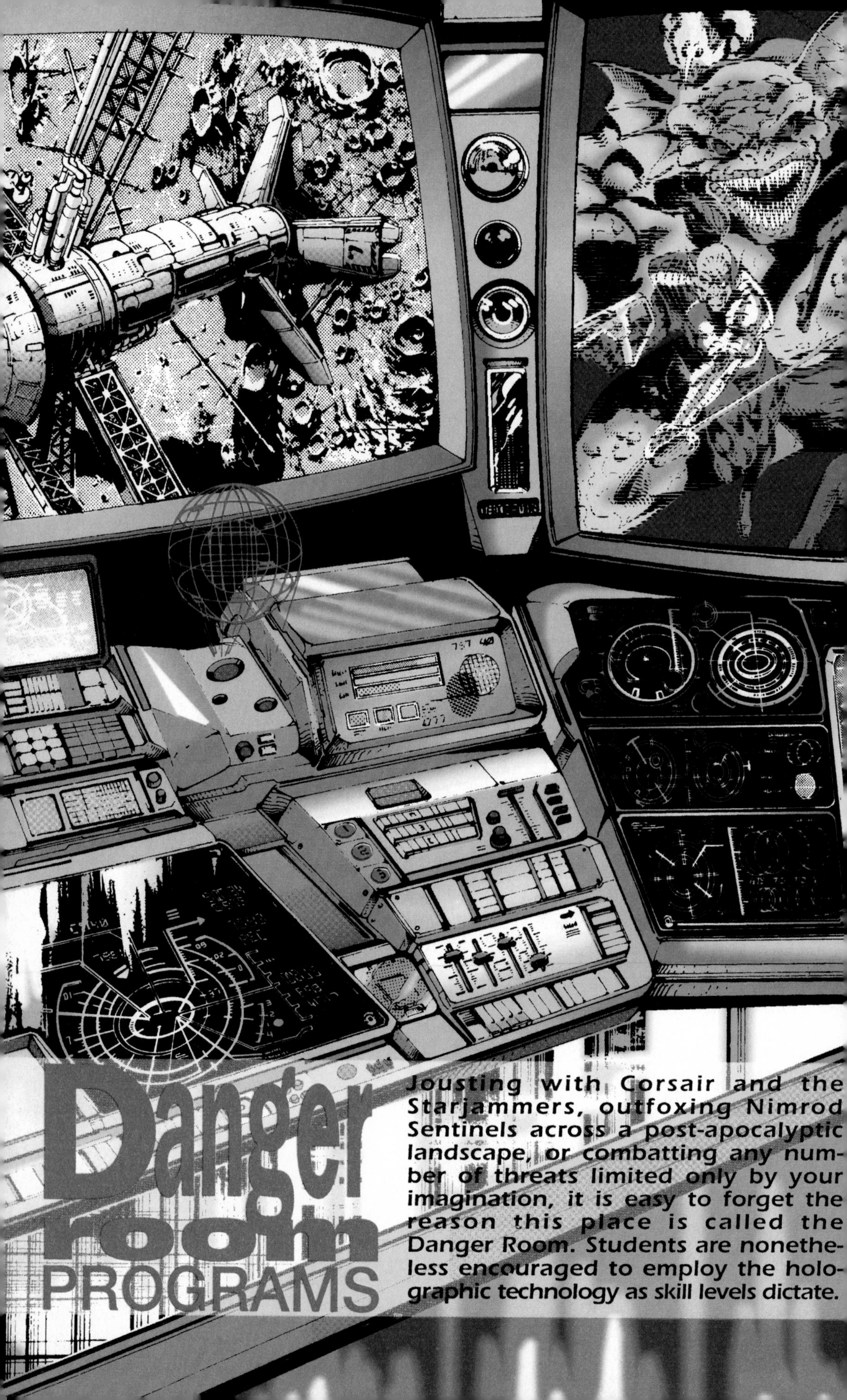

Danger room PROGRAMS

Jousting with Corsair and the Starjammers, outfoxing Nimrod Sentinels across a post-apocalyptic landscape, or combatting any number of threats limited only by your imagination, it is easy to forget the reason this place is called the Danger Room. Students are nonetheless encouraged to employ the holographic technology as skill levels dictate.

The Danger Room World View Library can be used for basic gymnastic workouts which include no holographic display (primary level Alpha 1). This is the most basic program designed with novices in mind. There are over 120 levels of increasing difficulty in the Danger Room computers. The hologram library files begin on level 21 Beta.

NOTE: While I do not subscribe to this theory myself, Dr. MacTaggert argues that continued exposure to reality simulation may dull one's sensitivity to danger rather than sharpen it. In deference to her expertise on combat related stress and post-trauma orientation, Holo-specific Danger Room participation is restricted to thirteen hours a week.

COMBAT OPERATIONS CENTER
Organizational Component Breakdown

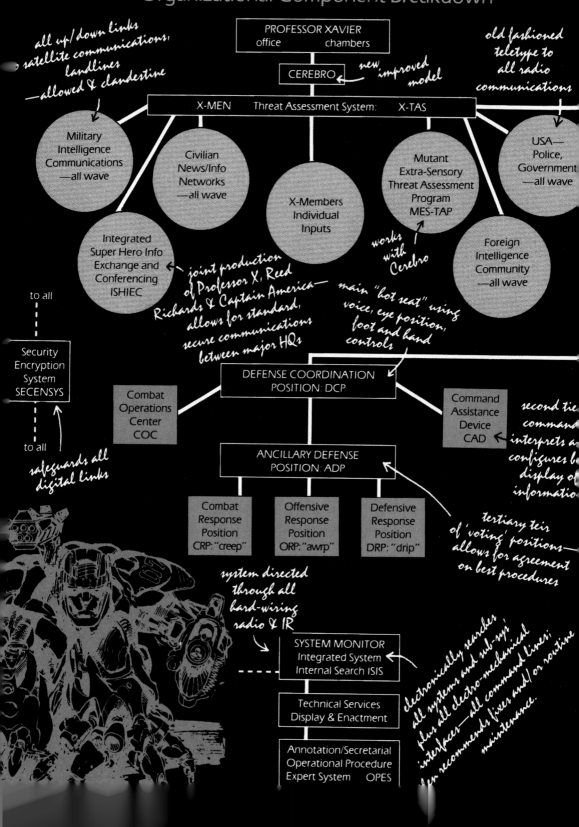

PROFESSOR XAVIER
office   chambers

CEREBRO

new improved model

X-MEN   Threat Assessment System: X-TAS

all up/down links to satellite communications, landlines —allowed & clandestine

old fashioned teletype to all radio communications

Military Intelligence Communications —all wave

Civilian News/Info Networks —all wave

X-Members Individual Inputs

Mutant Extra-Sensory Threat Assessment Program MES-TAP

USA— Police, Government —all wave

Integrated Super Hero Info Exchange and Conferencing ISHIEC

Foreign Intelligence Community —all wave

joint production of Professor X, Reed Richards & Captain America— allows for standard, secure communications between major HQs

works with Cerebro

main "hot seat" using voice, eye position, foot and hand controls

to all

Security Encryption System SECENSYS

to all

safeguards all digital links

DEFENSE COORDINATION POSITION: DCP

Combat Operations Center COC

Command Assistance Device CAD

second tier command interprets and configures best display of information

ANCILLARY DEFENSE POSITION: ADP

Combat Response Position CRP: "creep"

Offensive Response Position ORP: "awrp"

Defensive Response Position DRP: "drip"

tertiary tier of 'voting' positions— allows for agreement on best procedures

system directed through all hard-wiring radio & IR

SYSTEM MONITOR Integrated System Internal Search ISIS

Technical Services Display & Enactment

Annotation/Secretarial Operational Procedure Expert System   OPES

electronically searches all systems and sub-systems plus all electro-mechanical interfaces—all command lines; then recommends fixes and/or routine maintenance.

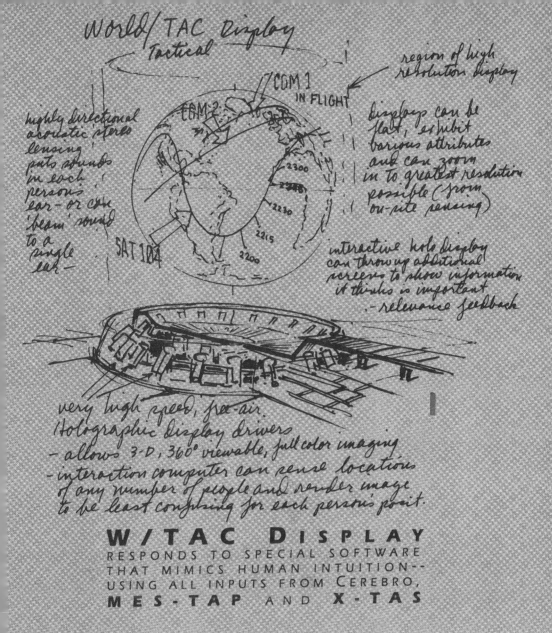

World/TAC Display

Tactical

region of high resolution display

CAM 1 IN FLIGHT

CAM 2

highly directional acoustic stereo lensing puts sounds in each person's ear — or can 'beam' sound to a single ear —

SAT 184

2300
2245
2230
2215
2200

displays can be flat, exhibit various attributes and can zoom in to greatest resolution possible (from on-site sensing)

interactive holo display can throw up additional screens to show information it thinks is important — relevance feedback

very high speed, free-air. Holographic display drivers
– allows 3-D, 360° viewable, full color imaging
– interaction computer can sense locations of any number of people and render image to be least confusing for each person's posit.

W/TAC DISPLAY

RESPONDS TO SPECIAL SOFTWARE THAT MIMICS HUMAN INTUITION-- USING ALL INPUTS FROM CEREBRO, **MES-TAP** AND **X-TAS**

WAR ROOM

I have spent an inordinate amount of time trying to derive an alternate designate for the "War Room." It has been my fervent wish, long before the formation of the X-Men, that hostilities be avoided at all costs, be it human vs. mutant or mutant vs. mutant. In recent years, however, I have become painfully aware that a war is being waged across the planet Earth — and that we are the first, quite possibly the final, line of defense.

Since the last printing of this manual, the number of mutant fringe groups have increased disproportionately to the membership of the X-Men (X-Factor, X-Force notwithstanding). Where there was once the Brotherhood of Evil Mutants, Factor Three, the Inner Circle of the Hellfire Club, and later the Morlocks, we have recently witnessed the introduction of the Horsemen of the Apocalypse, the Upstarts, the Acolytes, the Mutant Liberation Front, the so-called Nasty Boys, and the Dark Riders. This does not even include the ever-evolving army of government manufactured Sentinels, the threat of Project: Wideawake, or the paramilitary mutant-hating "Friends of Humanity." To pretend we are not at war — to hide behind euphemisms — would be misleading and, worse case scenario, fatal.

the WAR room

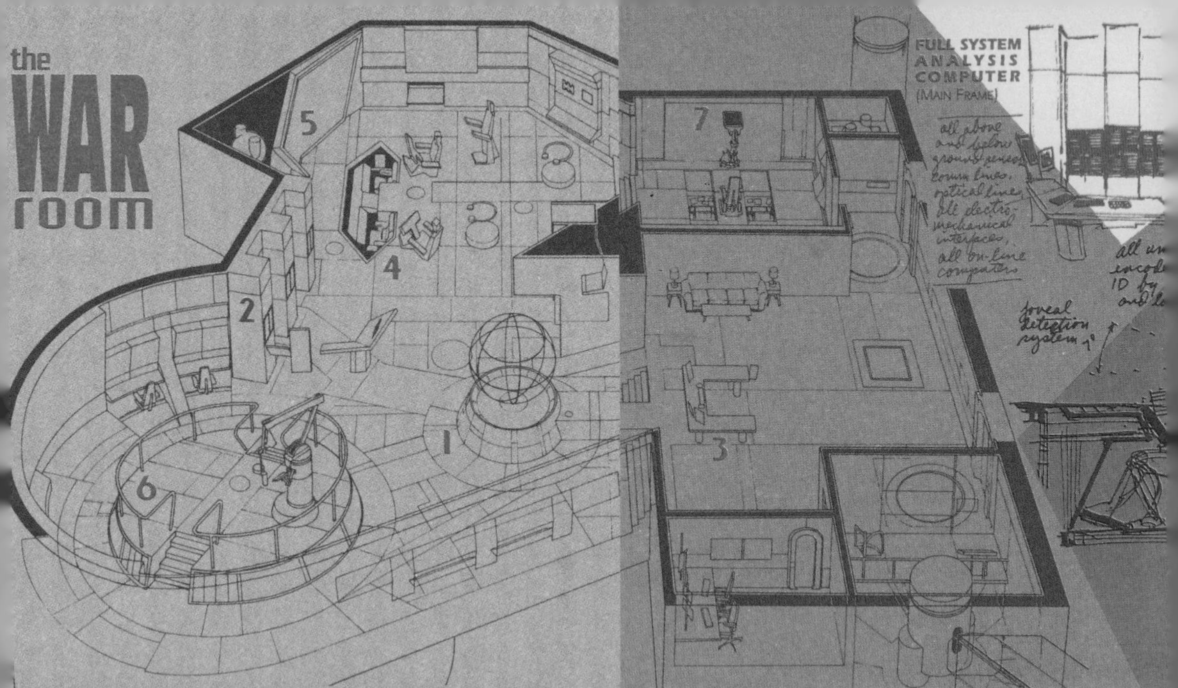

5
4
2
1
6
7
3
FULL SYSTEM ANALYSIS COMPUTER
(MAIN FRAME)
all above and below ground sensors, comm lines, optical lines, all electro-mechanical interfaces, all on-line computers
foveal detection system

The War Room itself constantly monitors all broadcast information networks, ranging from NORAD Central Command to S.H.I.E.L.D. Intelligence, to the nightly news. From the F.A.A. flight patterns for every airport in the United States, to personnel files for England's MI6, and the former Soviet Union's KGB. High speed scans extract that information from these sources which is applicable to our mission and our goals. I have every confidence that the intelligence system we have at our disposal is second to none.

While it may appear unseemly and disturbing that we are engaged in the borrowing of such information, it must be stressed that accessing this data has proven vital to our survival on many occasions. We live in difficult times and moral choices of questionable nature are unfortunately the result. Rest assured this information is never used in any illegal manner.

SECURITY NOTE: Various safeguards have been built into the system ranging from varying frequency modulators and computer viruses to nanotechnology. Most are based on Shi'ar design and augmented by the X-Man, Forge, to act as buffers between our information systems and our network of infotaps. In this way we are assured no intelligence gathering organization can trace their security leaks back to us.

SIDENOTE: The War Room computer is on constant interface with the secured computer in the ready room where more private sources of information are processed.

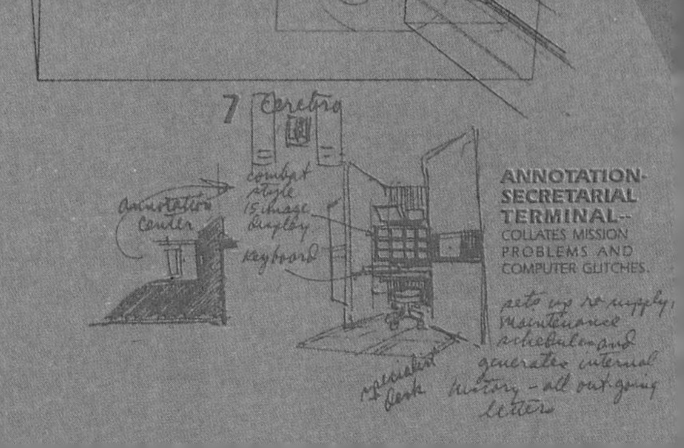

7 Cerebro
Annotation Center
combat style 15 image display
keyboard
specialist desk
ANNOTATION-SECRETARIAL TERMINAL--
COLLATES MISSION PROBLEMS AND COMPUTER GLITCHES.

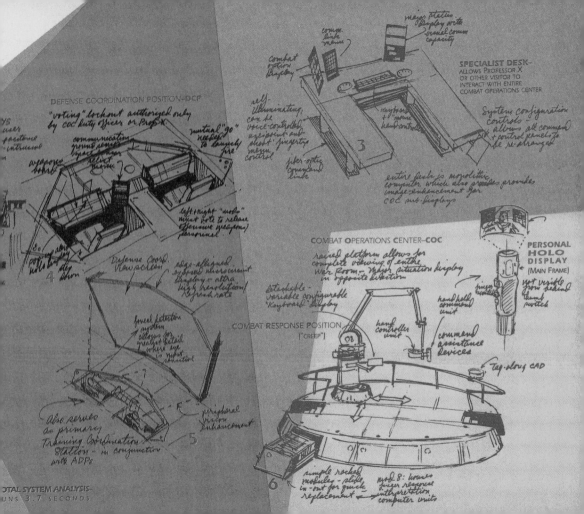

DEFENSE COORDINATION POSITION-DCP

"voting" lockout authorized only by COC duty officer or Prof. X

communication round sensor reject sensor reject menu

mutual "go" needed to launch fire

YS user positive intrusive

weapons search

left + right "mode" must vote to release (offensive weapons) personnel

So prog. also will display

4 dep down

Defense Coord. view screen

edge-aligned exposed microsecond display + ultra high resolution/refresh rate

freeze detection system allows for greatest detail where eye is most sensitive

peripheral vision enhancement

Also serves as primary Training Coordination Station - in conjunction with ADPs

5

self-illuminating, can be voice-controlled, viewpoint and object "finger-tip" menu control

fiber-optic command link

3

comm. link menu

combat option display

major status display with visual comm. capacity

SPECIALIST DESK-
ALLOWS PROFESSOR X OR OTHER VISITOR TO INTERACT WITH ENTIRE COMBAT OPERATIONS CENTER

keyboard + "menu" hand controls

System configuration controls - allows all command + control panels to be re-arranged

entire desk is monolithic computer which also provides image-enhancement for COC sub-displays

COMBAT OPERATIONS CENTER-COC

raised platform allows for complete viewing of entire War Room - Major situation display in opposite direction

detachable - variable configurable "keyboard" display

COMBAT RESPONSE POSITION ("CREEP")

hand controller unit

hand held command unit

command assistance devices

PERSONAL HOLO DISPLAY (MAIN FRAME)

finger controls

not visible from behind

thumb switch

Tag-along CAD

simple rocket modules - slide in-out for quick replacement

mod 8: houses finger response interpretation computer units

6

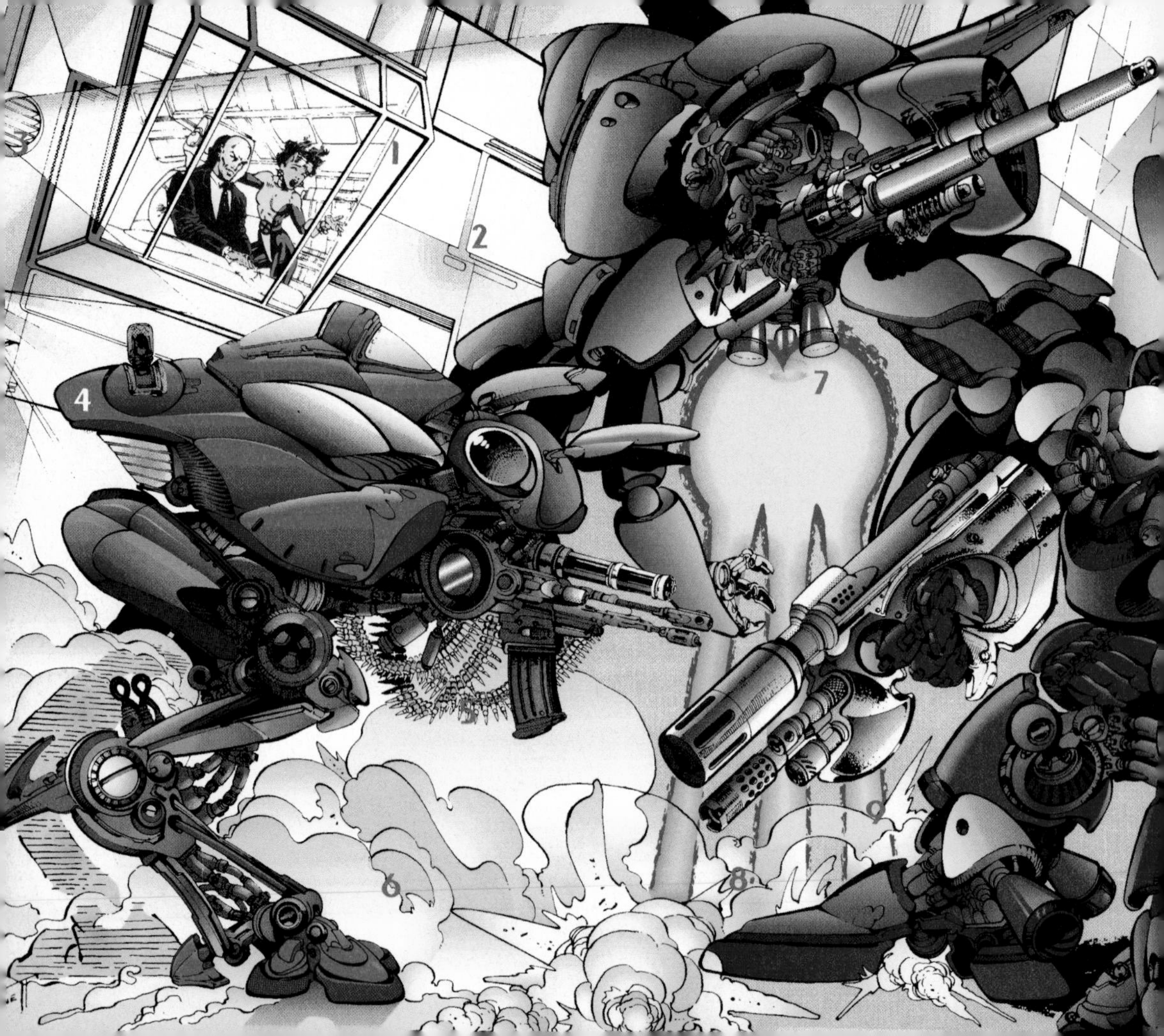
1
2
4
7
9
6
8

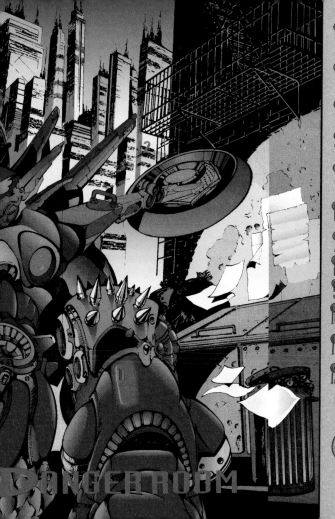

1. **DANGER ROOM MASTER CONTROL**--Direct Viewport. Viewing is 'one way' with highly directional active photon filtering (APF). APF functions by tuning a forcefield so that the incident wavefront is altered to follow the room programming.

2. The basic Danger Room in/out system is maintained in the original **SHI'AR FAST PROCESSING COMPUTERS**–parts of which cover the entire inner surface of the Danger Room. Heating and cooling is all electronic.

3. **MOBILE LASER CLUSTER HEADS** are moved over the Danger room's surface to facilitate the placement of gravity lenses and associated effects.

4. Solid surfaces with thoroughly realistic appearances are achieved with accurate surface texture modeling laid on polygonal surfaces of **OVERLAPPING GRAVITY FIELDS.**

5. 'PROJECTILES' are composed of rapidly moving and tightly focused pressor beams (force fields). Can be made non-lethal by reducing momentum signature–thus awareness of being hit is maintained without loss of life.

6. **EXTENSIVE FILES AND MODELLING PROGRAMS** allow for a great variety of realistic environmental as well as atmospheric and dust effects.

7. **PROGRESSIVE WAVED TRACTOR/PRESSOR BEAMS** allow for realistic exhaust/wind effects.

8. Projected **PINPOINT GRAVITY LENSES** allow simple laser beams to be redirected as other light sources.

9. **PRESSER BEAM ACOUSTIC ENGINES AND LENSING** allows for accurate noise level and frequencies.

10. **TARGETING AND COMMUNICATIONS ANTENNAE** accurately modeled using gravity lensing–allows for direction-finding and ranging.

11. The Danger Room can synthesize random danger elements from its **INTERNAL LIBRARY** of weapons files, alien combat files, or random danger generator.

12. **DANGER ROOM WORLD VIEW MODEL LIBRARY** has digital models of over 50 million objects and their attributes, included are: garbage cans (plus sub-elements) and buildings.

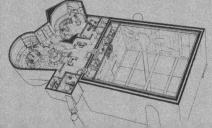

DANGER ROOM

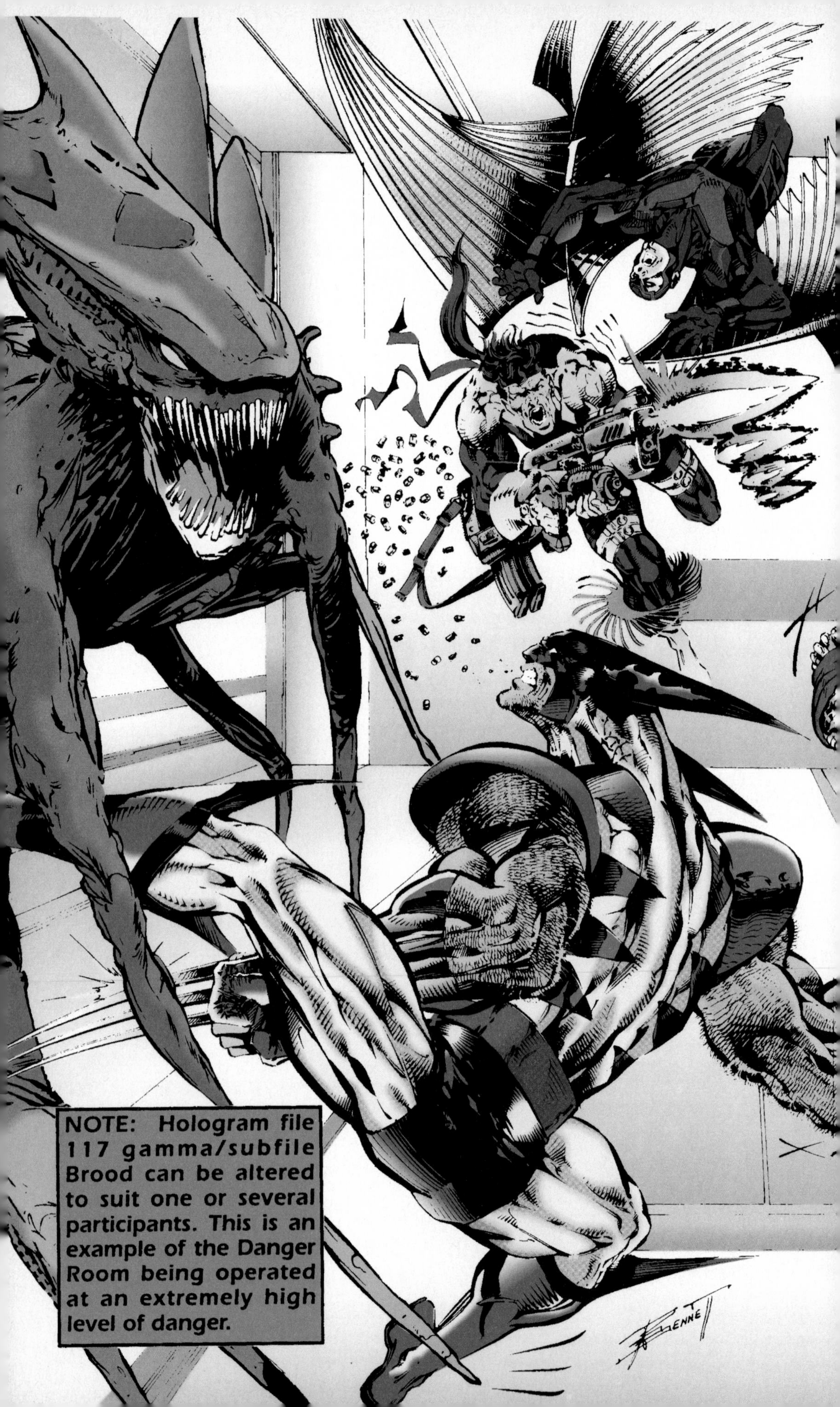
NOTE: Hologram file 117 gamma/subfile Brood can be altered to suit one or several participants. This is an example of the Danger Room being operated at an extremely high level of danger.

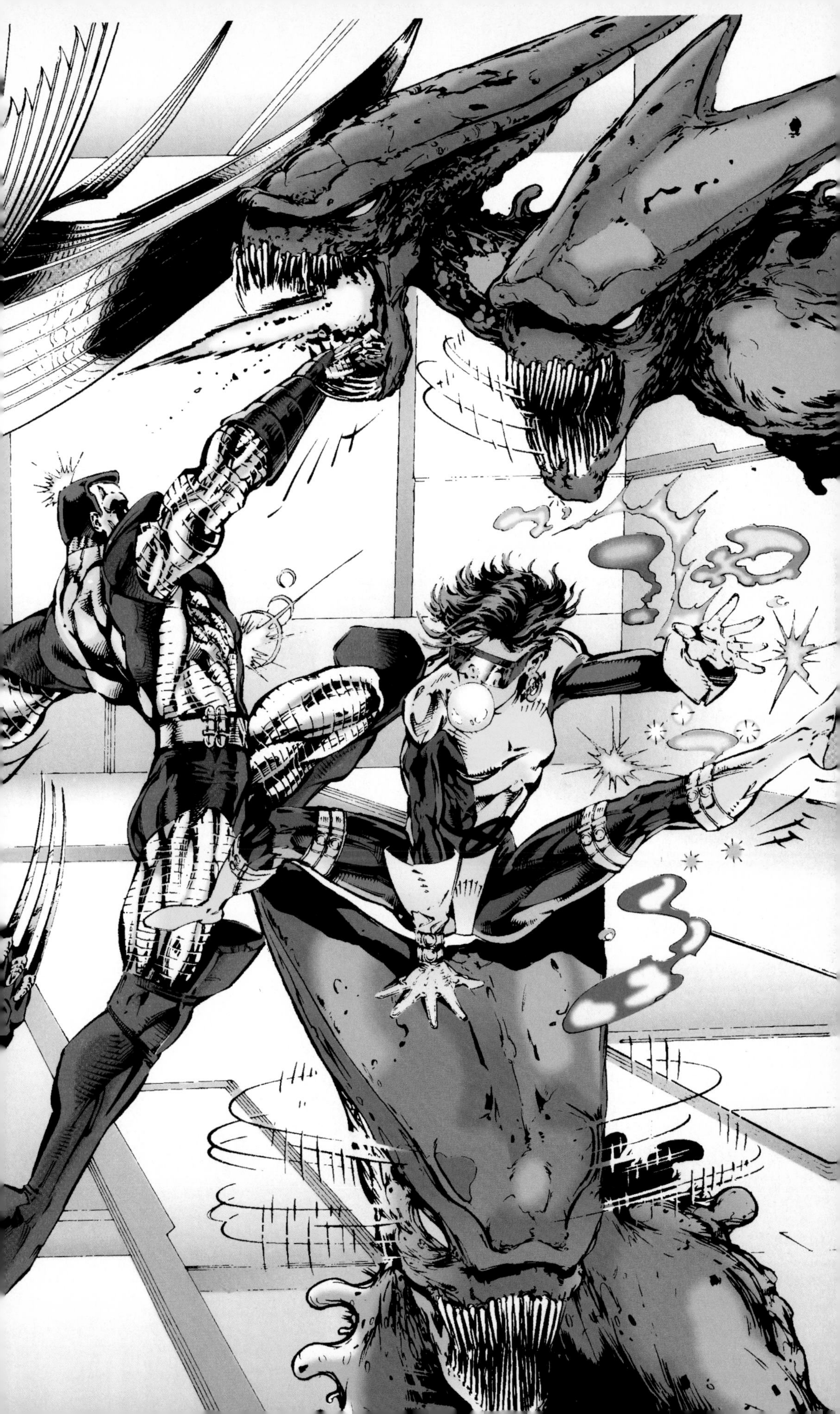

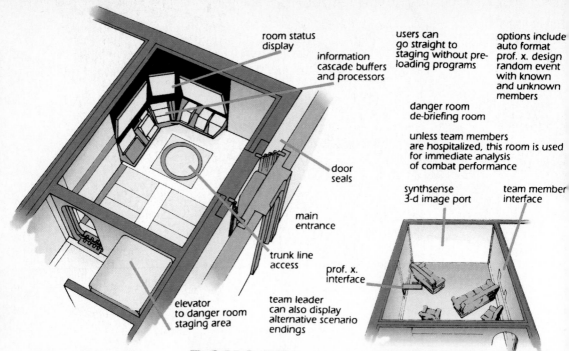

room status display

information cascade buffers and processors

users can go straight to staging without pre-loading programs

options include auto format prof. x. design random event with known and unknown members

danger room de-briefing room

unless team members are hospitalized, this room is used for immediate analysis of combat performance

door seals

main entrance

synthsense 3-d image port

team member interface

trunk line access

prof. x. interface

elevator to danger room staging area

team leader can also display alternative scenario endings

DANGERroomCONTROLannex

To the untrained eye it is a featureless room. To anyone who enters it, however, and engages its systems–it is clear that the Danger Room is the ultimate battle simulator.

Behind unassuming gray paneled walls exist a multitude of exercise and combat paraphernalia designed to put even the most well-trained mutant through their paces. (Laser cannons, omnium spring vices, pyrotechnic extension lances and sensory deprivation cocoons are only a handful of Shi'ar based hardware secreted within.) Recently combined with Shi'ar holographic technology, the Danger Room can assume a three dimensional interactive environment conducive to the constant refinement of teamwork vital to the X-Men's daily operations.

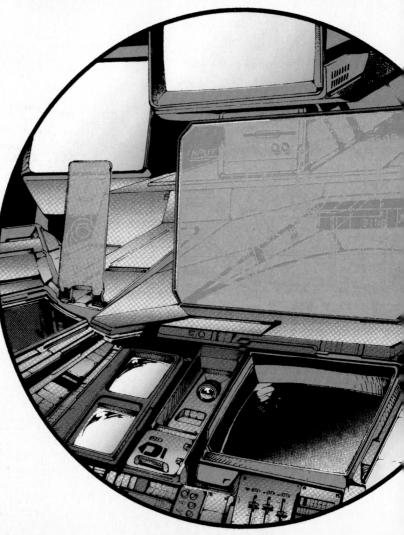

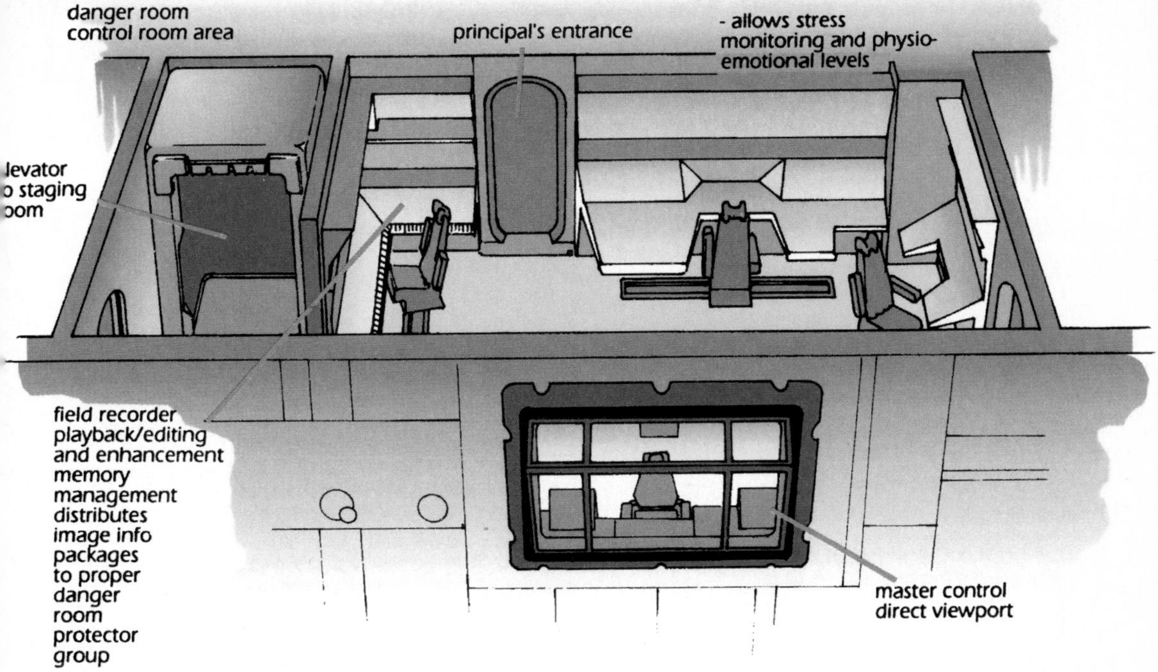
danger room
control room area
principal's entrance
- allows stress
monitoring and physio-
emotional levels
levator
o staging
oom
field recorder
playback/editing
and enhancement
memory
management
distributes
image info
packages
to proper
danger
room
protector
group
master control
direct viewport

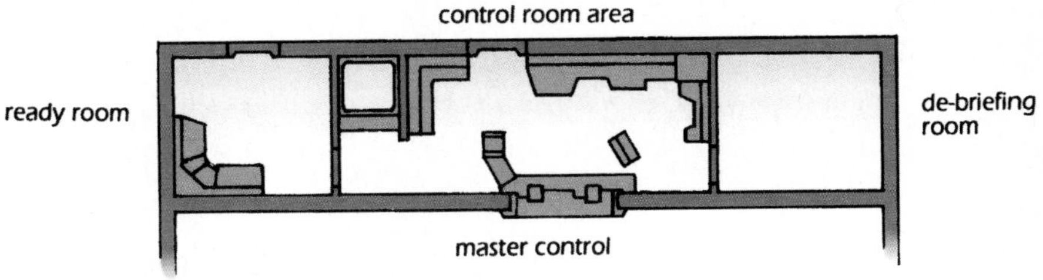
control room area
ready room
de-briefing
room
master control

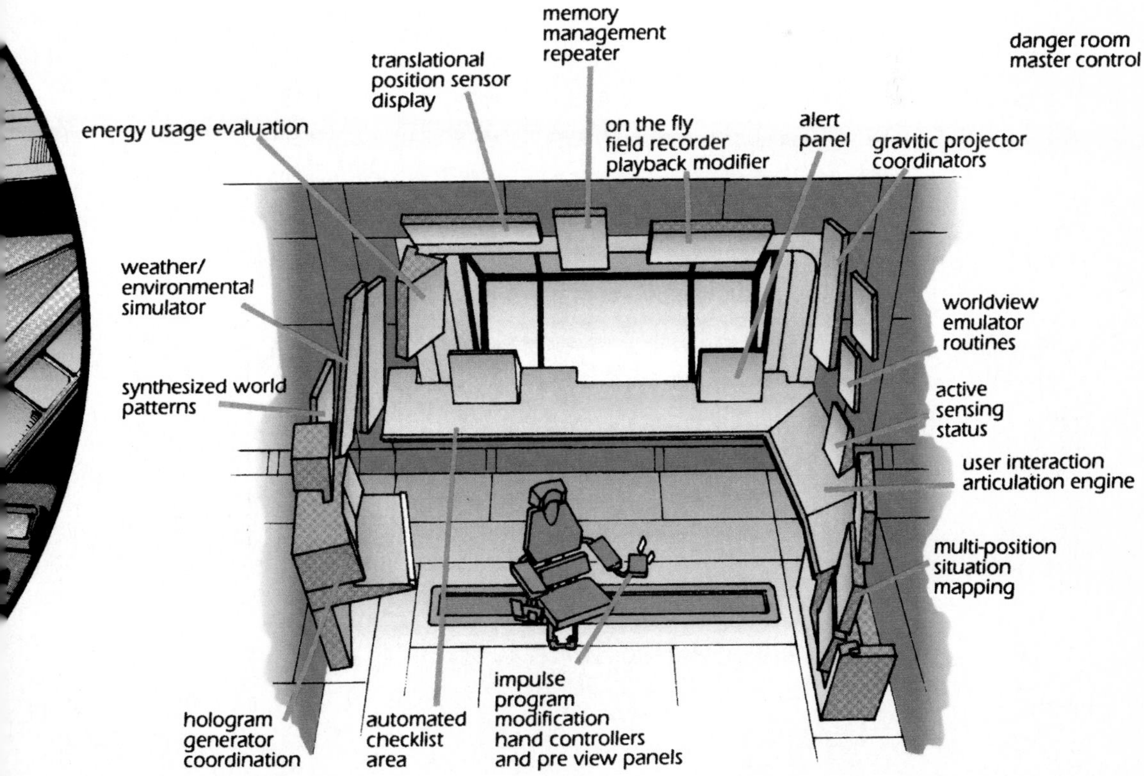
memory
management
repeater
translational
position sensor
display
danger room
master control
energy usage evaluation
on the fly
field recorder
playback modifier
alert
panel
gravitic projector
coordinators
weather/
environmental
simulator
worldview
emulator
routines
synthesized world
patterns
active
sensing
status
user interaction
articulation engine
multi-position
situation
mapping
impulse
program
modification
hand controllers
and pre view panels
hologram
generator
coordination
automated
checklist
area

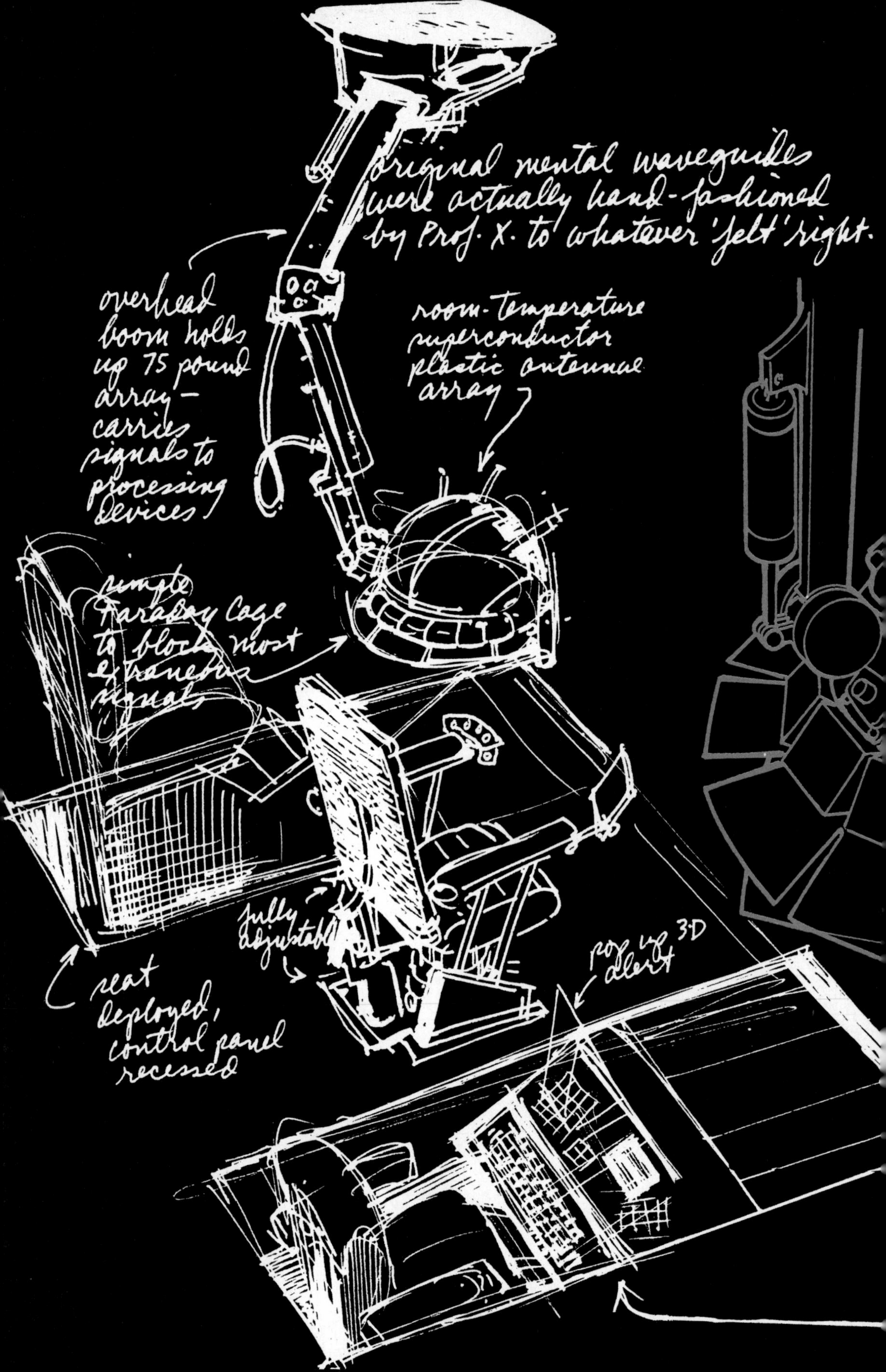
original mental waveguides were actually hand-fashioned by Prof. X. to whatever 'felt' right.
overhead boom holds up 75 pound array—carries signals to processing devices
room-temperature superconductor plastic antennae array
simple Faraday cage to block most extraneous signals
fully adjustable
pop up 3-D alert
seat deployed, control panel recessed

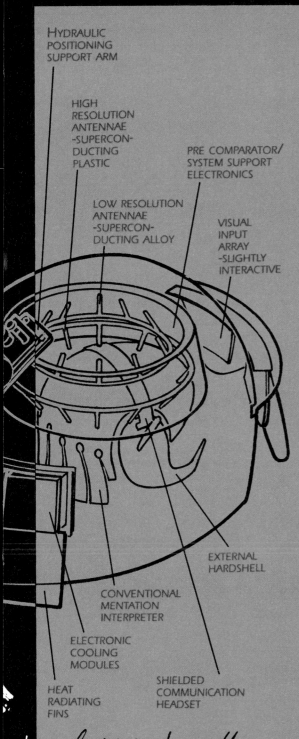

HYDRAULIC
POSITIONING
SUPPORT ARM

HIGH
RESOLUTION
ANTENNAE
-SUPERCON-
DUCTING
PLASTIC

PRE COMPARATOR/
SYSTEM SUPPORT
ELECTRONICS

LOW RESOLUTION
ANTENNAE
-SUPERCON-
DUCTING ALLOY

VISUAL
INPUT
ARRAY
-SLIGHTLY
INTERACTIVE

EXTERNAL
HARDSHELL

CONVENTIONAL
MENTATION
INTERPRETER

ELECTRONIC
COOLING
MODULES

HEAT
RADIATING
FINS

SHIELDED
COMMUNICATION
HEADSET

heavily re-configurable control panel - allows for max. user compatibility - entire display can be devoted to one image plus limited menu coupled with point-and-shoot interaction.

Since the earliest days of its creation, Cerebro was thought to be the ultimate means with which to catalogue and track genetic anomalies anywhere in the world. Constantly sweeping the globe by piggy backing pre-existing satellite projections, this ultimate mutant detector is sensitive to aberrations in electromagnetic brain wave activity most often attributed to biological mutations. Whether due to the prolific increase in the range of mutations over recent years, environmental deteriorations such as the erosion of the ozone layer, or the improbable event of orchestral machinations by any number of saboteurs, we have become painfully aware of the limitations of Cerebro.

For your protection—as well as the classified subjects currently identified by Cerebro—unauthorized use is strictly forbidden. (In the unlikely event that the computer's integrity has been compromised, any attempt at first contact with a suspected mutant could conceivably serve as a beacon to an outside agency eager to establish a less than fortuitous relationship.)

While the computer's interactive headpiece is more easily wielded by psi-sensitive mutants, Cerebro is also user friendly to non-mutants with proper training.

NOTE: Extended use of Cerebro may result in a low-grade REM sleep irritation. If that should happen, please consult a campus physician before further use.

CEREBRO

Professor X's Ready Room

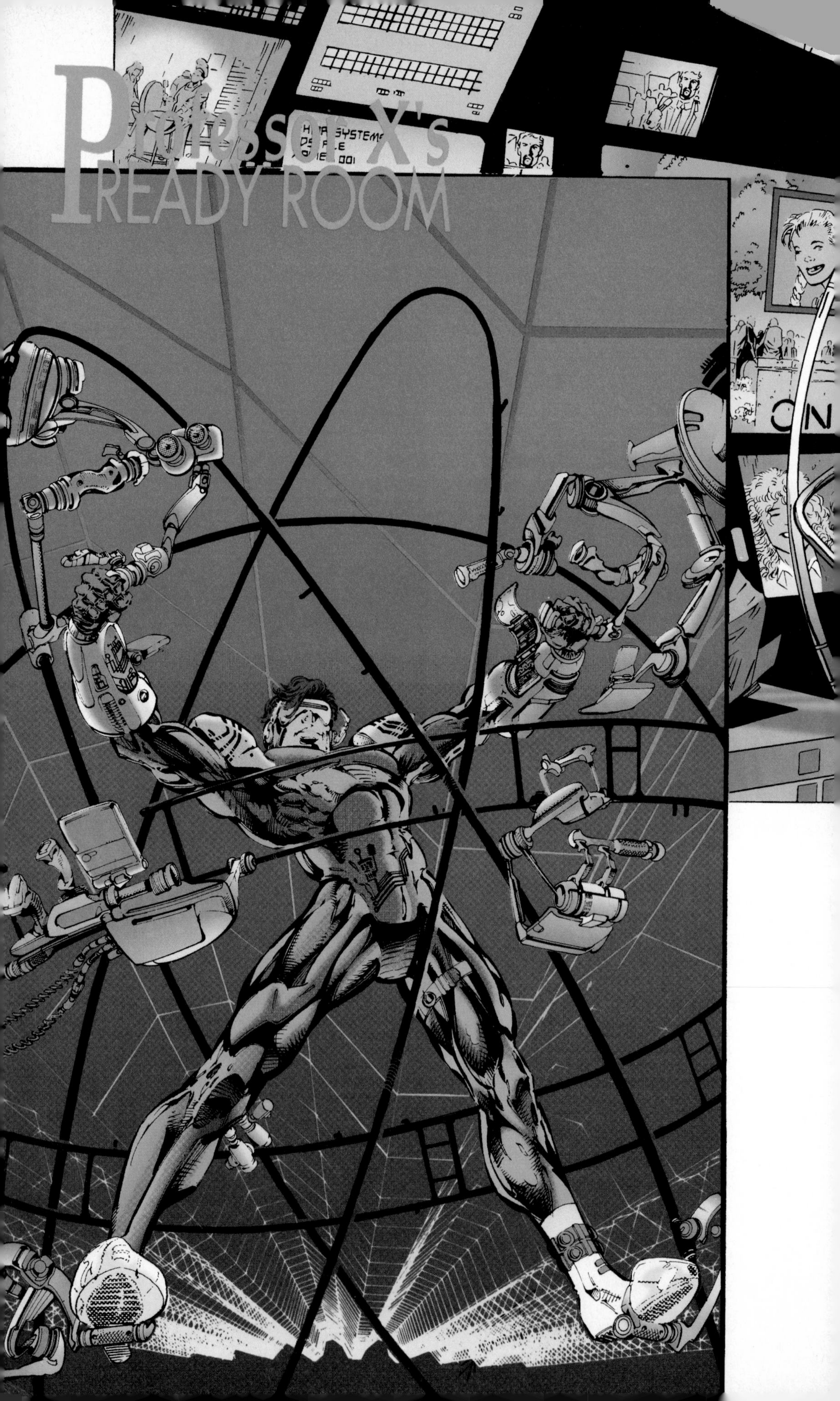

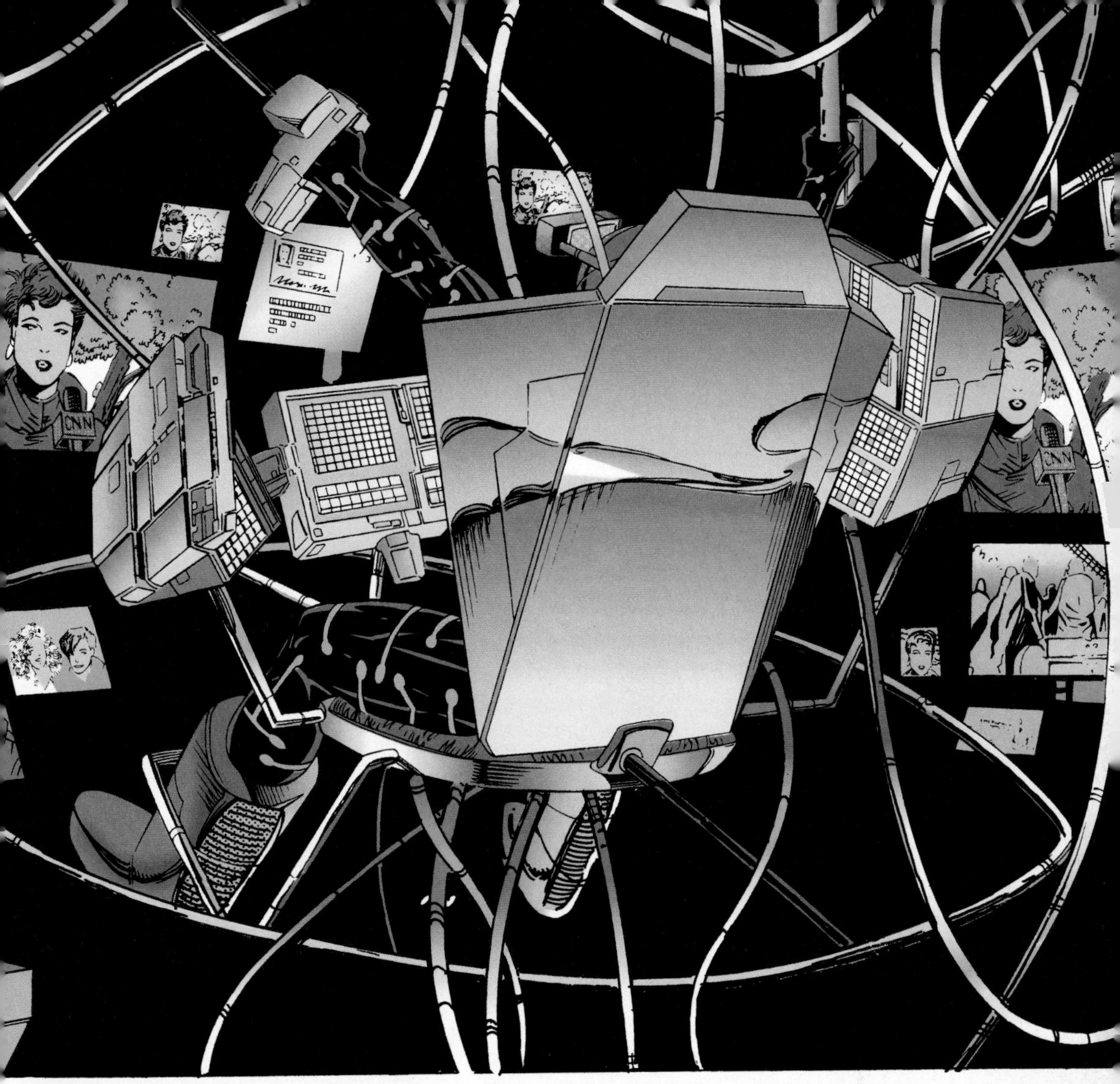
CNN
CNN

THE NERVE CENTER

The mansion's most highly secured location provides instant access to everything from the Danger Room failsafe programs, to the War Room information override, to Mansion Security parameters. It's most important feature, however, is the interactive-CEREBRO augmentation chamber.

Highly sensitive files and documents from allies, both human and mutants, are stored here. There are several failsafe devices to ensure that these files will not be accessed. All computer coded messages coming in from underground operatives are filtered through here. So as not to betray the confidences of people who risk much for me and mine, no other computer in the mansion can accept or decode these messages. So sensitive is this area it is the only chamber equipped with self-destruct sequences. Any unauthorized entry will result in expulsion.

Until recently, I was the only resident of the mansion aware of the existence of the Ready Room. . .preferring to use the facility as a private study, a sanctum sanctorum from which to occasionally escape the mantle of leadership. With the ever escalating confrontations between increasingly volatile mutant factions, I have come to appreciate the need for an open door policy between myself and senior members of the X-Men.

This room has been designed for a psi-sensitive. Non psi-sensitive individuals can utilize some of this equipment with special psionic enhancers. This room is restricted and will only allow entrance to field commanders who have been trained to utilize this room at its highest functioning level.

If it is true, and I believe it is, that "knowledge is power" — the Ready Room is, unequivicably the most powerful room in the mansion.

MED LAB

ORIGINALLY CONSTRUCTED TO HOUSE A SCRUB ROOM, AN OPERATING THEATRE, A BURN UNIT, AN INTENSIVE CARE WARD, AND A HOMO-SUPERIOR SENSITIVE PHYSICAL AND OCCUPATIONAL THERAPY DEPARTMENT, THE X-MEN'S ONGOING RELATIONSHIP WITH THE SHI'AR EMPIRE HAS PROPELLED THE MED-LAB'S CAPABILITIES FARTHER THAN I HAD EVER IMAGINED. RECENT ADDITIONS OF THE ALIEN TECHNOLOGY INCLUDE HOLOGRAPHIC DIAGNOSTICS, SUB-EPIDERMAL CLONING, AND TECHNO-ORGANIC TISSUE BONDING.

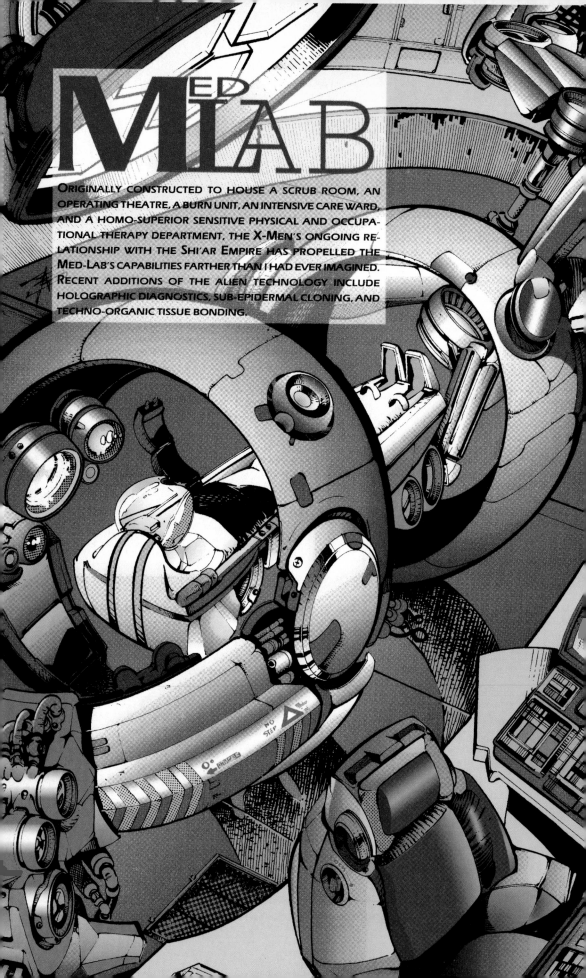

Ideally, this is the room in which the residents of the mansion should spend the least amount of time (outside the context of a teaching environment). Should circumstances arise that necessitate a visit to the Med-Lab as a patient, you'll discover it is a full service facility capable of accommodating every aspect of the medical arts and science known to man — and several that are not.

Though any number of specialists are on call twenty-four hours a day, we have discovered over the years that there is very little that cannot be handled "in house." NOTE: All extraneous off-campus medical personnel have been cleared on a Tertiary Security Level and should be considered "mutant friendly."

Every undergraduate student will be required to spend seventy-two hours a semester interning in the Med-Lab. This will count as 23% of your final grade. Extra-credit assignments in the past have included such research essays "Designer Genetics" by Henry McCoy, "Why?" by Katherine Pryde, and "Binary Diagnostic Encoding" by Douglas Ramsey.

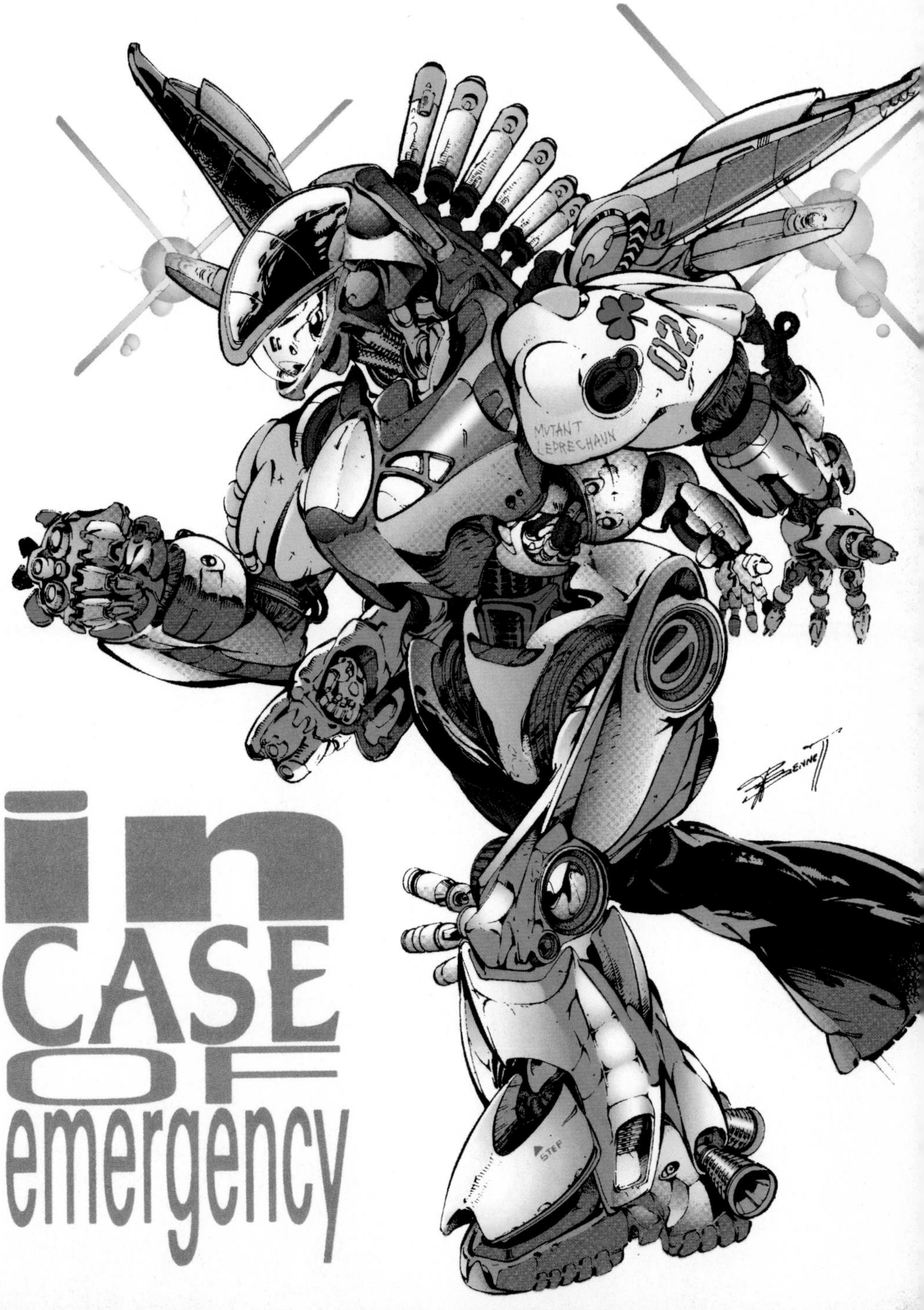
02
MUTANT LEPRECHAUN
STEP

in CASE OF emergency

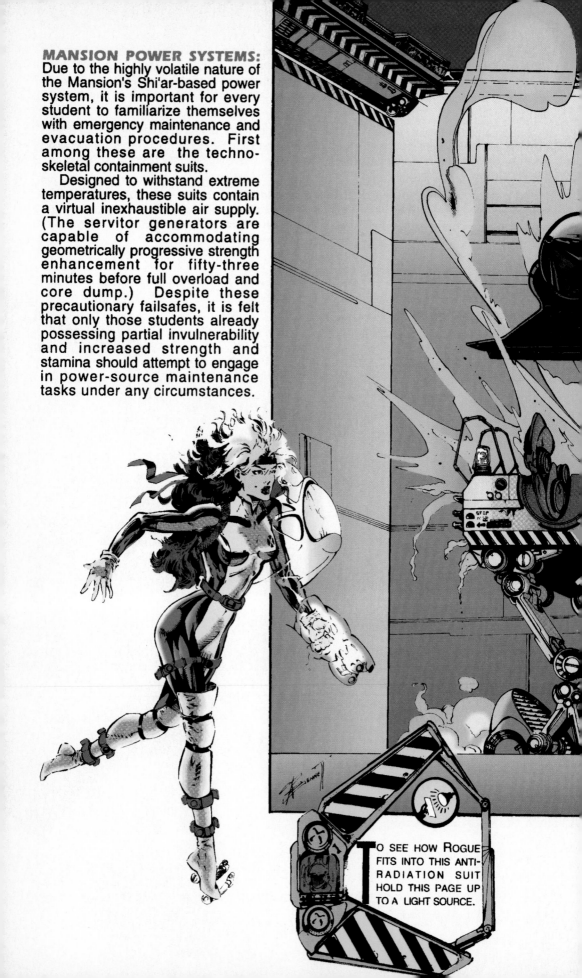

MANSION POWER SYSTEMS: Due to the highly volatile nature of the Mansion's Shi'ar-based power system, it is important for every student to familiarize themselves with emergency maintenance and evacuation procedures. First among these are the techno-skeletal containment suits.

Designed to withstand extreme temperatures, these suits contain a virtual inexhaustible air supply. (The servitor generators are capable of accommodating geometrically progressive strength enhancement for fifty-three minutes before full overload and core dump.) Despite these precautionary failsafes, it is felt that only those students already possessing partial invulnerability and increased strength and stamina should attempt to engage in power-source maintenance tasks under any circumstances.

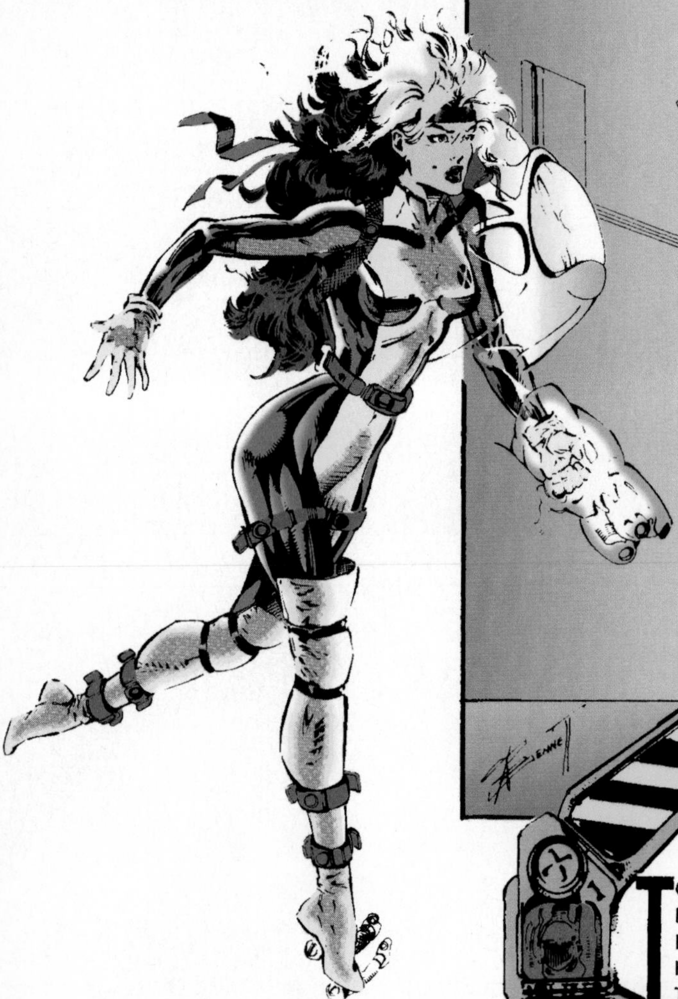

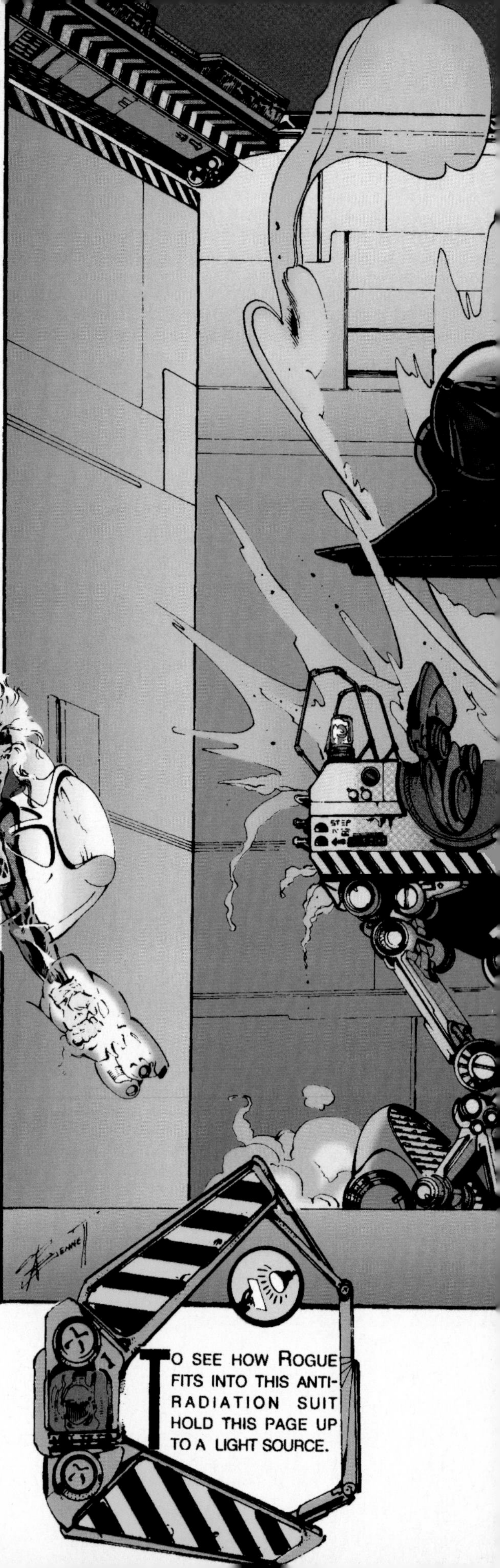
TO SEE HOW ROGUE FITS INTO THIS ANTI-RADIATION SUIT HOLD THIS PAGE UP TO A LIGHT SOURCE.

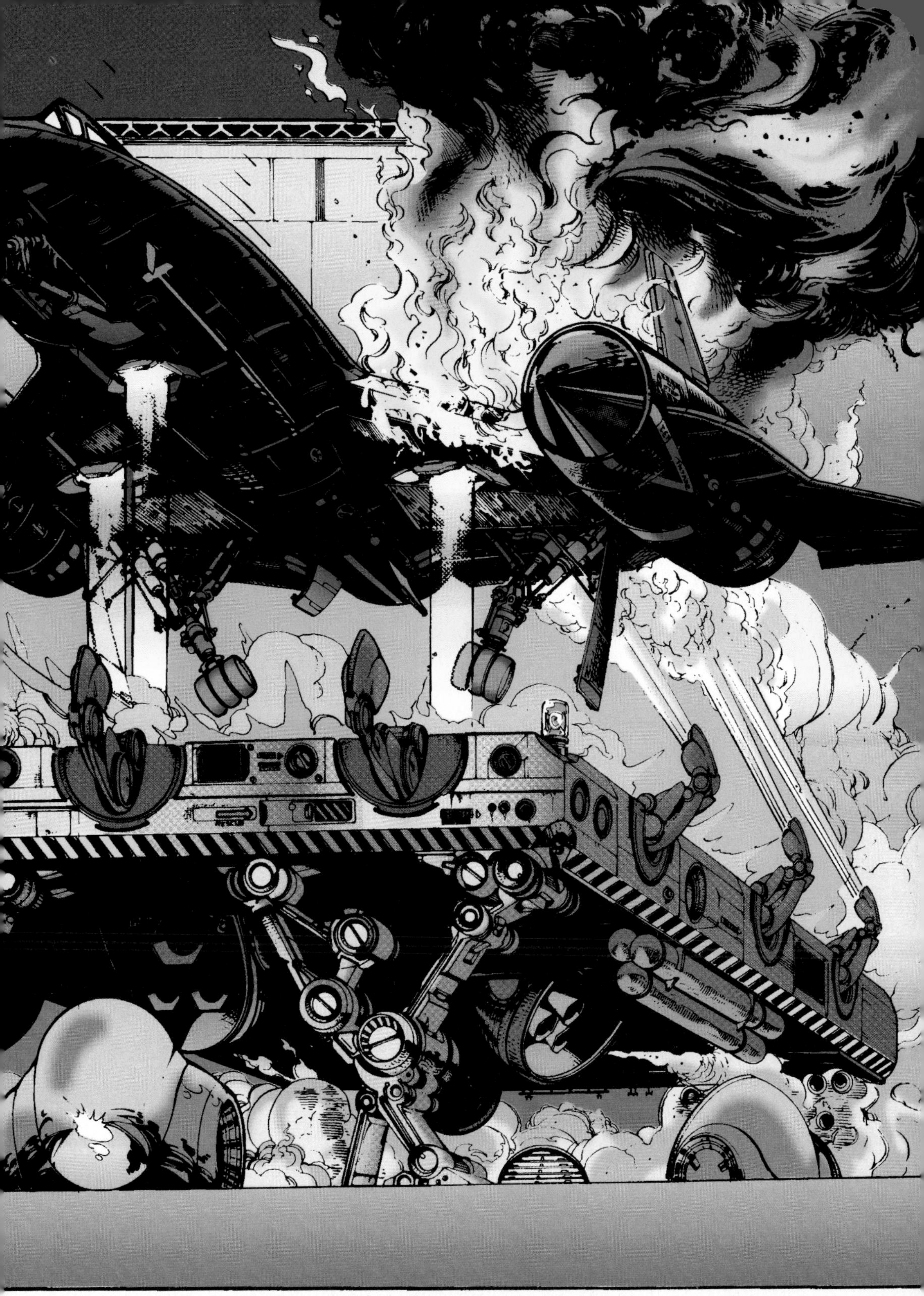

FIRE HAZARDS: The mansion is equipped with multiple redundant safety systems. Almost all possible fire hazards have been envisioned and computers are self sufficient. Pictured here is an example of the mansion's ability to be 94% energy recycling. All expelled sources of energy are recycled into the mansion's Shi'ar designed processing system for future use.

MUIR ISLAND

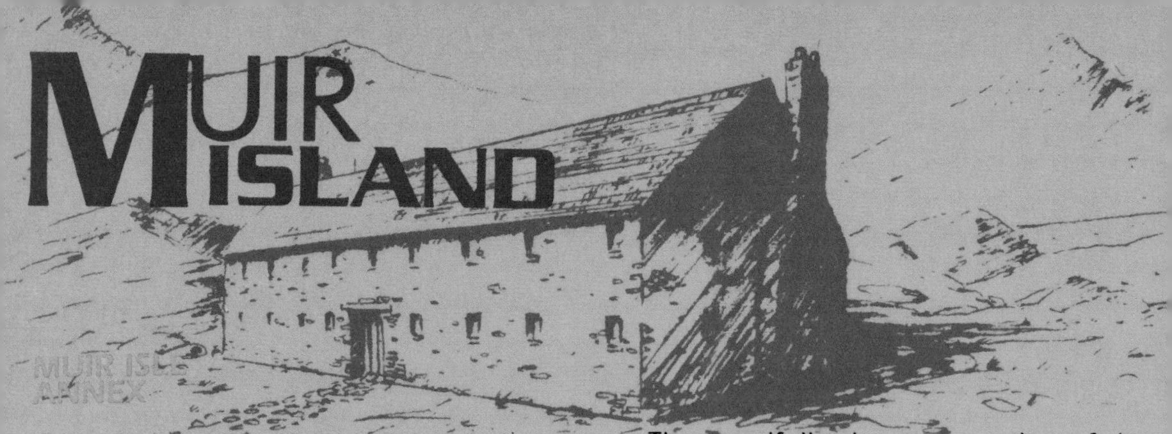
MUIR ISLE
ANNEX

Since its inception, Muir Isle, located off the northwestern crest of Scotland has been the linchpin of the X-Men's support operations. Under the auspices of Dr. Moira MacTaggert and the European Cooperative of Biological Arts and Sciences, the genetic research facility is recognized around the world as the primary information warehouse for mutant related studies. Unfortunately, the ever prevalent state of human/mutant relations precludes any public affiliation between ourselves and this organization short of the high profile correspondence accepted between Muir Isle and the Xavier Institute.

The mercifully slow progression of the mutagenic deceleration disorder known as the Legacy Virus has become paramount to Dr. MacTaggert and her staff. Working closely with our own Dr. Henry McCoy, and Forge out of Washington, D.C., everyone agrees the first priority is discovering how the disease is spread among the mutant populace. Muir Isle is also heavily involved in the treatment of the disease in the sincere hope they can contain the genocidal aspects of the Legacy Virus before it mutates to a point capable of infecting homo sapiens.

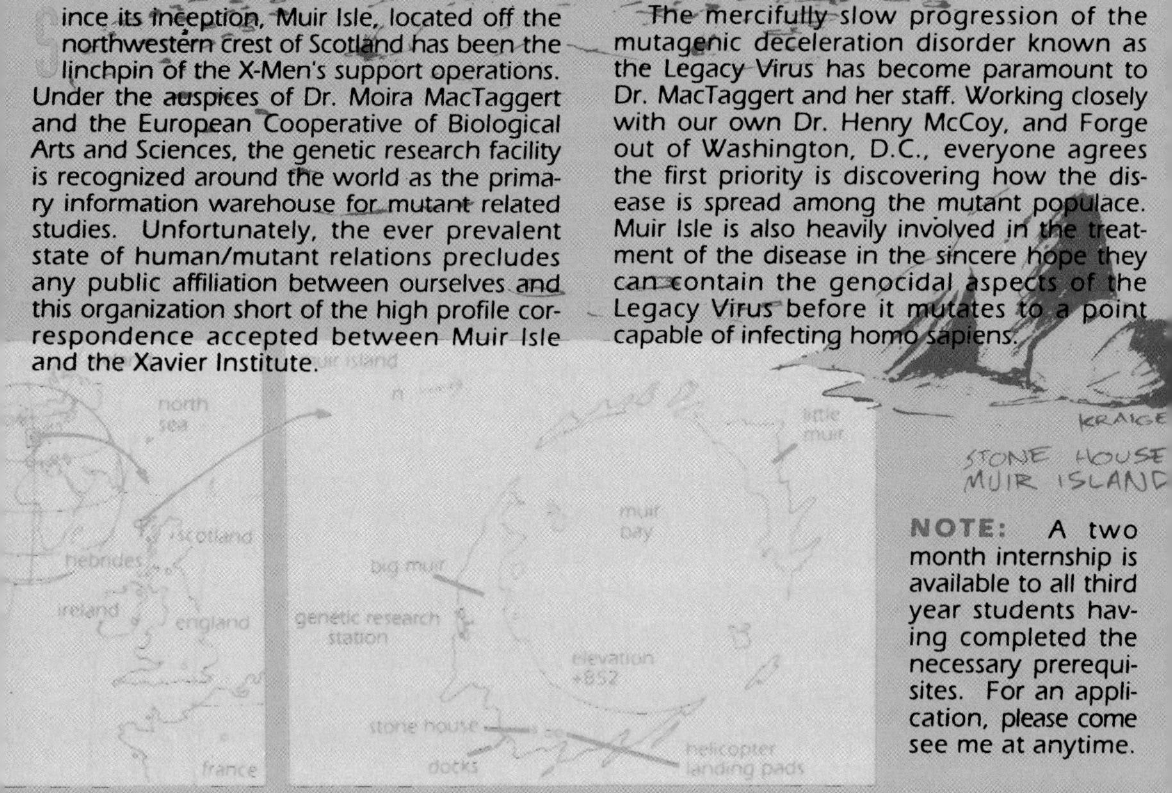
muir island
north sea
scotland
hebrides
ireland
england
france
n
little muir
muir bay
big muir
genetic research station
elevation +852
stone house
docks
helicopter landing pads

KRAIGE

STONE HOUSE MUIR ISLAND

NOTE: A two month internship is available to all third year students having completed the necessary prerequisites. For an application, please come see me at anytime.

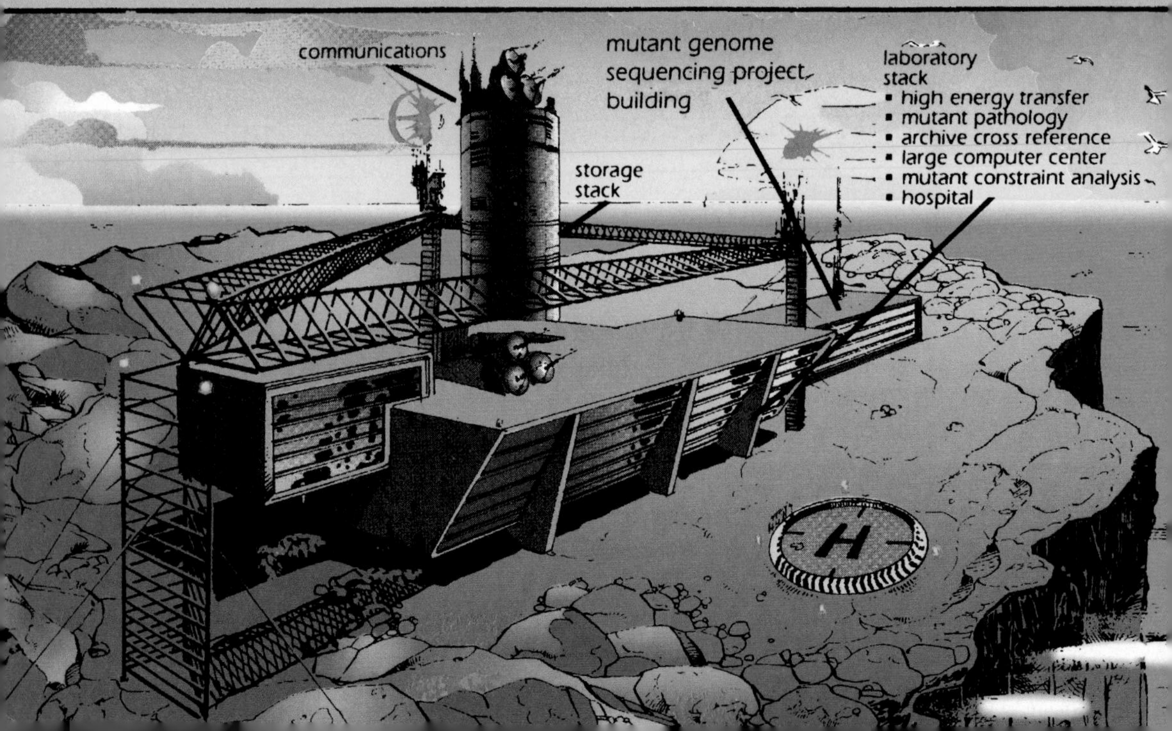
communications
mutant genome sequencing project building
storage stack
laboratory stack
• high energy transfer
• mutant pathology
• archive cross reference
• large computer center
• mutant constraint analysis
• hospital

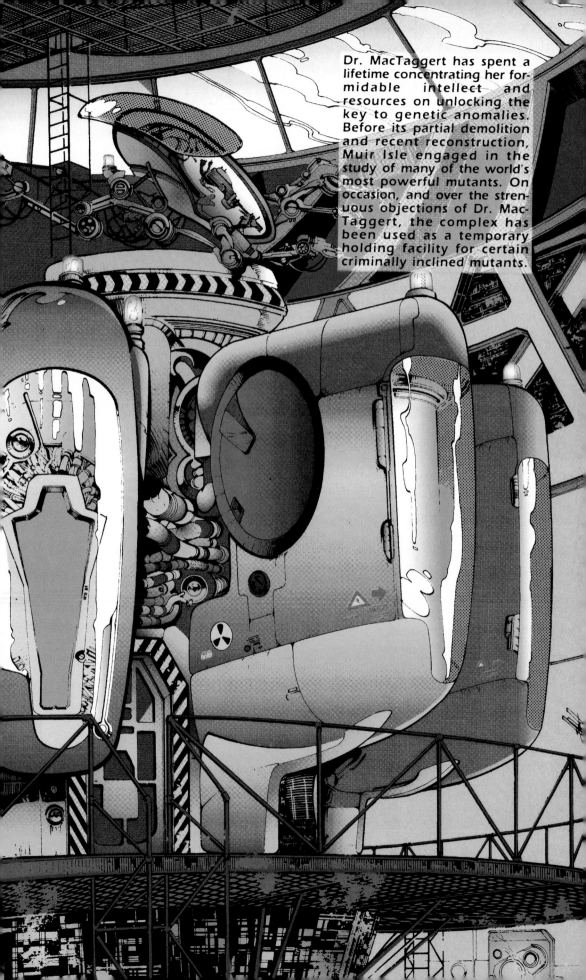

Dr. MacTaggert has spent a lifetime concentrating her formidable intellect and resources on unlocking the key to genetic anomalies. Before its partial demolition and recent reconstruction, Muir Isle engaged in the study of many of the world's most powerful mutants. On occasion, and over the strenuous objections of Dr. MacTaggert, the complex has been used as a temporary holding facility for certain criminally inclined mutants.

MASSACHUSETTS ACADEMY

Under our current expansion plans, the Xavier School for Gifted Youngsters is scheduled to relocate to the former Massachusetts Academy shortly. Once a private school in Snow Valley, nestled away in the Berkshire Mountains, this new complex will now act as the new cornerstone in the next stage of the dream, Generation X. Current plans call for Sean Cassidy, long time adjunct member of the X-Men, to take over as headmaster for our Massachusetts campus.

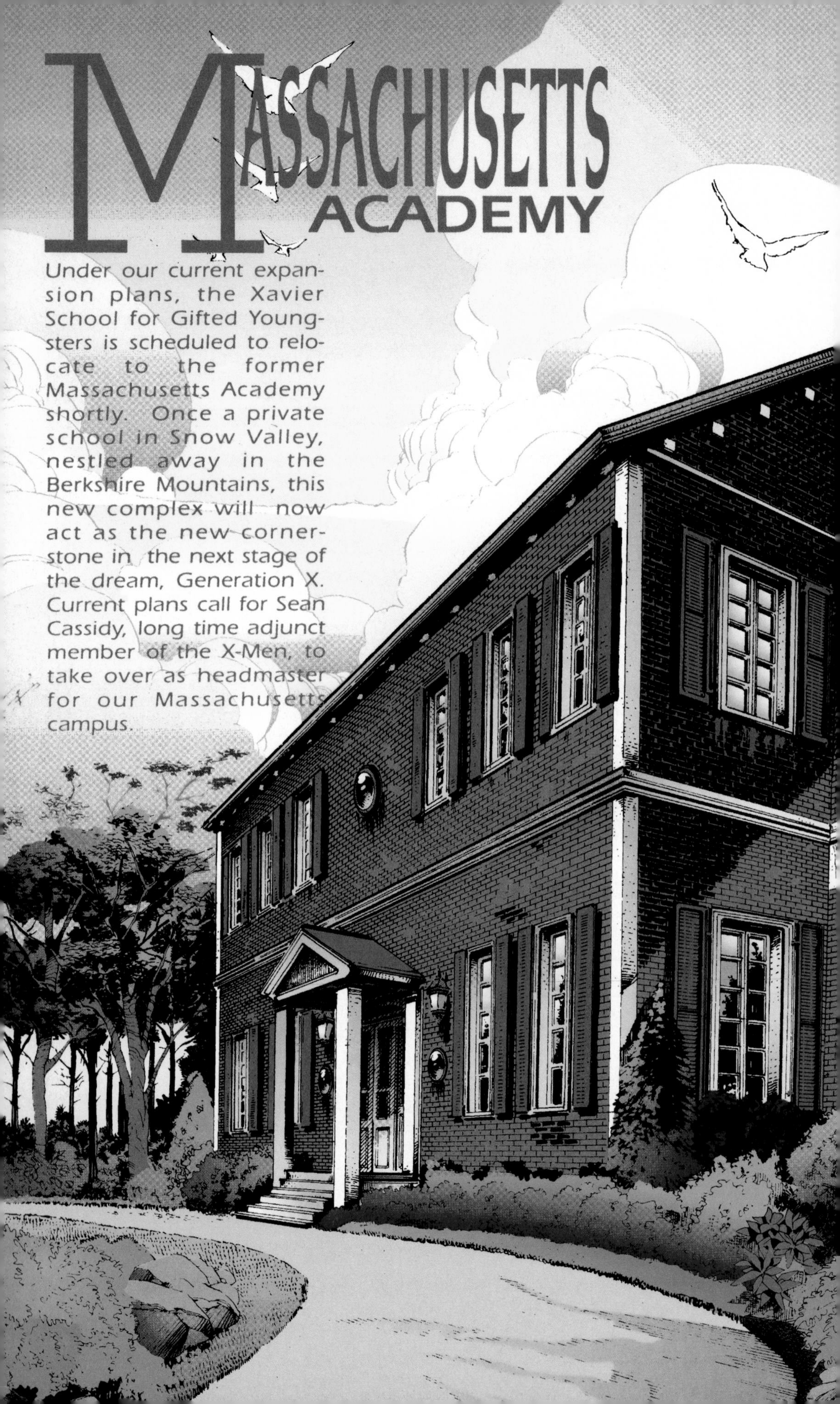

It's your first day at the Xavier Institute for Higher Learning, the Westchester mansion which serves as the home and training center of the X-Men. You've been introduced to Headmaster Professor Charles Xavier, toured the public areas of the estate, and met some of your fellow students.

Now, prepare yourself to travel behind mansion walls to a place that the outside world never sees. Explore the alien technology of the War Room, feel the heat of the Danger Room, and experience first-hand the inner workings that are Cerebro. In short, welcome to the

X-MEN!

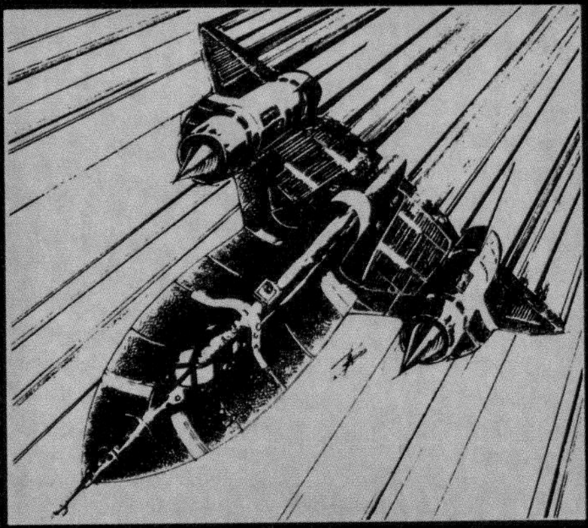

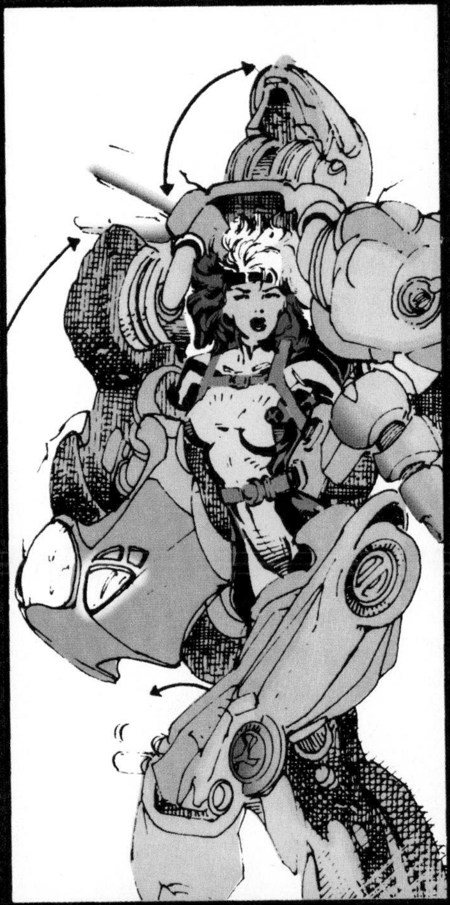

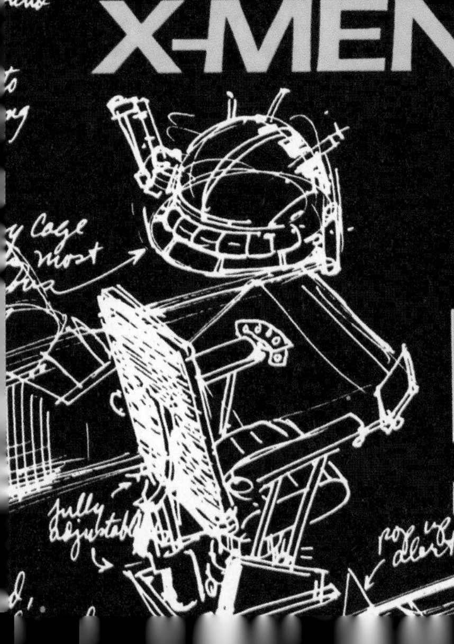

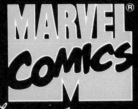

fully adjustable
group movements – stations allow for "mechanical"

MARVEL COMICS

$6.95 U.S./$8.70 CAN.

Several other pinups showcasing X-Men-related equipment and locations were published following the *Survival Guide to the Mansion.*

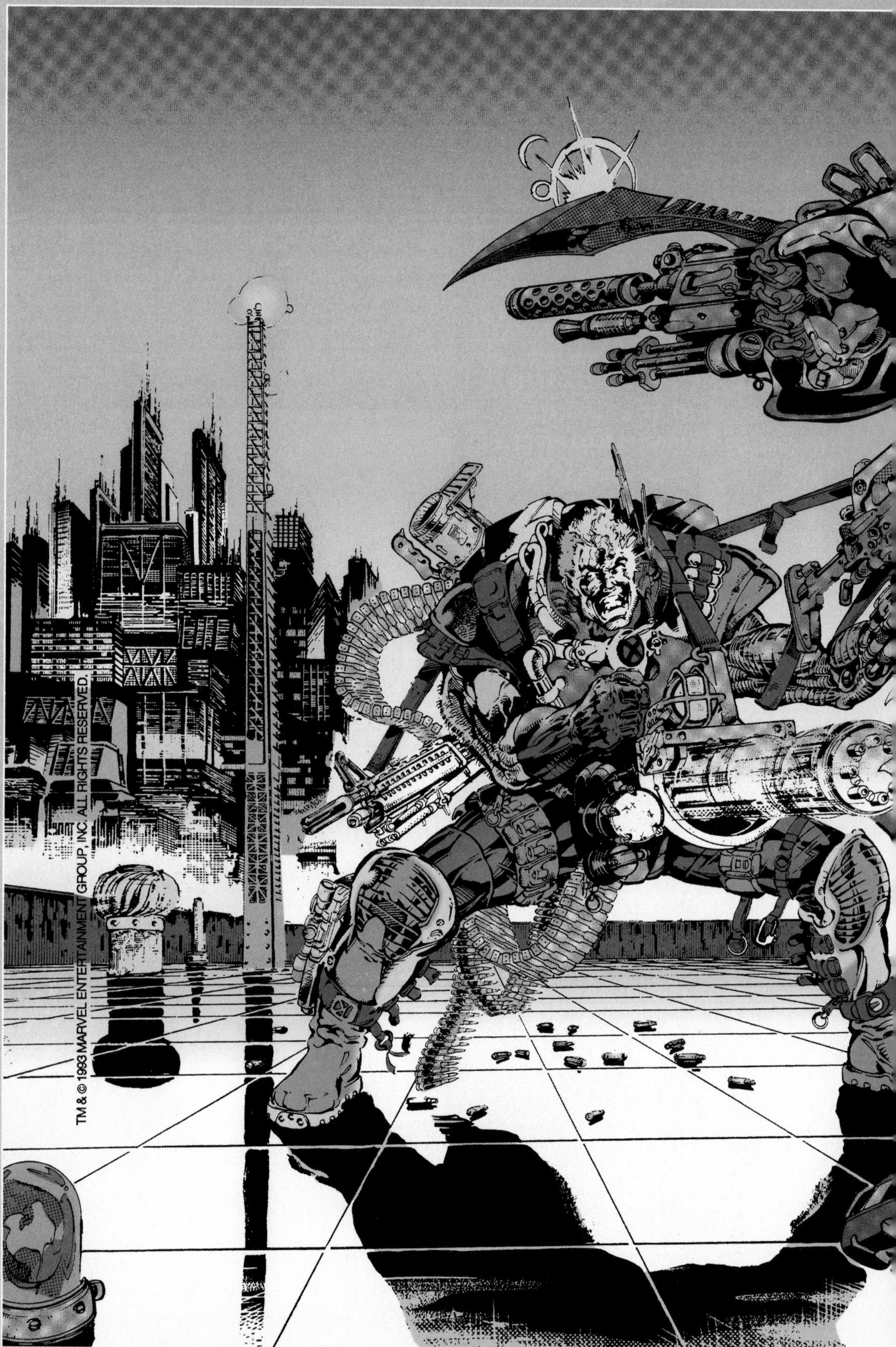

TM & © 1993 MARVEL ENTERTAINMENT GROUP, INC. ALL RIGHTS RESERVED.

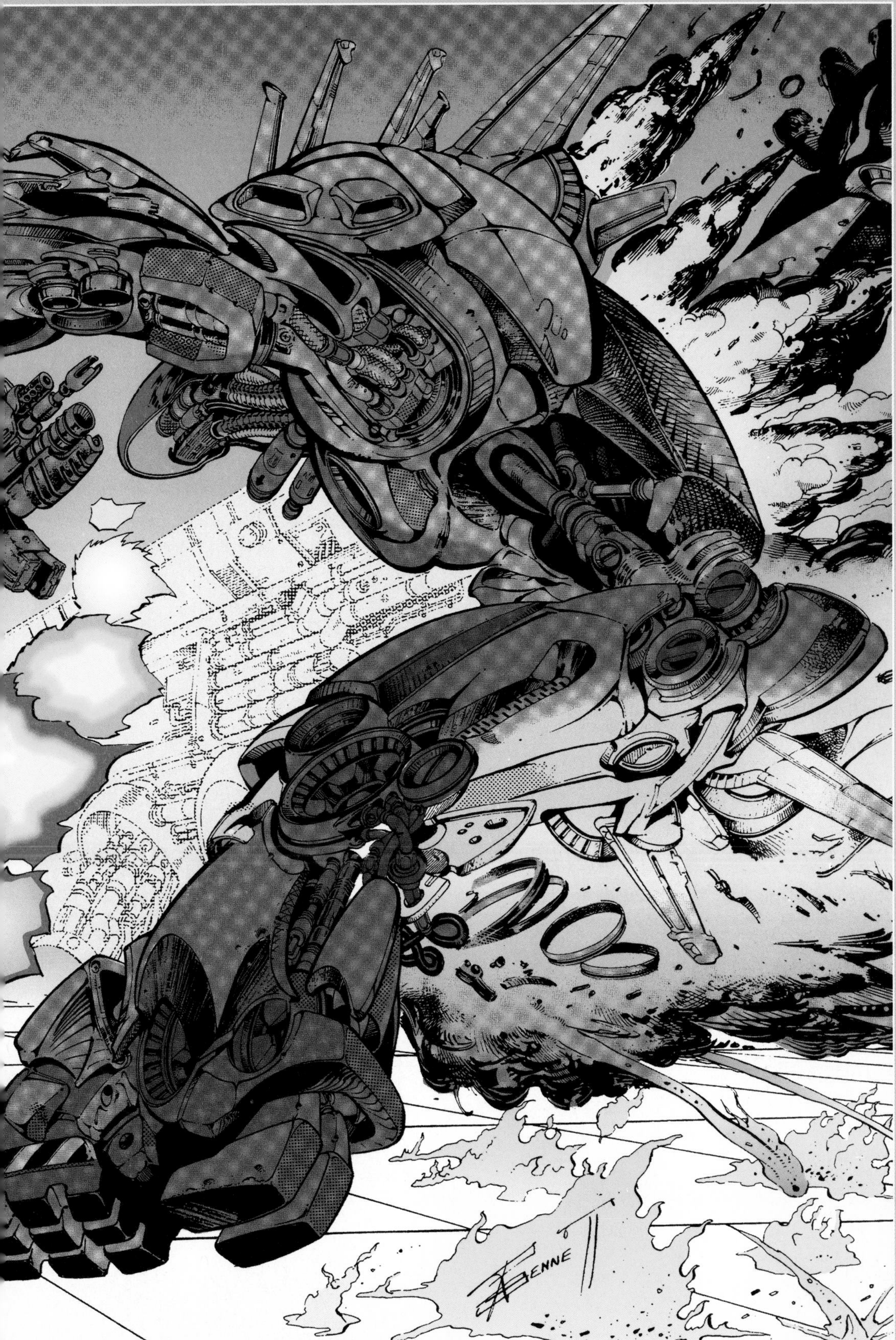
BENNETT

X-Men Poster Magazine #2 pinup by Richard Bennett

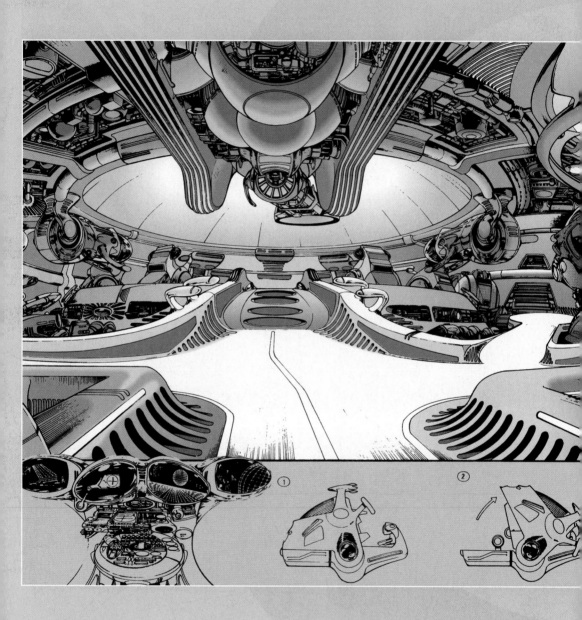

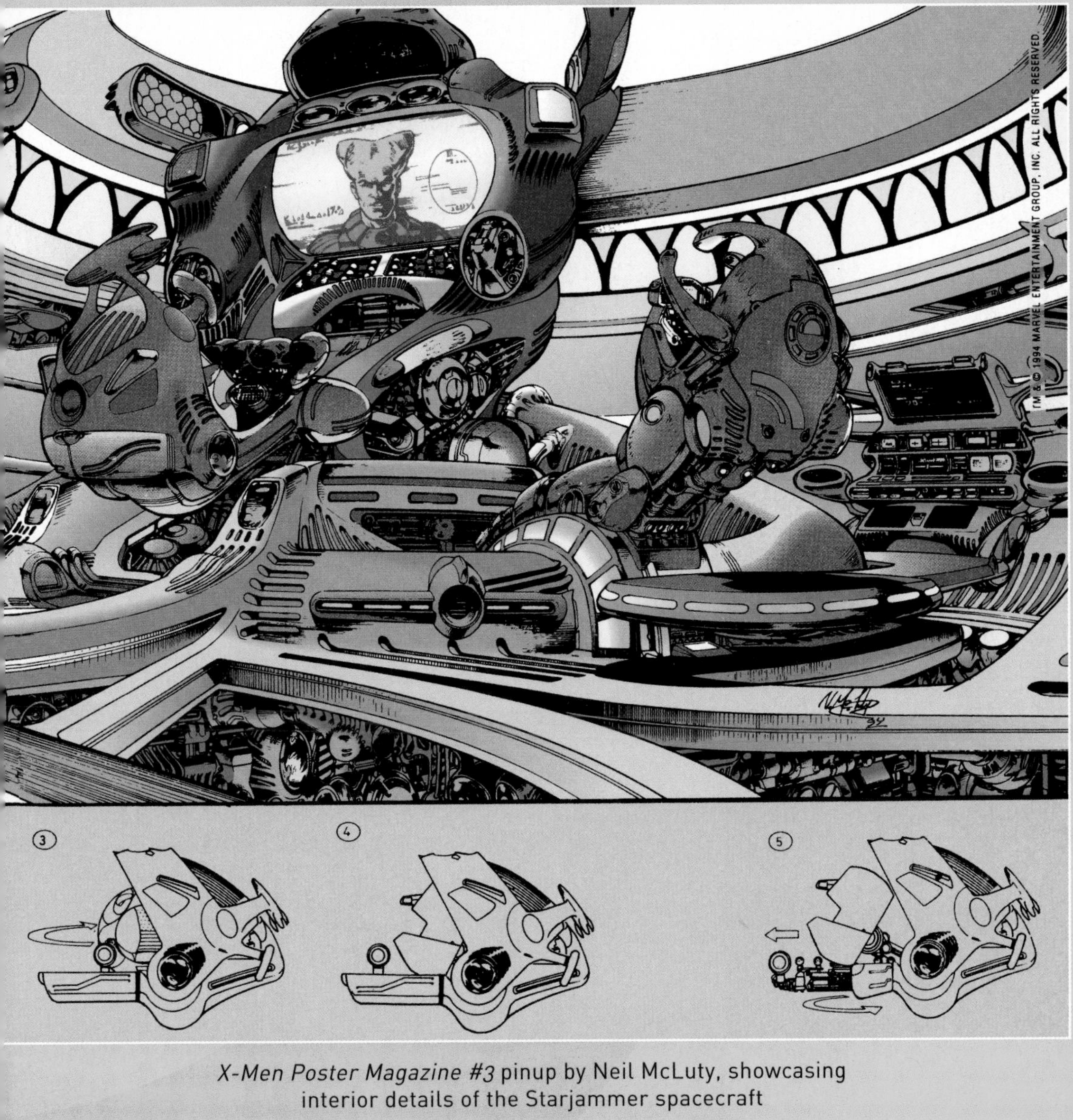
TM & © 1994 MARVEL ENTERTAINMENT GROUP, INC. ALL RIGHTS RESERVED.
3
4
5

X-Men Poster Magazine #3 pinup by Neil McLuty, showcasing interior details of the Starjammer spacecraft

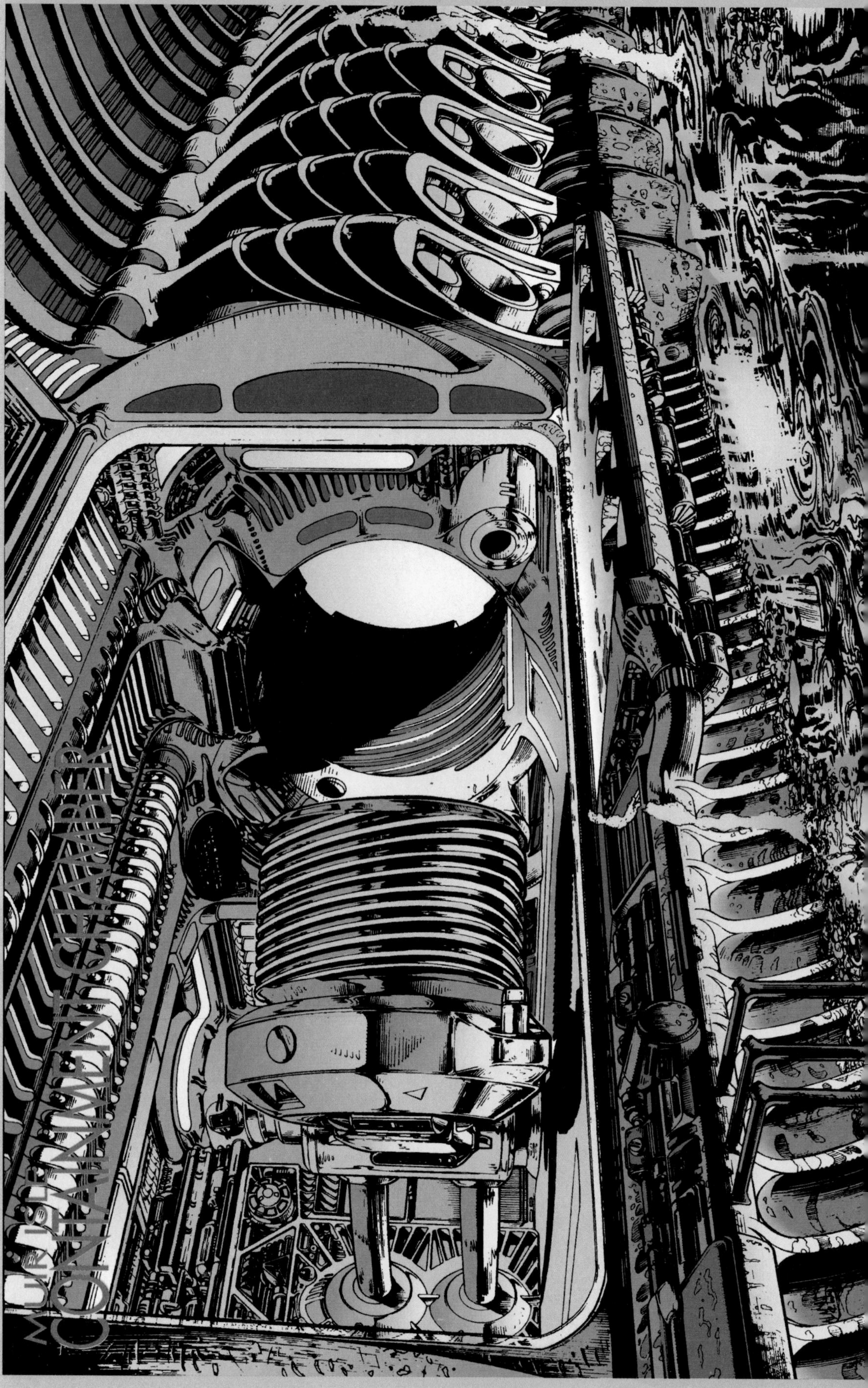
MUIR ISLE
CONTAINMENT CHAMBER

Excalibur Annual #2 pinup by Neil McLuty & Joe Rosas

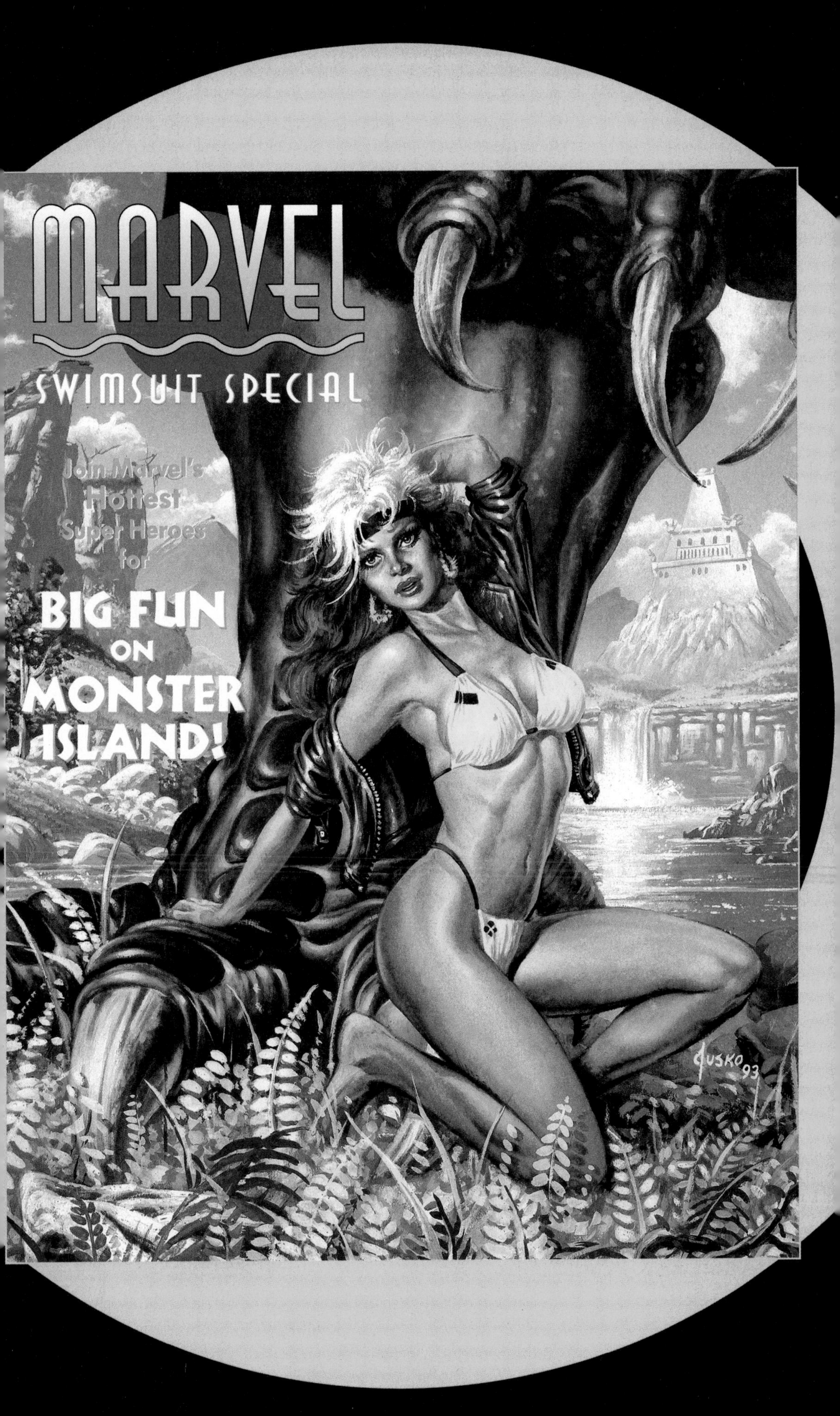
MARVEL
SWIMSUIT SPECIAL
Join Marvel's Hottest Super Heroes for
BIG FUN ON MONSTER ISLAND!
JUSKO 93

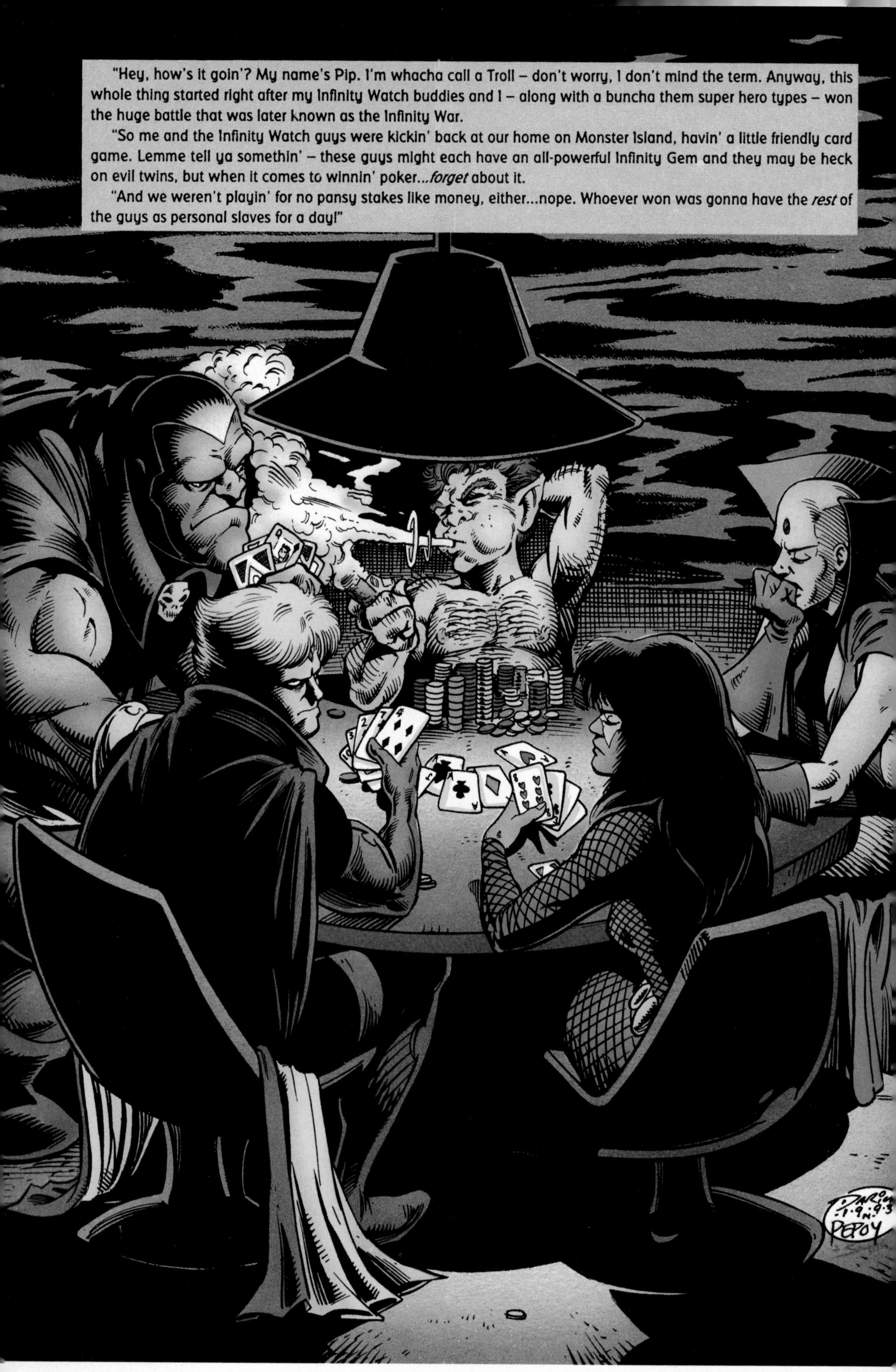
"Hey, how's it goin'? My name's Pip. I'm whacha call a Troll – don't worry, I don't mind the term. Anyway, this whole thing started right after my Infinity Watch buddies and I – along with a buncha them super hero types – won the huge battle that was later known as the Infinity War.
"So me and the Infinity Watch guys were kickin' back at our home on Monster Island, havin' a little friendly card game. Lemme tell ya somethin' – these guys might each have an all-powerful Infinity Gem and they may be heck on evil twins, but when it comes to winnin' poker...*forget* about it.
"And we weren't playin' for no pansy stakes like money, either...nope. Whoever won was gonna have the *rest* of the guys as personal slaves for a day!"
PEPOY

Writer: Dan Slott • Penciler: Darick Robertson • Inker: Andrew Pepoy • Colorist: Tom Smith • Designer: Dawn Geiger • Editor: Evan Skolnick • Group Editor: Bobbie Chase

"Well, you can guess which way the chips fell – *my* way! So I told 'em how it was gonna be...and man, you shoulda seen their faces! They had no idea that they'd be usin' their Infinity Gems to help me arrange somethin' I thought was long overdue...

"...a *party!* I mean, what's the point of winnin' a war if you ain't gonna celebrate afterwards? Yeah, sure, my pals were a bit reluctant at first...but a deal's a deal..."

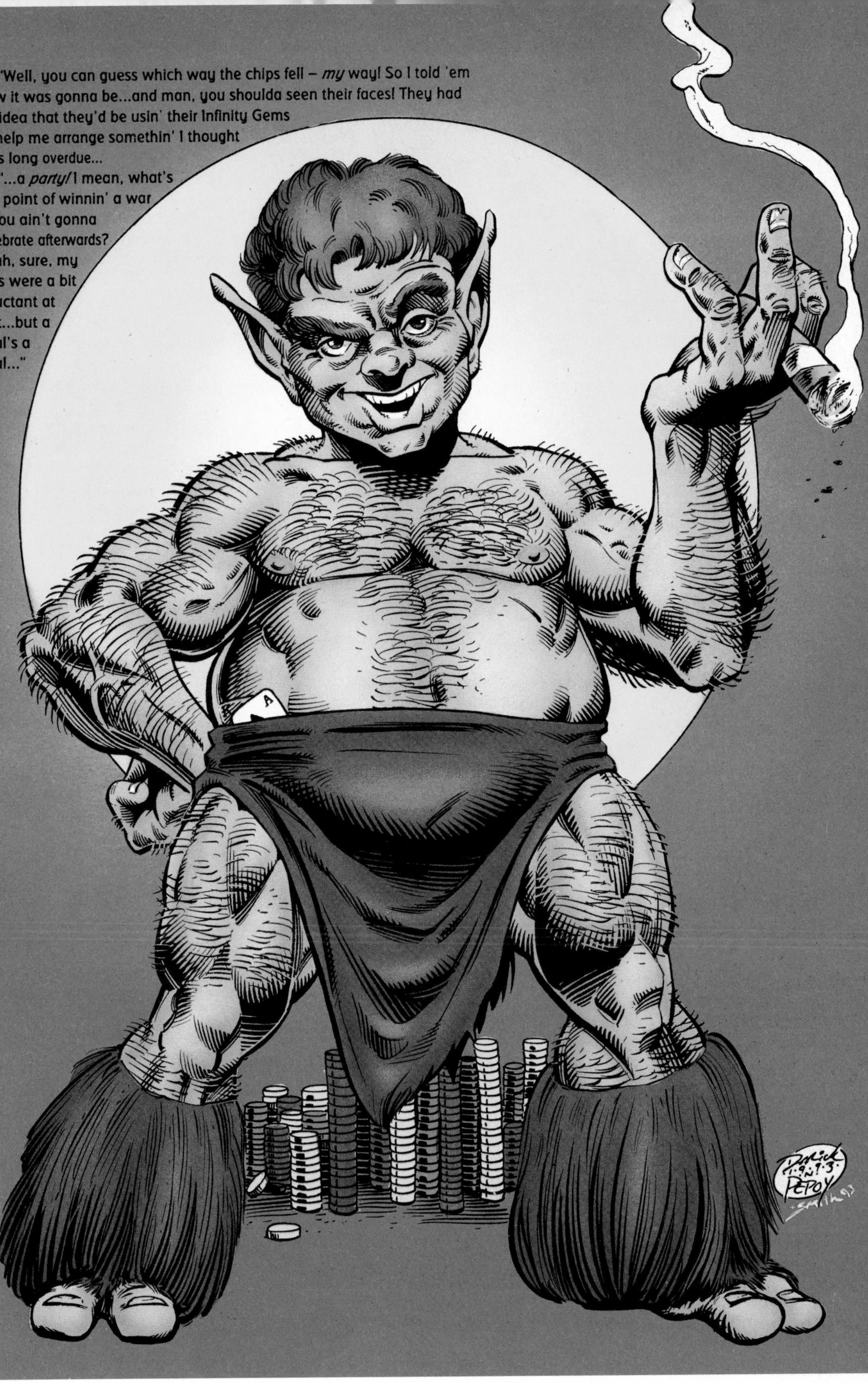

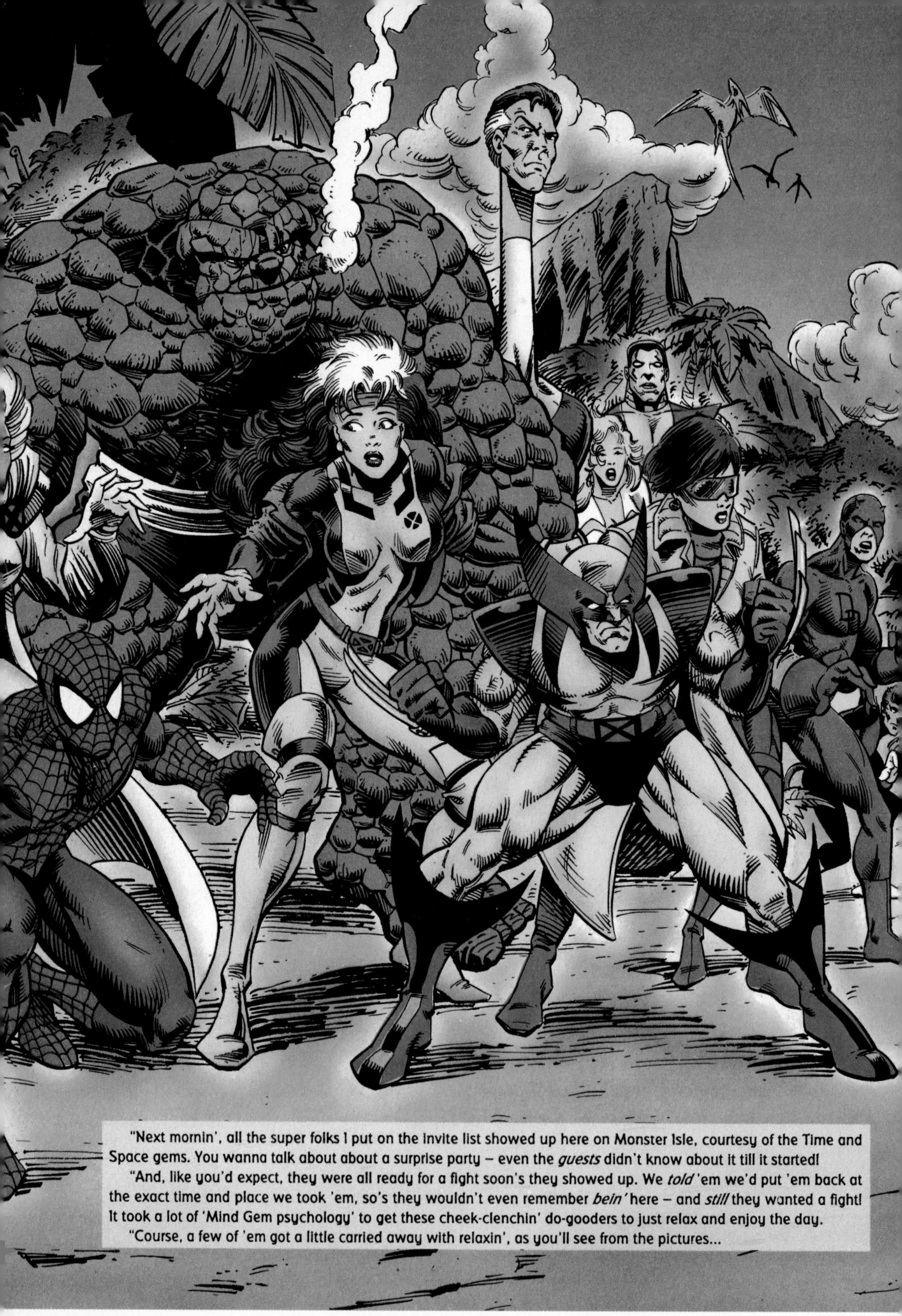
"Next mornin', all the super folks I put on the invite list showed up here on Monster Isle, courtesy of the Time and Space gems. You wanna talk about about a surprise party – even the *guests* didn't know about it till it started!
"And, like you'd expect, they were all ready for a fight soon's they showed up. We *told* 'em we'd put 'em back at the exact time and place we took 'em, so's they wouldn't even remember *bein'* here – and *still* they wanted a fight! It took a lot of 'Mind Gem psychology' to get these cheek-clenchin' do-gooders to just relax and enjoy the day.
"Course, a few of 'em got a little carried away with relaxin', as you'll see from the pictures...

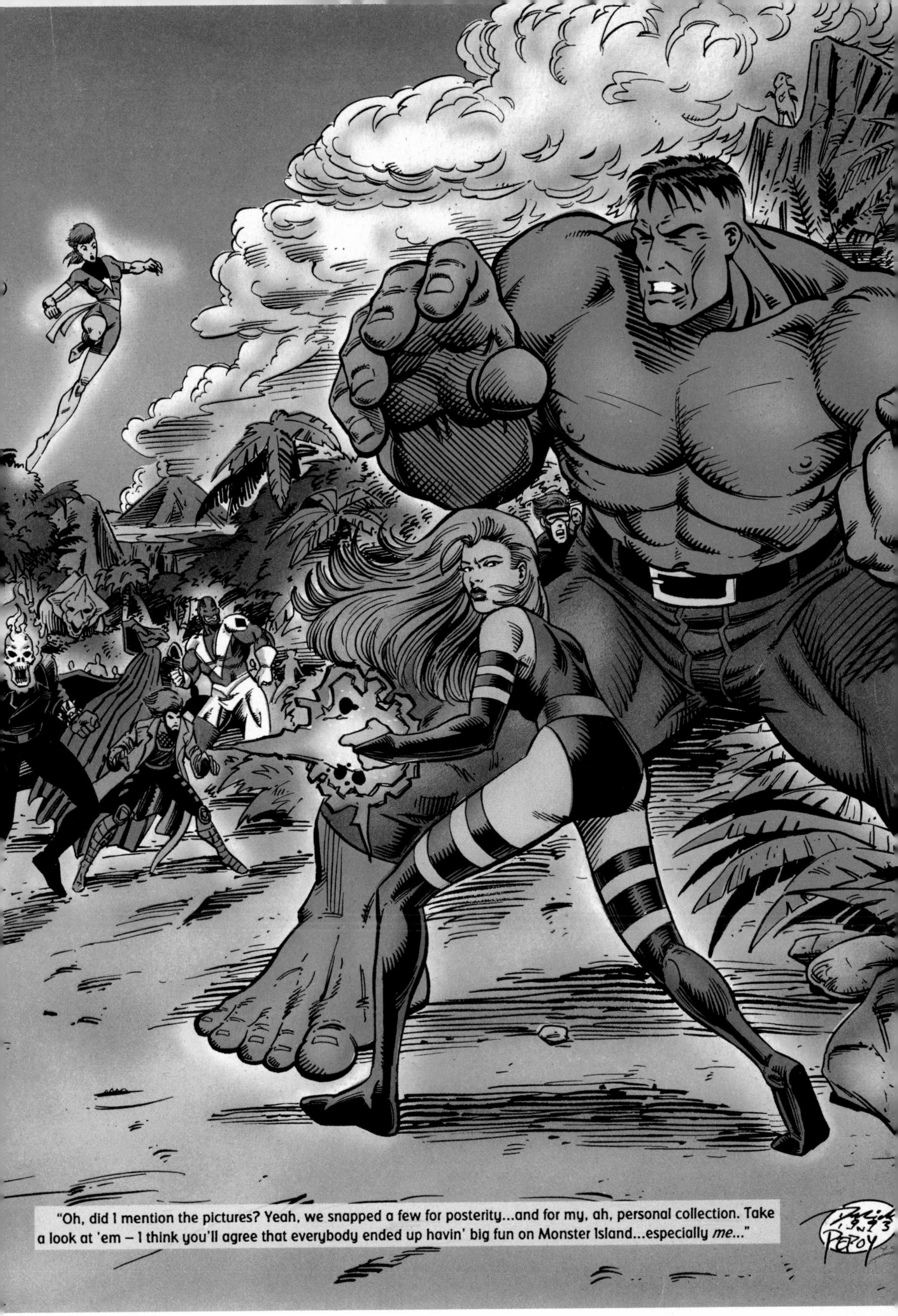
"Oh, did I mention the pictures? Yeah, we snapped a few for posterity...and for my, ah, personal collection. Take a look at 'em – I think you'll agree that everybody ended up havin' big fun on Monster Island...especially *me*..."

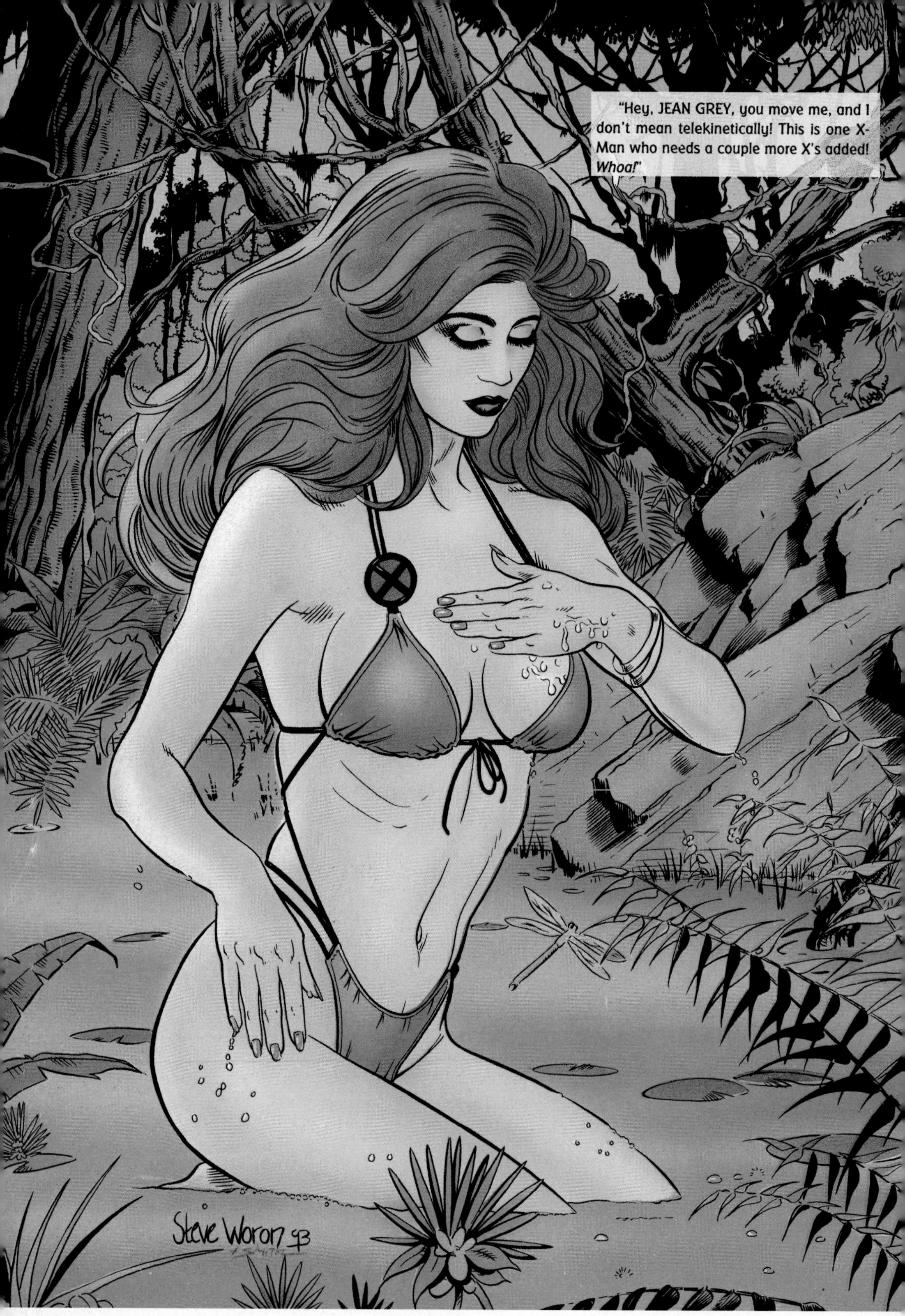
"Hey, JEAN GREY, you move me, and I don't mean telekinetically! This is one X-Man who needs a couple more X's added! *Whoa!*"
Steve Woron 93

Pinup by Steve Woron & Tom Smith

Pinup by Art Thibert & Paul Mounts (facing page)

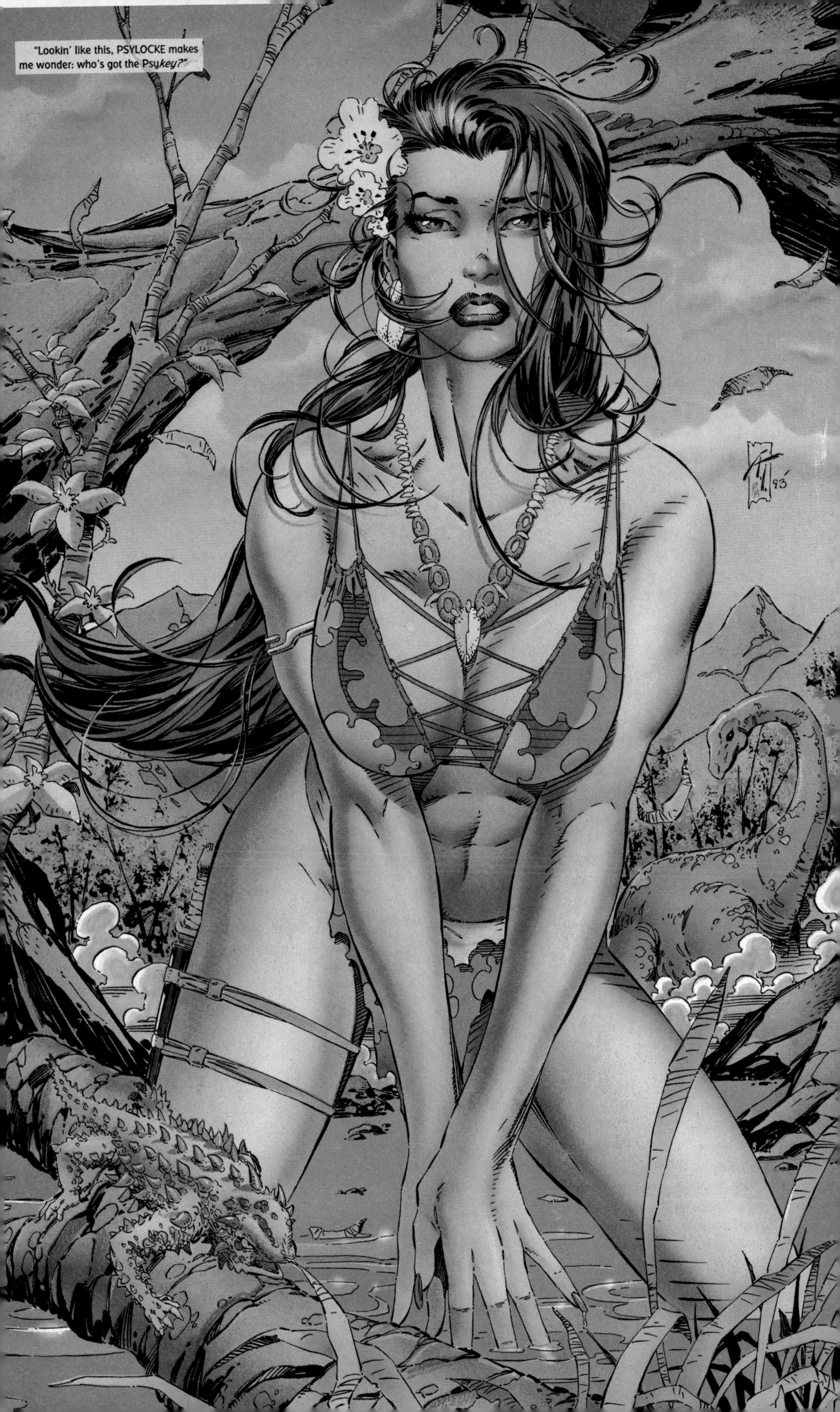
"Lookin' like this, PSYLOCKE makes me wonder: who's got the Psy*key?*"

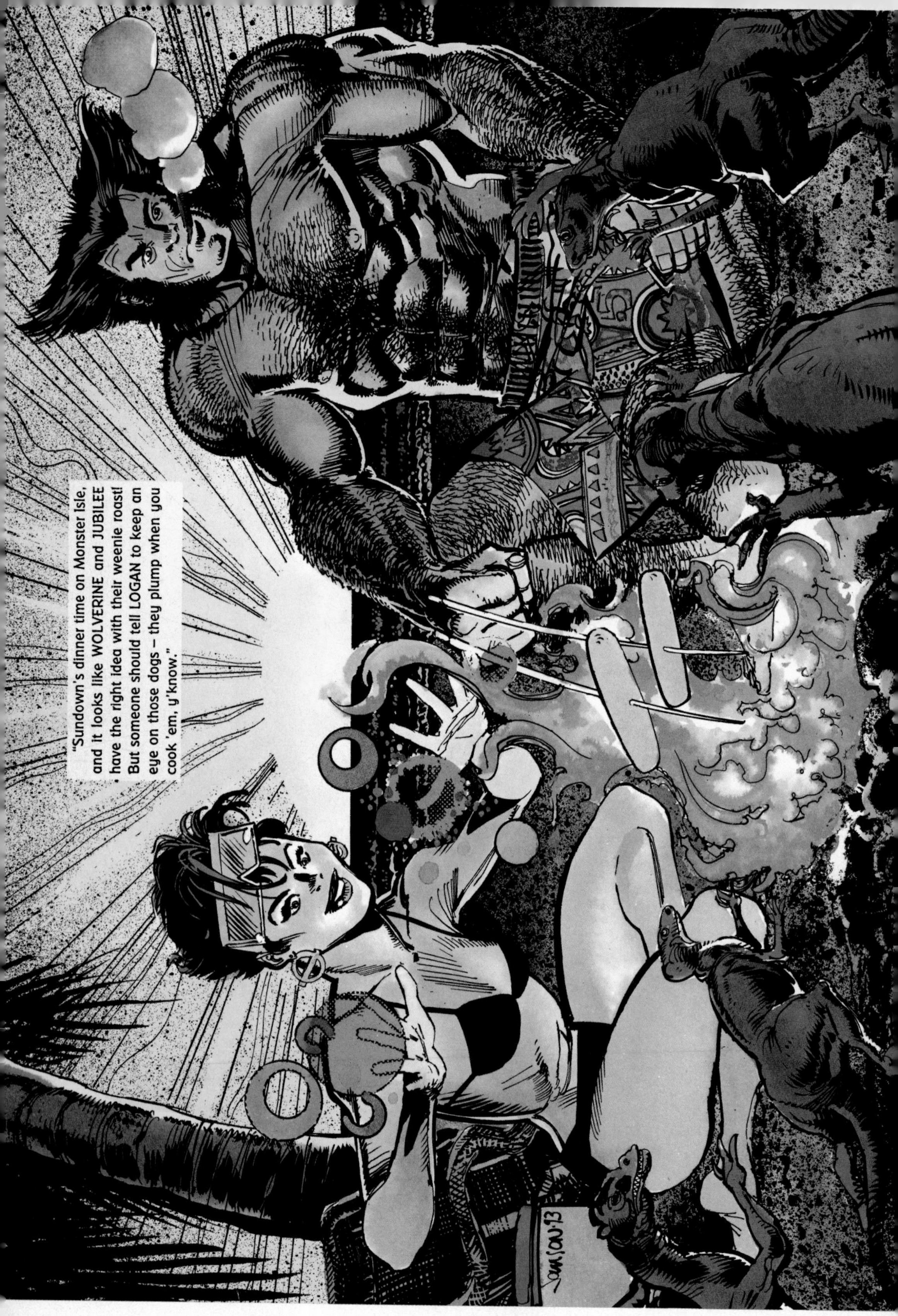
"Sundown's dinner time on Monster Isle, and it looks like WOLVERINE and JUBILEE have the right idea with their weenie roast! But someone should tell LOGAN to keep an eye on those dogs – they plump when you cook 'em, y'know."

Pinup by Klaus Janson

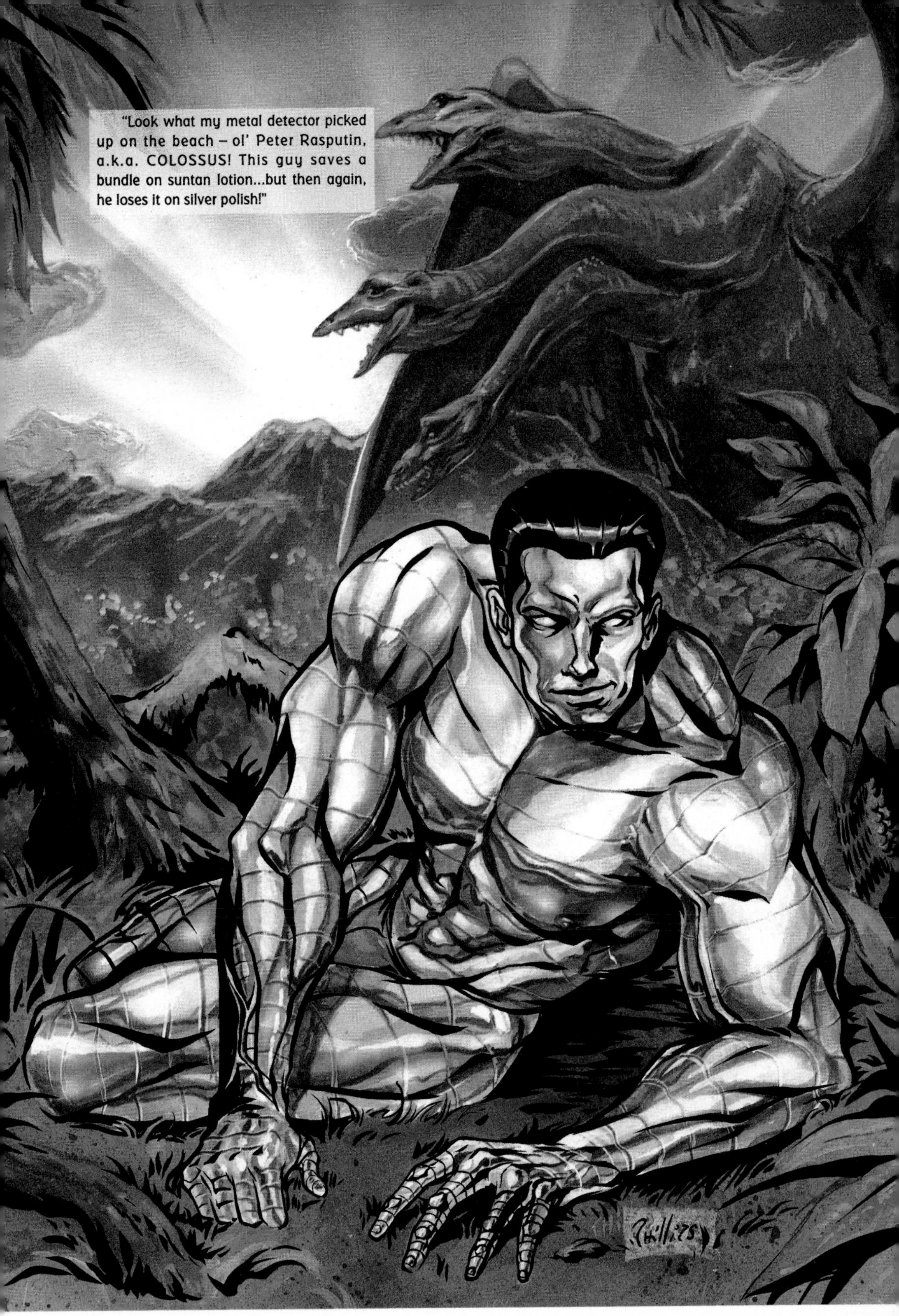
"Look what my metal detector picked up on the beach – ol' Peter Rasputin, a.k.a. COLOSSUS! This guy saves a bundle on suntan lotion...but then again, he loses it on silver polish!"
Phillips '95

Pinup by Joe Phillips

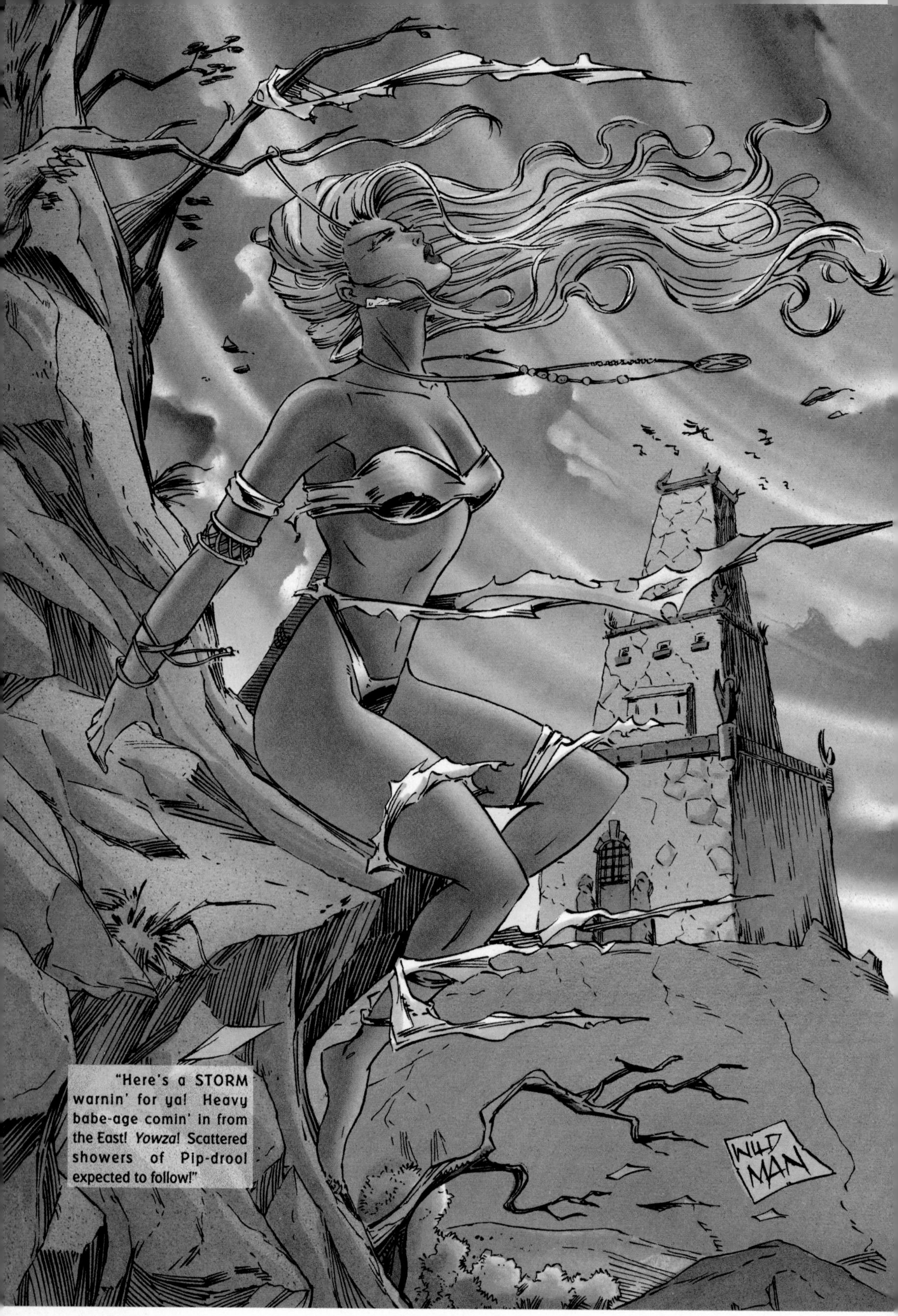
"Here's a STORM warnin' for ya! Heavy babe-age comin' in from the East! *Yowza!* Scattered showers of Pip-drool expected to follow!"
WILD MAN

Pinup by Andrew Wildman & Paul Mounts

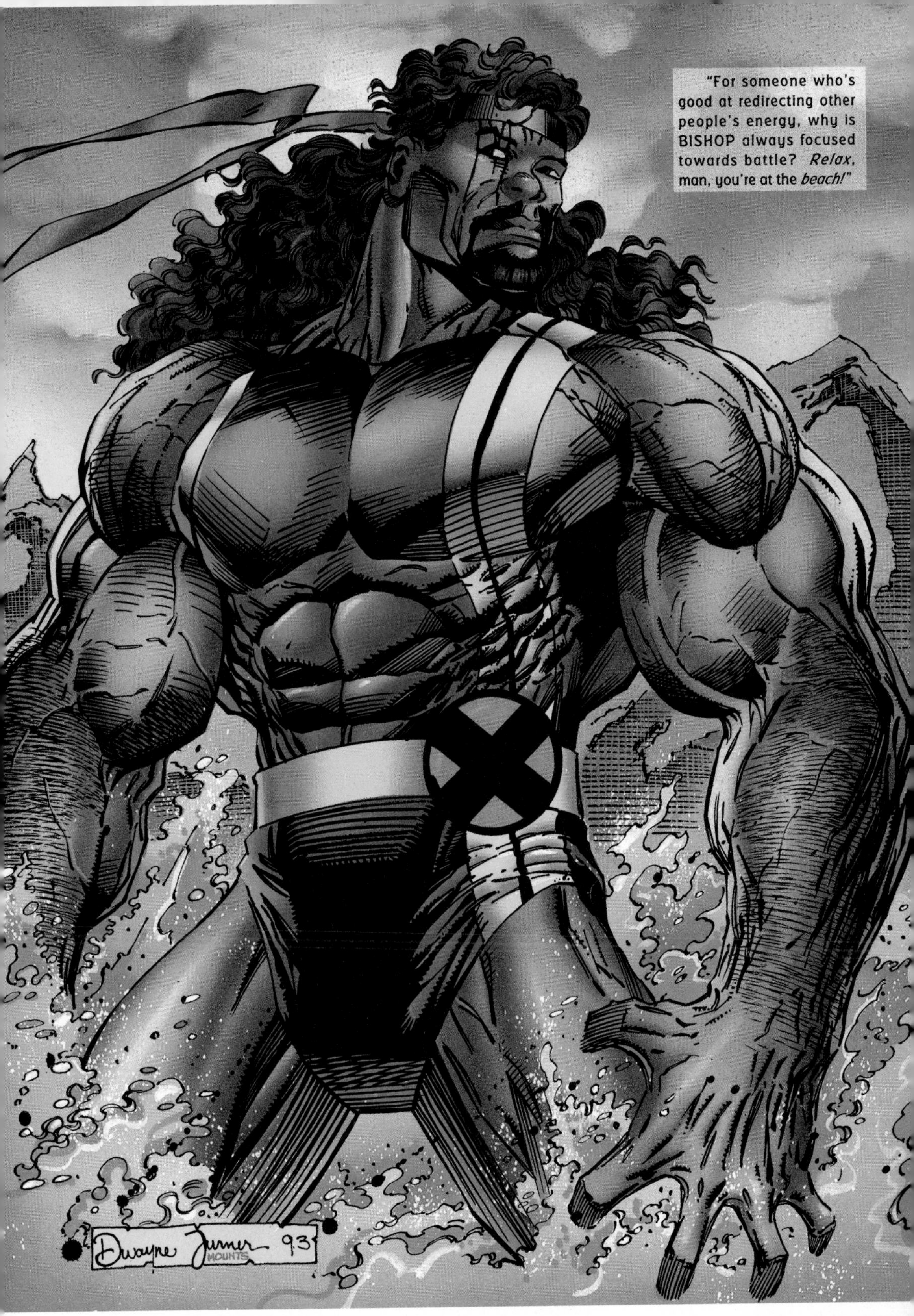
"For someone who's good at redirecting other people's energy, why is BISHOP always focused towards battle? *Relax*, man, you're at the *beach!*"
Dwayne Turner 93
MOUNTS

Pinup by Dwayne Turner & Paul Mounts

JIM LEE & SCOTT WILLIAMS • MARK TEXEIRA • JOHN ROMITA JR. • ANDY KUBERT & MARK PENNINGTON • WHILCE PORTACIO & ART THIBERT • BILL SIENKIEWICZ • JOE MADUREIRA & HARRY CANDELARIO • JACK KIRBY & CHIC STONE • LARRY STROMAN & MARK FARMER • JOE QUESADA & JIMMY PALMIOTTI • ADAM HUGHES • MIKE MIGNOLA • JOE RUBINSTEIN • MARC SILVESTRI & DAN GREEN • JIM STERANKO • BARRY WINDSOR SMITH • JOHN BYRNE & TERRY AUSTIN • ALAN DAVIS • NEAL ADAMS & TOM PALMER • PAUL SMITH • DAVE COCKRUM • ROB LIEFELD • ART ADAMS •

30TH ANNIVERSARY 1962 1992

THE AMAZING SPIDER-MAN

02078

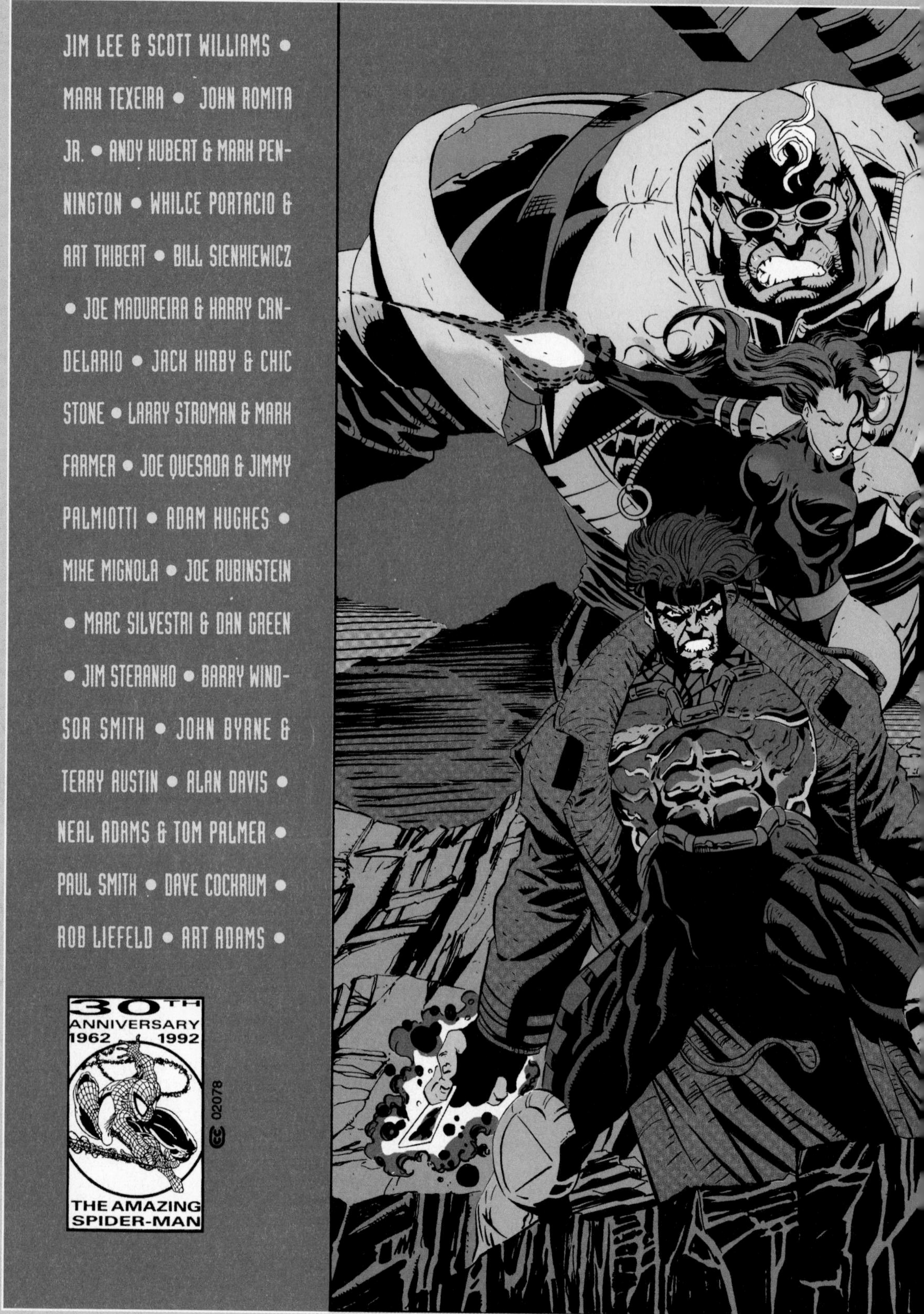

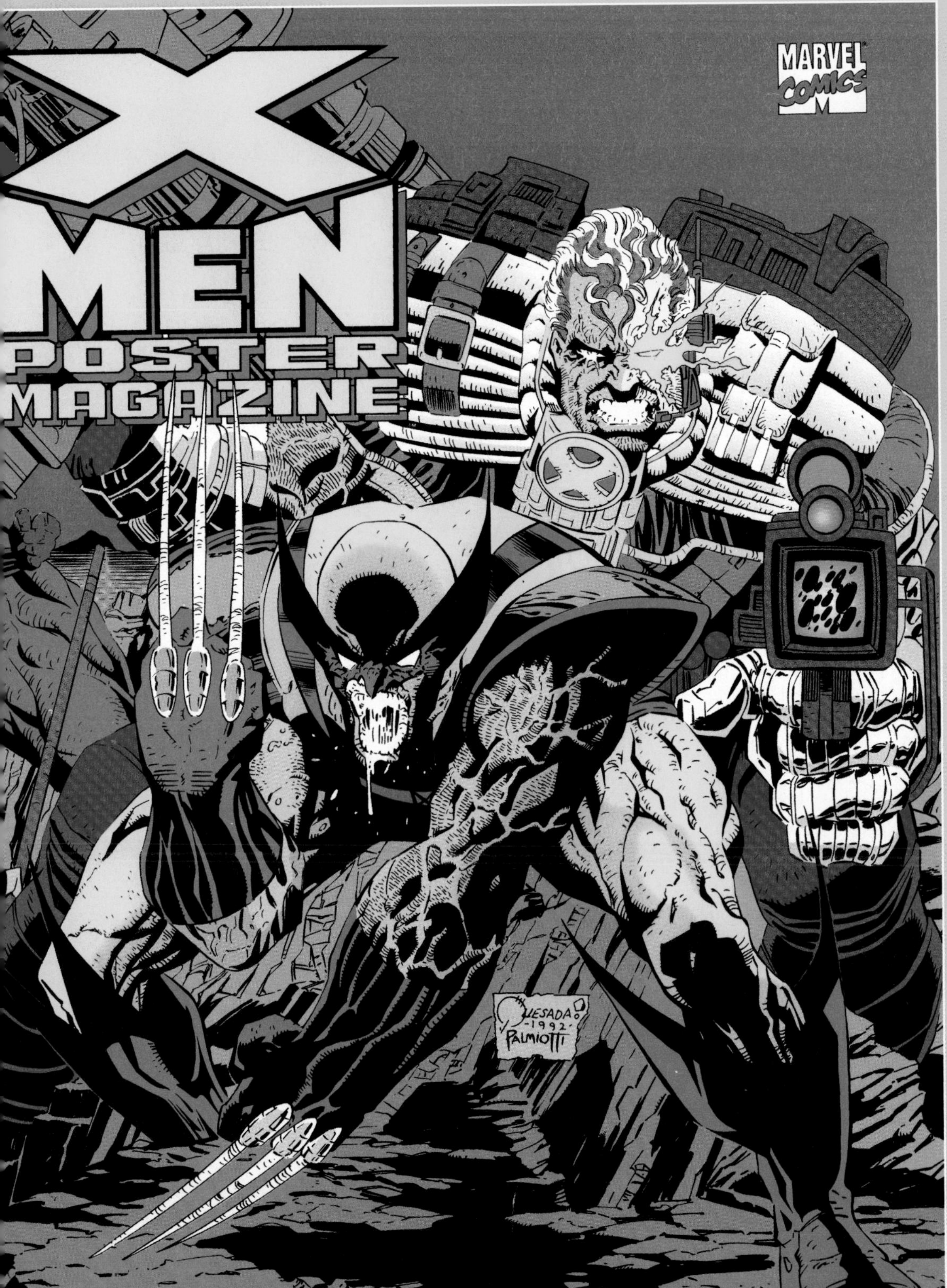

X-MEN
POSTER
MAGAZINE
MARVEL COMICS
QUESADA 1992 PALMIOTTI

X-Men Poster Magazine #1 cover art by Joe Quesada & Jimmy Palmiotti

ANDY KUBERT • GREG CAPULLO • MARK TEXEIRA • DWAYNE TURNER • ART THIBERT • JOE QUESADA • AL MILGROM • ROB LIEFELD • JOHN ROMITA JR. • DAN PANOSIAN • CHRIS BACHALO • JIM LEE • SCOTT WILLIAMS • RICHARD BENNETT • JOE MADUREIRA • MARK FARMER • BRANDON PETERSON • JACK KIRBY • MICHAEL GOLDEN • JOHN BYRNE • TERRY AUSTIN • BILL SIENKIEWICZ • JIM STERANKO • TED McKEEVER • LEE WEEKS • KENT WILLIAMS • JAE LEE • ALAN DAVIS • MARK PENNINGTON • HARRY CANDELARIO • PAUL SMITH • LARRY STROMAN • JIMMY PALMIOTTI •

$4.95US $6.25CAN £3.70UK

CC 02078

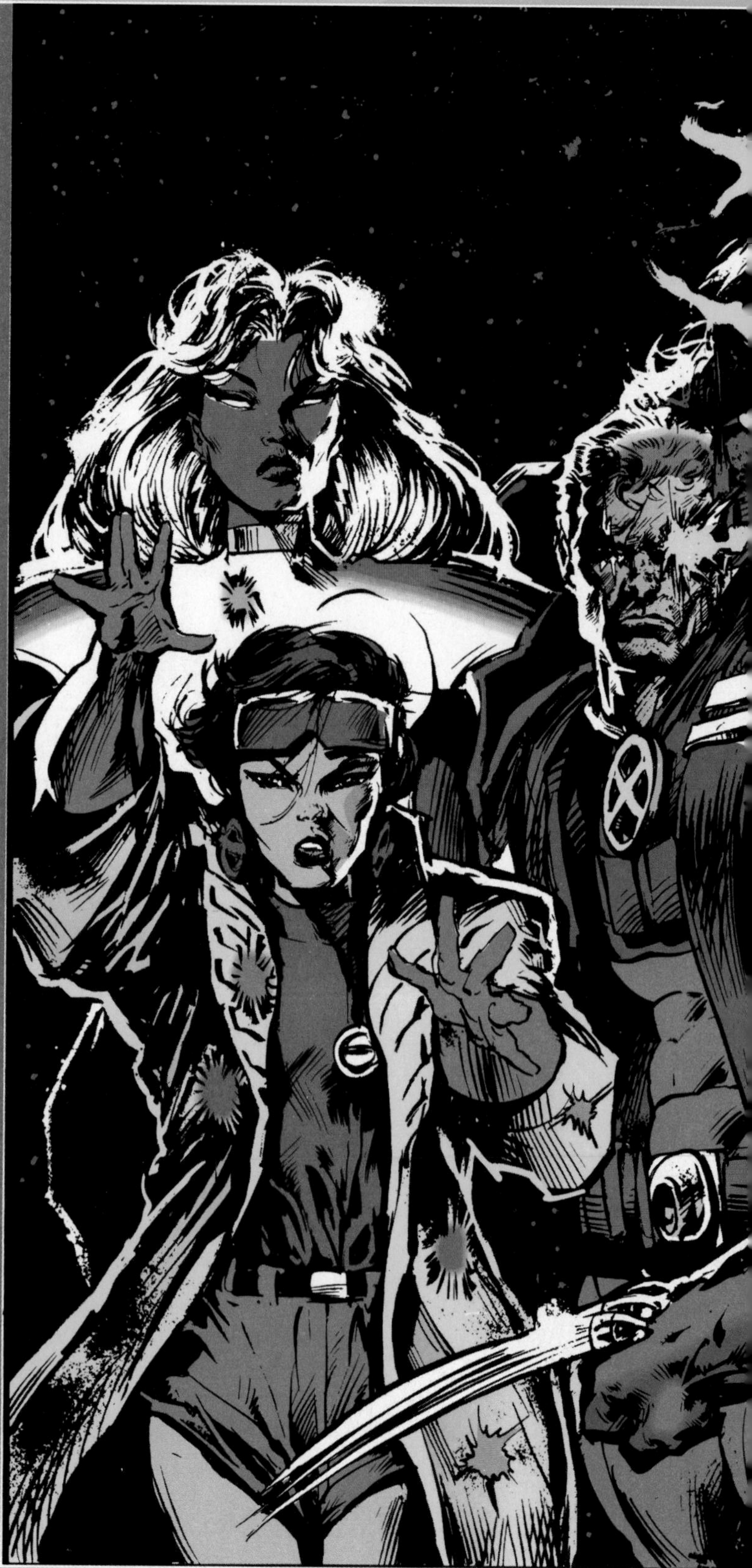

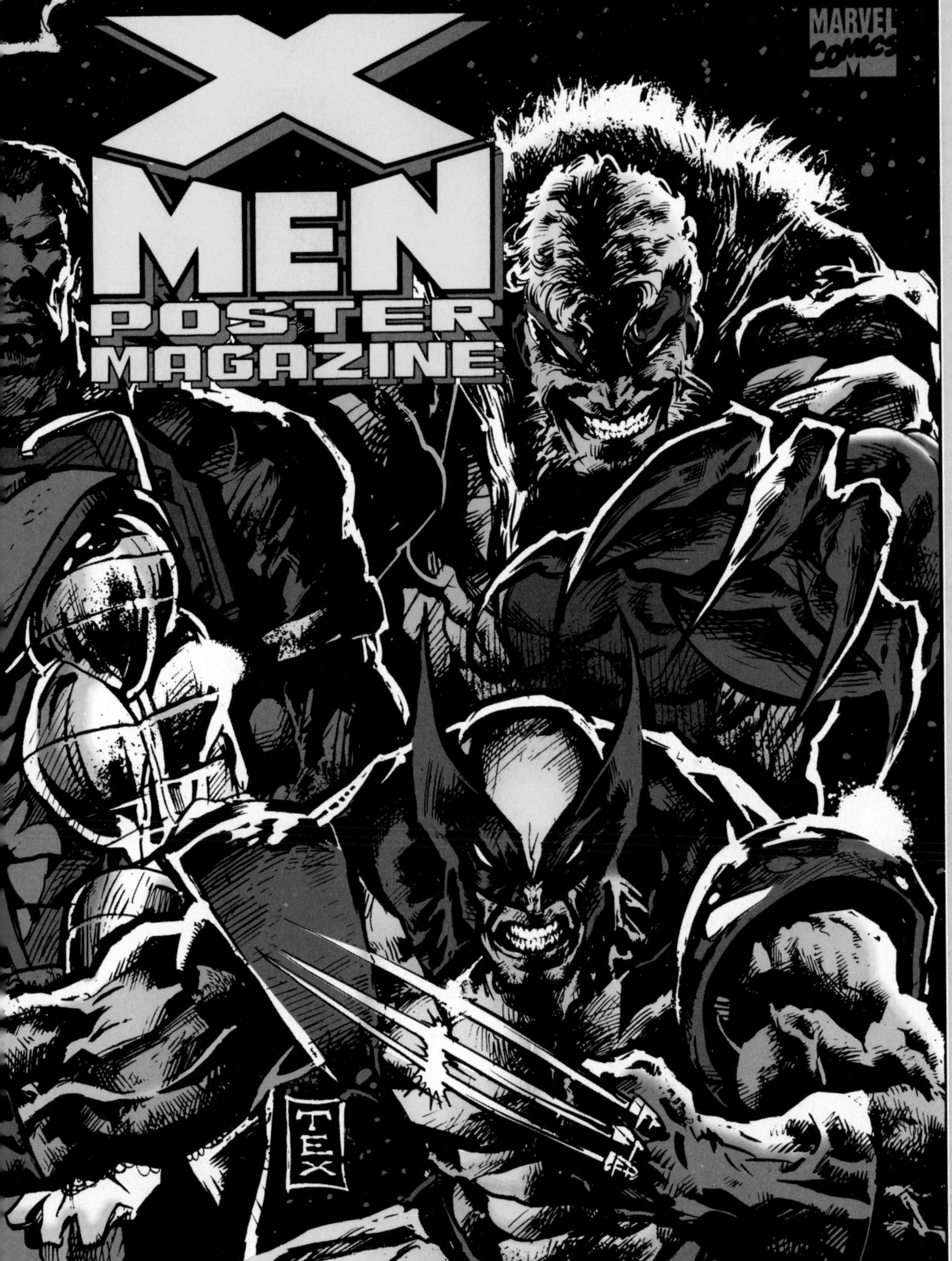
MARVEL COMICS
X-MEN
POSTER MAGAZINE
TEX

X-Men Poster Magazine #2 cover art by Mark Texeira

ANDY KUBERT • MATT RYAN • CARLOS PACHECO • CAM SMITH • STEVE SKROCE • MIKE SELLERS • LEE WEEKS • DOUG ALEXANDER • JOE MADUREIRA • DAN GREEN • KEN LASHLEY • RANDY ELLIOTT • ADAM KUBERT • IAN CHURCHILL • JASON MINOR • GARY FRANK • JAN DUURSEMA • AL MILGROM • RICHARD BENNETT • LIAM SHARP • LARRY STROMAN • JAE LEE • NEIL MCLUTY • ANTONIO DANIEL • KEVIN CONRAD • HARRY CANDELARIO • TIM SALE • GENE HA • AL VEY • ADAM HUGHES • BILL SIENKIEWICZ

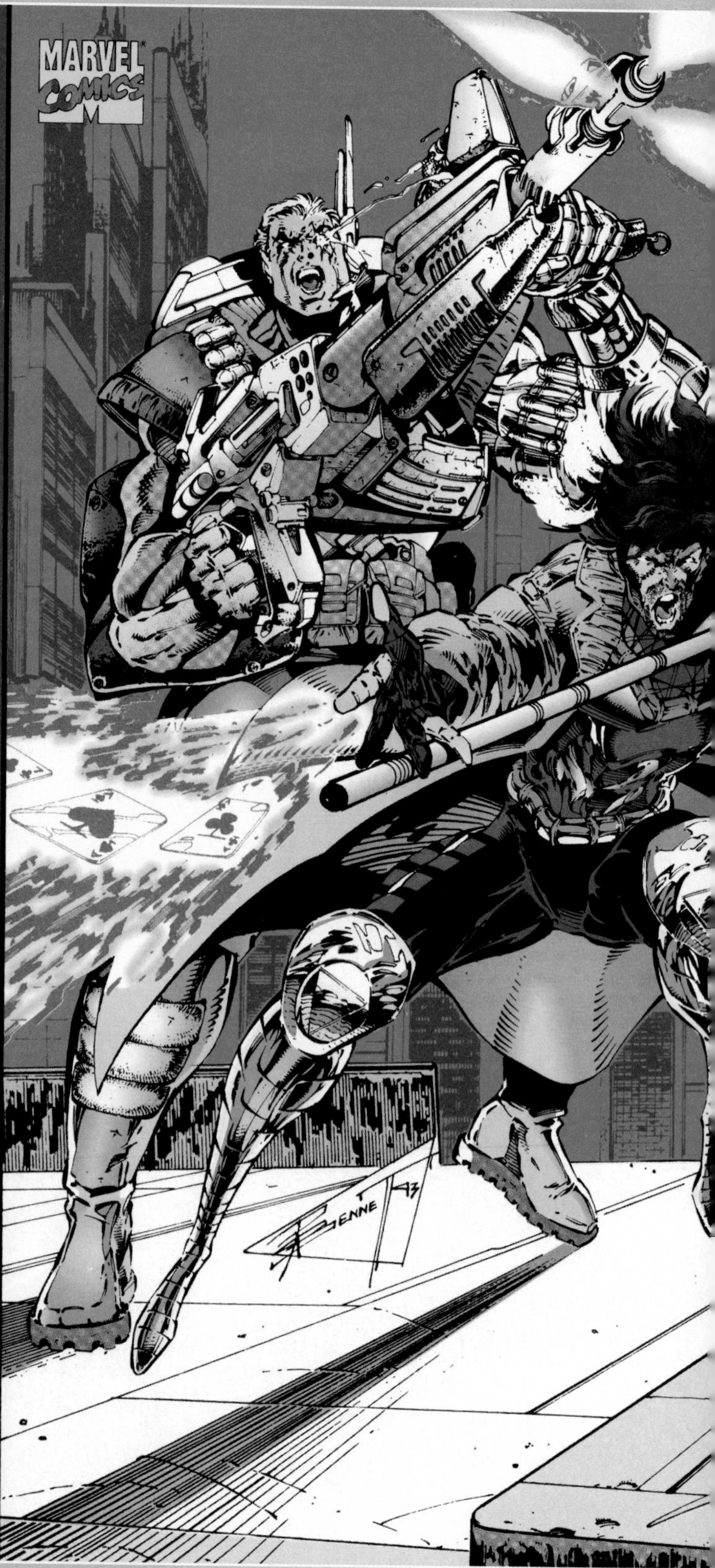

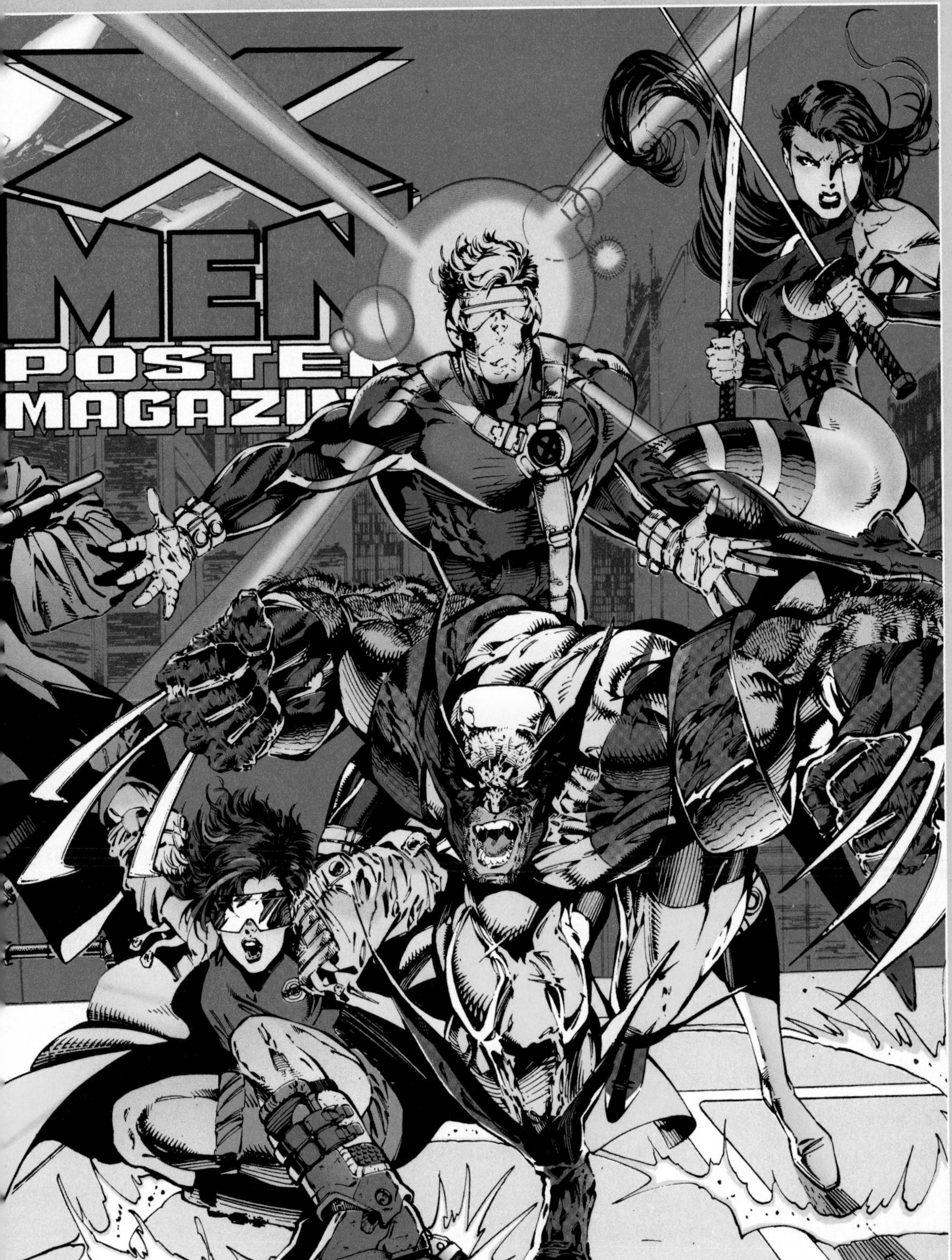
X
MEN
POSTER
MAGAZIN

X-Men Poster Magazine #3 cover art by Richard Bennett

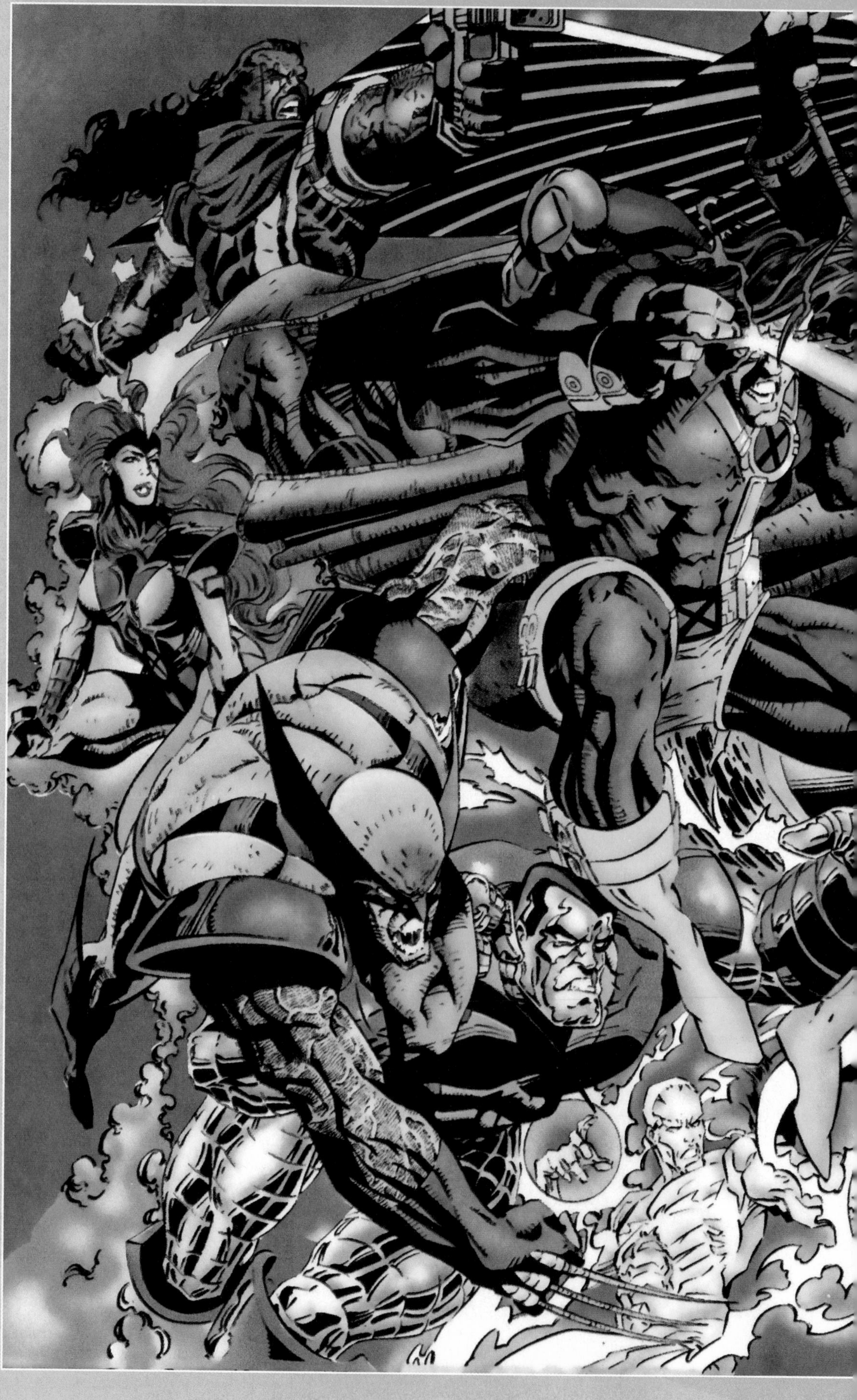

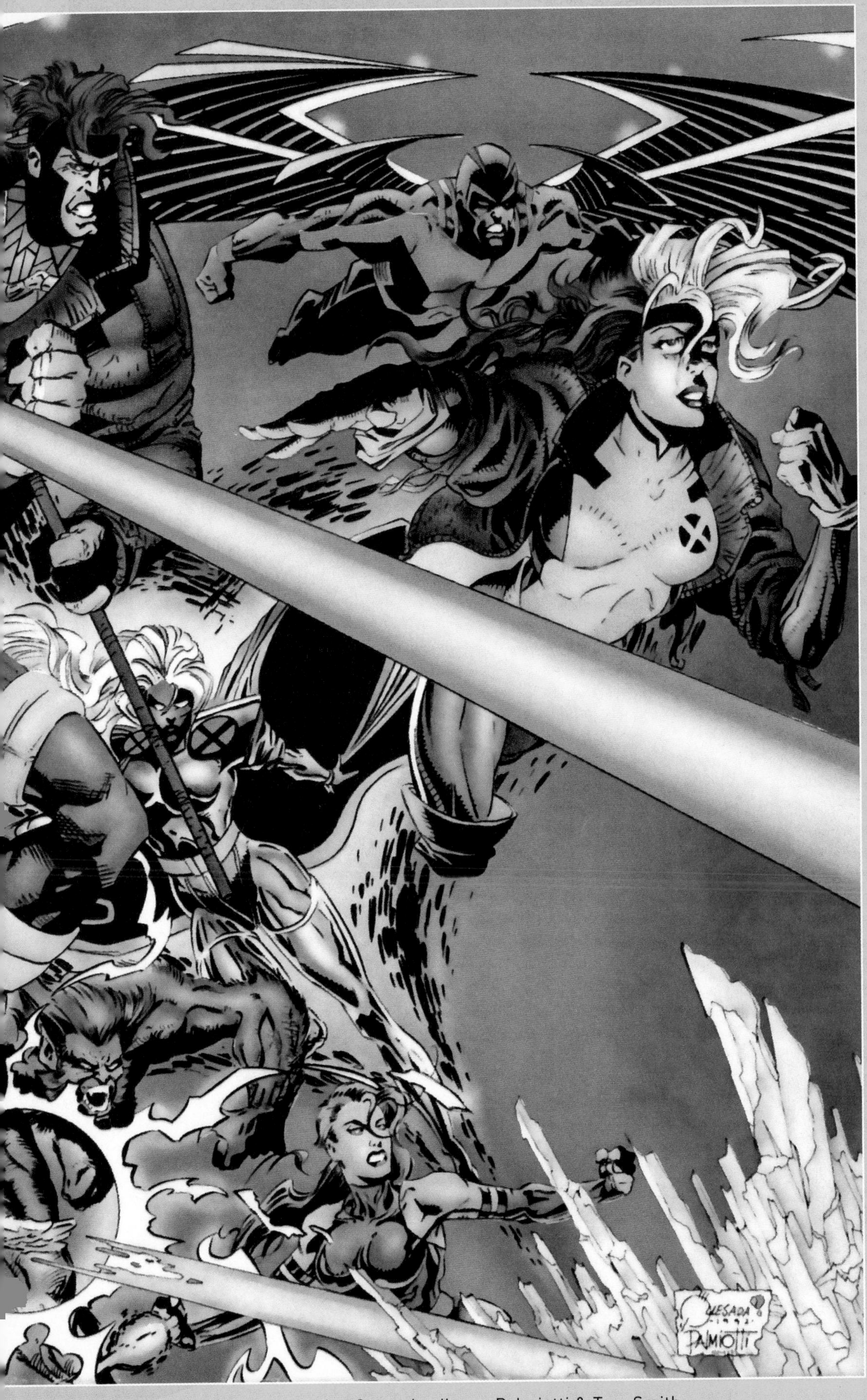
QUESADA
PALMIOTTI

X-Men pinup by Joe Quesada, Jimmy Palmiotti & Tom Smith

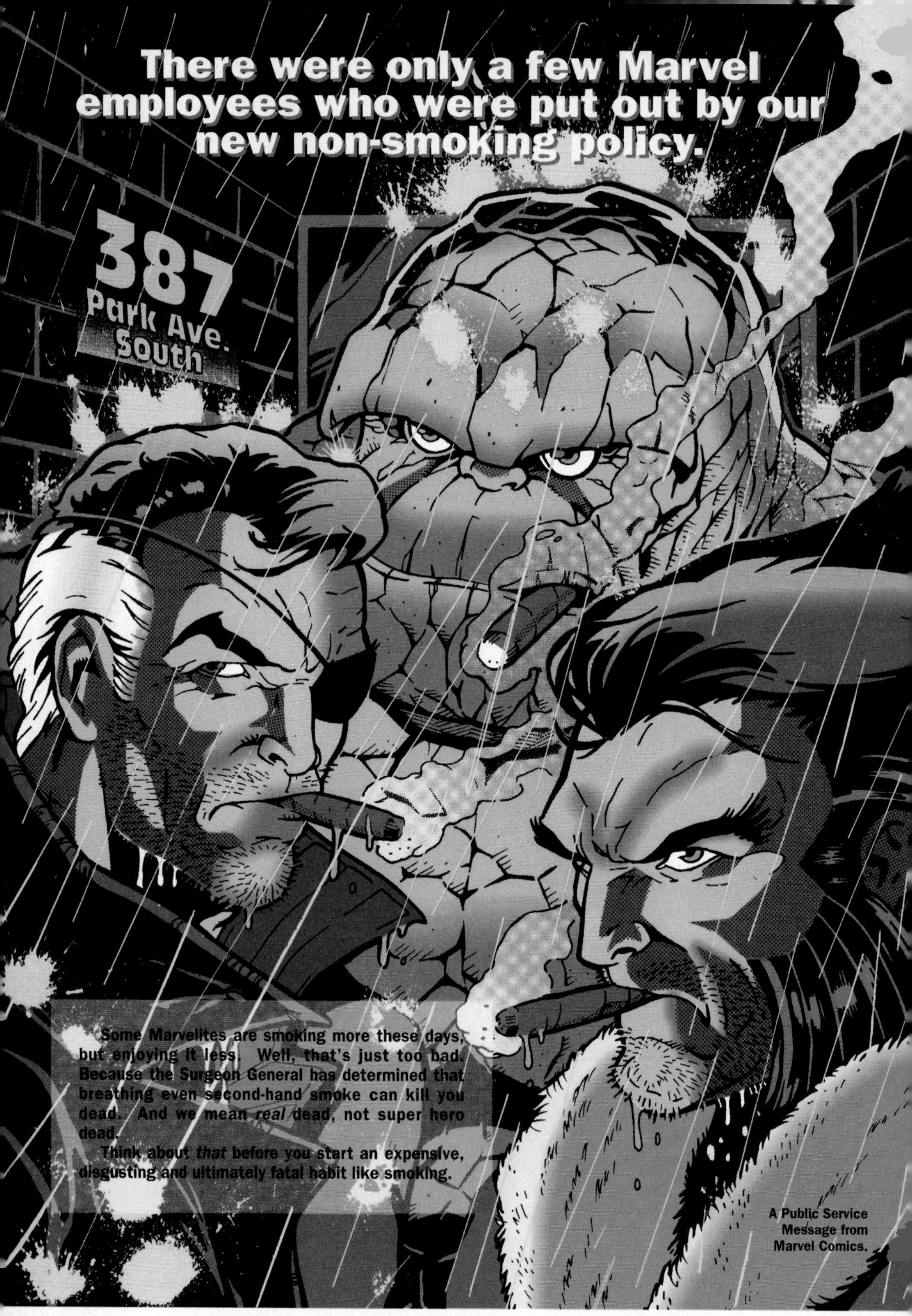

There were only a few Marvel employees who were put out by our new non-smoking policy.
387 Park Ave. South
Some Marvelites are smoking more these days, but enjoying it less. Well, that's just too bad. Because the Surgeon General has determined that breathing even second-hand smoke can kill you dead. And we mean *real* dead, not super hero dead.
Think about *that* before you start an expensive, disgusting and ultimately fatal habit like smoking.
A Public Service Message from Marvel Comics.

Marvel Year-In-Review '93 parody ad by Clay Griffith, Manny Galàn & Gregory Wright

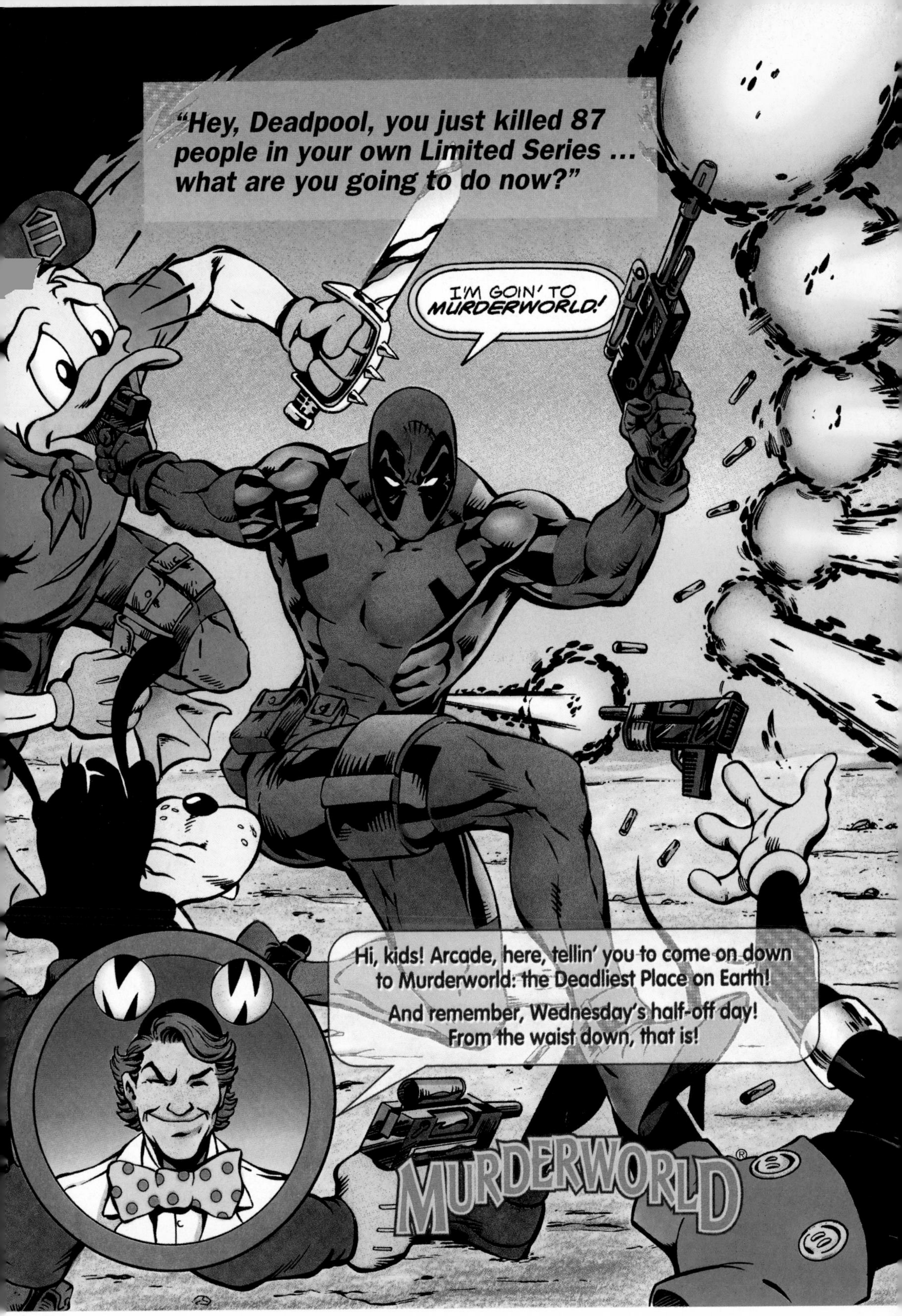
"Hey, Deadpool, you just killed 87 people in your own Limited Series ... what are you going to do now?"
I'M GOIN' TO MURDERWORLD!
Hi, kids! Arcade, here, tellin' you to come on down to Murderworld: the Deadliest Place on Earth!
And remember, Wednesday's half-off day! From the waist down, that is!
MURDERWORLD®

Marvel Year-In-Review '93 parody ads by Dan Slott, Manny Galàn, Scott Koblish, Gregory Wright & Paul Mounts

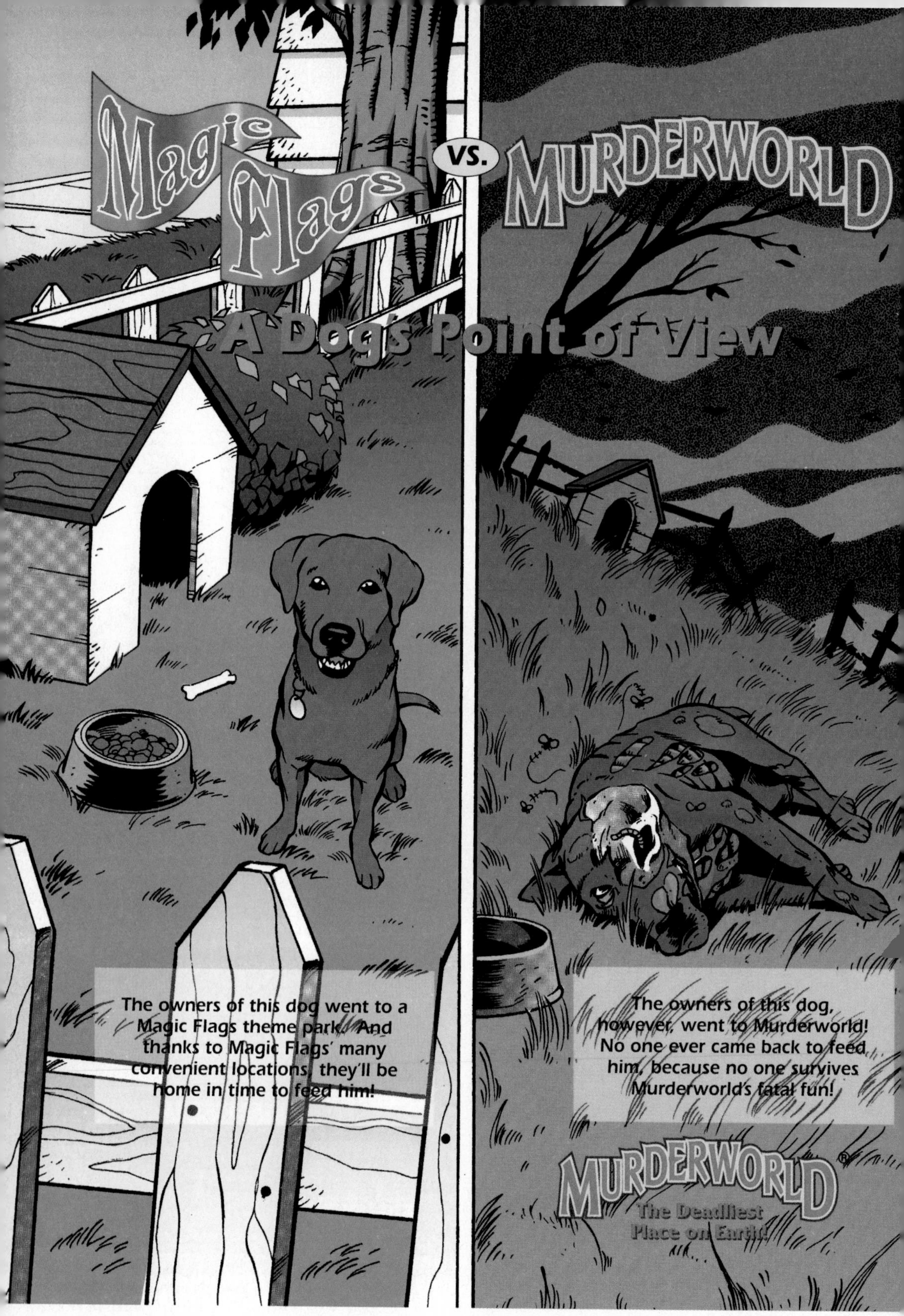
Magic Flags™
vs.
MURDERWORLD
A Dog's Point of View
The owners of this dog went to a Magic Flags theme park. And thanks to Magic Flags' many convenient locations, they'll be home in time to feed him!
The owners of this dog, however, went to Murderworld! No one ever came back to feed him, because no one survives Murderworld's fatal fun!
MURDERWORLD®
The Deadliest Place on Earth!

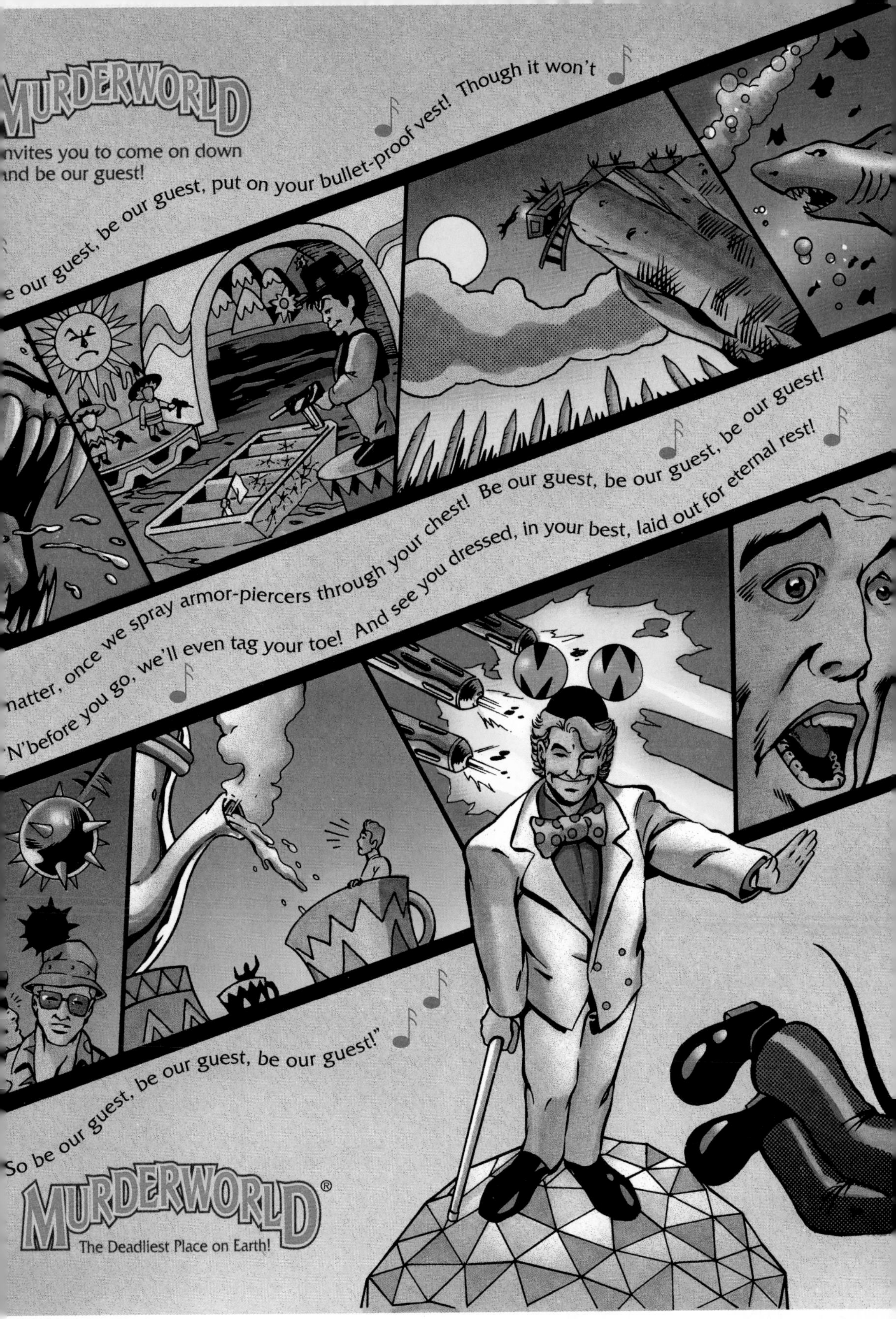
MURDERWORLD
invites you to come on down
and be our guest!
Be our guest, be our guest, put on your bullet-proof vest! Though it won't
matter, once we spray armor-piercers through your chest! Be our guest, be our guest, be our guest, be our guest!
'N'before you go, we'll even tag your toe! And see you dressed, in your best, laid out for eternal rest!
So be our guest, be our guest, be our guest!"
MURDERWORLD®
The Deadliest Place on Earth!

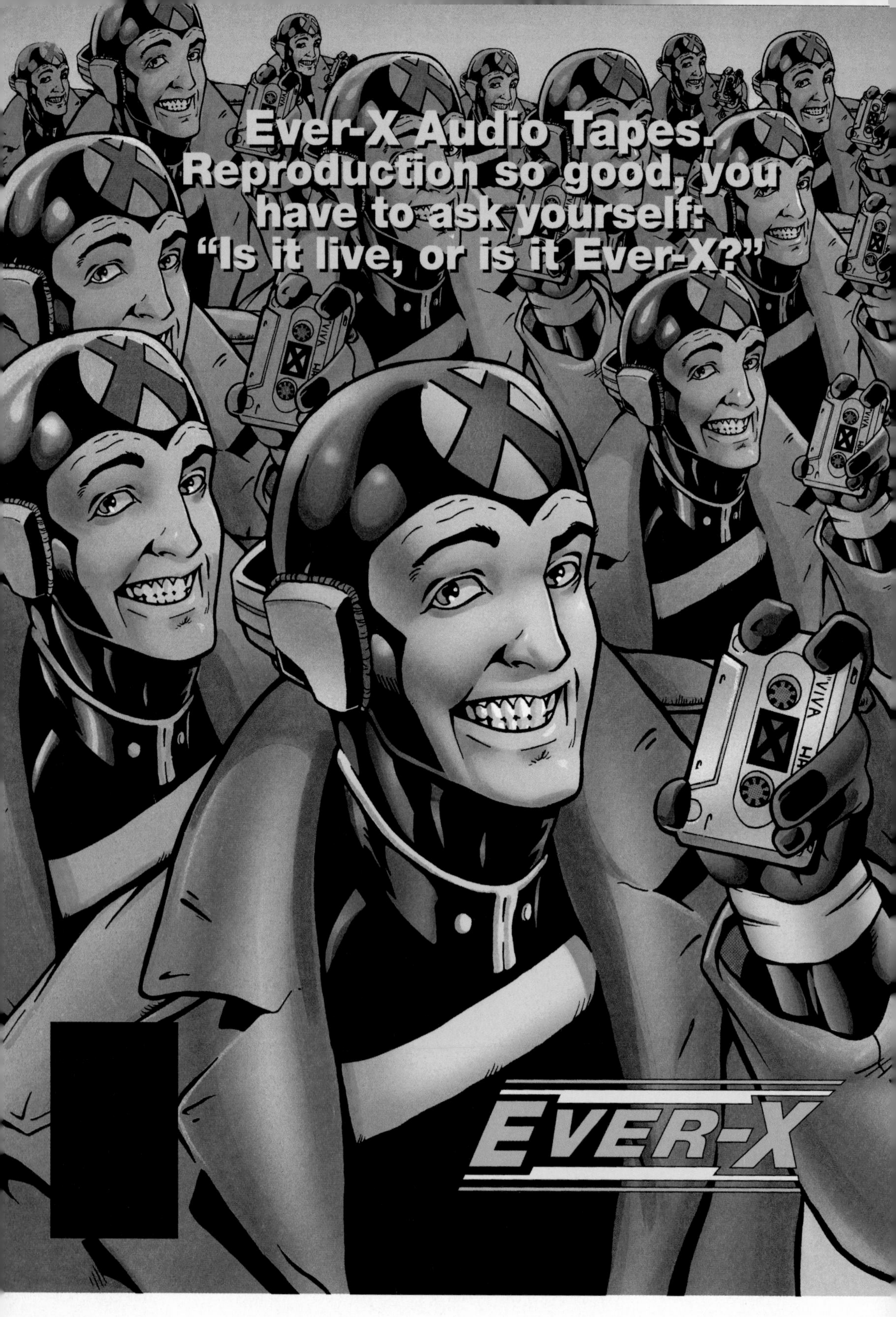
Ever-X Audio Tapes.
Reproduction so good, you have to ask yourself:
"Is it live, or is it Ever-X?"
EVER-X

Marvel Year-In-Review '93 parody ad by Manny Galàn & Paul Mounts

X-Men #22, page 5 pencils by Andy Kubert, inks by Mark Pennington & color guide by Joe Rosas

X-Men/Avengers pinup by Jeff Johnson, Mark McKenna & Tom Smith

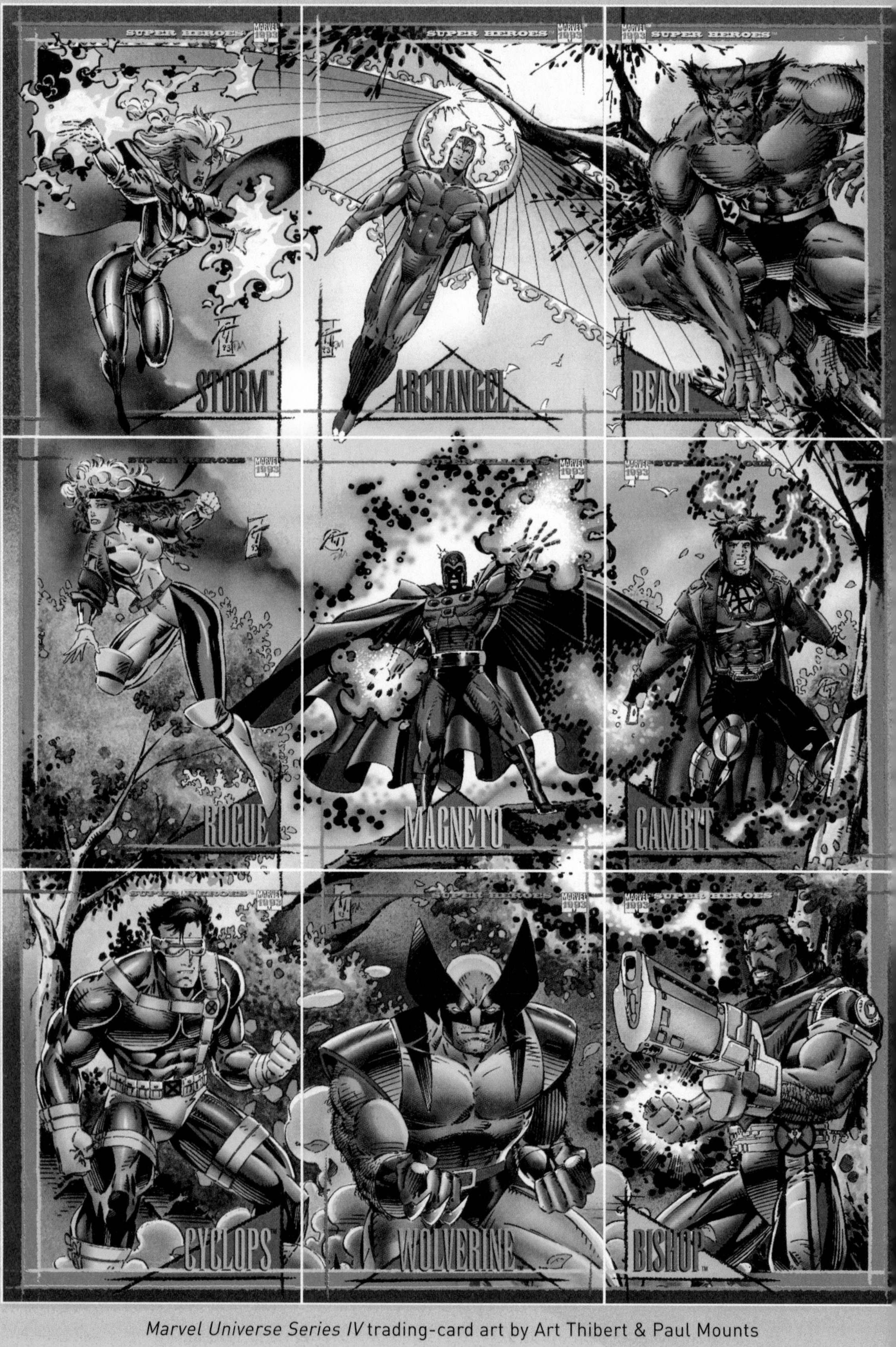
SUPER HEROES
STORM
SUPER HEROES
ARCHANGEL
SUPER HEROES
BEAST
ROGUE
MAGNETO
GAMBIT
CYCLOPS
WOLVERINE
BISHOP

Marvel Universe Series IV trading-card art by Art Thibert & Paul Mounts

ARCHANGEL
SUPER HEROES
X-MEN: SERIES 2
BEAST
SUPER HEROES
X-MEN: SERIES 2
SUPER HEROES
X-MEN: SERIES 2
COLOSSUS
SUPER HEROES
X-MEN: SERIES 2
CYCLOPS
SUPER HEROES
X-MEN: SERIES 2
GAMBIT
SUPER HEROES
X-MEN: SERIES 2
JEAN GREY
SUPER HEROES
X-MEN: SERIES 2
ICEMAN
SUPER HEROES
X-MEN: SERIES 2
JUBILEE
SUPER HEROES

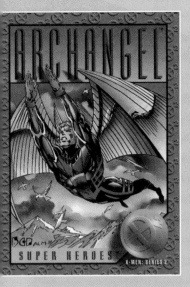

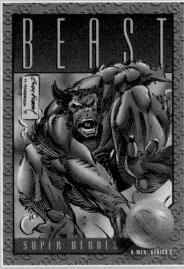

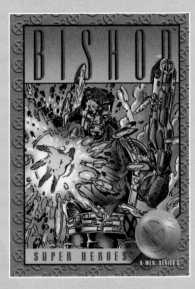

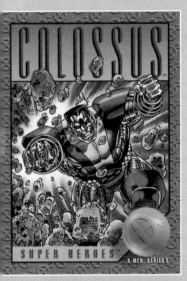

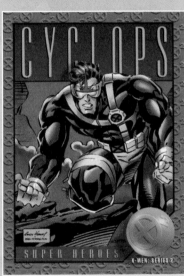

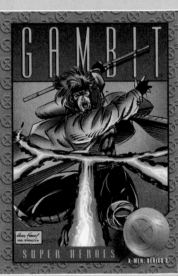

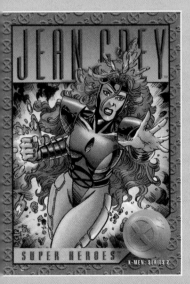

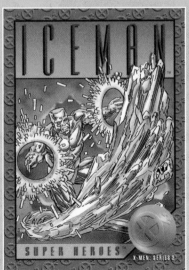

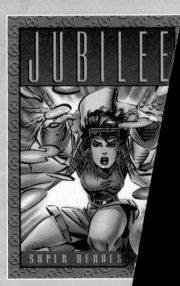

X-Men: Series 2 trading-card art by Brandon Peterson & Al Milgrom, Andy Kubert & Mark Pennington, and Paul Mounts

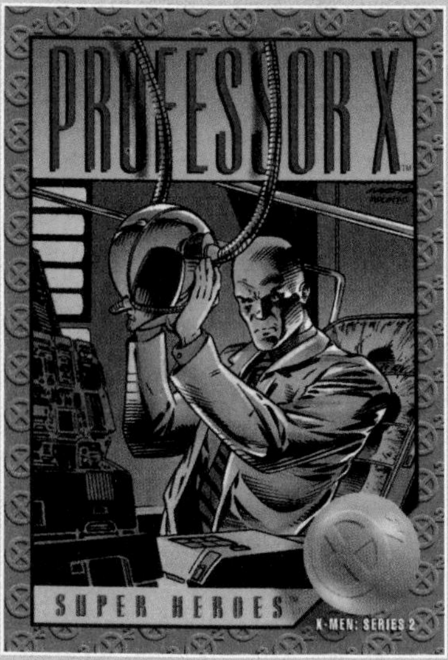
PROFESSOR X
SUPER HEROES
X-MEN: SERIES 2

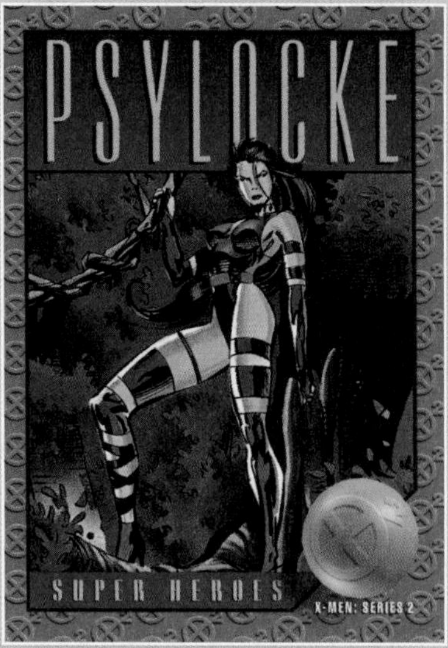
PSYLOCKE
SUPER HEROES
X-MEN: SERIES 2

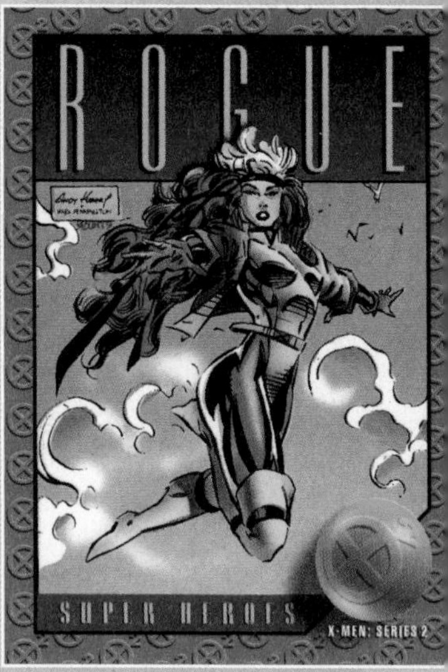
ROGUE
SUPER HEROES
X-MEN: SERIES 2

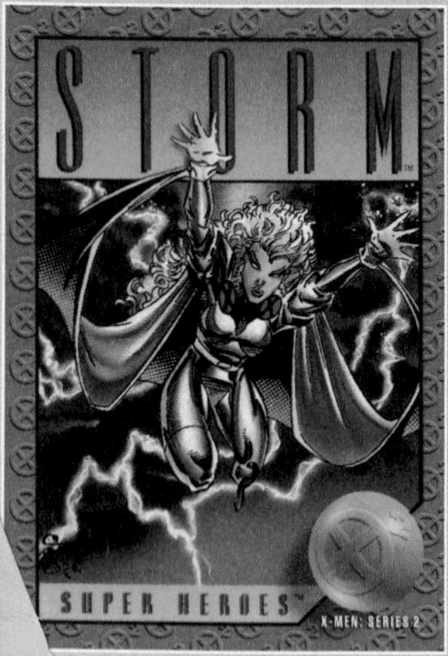
STORM
SUPER HEROES
X-MEN: SERIES 2

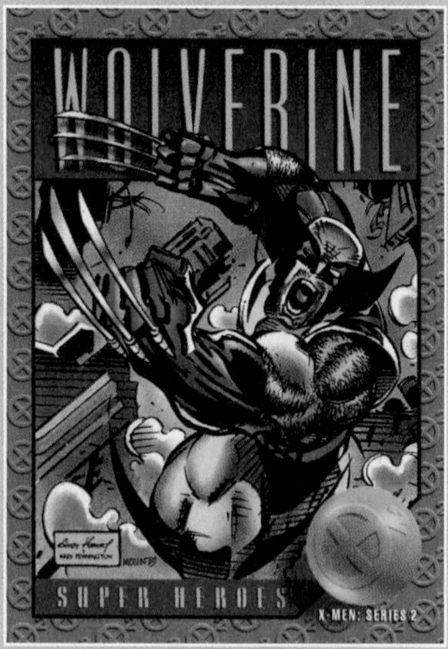
WOLVERINE
SUPER HEROES
X-MEN: SERIES 2

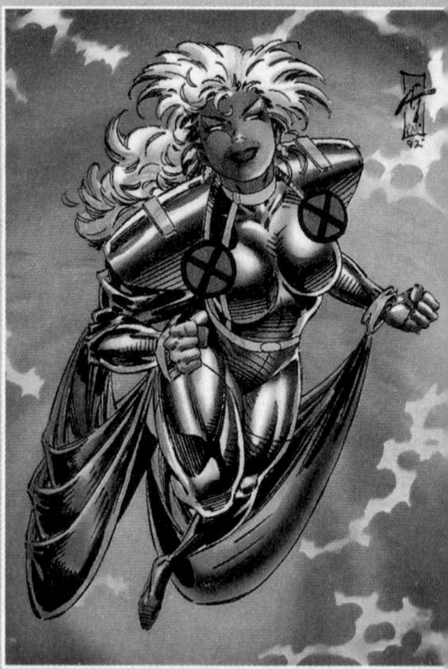

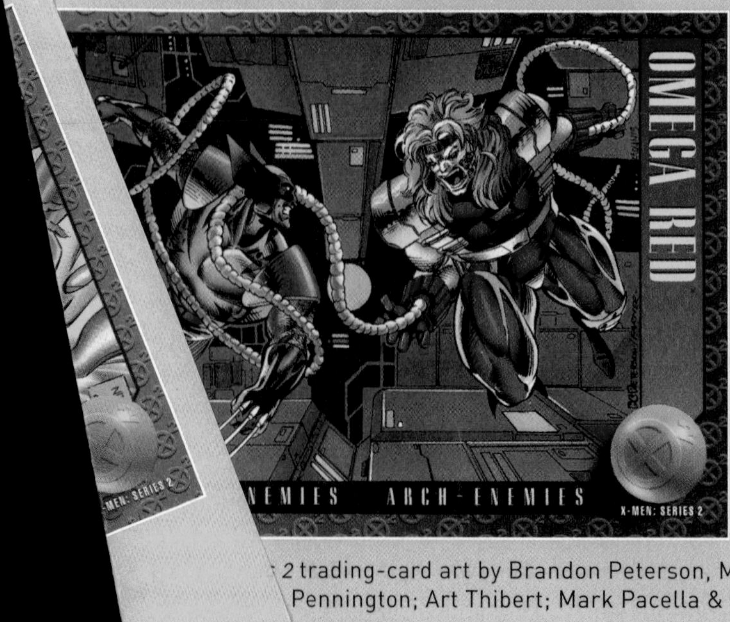
OMEGA RED
ARCH-ENEMIES
X-MEN: SERIES 2

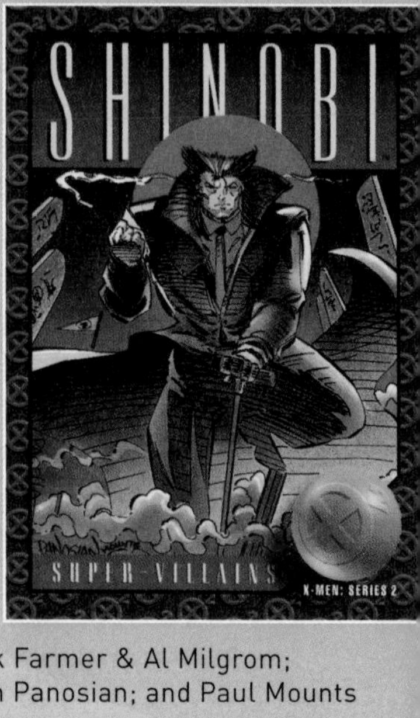
SHINOBI
SUPER-VILLAINS
X-MEN: SERIES 2

2 trading-card art by Brandon Peterson, Mark Farmer & Al Milgrom;
Pennington; Art Thibert; Mark Pacella & Dan Panosian; and Paul Mounts

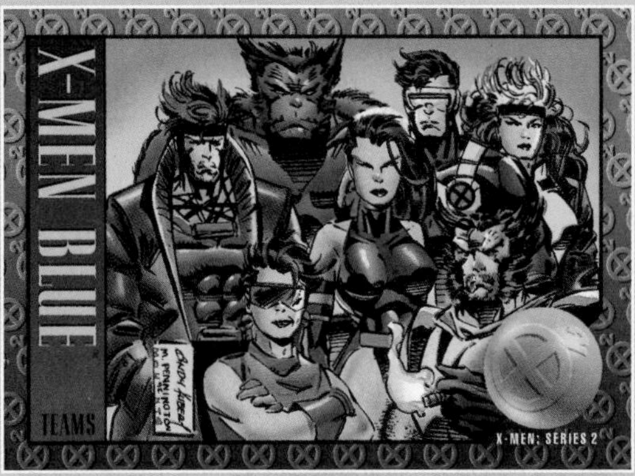
X-MEN BLUE
TEAMS
X-MEN: SERIES 2

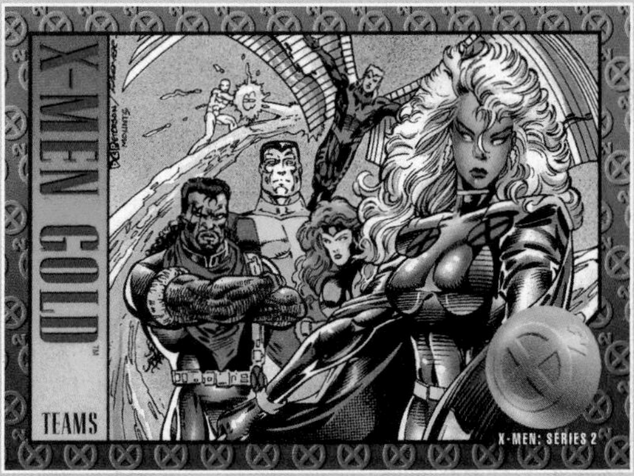
X-MEN GOLD
TEAMS
X-MEN: SERIES 2

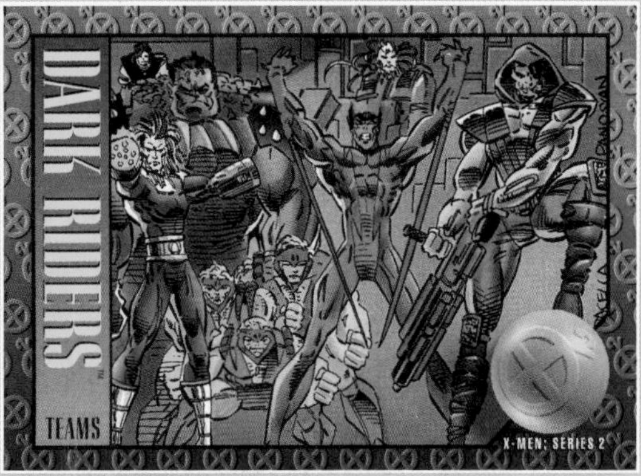
DARK RIDERS
TEAMS
X-MEN: SERIES 2

X-Men: Series 2 trading-card art by Andy Kubert & Mark Pennington, Brandon Peterson & Mark Farmer, Mark Pacella & Dan Panosian, and Paul Mounts

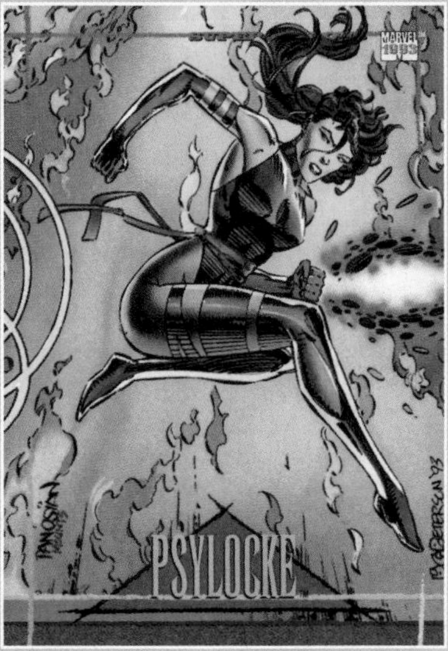
PSYLOCKE

Marvel Universe Series IV trading-card art by Brandon Peterson, Dan Panosian & Paul Mounts

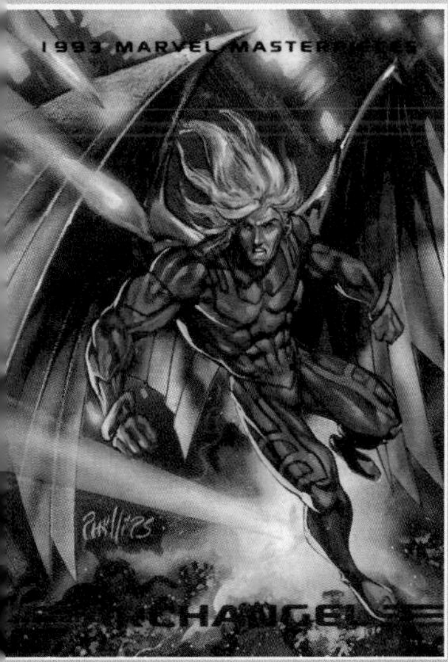

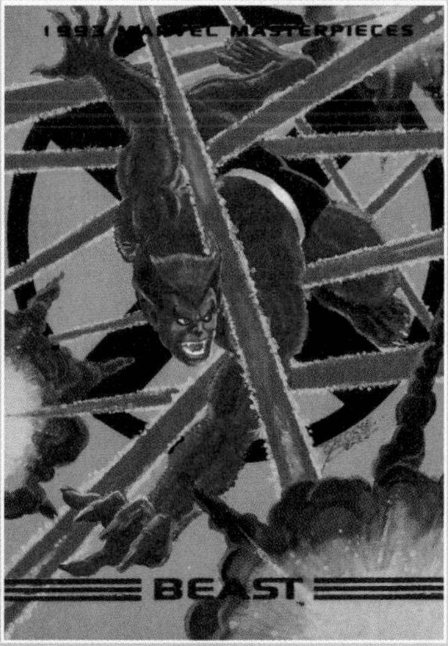
BEAST

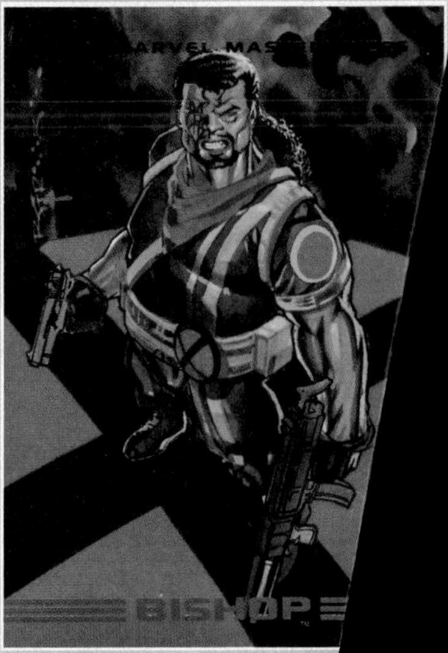

Marvel Masterpieces 1993 trading-card art by Joe Phillips, George Pérez & Brian Stelfreez

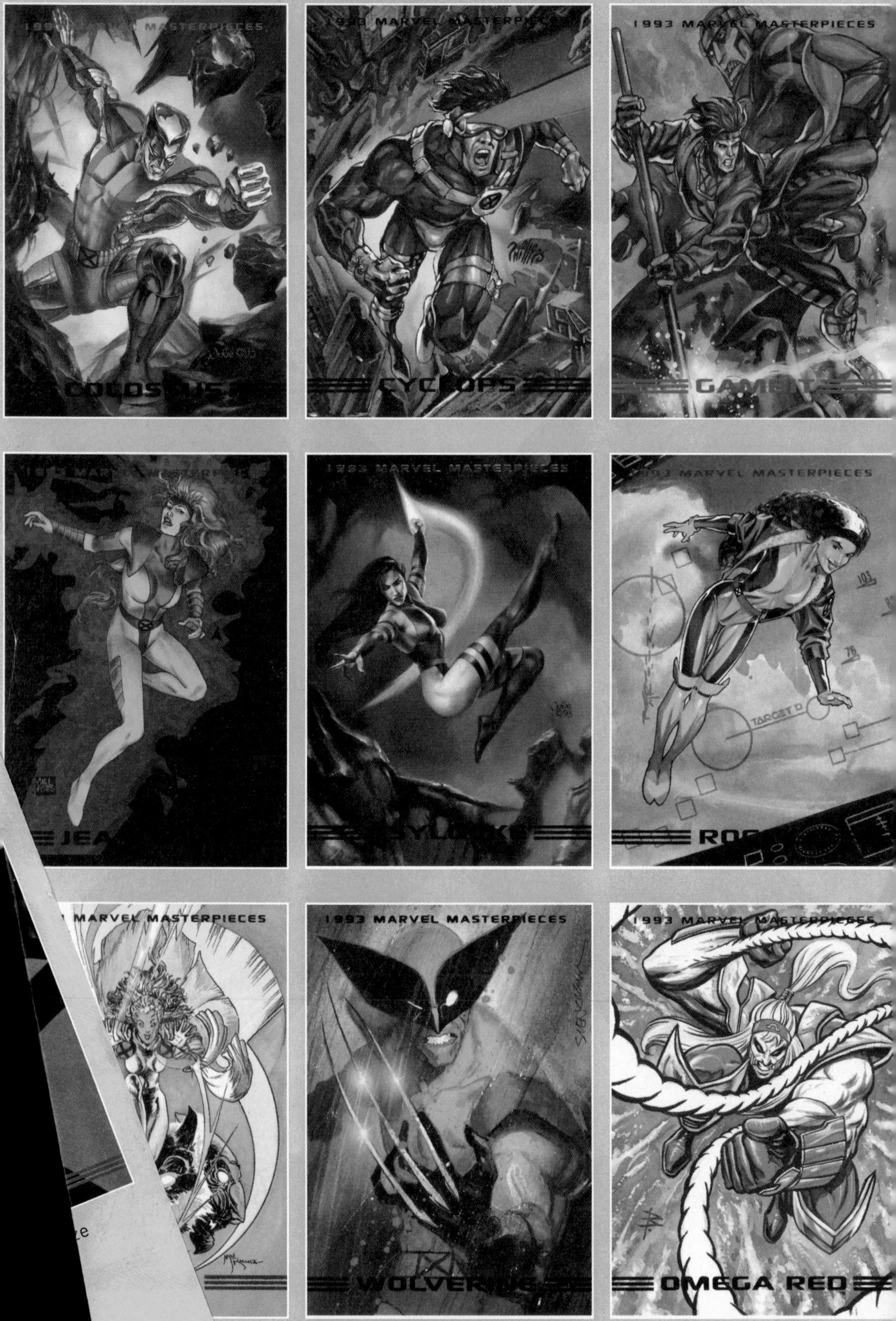
1993 MARVEL MASTERPIECES
CYCLOPS
1993 MARVEL MASTERPIECES
1993 MARVEL MASTERPIECES
1993 MARVEL MASTERPIECES
OMEGA RED

rpieces 1993 trading-card art by Julie Bell, Joe Phillips, Carl Potts, freeze, Michael William Kaluta, Bill Sienkiewicz & Bret Blevins